If you're making the move from Jet to SQL Server, but want to have Access as your front end, this is the book for you! In a clear concise manner, Mary and Andy manage to convey the necessary knowledge to get you thinking SQL Server, while not overburdening you with unnecessary details. This book belongs in any serious VB/Access developer's library.

F. Scott Barker
Former Microsoft Access team member
Author of *Microsoft Access 2000 Power Programming*

An invaluable resource for the Access developer moving to SQL Server. This book fills a great void.

Stephen Forte
Technical Editor, Access/VB/SQL Advisor

Mary and Andy's work on this subject is methodical, thorough, and excellent.

If you are a serious developer, you must have this book in your library!

Michael J. Hernandez
Owner of DataTex Consulting Group
http://www.datatexcg.com
Author of *Database Design for Mere Mortals* and *SQL Queries for Mere Mortals*

If you are considering moving your Access database to SQL Server, this is a must-have book. Andy and Mary cover the subject with grace and depth, demonstrating their deep technical knowledge about developing rich applications using the latest Microsoft technologies. This book is easy to read while providing clear technical examples of important concepts.

Clint Covington
Access Program Manager
Microsoft Corporation

Microsoft® Access Developer's Guide to SQL Server

Mary Chipman and Andy Baron

201 West 103rd St., Indianapolis, Indiana, 46290 USA

Microsoft® Access Developer's Guide to SQL Server

Copyright ©2001 by Sams Publishing

International Standard Book Number: 0-672-31944-6

Library of Congress Catalog Card Number: 00-101899

Printed in the United States of America

First Printing: December 2000

03   02   01   4   3   2

Trademarks

Warning and Disclaimer

ASSOCIATE PUBLISHER
Bradley L. Jones

ACQUISITIONS EDITOR
Sharon Cox

DEVELOPMENT EDITOR
Kevin Howard

EXECUTIVE EDITOR
Rosemarie Graham

MANAGING EDITOR
Charlotte Clapp

PROJECT EDITOR
Carol Bowers

COPY EDITOR
Bart Reed

INDEXER
Greg Pearson

PROOFREADER
Katherin Bidwell

TECHNICAL EDITOR
Don Rainwater

TEAM COORDINATOR
Pamalee Nelson

MEDIA DEVELOPER
J.G. Moore

INTERIOR DESIGNER
Anne Jones

COVER DESIGNER
Anne Jones

LAYOUT TECHNICIANS
Ayanna Lacey
Heather Hiatt Miller
Stacey Richwine-DeRome

Overview

Contents

Foreword

The software world is continually changing, and at Microsoft we understand the importance of Access changing with it. With Access 2000 and in the future versions, Microsoft delivers a host of new features designed to help developers build a new class of solutions using the latest database and Web technologies. Beginning in Access 2000, you can employ SQL Server as your native database engine, build browser-based solutions using Data Access Pages (DAPs), and take advantage of even greater integration with the rest of the Office family of applications.

One of the most powerful and exciting changes presented in Access 2000 was the introduction of Access projects (ADPs). Microsoft Access projects allow developers to build solutions tied directly to SQL Server using Access's familiar, friendly design environment and tools, thereby opening up an entirely new avenue of development to Access users. The Access team was very focused on integrating this new functionality into Access in a seamless fashion. We wanted you to be able to leverage the knowledge and skill you have acquired working with Access in the past, while at the same time taking full advantage of the power and scalability of Microsoft SQL Server. This is where the authors of *Microsoft Access Developer's Guide to SQL Server* come in.

Mary Chipman and Andy Baron have created a book that eloquently covers every aspect of creating well-architected applications using Access and SQL Server, whether you are using the new ADP format or sticking with MDBs. This book covers wide ground—from how to leverage powerful new features, such as ADPs and DAPs, to correctly designing and implementing SQL Server applications. They also offer clever techniques for creating efficiently linked MDBs and cover various strategies for effectively upsizing your existing Access applications. Mary and Andy provide lucid explanations of the concepts underlying successful database applications, and their book describes the background and history of many of the technologies that Access and SQL Server are built upon. Additionally, Mary and Andy provide a great in-depth introduction to SQL Server, including thorough coverage of security, Transact-SQL, and SQL Server's maintenance, tuning, and administration tools. The authors provide up-to-date coverage of the new features added to SQL Server 2000, such as native XML support, and they show you how to take advantage of them in your Access application. Finally, Mary and Andy provide an abundance of useful tips, tricks, and workarounds scattered throughout every chapter. They tell you what works well, where different technologies can be used to their greatest effect, and how to effectively handle commonly faced design issues. Throughout their coverage, they assume that scalability is paramount, and they always guide you toward solutions that will impose the least burden on your server and your network while providing the richest possible experience for the user.

Mary and Andy are leaders in the Access development community. They have extensive experience developing Access and SQL Server applications, and they have a long history with the products as speakers, trainers, Access MVPs, and authors. They are key participants in

Microsoft's Access Insiders group, whose members provide the Access development team with product guidance and feedback. They know Access, and they know what Access developers will face when migrating solutions from Jet to SQL Server. They understand the advantages of continuing to build apps in Access, as well as the challenges you'll face, and they tell you how to go about it successfully. If you are looking for an articulate, practical book on building powerful and efficient applications using Access and SQL Server, look no further—this book should be considered an essential resource.

Jon Sigler and Dave Gainer
Program Managers, Microsoft Access Development Team

About the Authors

Mary Chipman and **Andy Baron** are Senior Consultants with MCW Technologies, a Microsoft Certified Solution Provider. Mary and Andy specialize in application development, training, and writing about Microsoft Access, SQL Server, Visual Basic, the .NET framework, and related technologies. They are contributing editors at *Access/VB/SQL Advisor* magazine from Advisor Media and the *Smart Access* newsletter from Pinnacle Publishing, Inc., and they speak frequently at industry conferences. Mary and Andy have both received Microsoft's Most Valuable Professional (MVP) award every year since 1995, based on their contributions to Microsoft's online support newsgroups. They coauthored training courses covering Access and SQL Server for Application Developers Training Company (http://www.appdev.com), and they appear in AppDev's training videos and CD-ROMs. Mary and Andy have both contributed to many other successful technical books, and Mary coauthored the *Access and SQL Server Developer's Handbook* (for Access 95 and SQL Server 6), and *SQL Server 7.0 in Record Time*, both published by Sybex. When they're not at their computers or on the lecture circuit, the authors enjoy scuba diving and walking on the beach at their home in Singer Island, Florida.

Dedication

We dedicate this book to our parents. As members of dynamic,
modern families, we're blessed with lots of them:

Kathy and Harvey; John; Isadora and Al; Henry and Ina

Now there's something in this book that all of you can understand:

We love you.

Acknowledgments

We couldn't have written this book without the help and cooperation of our friends and colleagues on the Access and SQL Server teams at Microsoft. Particular thanks to Dave Gainer for reading chapters, coordinating Microsoft feedback, and generally being there to help us in any way he could. Thanks also to Bill Ramos for reading chapters and clearing up a lot of the gray areas concerning how Access interacts with SQL Server. We truly could not have made several important deadlines if Dave and Bill hadn't heeded our pleas and taken the trouble to send us a CD as soon as SQL Server 2000 was released to manufacturing. Sumit Chauhan is a brilliant member of the Access development team who was very generous with her time and shed invaluable light on the inner workings of ODBC and OLE DB. Clint Covington was a big help, showing us how useful DAPs can be once you figure out how to make them work. Tom Casey, on the SQL Server team, provided much appreciated encouragement and put us in touch with the right people when we needed clarification. Balaji Rathakrishnan clarified several OLAP-related issues. Roger Wolter sent us sorely needed DLLs for testing late in the SQL Server 2000 beta, and he was kind enough to review our coverage of SQL Server's exciting new XML features. Richard Waymire was a big help in clearing up obscure SQL Server issues, and Jeff Ressler was also very helpful. We are truly lucky to be writing about products from two of the greatest teams at Microsoft, and we hope we've done their products justice.

At Sams, our publisher, we'd like to thank our Acquisitions Editor, Sharon Cox, our Development Editor, Kevin Howard, and our Copy Editor, Bart Reed, whose deft changes to the text we always appreciated. Thanks also to our Technical Editor, Donald Rainwater, and to Carol Bowers, our Project Editor. These folks were always there for us when we needed them, and we're very glad we chose Sams as our publisher.

We'd like to thank the many friends and colleagues who provided invaluable support along the way. If your name doesn't appear here, please know that your contributions and encouragement were no less valued and appreciated.

Several folks with much more experience using SQL Server than we have were kind enough to review chapters and offer improvements. Particular thanks to Leslie Koorhan, who provided detailed feedback and set us straight on several important SQL Server issues. Steve Thompson took time to read early chapters and gave us very helpful comments and examples. Thanks to Michael Hotek for reviewing several of our chapters and providing a treasured resource to all SQL Server developers—his Web site, `www.mssqlserver.com`—and thanks to Sue Hoegemeier, who offered advice and insight on real-world issues involving the perils of Access/SQL Server applications; her war stories were always both amusing and instructive.

Our friends in the Access community, John Viescas, Steven Forte, Mike Hernandez, Alison Balter, and Scott Barker, all took time to read chapters and to offer corrections and suggestions that were very much appreciated. Mike Hernandez shared an early chapter from the book he coauthored with John Viescas, *SQL Queries for Mere Mortals*, and allowed us to draw upon the work he'd done, piecing together a history of SQL. Thanks to all of you. And thanks to Michael Kaplan, another old Access friend who was working on a book of his own, *Internationalization with Visual Basic*, and who helped us get straight on the related collation issues in SQL Server. Our buddy in Sydney, Australia, Adam Cogan, also gave us some valuable upsizing tips.

We've been fortunate to share membership in MCW Technologies, LLC, with Mike Gunderloy, Ken Getz, Paul Litwin, and Brian Randell (and with Mike Gilbert before he moved on to do great things at Microsoft). What a group! Ken Getz is a close friend who's companionship we treasure; the fact that Ken knows so much and shares his knowledge with us so readily is just icing on the cake. Mike Gunderloy is so smart that he sometimes appears to be of another species, and his brains are matched by a bountiful heart. Mike, too, was working on a book while we were—*Mastering SQL Server 2000*—and he was always available with answers when we needed him. Paul Litwin has been a pioneer in deciphering and clearly explaining Access issues since version 1. Paul's work on ADPs and DAPs in volume 2 of the *Access 2000 Developer's Handbook* served as a valued foundation for our own research. And Brian Randell's expertise in the gnarly world of COM and COM+, not to mention his constant good humor, was a comfort to us anytime we needed help with *n*-tier issues.

In addition, we'd like to thank all our fellow MVPs on Microsoft's public newsgroups, who provide free help and information every day to users around the world. They may not all have contributed directly to this book, but without their presence the sum total of our ignorance would be much greater than it is.

We've tried hard to be accurate, but if we got anything wrong it certainly wasn't anyone's fault but our own. Had we listened better, we'd have gotten it all right.

And, finally, although they contributed nothing of technical merit whatsoever, we'd like to thank George McLafferty and all of our dive buddies aboard *Sea Fever* for being there on Wednesdays and Saturdays when we just had to get away from it all and go commune with the fishes.

Tell Us What You Think!

As the reader of this book, *you* are our most important critic and commentator. We value your opinion and want to know what we're doing right, what we could do better, what areas you'd like to see us publish in, and any other words of wisdom you're willing to pass our way.

I welcome your comments. You can email or write me directly to let me know what you did or didn't like about this book—as well as what we can do to make our books stronger.

Please note that I cannot help you with technical problems related to the topic of this book, and that due to the high volume of mail I receive, I might not be able to reply to every message.

When you write, please be sure to include this book's title and author as well as your name and phone or fax number. I will carefully review your comments and share them with the author and editors who worked on the book.

Email: Rosemarie.Graham@samspublishing.com

Mail: Rosemarie Graham
         Executive Editor
         Sams Publishing
         201 West 103rd Street
         Indianapolis, IN 46290 USA

Introduction

Are You Nuts?

What are you doing reading this book? Haven't you heard that Access is dead? Didn't you know that Access has never been more than a toy? Don't you realize that once you move your data to SQL Server, you need to use Visual Basic or some other "real" programming tool to build your application?

Even if you haven't succumbed to believing those myths, you probably do have some serious doubts about whether you should stick with Access as you make the transition to using SQL Server. And those doubts are well founded. The techniques and strategies that work well for building Access/Jet applications could indeed get you into trouble as you move to building SQL Server applications. Even if you don't anticipate needing to support a larger group of users or bigger tables, SQL Server offers many advantages that you won't benefit from unless you understand how they work and how to use them effectively.

Access is a delightful development environment. Access forms and reports make it easy to build friendly and powerful user interfaces for entering and presenting data, and the VBA language helps you make those forms and reports really sing and dance. You've probably already hit the Access "wall" that forced you to dig in and learn about things such as the NotInList event and the use of recordsets to get beyond just relying on wizards, macros, and simple drag-and-drop techniques. There are great books and Internet resources available to help you break through that wall, but when it comes to moving your Access applications to SQL Server, there are far fewer resources available. And if you continue to use the same techniques that worked well in an all-Access application, you'll end up with very little benefit from migrating your database to SQL Server. Just "upsizing" the tables isn't enough. You need to upsize the entire application by rethinking its basic data-access architecture, and no wizard can do that for you.

Some Access programmers have been struggling with this since the early days of Access, but that struggle has become much more common lately. The Internet has caused almost every business to consider exposing at least part of its data to potentially thousands or even millions of users, and SQL Server itself has become much more inviting.

Questions, Questions

The SQL Server team at Microsoft did a terrific job of completely rewriting the product for version 7.0, and SQL Server 2000 has even more great features. Not least among these features is the stuff you don't see, and that's the point. It no longer takes a full-time database administrator to keep most SQL Server databases running efficiently. A lot is handled for you automatically that used to require continual tweaking, and now when you do need to adjust or create something, there are a host of well-designed wizards to guide you along.

On the Access side, there has also been an increased push to move you toward using SQL Server. A version of SQL Server called *MSDE* began shipping with Access 2000. Also, a new kind of Access application, the ADP, allows you to work directly with SQL Server without going through the Jet database engine.

This new push toward SQL Server has, however, caused a lot of confusion. Should you keep your front-end Access objects in an MDB file or convert to using the new ADP format? What exactly are those new ADPs anyway, and what new features do they provide? Do those new features really work as advertised? Does all your DAO code need to be converted to ADO? What version of SQL Server should you be using? What exactly are triggers and stored procedures, and when should you use them? What's the MSDE and what exactly can or can't it do? What if you're happy with Access 97 and don't want to upgrade to Access 2000? In MDBs, should you use ODBC to link to SQL Server tables or somehow start relying on pass-through queries? Do you continue to create bound forms and controls, or should everything be unbound? What does "*n*-tier" mean, and can your Access application become part of an *n*-tier architecture? And what happens if you want to migrate the whole thing to the Internet and still maintain an Access front end?

We wrote this book to address all those concerns and to give you a thorough introduction to SQL Server 2000. Regardless of the version of Access you're using, you'll find useful, detailed examples of how to create applications that make efficient use of the server. All the examples were created using Access 2000 and SQL Server 2000, which both added significant new features for application developers. But even if you are still working with SQL Server 7.0, we're confident you'll find this introduction to SQL Server useful.

What You'll Find in this Book

We start off by examining what's involved in upsizing your database to SQL Server. You have several options for upsizing, and we cover the strengths and weaknesses of each.

Next we tackle SQL Server fundamentals, focusing on how to use the graphical tools that provide the easiest gateway to SQL Server features. We explain several important but potentially confusing options that were added in SQL Server 2000, such as the ability to install and run multiple simultaneous instances.

The third chapter deals with security. In order to work effectively with SQL Server, you must understand security; otherwise, it will trip you up at every turn. You'll learn how to create logins, how to assign fixed-server and database roles, how to work with application roles, and how you can manage it all from an Access 2000 project (ADP), if that's your preference.

The next chapter digs into the capabilities of Access projects—those new ADP files. You'll learn how you can use Access projects to manage SQL Server database objects and how to take advantage of the new properties in ADP forms and reports.

Chapter 5 deals with linking an Access database (MDB) to SQL Server tables. You'll learn how Access uses ODBC and how to work efficiently in a linked table application. These techniques will be useful in any version of Access, and we explain why you may want to use MDB databases to connect to SQL Server, even in Access 2000 or later versions.

Chapter 6 introduces ActiveX Data Objects (ADO), a library of objects that you can use to work with SQL Server data programmatically. ADO can be confusing, especially if you're experienced with the older object model, DAO. We cover the differences and provide guidance on how to use ADO efficiently. But we also tell you where DAO may continue to be your best choice.

Chapter 7 takes you through the steps of designing and creating a SQL Server database. We review database design and normalization concepts and then build a database in SQL Server. You'll learn about creating defaults, constraints, rules, triggers, indexes, and database diagrams, with emphasis on areas that are significantly different from what you're used to in Access.

Chapter 8 introduces you to Transact-SQL. As an Access developer, you've been shielded from having to know much about the guts of the SQL query language, but as a SQL Server developer, you really need to know how to use it to create views, stored procedures, and, in SQL Server 2000, user-defined functions. You'll learn the syntax of Transact-SQL and how to use the query-building tools that SQL Server provides. Unlike Access SQL, Transact-SQL contains many programming features, such as variables and conditional execution. These programming capabilities are introduced here and then explained in detail in Chapter 10.

In Chapter 9 you'll learn how to create and optimize SQL Server views, which are similar to the SELECT queries you've built in Access. You'll learn about the new capabilities of views in SQL Server 2000, such as how to add indexes to views and how user-defined functions allow you to create "parameterized" views.

Chapter 10 covers the essentials of programming effective stored procedures, which is an art form in itself. You'll learn the difference between a batch, a script, and a stored procedure. You'll also understand transactions and how you can implement your own transactions in SQL Server, as well as how SQL Server locks records. Stored procedures go way beyond the capabilities available in Access queries, and this chapter includes sections on using temp tables, cursors, error handling, and system functions. You'll also learn how to debug your stored procedures, just in case you don't get things right on the first try.

Chapter 11 shows you how to create an unbound Access application. You'll learn why this is the best choice if you need to scale to accommodate many users as well as what the trade-offs are in deciding between an Access MDB and an ADP. You'll learn how to handle all data access through ADO code and to take advantage of local storage for filling list boxes and combo boxes. Examples show how to load and update data, while avoiding multiuser concurrency problems, and how to use batch processing to add efficiency. Detailed code listings are provided, including examples of how you can use XML to provide local storage for ADPs.

Chapter 12 covers building Access reports based on SQL Server data. You'll learn about new report properties in Access 2000 ADPs and how to base reports on SQL Server 2000's new user-defined functions. You'll also see examples of techniques you can use with any version of Access to make efficient use of the server. Advanced-level examples show how to build a crosstab report based on SQL Server data and how to return data to an Access report from an OLAP cube.

Chapter 13 discusses Internet features in Access and SQL Server. You'll learn about the Web Assistant Wizard in SQL Server and the Web system stored procedures. The chapter also explains how to take advantage of the rich support for XML that was added in SQL Server. You'll learn how to create Data Access Pages (DAPs) in Access 2000, how to use the Office Web Components, and how to deploy your DAP over the Internet using Remote Data Services (RDS).

Chapter 14 brings you into the world of *n*-tier applications. Learn about why *n*-tier architectures make applications easier to deploy and maintain, and how Access can be used to build presentation-tier objects that work well in an *n*-tier solution. You'll see how to use Visual Basic and Microsoft Transaction Server (MTS) to migrate your Access class modules into stateless middle-tier components and how this all looks using COM+ in Windows 2000. A detailed example takes the sample application from Chapter 11 and transforms it into a true *n*-tier design.

Chapter 15 explores the issues you'll face when tuning, deploying, and maintaining your SQL Server database. It shows you the tools you can use to support these tasks. You'll learn how to work with the SQL Server Profiler to monitor performance and to see the exact effect that your Access application is having on the server. You'll also learn how to use the Windows Performance Monitor and how to set up maintenance jobs and alerts in SQL Server. This chapter also covers the important topics of how to perform regular backups of your SQL Server data and how to restore from a backup if you ever need to. On the topic of deployment, you'll learn how to distribute your application with a runtime version of Access, using Microsoft Office Developer (MOD) and the Package and Deployment Wizard as well as how to copy and move a SQL Server or MSDE database.

As trainers, conference speakers, writers, and consultants, we've seen, first hand, the problems that Access developers face when moving to SQL Server. Even experienced Access pros often end up confused and frustrated, because the path is poorly marked and there have been few sources of guidance along the way. We hope this book provides maps you can use to avoid the marshes and scale the hilltops. We think the journey is worth taking. With Access and SQL Server you really can build reliable, scalable, friendly systems, and have fun doing it.

All the sample code and applications presented in this book are available for download at `http://www.SamsPublishing.com`.

Converting Your Access Database to SQL Server

IN THIS CHAPTER

Microsoft Access is really two products in one. It's a tool for creating the forms, reports, and VBA code that comprise a front-end application for viewing and manipulating data. Behind the scenes, however, Access also supplies a database engine that performs the actual data retrieval, manipulation, and storage. The database engine that has been an integrated part of Access since version 1.0 is called the *Jet database engine*, and its native file format is the familiar .MDB file.

It is possible, however, to use Access for building the front-end application while relying on SQL Server (or another database engine) to perform the data management. Microsoft has made this option more readily available in Access 2000 by including a free version of the SQL Server database engine, called the *Microsoft Data Engine* (MSDE). In SQL Server 2000, this version is called the SQL Server 2000 Desktop Engine.

Chapter 2, "SQL Server Fundamentals," compares the MSDE/Desktop Engine with the full versions of SQL Server that are available, and later chapters suggest various strategies you can pursue to create or convert front-end Access applications to work well with the SQL Server database engine. But first, take a moment to consider why you might want to use SQL Server rather than Jet.

Many people think that upsizing from the Jet database engine to SQL Server is a universal panacea for whatever is ailing their Access databases. It's not. In fact, just the opposite is usually true. If your Access application is a dog, then most likely it will still be a dog after you upsize it to SQL Server—perhaps an even bigger, uglier, shaggier dog! Even a well-designed Jet database often won't run any faster after the tables are upsized to SQL Server if you are using the same data access methods you used for your Access database. In order to successfully convert your Access database, you have to be clear about why it needs to be upsized, and you need to understand how to take advantage of the strengths of SQL Server by reworking the data access elements of your Access application.

This chapter discusses two different techniques for upsizing your Access 2000 database. You can use the Upsizing Wizard, which is built into Access, or you can use the Data Transformation Services (DTS) Import Wizard, which is available from the Enterprise Manager in SQL Server. You'll also look at how you can keep some data in Access if you need to, by setting up your Access database as a linked server in SQL Server. Before digging into the mechanics of upsizing, however, you need to consider why you'd want to.

Reasons to Upsize

People come up with a lot of reasons to upsize, and sometimes not all of them are good ones. Upsizing won't solve whatever happens to be wrong with your Access database. You need to have a clear understanding of the strengths and weaknesses of both Access and SQL Server before you start.

Number of Users

The generally accepted number of concurrent users that Access can handle comfortably is about 15 to 20. This number is open to debate. Some experts will tell you that the number is much smaller. Other experts will report successful Access implementations with 100 or even 200 users. A lot depends on what kind of application it is and how the database is being used. For example, an application in which users are not editing the same records concurrently will support many more users than applications where there is a good deal of contention for the same records. An application where users simply browse and report on data, without performing any edits, can theoretically support up to the absolute limit of 255 users.

Factors unrelated to the application, such as network hardware and even certain antivirus programs, can also have a negative impact on multiuser performance. Most experienced Access developers agree, however, that even under the best conditions, the average business application will start to degrade in performance if the Jet database engine, running concurrently on each user's machine, is asked to manage more than a couple dozen users.

So, one good reason to upsize to SQL Server is the need to support many users who are simultaneously updating, adding, and deleting records. This also means that most public Web sites using an Access database are good candidates for upsizing.

SQL Server is capable of scaling to support thousands of simultaneous users.

Size of the Database

Access 2000 databases have a maximum size of 2GB, and previous version allowed only 1GB. However, SQL Server databases can grow to sizes measured in terabytes (see `http://terraserver.microsoft.com` for an interesting example of a huge SQL Server database).

Access programmers can work around the size limitation of Jet by splitting databases—tables can be linked from multiple databases in a single Access linked-table application, allowing the 1GB or 2GB limit to be applied to each table in its own separate database rather than to an entire database containing multiple tables. Nevertheless, compacting a very large Jet database regularly is necessary and can take many hours to complete. Indexed searches are amazingly fast in large Jet databases, but some operations, such as complex multijoin queries, can be agonizingly slow.

Two gigabytes, or even a more conservative 500MB to 700MB, is still, however, a whole lot of data, and so it is rare that Access developers need to move to SQL Server based on the size of their databases alone.

It is nice to know that you don't have to worry about outgrowing SQL Server, but this by itself is rarely a reason to upsize.

Performance

Performance is a frequently misunderstood reason for converting to SQL Server. There is an assumption that, no matter how slow the Access database is, upsizing will magically speed things up. Often, just the opposite is true, and upsizing results in even slower performance. Performance has as much to do with database design and application design as it does with the platform.

SQL Server can, however, be more efficient at retrieving and updating records in large databases, and later in the chapter, ways are discussed to speed things up even further. Also, if you have the hardware to support it, upsizing to SQL Server lets you take advantage of parallel query execution across multiple processors. By concentrating execution of data operations on one powerful machine, or even on a cluster of machines, SQL Server makes it possible to throw lots of hardware resources at the server for less money than it would take to upgrade each Access user's workstation. But as a rule, Access developers who upsize mainly in the hope of improving performance are often disappointed, unless they significantly reengineer their applications.

Transaction Logging

Because the Jet database engine runs on each user's system, it cannot possibly keep a comprehensive record of all the data changes that are made by multiple users. SQL Server, on the other hand, processes all data changes centrally, so it maintains a complete and up-to-the-moment log of everything that has happened in the transaction log.

If you need to be able to recover data up to a point of failure, in the event of a crash or a serious user error, Access does little for you. Some basic data repair capabilities are built into the Jet engine, but most recovery scenarios will require that you resort to a backup and will at best result in the loss of some data. SQL Server's transaction log, however, lets you recover fully to the point of failure by "rewinding" and/or "replaying" all database activity. What's more, SQL Server supports backups in real time as well as device mirroring for full redundancy.

The ability to recover fully from a hardware or application failure is an important reason to consider upsizing.

Data Integrity

Another issue is database corruption. Network errors or problems on individual user's machines can leave an Access database in a corrupted state, because all data changes are sent over the network from the user's desktop to the file server. Users can corrupt the database simply by turning their systems off while in the middle of a critical operation, or by simply opening a database in Microsoft Word, which irretrievably corrupts a database (even if it's not saved in Word).

On the other hand, it's very difficult to corrupt a SQL Server database, and the server can more easily be protected from untrained users. Network problems are also much less of a threat to SQL Server, because data changes are always performed on the server, and the network is only used to send requests to the server or to send results back to the users.

Security

Another important reason to upsize to SQL Server is to take advantage of the more robust, and even more convenient, security that comes with SQL Server's strong integration with Windows NT and Windows 2000 security.

If you employ integrated security with NT/2000, your users won't have to log on twice the way they do when you activate Access security logins. You can assign permissions to NT/2000 users and groups and then easily track which users are doing what in each SQL Server database.

An added source of security is the fact that the actual files SQL Server uses for data storage are not accessible. You don't need to worry about someone deleting or copying a database file the way you do with Jet, which requires that users have read, update, and delete privileges to the network share where your data is stored. SQL Server will not offer much help in securing the forms, reports, and code in your applications, but the data itself can be made very secure. SQL Server offers an interesting array of security options. SQL Server security is discussed in detail in Chapter 3, "Understanding SQL Server Security."

Administration

SQL Server's tight integration with Microsoft's server operating systems also allows you to use Windows NT or Windows 2000 for event logging, messaging, and performance monitoring. The SQL Server Enterprise Manager makes it possible to centrally administer local and remote servers, and you can add linked servers for distributed querying. Although Jet databases are easier to administer, that's only because they severely limit your administrative options.

SQL Server Tools

Apart from the core components for managing your data, SQL Server includes a number of very powerful auxiliary tools that may motivate you to upsize your data. You'll find entire books devoted to each of these powerful tools, but here is a brief overview.

Data Transformation Services (DTS) is a fully programmable set of services for creating and executing operations that move your data from virtually any source to any destination. The data does not even have to pass through SQL Server itself, so you can make use of this tool to work with your data even if you don't upsize. But it is one good reason to start using SQL Server. Later in this chapter, you'll see how DTS can be used as one way to upsize your Access database to SQL Server.

Online Analytical Processing (OLAP) services allow you to build sophisticated decision support systems that can slice and dice data according to dimensions that you define. Summary calculations that would normally take a long time to perform can run very quickly with OLAP. Again, these services can be combined with DTS to work with data that's not native to SQL Server, but they certainly give you an extra reason to become a SQL Server developer.

English Query allows you to create forms or Web pages where your users can type in natural language questions about your SQL Server data. With the help of powerful wizards, you define the semantic relationships in your database, and English Query does the hard work of parsing out users' questions and translating them into SQL queries.

SQL Server Agent is a powerful management tool that allows you to create and schedule administrative jobs consisting of multiple steps. You can also define alerts that are triggered automatically when certain errors occur, and you can specify which operators should be notified.

SQL Mail allows you to write stored procedures that call directly into your email system. Also, SQL Server 2000 has added a number of new features for generating XML documents from within your stored procedures.

Okay, so you're convinced that you want to upsize. How should you go about it?

Getting Started with the Upsizing Wizard

The Upsizing Wizard can give you a good start in the process of migrating your Access application to SQL Server. It helps you convert your tables, and, if you intend to use an Access Project (ADP), it will migrate queries in your Microsoft Access (Jet) database to views and stored procedures in SQL Server or MSDE. In addition, it will point your Access forms and reports at the new SQL Server data.

Versions of SQL Server Supported by the Upsizing Wizard

You can upsize to any version of SQL Server 7.0 or SQL Server 2000, including the Standard, Personal, Developer, and Enterprise editions. You can also upsize to all versions of the SQL Server 2000 Desktop Engine (formerly known as MSDE). The renaming of the SQL Server versions between SQL Server 7.0 and SQL Server 2000 is confusing, to say the least. The Desktop edition of SQL Server 7.0 is now the Personal edition, and a new Developer edition has been added which allows a developer to build any kind of application, but prohibits deployment. Access 2000 was released before SQL Server 2000 and its documentation refers frequently to the MSDE, as we do in various places throughout this book. If you're using SQL Server 2000 (and we recommend that you do), just remember that MSDE equals the SQL Server 2000 Desktop Engine. The SQL Server versions are discussed in more detail in Chapter 2.

CHAPTER 1

Access 2000-SQL Server 2000 Compatibility Issues

Because SQL Server 2000 was released subsequent to the release of Access 2000, there was no way for the Access team to anticipate what would be in the product. Therefore, there are some incompatibilities between Access projects (ADPs) and SQL Server 2000. Several features don't work, such as creating new databases or saving revisions to existing database objects from an ADP. The Upsizing Wizard itself will fail to work, generating an "Overflow" error message when it tries to connect to SQL Server.

There isn't a single remedy for these problems; you need to take several steps:

- Install Microsoft Office 2000 SR-1, or Access 2000 SR-1 if you don't have the full Office suite. The SR-1 update is available on Microsoft's Web site at `http://officeupdate.microsoft.com`. If later server releases are available by the time you read this, follow Microsoft's instructions for upgrading to the latest service release.

- Install the SQL Server 2000 client tools on any user machines where you need the users to have the capability to create or save design changes to database objects.

- Check the OfficeUpdate Web site for a patch to be applied to the Upsizing Wizard, or a new version of the wizard. The version of the wizard that shipped with Access 2000 contained code that looked specifically for version 7.x of SQL Server and won't work with SQL Server 2000.

TIP

The Upsizing Wizard will work with a SQL Server 6.5 database as well as SQL Server 7.0 and SQL Server 2000 databases. However, you need to have SQL Server 6.5's Service Pack 5 installed for the Upsizing Wizard to work with SQL Server 6.5.

Unattended Upsizing

Unlike earlier versions, the Access 2000 Upsizing Wizard can run unattended because when it hits an error, it doesn't stop processing to report the error. Instead, it logs the error. The wizard creates a report listing its successes and failures, which you can view at the end of the process. If the wizard runs into any problems with duplicate table names, where a table already exists on the SQL Server database, it simply renames the upsized table, appending a number to the end of the table name.

TIP

The upsizing report will be saved as a snapshot report in the same folder as the database being upsized. Make sure you have a printer driver installed on the computer that runs the Upsizing Wizard; otherwise, the wizard will fail.

Upsizing Wizard Choices

Although upsizing tools have been available for all versions of Access, the Upsizing Wizard that's included with Access 2000 represents a significant improvement. Also, SQL Server underwent a complete rewrite prior to version 7.0, and the Access 2000 wizard is the only one geared toward working with the SQL Server 7.0 technology. So, your first step should be to move any data that may be in older versions of Access into Access 2000, if you choose to take advantage of the Access upsizing wizard. As noted earlier in this chapter, make sure that you have the latest patch available from Microsoft because the Upsizing Wizard that shipped with Access 2000 does not work with SQL Server 2000.

When you use the Access 2000 Upsizing Wizard, you have to make some decisions about how you want to proceed. Here are your options:

- You can create a new SQL Server database, upsize your tables, and link the new tables to your Access database (MDB). Only the tables will be created in SQL Server. For the most part, your application will continue to run normally. The original Access tables are not deleted; they are renamed with "_local" appended to their original names. Note that for some reason a space is added to the end of the table name after the word *local*. If you ever need to work with these tables programmatically, don't forget about that space!

- You can upsize the structure only and not make any changes in Access. You might choose this option if you'd like to modify the design in SQL Server before you load the data.

- You can upsize the structure and data to a new database in SQL Server and not do anything to the Access database.

- You can upsize to a new or existing database in SQL Server and create a new Access project (a file ending in the extension .adp). Your original Access database will be unchanged, and a new Access project will be created. The ADP file format is new in Access 2000 and is used by Access to store all your front-end objects, without running the Jet database engine. Queries will be converted to views (views are similar to Access SELECT queries) or stored procedures in SQL Server, and all forms, reports, data access pages (DAPs), macros, and modules will be copied into the new project file. The project file will be connected directly to SQL Server or MSDE. There is no such thing as local storage for tables and queries because there is no local database engine, so all data objects (tables and queries) must live on the server.

Chapter 4, "Introduction to Access Projects (ADPs)," and Chapter 5, "Linking to SQL Server Using Access Databases (MDBs)," cover how to get the most out of both kinds of Access 2000 applications—ADPs that directly use SQL Server for managing data, or MDBs, which still make use of the Jet database engine and link to SQL Server using Open Database Connectivity (ODBC). After reading these chapters, you'll have a better understanding of the advantages and sacrifices inherent to each development strategy. But for now, you'll just look at getting the data in place.

What Gets Upsized

The following elements can be upsized, depending on your choices when using the Upsizing Wizard:

- If you elect to upsize and link the SQL Server tables to your Access database, only the tables and any relationships between them will be affected.

- If you elect to upsize and create a new Access project (ADP), queries will also get upsized either to views or stored procedures. See the section "Upsizing Queries to an Access Project (ADP)," later in this chapter, for more details.

- Validation rules will get upsized to triggers in their respective tables. A trigger is a Transact-SQL statement that runs automatically when data is modified, and in this case it's used to validate data. Transact-SQL is the dialect of Structured Query Language (SQL) that SQL Server uses. However, you may instead want to implement the validation rule as a constraint. The reason why you'd want to go to this trouble is that for certain operations, triggers are ignored and won't fire. A table constraint will always validate incoming data. See Chapter 7, "Designing and Creating a SQL Server Database," for a full discussion of how triggers and constraints work.

- Linked tables also get upsized, although if you are working with heterogeneous data sources, you may want to upsize using DTS (Data Transformation Services). Using DTS will give you more control over the outcome. Using DTS to upsize is discussed later in the chapter.

What Gets Ignored

The Upsizing Wizard will ignore all of the following:

- If any table name contains an apostrophe or single quote ('), none of your tables will be upsized.

- If the Upsizing Wizard encounters errors from migrating the data in your tables, it will continue on and upsize the structure of the remaining tables, but not the data. If this is the case, you can use DTS to grab the data after the wizard has run.

- All Access-defined field properties, such as input masks, formats, captions, and descriptions, get ignored.

- If a function is used in a field validation rule that the Upsizing Wizard can't map to Transact-SQL the validation rule will be skipped but the rest of the table will be upsized. Transact-SQL is discussed in more detail in Chapter 8, "Introduction to Transact SQL (T-SQL)."

- The Validation Text property will not upsize if its accompanying validation rule fails to migrate. Single quotes in the Validation Text property will display as double quotes after upsizing.

- If a function is used in a field's Default Value property, the entire table is skipped.

- The Allow Zero Length field property is also ignored. The Upsizing Wizard does not attempt to create a trigger or CHECK constraint to enforce the rule.

- Any security settings you have configured in Access will be ignored. You'll need to configure SQL Server security for tables after upsizing. Chapter 3 covers setting up SQL Server security in detail.

- Hidden tables will be skipped.

- Unfortunately, you'll also find that if the Upsizing Wizard can't find a Transact-SQL equivalent for a default value expression in a field, it skips the entire table containing that field.

- Lookup fields, which display values from a lookup table in place of the key value, are ignored. The key value will be upsized, not the lookup value. SQL Server does not support this functionality.

How Indexes Are Handled

Primary keys are upsized as unique, nonclustered indexes. Clustered and non-clustered indexes are discussed in detail in Chapter 7. If you want to set an index to be a primary key or a clustered index, you need to do that after the wizard has run.

Regular indexes in Access are upsized as follows:

- Yes (Duplicates OK) indexes are upsized to nonclustered indexes.

- Yes (No Duplicates) indexes are upsized to unique, nonclustered indexes.

> **CAUTION**
>
> Access allows you to create a Yes (No Duplicates) index on a field and at the same time set the Required property to True if the field contains more than one null value. In this case, the wizard will upsize only the structure of the table and will leave the data behind. Make sure that all fields that contain more than one null value have the Required property set to No and don't have a unique index on that field. The problem is twofold: Access allows you to set these rules without applying them to existing data, but SQL Server won't let you import data that violates the rules. Also, Access allows multiple records with nulls in uniquely indexed fields, but SQL Server doesn't.

How Data Types Are Mapped

Table 1.1 shows how data types are mapped from Access to SQL Server by the Upsizing Wizard. If you don't like a choice the wizard makes, you can change the data type before the conversion or after the wizard has completed. You can also use DTS instead, which gives you complete control over the process. DTS is discussed later in the chapter.

TABLE 1.1   How the Upsizing Wizard Maps Data Types Between Access and SQL Server

Access	SQL Server
AutoNumber - Number (Long)	int (with the IDENTITY property set)
Byte	smallint
Currency	money
Date/Time	datetime
Hyperlink	ntext
Memo	ntext
Number (Decimal)	decimal
Number (Double)	float
Number (Integer)	smallint
Number (Long)	int
Number (ReplicationID)	uniqueidentifier
Number (Single)	real
OLE Object	image
Text	nvarchar
Yes/No	bit

SQL Server data types that have an *n* in front of them are Unicode data types. If you want to change these to non-Unicode types, you must do so after the wizard has run. Data types are discussed in more detail in Chapter 2.

Upsizing Queries to an Access Project (ADP)

Select queries are upsized to views, whereas action queries, such as append, delete, update, and make-table queries, are upsized to stored procedures. SQL statements that are the row sources of list and combo boxes also get upsized to views. Because they aren't publicly named in Access, they get arbitrarily named ut_qry1View, ut_qry2View, ut_qry3View, and so on, based on the order in which the Upsizing Wizard handles them.

Views in SQL Server don't support the same functionality as Access queries (for example, they can't have an ORDER BY clause), so the Upsizing Wizard may elect to upsize a single query to a stored procedure or to a view that feeds intermediate results to a stored procedure. So, on a sorted query, you'll end up with a view to select the data and then a stored procedure to handle the ORDER BY. If your original query was named MyQuery, you'll end up with a view named MyQuery and a stored procedure named MyQuery.

Parameter queries are upsized to stored procedures, which can handle input parameters in the WHERE clause.

The Upsizing Tools do not try to upsize every type of Microsoft Access query that you may have in your Access (Jet) database. Chapter 4 explains how to fill in these gaps. When you're upsizing to an ADP, the following queries will be ignored:

- Crosstab queries.
- Parameterized action queries.
- Action queries that contain nested queries. If any queries contain parameters, an ORDER BY clause, or any keywords that cause the query to upsize as a stored procedure, the queries will fail to upsize because views cannot have stored procedures as a data source.
- SQL pass-through queries.
- SQL Data Definition Language (DDL) queries.
- Union queries.
- Queries that reference values on a form.

You must manually re-create queries that the Upsizing Tools do not migrate. Bear in mind that Access-specific query syntax, such as the TRANSFORM and PIVOT syntax used in crosstab queries, is not supported in SQL Server.

Some action queries may upsize but not work. For example, a make-table query is upsized using a SELECT INTO statement to create a new table. SELECT INTO fails unless the Select

Into/Bulkcopy option for the database is turned on. By default, it's turned off because any bulk copy action truncates the Transaction log. SELECT INTO is discussed in more detail in Chapter 8.

Append queries that insert values into an Identity column will fail unless the IDENTITY_INSERT option for the table has been turned on. AutoNumber fields are upsized to integer columns with the Identity property set, which mimics AutoNumber field behavior in Access. Access will allow you to insert values in an AutoNumber field by running an append query, but SQL Server won't unless you set the IDENTITY_INSERT property first.

The following are all the Access query properties that won't upsize:

> Output All Fields
> Description
> Unique Values
> Unique Records
> Run Permissions
> Source Database
> Source Connect String
> Record Locks
> Recordset Type
> ODBC Timeout
> Filter
> Order By
> Max Records
> Subdatasheet Name
> Link Child Fields
> Link Master Fields
> Subdatasheet Height
> Subdatasheet Expanded

Upsizing Forms to an Access Project (ADP)

All your Access forms will be added into the new Access project by the Upsizing Wizard. The Record Source and Row Source properties of your forms and combo/list boxes will be handled differently, according to the options displayed in Table 1.2.

TABLE 1.2 How the Upsizing Wizard Handles Record Source and Row Source Properties

Record/Row Source Value	Wizard Creates
Table name	No change
SELECT statement	View
SELECT statement with ORDER BY	Stored procedure
Unsorted query	View
Sorted query	Stored procedure
Parameter query	Stored procedure

TIP

Before you upsize, make sure your forms use the TableName.FieldName syntax in any SQL statements used for the Record Source and Row Source properties; otherwise, your forms will fail to open after they have been added to the new Access project.

All chart objects will fail to work after upsizing because the wizard does not manage to migrate the Row Source property correctly. You'll also get a couple error messages. However, it's easy to fix the problem—simply copy the value in the Row Source property of the chart object in your original database and manually paste it into the Row Source property of the form in your new Access project.

Upsizing Reports to an Access Project (ADP)

Reports always get upsized and copied to the new Access project, no matter what errors may have occurred. However, that doesn't mean that they'll necessarily work when they arrive—you'll have to inspect them and fix any problems that may have occurred.

For the most part, the Upsizing Wizard will process reports in much the same way it does forms. The report's Record Source property will be replaced with either a view or a stored procedure, following the rules for forms, as shown in Table 1.2.

Here are some of the problems you may encounter with upsized reports:

- Charts appear blank until you manually reset the Row Source property.
- SELECT statements used in the Record Source property of a report must use the TableName.FieldName syntax; otherwise, the report won't open.
- If you use a SELECT statement in the Row Source property of your report, any values stored in the OrderBy and Filter properties will be discarded.

- If the FilterOn property is set to Yes, the report will not open. You can fix this by using the ServerFilter property instead.

Chapter 12, "Building Access Reports from SQL Server Data," presents several strategies for creating Access reports that are specifically geared toward working with SQL Server data.

Upsizing Gotchas: What to Watch Out For

It should come as no surprise that there are several traps you can fall into when upsizing. The Upsizing Wizard doesn't attempt to handle all possibilities, and, although it does print a report that tells you what failed, it won't tell you why something failed. Here are some things to watch out for:

- *Updateable queries*. Not all queries that are updateable in Access will still be updateable after being converted to SQL Server, particularly queries with multiple joined tables. The queries may upsize successfully, but you'll need to examine all your updateable queries, including all the queries behind your data entry forms, to make sure they still work.

- *Built-in functions*. Many VBA functions are handled automatically by the Access expression service and may be used in query criteria, aggregate expressions, grouping, sorting, validation rules, and default values. SQL Server has its own similar set of functions, but the Upsizing Wizard doesn't attempt to perform a translation. You'll need to do it yourself, and you'll need to watch out for objects that are skipped because they contain function calls.

- *System fields in replicas*. If you have implemented replication in your Access database, you'll need to remove all the replication system fields that were added by Access before you upsize. A good free utility for doing this is available at www.trigeminal.com.

- *Tables without a unique index*. Be sure that each table you upsize has a primary key or unique index, even if it's a table you're using to hold only one record. Without a unique index, you won't be able to update data in that table.

- *Unique indexes on fields with multiple nulls*. Access allows null values in multiple rows of a field with a unique index, but SQL Server doesn't.

- *Unequal field sizes in related fields*. It is possible in Access to have a relationship defined between two text fields of unequal length. You need to ensure that all related fields have the same length before you upsize.

- *Invalid dates*. SQL Server supports two data types for dates, and both of them have a range that is smaller than the range supported in Jet databases. If someone mistakenly entered a date in your database with a year of 199, which is a perfectly valid year in Access, you will be unable to upsize that row of data.

- *Hyperlinks*. The hyperlink field behavior that you see in Access won't persist once you upsize your data to SQL Server. You may still want to preserve the data and handle the hyperlinking programmatically. However, because Access hyperlink data is actually stored in Memo fields, your hyperlinks will be converted to SQL Server ntext data types, which are very resource intensive. If your hyperlinks are all less than 256 characters, you may want to convert them to simple text fields in Access before you upsize. Access text fields get converted to the much more efficient nvarchar data type.
- *Combo boxes and list boxes that don't work correctly*. Previously working combo boxes and list boxes may be empty or give an error message after the Upsizing Wizard runs. The reason is that the RowSource property of the combo box or list box contains a query that uses parameters, a query that references form controls in its WHERE clause, or a SELECT statement that does not fully qualify each column with the TableName.FieldName syntax. You need to fix these problems after you've upsized.

What About Security?

Unlike Access security, which by default allows anyone into your database, SQL Server security is always on and restrictive by default. The Upsizing Wizard will fail unless you are logged on to SQL Server with the CREATE TABLE, CREATE DEFAULT, CREATE DATABASE, and SELECT permissions on the systems tables in the master database. It's easiest if you're a member of the sysadmin role or if you log on as the sa user. SQL Server security is covered in Chapter 3, and you may want to take a peek ahead before you upsize if you don't already know the basics of how to create or enable a security login.

If you've implemented Access user-level security, you also need Read Design and Read Data permissions on all the tables in the Access database. It's easiest if you log on as a member of the Admins group, check the permissions on the tables, and give yourself any permissions that may be missing for that Admins account.

In Access 2000, you can place password protection on the VBA project in your MDB. If you've done this and you want to upsize to an ADP, you'll need to clear the VBA password first.

CAUTION

The Upsizing Wizard will simply skip upsizing any objects on which you do not have sufficient permissions. In addition, no errors will be logged in the upsizing report. If you have problems upsizing objects because you do not have sufficient permissions, you may need to de-secure the database in Access prior to upsizing. For more information on Access security and the steps to secure or de-secure an Access database, download the Access Security FAQ from Microsoft's Web site.

Using the Upsizing Wizard to Create Linked Tables

Upsizing to SQL Server while linking the SQL Server tables to your Access database is a good way to get started with SQL Server. The main advantage is that your application will mostly continue to work unchanged, so you don't have the burden of fixing problems in forms or reports while you're still trying to get familiar with how SQL Server operates.

Upsize and Link to an Access MDB

Getting going with the Upsizing Wizard is pretty straightforward—just choose Tools, Database Utilities, Upsizing Wizard from the menu bar. This will display the opening dialog, as shown in Figure 1.1. At this point you can select between using an existing SQL Server database and creating a new one. The first time through, you'll probably choose to create a new database. However, if your Access database is quite large, you may elect to upsize in smaller batches, upsizing only some of the objects at a time to a SQL Server database that already exists. Click Next to continue.

FIGURE 1.1
The Upsizing Wizard lets you choose between creating a new database and upsizing to an existing one.

The next wizard dialog lets you supply login information to SQL Server, as shown in Figure 1.2. If you leave the Login ID and Password text boxes empty, and if you're using Windows NT or Windows 2000, the wizard will use integrated security settings, logging you in as the current user. Make sure to use a security account that has the required permissions on SQL Server. A good choice is the sa account or any other account mapped to the sysadmin (system administrator) fixed server role. Security is discussed in detail in Chapter 3, and you'll find that, unlike with Access, it is hard to do much in SQL Server without understanding at least the basics of its security system. Type in a name for the new database that's different from any existing database names on that server. Click Next to move on.

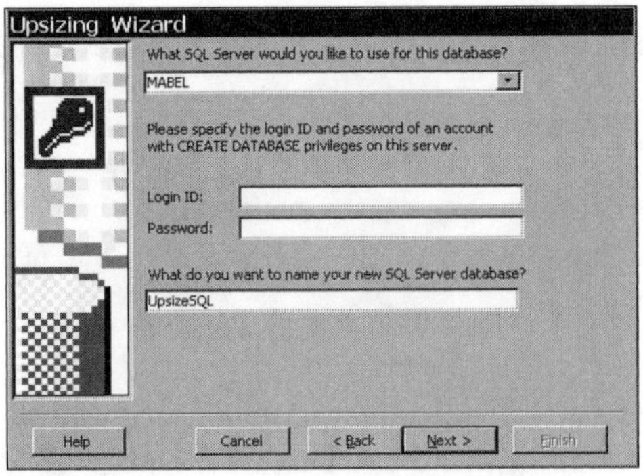

FIGURE 1.2

If you don't supply a login ID and password, the Upsizing Wizard will assume you're using Windows NT or Windows 2000 authentication.

You then need to select the tables that will be upsized. You can select some or all the tables. Figure 1.3 displays an example of selecting all the tables to be upsized.

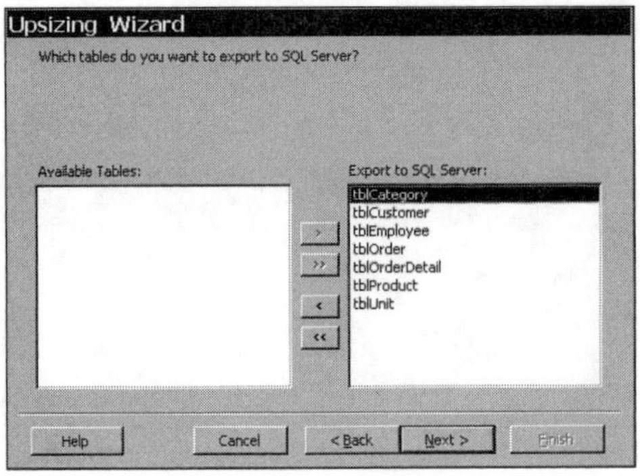

FIGURE 1.3

You can select some tables or all the tables in your Access database.

The next wizard dialog, shown in Figure 1.4, is probably the most important one, and the trickiest! This is where you specify which attributes you'd like upsized. Choices made here will have a significant impact on your SQL Server database and on the success of your attempt at upsizing.

FIGURE 1.4
These are important options you need to consider carefully when you upsize your database.

The following subsections provide a rundown of each option.

Indexes

The Upsizing Wizard will create indexes on your SQL Server tables corresponding to those you defined in Access. If you upsize a table with a unique index on fields that also don't have a required value, only the structure of the table will upsize, not the data.

Validation Rules

Any table-level and field-level validation rules will be implemented as UPDATE and INSERT triggers, unless they employ Access-specific functions. One good option is to skip all validation rules when you upsize and add them back later, because this is a frequent cause of upsizing problems. The techniques you can use to create the equivalent of validation rules in SQL Server are covered in Chapter 2.

Defaults

Default values will be carried over to the new tables; however, they will not be upsized as SQL Server default objects but as default constraints using Declarative Referential Integrity (DRI). Beware of values that include Access-specific functions.

Table Relationships: Use DRI or Use Triggers

Your best bet is to choose DRI here. This is essentially the same kind of referential integrity that you are accustomed to in Access, where you use the Relationships window to "declare" the referential integrity relationships you want to enforce. When you choose DRI, you'll receive what looks like an error message, but it's really not indicating an error. It's warning you that you will lose cascading updates/deletes, which were not supported in SQL Server 7.0 as an integrated part of DRI. In SQL Server 2000, Microsoft added support for cascading updates and deletes. In Chapter 7, you'll see how you can implement these new referential actions in SQL Server 2000.

Even if you're using SQL Server 7.0, you still should choose DRI rather than triggers. Triggers are an older technology that can cause problems for performance, data integrity, and locking, especially when a trigger created on one table causes changes to another table. In SQL Server 7.0, if you want both DRI and cascading updates/deletes, you can perform all updates and deletes using stored procedures that safely and efficiently handle the cascading operations. DRI and triggers are both discussed in Chapter 7, and stored procedures are covered in Chapter 10, "Programming Effective Stored Procedures."

Add Timestamp Fields to Tables

If you choose the option Yes, Let Wizard Decide when asked whether timestamp fields should be added to tables, the wizard will create a timestamp column in every table that contains a Memo field or an OLE object.

The timestamp (or rowversion) column in SQL Server isn't about keeping time, and the values that are used cannot even be translated into standard date/time values. Instead, it is simply an efficient binary field that's maintained automatically by SQL Server to uniquely identify progressive versions of each row in a table. SQL Server adds timestamps to tables with text (memo) or binary (OLE Object) fields so that it can figure out if a record has been edited without having to load the potentially huge amount of data stored in the field itself. Adding timestamps enhances performance with tables containing floating-point numbers, OLE Object (binary) fields, or Memo (text) fields. Don't be confused by the new terminology, rowversion. This is the Microsoft SQL Server 2000 alias to the timestamp data type, which means it has the same functionality as timestamp. This new term, rowversion, is actually a much more accurate description of how this type of column is used.

NOTE

You can't view or edit the values in timestamp fields from Access.

Only Create the Table Structure; Don't Upsize Any Data

Upsizing data will build an empty database in SQL Server. You might choose this option if you want to work on the database structure before loading the data.

Figure 1.5 displays the wizard dialog where you choose whether you want to create tables in SQL Server and link them to an existing Access database (MDB) or connect to the created SQL Server tables using a new Access project (ADP). You can also choose to create the new tables and do nothing else.

If you choose to link, your existing tables will be renamed, and the newly created SQL Server tables will be linked to your Access MDB.

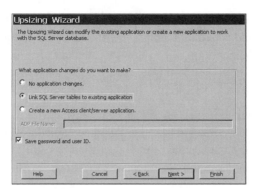

FIGURE 1.5
You can choose to link tables to your existing Access database or to create a new Access project.

Save Password and User ID

The default is not to save the user ID and password. If you enable this option, then in an Access database with linked tables users will be able to access data on the server without specifying a password. In an Access project, the username and password will be saved in the connection string used to connect to the server.

Don't elect to save the user ID and password unless you want your user ID and password cached with the linked tables. If you're using integrated Windows NT/2000 security, this setting will be ignored. If not, this option will determine whether a login dialog pops up every time one of the new tables is accessed.

What Application Changes Do You Want to Make?

Chapters 4 and 5 discuss in detail the differences between using Access MDBs and ADPs to build your SQL Server applications. Both have their distinct advantages. In a nutshell, MDBs, which use ODBC (Open Database Connectivity) to connect to SQL Server, offer all the benefits of having the Jet database engine around to manage local data and queries. ADPs, on the other hand, efficiently use a single OLE DB connection to just one SQL Server database. Because ADPs were first introduced in Access 2000, they are still somewhat limited in what they can do, but they hold great promise for the future and may already be your best choice. In Chapters 4 and 5, you'll see that for now MDBs still tend to be favored.

You can click the Finish button here. The next wizard dialog doesn't offer any more choices.

The Upsizing Report

The wizard will create an upsizing report when it's finished. This report is automatically saved in snapshot format in the current directory, so you won't lose it when you close the report. This report contains all the information you need to keep track of what the Upsizing Wizard actually did, where it succeeded, and where it failed. This will give you a pretty good idea of where to start with the inevitable cleanup. Figure 1.6 shows a fragment of an upsizing report where the table validation rule failed to upsize. You would need to implement this rule in SQL Server manually.

You'll note that even though the report shown in Figure 1.6 tells you what failed, it doesn't tell you why. In this case the validation rule that failed contained a VBA function, `DateAdd`. Even though Transact-SQL (T-SQL), the SQL dialect used by SQL Server, has its own `DateAdd` function, the syntax is slightly different and the wizard wasn't equipped to make the translation.

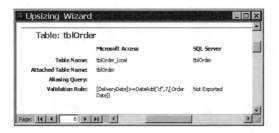

FIGURE 1.6
The upsizing report gives you crucial information about every aspect of your conversion.

Testing the Result

After the wizard is finished, you can put your application through its paces to see if it still works. One thing you may want to do is check the tables to see that they contain the same number of rows as the original! They won't always, and the wizard report won't tell you about it. All of your original tables have been renamed with "_local" appended to the original name, as shown in Figure 1.7, if you chose to create linked tables. Your queries, forms, and reports will be pointing to the SQL Server tables now, not the Access tables. If you decide to undo the upsize, simply delete the linked tables in the MDB, rename your local Access tables back to their original names, and delete the new SQL Server database. In Chapter 2, you'll learn how to manage SQL Server objects.

Upsize to an Access Project

If you choose to create a new project, your original Access database will not be modified in any way. Your tables and queries will be upsized to SQL Server, and a new Access project (ADP) file will be created. When you run the wizard, you'll choose all the same options as for upsizing to linked tables. However, the results will be quite different:

- All the newly upsized SQL Server tables will be displayed as native tables in the new Access project.

- Queries will be converted to views and stored procedures.

- All your forms, reports, data access pages, macros, and modules will be copied into the new Access project.

- SQL statements used as the record sources or row sources of forms, list boxes, and combo boxes will be upsized to views.

FIGURE 1.7

The Upsizing Wizard won't delete your original Access tables; it will just rename them.

When the Upsizing Wizard is finished, you'll be prompted for the connection information for your new Access project file, as shown in Figure 1.8. You can click the Test Connection button to make sure your settings work.

The report created for an Access project (ADP) has an additional section that contains the new views and stored procedures the wizard created as well as their definitions. Figure 1.9 shows a fragment of an upsizing report. Note that the wizard successfully upsized a plain totals query to a view, but its attempt to upsize a parameterized totals query to a stored procedure failed.

By the time you finish this book, you should be well on your way to being able to complete any upsizing tasks that the wizard couldn't handle successfully.

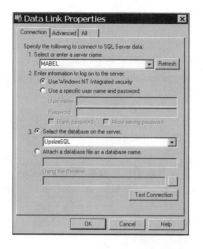

FIGURE 1.8

When you upsize to a new Access project, the final step is specifying connection information.

```
Query Name    qryTotal

              Upsized using SQL:

              CREATE VIEW qryTotal
              AS
              SELECT tblOrder.OrderID, sum(SalePrice*Quantity) AS Total
              FROM tblOrder INNER JOIN tblOrderDetail ON (tblOrder.OrderID = tblOrderDetail.OrderID)
              GROUP BY tblOrder.OrderID

Query Name    qryTotalParam

              Failed to upsize. Attempted to use SQL:

              CREATE PROCEDURE qryTotalParam @Enter_Pay_Meth varchar (255)
              AS
              SELECT tblOrder.OrderID, tblOrder.PaymentMethod, sum(SalePrice*Quantity) AS Total
              FROM tblOrder INNER JOIN tblOrderDetail ON (tblOrder.OrderID = tblOrderDetail.OrderID)
              GROUP BY tblOrder.OrderID, tblOrder.PaymentMethod
              HAVING (((tblOrder.PaymentMethod)="Enter Pay Meth"))
```

FIGURE 1.9

The upsizing report for an Access project has an additional section displaying how queries were handled.

Upsizing with Previous Versions of Access

If you're upsizing from Access 97 to SQL Server 7.0, you can download the Upsizing Wizard from the following location:

```
http://www.microsoft.com/products/developer/officedeveloper/Access/
prodinfo/exe/wzcs97.exe
```

> **CAUTION**
>
> Make sure you get the right version of the Upsizing Wizard. There's an older Upsizing Wizard that works from Access 97 to SQL Server 6.5, and if you try to use it to upsize to SQL Server 7.0 or higher, it will try, but fail.

Upsizing Using Data Transformation Services (DTS)

If you're using SQL Server 7.0 or SQL Server 2000, you can also use the Data Transformation Services (DTS) Import Wizard to upsize. It won't do anything Access specific, such as linking your tables to an existing Access database or creating a new Access project, but it will get your Access tables into SQL Server, and as an added bonus, it will let you perform custom transformations on the data. For example, if you want to change the data type of an integer field in Access to accommodate a long integer in SQL Server, you can transform the data while it's being imported. You can also write VBScript to conditionally import some rows and not others.

Although the DTS engine is included with MSDE versions of SQL Server, the DTS Import Wizard user interface is only available as part of a full retail version. The technique described here will only be available to you if you have a full version of SQL Server. As a developer, you'll want to have this anyway. Because using the DTS Import Wizard requires you to work from within the SQL Server user interface, if you're new to SQL Server, you may want to read Chapter 2, which covers the basics of how to work in SQL Server, before attempting this technique.

Before you start using the DTS Import Wizard, you need to create a new, empty SQL Server database. You can then launch the wizard from the SQL Server Enterprise Manager by choosing Tools, Data Transformation Services, Import Data from the menu bar. The first dialog of the DTS Import Wizard lets you know that you can use it to import data from all kinds of different files, ranging from database and spreadsheet files to text files.

The second dialog asks you to specify the source type and filename, as shown in Figure 1.10. If your Access database is secured, you can type the username and password required. Clicking the Advanced button will give you another set of options where you can specify the workgroup file.

The next step is to specify the destination, as shown in Figure 1.11. You need to specify the SQL Server OLE DB Provider, the name of the server, and the destination database. You'll learn more about OLE DB in Chapter 6, "ActiveX Data Objects (ADO) Fundamentals."

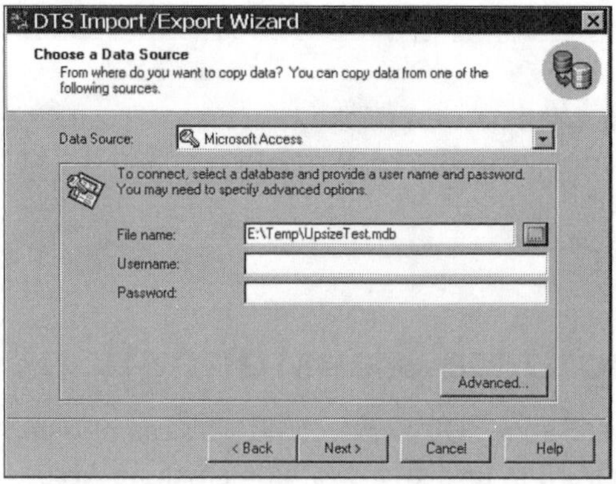

FIGURE 1.10

Choosing a data source involves setting the type of source and the filename, plus any needed security information.

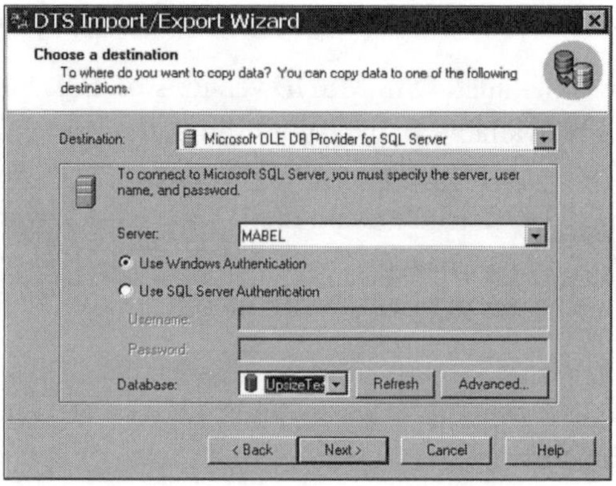

FIGURE 1.11

Specifying the destination database on SQL Server.

You then have the option of copying the tables or using a query, as shown in Figure 1.12. If you choose to use a query, you can select specific rows or columns to be upsized.

The next DTS Wizard dialog is where things get interesting. You select the tables you want to convert and optionally create your own transformations. You can also choose to include all primary and foreign keys. Figure 1.13 shows this wizard dialog, with the tblProduct table selected.

FIGURE 1.12

The DTS Import Wizard gives you the option of creating your own query to import the data.

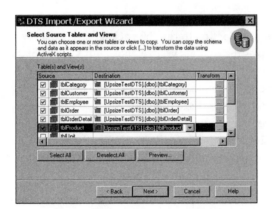

FIGURE 1.13

The DTS Import Wizard allows you to import primary and foreign keys as well as the tables.

If you click the Transform button, another dialog will open that allows you to modify your data while it is being imported. You can reset column mappings, build table constraints, or script data transformations. Figure 1.14 shows changing the column data type of the new table to var-char. The source in Access is a Hyperlink data type, which if left alone would be translated to ntext. The varchar data type is a more efficient data type that does not have the overhead associated with ntext. This is a definite advantage over the Access Upsizing Wizard, where you have no control over the data type translations.

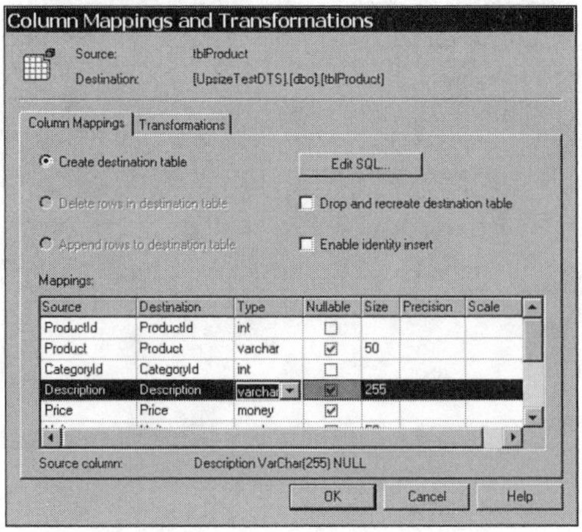

FIGURE 1.14
You can change the destination column data type.

The next dialog gives you the option to run the package immediately or to schedule it, and then the final dialog summarizes the options you've chosen. It's possible that you may get some errors. If so, you'll need to fix the errors in Access and import those tables again. One possible cause of failure might be that you created a primary key field in Access and didn't set the Required property to True. Access doesn't automatically set the Required property when you create a primary key, even though the field is always treated as a required field. SQL Server, however, will interpret this as permitting a null value in the primary key, which would be disallowed. In this case, you'd need to go back into Access, set the Required property on all primary keys, and then run the DTS Import Wizard again.

This only scratches the surface of what you can do using the very powerful DTS tools that are built into SQL Server. If you are required to perform any complex import or export operations, you should dig deeper into this terrific set of services. In addition to the wizard, you can use VBA code to create and schedule DTS packages by working with the Microsoft DataPump and Data Package object libraries. DTS may well be the preferred method of upsizing your Access database because of the level of control that it offers.

Using Linked Servers for Data Access

A final alternative to upsizing or converting your Access database to SQL Server is just to leave it where it is and link to it from SQL Server. One of the advantages of using Access databases is that Access has always been very good at linking to data sources other than Access. You can link to text files, spreadsheets, HTML tables, ISAM databases such as Paradox and FoxPro, or to ODBC data sources. SQL Server also lets you link to heterogeneous data sources by setting up a linked server.

In the Enterprise Manager in SQL Server, select the Security folder and expand it so that you can see the icon for Linked Servers. (The use of Enterprise Manager in SQL Server is explained in Chapter 2.) Right-click and select New Linked Server from the pop-up list. This will display the Linked Server Properties dialog with the General tab active, as shown in Figure 1.15. The required items include a name for the linked server (this can be anything you want), the provider name, and the data source.

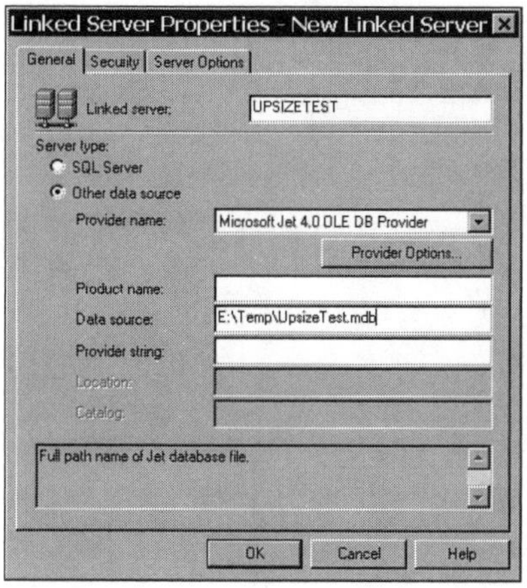

FIGURE 1.15
You need to set a name, provider, and data source for an Access linked server.

The Security tab defaults to no security, which is the simplest option for an Access database. If your Access database is secured using user-level security, then you must place the name and location of the workgroup file in the following registry key:

```
HKEY_LOCAL_MACHINE\SOFTWARE\Microsoft\Jet\4.0\Engines\SystemDB
```

Note that this registry location is not the same location that the Workgroup Administrator utility writes to in the registry, so even if the secured workgroup file is the default for Access, it will be ignored by the linked server. There is no facility for specifying the workgroup file location other than this registry key, and there is no provision for linking to more than one workgroup file at a time.

Figure 1.16 shows the linked server expanded to display all the tables in the Access database. This is as far down as you can drill using the Enterprise Manager.

You can now write queries against the linked server, but the Transact-SQL syntax for referring to a table in a linked server is a little different from what you use with regular tables. Transact-SQL syntax is covered in Chapter 8, but here's the syntax to use with linked tables:

```
ServerName.[table_category].[table_schema].TableName
```

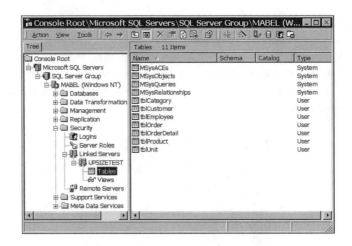

FIGURE 1.16

Viewing the tables of a linked Access server.

For an Access database, `table_category` and `table_schema` don't apply, so a real query against a linked server would look like the following:

```
SELECT EmployeeId, LastName, FirstName
FROM upsizetest...tblEmployee
```

Using linked servers certainly should not be regarded as a substitute for upsizing. However, if you need to keep some data in Access, or if your database currently uses information linked from other data sources, you may find the use of linked servers to be a valuable component of your overall upsizing strategy. Linked servers are discussed in more detail in Chapter 8.

Beyond Upsizing: What's Next?

It would be nice if you could just dust off your hands and walk away once you've gotten your data upsized to SQL Server. However, unless your application is extremely simple or only needs to support one user, your work has only just begun. Techniques that worked well in Access don't necessarily work well with SQL Server. Most of the rest of this book is going to deal with various ways to handle these differences, but here's an overview of some of the issues you'll face.

How Access Handles Linked SQL Server Data

When you upsize to linked tables, Access uses Open Database Connectivity (ODBC) to handle the translation between SQL Server and Access. The benefit to you as a developer is that you don't need to learn how to program in Transact-SQL (T-SQL) right away because ODBC is taking care of translating your Access SQL queries into syntax that SQL Server understands.

The ease of use of ODBC comes at a price, however. You won't be taking full advantage of all the features that SQL Server has to offer, and some techniques that worked well for you before may no longer be efficient.

To make the best use of SQL Server, you'll want to move as much data processing as possible to the server. With linked tables, the Jet database engine will still be operating on each user's desktop, but you'll want to avoid moving all the data in your tables across the network to the user's machine (the client machine) to be processed by Jet.

For example, an Access query that has a user-defined function in one of its criteria will not be able to be processed on the server because SQL Server has no way of running your VBA functions. Instead, all the data will be sent over the wire to your user, where the Jet engine will apply your function to each record. Instead, it would be more efficient to translate the logic in your VBA function into Transact-SQL that could be run in a stored procedure on the server. Then only the results would be sent to your user.

By eliminating the option of having Jet perform queries locally, ADPs force you to do all your query processing on the server, although some basic data processing can be performed in your VBA code, using ADO, as you'll see in Chapter 6.

New Data Type Choices

You may find that you disagree with some of the choices that the Upsizing Wizard makes when converting Access data types to SQL Server (refer to Table 1.1). For example, all text fields are upsized to the nvarchar data type in SQL Server. This is a data type that allocates an additional two bytes per character and can therefore accommodate all Unicode characters. In other words, text from almost all the languages in use in the world, including Korean, Arabic, Yiddish, Hindi, and even Klingon (really!), can be represented in nvarchar fields. If your data will only contain Western alphabet characters, it would be more efficient to use varchar.

Similarly, the date/time data type that the wizard uses is datetime, which can handle values between January 1, 1753 and December 31, 9999 to a precision of 3.33 milliseconds. But if you can make do with a range of January 1, 1900 to June 6, 2079, with precision just to the minute, you can use the smalldatetime data type, which uses only half the storage of datetime.

Code Cleanup

Whether you're using an Access database (MDB) or an Access project (ADP), you'll need to do some code cleanup to get rid of unsupported objects and methods that don't apply to SQL Server. If you've used Data Access Objects (DAO) to work with your data in VBA code, your code will automatically be loading and using the Jet database engine. To make the most efficient use of SQL Server, you'll want to modify the code to use ADO, which is covered in Chapter 6. If you've upsized to an ADP, any DAO code using the default workspace will not work because no Jet workspace is created in an ADP. For example, any references to CurrentDB will fail.

However, it is not just a matter of translating code that worked with one type of recordset to now work with another type of recordset. Some basic programming strategies will have to be modified. For example, DAO allows you to nest transactions up to five levels deep, but SQL Server supports only one transaction at a time. If your Access code includes nested transactions, only the outermost transaction is sent to the server and the other transactions are ignored. Because the inner transactions are never sent to the server, no error is returned—the transactions just fail silently. Your best bet here is to write stored procedures on the server to meet your transaction needs. Transactions in stored procedures are covered in Chapter 10.

Forms and Reports

You'll probably want to change many of the techniques that you're using in your Access forms and reports to take better advantage of SQL Server and to make your application more scalable. In general, you'll want to fetch less data. Here are a couple quick tips:

- If you're upsizing to an Access database (MDB), don't base forms on entire tables or on queries that return result sets from entire tables. Instead, populate the form on demand and don't load data when the form opens. You can also take advantage of local Jet tables to cache data instead of working directly with server data.

- There are no local tables if you're upsizing to an Access project file (ADP), but you can use the MaxRecords, ServerFilter, and ServerFilterByForm properties of the form to restrict the number of records that are returned.

All the remaining chapters in this book will directly or indirectly come to bear in helping you decide on the approaches that are best for building scalable applications. They provide a range of options and a balanced view of each set of techniques, but whichever path you follow, you'll probably decide that many of the tried and true methods you have been using are no longer the optimal choices.

Security

Last but not least, you'll need to implement security. Unlike Access, SQL Server security prevents users from accessing your database until you specifically grant them the right to do so. See Chapter 3 for detailed coverage of how SQL Server security works.

Summary

In this chapter you've looked at the reasons for upsizing an Access application to use SQL Server, and you've seen the various ways you can accomplish the task.

You can use the Upsizing Wizard, which will convert your tables and, in ADPs, your queries as well. Alternatively, you can use the DTS Import Wizard, which gives you a much finer level of control and the capability to perform complex transformations on the data you're upsizing. If you want to leave some of your data in Access, or if you need to make heterogeneous data available in SQL Server, you can also set up one or more linked servers.

Simply getting your data into SQL Server, however, is just the beginning. To take full advantage of the benefits that SQL Server can offer, and to allow your database to grow in size and in the number of users, you'll need to modify all aspects of your application. The remainder of this book provides you with the knowledge and perspective you'll need to do just that.

SQL Server Fundamentals

IN THIS CHAPTER

SQL Server is a big product, and it can be overwhelming at first glance. Several pieces of the puzzle need to fit together conceptually in order for you to work successfully with SQL Server. This book makes no attempt to delve into the details of the engine internals—there are entire books out there devoted to that topic. One book we, the authors, have found useful is *Inside SQL Server 7.0* by Soukup and Delaney, Microsoft Press. The updated version for SQL Server 2000 was not out at the time of this writing, but it should be every bit as useful as its predecessor. This chapter is intended to give you a bird's-eye view of the product as a whole and explain the various components and how they all fit together. Of course, which components are present depends on the SQL Server edition you install. So, this chapter starts with a description of those options.

SQL Server Editions

SQL Server comes in several different flavors and is therefore able to scale from hand-held devices up to multiterabyte servers. The editions of SQL Server 2000 are named somewhat differently from prior versions, so you could easily get confused if you're already familiar with the editions in SQL Server 7.0 (Enterprise, Standard, Desktop, and MSDE). Here's a list of the new editions and the capabilities of each one:

- *Enterprise Edition.* This edition supports all features and scales up to support the largest Web sites, enterprise systems, and data warehousing systems.
- *Standard Edition.* The Standard Edition is used for smaller workgroups and departmental databases.
- *Personal Edition.* The Personal Edition is the new name for what was the Desktop version in SQL Server 7.0. It is designed for standalone applications and for users who are disconnected a lot of the time from their main SQL Server.
- *Developer Edition.* The Developer Edition supports all the features of the Enterprise Edition and allows developers to write and test applications using those features. The licensing agreement prohibits use as a production server.
- *Desktop Engine.* The Desktop Engine is the edition formerly known as MSDE. This makes it somewhat confusing because, in SQL Server 2000, what was the Desktop Edition has been renamed *Personal Edition*. The Desktop Engine edition is redistributable and is designed for software vendors to package with their applications. SQL Server 2000's multi-instancing capability was created partly to allow users to install the Desktop Engine as part of a software package without having to worry about conflicts with an existing installation of SQL Server.
- *Windows CE Edition.* This flavor is designed to be used with Windows CE or Pocket PC devices. It supports most standard queries and is able to synchronize data with SQL

Server Enterprise and Standard Editions. Although the other editions all use the same core database engine, this one does not. It uses its own engine (built mostly by our friends from the Jet team), which is optimized to work well in a small memory footprint.

- *Enterprise Evaluation Edition.* This edition is a full-featured, free download that quits 120 days after downloading.

Features Supported

The Enterprise Edition, Developer Edition, and Enterprise Evaluation Edition support all the features of SQL Server 2000. Here's the complete feature list:

- Multiple instance support
- Failover clustering (up to four nodes)
- Failover support in Enterprise Manager
- Log shipping
- Parallel DBCC
- Parallel CREATE INDEX
- Enhanced read-ahead and scan
- Indexed views
- Federated database server
- Graphical DBA and developer utilities and wizards
- Full-text search

The Standard and Personal Editions support the following features:

- Multiple instance support
- Graphical DBA and developer utilities and wizards
- Full-text search

Finally, the Desktop Engine and Windows CE Editions provide multiple instance support.

In addition to these listed features, editions other than Enterprise, Standard, Developer, and Enterprise Evaluation have limited capabilities as far as supporting SQL Server replication, DTS, and Analysis Services. These limitations are fully documented in SQL Server Books Online under the topic "Editions of SQL Server 2000." Analysis Services (formerly know as *OLAP*) and English Query are really separate products that are bundled with the Standard, Developer, Enterprise, and Enterprise Evaluation Editions. These editions all run only on Windows NT Server or Windows 2000.

Pricing and Licensing

Microsoft has introduced a new, processor-based licensing model for its server products. This is designed to accommodate the needs of customers who are building e-commerce and Web solutions. This new licensing model comes as a huge relief for those who had to wrestle with the complex licensing and pricing model that exists for SQL Server 7.0. The old per-server and Internet Connector Licenses have been eliminated.

Under the new processor-based licensing model, a customer purchases a processor license for each processor running the software. This includes access for an unlimited number of users to connect either from a LAN, WAN, or outside the firewall, or through tin cans on a string (only kidding). There's no need to purchase any additional licenses with the processor model.

In addition, Microsoft will continue to offer server licenses and per-seat Client Access Licenses (CALs) for customers using SQL Server in non-Web-based scenarios. These two models replace licensing options used with SQL Server 7.0, most notably the SQL Server Internet Connector License and the licensing based on running SQL Server in per-server mode.

Upgrades are available for existing customers at a reduced cost, at approximately 50 percent of the product price.

The following is the price list for the server and processor licensing options at the time of this writing:

Licensing Option	Price
SQL Server 2000 Standard Edition, five CALs	$1,489
SQL Server 2000 Standard Edition Processor License	$4,999
SQL Server 2000 Enterprise Edition Server License, 25 CALs	$11,099
SQL Server 2000 Enterprise Edition Processor License	$19,999

These prices do not take into account any volume or other discounts you may receive, so your mileage may vary. The cost of purchasing SQL Server is generally lower than for other comparable relational database systems.

SQL Server Graphical Components

SQL Server 2000 provides a very rich selection of tools that provide graphical user interfaces, which makes it easy to perform just about any task—from administrative chores to creating databases and querying the data in them. The graphical tools provide a good way to get familiar with how SQL Server works because they fully expose SQL Server's features and functionality. The graphical tools let you explore the environment and are an invaluable aid to understanding what's available with SQL Server.

If you are coming from an Access environment, one thing about SQL Server you'll notice right away is that more of its guts are exposed. Access is fairly inscrutable—there is no way of peering inside msaccess.exe and the Jet DLLs to see how they're behaving. SQL Server gives you many helpful windows into its inner workings by exposing its operations through system stored procedures, system tables, and Transact-SQL. Plus, wizards are available to help you with complex tasks, such as setting up replication, developing a backup and maintenance plan, and tuning performance.

The central work area in the graphical tool set is the Enterprise Manager.

Enterprise Manager

Using the Enterprise Manager, you can perform almost all the tasks necessary for managing and administering SQL Server. It is based on the Microsoft Management Console (MMC), which is a common server-management environment with a tree view on the left and a multi-purpose area on the right, as shown in Figure 2.1. You can use the Enterprise Manager to perform the following tasks:

- Register, manage, configure, and secure servers and remote servers
- Create and modify databases, logins, users, permissions, and other objects in each registered server
- Query, import, and export data
- Back up and restore databases
- Configure and administer replication
- Manage alerts, operators, error logs, and maintenance jobs
- Create and manage full-text indexes and Web Assistant jobs

Figure 2.1 shows the main window of the Enterprise Manager. The Enterprise Manager presents the SQL Server objects in a hierarchical view, where each node can be expanded to display child nodes. In this view, the server node is expanded and, in the right pane, the Wizards option is selected. You can perform actions by clicking a shortcut in the right pane or by selecting a node in the left pane and choosing a menu item. The right-click mouse button also presents a context-sensitive menu of options to choose from for each node in the hierarchy.

One of the benefits of using the Enterprise Manager when you're first getting started is that there's a wizard for just about anything you could conceivably want to do in SQL Server.

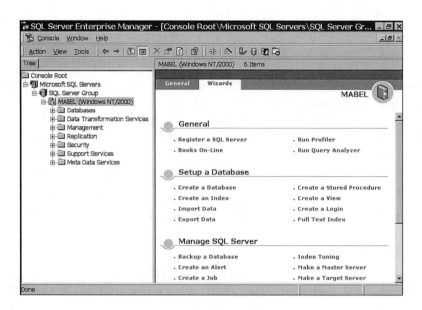

FIGURE 2.1

The Enterprise Manager with the Wizards option selected in the right pane.

The Wizards

All the wizards are listed in the Tools, Wizards menu option as well as in the Run a Wizard toolbar button (it's the one with the magic wand icon). Here's a list of the wizards:

- Register Server Wizard
- Create Database Wizard
- Create Index Wizard
- Create Login Wizard
- Create Stored Procedure Wizard
- Create View Wizard
- Full-Text Indexing Wizard
- Data Transformation Services (DTS) Import Wizard
- DTS Export Wizard
- Backup Wizard
- Copy Database Wizard
- Create Alert Wizard

- Create Job Wizard

- Database Maintenance Plan Wizard

- Index Tuning Wizard

- Make Master Server Wizard

- Make Target Server Wizard

- Web Assistant Wizard

- Configure Replication Publishing and Distribution Wizard

- Create Publication Wizard

- Create Pull Subscription Wizard

- Create Push Subscription Wizard

- Disable Publishing and Distribution Wizard

Although some of these terms may be unfamiliar to you, you can see that it's quite a list. In addition to these full-blown wizards, there many helpful dialog boxes that pop up when you select particular tasks. Not very long ago relational databases required you to type in and execute SQL statements to accomplish these tasks.

Keyboard and Menu Options

Dialog boxes besides the wizards are available from the toolbar and the menu bar in the Enterprise Manager. The menu choices depend on which node is currently selected. In Figure 2.1, only options that apply to the context of the server are displayed. The right-click menu choices naturally also reflect the node selected.

The Tools menu, shown in Figure 2.2, provides a list of other actions that can be taken from the server node context. Note that the Generate SQL Script option is grayed out because it would only be valid for a specific database, and there is no database highlighted.

Right-clicking an object in the Enterprise Manager generates the context-sensitive menu that applies to the object. Figure 2.3 shows the right-click menu for the server object with the All Tasks flyout menu selected. This gives you a pretty good idea of which tasks are easily performed at the server level.

As you explore the Enterprise Manager, expanding the various nodes, pay attention to the right-hand pane, the right-click menu selections, and the Tools menu, which can be used to launch the Query Analyzer, among other things.

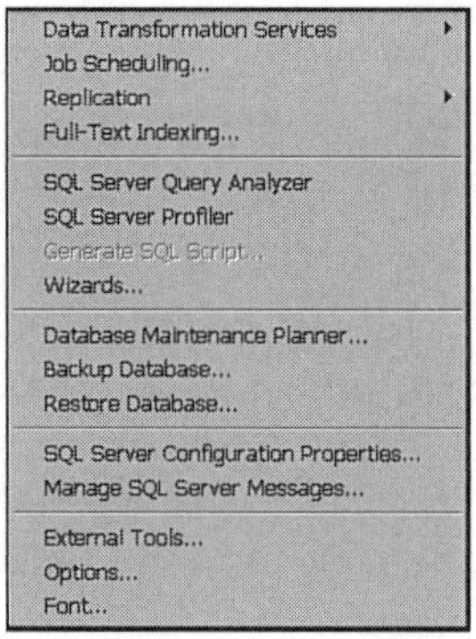

Data Transformation Services ▶
Job Scheduling...
Replication ▶
Full-Text Indexing...

SQL Server Query Analyzer
SQL Server Profiler
Generate SQL Script...
Wizards...

Database Maintenance Planner...
Backup Database...
Restore Database...

SQL Server Configuration Properties...
Manage SQL Server Messages...

External Tools...
Options...
Font...

FIGURE 2.2

The contents of the Tools menu from the server context.

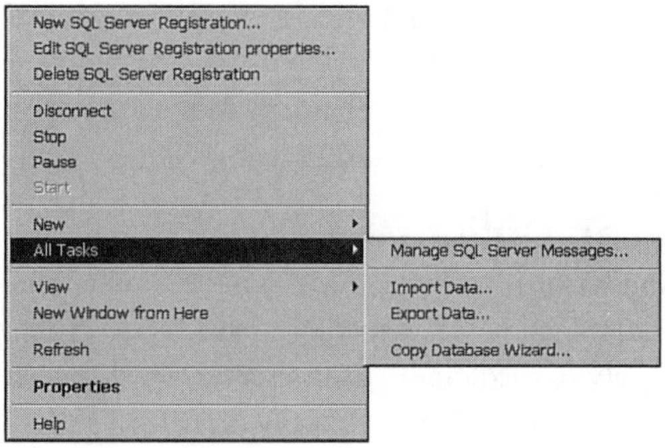

New SQL Server Registration...
Edit SQL Server Registration properties...
Delete SQL Server Registration

Disconnect
Stop
Pause
Start

New ▶
All Tasks ▶   Manage SQL Server Messages...

View ▶   Import Data...
New Window from Here   Export Data...

Refresh   Copy Database Wizard...

Properties

Help

FIGURE 2.3

The right-click menu for the server object.

Query Analyzer

The Query Analyzer has been beefed up considerably from previous versions of SQL Server, with more features to make it a robust tool for creating and testing queries, stored procedures, and views. These tasks are covered in detail in later chapters. The Query Analyzer gives you a graphical user interface that allows you to create and run Transact-SQL statements interactively. Transact-SQL is the dialect of Structured Query Language that's used in SQL Server.

That, too, is covered in detail later in the book. Here are some of the other features available in Query Analyzer:

- The ability to use multiple connections with different security and database contexts for testing and debugging.
- User-configurable color-coding of Transact-SQL syntax, much like the Visual Basic Editor.
- An Object Browser and Search object to make it easy to find objects and explore their structure.
- Template files that include the basic Transact-SQL statements needed to create objects and perform programming tasks.
- The Transact-SQL Debugger, which allows you to step through stored procedure code, much like in the Visual Basic Editor. (Transact-SQL goes beyond the syntax available in Access SQL and incorporates procedural programming capabilities such as flow control, conditional processing, viewing variable values, and error handling.)
- A graphical diagram of the showplan information for the execution of Transact-SQL queries, which allows you to troubleshoot poorly performing queries.
- The Index Tuning Wizard, which analyzes Transact-SQL statements and their underlying tables to determine whether adding additional indexes will improve performance.

The Query Analyzer is shown in Figure 2.4, with the Object Browser loaded. You can navigate the functionality from the menus or by right-clicking in the Object Browser. Note that the Object Browser has two tabs: The right tab (not shown) allows you to load templates that simplify the process of writing complex Transact-SQL code. The left tab (shown) also helps you write code—right-click any object in the browser to see the menu for creating code. The SQL text shown in Figure 2.4 was created by right-dragging DATENAME and choosing Execute from the menu. You'll have different choices depending on whether you choose a database object (such as a table) or one of the common objects, such as the DATENAME function shown here.

You'll probably be spending a great deal of time in the Query Analyzer. Microsoft has put in a lot of development time making the user interface as friendly as possible, and it's now even better than it has been in past versions. If you are familiar with SQL Server 7 and new to SQL Server 2000, you're in for a treat, with the Object Browser, templates, and the Debugger standing by to help you create robust Transact-SQL code. The Query Analyzer is covered in

2

SQL SERVER
FUNDAMENTALS

more detail in Chapter 8, "Introduction to Transact SQL (T-SQL)," Chapter 9, "Creating and Optimizing Views," Chapter 10, "Programming Effective Stored Procedures," and Chapter 15, "Deployment, Tuning, and Maintenance."

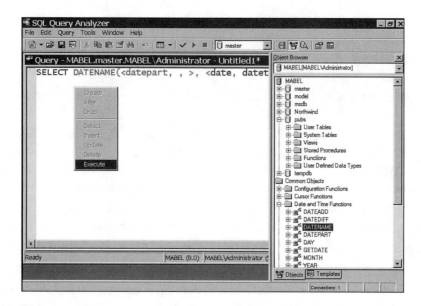

FIGURE 2.4
The Query Analyzer.

Performance Monitor

The Windows Performance Monitor is actually part of Windows NT or Windows 2000, but SQL Server ships with a set of counters that make it easy to monitor computer resources. A *counter* measures some resource on the computer, and the SQL Server counters allow you to track SQL Server–specific items, such as the following:

- SQL Server I/O
- SQL Server memory usage
- SQL Server user connections
- SQL Server locking
- Replication activity

You can launch the Performance Monitor from the Windows NT or Windows 2000 Start menu by choosing Programs, Administrative Tools and then clicking Performance Monitor (Windows NT) or just Performance (Windows 2000).

This launches a blank window—you need to add some counters to have something to monitor. Right-click the empty pane, and choose Add Counters. Figure 2.5 shows the Performance Monitor in Windows 2000 with the Add Counters dialog box loaded and the list of SQL Server counters displayed.

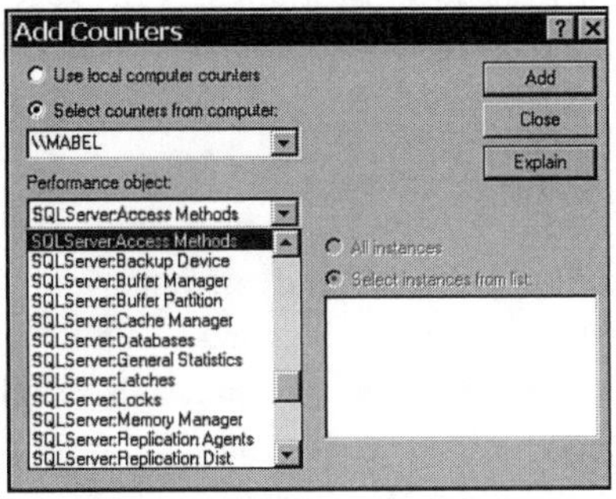

FIGURE 2.5

Adding SQL Server counters to the Performance Monitor in Windows 2000.

You probably won't want to load all the available counters. As you're browsing the list, clicking the Explain button will tell you what specifically each one does. Expect some performance overhead when monitoring SQL Server with the Performance Monitor, although the impact will vary according to the hardware platform, the number of counters, and the selected update interval.

The Performance Monitor is covered in more detail in Chapter 15.

You'll find that, although several tools are provided to help you check and improve the performance of SQL Server, excellent performance can be achieved simply by letting SQL Server tune itself. Once you have created a database with a good relational structure and adequate indexing, SQL Server 2000 does a lot to adjust its own settings based on experience. This is in stark contrast to older versions and current competing products, which require you to set lots of "knobs" to achieve optimum performance.

Data Transformation Services (DTS)

As shown in Chapter 1, "Converting Your Access Database to SQL Server," Data Transformation Services (DTS) is a champ at importing, exporting, and transforming data from many different data sources. It can also be used for transferring indexes, views, logins, stored procedures, triggers, rules, defaults, constraints, and user-defined data types, in addition to the data.

2

SQL SERVER
FUNDAMENTALS

DTS does a lot more than the Access Import/Export Wizard you may be familiar with. Going into DTS at the level of detail it deserves is beyond the scope of this book, but here are a few of the core concepts:

- A *DTS package* is an editable object that contains collections of connections, DTS tasks, DTS transformations, and workflow constraints. A package contains one or more steps that are executed when the package runs. Steps include connecting to a data source, copying data or objects, transforming data, and notification of processes or events. Packages can also be scheduled for execution.

- A *DTS task* is a unit of work that's executed as a single step in a package. Tasks define the item of work that's to be performed and encompass a wide variety of operations, including copying data or database objects, data transformations, and even the Send Mail task, which sends an email if a package step succeeds or fails. DTS includes the Execute Package task, which allows one package to run another as a package step, and the Message Queue task, which allows you to use Microsoft Message Queuing to send and receive messages between loosely coupled packages. DTS also allows you to create your own custom tasks.

- A *DTS transformation* operates on a piece of data before it arrives at its destination. You can change the attributes (size, data type, and so on), as well as manipulate the data itself, by extracting substrings, for example. You can also write ActiveX scripts to include conditional logic when transforming the data or to create your own COM objects and use them to manipulate column data.

- A *DTS package workflow* allows you to define the order of execution of the various tasks in the package. Using precedence constraints, you build conditional branches in a workflow, linking tasks based on whether the first task in the sequence executes successfully. Steps without constraints are executed immediately, and several steps can execute in parallel. Workflows can also be programmed with ActiveX scripts.

Once you've run the wizard to create a DTS package, you are able to edit the package in the DTS Package Designer. You can also create a package from scratch using the designer, but when you're first getting started, it's probably easier to use the Import/Export Wizard. Figure 2.6 shows a package for exporting data with the Transformations tab displayed.

Profiler

The SQL Server Profiler gives you a graphical user interface for capturing SQL Server events, which are then saved in a trace file. The trace file can be analyzed later or replayed to reproduce a problem in order to diagnose and fix it. The Profiler is useful for the following tasks:

- Examining queries to find the cause of slow-running queries or other problems.

- Capturing a series of Transact-SQL statements that cause a problem. A saved trace can be replayed on a test server, where the problem can be isolated and diagnosed.

- Monitoring the performance of SQL Server to tune workloads.

- Security auditing to record actions for later review.

- Examining locks to determine the cause of deadlocks or blocking.

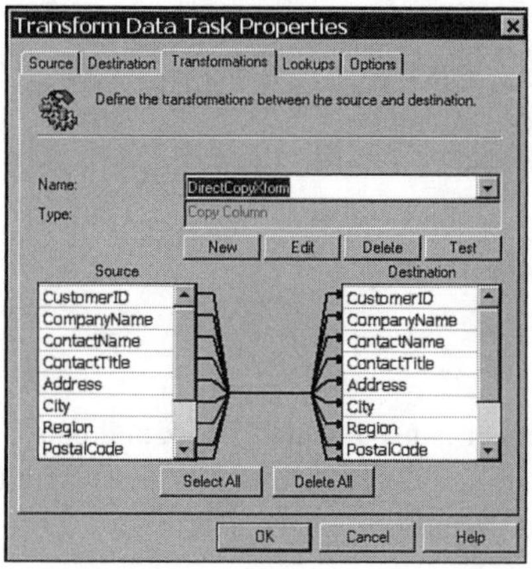

FIGURE 2.6
Editing a package in the DTS Package Designer.

The Profiler is a valuable tool for determining the resources used by your Access/SQL Server application as well as the exact SQL statements Access is sending to SQL Server. Have you ever wondered what exactly happens on the server when you update a row in an Access form? Profiler can show you.

To create a trace, choose Tools, SQL Server Profiler from the Enterprise Manager menu (or launch it from the Windows Start menu). You can then define a trace from scratch by choosing the columns and counters you want to display, as shown in Figure 2.7, in which a security audit trace is being created.

The Profiler ships with a group of templates to help you define your trace, or you can create your own template and open it. The Profiler is covered in more detail in Chapter 15.

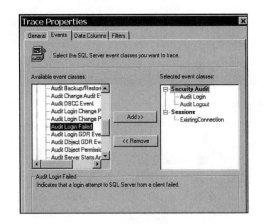

FIGURE 2.7

Creating a trace to perform a security audit.

Service Manager

The SQL Server Service Manager is used to start, stop, and pause the Microsoft SQL Server 2000 components on the server. You double-click it in the system tray on your taskbar (next to the clock) or launch it from the Windows Start menu. Figure 2.8 displays the Service Manager in its maximized form.

FIGURE 2.8

The SQL Server Service Manager.

Client Network Utility

You may never actually need to use the Client Network Utility. Users can specify the network name of the server on which SQL Server is running, and you really don't need to take any action to make that possible. The Client Network Utility is used to manage the client Net-Libraries and to define server alias names. It can also be used to set the default options used by DB-Library applications. Unless you are a C or C++ programmer, it is highly unlikely that you'll be writing a DB-Library application.

Here are other tasks you might perform using the Client Network Utility:

- Configuring a SQL Server installation to listen on an alternate network address
- Setting up an alias to use in place of the server network name in a connection request

Launch the Client Network Utility from the Windows Start menu. Figure 2.9 shows the Client Network Utility with the General tab selected.

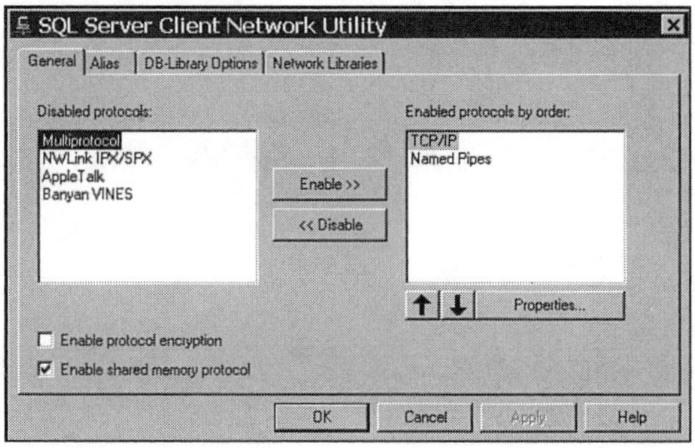

FIGURE 2.9
The Client Network Utility.

Server Network Utility

You would use the Server Network Utility to manage the server Net-Libraries. It is used to specify the network protocol stacks on which an instance of SQL Server listens for client requests, the sequence in which network libraries are considered when establishing connections from applications, and new network addresses on which SQL Server 2000 listens. Because these options are specified during SQL Server setup, it is unlikely you'll ever need to use the Server Network Utility. Figure 2.10 shows the General tab of the SQL Server Network Utility.

Books Online

Last, but not at all least, SQL Server Books Online may be the most important graphical component of all. It's your primary resource for information on SQL Server. Because SQL Server is such an enormous product, even the most experienced developers use this tool regularly, and fortunately the quality of this online documentation is excellent. Figure 2.11 shows Books Online with all the chapters displayed in the left pane in the Contents tab and jumps to Web links and other sources of information in the right pane. Expand the plus sign in the Contents pane to drill down to a selected topic.

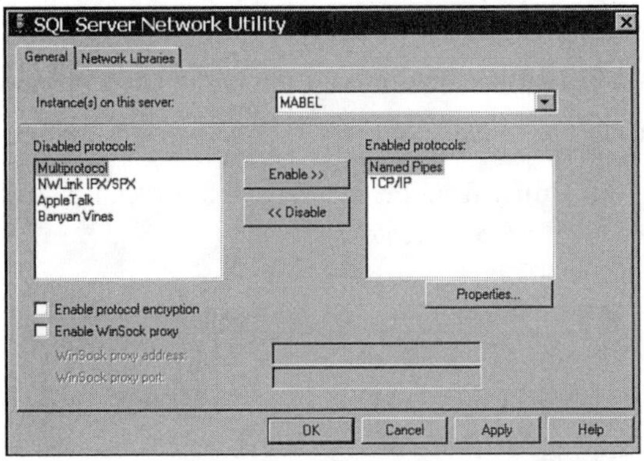

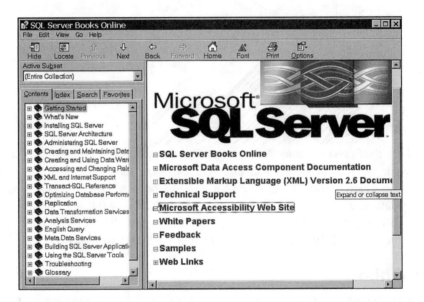

FIGURE 2.10
The Server Network Utility.

FIGURE 2.11
Books Online.

If you've used Help in any recent Microsoft products, you'll find Books Online very familiar. However, you may not recognize or understand some of the features. So, here's a quick tour that will save you time when you need to find information in a hurry.

The Active Subset

The Active Subset drop-down list in the upper-left corner allows you to drill down to a topic that interests you instead of browsing the full contents. When you select a topic, the entire table of contents reflects the change, as shown in Figure 2.12, where Analysis Services is selected. Only the items that have some relevance to the active subset are displayed. Clicking an item in the left pane loads it into the right pane.

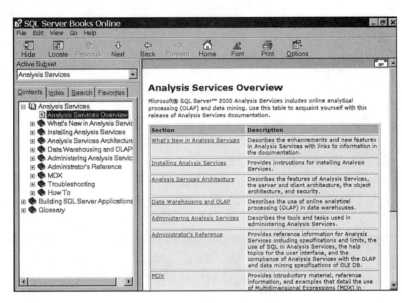

FIGURE 2.12
Selecting an active subset.

The Index Tab

The Index tab lets you search on keywords by typing in the first few letters of the item you're looking for. To load a selected item into the right pane, double-click it. Figure 2.13 shows loading the System Administrator (sa) Login topic from the Index tab. Note the icon in the upper-right corner for viewing related topics as well as the jumps at the bottom of the item for related topics. This helps you move quickly to items that may be of relevance.

The Search Tab

The Search tab lets you search for topics using keywords and wildcard characters. Figure 2.14 shows searching for the string "sp_add*" and looking in titles only. Selecting the Search Titles Only option is usually a good way to start a search because it returns a smaller result set. You can also use the Active Subset dialog box in a search to narrow down the number of items returned. Double-clicking loads the selected item into the right pane.

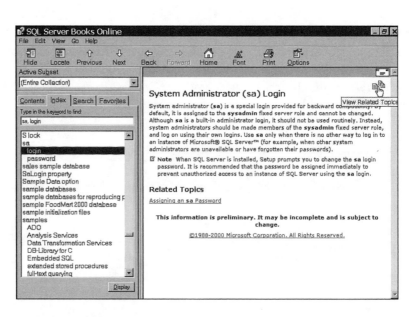

FIGURE 2.13

Finding an entry from the Index tab.

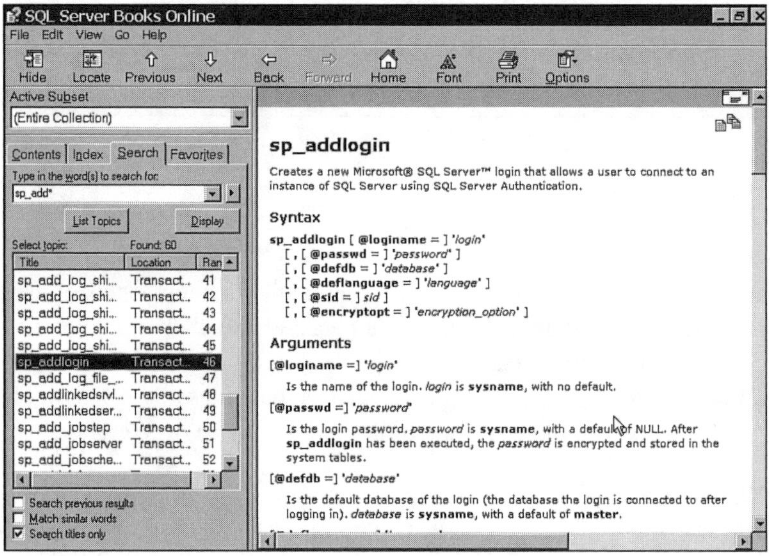

FIGURE 2.14

Using the Search tab.

The Favorites Tab

When you come across an item that you know you are going to need later, add it to your Favorites tab. Simply click the Add button on the bottom of the screen, as shown in Figure 2.15. The next time you click the Favorites tab, your topic will show up in the list, and you can load it by clicking the Display button. When you no longer need a topic, remove it by clicking the Remove button.

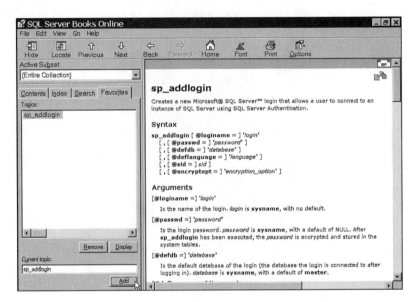

FIGURE 2.15

Adding a topic to the Favorites list.

When you load an item in the right pane by using the Index, Search, or Favorites tab and then click the Contents tab, you see the item highlighted in the table of contents. This helps you understand how the table of contents is structured. For other tips on using Books Online, see the Books Online topic *Using SQL Server Books Online*. The sooner you become familiar with Books Online, the sooner you'll become proficient with SQL Server.

The Server

The Enterprise Manager can be used to register servers and create SQL Server groups. SQL Server groups provide a way to organize servers if you're managing multiple installations from one central server. If not, you'll probably find the default SQL Server Group node sufficient. You can create additional server groups, which are meant to be a convenient way of organizing multiple servers. The default SQL Server Group node has your local SQL Server listed under it if you are managing only one server.

Registration Properties

If you right-click your SQL Server node and choose Edit Registration Properties from the menu, you'll see the dialog box shown in Figure 2.16. This allows you to change connection settings, such as whether to use NT authentication or SQL Server authentication. The options at the bottom of the dialog box allow you to determine whether to poll the SQL Server services and show their state in the console (Enterprise Manager itself is referred to as the *console*), whether to display system databases and system objects, and whether to start SQL Server automatically when connecting.

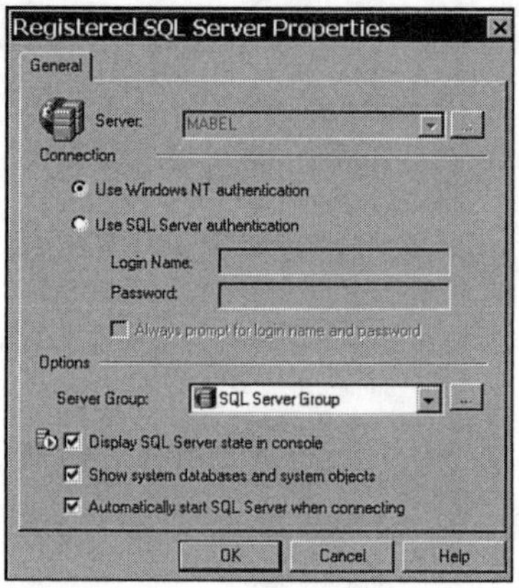

FIGURE 2.16
The Registered SQL Server Properties dialog box.

The other configurable server properties are located in the Server Properties dialog box.

Server Properties

To load the Server Properties dialog box, right-click your server node and choose Properties from the list. This will open the Server Properties dialog box with the General tab displayed, as shown in Figure 2.17. This shows you many properties that are not configurable, such as the operating system and number of available processors. Other options, such as the default server collation, are only configurable when SQL Server is installed. The Startup Parameters button at the bottom of the dialog box displays the Server Parameters dialog box, which lists the parameters currently being used with SQL Server. The Network Configuration dialog box loads the SQL Server Network Utility described earlier in this chapter.

FIGURE 2.17
The options on the General tab of the SQL Server Properties dialog box.

The following subsections cover the configurable options on the remaining tabs. Fortunately, you can be productive with SQL Server without needing to worry about these settings. SQL Server makes intelligent choices for you. However, reviewing them briefly will give you an idea of what's going on behind the scenes as well as where to go if you do want to take more direct control of your server.

Memory

The Memory dialog box allows you to configure SQL Server memory.

Here's a list of your options:

- *Use a fixed memory size.* This allows you to specify a fixed memory size for SQL Server instead of the default, which is to let SQL Server dynamically configure its own memory.

- *Reserve physical memory for SQL Server.* This reserves the amount of memory specified for SQL Server instead of swapping out SQL Server's pages when the server is idle.

- *Minimum query memory.* This specifies the minimum amount of memory allocated per user for query execution.

- *Configured values.* This allows you to change the values for the options on the Memory tab.

- *Running values.* This shows you the options that are currently running and can be used to see whether the configured values have taken effect. If you have changed any settings on this tab and the running values are not the same as the configured values, you need to restart the server for them to take effect.

For the most part, leave these settings alone unless you have a good reason to change them. SQL Server does an excellent job of managing its own memory.

Processor

The Processor tab has options that apply if you're using multiple processors. On a single-processor machine, many of these will have no meaning. Here are the options you'll find:

- *Maximum worker threads.* Allows you to specify the maximum worker threads available to SQL Server processes.

- *Boost SQL Server priority on Windows NT/2000.* Allows you to specify whether SQL Server can run at a higher priority than other processes running on the same computer. You should turn this option on only if you have a computer dedicated to SQL Server only.

- *Use Windows NT fibers.* Lets you specify that SQL Server uses fibers instead of threads. This means that SQL Server allocates one thread per CPU and one fiber per concurrent user, up to the maximum worker threads value. You need to restart the server for this to take effect.

- *Use all available processors.* Tells SQL Server that you want it to use all available processors when executing parallel queries.

- *Use n processors.* Lets you specify a finite number of processors to use when executing parallel queries.

- *Minimum query plan threshold for considering queries for parallel execution.* Specifies the threshold at which SQL Server will consider a query for a parallel execution plan. Queries are executed in parallel only when the estimated cost to execute a serial plan for the same query is higher than the value set for this option.

- *Configured values.* Works the same way here as it does in the Memory tab.

- *Running values.* Works the same way here as it does in the Memory tab. If you've made changes and the running values are not the same as the configured values, you need to restart the server.

Security

The Security tab allows you to set the following server-wide security options:

- *Authentication.* This option shows two choices: SQL Server and Windows NT/2000, and Windows NT/2000 only. In SQL Server 2000, the default is Windows NT/2000 only, which disallows SQL Server logins. This is a big change from previous versions of SQL Server, which automatically enabled SQL Server logins—most notably the sa login, which usually had no password and allowed anyone using it to log on as an administrator.

- *Audit level.* This option is set to None to disable auditing of logins by default. You can turn on auditing by choosing Success to audit successful login attempts, Failure for failed login attempts, or All to audit both successful and failed login attempts. The log records show up in the Windows NT/Windows 2000 application logs or the SQL Server error log, or both, depending on your logging configuration. You need to restart the server for auditing options to take effect.

- *Startup service account.* This option allows you to specify the system account and password that the SQL Server service account uses. Make sure that if you choose the This Account option, the password for the account is set to Never Expires in Windows NT/Windows 2000. The account must also be a member of the Windows NT/Windows 2000 Administrators group.

As these settings make clear, security in SQL Server, unlike Access security, is very tightly integrated with the security settings in Windows NT/2000. Security is covered in detail in Chapter 3, "Understanding SQL Server Security."

Connections

The Connections tab lets you set options to configure defaults for connections, as shown in Figure 2.18.

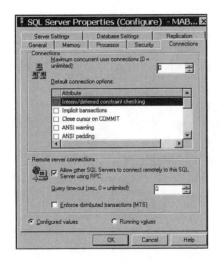

FIGURE 2.18

The Connections tab on the SQL Server Properties dialog box.

Here's a description of the various options:

- *Maximum concurrent user connections.* The default for this option is zero (0), which, paradoxically, means an unlimited number of users can connect. You'll find that a default value of zero means *unlimited* in other SQL Server options as well.

- *Default connection*. This options list shows the default options that will be applied to all connections for query processing for the selected server.

- *Allow other SQL Servers to connect remotely to this SQL Server using RPC*. This option allows other instances of SQL Server to connect remotely to the server.

- *Query time-out (sec)*. This option specifies the number of seconds before a remote query times out. The default is zero (0), unlimited.

- *Enforce distributed transactions (MTS)*. This option forces the server to use the Microsoft Distributed Transaction Coordinator (MS DTC) to coordinate distributed transactions. In Windows 2000, this service is actually part of COM+, but the older terminology remains in this dialog box. The COM+ transaction coordinator is discussed in Chapter 14, "Architecting Distributed *n*-Tier Applications."

- *Configured values*. This option works the same way here as it does in the other tabs.

- *Running values*. This option works the same way here as it does in the other tabs.

Server Settings

The Server Settings tab allows you to set these options:

- *Default language for user*. This option specifies the language used for server messages.

- *Allow modifications to be made directly to the system catalogs*. This option allows modifications to the system catalogs, or *system tables*. The default value is to disallow such modifications, and you should probably leave it that way. Inappropriate modifications to the system catalogs could easily cause your server to crash or become inoperable.

- *Allow triggers to be fired which fire other triggers (nested triggers)*. This option allows for nested triggers (triggers that fire other triggers). The default here is to disallow nested triggers. Because a trigger is an action that fires when data is modified, a trigger extends the duration of the transaction that it is firing in. Nested triggers extend those transactions even further and may cause unintended results in the data as well as impose a performance penalty. Avoiding nested triggers is generally a good idea, and this option makes that easy. Triggers are covered in Chapter 7, "Designing and Creating a SQL Server Database."

- *Use query governor to prevent queries exceeding specified cost*. This option is useful if you allow ad hoc querying of your databases. The query governor will prevent a query from executing if it exceeds the specified cost. This prevents the execution of expensive queries, such as `SELECT * FROM MyMillionRowTable`. But be careful—this could also prevent the execution of an expensive but necessary query (for example, the record source of a long, complex report).

- *SQL Mail Start session using profile*. This option lets you specify a valid MAPI profile name for the mail client. This feature allows you to automatically send email when certain server events occur.

- *When a two-digit year is entered, interpret as a year between.* This option lets you specify how SQL Server interprets dates when only two digits of the four-digit year are entered. The default spans 1950 to 2049 as the current century. For example, if 49 is entered for a year value, it will be entered as 2049. If 50 is entered, it will be entered as 1950.
- *Configured values.* This option works the same way here as it does in the other tabs.
- *Running values.* This option works the same way here as it does in the other tabs.

Database Settings

The Database Settings tab allows you to configure database-specific options, as shown in Figure 2.19.

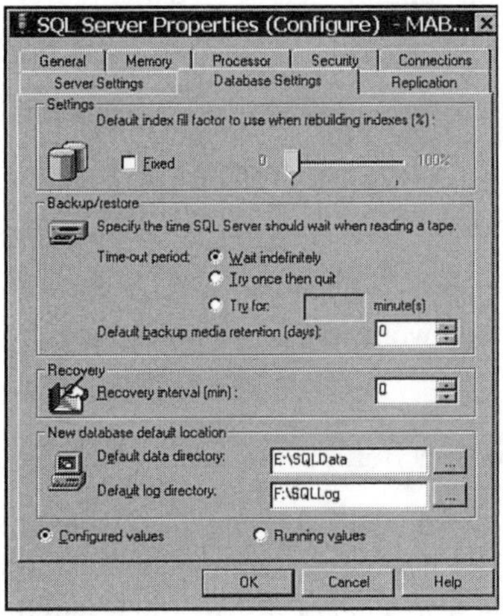

FIGURE 2.19

The Database Settings tab in the SQL Server Properties dialog box.

Here's a description of the options:

- *Default index fill factor to use when rebuilding indexes (%).* This option can be set to a fixed amount. The index fill factor determines how full each index page is when it creates a new index. This only applies to indexes created on tables where there is existing data. If you leave this option blank, SQL Server will select the optimal setting. SQL Server indexing is covered in Chapter 7.
- *Backup/restore time-out period.* This can be set to Wait Indefinitely, Try Once Then Quit, or Try for *n* Minutes.

- *Default backup media retention (days).* This option specifies the default length of time to retain each backup after the backup has been used for a database or a transaction log backup.

- *Recovery interval (Min).* This option is the maximum number of minutes per database that SQL Server needs in order to complete its recovery procedures. What this means is that each time an instance of SQL Server starts, it recovers each database, rolling back transactions that did not commit and rolling forward transactions that did commit but whose changes were not yet written to disk when the server stopped. The default is zero (0), which means that SQL Server will configure it automatically. You should probably leave it at zero unless you have a good reason to set an upper limit on the time it should take. Backups, recovery, and the transaction log are covered in Chapter 15.

- *Default data directory.* This option specifies a default directory where the data files are located when a new database is created. When you create a new database, you can alter this setting.

- *Default log directory.* This option specifies a default directory where the log files are located when a new database is created. When you create a new database, you can alter this setting.

- *Configured values.* This option works the same way here as it does in the other tabs.

- *Running values.* This option works the same way here as it does in the other tabs.

Replication

The Replication tab allows you to perform actions using the following buttons:

- *The Configure button.* Lets you configure publishing and distribution on the server by launching the Configure Publishing and Distribution Wizard. If you already have your server configured as a publisher and/or distributor, it will display the Publisher and Distributor Properties dialog box.

- *The Disable button.* Launches the Disable Publishing and Distribution Wizard if you have configured your server as a publisher/distributor. Chapter 15 briefly discusses the basic concepts of replication in SQL Server 2000.

The System Databases

The first node under the Server node is the Databases node. The Databases node contains all the user databases as well as the system databases. SQL Server also installs with two sample databases:

- *The pubs database*. This is a sample database based on publishing. It contains authors, titles, stores, and various other tables relating to publishing. It's used for much of the sample code found in Books Online.

- *The Northwind database*. This is the SQL Server version of the Northwind database found in Access. Its basic structure and much of the sample data should be familiar to all Access users (has any Access developer *not* heard of Nancy Davolio?). It's also used for the sample code found in Books Online.

However, the really important databases you'll find here before adding any of your own are the system databases—master, tempdb, model, and msdb. They are crucial to the operation of SQL Server itself. The physical data files for each of the system databases are installed in the `Program Files\Microsoft SQL Server\Mssql\Data` folder. You should not delete or move these files; otherwise, you'll probably have to reinstall SQL Server.

Here's a brief overview of how each of the system databases is used by SQL Server.

master

The master database records all the system-level information, including login accounts and all system configuration settings. Information about each database created in SQL Server is recorded in the master database, along with the location of the data files associated with that database. Because master records the initialization information for SQL Server itself, it is very important that you always have a current backup of master on hand. If master is corrupted, lost, or damaged, you'll be unable to start the server.

If the worst should happen and you cannot restore a backup of master, you can run a rebuild master utility (`rebuildm`) to rebuild the master database. However, in order to rebuild master successfully, you'll need to have one of two things:

- The scripts to rebuild the database objects and a backup to reload the data.

- The data and log files to use with the `sp_attach_db` stored procedure. `sp_attach_db` "attaches" a database by inserting entries into the systems tables in master, thus informing SQL Server that the database exists.

The master database also contains all the system stored procedures and extended stored procedures, which are discussed later in this chapter.

tempdb

The tempdb database is one system database you don't need to worry about backing up—it is automatically created when SQL Server starts and is destroyed when the server shuts down. tempdb holds all temporary tables and temporary stored procedures and fulfills the temporary storage needs of SQL Server itself, such as temporary work tables needed for complex queries, and so on. All users who can connect to SQL Server have access to tempdb—any temp tables or stored procedures created by a user's connection are automatically dropped when the user disconnects. Nothing is permanent in tempdb.

The default setting for tempdb is autogrow. Because the autogrow database option consumes some overhead, you can increase the size of tempdb by using a query containing ALTER DATABASE to increase its size or by changing the database options in the model database (discussed next).

model

The model database is the template for all databases created on a system, including tempdb. All objects in the model database are copied to the new database at the time it is created, including database properties. In other words, all new databases, including tempdb, are exact copies of model at the time they are first created. If you want any of your own tables, views, stored procedures, functions, user-defined data types, and database options to be automatically included in every database you create, place those objects in the model database.

Because tempdb is created every time SQL Server is started, the model database must always exist on a SQL Server system. If you have created custom objects in your model database and you cannot restore from a backup, you'll need to re-create all that information by hand.

msdb

The msdb database is used to store historical information about backups and restores, down to the details of who performed the backup, at what time, and to which devices or files. Backup events for all databases are recorded even if they were created with custom applications or third-party tools. This is, of course, very different from Access, where backups are performed at the operating system level and the Jet database engine knows nothing about them.

The msdb database is also used for scheduling alerts and jobs as well as for recording operators. If msdb is irretrievably lost, all the information it contained would need to be re-created by hand. Alerts, jobs, and backups are covered in Chapter 15.

distribution

You won't see the distribution database along with the other system databases unless you configure your server as a publisher or distributor for replication. The distribution database is used only to store data pertaining to replication, including transactions, snapshot jobs, synchronization status, and replication history information. A server configured to participate either as a remote distribution server or as a combined publisher/distributor has a distribution database. Replication concepts are covered in Chapter 15.

Backing Up the System Databases

As you can see, backing up the master, model, msdb, and distribution databases (if you are using replication) is crucial to the security and integrity of your SQL Server. Things aren't as simple as they were in Access, where all you had to worry about was your MDB file and your workgroup file (MDW). Be sure to get comfortable with the material in Chapter 15 on backups and restores before you go too far with SQL Server.

System Stored Procedures

The system stored procedures stored in the master database are used for administrative and informational tasks. If you were wondering how the Enterprise Manager performs its work, look no further—the system stored procedures are what's under the hood (as well as some direct Transact-SQL code). The Enterprise Manager itself is simply a graphical user interface that calls the system stored procedures to get its work done. Understanding the system stored procedures, or at least becoming familiar with them, can take a lot of the mystery out what's going on behind the scenes when you're working with SQL Server. The Transact-SQL code in the system stored procedures is exposed and fully documented—you can examine any of it by expanding the master database node and then expanding the Stored Procedures node and double-clicking the stored procedure of your choice. Many of these stored procedures, such as the sp_catalogs stored procedure shown in Figure 2.20, are called by other stored procedures or by other applications, and you won't have much need to call them directly yourself.

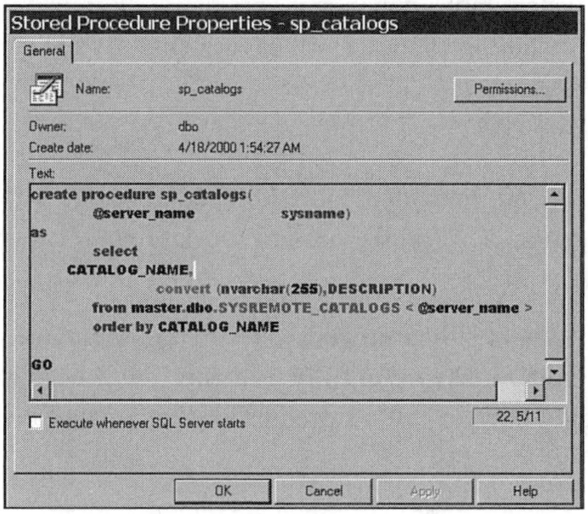

FIGURE 2.20
The sp_catalogs *stored procedure.*

There are many useful system stored procedures you can call at any time, such as the sp_helptext stored procedure, which will print out the text of a rule, a default, or an unencrypted stored procedure, trigger, or view. For example, executing sp_helptext 'sp_catalogs' in the Query Analyzer gives the following results:

```
Text
- - - - - - - - - - - - - - - - - - - - - - - - - - - - - - - - - - - - - - - - - - - - - -
create procedure sp_catalogs(
    @server_name sysname)
as
    select
        CATALOG_NAME,
        convert (nvarchar(255),DESCRIPTION)
    from master.dbo.SYSREMOTE_CATALOGS < @server_name >
    order by CATALOG_NAME
```

As you can see, the sp_catalogs stored procedure is meant to be a wrapper around the SYSREMOTE_CATALOGS system table, which holds information about linked servers. Linked servers are explained in Chapter 8. Many of the system stored procedures are there so that you don't have to query the system tables directly to find out information about your SQL Server or your database objects. Others let you work more directly with SQL Server objects. As in Access, queries you write that work directly with the system tables are not guaranteed to work in future versions because the makeup of those tables could changes. The system stored procedures, however, will be revised to work correctly with each version of SQL Server, and any obsolete ones will be fully documented. The system tables could change in myriad, undocumented ways, leaving a system table–dependent application high and dry when it comes to upgrading. Many of the remaining chapters will cover using system stored procedures to perform tasks or to get information.

The sp_ Prefix

You may be wondering why all the system stored procedures start with the sp_ prefix. This isn't just a naming convention. That prefix confers special features to any stored procedure with a name that uses it.

The sp_ prefix enables a system stored procedure located in the master database to be called from any other database without having to fully reference the procedure name or the database name. Normally, you would have to call a stored procedure located in another database with the following syntax:

```
EXEC [database name].[owner name].[stored procedure name]
```

The system stored procedures with an sp_ prefix located in master can be called from any database using this syntax:

```
EXEC [stored procedure name]
```

The other reason that the sp_ prefix is special is that any systems tables referenced in the system stored procedure will refer to the tables in the database from which the system stored procedure was called, not the tables in the master database, which would be the case without the sp_ prefix. Many of the system stored procedures are designed to return information about the current database, not the master database that contains them, which has different systems tables from the user databases. Of course, if the system table being referenced by a particular stored procedure belongs to the master database, that's the one that will be used.

If you want to write your own system stored procedures and have them work the same way the built-in system stored procedures work, simply use the sp_ prefix and place them in the master database. You can also modify the built-in system stored procedures. However, if you do so, you should copy the stored procedure you want to modify and save it under a new name, leaving the original alone. It's conceivable that you could break things both inside and outside of SQL Server by monkeying around with the built-in system stored procedures.

You are encouraged, however, to explore the system stored procedures fully. You can learn a lot about how SQL Server works and about how to write good stored procedures. The techniques used in the system stored procedures will come in handy when you write your own. Stored procedures are covered in Chapter 10.

Extended Stored Procedures

Unlike the system stored procedures, the extended stored procedures are not written in Transact-SQL. Instead, they are written in a programming language such as C or C++ using the Open Data Services API. Extended stored procedures are DLLs that are dynamically loaded by SQL Server and run directly in the address space of SQL Server itself.

You can't use Visual Basic to write an extended stored procedure, but if you're a C programmer, you can extend the functionality of SQL Server by writing your own extended stored procedures. You just have to make sure to add error and exception handling and to carefully debug and test your extended stored procedures because they have the potential to crash SQL Server if they fail (remember, they're running in SQL Server's address space).

Some extended stored procedures have the sp_ prefix, but most have an xp_ prefix and are located in the Extended Stored Procedures node in the master database. There are no special properties associated with the xp_ prefix, and you can't count on the name alone for determining whether a stored procedure is a regular system stored procedure or an extended stored procedure. If you double-click an extended stored procedure, you'll see the name of the extended stored procedure and the name of the DLL it calls, as shown in Figure 2.21. The xp_cmdshell extended stored procedure allows you to shell out to execute an operating system command from within a SQL Server query.

Management

The Management node contains child nodes for SQL Server Agent, Backup, Current Activity, Database Maintenance Plans, and SQL Server Logs. Here's an overview of these features.

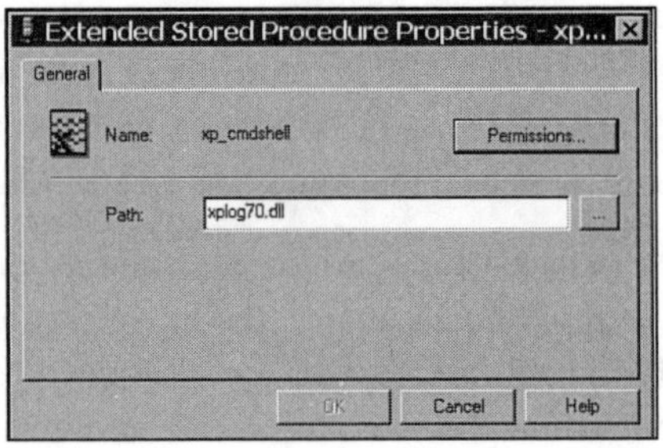

FIGURE 2.21
The definition of the xp_cmdshell *extended stored procedure.*

SQL Server Agent

The SQL Server Agent node shows three subnodes: Alerts, Operators, and Jobs. SQL Server Agent is responsible for running automated maintenance tasks in SQL Server—executing jobs, firing alerts, and notifying operators. SQL Server Agent must be started before any of these administrative tasks can run. This option is controlled in the SQL Server Service applet or by setting the Server Registration properties. If the agent is stopped, you can also start it manually by right-clicking the SQL Server Agent node and choosing Start.

You can create a new alert, operator, or job by right-clicking the node and choosing the New option. The appropriate dialog box will then be loaded.

Backup

The Backup node displays any backup devices you may have configured. If you right-click Backup, you'll see two options:

- *New Backup Device*. Backups can be made to a disk backup device, which is a named location on a disk, or to a tape backup device.
- *Back up a Database*. This launches a dialog box that lets you create a database backup. The backup can be placed on a backup device (if there is one), or you can specify a path and filename for the backup.

A more complete solution is to use a database maintenance plan, discussed later, to handle your backup needs.

Current Activity

The Current Activity node displays information about current activity in SQL Server. The activity being monitored includes the following:

- Current user connections and locks
- Process number, status, locks, and commands that active users are running
- Objects that are locked and the kinds of locks that are present

The icons and properties shown in this node are fully documented in Books Online under the topic "Monitoring with SQL Server Enterprise Manager."

The sp_who and sp_lock system stored procedures can also be used from the Query Analyzer to monitor server activity. Viewing current activity in the Current Activity node will not necessarily show you what is actually current—locks are measured in millionths of a second, so what you are seeing is not necessarily what is currently happening. Running traces via the SQL Server Profiler is probably a better choice for getting a comprehensive picture of activity and locking on your server.

Database Maintenance Plans

The Database Maintenance Plans node shows you all the database maintenance plans you have created. Database maintenance plans enormously simplify the day-to-day drudgery of maintaining and backing up your SQL Server databases. This is a long way from Access, where all you had to do was compact the database and run a simple backup.

Each database maintenance plan contains options for selecting the databases to be included, whether optimizations and data integrity checks are run, backup and log backup options, and reporting options. Figure 2.22 shows a database maintenance plan that includes the pubs and Northwind databases.

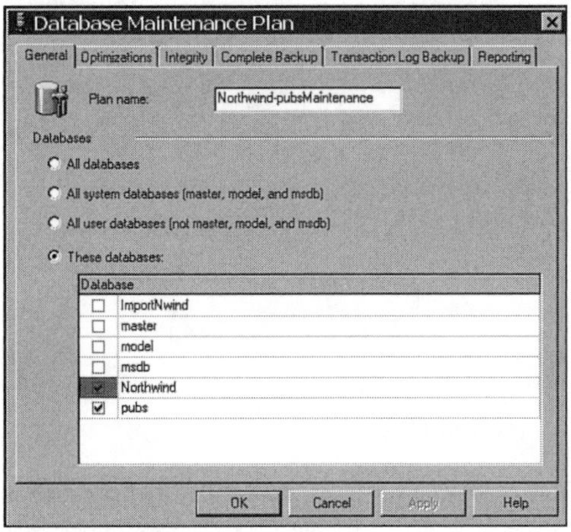

FIGURE 2.22
The Database Maintenance Plan dialog box.

The first time you create a plan, the Database Maintenance Plan Wizard runs, taking you through the options. Once the wizard is finished, the plan shows up in the Database Maintenance Plan folder, where you can modify it as needed.

Database maintenance plans are covered in more detail in Chapter 15.

SQL Server Logs

The SQL Server Logs node contains the SQL Server error log. Don't be mislead by the name—this log gives you information about processes that have run and whether they completed successfully. The error log itself is a text file that's located in `\Program Files\Microsoft SQL Server\MSSQL\LOG\Errorlog` (no filename extension), so it can be opened with Notepad or any text editor as well as the Enterprise Manager.

Each time an instance of SQL Server is started, a new error log is created. SQL Server retains backups of the previous six logs, with the most recent log having a filename extension of `.1`, the second most recent an extension of `.2`, and so on. Figure 2.23 shows the SQL Server error log.

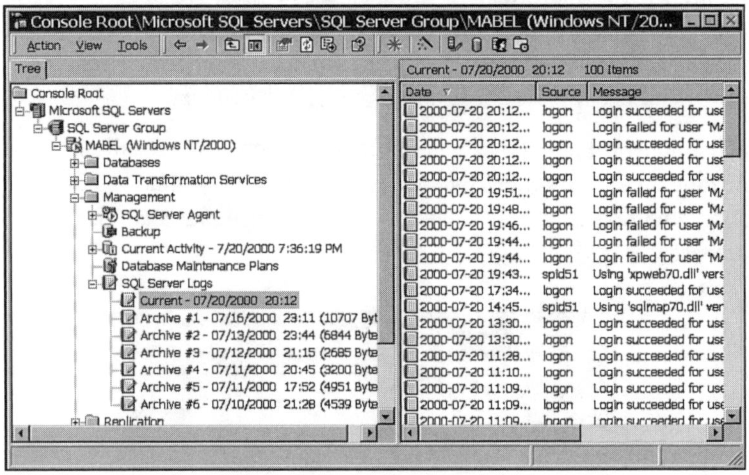

FIGURE 2.23
The SQL Server error log viewed from the Enterprise Manager.

Replication

The Replication node has two child nodes:

- *Publications*. A *publication* is a collection of one or more articles from one database. This grouping of multiple articles makes it easier to specify a logically related set of data and database objects that you want to replicate together.

- *Subscriptions*. A *subscription* is a request for a publication from another database or server. The subscription can be requested by the publisher (a push subscription) or by the subscriber (a pull subscription).

Unless you've implemented replication, these nodes will be empty. Replication is covered fully in SQL Books Online, and wizards are available to take you through every step in configuring and setting up replication.

Security

The Security node contains the child nodes Logins, Server Roles, Linked Servers, and Remote Servers.

Logins

A SQL Server login is saved in SQL Server, and a user logs in by supplying a name and password. A Windows NT (or Windows 2000) login is a preexisting login that's enabled for use in SQL Server. There is no additional login dialog box when an enabled user accesses SQL Server.

Security in SQL Server 2000 has two basic parts:

- *Authentication.* A user logs onto the server and is authenticated. The user can then perform any actions at the server level based on membership in fixed server roles (discussed next).

- *Permissions.* In order to work with a database, a user has to be granted permission to open the database and permission to work with the data or objects in the database. Only authentication and server roles are configurable at the server level; permissions are assigned at the database level.

Security is covered in detail in Chapter 3.

Server Roles

You can assign members to fixed server roles. Fixed server roles allow users to perform strictly defined server tasks without necessarily granting them broad-based powers to administer the entire server. The sysadmin fixed server role is the system administrator, and it has unlimited powers. The other fixed server roles are limited to performing specific tasks:

- *serveradmin.* Can set server-wide configuration options and shut down the server.

- *setupadmin.* Can manage linked servers and startup procedures.

- *securityadmin.* Can manage logins and CREATE DATABASE permissions as well as read error logs. This role cannot promote itself or others to sysadmin or set permissions inside individual databases.

- *processadmin.* Can manage processes running in SQL Server.

- *dbcreator.* Can create, alter, and drop databases.

- *diskadmin.* Can manage disk files.

You can think of these roles as groups that users can be made members of. A user who is made a member of the role automatically inherits the capabilities granted to the role. There are also fixed database roles, which grant permissions for set tasks at the database level. However, unlike the security groups in Access, the built-in fixed roles cannot be modified or deleted.

Linked Servers

Linked servers let you use SQL Server as a gateway to other data sources for distributed querying. This provides the ability to create heterogeneous queries that combine data from any data store that has an OLE DB provider (including all ODBC data sources), such as Oracle, Access, and even a text file. OLE DB is covered in Chapter 6, "ActiveX Data Objects (ADO) Fundamentals," and the steps for setting up linked servers and creating distributed queries are covered in Chapter 8.

Remote Servers

A remote server configuration allows a client connected to one instance of SQL Server to execute a stored procedure on another instance of SQL Server without establishing another connection. A remote server must be a SQL Server.

Support Services

The Support Services node contains the child nodes Distributed Transaction Coordinator, Full-Text Search, and SQL Mail.

Distributed Transaction Coordinator

The Microsoft Distributed Transaction Coordinator (MS DTC) manages transactions that span data sources, allowing client applications to include several different data sources in one transaction by coordinating the transaction across all the involved servers. The MS DTC service coordinates the proper completion of the distributed transaction to ensure that either all the updates on all the servers are made permanent or, in the case of errors, all rolled back.

Full-Text Search

Full-Text Search allows you to create full-text indexes for word searches in character string data. The full-text index stores word information for a given column, which is used to complete full-text queries that search for particular words or combinations of words. The full-text index is contained in a full-text catalog, and each database can have one or more full-text catalogs. These catalogs are managed by the Search service, not contained in the databases themselves. To create a full-text catalog, right-click the database and choose New, New Full-Text Catalog from the menu. Full-text searching is fully documented in SQL Books Online.

SQL Mail

SQL Mail allows SQL Server to send and receive email by establishing a client connection with a mail server. These messages can be generated by stored procedures, triggers, jobs, and alerts to provide status or warning messages. SQL Mail consists of a number of stored procedures, which are used by SQL Server to process email messages that are received in the designated SQL Mail account mailbox or to process email messages generated by the stored procedure xp_sendmail. SQL Mail requires a post office connection, a mail store (mailbox), a mail profile, and the Microsoft Windows NT 4.0 or Windows 2000 domain user account used to log into an instance of SQL Server. SQLAgentMail can be configured to send an email when an alert is triggered or when a scheduled task either succeeds or fails.

Meta Data Services

Meta Data Services provides storage service for SQL Server meta data (data about data) that's stored in a registered repository database, including meta data associated with specific Data Transformation Services (DTS) packages and all Online Analytical Processing (OLAP) meta data. Repository tables are included in the SQL Server msdb system database to support management and storage of SQL Server meta data. To run the browser, click Meta Data Services.

When you use the Meta Data Browser in SQL Server Enterprise Manager, you function in End User mode. End User mode provides read-only access to the repository database. You can view any meta data that you store in the repository.

SQL Server Enterprise Manager purposely restricts the functionality of the Meta Data Browser to protect the meta data. Modifying or deleting native meta data can corrupt your SQL Server installation. For this reason, actions that put your meta data at risk are not supported in this mode.

About Multiple Instances of SQL Server

SQL Server 2000 supports multiple instances of SQL Server running concurrently on the same machine. These instances can be SQL Server 2000 or a mixture of SQL Server versions. Each instance of the SQL Server database engine has its own completely separate set of system and user databases. Applications can connect to each SQL Server instance pretty much the same way they connect to different SQL Servers running on different computers.

The Default Instance

When you install multiple instances, only one default instance exists. The default instance is identified by the name of the computer, the same way it always has been. A client application connects to the default instance the same way it would if that SQL Server were the only instance running. The following configurations can operate as a default instance:

- SQL Server 2000
- SQL Server version 7.0
- SQL Server version 6.5 (with SQL Server 6.5 Service Pack 5)

- A default instance of SQL Server 2000 that can be version switched with an installation of SQL Server version 6.5 (SQL Server 6.5 Service Pack 5) using the SQL Server 2000 `vswitch` utility.

- An installation of SQL Server version 7.0 that can be version switched with an installation of SQL Server version 6.5 using the SQL Server version 7.0 `vswitch` utility.

Named Instances

Every other instance of SQL Server on the computer (or cluster) must be a named instance of SQL Server 2000. The name is specified during installation of that instance. When connecting to a named instance, an application must provide both the computer name and the instance name using this syntax:

`MyComputer\MyInstance`

You are not required to pick a default instance—you can run only named instances without a default instance if you choose.

Mixing SQL Server Versions with Instances

If you want to mix different SQL Server versions on a computer or a clustered group of computers, the default version must be the older version. In other words, only SQL Server 2000 can operate as a named instance. Also, because you only get one default, there can only be one instance of SQL Server 7.0 or 6.5.

What Each Instance Gets

Each instance gets its own database engine, supporting components, and system and user databases; however, you only get one set of client tools to service all instances. In other words, only one Enterprise Manager, Query Analyzer, Profiler, and so on.

The default instance keeps the names MSSQLServer and SQLServerAgent for the SQL Server and Agent services. For named instances, the service names are changed to MSSQL$*InstanceName* and SQLAgent$*InstanceName*, where *InstanceName* is the name of the instance. This allows them to be started and stopped independently of other instances on the same server, and it allows events, schedules, and notifications to be managed separately. You can start and stop each of the instances from a single copy of the SQL Server 2000 Service Manager. You can use a single copy of the Enterprise Manager to control objects in all instances on the computer or cluster, and you use a single copy of the SQL Server 2000 Server Network Manager to manage the network addresses for all the instances.

When multiple instances are installed, there's only one SQL Server 2000 program group (Microsoft SQL Server) on the computer or cluster, only one copy of each of the SQL Server 2000 utilities represented by the icons in the program group, and only one copy of Books Online.

If you run SQL Server version 6.5 as a default instance and run one or more named instances of SQL Server 2000, you need two SQL Server program groups. The SQL Server 2000 program group executes the SQL Server 2000 tools, and the SQL Server version 6.5 program group runs the SQL Server 6.5 tools.

If you are running SQL Server version 7.0 with SQL Server 2000, the icons in the SQL Server 7.0 program group will execute the SQL Server 2000 tools.

Benefits and Drawbacks of Multiple Instancing

You can have any number of named instances of SQL Server in addition to the default instance.

Here are some of the benefits of installing multiple instances:

- You can continue to run older versions and work with a current version on the same machine.
- You can support SQL Server in a fully clustered environment, where you can run multiple instances of SQL Server on the virtual server of a SQL Server failover cluster. When you install an instance of SQL Server 2000, you can specify up to four computers that make up the cluster for that instance. The cluster looks like a single computer to applications connecting to that instance of SQL Server. Clustering is described fully in "Failover Clustering Architecture" in SQL Books Online.
- You can maintain a separate independent SQL Server environment for development and testing on the same computer that holds your production server.
- You can roll out a secured SQL Server database in a sandboxed environment, where administrative rights are curtailed. In other words, you can structure security differently for each instance, with different administrators for each instance. Security is covered in Chapter 3.
- You can install software that comes bundled with the Desktop Edition of SQL Server (MSDE) on a machine that already has a server running.

The principal drawbacks are that administration becomes more complex, and multiple instances will consume more resources than a single installation. There is no free lunch.

The Database

A SQL Server database consists of a collection of tables, which store data, and other supporting objects that are organized into logical components. A database is physically implemented as two or more files on disk.

2

**SQL Server
Fundamentals**

Files and File Groups

When you create a new database, SQL Server creates a set of files to store all data and objects in that database. Database files cannot span databases—they contain objects from only a single database. Here are the files it creates:

- *Primary*. The primary file contains startup information as well as data. Every database has one primary data file, which can be defined to "autogrow" as needed. The filename extension for the primary data file is `.mdf`.

- *Secondary*. The secondary file holds additional data not in the primary file. A secondary file is optional and can also be defined to autogrow as needed. In SQL Server 2000, you can designate a secondary file group to be read-only. Secondary files are useful in situations where you have a very large database or you want to locate data on separate disk drives. You can have as many secondary files as you want. The filename extension for secondary data files is `.ndf`.

- *Transaction log*. The transaction log holds information used to recover the database. Each database must have at least one transaction log file, although the transaction log can be implemented across several files, which can be defined to autogrow as needed. This reduces the potential of running out of space in the transaction log while at the same time reduces administrative overhead. The filename extension for log files is `.ldf`.

Files, file groups, and data storage are covered more fully in Chapter 7.

The Transaction Log

The transaction log is one of the most important components of SQL Server and one of the most important differences between SQL Server and the Jet database engine. Jet couldn't possibly maintain a complete transaction log because the database engine can run simultaneously in many instances on multiple users' machines. Jet can check the state of the database for changes, but it really can't know all the steps that brought those changes about. SQL Server, of course, runs centrally and therefore can keep a unified, complete record of all changes to the data.

The transaction log guarantees the consistency and integrity of your data by using a write-ahead strategy. In other words, every transaction is recorded in the transaction log before it is written to the main data buffer and files. The log cache is managed separately from the buffer cache for data pages, resulting in simple, fast, and robust performance within the database engine. Here's what you get with the transaction log:

- The transaction log records all data modifications, preserving the atomicity of any transactions. In other words, if several actions need to succeed or fail together as a group, that fact is recorded in the transaction log.

- Whenever there is an error that might cause incomplete data to be committed to a table, the log records are used to roll back the modifications, thus keeping the data in a consistent state.

- In the event that SQL Server fails, a database could be left in a state where modifications were never written from the buffer cache to the data files. When SQL Server starts up again, it runs a recovery of each database, and modifications recorded in the log are rolled forward and committed to disk, whereas transactions that were incomplete are rolled back.

- Should you ever need to restore from a database backup, recovery is run to roll back any incomplete transactions. The transaction log can then be rolled forward to catch all completed transactions from the log backup. This allows you to restore a database up to any point in time. This doesn't only apply to failures on the server. If you discover, for example, that a new operator ran a payroll incorrectly, you could choose to roll the database back to the point before that operation began and start over. You would also have a record of all other activity that occurred while that bad payroll was running, but this would have to be reentered manually—rolling the transaction log backward or forward is an all-or-nothing deal that affects every transaction in the log.

Transactions are covered in more detail in Chapter 10, and using the transaction log is covered in Chapter 15.

Database Components

The following sections cover components that are specific to databases. Each database contains its own set of system tables, user tables, users, roles, and other database objects.

System Tables

Each SQL Server database contains system tables that store database-level system information for each database (see Figure 2.24). Because SQL Server depends on the integrity of the information in these system tables, you should not try to directly update the information in them.

Most of the information in the system tables that would be of use can be obtained through certain system stored procedures and special built-in queries called *information schema views*. You could build your own views to query data in the database system tables, but there's no guarantee that their organization won't change in future versions.

Tables

Tables contain a collection of rows (records) and columns (fields). Tables have several mechanisms for controlling the data that is entered into them—data types, constraints, rules, triggers, and defaults. Tables can also have indexes, which allow rows to be located quickly. Multiple tables can have declarative referential integrity (DRI) constraints added to ensure that related data in different tables remains consistent. For example, DRI might ensure that no products can be entered on orders without a related product record existing. Designing and creating tables is covered in Chapter 7, "Designing and Creating a SQL Server Database."

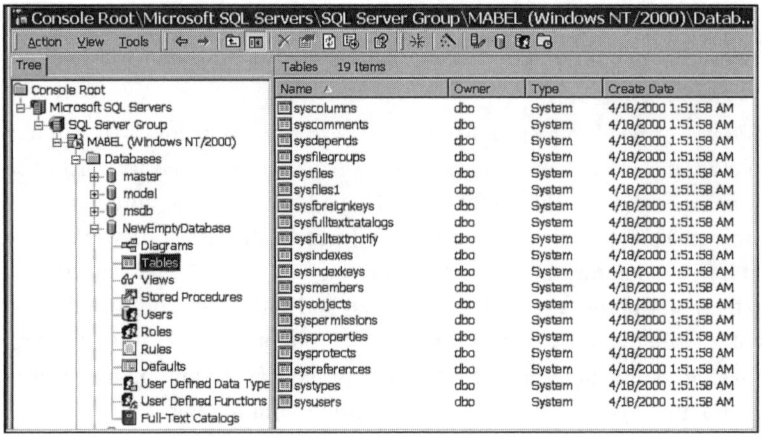

FIGURE 2.24
The systems tables in an otherwise empty database.

Indexes

Indexes on tables work much the same way an index in a book works—you look up a value in the index and go to that page. SQL Server 2000 also supports creating indexes on views. The two types of indexes are nonclustered and clustered. A table can have only one clustered index, and it reflects the actual order the data is stored in. You can think of a nonclustered index as analogous to a book index and a clustered index as analogous to the page numbers in the book. Indexes are covered in Chapter 7 and Chapter 9.

Triggers

Triggers can be defined in tables to fire on an INSERT, UPDATE, or DELETE statement. You can think of a trigger as an event procedure for data. In Access, events only happen on forms or reports, but in SQL Server, events can happen on data whenever it is modified. There is no such thing as a SELECT trigger because SELECT statements don't modify data. Here are the two types of triggers:

- INSTEAD OF triggers are executed instead of the usual triggering action (the triggering action is the INSERT, UPDATE, or DELETE statement). INSTEAD OF triggers, which are new in SQL Server 2000, can also be defined on views, where they can extend the types of updates a view can support.

- AFTER triggers are executed after any declarative referential actions that may be defined for a table, and they can be specified only on tables—views are not allowed for AFTER triggers. Specifying AFTER is the same as specifying FOR, which was the only option available in earlier versions of SQL Server. This means that any triggers that were defined in earlier versions of SQL Server are considered to be AFTER triggers. SQL Server 2000 allows you to specify which AFTER triggers you want executed as the first and last AFTER triggers for a table. You have no control over the order of the ones in the middle.

Triggers are covered in Chapter 7.

Constraints

A constraint in SQL Server is similar to a validation rule in Access. For example, suppose you want to limit the discount given to a customer. You can create a constraint that says a valid discount is between 0 and 20 percent. Each table has its own set of constraints.

Constraints are covered in Chapter 7.

Rules

Rules are constraints that can be applied, or *bound*, to more than one table. Rules have a database-wide scope but cannot be applied across multiple databases.

Rules are covered in Chapter 7.

Defaults

You can create a default when you want a value to be supplied automatically when a new row is created. For example, the order date in the Orders table can be defined to have a default of today's date, which means the date is automatically supplied on a new order and takes effect unless another value is entered for that column.

Defaults are covered (you guessed it!) in Chapter 7.

Views

You can think of a view as a virtual table, or a saved SELECT statement. In this respect, it is very much like an Access SELECT query. The main difference is that views do not support parameters, whereas Access queries do. Views are useful for performing the following tasks:

- Restricting users to specific columns and rows in a table.
- Joining columns from multiple tables so that they appear to be a single table. This keeps users from having to write complex queries.

- Aggregating data to produce summaries instead of providing detail data to be aggregated on the client. This speeds up reporting.

Although views don't usually cause any extra data to be saved, SQL Server 2000 introduces a feature called *indexed views* (also called *materialized views*), which enhances performance by persisting and indexing the results of a view. These indexes are automatically maintained when changes are made to the underlying tables.

Views are covered in Chapter 9.

Stored Procedures

Stored procedures are a cross between queries and programming code that are written in Transact-SQL. In addition to parameters, which are available in Access queries, stored procedures can contain complex logic and can return more than one result set.

Stored procedures also improve performance because they are compiled and cached in memory on the server after first being executed. For developers moving from Access to SQL Server, writing stored procedures is probably the single most important new skill to develop.

Transact-SQL is covered in Chapter 8, and stored procedures are covered in Chapter 10.

User-Defined Functions

User-defined functions are new in SQL Server 2000. They combine many of the benefits of both views and stored procedures.

User-defined functions can have input parameters, and they can return a single, scalar value, such as a number or text. They can also, however, return a set of rows of data, referred to as a *table*, which makes them much like views with parameters. User-defined functions can be used in any Transact-SQL expression and in any clause of a SELECT statement.

User-defined functions are covered in Chapter 9 and in Chapter 12, "Building Access Reports from SQL Server Data."

User-Defined Data Types

User-defined data types allow you to extend the core data types that are part of SQL Server by adding your own custom limitations to a base type. You can specify the length, nullability, rules, and default value of a base type to create your own user-defined type. For example, you could define a data type named *StateCode* as character data with a length of two characters, and this type would then show up on the standard list of data types anytime you add a new field to a table.

User-defined data types are covered in Chapter 7.

Collations

A *collation* represents the physical storage of character strings and specifies the rules by which characters are sorted and compared. In earlier versions, this was set once, when SQL Server was installed. At that time, you selected a language, code page, and sort order, and only one collation for each instance of SQL Server was supported. It was a big hassle to change the collation once SQL Server was installed. In SQL Server 2000, columns in a table can have different collations. For example, you could have an English-based column and a Kanji-based column, each with their own sorting and comparison rules.

Collations in SQL Server 2000 allow you, for example, to support multinational Internet applications, where many client computers are running on different languages.

Collations are fully documented in SQL Books Online under the "Collations" topic.

Extended Properties

Extended properties are new in SQL Server 2000, but as an Access developer, you are probably already familiar with them. In Access tables, extended properties are used to allow you to specify things like formatting of fields, input masks, and datasheet formatting. One of the reasons the SQL Server team added extended properties in SQL Server 2000 is to allow future versions of Access to continue to support the properties that Access users have come to rely on, when working with SQL Server rather than Jet.

Extended properties can be used to store additional information about database objects. The property is stored in the database and can be read by all applications accessing the database.

Each extended property has a user-defined name and value. The value of an extended property is a sql_variant value (a new data type in SQL Server 2000) that can contain up to 7,500 bytes of data. Individual database objects can have multiple extended properties.

Several stored procedures and a system function are available for working with extended properties:

- `sp_addextendedproperty` adds a new extended property to a database object.
- `sp_updateextendedproperty` updates the value of an existing extended property.
- `sp_dropextendedproperty` drops an existing extended property.
- `fn_listextendedproperty` retrieves the value of an existing extended property.

Extended properties are covered in the SQL Books Online topics "Property Management" and "Using Extended Properties on Database Objects."

2

SQL SERVER FUNDAMENTALS

What's New in SQL Server 2000

Throughout this chapter, and in other parts of the book, the various features and capabilities new in SQL Server 2000 are noted. Here, gathered in one place, is a summary of most of these new features:

- *Multiple instances of SQL Server*. A single computer can now host multiple instances of the relational database engine. Each computer can run one instance of the relational database engine from SQL Server version 6.5 or 7.0, along with one or more instances of the database engine from SQL Server 2000. Each instance has its own set of system and user databases. Applications connect to each instance the same way they connect to different instances running on different computers, with a new naming convention (server\instance) to specify nondefault instances.

- *Cascading referential integrity constraints*. Access developers have been used to having cascading updates and deletes ever since Access 2.0. SQL Server 2000 finally has them too. Referential integrity is covered in Chapter 7.

- *User-defined functions*. Transact-SQL has been extended to allow you to create your own user-defined functions. A user-defined function can return a scalar (single) value or a table. User-defined functions are covered in Chapter 9 and in Chapter 12.

- *New data types*. The three new data types in SQL Server 2000 are bigint, an 8-byte integer (twice the storage of long integers), sql_variant, which allows storage of different data types, and the table data type, which allows applications to temporarily store results for later use. Data types are covered in Chapter 7.

- *Text in row data*. This is the ability to store small text, ntext, and image values (comparable to Jet memo and OLEObject data types) directly in the rows in the table instead of storing them separately as was always done in previous versions. This reduces not only the overall amount of space needed to store these values but also the amount of disk I/O needed to process them.

- *Collation enhancements*. Collations in SQL Server 2000 replace the old code pages and sort orders and can be based on Windows collations. In earlier versions of SQL Server, code pages and sort orders could only be specified at the server level and applied to all databases on the server—collations can now be specified at the database or column level.

- *Index enhancements*. Indexes can be created on computed columns. You can also specify the sort order for an index and whether the database engine should use parallel scanning and sorting during index creation. Indexes are covered in Chapter 7 and Chapter 9.

- *Indexed views.* In earlier versions of SQL Server, you could create indexes only on tables. Indexed views in SQL Server 2000 can improve performance for views performing complex aggregations and joins. Indexed views are covered in Chapter 9.

- `INSTEAD OF` *and* `AFTER` *triggers.* A trigger is executed on an action statement (for instance, `INSERT`, `UPDATE`, or `DELETE`). An `INSTEAD OF` trigger executes instead of the action statement. `AFTER` triggers fire after the action statement. SQL Server 2000 allows you to specify which `AFTER` trigger fires first and which one fires last. Triggers are covered in Chapter 7.

- *XML support.* SQL Server can return data as XML documents. XML can also be used to insert, delete, and update values in a SQL Server database. XML support is covered in Chapter 13.

- *Backup and restore enhancements.* SQL Server 2000 introduces support for recovery to specific points of work using named log marks in the transaction log and the ability to perform partial database restores. Overall, backup and restore options are easier to understand than in earlier versions. Backing up is covered in Chapter 15.

- *Kerberos and security delegation.* SQL Server 2000 uses Kerberos and delegation to support both integrated authentication as well as SQL Server logins in Windows 2000. Kerberos allows mutual authentication between the client and the server as well as the ability to pass the security credentials of a client between computers so that work on a remote server can proceed using the credentials of the impersonated client.

- *Federated SQL Server 2000 servers.* No, SQL Server hasn't formed its own government to take over the universe (yet). A group, or *federation*, of SQL Servers is designed to support the data storage of very large Web sites and enterprise systems by allowing enhancements such as distributed partitioned views and horizontal partitioning of tables across multiple servers. This allows you to scale out one database server to a group of database servers that cooperate to provide the same performance levels as a cluster of database servers. This scale-out, or *shared-nothing*, capability makes SQL Server competitive with any other product on the market when it comes to providing optimum performance for very large databases.

- *Failover clustering enhancements.* Failover cluster administration has been improved to simplify installation, configuration, and maintenance. Additional enhancements include the ability to fail over to or fail back from any node in a SQL Server 2000 cluster, the ability to add or remove a node from the cluster through SQL Server 2000 Setup, and the ability to reinstall or rebuild a cluster instance on any node in the cluster without affecting the other cluster node instances.

- *Net-Library enhancements*. The Net-Libraries have been rewritten to eliminate the need to administer Net-Library configurations on client computers, to support connections to multiple instances of SQL Server on the same computer, and to support Secure Sockets Layer encryption over all Net-Libraries.

- *Distributed query enhancements*. Distributed queries—queries that go against data sources outside of SQL Server—have been enhanced with new methods that OLE DB providers can use to report statistics and the level of SQL syntax supported. The distributed query optimizer can then use this information to reduce the amount of data that has to be sent from the OLE DB data source. SQL Server 2000 delegates more SQL operations to OLE DB data sources than earlier versions of SQL Server. Distributed queries also support the other functions introduced in SQL Server 2000, such as multiple instances, mixing columns with different collations in result sets, and the new bigint and sql_variant data types.

- *Scalability enhancements for utility operations*. Utility operations such as differential backups, parallel database consistency checking (DBCC), and parallel scanning now run much quicker. DBCC can also now take advantage of multiple processors.

SQL Server 2000 is an incremental upgrade to SQL Server 7.0, which was a major release that represented a complete rewrite of the product. In fact, originally this version was called *SQL Server 7.5*. Few dramatic new features have been added, but every area of the product has been significantly improved. This is definitely the best-ever version of SQL Server, and if your company or client hasn't yet upgraded, you won't go wrong advising them to do so.

Installing SQL Server

SQL Server 2000 is one of the easier products to install, but it still takes some planning and preparation, especially if you are upgrading from a previous version. If you are doing a clean install on a machine that has never had SQL Server installed on it, you probably won't need to do much preparation besides making sure you have plenty of disk space and that you meet the hardware and software requirements. However, if you are upgrading from an earlier version, you need to study the SQL Books Online topic "Backward Compatibility." A subset of Books Online dealing with installation issues is available on the SQL Server Setup CD—you don't have to install SQL Server first to gain access to it.

Before Installing SQL Server

The hardware and software requirements for installing SQL Server can be found in the SQL Books Online topic, "Hardware and Software Requirements for Installing SQL Server 2000." Table 2.1 shows the minimum hardware, memory, and disk space requirements. Bear in mind that the memory and hard disk space numbers are the minimum requirements, not the optimal numbers.

2

SQL SERVER
FUNDAMENTALS

TABLE 2.1   Hardware, Memory, and Disk Space Requirements for SQL Server 2000

Computer	Intel or compatible. Pentium 166MHz or higher, Pentium Pro, Pentium III, or the minimum processor required for your operating system, which varies for SQL Server editions.
Memory (RAM)	Enterprise Edition: 64MB minimum 64GB, 2GB
	Standard Edition: 32MB minimum
Hard disk space	SQL Server 2000: 180MB full install 170MB typical install 65MB minimum install 90MB client tools only Analysis Services: 50MB English Query: 12MB

Table 2.2 shows the operating system requirements for the various versions of SQL Server.

TABLE 2.2   Operating System Requirements for SQL Server 2000

SQL Server Edition	*Operating System*
Enterprise Edition	Microsoft Windows NT Server 4.0, Microsoft Windows NT Server Enterprise Edition 4.0, Windows 2000 Advanced Server, and Windows 2000 Data Center Server. Microsoft Windows 2000 Server is required for some SQL Server 2000 features.
Standard Edition	Microsoft Windows NT Server 4.0, Windows 2000 Server, Microsoft Windows NT Server Enterprise Edition, Windows 2000 Advanced Server, and Windows 2000 Data Center Server.
Personal Edition	Microsoft Windows 98, Windows NT Workstation 4.0, Windows 2000 Professional, Microsoft Windows NT Server 4.0, Windows 2000 Server, and Windows ME.
Developer Edition	Windows NT Workstation 4.0, Windows 2000 Professional, and all other Windows NT and Windows 2000 operating systems.
Client Tools Only (includes the option to select components)	Windows NT 4.0, Windows 2000 (all versions), and Windows 98.
Connectivity Only	Windows NT 4.0 or Windows 2000, Windows 98, and Windows 95.

The Internet software required is Microsoft Internet Explorer 5.0 or higher for all installations of Microsoft SQL Server 2000, except for the Connectivity Only option, which requires Microsoft Internet Explorer 4.01 with Service Pack 2. Internet Explorer is required for Microsoft Management Console (MMC) and HTML Help. A minimal install is sufficient, and Internet Explorer does not need to be your default browser.

If you are writing XML applications, the requirements are a little more extensive. The Internet Information Server (IIS) Virtual Directory Management for SQL Server utility can run on any edition of Microsoft Windows NT 4.0 or Microsoft Windows 2000.

Computers running Windows NT 4.0 require the following components:

- Microsoft Internet Information Server 4.0 or higher (or Peer Web Services 4.0 or higher on Windows NT Workstation 4.0)
- Microsoft Management Console 1.2 (installed by the Windows NT Option Pack and by SQL Server 2000 Setup)

For computers running Microsoft Windows 2000 Professional, the Administrative Tools pack (`Adminpak.msi`) must also be installed. This file is located in the System32 folder of the Windows 2000 Server editions.

Network Software Requirements

Microsoft Windows NT, Windows 2000, Windows 98, and Windows 95 have built-in network software. No other network software is required unless you are using Banyan VINES or AppleTalk ADSP.

Novell NetWare client support is provided by NWLink.

Supported Clients

Microsoft SQL Server 2000 supports the following clients: Windows NT Workstation, Windows 2000 Professional, Windows 98, Windows 95, Apple Macintosh, OS/2, and UNIX. UNIX requires ODBC client software from a third-party vendor.

Other Microsoft Product Issues

Both Access 2000 and Visual Studio 6.0 have issues with SQL Server 2000 mainly because both products were released well in advance of SQL Server 2000. Here are the particulars:

- *Access 2000*. Microsoft Access 2000 requires the installation of either Microsoft Office 2000 Service Release 1 or Access 2000 Service Release 1 to operate correctly with SQL Server 2000. And even then, there are problems with Access projects (ADPs). You can't create database diagrams, tables, or views. With SR1, you can alter database diagrams, table designs, and view designs, but you can't save any changes.

- *Visual Studio 6.0*. Same problems. Visual Studio 6.0 Service Pack 4 allows you to alter database diagrams, stored procedures, table designs, and view designs, but you cannot save them. A future Visual Studio service pack will allow a limited ability to save changes.

The workaround is to use the tools provided with SQL Server—the Enterprise Manager and the Query Analyzer—to create and modify your database objects.

Setting Up the System Accounts

SQL Server needs to have its own operating system accounts for the SQL Server service and the SQL Server Agent service. You can assign both services the same account. If you are installing on Windows 98/ME, you can skip this section. Windows 98/ME does not support Windows services; instead, SQL Server simulates the SQL Server and SQL Server Agent services, so no accounts are necessary.

The services can have either a local system account or a domain user account. The local system account does not require a password, does not have network access rights in Windows NT 4.0 and Windows 2000, and restricts your SQL Server installation from interacting with other servers. Because this is so limiting, a domain user account is generally used. Activities that can only be performed with a domain user account include the following:

- Remote procedure calls (RPCs)
- Replication
- Backing up to network drives
- Heterogeneous joins that involve remote data sources
- SQL Server Agent mail features and SQL Mail

Domain User Account Requirements

It's recommended that the domain user account you set up be a member of the Administrators group. If not, you need to ensure that the account has permissions to perform the following tasks:

- Access and change the SQL Server directory (`\Program Files\Microsoft SQL Server\Mssql`).
- Access and change the `.mdf`, `.ndf`, and `.ldf` database files.
- Log in as a service.
- Read and write Registry keys at and under `HKEY_LOCAL_MACHINE\Software\Microsoft\MSSQLServer`.
- Or, for any named instance read and write the following registry keys at and under: `HKEY_LOCAL_MACHINE\Software\Microsoft\Microsoft SQL Server`.

```
HKEY_LOCAL_MACHINE\System\CurrentControlset\Services\MSSQLServer.
```
Or, for any named instance:
```
HKEY_LOCAL_MACHINE\System\CurrentControlset\Services\MSSQL$Instancename.
HKEY_LOCAL_MACHINE\Software\Microsoft\Windows NT\CurrentVersion\Perflib.
```

Several servers running SQL Server can share the same user account. When you're setting up replication, it's recommended that a publisher and all its subscribers share the same SQL Server service account.

Running the Install—Before You Start

Installing SQL Server is quite simple if you're running the setup interactively. The option Browse Setup/Upgrade Help (in the first dialog box in the SQL Server Setup CD) loads the portion of SQL Server Books Online with all the relevant topics for installing and upgrading from previous versions of SQL Server. Here's the topic list:

- Overview
- Basic Installation Options
- Advanced Installation Options
- Working with Named and Multiple Instances of SQL Server 2000
- Working with Instances and Versions of SQL Server
- Failover Clustering
- How to Install Failover Clustering
- Collation Options for International Support
- After Installing or Upgrading to SQL Server 2000
- Upgrading to SQL Server 2000: Overview
- How to Install
- Related Topics
- Installing Analysis Services
- Microsoft SQL Server 2000 Copyright and Disclaimer
- Additional SQL Server Resources

You should be able to find any information you need prior to installing SQL Server from browsing this subset of Books Online. If you are upgrading from an earlier version of SQL Server, make sure to read the topic "Backward Compatibility." There are four levels of backward compatibility issues:

- Level 1: Handling Discontinued Functionality
- Level 2: Handling Major Changes to Behavior

- Level 3: Updating to Improve Earlier Functionality
- Level 4: Handling Minor Changes to Behavior

If you are upgrading from SQL Server 7.0, you don't have that much to worry about because SQL Server 7.0 and SQL Server 2000 are compatible in most ways. The Copy Database Wizard allows you to move a SQL Server 7.0 database to SQL Server 2000.

The real backward-compatibility issues come in when you upgrade from SQL Server 6.5 and you've made modifications to the systems catalogs to accommodate your application. The SQL Server Upgrade Wizard will assist you in moving your database from 6.5 to SQL Server 2000. Upgrading from earlier versions of SQL Server is not supported—you must upgrade any earlier versions to SQL Server 6.5 and then upgrade to SQL Server 2000.

Installing Database Components

When you select the Install SQL Server Components option when installing the SQL Server Personal Edition, the Install Components dialog box gives you three options:

- *Install Database Server.* This is the setup for SQL Server and must be run before installing any of the other options.
- *Install Analysis Services.* Analysis Services (formerly known as *OLAP Services*) is for online analytical processing and data warehousing.
- *Install English Query.* English Query is a tool for building applications that let users write queries in plain English instead of Transact-SQL.

When you select Install Database Server, the next dialog box is an informational screen that informs you that the Installation Wizard allows you to install a new instance of SQL Server or modify an existing instance. Click Next to continue with the installation.

Figure 2.25 shows the Computer Name dialog box where you can enter the name of the computer that SQL Server will be installed on. If you choose Local Computer, the correct name is filled in automatically. Click Next to continue.

The next dialog box, Installation Selection, lets you choose to create a new instance of SQL Server, upgrade, remove, or add components to an existing instance, or select Advanced options, as shown in Figure 2.26. Advanced options include support for cluster maintenance, unattended setup, and rebuilding the Registry.

The next few pages of the wizard prompt for user and company name and allow you to accept the license agreement and select the type of installation you want to perform.

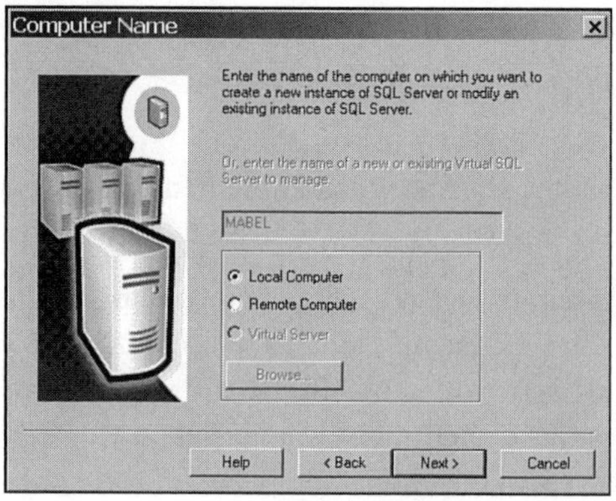

FIGURE 2.25

SQL Server can be installed on a local or remote computer.

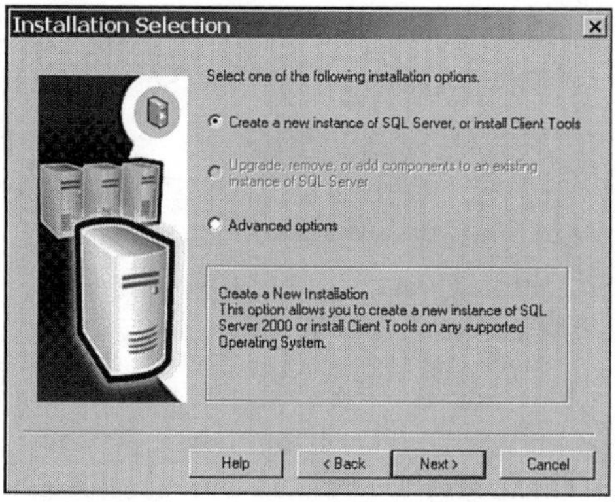

FIGURE 2.26

Selecting options for installation.

Installation Type Choices

Here are the three choices for Installation type:

- *Client Tools Only.* This option means that you will not install SQL Server itself. Use this option if you are connecting to a SQL Server on another machine. The client tools allow you to administer an existing SQL Server.

- *Server and Client Tools.* This is the default option. It will install both SQL Server and the client tools.

- *Connectivity Only.* This will install only the necessary Microsoft Data Access Components (MDACs) and network libraries needed to connect to SQL Server. Use this option for end users who do not need to administer the SQL Server.

Figure 2.27 shows the dialog box with the default Server and Client Tools option selected. Click Next when finished.

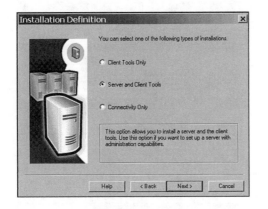

FIGURE 2.27
Choosing the installation type.

Selecting SQL Server Components

The SQL Server components are broken into several categories, as shown in Figure 2.28:

- Server Component
- Management Tool
- Client Connectivity
- Books Online
- Development Tool
- Code Samples

Choose the components and subcomponents you want to install. Options for a typical installation are selected by default. This dialog box allows you to reinstall components if you didn't install them the first time. However, you can't remove components by clearing the check boxes here—the only way to remove SQL Server components is to remove SQL Server entirely and reinstall without those components selected.

Instance Name

The wizard allows you to create either a default or a named instance, as shown in Figure 2.29. Remember that only SQL Server 2000 can function as a named instance, so if you want to run an instance of an earlier version of SQL Server, it must be the default instance. SQL Server 2000's new multi-instancing capabilities were discussed earlier in this chapter.

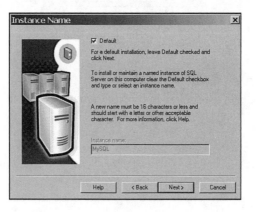

FIGURE 2.28
Selecting SQL Server components.

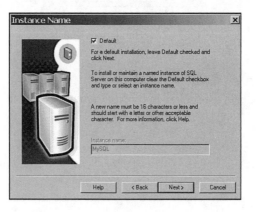

FIGURE 2.29
Installing SQL Server as the default instance.

Setup Type

The Setup Type dialog box lets you choose which options you want to install (see Figure 2.30). It also lets you specify different locations for the SQL Server system and the SQL Server data files.

Services Accounts

The dialog box for setting up the services accounts is shown in Figure 2.31. The local system account does not require a password, does not have network access rights in Windows NT 4.0, and may restrict your SQL Server installation from interacting with other servers. If you are running Windows 2000, the system account does allow network access. A domain user account uses Windows Authentication to set up and connect to SQL Server. By default, account information appears for the domain user account currently logged onto the computer. However, you can set up any domain account to use here, as long as it is a member of the NT Administrators group. You can configure separate accounts for SQL Server and SQL Server Agent, or you can use the same account.

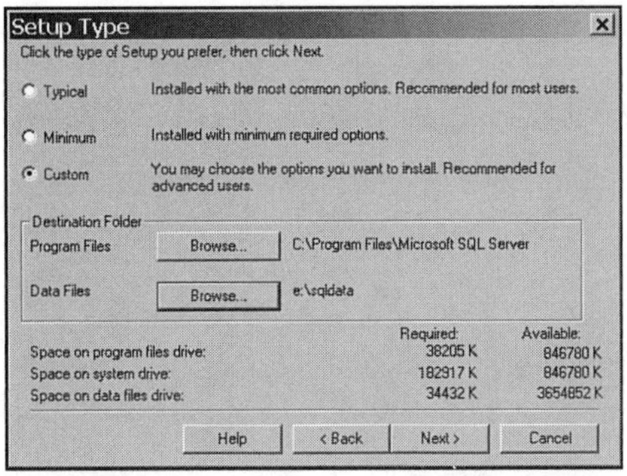

FIGURE 2.30
Choosing the setup type.

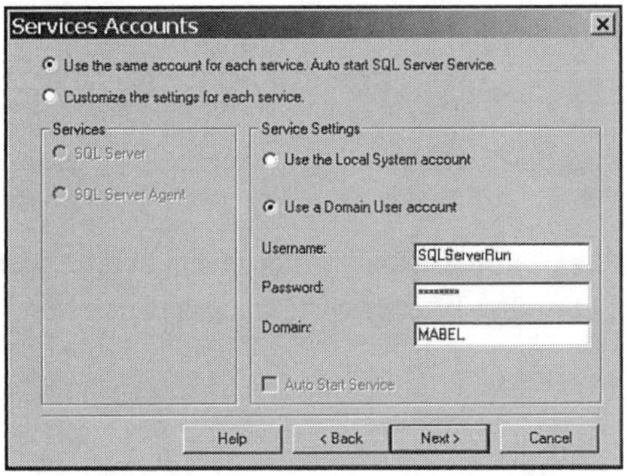

FIGURE 2.31
Setting up the services accounts.

Authentication Mode

SQL Server can authenticate users in Mixed Mode, which supports both SQL Server and Windows NT logins, or in Windows Authentication Mode, which validates a user through the operating system only, using trusted connections, as shown in Figure 2.32.

If you choose Mixed Mode, you can fill in a password for the sa (system administrator) user account. The sa account has complete and irrevocable permissions on every aspect of SQL Server and every SQL Server database located in that instance, so leaving this account with a blank password constitutes a considerable security hole. SQL Server authentication and security is discussed in Chapter 3.

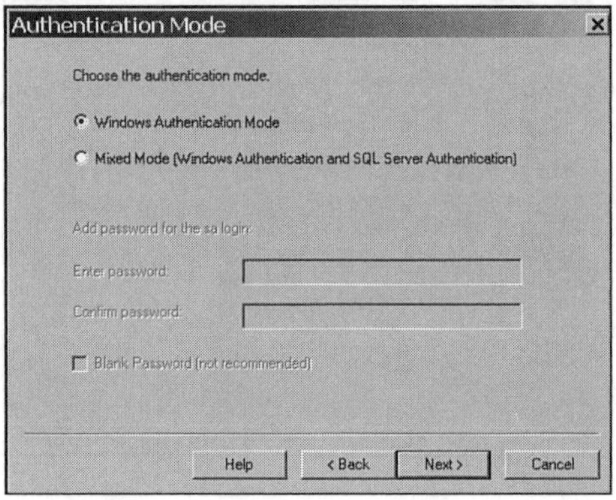

FIGURE 2.32
Choosing an authentication mode.

Licensing Mode

Here are the two choices for Licensing Mode:

- *Per Seat*. This option requires a CAL (Client Access License) for each device that will access SQL Server.
- *Processor License*. This option allows you to have a single license for each processor, which then allows any number of devices to access the server.

In the edit box, select the number of processors to license.

Collation Settings

The Collation Settings dialog box allows you to change the default setting to match the collation of another instance of SQL Server or the Windows locale of another computer.

Network Libraries

The Network Libraries dialog box allows you to select the network libraries to use when connecting to the server. The default is for SQL Server to listen on named pipes; however, you can also specify NWLink IPX/SPX, Apple Talk ADSP, or Banyan VINES.

Finishing Up

Once you've run through the options, click the Finish button, and SQL Server will be installed according to your selections. For such a powerful and versatile product, you'll find SQL Server's installation process to be quite quick and painless.

Summary

SQL Server 2000 comes in different editions from SQL Server 7.0, along with a new pricing and licensing model. The graphical components of SQL Server 2000 make it easy to learn and easy to use. The Enterprise Manager allows you to perform most of the tasks you will need, both for administering your SQL Server and for creating and modifying SQL Server database objects. Wizards are available to help get you started for just about any task you need to perform. The Query Analyzer has been enhanced in SQL Server 2000, with many features similar to those found in the Visual Basic Editor. The Performance Monitor is run from Windows NT or Windows 2000 and allows you to monitor server performance and security. Data Transformation Services (DTS) gives you the ability to import and export data and SQL Server database objects as well as to work with DTS packages using the DTS Designer in the Enterprise Manager. Other graphical tools—the Service Manager, Server Network Utility, and Client Network Utility—let you start and stop the SQL Server service and manage server and network connections. The SQL Server Profiler is a graphical tool for looking at SQL Server activity from the inside, and it's invaluable in tracking down performance bottlenecks, deadlocks, locking and blocking issues, as well as for discovering exactly how your Access application is interacting with SQL Server. SQL Books Online is where information about SQL Server is located, and it's the first place to look when a question or problem comes up. In the Enterprise Manager, the Server Registration and Server Properties dialog boxes let you configure most server options. The systems databases—master, msdb, tempdb, and model—store information that SQL Server itself uses. The system stored procedures in master are used by SQL Server, and along with Transact-SQL statements, they are what Enterprise Manager runs under the hood. Extended stored procedures are COM components that are called from inside SQL Server to extend the functionality of SQL Server. The management tools in SQL Server make it easy to create a database-maintenance plan for backing up and maintaining SQL Server, scheduling jobs, viewing error logs, and monitoring current activity. Logins, fixed server roles, linked servers, and remote servers can be configured from the Enterprise Manager. Support services include the Distributed Transaction Coordinator, Full-Text Search, and SQL Mail. SQL Server 2000 supports multiple instances, which allows you to have multiple SQL Server engines running on the same machine at the same time. Databases are stored in operating system files and can be configured across multiple files. All database components can be created and modified using the Enterprise Manager. Installing SQL Server is fairly straightforward—just make sure to read up on the Setup/Upgrade topic on the installation CD before you dive in. If you're upgrading from an earlier version, make sure you understand all the backward-compatibility issues that may apply to you.

Understanding SQL Server Security

IN THIS CHAPTER

Why Security Is Important

In most books about Microsoft Access, you'll find a section on security buried somewhere in the back of the book, if security is covered at all. In SQL Server, however, you really need to understand security before you go too far, unless you want everyone to have unrestricted access to all the databases on your server. You can easily provide that unrestricted access by using the sa system administrator login for everything, with no password assigned to sa. A recent study found that an alarming number of SQL Server databases that have been compromised by hackers over the Internet have done just that. Therefore, you should take the time to understand SQL Server security so that you can implement it properly from the moment you start building your database.

Access Security Versus SQL Server Security

Access user-level security is always present, even if you never make use of it. When you install Access, a workgroup information file named System.mdw is also installed. User, group, and password information is stored in that workgroup file, but Access makes it easy for you to ignore all that by silently logging in all users as the Admin user with no password. Securing an Access database involves taking about 10 nonobvious steps, but when you're done, you can create your own users and groups, assign various levels of permissions to them, and force users to log in before they can work with your database. However, at the end of the day even the most carefully secured Access database isn't really very secure. It is necessary to grant read, write, and delete permissions on the network share where the database and workgroup files reside, making Access databases vulnerable to being copied, hacked or stolen. Because Access does not support any kind of integrated security with the operating system, features such as password ageing, account lockout after invalid login attempts, and logging user activities are not supported. At its best, Access security is good for deterrence only.

On the other hand, SQL Server security can be very tightly integrated with NT/Windows 2000 security. It is not necessary to grant any permissions on the network shares containing SQL Server system or data files—all data access goes through SQL Server itself and users do not require direct access to the physical files.

The first step a user goes through when attempting to use a SQL Server database is authentication. After the user is authenticated, then access to databases on the SQL Server is determined by the permissions that are assigned to that user in a particular database. Authentication takes place at the server level, and permissions validation at the database level. In other words, you can allow a user to log on to SQL Server, but if you don't grant that user access or permissions to any databases, he or she won't get very far. Granting users access to databases and then assigning permissions inside of the databases allows them to interact with database objects in ways that you determine. Permissions can be directly assigned to users, to Windows

NT/Windows 2000 users and groups, or inherited through database roles, which are analogous to groups in both Windows NT/Windows 2000 and Access security.

Perhaps the most significant (and most welcome) difference between Access and SQL Server security is that if you are using Windows NT or Windows 2000, you can use integrated security. The same users and groups that were defined for your Windows NT/2000 network operating system can be automatically enabled to work in SQL Server without having to log on a second time. Although Windows 2000 added a few interesting new security features that weren't in NT, the basics haven't changed much as far as SQL Server is concerned. In this chapter, when integrated security is discussed, you can assume that the comments apply equally to Windows 2000 and Windows NT.

SQL Server logins are separate from the security accounts in the operating system, and to use them users have to log on once to the operating system and then again to SQL Server. Using integrated security, however, Windows NT/Windows 2000 accounts can be enabled so that users don't have to log on twice, and permissions can be assigned directly to Windows NT/Windows 2000 groups and users. In addition, Windows NT and Windows 2000 have auditing features that track user activity.

The major drawback of Access security is that it is file based. All Access workgroup files and databases are quite exposed because read, write, and delete permissions must be granted to all users for the network file shares where the Access files are stored if you want your users to be able to update the data. These files can, therefore, easily be copied, deleted, or hacked. Regular backups are your only defense against lost data, and there really is no defense against exposing your Access data to a determined and skilled hacker. SQL Server does not have those vulnerabilities. Its files can be protected on the server or on shared resources to which users have no direct access.

Letting Users In

There are two basic phases a user goes through when attempting to work with SQL Server data: authentication and permissions validation. Authentication involves logging on to the server itself, while permissions validation determines the allowed scope of a user's activities inside a particular database.

Authentication Basics

SQL Server supports two modes of user authentication:

- *SQL Server and Windows (mixed).* Both SQL Server and Windows NT/Windows 2000 logins are supported.
- *Windows Only.* Only Windows NT/Windows 2000 logins are allowed.

When you select SQL Server and Windows authentication mode on the Security tab of the server properties dialog box in the Enterprise Manager, as shown in Figure 3.1, users can employ either a SQL Server login or a Windows NT/Windows 2000 login to access the server.

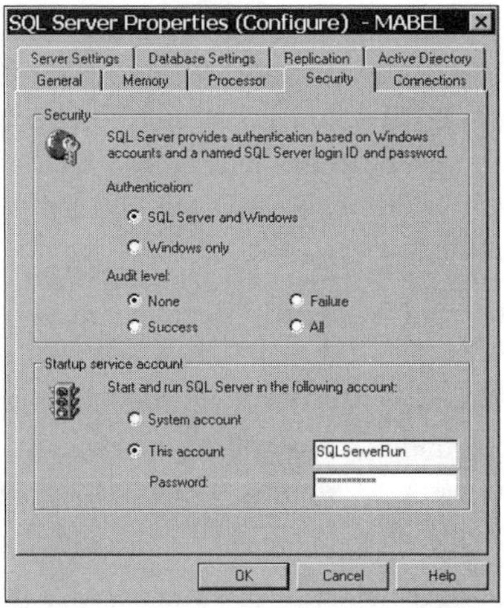

FIGURE 3.1

The Security tab on the Server Properties dialog box determines whether your server operates in mixed mode, allowing both SQL Server and Windows NT/Windows 2000 logins, or requires Windows NT/Windows 2000 logins only.

Windows NT/Windows 2000 logins can be defined for both Windows NT/Windows 2000 users and groups. For example, you can create a custom Developers group in Windows, enable a SQL Server login for that group, and not have to worry about enabling separate logins for all members of the Developers group. Windows NT/Windows 2000 user or group logins will not be prompted for a password when connecting to SQL Server.

SQL Server logins are not part of Windows NT/Windows 2000—they are saved in SQL Server itself. A user connecting to SQL Server using a SQL Server login will be prompted for a login name and password. If you select the Windows Only mode of authentication, then all SQL Server logins will be disabled and users will only be able to connect using their Windows NT/Windows 2000 logins. Mixed mode is much more flexible and it supports users on Windows 9x computers, but it is also less secure, because the logins and passwords are saved in the systems tables in SQL Server. If you configure your SQL Server to support SQL Server logins, then there is one built-in SQL Server login that you need to watch out for: the sa login.

The sa Login

The sa, or system administrator, is a SQL Server account that has unlimited powers if you install SQL Server in mixed mode. It cannot be modified or deleted. If you choose to allow both Windows and SQL Server logins, then the sa account is active. Anyone possessing the password for the sa login can perform all actions in all databases located on that SQL Server. In earlier versions of SQL Server, the sa login defaulted to having a blank password. You will be prompted to set a password for the sa login when installing SQL Server 2000 if you elect mixed mode authentication. Because the sa account is all-powerful, leaving it with a blank password constitutes a considerable security hole.

Logins and Permissions

Simply having a SQL Server login doesn't get a user very far unless he has permissions granted to him in individual databases. Permissions determine the scope of a user's activities within the database in which they are granted.

The two stages users pass through when working with SQL Server are authentication at the server level and permissions validation in relation to particular databases. Here's what happens when a user tries to work with SQL Server data:

- *Stage 1.* A user logs on, supplies a user ID and password, and is allowed to access the SQL Server.
- *Stage 2.* A user can work with specific database objects only if permissions have previously been granted on those objects.

It is possible for you to grant users the ability to log in to SQL Server and not to be able to do anything. Granting users permissions to work with database objects is a separate step. If you neglect to grant users access to database objects, they can log on but have nowhere to go. Permissions can be granted directly to users, or to database roles. Users then inherit permissions from the roles they belong to. Granting permissions is covered later in this chapter.

Users and Roles

SQL Server supports two different kinds of roles:

- *Fixed Server Roles.* Fixed server roles exist at the server level only, and allow users to perform server administrative tasks. Fixed server roles can't be modified or deleted, and you can't add new ones. Users inherit the capabilities of the roles by being added to the role.
- *Database Roles.* Fixed database roles exist in each database and allow role members a range of activities when they are added to that role. Like fixed server roles, fixed database roles can't be modified or deleted. However, you can also create your own custom user-defined database roles to simplify the process of granting and administering permissions in the database.

Roles are similar to Access security groups. Users inherit the permissions of the roles to which they are assigned. Administering permissions for database roles is much less complicated than for individual users. Setting permissions for users and roles is covered later in this chapter.

The Security Components As Exposed in Enterprise Manager

One good way to get a better understanding of the terms used in SQL Server security is to look at how they are represented in Enterprise Manager. (Enterprise Manager was introduced in Chapter 2, "SQL Server Fundamentals.")

At the server level, you'll find the following components in the Security node:

Logins. All users need logins in order to access SQL Server. These can be NT user or group logins or SQL Server logins.

Server roles. Logins can be assigned to server roles to enable users to perform administrative tasks.

At the database level, you find the following security components displayed under the individual database node:

Users. The Users node displays the database users. Add or configure database users from the right-click mouse button menu. Database users can be enabled logins, where the name of the user is the same as the login name, or you can create a different name. You can also have a user account called "guest" that is not mapped to a particular login. Any user who can get into the server can use the guest account.

Roles. The Roles node displays fixed database roles and user-defined roles. As with database users, right-click to add or configure the properties for both fixed and user-defined roles. All database users automatically belong to the built-in public role, and users can belong to multiple roles. Roles are the same as groups in Access or NT; users inherit permissions granted to the roles they belong to.

The Benefits of Windows NT/Windows 2000 Authentication (Integrated Security)

In pure security terms, Windows NT/Windows 2000 authentication is far more robust than limiting your database to SQL Server authentication. In addition to not having users log on twice—once to the operating system and then again to SQL Server—you also have the following benefits:

- Superior validation and encryption of passwords.
- NT auditing features.
- Enforcement of password expiration and minimum password length.

- Account lockout after invalid password attempts.

- Automatic updating of SQL Server security when changes are made in the operating system. Changes to NT users and groups take effect the next time a user logs on to SQL Server.

Integrated security is not available if you have installed SQL Server on a Windows 95/98 or Millenium machine.

The Benefits of SQL Server Authentication

SQL Server authentication is often sufficient for simple applications such as single-user databases and environments where the mapping of NT users and groups has a low correlation to the mapping of SQL Server accounts. The overhead of administering Windows NT/Windows 2000 users and groups might not be worth it if the security schema is very simple. In some cases, you might need to run SQL Server or the Desktop Engine on an operating system such as Windows 98 or Millennium, where NT security won't be available.

How NT Authentication and SQL Server Authentication Work Together

Setting your server to use both NT and SQL Server logins gives you the maximum amount of flexibility. Windows users and groups as well as SQL Server logins can be added to SQL Server fixed-server and database roles.

Figure 3.2 shows mapping NT users and groups as well as SQL Server users to SQL Server roles, where they will inherit the permissions granted to the roles.

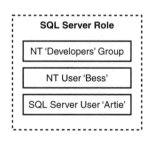

FIGURE 3.2

You can assign permissions to Windows NT/Windows 2000 groups and users in SQL Server by adding them to SQL Server roles.

Being able to add NT users and groups—as well as SQL Server users—to roles simplifies managing security because you need to apply settings only once to the roles.

3

UNDERSTANDING SQL SERVER SECURITY

It's always better to create a role and assign permissions to that role rather than assigning permissions explicitly to users. This simplifies administration, even if the role has only a single member. Consider a scenario in which a user leaves your company on Friday and a replacement is hired to start on Monday, but nobody bothered to tell you until late Friday afternoon. If you assigned permissions directly to the user, you must reconstruct the entire set of permissions and apply them to the replacement user account, sacrificing your weekend activities (or at least your Friday night) in order to get the job done in time. However, if you use roles, you simply delete the user account of the employee who left, create a login for the new user, and add the new user to the role. The new user will be able to take over where the old user left off, and nothing will stop you from getting out of work on time Friday evening.

Logins and Built-in Accounts

When you install SQL Server using Windows NT/Windows 2000, a login is automatically created for your NT account and the NT Administrators group as a whole. If you install SQL Server on a Windows 9x machine, you will be logged on using the sa user account. Figure 3.3 displays the Logins folder in SQL Server after installing SQL Server on a Windows NT server named *Mabel*. In addition to the BUILTIN\Administrators account and the sa account, there is also an account used to run the SQL Server services.

You need to be logged on as a member of the built-in NT Administrators group just to install SQL Server, so the login created is mapped to the NT BUILTIN\Administrators group. This means that any member of the NT Administrators group is automatically enabled to log on to SQL Server. You'll learn how you can disable this later in the chapter.

The MABEL\SQLServerRun account is the NT user account that SQL Server and its related services are running under. For SQL Server and SQL Server Agent to run as services in Windows, they must be assigned a Windows user account. It's common practice to use the same account for both SQL Server and SQL Server Agent. The account can be either the local system account or a domain user account. The local system account does not require a password. However, if you use the local system account instead of creating a domain user account specifically for the services, then your SQL Server will not have network access rights in Windows NT 4.0 and Windows 2000 and it will be restricted from interacting with other servers.

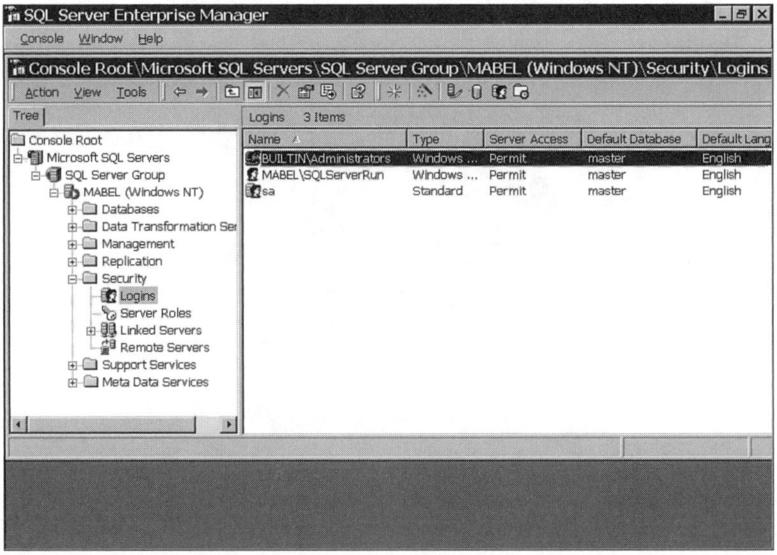

FIGURE 3.3
The Logins folder displays the accounts used when installing SQL Server on Windows NT/Windows 2000.

How Windows Authentication Works

When you configure your SQL Server to operate in Windows authentication mode, SQL Server assumes a trust relationship with the Windows NT/Windows 2000 Server. Windows takes care of authenticating user account names and checking passwords when logging on to the network, eliminating the need for a second login to SQL Server. Windows also keeps track of which security groups the user belongs to and passes this information along to SQL Server if a Windows NT/Windows 2000 user or group login has been enabled for SQL Server.

Enabling Windows NT/Windows 2000 Logins

To give a Windows NT/Windows 2000 login access to your server, right-click the Logins icon shown in Figure 3.3 and choose New Login from the menu. Figure 3.4 displays the General tab of the SQL Server Login Properties dialog box with a custom group named Developers selected. To grant access to the Windows NT/Windows 2000 Developers group, simply select the domain, type the username or group name, and select Grant Access. Note that this dialog box can also be used to deny access to any NT users or groups.

The Server Roles tab on the login dialog box allows you to assign a fixed server role to the login, and the Database Access tab allows you to assign database access and role membership. Make sure that the default database option selected on the General tab is also selected on the Database Access tab or you'll get an error message when you try to save the new login. Any

Windows NT/Windows 2000 users who are members of the Developers group will now be able to access SQL Server.

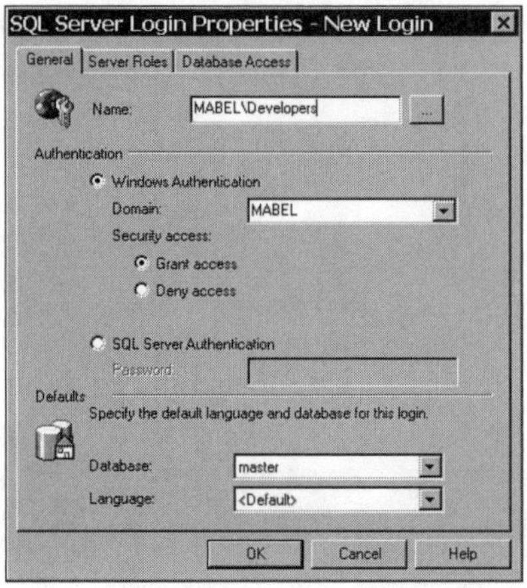

FIGURE 3.4
You can enable Windows NT/Windows 2000 logins and assign database access rights at the same time.

> **NOTE**
>
> When you make changes to Windows NT/Windows 2000 user and group accounts, the changes are automatically reflected in SQL Server. However, if an NT user is connected to SQL Server while changes are made to his account, the changes don't become effective until the next time the user connects to SQL Server.

As explained in Chapter 2, system stored procedures can be used to accomplish any task that you can perform using the Enterprise Manager. The system stored procedure `sp_grantlogin` is used to enable an NT login. This stored procedure can be run from the Query Analyzer or from your Access application by using a pass-through query or VBA code. (We give examples of how to run stored procedures from Access in several of the subsequent chapters of this book.) The syntax requires you to specify the domain or computer name, followed by a backslash and then the group or user name. Here's an example:

```
sp_grantlogin 'MABEL\AndyB'
```

If you are granting access to one of the Windows NT/Windows 2000 built-in accounts, you use the word BUILTIN instead of the server name:

```
sp_grantlogin 'BUILTIN\Administrators'
```

How SQL Server Authentication Works

SQL Server authentication requires creating logins within SQL Server rather than enabling operating system logins. To make use of a SQL Server login, users must log on to SQL Server as a separate action, even if they are already logged on to Windows. SQL Server manages these accounts internally, without reference to Windows. These accounts are stored in the master database and can be viewed by using the Enterprise Manager or by running the `sp_helplogins` system stored procedure, which has no parameters and displays all the logins and their properties:

```
sp_helplogins
```

The result set after running the `sp_helplogins` will display the properties of both SQL Server and Windows NT/Windows 2000 logins.

SQL Server logins are required if you are running on an operating system other than Windows NT or Windows 2000.

Creating SQL Server Logins

To create a SQL Server login, right-click the Logins icon shown earlier in Figure 3.3 and choose New Login from the menu. Select SQL Server Authentication. Figure 3.5 shows the creation of a SQL Server user named *Dudley*. The password you set will not be displayed, and you will be prompted to confirm it by typing it a second time when you click the OK button.

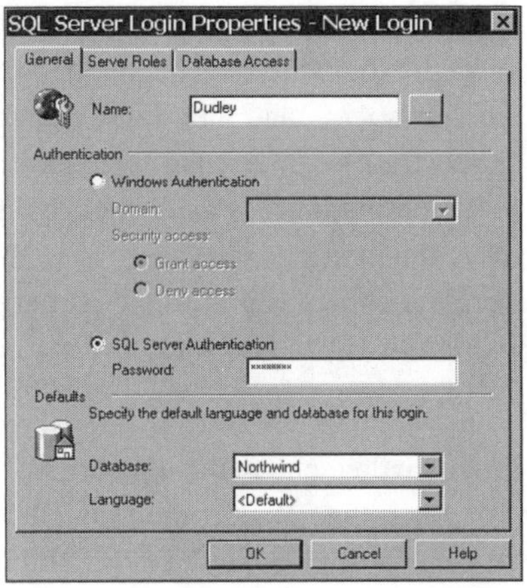

FIGURE 3.5

When creating a SQL Server login, you can assign a password as well as a default database.

The `sp_addlogin` system stored procedure is used to create a SQL Server login by passing in the login name, password, and default database. Here's an example:

```
sp_addlogin 'Buster', 'SecretPW', 'Northwind'
```

If you omit all the arguments except the login name, the password will default to NULL and the default database for that user will be the master database.

Rules for Naming SQL Server Logins, Users, Roles, and Passwords

Logins, users, roles, and passwords can contain from 1 to 128 characters. You can use letters, symbols, and numbers as long as the name does not contain a backslash and is not an empty string or null. If you elect to use special characters, you will have to use delimiters (double quotation marks or square brackets) when writing Transact-SQL statements. Delimiters are required if the login, user, role, or password contains a space or begins with a dollar sign ($), the at character (@), or a space.

Granting Database Access to Logins

After you've created logins for your users, you must give them the database permissions they will need to access data. You can do this at the time you create the logins on the Database Access tab of the New Login dialog by assigning them to database roles, or you can do it later by selecting a database and adding the logins to its Users collection. Expand the database node in Enterprise Manager, select the Users icon, and then right-click and choose New Database User from the list. Figure 3.6 shows the New User dialog box with the Login Name list dropped down. When you enable a login to access a database by making the login a user of that database, you can also grant membership in database roles, thereby giving the user a specific set of permissions. However, you can't assign individual permissions until after you've finished adding the user by clicking OK. Database roles and setting permissions are covered later in this chapter.

The system stored procedure `sp_grantdbaccess` adds the new user to a database. The name of the database user doesn't have to match the name of the login. The following example will add a database user named Buster to the Northwind database which is mapped to a login named Buster.

```
Use Northwind
sp_grantdbaccess 'Buster'
```

If, later on, you want to remove an account, you can run the `sp_revokedbaccess` stored procedure, which reverses the process and removes a database user.

FIGURE 3.6
You can enable database access from the database's Users node.

Database Users

The permissions assigned to your database users govern which activities they are allowed to perform and whether they are running ad-hoc queries, working through a front-end application, or choosing menu options in SQL Server. Permissions can also be inherited through membership in roles, which are discussed in the next section.

Each login is prevented from doing anything with databases where that login has not been explicitly enabled as a user, with one important exception: the guest user account.

The guest Account

You can create a special account named *guest* in any database. The guest account is not mapped to any particular login. Its purpose is to enable users who do not have access to a database under their own login to work with the database by using the permissions granted to guest. If you do not define a guest user account, logins that do not have user accounts assigned to them are prevented from working with the database. The guest account is most useful for Internet connections and anonymous connections where you do not need or want to track individual user activity.

Understanding Fixed Server Roles

Fixed server roles exist mainly to split up the tasks of administering the server. They exist outside of individual databases, although some include rights to create and alter databases. Table 3.1 displays the list of fixed server roles and a description of the permissions granted for each one. Note that the sysadmin fixed server role encompasses the rights of all the other fixed server roles.

TABLE 3.1 Fixed Server Roles

Role	Description
bulkadmin	Can execute BULK INSERT statements.
dbcreator	Can create and alter databases.
diskadmin	Can manage the disk files.
processadmin	Can manage the processes running in SQL Server.
serveradmin	Can configure the server-wide settings.
setupadmin	Can add, drop, and configure linked servers, manage extended procedures, and mark a stored procedure as startup.
securityadmin	Can manage the logins for the server (cannot administer database security).
sysadmin	Can perform any activity in the SQL Server installation. This role spans all the other roles.

CAUTION

Granting membership in sysadmin automatically grants unrestricted powers in a SQL Server and in all the databases it contains. This is an important point that cannot be emphasized enough. The sysadmin server role (or the sa user account) is omnipotent inside a SQL Server and has irrevocable permissions to do absolutely anything to all databases and objects in the SQL Server. There is no way to shield sensitive objects or data from a member of the sysadmin role, so be very careful who you let in as a member. Also bear in mind that any sysadmin member has access to the Windows NT/Windows 2000 administrative account that the SQL Server services use. This is the same as granting them administrative privileges on your Windows NT/Windows 2000 server. Members of sysadmin have access to the `xp_cmdshell` system stored procedure, which executes commands at the operating system level.

Adding a Login to a Fixed Server Role

Logins can be added to fixed server roles at the time the logins are created, or at any time thereafter, by going into the Properties dialog box for the login or by adding it through the Server Roles Properties dialog box. To add a login to a fixed server role, expand the server in Enterprise Manager and click Server Roles. Select the role to which you want to add a user, right-click the role, and select Properties from the menu. Click the Add button and select the logins you want to add. Figure 3.7 shows the members of the dbcreator fixed server role. Note that it is unnecessary to add any of the administrative accounts that are already mapped to the sysadmin fixed server role.

FIGURE 3.7
You can add members to a fixed server role by clicking the Add button in the Server Role Properties dialog box.

The sp_addsrvrolemember stored procedure will add a user to a fixed server role. Here's an example:

```
sp_addsrvrolemember 'MABEL\AndyB', 'dbcreator'
```

The sysadmin Fixed Server Role and the Windows NT Administrators Group

The Windows NT Administrators group is automatically added as a member of the sysadmin role when you install SQL Server. So, all users who are members of the NT Administrators group will have full rights in SQL Server. It is not possible to keep the NT Administrators group as an enabled login without having it mapped to the sysadmin role. If you want to remove the mapping between the NT Administrators group and the sysadmin role, you must disable the NT Administrators group from logging on to SQL Server. You can then enable individual NT accounts and grant them membership in the sysadmin role without letting in everyone who is in the NT Administrators group. Another option is to deny access to individual members of the NT Administrators group. The Deny access specified in the Logins dialog box for an individual login will always override the Allow access specified for the group.

Viewing Permissions for Fixed Server Roles

You can click the Permissions tab in the Server Role Properties dialog box to view specific permissions associated with a fixed server role, as shown in Figure 3.8.

To view individual permissions granted to fixed server roles, use the sp_srvrolepermission stored procedure. Running sp_srvrolepermission displays a list of roles and their associated permissions. If you run sp_srvrolepermission and pass a specific role name as a parameter, only the permissions associated with that role are listed:

```
sp_srvrolepermission 'diskadmin'
```

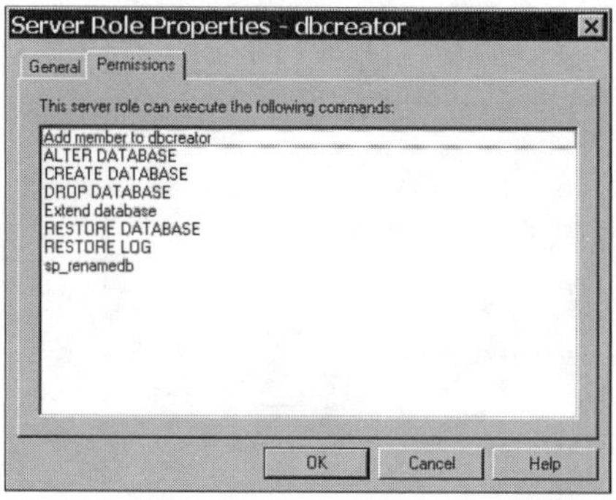

FIGURE 3.8
The permissions for each fixed server role are displayed on the Permissions tab.

Understanding Fixed Database Roles

The scope of fixed database roles is local to a particular database. As with fixed server roles, fixed database roles cannot be deleted and their permissions cannot be altered. Table 3.2 displays a list of fixed database roles with a brief description of each.

TABLE 3.2   Fixed Database Roles

Role	Description
db_accessadmin	Can add or remove NT users and groups and SQL Server users in the database
db_backupoperator	Can back up the database
db_datareader	Can see any data from all user tables in the database
db_datawriter	Can add, change, or delete data in all user tables in the database
db_ddladmin	Can add, modify, or drop objects in the database
db_securityadmin	Can manage role membership and can manage statement and object permissions in the database
db_denydatareader	Cannot see any data in the database
db_denydatawriter	Cannot change any data in the database
db_owner	Can perform the activities of all the database roles as well as maintenance and configuration activities

Adding a User to a Fixed Database Role

Users can be added to a fixed database role through either the Users properties dialog box or through the Roles properties dialog box. To add a user to a fixed database role, expand the database in Enterprise Manager and click the Roles folder. Right-click the role to which you want to add a user and select Properties from the menu. Click the Add button to make selections from the list of users who are enabled to use the database. Figure 3.9 shows a user added to the db_backupoperator fixed database role. Note that you can't view or set permissions here.

Fixed database roles can be used to greatly simplify the task of defining user permissions because they include some of the most common sets of permissions with which you will need to work. For example, the user shown in Figure 3.8 is now able to back up the database but won't necessarily be able to read, modify, or delete data in the database.

FIGURE 3.9
Adding a user to the db_backupoperator fixed database role.

The sp_addrolemember stored procedure is used to add a user to a role. Here's an example:

```
sp_addrolemember 'db_backupoperator', 'MaryC'
```

Unfortunately, within the Enterprise Manager there's no way to view the individual permissions assigned to a fixed database role as there is with a fixed server role. However, running the sp_dbfixedrolepermission stored procedure lists all the fixed database roles and their associated permissions. If you run sp_dbfixedrolepermission and pass a specific role name as a parameter, only the permissions associated with that role are listed. Here's an example:

```
sp_dbfixedrolepermission 'db_ddladmin'
```

The Public Role

The public role is the one built-in role for which you can actually modify the permissions. You don't need to make users members of the public role; they are already members. When you grant access to a database, every user is automatically added to the public role. You can't delete the public role, and you can't remove users from it. Every SQL Server database contains the public role, including the systems databases. The public role is useful for granting permissions that you want all users to have because everyone who can get into the database is a member of public. Always bear in mind that permissions granted to the public role are permissions that are granted to everyone, including the guest user account.

Object Owners

All objects in a database—tables, views, stored procedures, rules, defaults, and user-defined types—have an owner. If the user who created the object is a member of the sysadmin role, the object is owned by dbo. If the user is not a member of sysadmin, that individual user owns the object.

The Effects of Ownership

An object's ownership has two different effects on the object. It affects who can control permissions on the object (the owner always can set permissions), and it affects the identity of the object. Two tables named tblCustomer can exist in a database if each table has a different owner. The fully qualified way to refer to a database object is *database.owner.object*. Prepending the database and owner name is not necessary in most cases unless you are writing remote queries. It is common practice for database objects to be owned by a single user because that considerably simplifies administration and data access. In addition, any user who is the owner of an object in a database cannot be removed from the database. However, ownership can always be transferred if necessary. Any object owner, or member of the sysadmin fixed server role, or a member of both the db_ddladmin and db_securityadmin roles can run the sp_changeobjectowner stored procedure. To change the owner of a database, run the sp_changedbowner stored procedure. The following example will change the owner of the Customers table in the Northwind database from dbo to Dudley:

```
sp_changeobjectowner 'dbo.Customers', 'Dudley'
```

To change it back to dbo, use the following syntax:

```
sp_changeobjectowner 'Dudley.Customers', 'dbo'
```

dbo

The dbo is a special user that's mapped to the sysadmin fixed server role inside each database. If you are logged on as a user who is a member of the sysadmin role, all objects you create will be owned by dbo, not by your individual user account. You can't delete the dbo user account, and it is mapped exclusively to sysadmin. Don't confuse dbo with the db_owner fixed database role. The db_owner role actually has little to do with ownership of the objects in a database, other than the fact that members of that role are able to create objects and can, therefore, become owners without needing to be members of sysadmin. If users are members of sysadmin, any object they create will be owned by dbo. Any member of the sysadmin role can change ownership after the object has been created if you want dbo to be listed as the owner of all your database objects. However, make sure that you save any permissions that may exist for an object before you change owners, because all existing permissions are removed.

Working with User-Defined Database Roles

Database roles enable you to fine-tune the permissions assigned in individual databases. Because everyone belongs to the public role (and you probably don't want to grant permissions to everyone), your own user-defined roles can make administering security easier than it would be if you granted individual permissions for each user. Remove all permissions from public (or at least grant only permissions you want all users of the database to have) and then create your own roles, assigning them a more specific set of permissions.

User-defined roles allow you a great deal of flexibility in the administration of your databases. For example, suppose you hire a consulting company to work on your database, but you don't want the consultants to view sensitive data. You can create a special role, granting that role only the permissions that the consultants need to do their work. As the consultants come and go, all you need to do is add and remove them from that role.

Roles can be nested by adding user-defined roles as members of fixed database roles or other user-defined roles. For example, if you make the Payroll role a member of the Clerical role, a member of the Payroll role will be able to do everything that members of the Clerical role can do. You can then assign additional rights to the Payroll role that haven't been given to the Clerical role. Just bear in mind that there's a performance penalty if your nesting scheme gets too complex.

Creating a User-Defined Database Role

To create a new database role, expand the database in Enterprise Manager and right-click the Roles icon. Choose New Database Role from the menu. Now type in the name of the new role and add users to it by clicking the Add button. Figure 3.10 shows the New Role dialog. Note that you won't be able to assign permissions to the role until after you've saved it.

NOTE

After you've created your own database roles, add them to any fixed database roles. Database roles show up on the list along with the users when you click the Add button. However, you can't go the other way around and add fixed database roles to your custom roles.

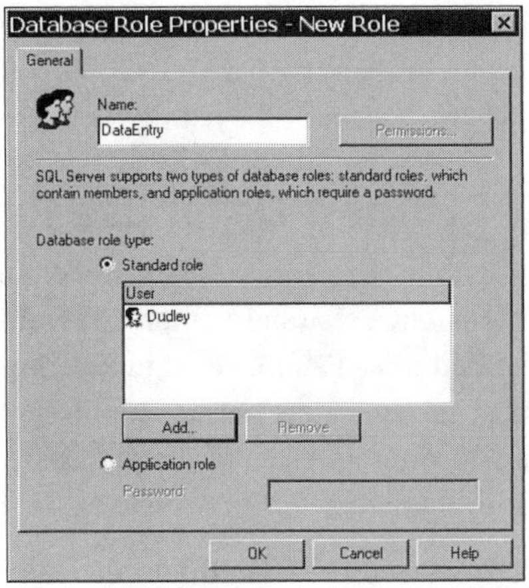

FIGURE 3.10
Adding a user-defined database role.

Understanding Application Roles

An *application role* is a special role that exists inside of a database and is designed to allow an application to log on independently of the users who are using it. In fact, you can't even add users to an application role. An application (Visual Basic, Excel, Access, Word, or whatever) activates the application role, and users of that application gain permissions that are granted to the application role. In the meantime, any permissions the users might have on their own are suspended, and only the application role's permissions are considered. For example, user AndyB is a member of the sysadmin role and has full permissions on the SQL Server. AndyB connects using an application role that has SELECT permissions only. AndyB will now have only SELECT permissions. For the duration of his connection with the application role, his full sysadmin privileges will be suspended.

Because application roles don't have authenticated users as other database roles do, a password must be supplied when the application role is activated. Once activated, the permissions of the application role apply for the duration of that connection. This makes application roles appropriate for applications that use only a single connection. Applications that use multiple connections or connection pooling don't work well with application roles because you can never be sure whether the application role is activated for that particular connection.

An application role is an excellent way to keep users from working directly with data. For example, you don't want users of an Excel application to use Excel's querying tools to write their own ad-hoc queries. By limiting the users to an application role, you can prevent them from either unintentionally or maliciously modifying data. You can also prevent them from writing SELECT queries that return too much data or data to which they shouldn't have access.

> **NOTE**
>
> Windows NT/Windows 2000 auditing of users will still be in effect, even for those users connecting through an application role. However, auditing does not cover SQL Server users. So, if auditing is required, use application roles only with NT authentication.

Creating an Application Role

To create an application role by using the Enterprise Manager, expand the Database folder and then right-click the Roles icon in the database in which you want to create the application role. Select New Database Role and enter the name of the new role. Select the Application Role option, fill in the name, and enter the password, as shown in Figure 3.11. You must save the new application role before setting permissions on it.

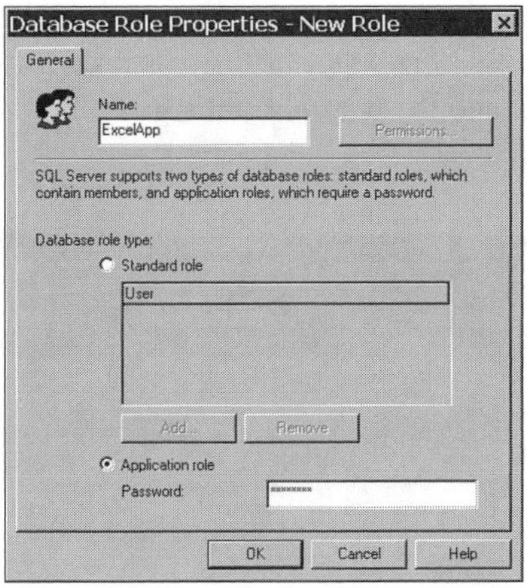

FIGURE 3.11

Creating an application role and supplying the application role's password.

The `sp_addapprole` stored procedure enables you to create an application role using Transact-SQL. Here's an example:

```
sp_addapprole 'ExcelApp', 'password'
```

Implementing an Application Role

After creating a new application role, you must follow these steps:

1. Set permissions for the application role. Remember that the application role inherits any permissions you have assigned to the public role. Permissions are covered in detail a little later in this chapter.

2. Make sure that users of the application role can log on to SQL Server. If you are using SQL Server authentication, create a login for the application role to use. If you are using NT authentication, your NT users might already have valid logins. If not, create a SQL Server login specifically for the application role.

3. Chapter 6, "ActiveX Data Objects (ADO) Fundamentals," discusses the use of ActiveX Data Objects to connect to a database from within a VBA program. When you use ADO to connect through an application role, you will create and open a connection object. After you have opened the connection, run the `sp_setapprole` stored procedure, supplying the application role name and password. This activates the application role until the connection is closed. Here's an example:

```
cnn.Execute "sp_setapprole 'ExcelApp', 'password'"
```

Keeping Track of Logins and Roles

After you've set up your logins and roles, you need a way to determine who is a member of what. The `sp_helplogins` stored procedure returns information about a login. Figure 3.12 shows the Query Analyzer running the `sp_helplogins` stored procedure. The top results pane displays the login information, and the bottom results pane shows the database users and roles to which the login is mapped.

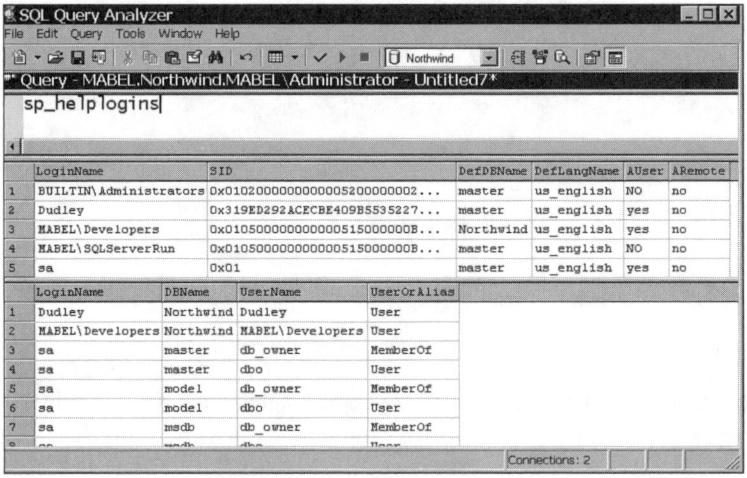

FIGURE 3.12

The sp_helplogins *stored procedure helps you keep track of who's who in your SQL Server.*

You can also run the `sp_helpuser` system stored procedure on both users and database roles to display their membership.

Removing Users and Logins

If you need to delete a user, removing the login automatically removes any accounts for that login in individual databases. Removing a user account from a database automatically removes any permissions the user might have had. However, you can't remove users who own objects. As noted earlier, you can transfer object ownership by running the sp_changeobjectowner system stored procedure, and then you can remove the user.

Make sure to remove both the user account and the login for a user you want to remove entirely. If you remove the user account from the database and neglect to remove the login, the user can still use the database through the guest user account, if one exists.

Database users and server logins can be removed simply by deleting them in the Enterprise Manager. You can also use system stored procedures for removing users and logins.

The sp_dropuser system stored procedure will remove a user from a database:

```
sp_dropuser 'MaryC'
```

The sp_droplogin system stored procedure will remove a SQL Server login:

```
sp_droplogin 'MaryC'
```

The sp_revokelogin system stored procedure will remove a Windows NT login:

```
sp_revokelogin 'MABEL\AndyB'
```

The sp_droprolemember stored procedure will remove a user from a role:

```
sp_droprolemember 'NewUsers', 'MaryC'
```

The sp_droprole stored procedure will delete a role:

```
sp_droprole 'NewUsers'
```

> **NOTE**
>
> You can't delete any of the fixed server roles or fixed database roles. You also can't delete a role if it has members. Therefore, remove the members first and then delete the role.

Resetting SQL Server User Passwords

If you are using SQL Server authentication, you can change or clear a user password in the Enterprise Manager by going into the properties for the login or by executing the sp_password stored procedure. Only members of the sysadmin role can change passwords without knowing the old password by passing NULL for the old password parameter. Invoking the sp_password stored procedure as shown here changes the forgotten password of user MaryC to newpassword:

```
sp_password NULL, 'newpassword', 'MaryC'
```

You can't change passwords or otherwise administer Windows NT or Windows 2000 logins from within SQL Server—you must use NT's User Manager for Domains utility or the security management tools in Windows 2000.

Understanding Permissions

In SQL Server, you must assign permissions for users to be able to interact with SQL Server objects. By default, no permissions are set. You can set permissions on objects and on Transact-SQL statements.

Object permissions are permissions set on objects, such as tables and views, that enable users to interact with these objects. Statement permissions are applied to a Transact-SQL statement, such as a CREATE TABLE statement. This enables a user to create a table. Inherited or implied permissions are those permissions that a user possesses by being a member of a role or by being the owner of an object. Object owners can perform any action on the object, including altering its definition, modifying its data, and controlling the way other users work with it.

As noted earlier in this chapter, users must have the appropriate permissions to perform any database activity on the server. Because most databases have many users, it makes sense to grant permissions only to roles and to let users inherit those permissions by being members of roles.

The Three Types of Permissions

Here are three Transact-SQL statements that cover the types of permissions you can assign:

- GRANT. Grants a permission.
- REVOKE. Revokes permission. This is the default state of affairs. If a permission is revoked, a user might still inherit it through membership in a role.
- DENY. Revokes a permission with no possibility of inheritance. DENY takes precedence over all other permissions, except permissions that come from being a member of sysadmin or from being the owner of an object.

How DENY Works

Imagine a scenario in which you have a Developers role that has been granted full permissions on all tables. You hire a new contractor to act as a developer, but you're reluctant to grant the contractor permission to view sensitive data. You add the contractor to the Developers group but deny the contractor permissions on just the tables containing the sensitive data. The contractor then can operate with the full permissions of the Developers group but can't see the sensitive data because the DENY on those tables overrides the full permissions the contractor would normally inherit from the Developers role.

Assigning Permissions

Members of the sysadmin and db_securityadmin roles can set any permission in the database. Owners of objects can set permissions on any of the objects they own.

> **TIP**
>
> When you want to assign multiple permissions, start at the bottom of your permission hierarchy. Grant basic permissions to the public role because everyone is a member of public. You can fine-tune this by granting additional permissions to specific roles and adding users to those roles. For example, grant SELECT to the public role if you want everyone to be able to read data. Grant INSERT, UPDATE, and DELETE only to more exclusive roles and add only trusted users to those roles. Alternatively, you can just revoke or deny permissions on all the tables and use views and stored procedures for data access. This is discussed in the next section.

Granting Permissions

You can use the Transact-SQL GRANT statement to grant permissions on objects, or you can use the Enterprise Manager. Select the object, user, or role and then right-click and bring up the Properties dialog box. Clicking the Permissions button displays the permissions settings. Figure 3.13 shows granting full permissions on the Categories table to the DataEntry database role.

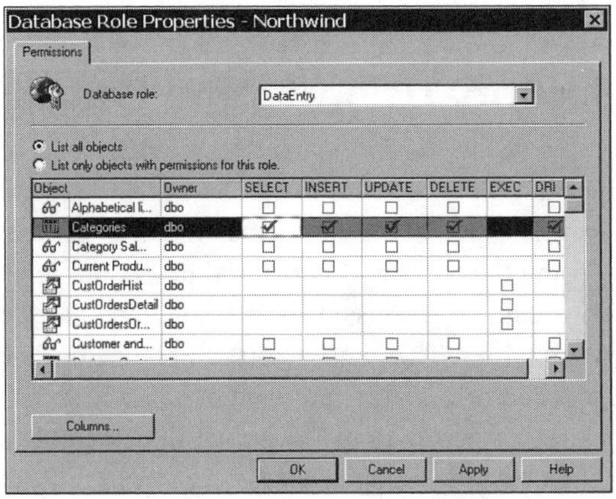

FIGURE 3.13

You can set permissions from the Properties dialog of a role, user, or object.

Revoking Permissions

Revoking a permission involves clearing the check box associated with that permission. All the cleared check boxes shown in Figure 3.13 are revoked permissions.

Denying Permissions

Denying a permission means that the permission is revoked and can't be inherited. Figure 3.14 shows denying permissions to the Categories table for the DataEntry role. That means members of DataEntry cannot inherit permissions to do anything with the Categories table, no matter which other roles they are members of. The only exceptions are members of the sysadmin role and object owners, who always have permissions.

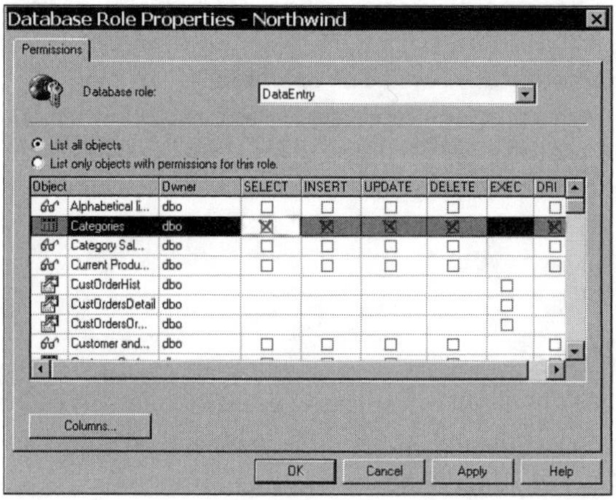

FIGURE 3.14
Denying permissions to the Categories table for the DataEntry role.

Implementing Security Using Stored Procedures

One plan you might want to consider for implementing security on your SQL Server database is to take advantage of the natural permissions hierarchy in SQL Server. Any permissions on tables are superceded by permissions set on views and stored procedures. Figure 3.15 shows setting EXECUTE permissions on the Sales by Year stored procedure in the Northwind database. Stored procedures have only a single permission—EXECUTE. The Sales by Year stored procedure selects data from several tables. This means you can revoke or deny all permissions on all the tables for the listed users and roles. Users are then not able to write ad-hoc queries against those tables because they have no permissions. However, they are able to execute the stored procedure. Removing all direct access to tables and using stored procedures is an excellent way to protect the data and the server. This prevents users from writing queries that inappropriately update or delete data. A simple ad-hoc query such as UPDATE Customers SET City = 'NYC' will result in every City field in the Customers table having a single new value: NYC. Cleaning up the mess could take a while, depending on the amount of data in the table and the time of the last backup. If written correctly, stored procedures protect you against this sort of situation.

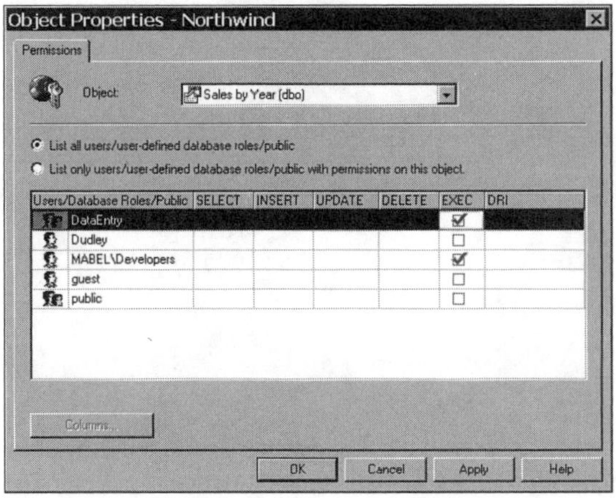

FIGURE 3.15
Stored procedures have a single permission, EXECUTE, which takes precedence over table permissions.

Removing permissions from tables and using stored procedures is also useful in situations where there might be large amounts of data returned in a SELECT query. Consider the effect on your SQL Server and your network if you allow users to write their own queries, and they construct something like SELECT * FROM MyMillionRowTable. In fact, the table doesn't even have to have a million rows; probably ten thousand or so would be enough to have a significant negative impact on server performance and network traffic. If several users run these types of queries at the same time, the server and the network could be easily be brought to their knees.

However, if you grant permissions only to stored procedures and not to tables, make sure that all objects have the same owner. If the table has one owner, and the stored procedure another, this technique won't work. Users will be required to have the necessary permissions on the underlying tables to execute the stored procedure.

Implementing Security Using Views

The permissions assigned to views also override those assigned to tables. Unlike row-returning stored procedures, views generally enable you to modify data. Figure 3.16 shows setting permissions for the CurrentProductList view in SQL Server. This view selects data from the Products table, so you can remove all permissions from the Products table and assign INSERT,

UPDATE, and DELETE permissions to the view instead. Only members of the NewUsers group will be able to update product data. The ExcelApp application role has read-only permissions on the view.

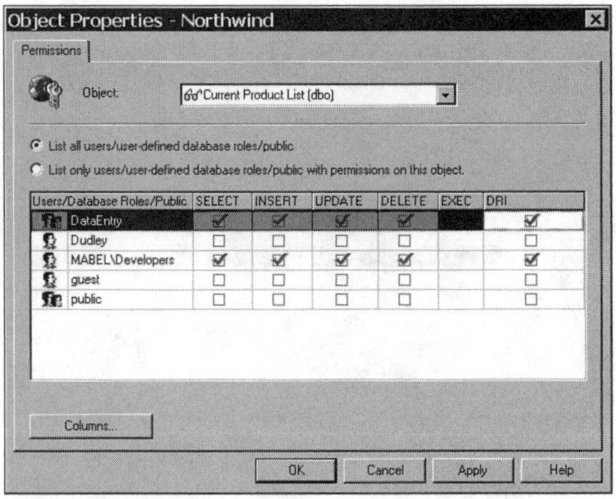

FIGURE 3.16

Permissions set in a view take precedence over table permissions.

Implementing Security Using User-Defined Functions

User-defined functions that return tables, a new feature in SQL Server 2000, can be used in much the same way as stored procedures and views for returning data. As long as users have permissions on the function, they don't need permissions on the base tables. However, functions suffer from a limitation that neither views nor stored procedures have—they are never updateable. Although you can base Access forms and reports on SELECT statements that call functions, the data can never be updateable. This isn't true of record sources based on views and stored procedures. The following SQL statement used as the record source for a form will execute the fnCategories function and return records matching the parameter value of 5, but the user won't be able to do anything except read the data:

```
SELECT * FROM dbo.fnCategories(5)
```

NOTE

Make sure that you fully qualify all object references with the owner name when working with SQL Server objects from an Access Project (ADP). You can base forms and reports directly on SQL Server tables, views, functions and stored procedures, and if you are logged on as a member of the sysadmin role, you will not need to qualify them with the <ownername.objectname> syntax. However, any users of your application who are not members of the sysadmin role will get errors if the owner name is not supplied as part of the object name. And because it is unlikely that you will want all your users to administer your SQL Server, fully qualifying all objects directly referenced with the owner name at the time you build your forms and reports will save you from having to revise them later.

Implementing Column-Level and Row-Level Security

SQL Server enables you to grant column-level permissions using the GRANT statement or the Columns button in the Permissions dialog box. The column-level permissions that are available are SELECT and UPDATE for the selected columns. The downside of granting column-level permissions is that they are not displayed unless you drill down into the Permissions dialog box and re-display the Columns button, making them difficult to administer. Setting column-level security using the Enterprise Manager is a new feature in SQL Server 2000 and did not exist in SQL Server 7.0.

However, you can also use views and stored procedures to achieve the same effect. To implement column-level security, revoke or deny all permissions to tables. Create stored procedures and views for users to work with that do not include the columns you do not want the users to see. As long as the views, stored procedures, and functions have the same owner as the underlying tables, users will be able to work with the data using those objects instead of working directly with the tables.

The only way to implement row-level security on a single table is to remove all permissions to the tables and use a WHERE clause in a view, function, or stored procedure that limits the rows returned. Grant permissions on the view, function, or stored procedure to allow the user to work with the data.

Encrypting Functions, Views, and Stored Procedures

SQL Server also enables you to encrypt views and stored procedures to scramble the definition so that it can't be read. You need to use the WITH ENCRYPTION option in Transact-SQL to encrypt a view or a stored procedure at the time you create it. This option is not available in the Enterprise Manager unless you type it in part of the Transact-SQL that defines the function, view, or stored procedure.

Use WITH ENCRYPTION in Transact-SQL to encrypt a function, view, or stored procedure. This obscures the definition itself, not the data. The following code creates an encrypted stored procedure:

```
CREATE PROCEDURE procEncrypted
WITH ENCRYPTION
AS
SELECT * FROM Customers
```

If you run the encrypted stored procedure, it works just fine and happily returns all the rows in the Customers table. However, if you try to use the sp_helptext system stored procedure to read the definition, all you will get is the message The object comments have been encrypted.

Encryption is useful if you want to hide both the structure and the implementation of your SQL Server database from prying eyes.

What About Access Security?

If you've implemented Access security, you must start over again in SQL Server. Access security maintains user and group information in the workgroup information file, for which there is no equivalent in SQL Server and no supported method of upsizing.

In addition, there is no automatic way to transfer permissions set on your Access tables to SQL Server. However, later in the chapter you'll learn how you can use VBA code to transfer your table permissions. Just be aware that the way permissions work in SQL Server is somewhat different from the way they work in Access. Access uses the "least restrictive" rule to grant permissions to a user. If any of the groups of which the user is a member has those permissions, the user inherits those permissions even though the user might have had those permissions removed either explicitly or through membership in another group. This works the same way that it does in SQL Server: Users inherit permissions from any roles to which they belong. However, the DENY permission that exists in SQL Server, which overrides less-restrictive permissions and group inheritance, has no corollary in Access.

Security in an Access Database (MDB)

If you are so inclined, you can still keep Access security for your Access form, report, and macro objects if you use an Access database as your front end. The Jet database engine that Access uses handles permissions assigned in each database, and Jet is still present in an Access 2000 MDB. The downside to this approach is that users will most likely need two logins to work with the application: one for Access and one for SQL Server (or NT if you are using NT authentication). In Access 2000, modules are no longer included under the Jet umbrella—you can set a separate password on your VBA project instead.

You can also create an MDE file, which strips out all your source code and prevents design changes from being made to any objects that would affect your VBA project. To create an MDE, choose Tools, Database Utilities, Make MDE File from the menu bar. This creates a new MDE file that you can distribute to your users. Make sure to save the MDB file because you cannot make any design changes to the MDE file. If you need to make design changes later, you must recompile a new MDE from the MDB file. Making an MDE file has no effect on tables or data.

Security in an Access Project (ADP)

In an Access project, all you have is SQL Server security. There is no workgroup information file and no multilevel security for your forms, reports, DAPs, macros, and modules because Jet is not present. However, you can administer security on your SQL Server objects from Access as long as you have the necessary permissions to do so in SQL Server. Choose Tools, Security, Database Security from the menu. This will load the SQL Server Security dialog box. There are three tabs displayed:

- *Server Logins*. Use the Add button to create a new SQL Server login or enable a Windows login. Use the Edit button to bring up the same dialog box you'd get in the Enterprise Manager for setting the default database, server roles, database access and database roles. The Delete button removes the login. When you click the OK button here, changes are automatically saved back to SQL Server.

- *Database Users*. Use the Add button to add a selected user to a database role. The Edit button is used either to add a user to a role, or to assign permissions directly to the user by clicking the Permissions button. The Delete button removes the database user.

- *Database Roles*. Use the Add button to add a database role. The Edit button is used either to add users to the selected role, or to assign permissions to the role by clicking on the Permissions button. Figure 3.17 displays the dialog box for setting permissions for the DataEntry database role. This is the same dialog box that the Enterprise Manager displays for modifying permissions.

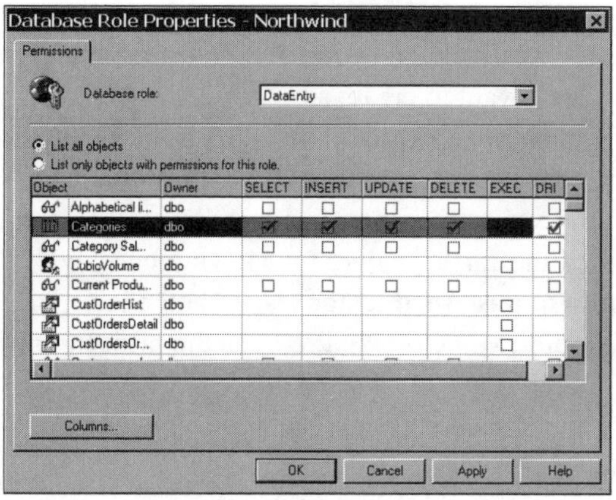

FIGURE 3.17
An Access ADP displays the same SQL Server dialog boxes for managing security that the Enterprise Manager does.

Stored Procedures and Views in an Access Project (ADP)

In Access projects (ADPs), you can use stored procedures that return records as the record sources of forms and reports. Normally row-returning stored procedures are not updateable, but Access enables you to add, update, and delete data on a form that's bound to a stored procedure, as long as the user doing the updating has ADD, UPDATE, and DELETE permissions on the underlying tables themselves. Views are also updateable as long as the user has permissions on the single table being updated using the view.

Unfortunately, the technique described earlier in this chapter of removing all permissions from tables and using only views or stored procedures won't work for Access forms that you want to be updateable. The reason for this is that when a form is based on a stored procedure, Access creates its own action query behind the scenes that attempts to make the data modification directly to the tables referenced in the stored procedure. If the user doesn't have permissions on the underlying tables, then the data will be read-only. You would need to use VBA code to perform updates using your stored procedures. We show how to do this in Chapter 11, "Scaling Up with Unbound Access Applications."

Creating an ADE from your Access Project (ADP)

Like the MDEs that can be created from Access databases, Access projects can be converted to ADE files, which have no source code and therefore offer no chance for users to modify the design of objects that would affect the VBA project. To create an ADE, choose Tools, Database Utilities, Make ADE File from the menu bar. This creates a new ADE file you can distribute to your users. Make sure to save the ADP file because you cannot make any design changes to the ADE file. If you need to make design changes later, you must recompile a new ADE from the ADP file. Making an ADE file has no effect on any of your SQL Server objects.

Setting a Password on the VBA Project

The VBA Project is not the same thing as an ADP or Access project, it refers to the collection of VBA modules in the database, including form and report modules, other class modules, and standard modules. If you don't want to create an MDE or an ADE, yet you still want to protect your code from prying eyes, set a password on the VBA project in Access 2000 in both Access databases and Access projects. Press Alt+F11 or Ctl+G to open a code window and select the database project name in the Project Explorer window. Right-click and select Properties. Click the Protection tab and check the **Lock project for viewing** checkbox. Type your new password in the **Password** and **Confirm password** textboxes as shown in Figure 3.18. The VBA project password won't take effect until you close and re-open the project. Once the password is set, anyone trying to read or modify the code will be prompted for the password. This provides some deterrence, but it is not as secure against hackers as creating an MDE or ADE file in which the source code no longer exists.

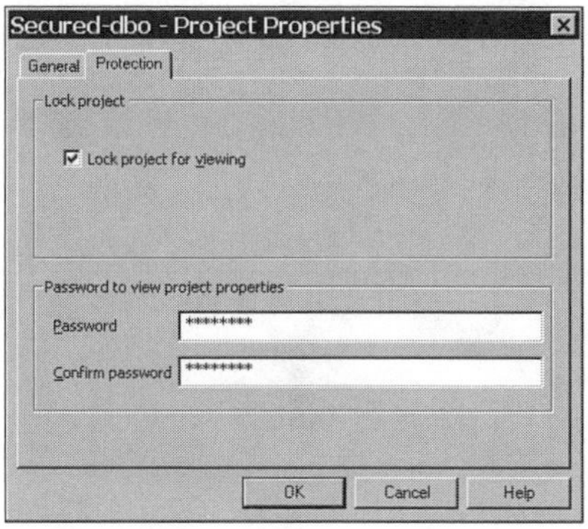

FIGURE 3.18
Setting a password on the VBA project.

Upsizing Access Security Permissions on Tables

If you have upsized an Access database that was secured with user-level security, then you're probably wondering what's the best way of transferring permissions over to the SQL Server database. One answer is to write code, retrieving the permissions that existed in the Access database using DAO (Data Access Objects), and then implementing the same permissions on the SQL Server tables. Retrieving and assigning permissions in either the Access user interface or the SQL Server Enterprise Manager is a tedious and time-consuming endeavor. This final section of the chapter presents an example of how you could use VBA code to transfer table permissions from an Access database to a SQL Server database. If you are not interested in working with security programmatically, you are welcome to skip to the "Summary" section and then move on to the next chapter.

Defining the Goal

It is impossible to anticipate every contingency, so we've designed a few procedures that will achieve a limited set of tasks. The following are the assumptions made:

- Custom groups were created and permissions were assigned only to groups, and not explicitly to users. Only permissions assigned to groups on tables will be migrated.

- New database roles will be created in the SQL Server database with the same names as the Access groups, and each group's permissions will be copied to the new role. The Access Users group will not be created—its permissions will be mapped to the SQL Server public role.

- Permissions set on Access tables are slightly different than permissions set on SQL Server tables. For example, there are no exact equivalents for the Access permissions

`Read Design`, `Modify Design`, and `Administer`, so those will be ignored. An additional SQL Server permission, `DRI`, does not exist in Access. This gives the user the ability to reference other tables that are related to the table with the `DRI` permission set. Permissions will be mapped as follows:

Access Permission	SQL Server Permission
Read Data	SELECT and DRI
Update Data	UPDATE
Insert Data	INSERT
Delete Data	DELETE

- Another wrinkle with transferring permissions comes with the way Access handles the `Read Data` permission. Access requires `Read Data` in order to grant `Update Data`, `Insert Data`, and `Delete Data`. SQL Server does not have that requirement; it is possible in SQL Server to grant the `INSERT` permission to a user to add data without letting that user browse the data later with a `SELECT` permission. After the code has run, you might want to review the permissions transferred to SQL Server and remove the `SELECT` permission where you think its removal is appropriate. You could also change the code to modify the mapping rules implemented.

Determining the Methods

The easiest way to retrieve permissions in Access is to use Data Access Objects (DAO). If you're wondering why ADOX (Microsoft ADO Extensions for DDL and Security) is not being used, it's because ADOX lacks critical functionality. ADOX implements many features that look good on paper but don't actually work, and retrieving separate permissions is one of them. So, for the time being, if you're going to tackle programming security tasks in Access, your best bet is to use DAO, Jet's original data access technology. DAO will not be covered in detail—just enough to retrieve individual permissions from the tables in the Access database. After the permissions are retrieved, ADO will be used to assign them to the upsized tables in SQL Server of the same name. Chapter 6 provides more background on the transition Microsoft has made from DAO to ADO, and it fully explains the major ADO objects.

Using DAO to Retrieve Access Permissions

The DAO object model is hierarchical in nature, and in order to retrieve permissions for tables, you must traverse the hierarchy. The workspace has a collection of groups you can use to retrieve group names. The database has a collection of containers for all Document objects where permissions are saved. If you're interested in table permissions, you need the Tables container. An individual table, such as tblOrders, is a document in the Tables container. You must point the User property of a Document object to a specific group in order to retrieve the permissions set for that group on the table. Figure 3.19 shows a diagram of how permissions are set on Container and Document objects for users and groups.

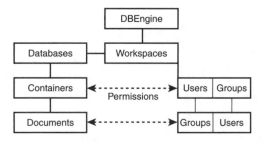

FIGURE 3.19

An abbreviated view of the DAO object model showing that permissions are set on Container and Document objects for users and groups.

In order to use DAO in Access 2000, you must set a reference to the DAO 3.6 object library by choosing Tools, References from the Visual Basic Environment. Figure 3.20 shows the DAO 3.6 reference as well as the ADO 2.5 reference, which is needed for the next section of code.

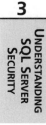

FIGURE 3.20

Setting references to the DAO 3.6 and ADO 2.5 object libraries.

After you've set the references, you can write the code. The top section of the `MigratePerms` procedure, where local variables are declared, uses the DAO object library name in front of all DAO objects so that there's no possible confusion between these DAO objects and the ADO objects that are used later. The `MigratePerms` procedure has a single parameter, `strDB`, which is the name of the SQL Server database to which you want to transfer the groups and permissions. Note that in addition to the Container and Document objects, there is also a TableDef object, which is needed to retrieve certain table properties. Here's the first section of code, where all of the variables are declared:

```
Public Sub MigratePerms(ByVal strDB As String)

    Dim ws As DAO.Workspace
    Dim db As DAO.Database
    Dim tdf As DAO.TableDef
    Dim grp As DAO.Group
    Dim con As DAO.Container
    Dim doc As DAO.Document
    Dim fPerm As Boolean
    Dim freturn As Boolean
    Dim strTable As String
    Dim strGrp As String
    Dim strMsg As String
```

The next step is to instantiate the object variables, pointing to the default workgroup (which is used to retrieve the group information), the default database, and the Tables container:

```
Set ws = DBEngine(0)
Set db = CurrentDb
Set con = db.Containers("Tables")
```

After the references are set for the Workspace, Database and Containers, you can walk the workspace object's Groups collection, pulling out each group name. For every group except the Users group, a new role is created in the SQL Server database using the same name. The CreateRole function takes the name of the SQL Server database and the name of the group. The CreateRole function is examined more closely in the next section when the ADO code is discussed.

```
For Each grp In ws.Groups
    strGrp = grp.Name
    ' Create a role for all groups except Users
    If strGrp <> "Users" Then
        freturn = CreateRole(strDB, strGrp)
    End If
```

It's time to walk through the database's collection of TableDef objects. Here, you need the name of the table and its attributes. If the attributes are zero, the table is a nonsystem, native Jet table. If the attributes are any nonzero value, the table's not a Jet table or a Jet system table, and it should be ignored. The table name is then set to a Document object. You need both the TableDef and the Document object because only the TableDef object gives you the attributes you need (it has to be a native Jet table) and only the Document object gives you the permissions that have been set for the table. You then set the Document object's UserName property to the name of the group:

```
For Each tdf In db.TableDefs
    ' If a table's attributes are 0, then it's a local table
```

```
If tdf.Attributes = 0 Then
    strTable = tdf.Name
    Set doc = con.Documents(strTable)
    doc.UserName = strGrp
```

After you have the Document object, you can retrieve the permissions set for the group by comparing the `Permissions` property with the permission in which you're interested. The `fPerm` Boolean variable returns `True` if the group has `Read Data` permission and `False` if the group doesn't have the permission:

```
fPerm = ((doc.Permissions And dbSecRetrieveData) = _
    dbSecRetrieveData)
```

If the group has `Read Data` permission, the `GrantPerm` function is called, and the database name, group name, table name, and permission to set are passed as arguments. Note that the `Trim()` function is applied to the name of the table. The Upsizing Wizard adds an extra space to the name of the table when it renames local tables. Because SQL Server tables aren't given this trailing space (thankfully!), you can use `Trim()` to come up with equivalent names:

```
If fPerm Then
    freturn = GrantPerm(strDB, strGrp, Trim(strTable), "SELECT")
End If
```

The rest of the procedure performs the same operations for the other permissions the group might possibly have on the table (`INSERT`, `UPDATE`, and `DELETE`):

```
fPerm = ((doc.Permissions And dbSecInsertData) = _
    dbSecInsertData)
    If fPerm Then
        freturn = GrantPerm(strDB, strGrp, Trim(strTable), "INSERT")
    End If

    fPerm = ((doc.Permissions And dbSecReplaceData) = _
    dbSecReplaceData)
    If fPerm Then
        freturn = GrantPerm(strDB, strGrp, Trim(strTable), "UPDATE")
    End If

    fPerm = ((doc.Permissions And dbSecDeleteData) = _
    dbSecDeleteData)
    If fPerm Then
        freturn = GrantPerm(strDB, strGrp, Trim(strTable), "DELETE")
    End If
End If
```

3

UNDERSTANDING
SQL SERVER
SECURITY

Using ADO to Set SQL Server Permissions

DAO is more efficient when working with Access security on Jet tables, but when it comes to SQL Server, then ADO is a better choice. An ADO Connection object creates a direct connection to SQL Server, bypassing Jet entirely. DAO requires Jet and/or ODBC, which adds unnecessary overhead when all you want to do is work with SQL Server.

Three procedures in basSecurity use ADO:

- OpenConnection. Initiates an ADO connection to the SQL Server database
- CreateRole. Creates roles in the SQL Server database
- GrantPerms. Assigns the permissions collected from DAO to the SQL Server tables

All three procedures use an ADO Connection object, which is declared as a private variable in the declarations section of the module. After the connection is opened, it stays active until it is explicitly closed or until the application is closed. Here's an example:

```
Option Compare Database
Option Explicit

Private mcnn As ADODB.Connection
```

The OpenConnection function takes a single parameter: the name of the database to open. OpenConnection returns True if it succeeds in connecting to SQL Server and False if it fails. OpenConnection is called from both the CreateRole and GrantPerms procedures. You might need to modify the connection string if you are not running your code on the server or if you are not using NT security. Here's the OpenConnection function:

```
Public Function OpenConnection( _
  ByVal strDB As String) As Boolean
On Error Resume Next
  Set mcnn = New ADODB.Connection
  mcnn.ConnectionString = "Provider=SQLOLEDB.1;" & _
  "Data Source=(local);" & _
  "Initial Catalog=" & strDB & ";" & _
  "Integrated Security=SSPI"
  mcnn.Open
  OpenConnection = (Err = 0)
End Function
```

The CreateRole procedure takes as parameters the name of the database and the name of the role to create. The procedure's first action is to check whether the Connection object is instantiated. If the Connection object is not instantiated, the OpenConnection function is called:

```
Public Function CreateRole(ByVal strDB As String, _
  ByVal strRole As String) As Boolean
On Error GoTo HandleErr
```

```
If mcnn Is Nothing Then
   Call OpenConnection(strDB)
     If mcnn Is Nothing Then
        MsgBox "Could not connect to server."
        GoTo ExitHere
     End If
End If
```

Once the connection is open, the Execute method runs the sp_addrole system stored procedure, passing it the name of the role to create:

```
mcnn.Execute "sp_addrole '" & strRole & "'"
CreateRole = True
```

The rest of the procedure involves error handling. Note that there's no MsgBox() here; if you run MigratePerms several times, errors will be returned that the role already exists. These errors can be safely ignored:

```
ExitHere:
  Exit Function

HandleErr:
  CreateRole = False
  Debug.Print "CreateRole", Err, Err.Description, Err.Source
  Resume ExitHere
End Function
```

The GrantPerm function assigns to the SQL Server tables the permissions retrieved earlier. Its parameters are the name of the database, the name of the role, the name of the table, and the permission to be set:

```
Public Function GrantPerm(ByVal strDB As String, _
  ByVal strRole As String, _
  ByVal strTable As String, _
  ByVal strPerm As String) As Boolean

  Dim strTemp As String

On Error GoTo HandleErr
```

This code tests to make sure that the Connection object is set. If it can't connect, it exits the procedure:

```
If mcnn Is Nothing Then
   Call OpenConnection(strDB)
     If mcnn Is Nothing Then
       MsgBox "Could not connect to server."
       GoTo ExitHere
     End If
End If
```

Your local tables might not have the string "_local " appended to them, depending on whether you used the Upsizing Wizard and whether you chose linked tables. If your tables have this string, it must be stripped off because the SQL Server tables will be named with the base table name, without the "_local " string appended. The Trim() function gets rid of the gratuitous space that the Upsizing Wizard adds:

```
strTemp = Right(strTable, 6)
If Trim(strTemp) = "_local" Then
   strTable = Mid(strTable, 1, (Len(strTable) - 6))
End If
```

If the Access group being passed in is the Users group, you'll want to assign its permissions to the SQL Server public role:

```
If strRole = "Users" Then strRole = "public"
```

Granting permissions in SQL Server is done through Transact-SQL with the GRANT statement. The ADO Connection object executes the SQL GRANT statement:

```
mcnn.Execute "GRANT " & strPerm & " ON " & _
    strTable & " TO " & strRole

  GrantPerm = True
```

The rest of the procedure involves error handling:

```
ExitHere:
  Exit Function
HandleErr:
  GrantPerm = False
    Debug.Print "GrantPerm", Err, Err.Description, Err.Source
  Resume ExitHere
End Function
```

Regardless of whether you choose to make use of this code, it's a good demonstration of how useful it is to know the system stored procedures used behind the scenes by SQL Server to carry out every task you perform in the Enterprise Manager. After you know the syntax of the system stored procedures, it's relatively easy to use ADO to execute the actions you want performed. In Chapter 6, you'll have a chance to get more comfortable with ADO (if it is new to you).

The entire module, basSecurity, is available, along with all the examples in this book, on the Sams Web site (samspublishing.com). You can import it into any Access 2000 database. The code can also be used in Access 97.

Summary

SQL Server has a rich and well-developed security model that offers enough options to accommodate most security needs. SQL Server's integration with Windows NT and Windows 2000 is especially welcome because it saves most users from confronting a second logon screen, and it helps make your data extremely secure.

Figure 3.21 shows the relationships between NT users, NT groups, SQL Server users, SQL Server logins, database users, database roles, application roles, and permissions.

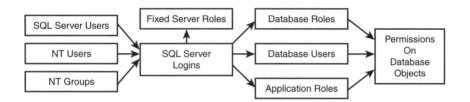

FIGURE 3.21
The SQL Server security model includes logins, users, roles, and permissions.

The first step in setting up security is to establish your SQL Server logins. Use Windows NT or Windows 2000 users and groups and create users within SQL Server. When your logins are in place, assign any of them that should perform administrative tasks on the server to fixed server roles. Enable logins as users in the individual databases on your server and assign them to fixed and custom database roles. Finally, assign permissions on your database objects to database users or, more conveniently, assign permissions to database roles. You can also establish application roles with their own passwords and define the permissions that are available to the users of those applications.

You also need to be aware of the importance of ownership of database objects. Any objects created by members of the sysadmin role are owned by dbo, but other objects are owned by the user who created them. Object ownership gives a user complete control over the permissions of that object and prevents the user from being removed from the database, but you can transfer ownership if you need to do so.

You can manipulate security settings by using Enterprise Manager or system stored procedures, and you can run those stored procedures by using ADO in code. SQL Server has the SQL-DMO object model, which you could use for setting security, but it too runs system stored procedures behind the scenes.

It is important to understand SQL Server security before you go too far in setting up a database. Whether you are running a lemonade stand or a nuclear submarine, getting security right is an essential part of building a successful database application.

3

UNDERSTANDING
SQL SERVER
SECURITY

Introduction to Access Projects (ADPs)

IN THIS CHAPTER

About Access Projects

Traditionally an Access application has consisted of a single MDB file that contains both the data objects (tables and queries) and the application objects (forms, reports, macros, and modules). You could split the database and move the tables into a separate MDB file, but at the end of the day, everything would still be managed by the Jet database engine and stored in an MDB file. With the introduction of Access 2000 came the Access project, which no longer has anything to do with the Jet database engine that has fueled all previous Access versions. Instead, all data objects (tables, views, and stored procedures) are SQL Server objects and reside on a SQL Server. Unlike Access databases, SQL Server has no forms, reports, macros, modules, or any other application objects. Access projects are designed to fill that need for SQL Server databases by providing storage for those application objects. An Access project also provides a way to store connection information to a single SQL Server as well as the capability of working directly with SQL Server data objects through the Access user interface. Although you can link to a SQL Server database through an Access MDB file, you can't work directly with SQL Server objects.

Access projects are not themselves databases, nor do they contain databases. An Access project can display objects and data by connecting to one of the following types of SQL Server databases:

- SQL Server 6.5 with Service Pack 5, running on Windows NT 4.0 or later.
- SQL Server 7.0 running on Windows NT 4.0 or later or Windows 95/98.
- MSDE (Microsoft Data Engine) running on Windows NT 4.0 or later or Windows 95/98. MSDE provides data storage compatible with SQL Server 7.0.
- SQL Server 2000 Enterprise Edition
- SQL Server 2000 Standard Edition
- SQL Server 2000 Personal Edition
- SQL Server 2000 Developer Edition
- SQL Server 2000 Evaluation Edition
- SQL Server 2000 Desktop Engine (MSDE)

TIP

It's recommended that you install SQL Server Service Pack 1 (or later service packs, if they're available when you read this), if you're running SQL Server 7.0 or MSDE.

An Access project connects to a server database through the SQL Server OLE DB provider. In addition to the data, all the tables, views, database diagrams, and stored procedures reside on the server, not in the Access project (ADP) file. The only things besides connection information saved in the Access project are forms, reports, data access pages, macros, and modules. Figure 4.1 shows the Object List in an Access project.

FIGURE 4.1
The objects in an Access project file.

Because the Access project is connected directly to SQL Server and all the data-containing objects live on the server, any changes you make to the design of tables, views, relationships, or stored procedures take place at the server, not in the ADP file.

Advantages of Access Projects

The main advantage of using an Access project for your client/server application is that you don't have to do any extra work to connect to SQL Server. You can base Access forms, reports, and data access pages directly on SQL Server tables, views, and stored procedures. You don't need Open Database Connectivity (ODBC) or the Jet database engine because you are working directly with SQL Server through its OLE DB provider.

In Access projects, a single efficient OLE DB connection is used for all data retrieval, data manipulation, and database design tasks. ADP forms use the ADO cursor engine to create and manage the forms' recordsets of data. These client-side recordsets impose a minimal load on the server, and consume no server resources when the forms are idle. OLE DB connections and ADO recordsets are defined and explained in Chapter 6, "ActiveX Data Objects (ADO) Fundamentals."

4

INTRODUCTION TO
ACCESS PROJECTS
(ADPs)

ADPs also provide graphical user interfaces for creating and modifying SQL Server objects. This is especially important if you are using MSDE as your database engine, because MSDE does not come with any design tools of its own.

Disadvantages of Access Projects

The biggest difference between Access databases (MDBs) and Access projects that will have an impact on you as an Access developer is that there is no built-in local storage for temp tables or queries. This can be difficult to get used to when you're used to having the flexibility of temp tables or allowing users to save their own local queries.

Projects limit you to a single connection to a single SQL Server database. Access databases use ODBC to link to any type of relational database, and a single Access database can link to a number of different data sources, not just SQL Server. You can work around this limitation in Access projects using SQL Server to connect to other data sources through OLE DB linked servers, but doing that is much more complex than creating links in an Access database. Linked servers are covered in Chapter 8, "Introduction to Transact SQL (T-SQL)."

No Local Storage

Because all data objects in an Access project are located on SQL Server, you cannot have local tables in your Access project because there is simply no place to put them. The Jet database engine is no longer present, so there is no mechanism with which to store them. This means you must fetch all the data your application uses from the server at runtime. For example, it's common practice in Access database client/server applications to populate local tables with static data (such as a list of states or the departments in your company). These local lookup tables can be used as the RowSource property for combo and list boxes, thus saving additional roundtrips to the server. In an Access project, all bound data must be fetched from the server, which results in increased network traffic. In Chapter 11, "Scaling Up with Unbound Access Applications," we show a workaround that uses VBA to populate combo and list boxes from locally stored XML files.

No Local Queries

In an Access database, the Jet engine provides a local query processor. With Jet not present, there is no mechanism to process local queries. Applications that allow users to create and save their own queries must allow users to save them as views or stored procedures, which are stored in SQL Server. Many database administrators prefer to restrict users from being able to store objects on the server.

The only workaround for this limitation is to install SQL Server or MSDE on each user's machine and set up linked servers to connect to other data sources. Queries (in the form of SQL Server views and stored procedures) could then be created and stored on the local SQL Server or MSDE. Linked servers are covered in Chapter 8.

Security Limitations

If you are used to working with Access user-level security to selectively allow users access to certain forms and reports, you will be very disappointed that there is no way to do this in an Access project. Jet handles user-level security for forms, reports, and macros in an Access database, and SQL Server security cannot be configured to handle security at the application level. Two options are available for application security:

- *Compile your Access project as an ADE.* This will protect the design of your forms, reports, and modules and prevent users from modifying or creating new Access objects.

- *Place a password on your module code.* This will prevent users from modifying code unless they know the password.

If you want to provide user-level security the way it's implemented in an Access database, you'll probably want to use an Access database instead of an Access project for your client/server application.

Creating a New Access Project

Create a new Access project by choosing File, New from the File menu. Figure 4.2 shows the New dialog box. Two options are available for creating Access projects:

- Create an Access project that's connected to an existing SQL Server database.

- Create an Access project that's connected to a new database (or rather a database that does not exist yet—an empty SQL Server database is created when you create the new project).

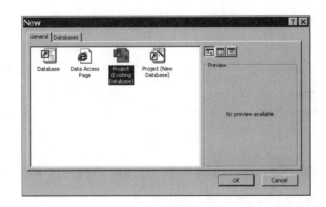

FIGURE 4.2

Creating a new Access project from an existing SQL Server database.

Connecting to SQL Server

When you click the OK button to create your new Access project, you will be prompted to fill in the connection information that the Access project will use to connect to your SQL Server database, as shown in Figure 4.3. The server name is the name of your SQL Server. You can use either integrated NT security or SQL Server security. Figure 4.3 shows connecting to a SQL Server named MABEL using NT authentication. The database selected is the Northwind database. Click the Test Connection button to make sure all the information you've specified works correctly.

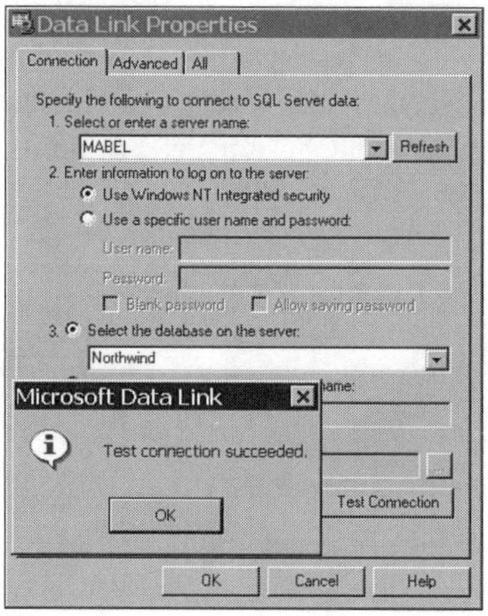

FIGURE 4.3
Connecting to an existing SQL Server database when creating a new Access project.

TIP

You can change the connection properties later by choosing File, Connection from the Access Project menu.

Designing SQL Server Objects in an Access Project

An Access project supplies you with the basic tools you need to create and modify SQL Server tables, database diagrams, views, and stored procedures. The following sections briefly cover each one.

Creating and Editing Tables

To create a new table, select Tables in the Object List and then select the Create Table in Design View option. You will be prompted for the name of your new table. Once named, the new table will be opened in the table designer in your Access project. Figure 4.4 shows columns being defined for a new table named tblProductGiveaways. The table designer in an Access project is very similar to the one in SQL Server's Enterprise Manager. (For coverage of using Enterprise Manager to create tables, see Chapter 7, "Designing and Creating a SQL Server Database.") You can work with the menu items or toolbar buttons to create and modify column definitions. When you save your changes, the SQL Server Northwind database will be updated and the new table added.

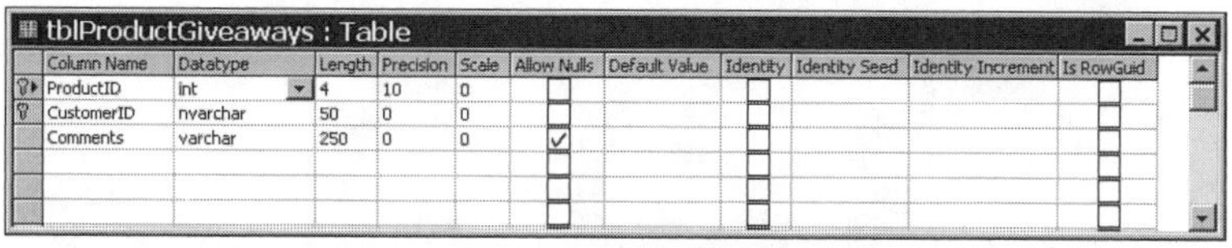

FIGURE 4.4
Creating a new table and defining the columns.

You can use the table designer to change any of the existing tables in the Northwind database by selecting the table in the Object List and clicking the Design button.

The Access project table designer is very similar to the one that exists in the SQL Server Enterprise Manager. It allows you to define the columns, specify the data types, and set other table properties the same way you would using the Enterprise Manager's table designer. Creating tables is discussed in more detail in Chapter 7.

You can view any table data in datasheet view after saving the table and choosing the View button or View, Datasheet from the menu bar. Like the table designer in the Enterprise Manager, most features are available using a right mouse click.

Working with Constraints, Relationships, and Indexes

The Properties dialog box allows you to work with constraints, relationships, and indexes. A SQL Server constraint is similar to a validation rule in Access, and constraints are discussed in detail in Chapter 7, along with relationships and indexes.

You can bring up the Properties dialog box using any of the following methods:

- Right-click anywhere in the table definition
- Choose View, Properties from the menu
- Click the Properties button on the toolbar

Figure 4.5 shows a constraint being created to limit the product IDs of products entered in the tblProductGiveaways table to the product IDs of specific products. There is no explicit Save button—when you close the dialog box, the constraint will be saved at the time you save the table.

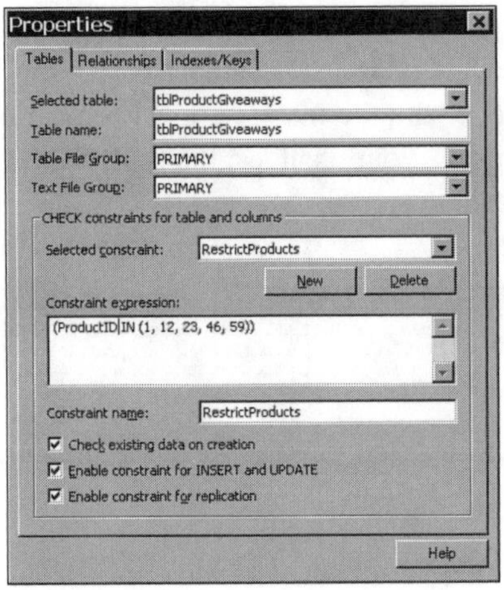

FIGURE 4.5
Creating a constraint to limit the products entered.

The Relationships tab lets you modify the properties of existing relationships if you have already created them. Figure 4.6 displays the Employees table relationships. Use a database diagram to create relationships from scratch. Creating and modifying database diagrams is covered in the next section, and relationships are discussed in detail in Chapter 7.

The Indexes/Keys tab lets you set indexes and primary keys, as shown in Figure 4.7. The usage of indexes and keys is also covered in detail in Chapter 7.

Creating and Editing Database Diagrams

Database diagrams are similar to the Edit, Relationships window in an Access database, but they possess many more features. You can also have more than one database diagram per database, which comes in handy if your schema is complex or has many tables. The main purpose of database diagrams is to allow you to create relationships between tables and configure referential integrity in your SQL Server database using a graphical user interface. Database diagrams also allow you to modify the schema and properties of your SQL Server tables by creating constraints and primary keys, and by modifying other table properties. When a database diagram is saved, all changes to objects modified during that session are saved as well. Use database diagrams to perform the following tasks:

- Create relationships between the tables in your SQL Server database. You can drag and drop columns between tables on the diagram to create relationships. You can also edit existing relationships by right-clicking the relationship join line and choosing Properties from the list.

- Store multiple diagrams, each with its own combination of tables. This is great when you have a large schema and want to work with the parts separately.

- Work with all properties of a table, not just the relationships. Data types, constraints, indexes, and other table properties can be modified through database diagrams.

- Create annotations (or labels) in your diagram. (They're known as *annotations* in the Enterprise Manager and *labels* in Access 2000.) Annotations are simply descriptive text that you can insert into your diagrams. They have no effect on the underlying tables or schema.

- Print diagrams.

- Save changes to the underlying tables.

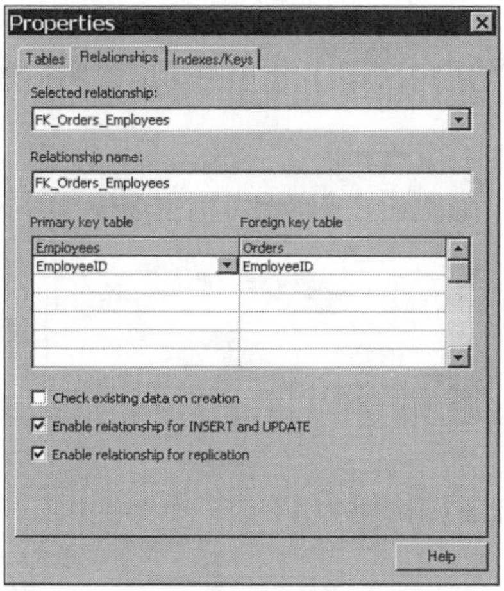

FIGURE 4.6
The Relationships tab showing relationships in the Employees table.

Database diagrams in Access projects have most of the features found in the database diagrams in the Enterprise Manager. There isn't 100-percent parity—for example, the ability to script objects is missing in Access—but you can do just about everything else. Figure 4.8 shows a database diagram of the Northwind database. The relationship label describing the relationship between the Products and the Order Details tables is displayed, which you can see when you linger your mouse over the join line between two tables. Note the annotation at the top of the diagram pane.

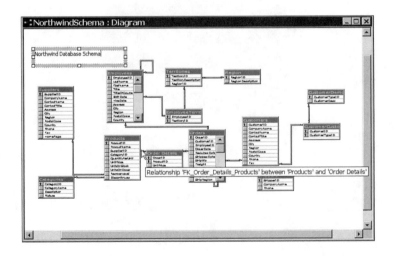

FIGURE 4.7

Creating/modifying indexes and keys in the Indexes/Keys tab.

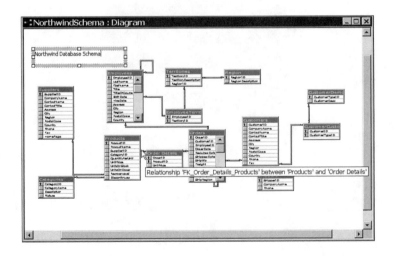

FIGURE 4.8

The database diagram for the Northwind database.

Using a Database Diagram to Modify a Table

To modify the design of a table using a database diagram, select the table and right-click it. This will display the pop-up menu shown in Figure 4.9. The top third of the menu changes the display characteristics of the database diagram. You can set a primary key and work with the tables and the rows of the table. If you choose the Properties option on the bottom of the menu with a table selected, you will load the same Table Properties dialog box as that shown in

Figures 4.5, 4.6, and 4.7. This will allow you to work with the table's constraints, relationships, and indexes.

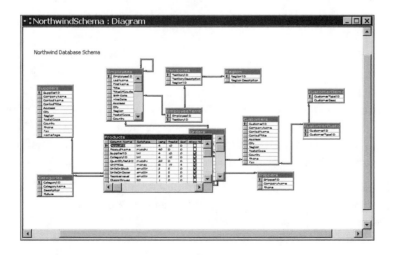

FIGURE 4.9

The context-sensitive menu available when a table is selected on the database diagram.

Changing Column Properties

The Column Properties option shown in Figure 4.9 displays the column definitions for the selected table, as shown in Figure 4.10. This allows you to modify the data type, length, precision, scale, and nullability of existing columns as well as define new columns. The column definitions are fully editable, and any changes made here will be saved back to the database when the database diagram is saved.

FIGURE 4.10

Working with column definitions in a database diagram.

If you right-click an empty area of the database diagram, you will get the menu options shown in Figure 4.11. These options allow you to configure the database diagram as a whole. You can add tables and labels as well as set other diagram properties.

The use of database diagrams is also discussed in Chapter 7.

FIGURE 4.11
Options for the database diagram as a whole.

CAUTION

Database diagrams differ from the Relationships window in Access databases in one crucial respect. If you delete a table from the Database diagram, it will be deleted from the SQL Server database. If you delete a table from the Relationships window in an Access database, neither the table nor its relationships are actually deleted (they're only removed from the Relationships pane). To remove a table from a database diagram without deleting it, right-click the table and choose Hide Table. This will safely remove it from the database diagram.

Creating and Editing Views

You can use an Access project to create or modify a view. Views are very similar to the select queries that you are used to creating in Access, but they have a couple of limitations. You can't include sorting in most views (view that select top values are an exception), and you also can't include parameters. Views are discussed in more detail in Chapter 9, "Creating and Optimizing Views," but the tools for working with them in ADPs are covered here.

To create a new view, select Views in the Object List and click the New button. This will create a new, empty view. Click the yellow plus sign (+) button to add tables to the view. This loads the Show Table dialog box, and you can drag and drop the tables you want to use in your view onto the top pane, as shown in Figure 4.12. When you add tables to your views that have established relationships, joins matching the relationships are created automatically for you. You can optionally choose to show any of the three panes of the design window—the tables, the columns grid, and the SQL text—by clicking the toolbar buttons corresponding to each pane. To see the results of the view, click the Datasheet View toolbar button in the upper left-corner.

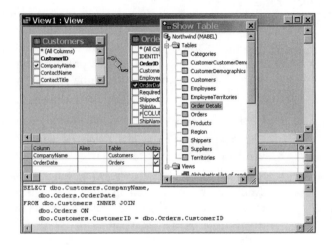

FIGURE 4.12
Creating a view in an Access project.

Creating Aggregate Views

To add a GROUP BY clause to your query, choose Query, Group By from the menu bar or click the Group By toolbar button. The following aggregate functions can be used to create aggregate views:

- Sum
- Avg
- Count
- Min
- Max
- StDev
- StDevP
- Var
- VarP

We discuss the use of aggregate functions in Chapter 8.

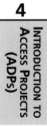

Setting View Properties

Additional view properties are available via the View, Properties menu, by right-clicking an empty area of the view, or by clicking the Properties button on the toolbar. Table 4.1 lists the available properties along with a brief description of each one.

TABLE 4.1 Additional Properties of Views

Property	Description
Top	Specifies a TOP clause, which can be either a number or a percent. This is the same as the Top property in Access queries, where it first appeared before being adopted in SQL Server.
Output all columns	Displays all columns, regardless of whether they're checked.
DISTINCT values	Duplicate results will be omitted and only unique rows displayed.
Encrypt view	The view will be encrypted. Once the view is saved and closed, you will never be able to display or edit its design again.
GROUP BY extension	Specifies that the WITH CUBE, WITH ROLLUP, and ALL options are available for views based on aggregate queries. These extended operators can be used to generate result sets that contain both detail rows for each item and summary rows for each group, similarly to an Access report.
WITH CUBE	Creates multidimensional summaries from all combinations of values in the selected columns.
WITH ROLLUP	Similar to WITH CUBE, WITH ROLLUP creates fewer summary results, limiting itself to a one-dimensional hierarchy of values.
ALL	Use GROUP BY ALL to see all groups in your results even if some include no rows. Otherwise, groups with no rows are omitted.

When you click the Save button or choose File, Save, the view is saved to the SQL Server database. Once you save the view, choose View, Datasheet from the menu bar or click the toolbar button to see the results shown in datasheet view. For more detailed information about what you can do with views, see Chapters 8 and 9. The summarization options are also discussed in Chapter 12, "Building Access Reports from SQL Server Data."

Creating and Editing Stored Procedures

Access ADPs also allow you to create and modify stored procedures, which are composed of Transact-SQL code. Stored procedures are compiled and executed in a somewhat similar way to how saved queries are handled in Access. Any saved SQL Server queries containing parameters must be created as stored procedures, not views. The Transact-SQL language contains many features that aren't available in Access SQL, and using those features in stored procedures allows you to do things with stored procedures that in Access would require VBA code. For a glimpse of the power available in Transact-SQL, see Chapter 10, "Programming Effective Stored Procedures."

To create a new stored procedure in an Access project, select Stored Procedures in the Object List and click the New button. This will load an empty shell for a stored procedure, as shown in Figure 4.13. Replace the `"StoredProcedure1"` name with a name of your choosing. The stored procedure shell provided contains comment blocks for specifying input and output parameters. Remove the comment characters ("/*" and "*/") and replace the existing text with your own parameters, data types, and default values. The SET NOCOUNT ON statement can be activated by removing the comment characters surrounding it. Type in your Transact-SQL statements after the AS statement and before the RETURN statement, which is optional, on the last line of the stored procedure. If you remove the RETURN statement, the stored procedure will terminate after the last statement.

Unfortunately, Microsoft hasn't yet tackled the task of providing a friendly graphical user interface for creating stored procedures. The only way to create one in Access is to type or paste the correct text into this window.

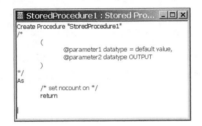

FIGURE 4.13
The empty stored procedure shell.

Figure 4.14 shows a completed stored procedure with a single input parameter for the CustomerID. If the `CustomerID` parameter is supplied, the name and total for each product the customer purchased is displayed.

FIGURE 4.14
A completed stored procedure in an Access project.

> **TIP**
>
> Because there are no visual data tools for generating the SQL statements used in stored procedures, you will probably want to use either the SQL Server Query Analyzer or the view designer in Access to construct Transact-SQL statements. This technique comes in handy for complex join syntax and aggregate queries that are difficult to type manually and therefore prone to error.

Stored procedures are covered in detail in Chapter 10.

Forms in Access Projects

For the most part, forms in Access projects have the same events and properties you're used to working with in Access databases, with the addition of some new properties specifically designed to work with SQL Server data and the modification of a few familiar properties that have different options. Certain other properties, such as Record Locks and the dynaset/snapshot Recordset Type options, have been removed entirely because they are not relevant to SQL Server.

One powerful new feature is the ability to bind forms to updatable ADO recordsets, which is not possible in an Access database. The following sections explore how you can use these new capabilities in your Access forms.

Using Form Properties

Most properties on a form are read/write both at design time and at runtime. In an Access project, the intelligent use of form properties is one way of controlling the amount of data that travels over the network from the server to the Access client application. Because SQL Server tables can become quite large, it's important to base forms on the smallest amount of data necessary to get the job done. The old Access bound form technique of basing forms on entire tables does not work efficiently with SQL Server or scale well for large numbers of users. In addition, it can cause the network to become overloaded. In general, you'll want to restrict the form's Record Source property so that only data the user really needs at the moment is fetched.

Record Source

The Record Source property has been a feature of Access forms since forms were invented. The Record Source property in Access projects can be set to the following data sources:

- Tables
- Views

- Stored procedures
- Transact-SQL statements that return records

You can set the Record Source property from the New Form dialog box for tables and views at the time the form is created or from a dialog box in the property sheet after the form has been created. A notable exception is stored procedures, which are not available until after you create the form.

Setting the Record Source to a Stored Procedure

Even though you can base forms on stored procedures, it's not readily apparent how to do so if you create a form from scratch. Figure 4.15 shows the drop-down list of available tables and views when you create a new form, but stored procedures are absent from the list.

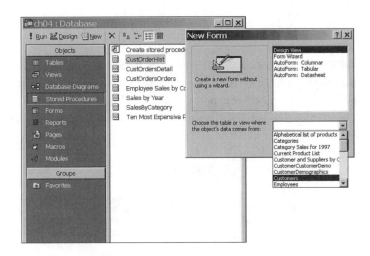

FIGURE 4.15

Where are the stored procedures? Creating a form from scratch.

The workaround for this problem is to create the form without a data source. Once the form is created, you can select the stored procedure from the form's Record Source property, as shown in Figure 4.16. For some reason, the form's Record Source property lists stored procedures, but the New Form dialog box doesn't.

One singular feature of setting a form's Record Source property to a stored procedure is that, contrary to what you might expect, the form is not necessarily read-only. If the form's Recordset Type property is set to Updatable Snapshot (as discussed in the next section), and the stored procedure returns a result set based on an updatable query, you can edit the data on the form, as shown in Figure 4.17. Normally the result set returned by a stored procedure is read-only. However, Access creates a recordset "under the hood" that's based on the stored procedure and uses that recordset to post changes back to the server.

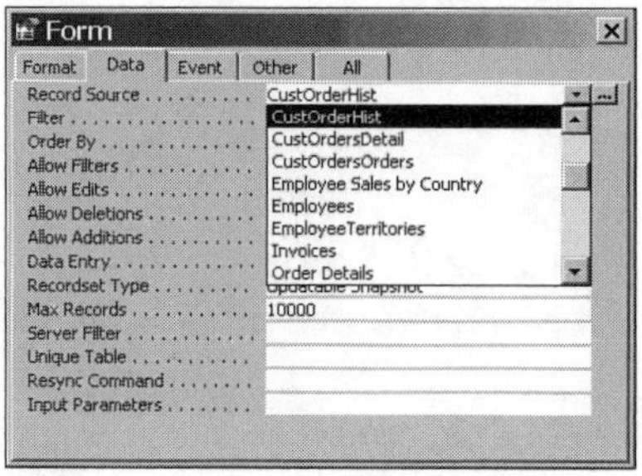

FIGURE 4.16
Setting the Record Source property of a form to a stored procedure.

The updatablility of a form based on a stored procedure will only be possible if the user has permission to update the base table. The only security permission you can set for a stored procedure is permission to run the procedure, and this alone will not enable a user to directly update the underlying tables. For a full discussion of SQL Server security, see Chapter 3, "Understanding SQL Server Security."

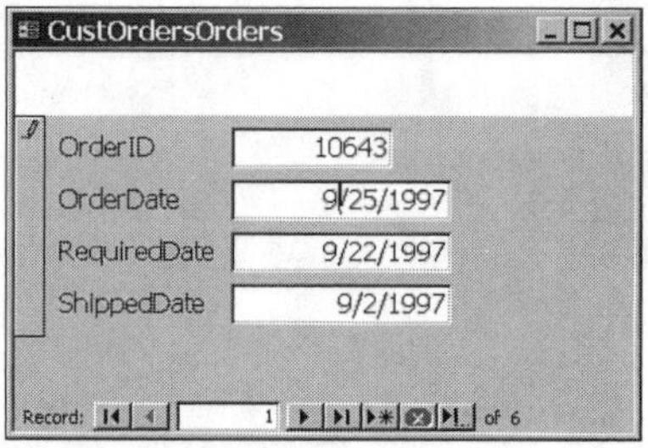

FIGURE 4.17
Updating a form based on a stored procedure.

Recordset Type

Figure 4.18 shows the form's Recordset Type property being set to either Snapshot or Updatable Snapshot. Updatable Snapshot is the default, and it allows you to use the form to modify data. The term *updatable snapshot* may be confusing because snapshots are read-only in Access databases. However, unlike the forms in Access databases, which have always been based on DAO recordsets, the forms in Access 2000 projects are based on ADO recordsets, and in ADO, snapshots can be updated. These two Recordset Type options—Snapshot and

Updatable Snapshot—replace the Dynaset and Snapshot recordset types available in an Access database.

Access projects use the word *snapshot* to refer to a static ADO recordset. Static recordsets in ADO can be made updatable by setting the lock type of the recordset. If you choose an updatable snapshot in an Access form, what you are actually getting is an ADO recordset with a cursor type of adOpenStatic, a lock type of adLockOptimistic, and a cursor location of adUseClient. In Chapter 6, ADO recordsets and their properties are discussed in detail.

The static ADO recordset used by the form behaves differently from a DAO recordset, which if set to Dynaset automatically shows changes made by other users. The ADO recordset requires you to explicitly invoke the Refresh method of the form in order to see changes made by other users. When you choose the updatable snapshot option, Access retrieves enough schema information to be able to update rows on the server later. If you don't intend to use the form to modify data, choosing the Snapshot recordset type will be more efficient, because Access doesn't have to go to all the trouble of caching information it will never need. The ADO cursor engine that maintains the recordset and, optionally, handles updates is fortunately quite efficient and places a minimal load on the server once the recordset has been opened.

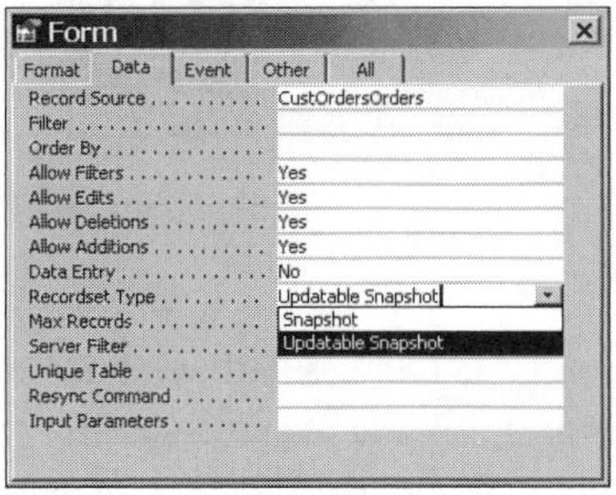

FIGURE 4.18
Setting the Recordset Type property.

Max Rec Button

The Max Records button on a form, located on the far right side of the built-in navigation buttons, displays a slider control that can be used to set the maximum number of records that the form will retrieve. When the Max Rec Button property is set to Yes, as shown in Figure 4.19, the form displays the button. If this property is set to No, the button is hidden.

When the Max Rec Button property is enabled, you or an end user can use the slider shown in Figure 4.20. The minimum number of records you can set using the slider is 100, but lower numbers can be typed directly in the Max Records text box. If you type 0 (zero), all records will be retrieved. If you type a negative number, the minus sign will be ignored, and the positive number of records will be returned.

4

INTRODUCTION TO
ACCESS PROJECTS
(ADPs)

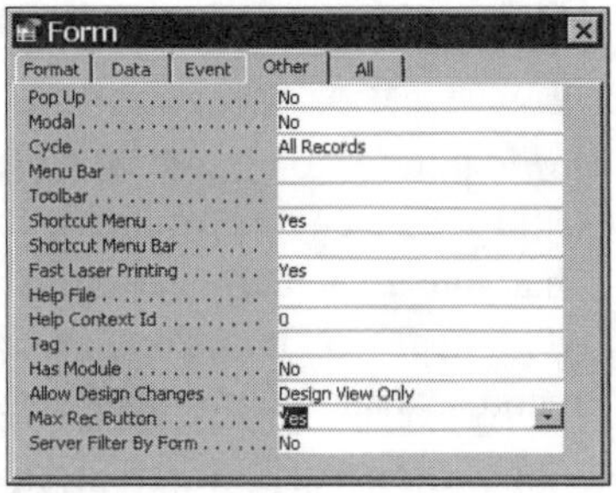

FIGURE 4.19

The Max Rec Button property controls the visibility of the Max Records button of the navigation buttons.

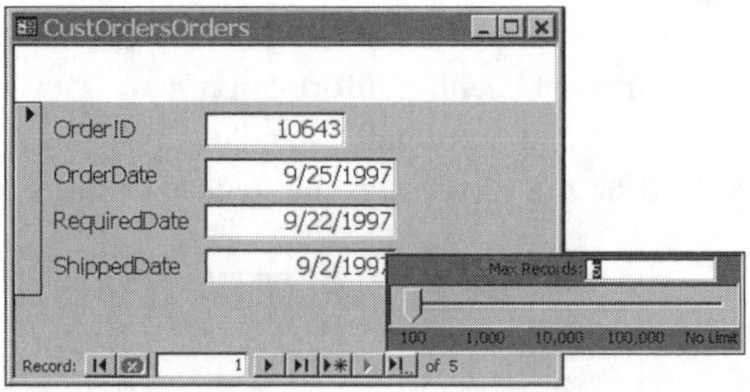

FIGURE 4.20

Setting the maximum number of records on a form.

Opening a form based on an entire table and then allowing the user to restrict the records using the Max Records slider isn't the most efficient way of working with SQL Server data. All the records would travel across the network and then the excess ones would be thrown away. To cut down on network traffic and minimize resources on the SQL Server, set the Max Records property before the form is opened.

Max Records

The Max Records property sets the maximum number of records to return, based on the sort order of the SELECT statement used in the form's record source. It truncates the rows returned based on the number chosen by using the Transact-SQL SET ROWCOUNT *n* statement, which causes SQL Server to stop processing the query once the specified number of rows has been retrieved. This property is useful in preventing forms from returning inordinately large amounts of data. If you set the Max Records property to 100, your form will only be able to work with the first 100 rows, even if the data source has 10,000 rows. The 101st row and beyond will be unavailable.

Setting Max Records Using VBA

You can set the Max Records property from the property sheet or dynamically at runtime by writing some code. Listing 4.1 shows the event procedure for the `Open` event of the frmCustomer form. The user is prompted for the maximum number of records to enter and then the form's `RecordSource` property is set to the Customers table.

LISTING 4.1 The `Open` Event Procedure Setting the `MaxRecords` Property

```
Private Sub Form_Open(Cancel As Integer)
    Dim strMaxRec As String
    strMaxRec = InputBox( _
      "Enter the maximum number of records.", _
      "Set MaxRecords", 10)
    If IsNumeric(strMaxRec) Then
      Forms!frmCustomer.MaxRecords = strMaxRec
      Me.RecordSource = "Customers"
    Else
      MsgBox "Invalid value for maximum records.", _
        vbOK, "Can't Open Form"
      Cancel = True
    End If
End Sub
```

The Customers table is used here to keep the example simple, but in a real-world application it rarely makes sense to use a table, rather than a view, stored procedure, or SQL string as your form's record source.

Input Parameters

The `InputParameters` property allows you to pass parameters to the form's record source. The `InputParameters` property can be used with stored procedures or with direct Transact-SQL statements. This requires you to set up the record source as a Transact-SQL statement with a `WHERE` clause or as a parameterized stored procedure. To use a SQL statement as the record source for the form, leave a question mark (?) as the placeholder for the parameter:

```
SELECT * FROM Orders WHERE CustomerID = ?
```

Specify the `InputParameters` property by using the parameter name, the data type, and the value, or a reference to where the form can obtain the value:

```
CustomerID nchar(5)=Forms!frmOrderInputParameter!cboCustomer
```

The parameter value the `SELECT` statement is expecting is the customer ID, which matches the ? placeholder. The CustomerID column in the Orders table has a data type of nvarchar(5). When a user selects an item from the cboCustomer combo box located in the header section of the frmOrderInputParameter form, the `AfterUpdate` event of the combo box fires. This requeries the form, displays the form's Detail section, enables the navigation buttons, and resizes the form, as shown in Listing 4.2.

LISTING 4.2   The cboCustomer `AfterUpdate` Event Requeries the Form

```
Private Sub cboCustomer_AfterUpdate()
    Me.Requery
    Me.Detail.Visible = True
    Me.NavigationButtons = True
    DoCmd.RunCommand acCmdSizeToFitForm
End Sub
```

When this sample form opens for the first time, it has no `RecordSource` property set and the detail section is hidden. Only the form header section is shown, with the cboCustomer combo box visible. The cboCustomer combo box has its bound column set to the customer ID, which supplies the parameter value for the form's record source. Once the user selects a customer from the combo box, the orders for the customer are loaded, the Detail section's `Visible` and `NavigationButtons` properties are set to `True`, and the form is resized. Figure 4.21 shows the form in form view after a customer has been selected. Only the order and order detail records for that customer will be loaded.

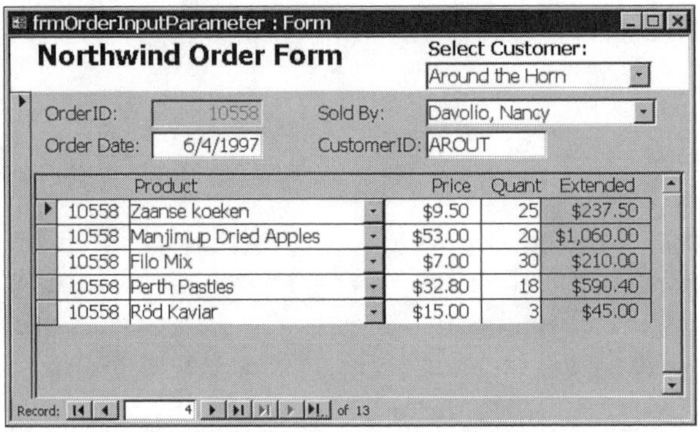

FIGURE 4.21
The frmOrderInputParameter form uses the Input Parameters property to limit the number of rows returned.

You can also use a syntax for the Input Parameters property on a form that is similar to syntax you may be familiar with from Access parameter queries. For example, you could create a customer form with the following setting for Input Parameters:

```
CustomerID nchar(5)= [Enter Customer ID:]
```

When this form opens, user will see the same Enter Parameter Value dialog box that pops up when a parameter query is run. The use types in a customer ID, and then the form opens showing data for just that customer. In some situations this may be acceptable, but using your own form to receive input parameter values allows you to present a much friendlier and more versatile user interface.

No matter how you choose to implement it, limiting the amount of data being loaded into a form is a good way to speed up your application and to minimize the load on both the server and the network.

> **NOTE**
>
> The syntax shown in online help for the `InputParameters` property is incorrect and does not work. The example shown uses `state char=[Form]![StateList]`. It should read `state char=[Forms]![frmMyForm]![StateList]` instead. Although `[Form]` can usually be used to refer to the current form in a property setting, that abbreviation just does not work in this context.

Server Filter

The `ServerFilter` property allows you to limit the amount of data returned by applying a filter at the server before data is fetched. The difference between the Server Filter property and the regular Filter property commonly found on Access forms is that the Filter property filters data after it has been fetched from the server, not before. If you use the Filter property, you are fetching all the rows across the network and then eliminating the ones you don't need. In terms of efficiency, the Server Filter property is a much better choice. It eliminates waste by reducing network traffic and minimizing server resources consumed.

You need to set the `ServerFilter` property before the form's `RecordSource` property is set. Listing 4.3 shows the `Open` event of frmProductListServerFilter. The `ServerFilter` property is set to the category ID based on the value returned by the `InputBox` function. The form's `RecordSource` property is then assigned, which executes the query with the server filter applied. The Detail section is then unhidden and the form resized. Creating a server filter is essentially the same as wrapping your record source in a SQL statement with a `WHERE` clause—something like:

```
SELECT * FROM MyRecordSource WHERE <My Server Filter>
```

4

LISTING 4.3   Setting the Form's ServerFilter Property

```
Private Sub Form_Open(Cancel As Integer)
    Dim strID As String

    ' Collect the CategoryID of products to load
    strID = InputBox( _
      "Enter CategoryID", "Enter 1 through 8", 1)

    ' Set the ServerFilter
    With Me
        .ServerFilter = "CategoryID=" & CLng(strID)
        .RecordSource = "SELECT * FROM Products"
        .Detail.Visible = True
    End With

    ' Resize the form
    DoCmd.RunCommand acCmdSizeToFitForm
End Sub
```

Figure 4.22 shows frmProductListServerFilter in Form view with only products matching the Confections category.

FIGURE 4.22
The frmProductListServerFilter form shows the product list filtered by category.

TIP

The Server Filter and Server Filter by Form properties (discussed next) do not work on forms based on stored procedures. If your form is based on a stored procedure, use the Input Parameters property discussed earlier. Use the Server Filter property only when a form's record source is based on a Transact-SQL statement, table, or view.

Server Filter by Form

The Server Filter by Form property allows users to define their own server filters at runtime, which are then processed by SQL Server before any data is returned to the form. Here are the steps Access follows while opening the form when the Server Filter by Form property is set:

1. The form is opened in Filter by Form view, and you can supply any value (or combination of values) to filter the data. Figure 4.23 shows a filter being set on the Reports To field in the frmEmployeeServerFormFilter form.

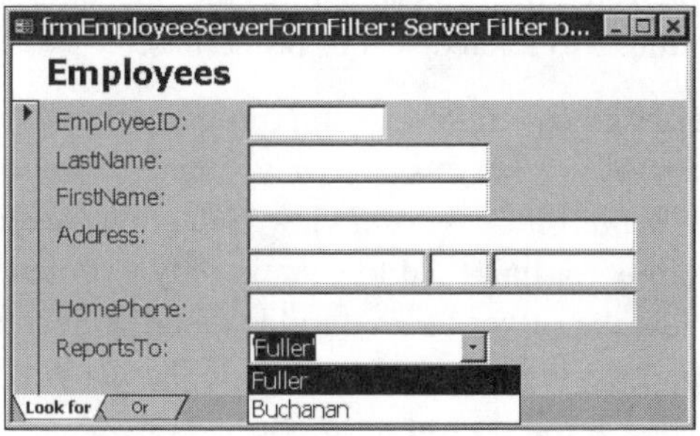

FIGURE 4.23

Opening a form in Server Filter by Form view.

2. When the user clicks the Apply Server Filter button, Access constructs a WHERE clause based on the filter and uses that as part of the SQL statement to populate the form.

3. The WHERE clause that Access creates is saved in the form's ServerFilter property, which now reads as follows:

```
((ReportsTo='2'))
```

Figure 4.24 shows the form opened in Form view, with the server filter applied. Only the employees reporting to Fuller ('2') are listed.

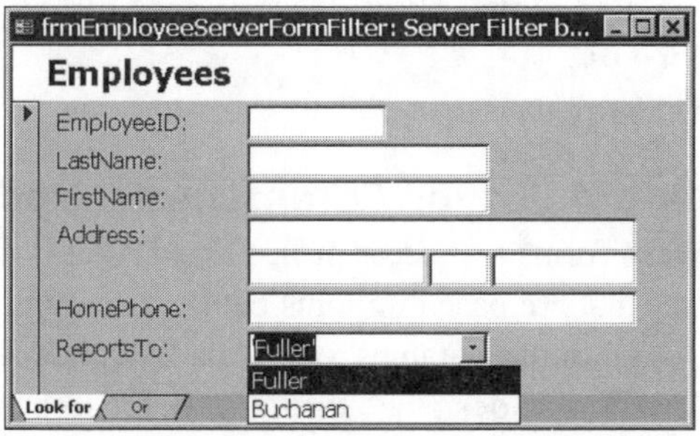

FIGURE 4.24

The frmEmployeeServerFormFilter form in Form view with the server filter applied.

4

INTRODUCTION TO ACCESS PROJECTS (ADPs)

As shown in Figure 4.23, when a form is in ServerFilterByForm view each field becomes a combo box allowing the user to select from the domain of possible values in the record source. The data to populate these dropdown lists must of course come from the server, which would seem to defeat the whole purpose of using a filter in the first place. To populate all those lists you would need to retrieve every bit of data in the record source, so what is the point of then applying a filter on the server and grabbing some of that data all over again? Well, clearly the point here is not to lessen the load on the server, because filling those lists is expensive. The point is to provide a useful friendly interface for your users that makes it easy for them to find the records that they are interested in. You can control the impact on the server of using ServerFilterByForm by setting two related sets of properties.

First, each text box on the form has a Filter Lookup property that you can set to Never, Database Default, or Always. If you set this to Always, then a combo box list of values will be created for that text box in ServerFilterByForm view. Selecting Never for the Filter Lookup property causes the combo box for that field to contain only two items: Is Null and Is Not Null. No query will be executed on the server for that field when the ServerFilterByForm view is loaded. The Database Default option will either populate the list will values or with the simple Is Null/Is Not Null based on a second set of properties.

The second set of properties that affects the behavior of ServerFilterByForm appears on the Edit/Find tab of the Tools, Options dialog box. Here, you can check off an option to Show List of Values in Records at Server. Checking this option causes fields that have their Filter Lookup property set to Database Default to get populated dropdown lists in ServerFilterByForm view. Clearing this checkbox causes those fields to get the simple Is Null/Is Not Null list. There is also a property on the Edit/Find tab of the Tools, Options dialog box that allows you to prevent dropdown lists in ServerFilterByForm view from displaying more than a specified number of rows.

NOTE

When you set the `ServerFilterByForm` property to `True`, the `Filter` property is not available.

Using Unique Table and Resync Command to Update Data

One major difference between forms in Access projects and Access databases concerns the updatability of data in forms that are based on joins between multiple tables. If you have a form that is based on data from multiple tables, only data from one table can be updatable. The Unique Table property allows you to designate the table that is to be updated. Only the table listed in the Unique Table property can be updated; data from all other tables is read-only.

The companion property to Unique Table is *Resync Command*. The *Resync Command* property is required if you want Access to perform row fixup and "look up" the new values from the other table when data in the unique table changes. Access does not automatically perform row fixup in Access projects the way it does in Access databases. If you do not specify the *Resync Command* property, the old values will continue to be displayed even though the related data in the unique table has changed, which is visually confusing to users.

The frmOrderUniqueTable form illustrates using the Unique Table and *Resync Command* properties. The form is based on the following SQL statement:

```
SELECT Customers.CompanyName, Orders.CustomerID,
  Orders.OrderID, Orders.OrderDate
FROM Customers
INNER JOIN Orders
ON Customers.CustomerID = Orders.CustomerID
ORDER BY Customers.CompanyName
```

The Unique Table property is set to the Orders table, as shown in Figure 4.25. Only the columns from the Orders table will be updatable in the form.

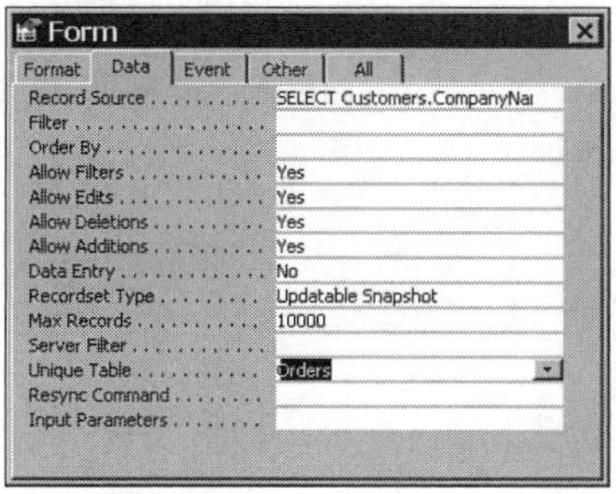

FIGURE 4.25

Setting the Unique Table property.

Although the columns will be updatable in the form, row fixup won't happen unless you also set the Resync Command property. For this property, you need to supply a SQL statement that is the same SQL statement used for the form's RecordSource property, with a WHERE clause added using the "?" parameter placeholder for every key field in UniqueTable (in this case, OrderID). The WHERE clause performs the row fixup by looking for the matching values based on a particular order ID:

```
SELECT Customers.CompanyName, Orders.CustomerID,
  Orders.OrderID, Orders.OrderDate
FROM Customers
INNER JOIN Orders ON
```

```
Customers.CustomerID = Orders.CustomerID
WHERE Orders.OrderID = ?
```

Figure 4.26 shows the CustomerID field in the process of being changed from "AROUT" to "ANTON". The change has not yet been committed, and the old value is still displayed in the Name column. Figure 4.27 shows the form after the record has been saved and the Name column has been "fixed up" to display the new value for the customer name.

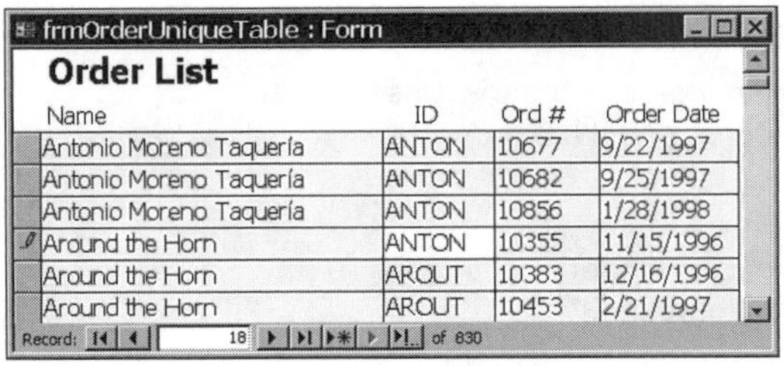

FIGURE 4.26
Editing the CustomerID field in the Orders table.

FIGURE 4.27
The Name column is fixed up after the record has been saved.

Using the Recordset Property to Bind a Form to a Recordset

One promising new feature of Access projects is the ability to bind a form to an ADO recordset. Instead of setting the form's RecordSource property, you can create an ADO recordset in code and then assign the form's Recordset property instead. The frmEmployeeRecordset form handles this in its Open event, as shown in Listing 4.4. The ADO recordset is created with a CursorType property of adOpenKeyset and a LockType property of adLockOptimistic so that the form is updatable. If you don't set the LockType property, the form will be read-only. Once the recordset is opened, it is assigned to the form's Recordset property. Note that the RecordSource property of the form is left blank because the Recordset property binds the data to the form. For detailed coverage of opening ADO recordsets and setting their properties, see Chapter 6.

LISTING 4.4   Binding the frmEmployeeRecordset Form to an ADO Recordset in the Form's Open Event

```
Private Sub Form_Open(Cancel As Integer)
    ' Opens the form based on an ADO recordset
    Dim rst As ADODB.Recordset

    ' Create recordset with Keyset cursor,
    ' and Optimistic locking so it's read/write
    Set rst = New ADODB.Recordset
    rst.ActiveConnection = CurrentProject.Connection
    rst.Open _
        Source:="select * from Employees", _
        CursorType:=adOpenKeyset, _
        LockType:=adLockOptimistic

    ' Pass recordset to form
    Set Me.Recordset = rst

    ' Once the recordset has been assigned to the
    ' form, the variable is no longer needed.
    rst.Close
    Set rst = Nothing
End Sub
```

Once the ADO recordset has been handed off to the form by setting the form's Recordset property, the object variable used to create it is no longer needed. The recordset variable can be set to Nothing, thus releasing the resources and memory it consumed.

Implementing Transactions in Bound Forms

One feature that has long been requested by Access developers is the ability to have transactions in forms. This is now possible in an Access project because you can set the form's Recordset property to an ADO recordset. Here's one way to make it work:

1. In the Declarations section of the form's module, declare two private Boolean variables, which will be set to True if the form is dirty (edits are happening) or there are pending changes. Declare private Connection and Recordset object variables to handle the connection and recordset, while making them available to multiple form procedures. The Connection object variable will control the transaction, and the Recordset will be the data source for the form.

4

INTRODUCTION TO
ACCESS PROJECTS
(ADPs)

2. In the Open event of the form, set the Connection object variable to CurrentProject.Connection and open the Recordset variable to assign it to the Recordset property for the form.

3. In the form's Dirty event, use the BeginTrans method of the Connection object. This will start an ADO transaction that will not be terminated until you either commit or rollback the transaction.

4. If an explicit transaction has been initiated, you need to explicitly commit or rollback the transaction. The form must be closed using the Close button, which sets a Boolean variable to True so that the Unload event of the form will either commit or rollback the transaction. The Unload event's Cancel parameter can be set to True, keeping the form open.

Listing 4.5 shows the complete code listing for frmProductTransaction.

LISTING 4.5 Implementing Transactions in Bound Forms

```
Option Compare Database
Option Explicit

' Boolean variables to track transaction
Private mfDirty As Boolean
Private mfPending As Boolean
Private mfOK As Boolean

' Connection and Recordset objects to be used
' to manage transactions
Private mcnn As ADODB.Connection
Private mrst As ADODB.Recordset

Private Sub cmdCommit_Click()
    ' Allow the transaction to commit
    ' or rollback, and the form to close.
    On Error GoTo HandleErr
    mfOK = True
    DoCmd.Close

ExitHere:
    Exit Sub
HandleErr:
    ' Cancelling the close action triggers
    ' runtime error 2501, which can be ignored.
    Resume ExitHere
End Sub
```

LISTING 4.5 Continued

```
Private Sub Form_AfterDelConfirm(Status As Integer)
    ' Set the status of the mfPending flag
    ' if records are to be deleted
    If Not mfPending Then
        mfPending = (Status = acDeleteOK)
    End If
End Sub

Private Sub Form_AfterUpdate()
    ' Set the mfPending flag to True
    mfPending = True
End Sub

Private Sub Form_Delete(Cancel As Integer)
    ' If a transaction isn't already started, then
    ' start one and set the mfDirty flag to True
    If Not mfDirty Then
        mcnn.BeginTrans
        mfDirty = True
    End If
End Sub

Private Sub Form_Dirty(Cancel As Integer)
    ' If this event happens, then someone started
    ' editing. If the mfDirty flag isn't set to
    ' True, then start the transaction.
    If Not mfDirty Then
        mcnn.BeginTrans
        mfDirty = True
    End If
End Sub

Private Sub Form_Open(Cancel As Integer)
    ' Open the connection object
    Set mcnn = New ADODB.Connection
    mcnn.Open _
      ConnectionString:=CurrentProject.Connection

    ' Open a read-write recordset
    Set mrst = New ADODB.Recordset
    mrst.Open _
      Source:="SELECT * from Products", _
      ActiveConnection:=mcnn, _
      CursorType:=adOpenKeyset, _
      LockType:=adLockOptimistic
```

LISTING 4.5   Continued

```
    ' Set the recordset to the form
    Set Me.Recordset = mrst
End Sub

Private Sub Form_Unload(Cancel As Integer)
    ' Checks to see if there's any pending
    ' transactions and either commits or
    ' rolls back
    Dim strMsg As String
    strMsg = "Click Yes to save all, No to roll " _
        & "back and Cancel to continue editing."

    ' If there's pending changes, commit/rollback
    If mfOK Then
        If mfPending Then
            Select Case MsgBox( _
                strMsg, vbYesNoCancel, "Save Products")
                    Case vbYes
                        ' Commit the transaction
                        mcnn.CommitTrans
                    Case vbNo
                        ' Roll back all changes
                        mcnn.RollbackTrans
                    Case vbCancel
                        ' Cancel the transaction and go
                        ' back to editing
                        Cancel = True
                        mfOK = False
            End Select
        End If
    Else
        MsgBox "Press the Close button to quit."
        Cancel = True
    End If
    ' If the transaction has been committed or rolled
    ' back, then allow the form to close and clean up
    ' the variables.
    If mfOK Then
        Set mrst = Nothing
        Set mcnn = Nothing
    End If
End Sub
```

Caveats on Transactions in Forms

Bear in mind that keeping transactions open and pending over a long duration will cut down on user concurrency. SQL Server needs to hold locks on the data being edited, which means that other users can't initiate transactions until the pending transaction either commits or rolls back. Although this technique may come in handy for certain kinds of forms, you certainly wouldn't want to construct all your forms to use explicit ADO transactions because the transactions could be pending for excessively long periods of time. Consider the scenario where a user has started editing a form, has opened a transaction with a `BeginTrans` statement, and then goes out to lunch. SQL Server will hold the necessary locks on the data until the user returns from lunch, and in the meantime, nobody else can work with the data. Therefore, this technique is useful if your application (or a particular form) only needs to support a few users at a time or if multiple concurrent users do not edit the same records. In Chapter 11, we show you alternative ways to allow users to cancel changes made to multiple rows of a subform.

Working with Multiple Recordsets

Another interesting feature of ADO recordsets is the ability to work with multiple recordsets using a single ADO recordset variable. The frmMultiple form contains two subforms—one based on the Employees table and the other based on the Customers table. The form's `Open` event procedure, shown in Listing 4.6, creates a single, read-only ADO recordset. The string used as the source of the recordset contains two separate `SELECT` statements, delimited by a semicolon. Once the recordset is opened and assigned to the first form object variable, the `NextRecordset` method is used to fetch the next recordset and assign it to the second form variable. If you don't use a separate form object variable for each subform, the first subform's recordset is invalidated when the `NextRecordset` method is invoked and the second recordset is assigned to the second form. Both of the recordsets are read-only.

LISTING 4.6   Creating Multiple Recordsets

```
Private Sub Form_Open(Cancel As Integer)
    Dim rst As ADODB.Recordset
    Dim frm1 As Form
    Dim frm2 As Form
    ' Create recordset
    Set rst = New ADODB.Recordset
    rst.ActiveConnection = CurrentProject.Connection
    rst.Open _
      Source:="SELECT * FROM Employees;" _
        & "SELECT * FROM Customers"

    ' Pass first recordset to form
    Set frm1 = Me!fsubEmployee.Form
```

LISTING 4.6   Continued

```
    Set frm1.Form.Recordset = rst

    ' Pass second recordset to form
    Set frm2 = Me!fsubCustomer.Form
    Set frm2.Form.Recordset = rst.NextRecordset

    ' Close the recordset
    rst.Close
    Set rst = Nothing
End Sub
```

Figure 4.28 shows the form opened in Form view with multiple recordsets.

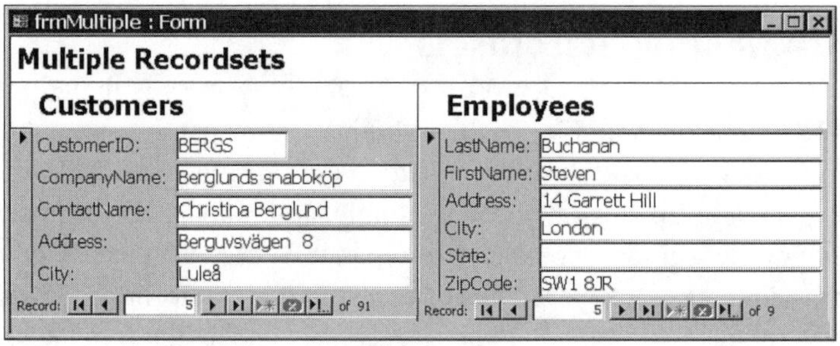

FIGURE 4.28
A form opened with multiple recordsets assigned to the subforms.

Working with the Form's Recordset

Access has always allowed you to bind a form to data by setting its RecordSource property. That record source can be the name of a table, a row-returning query, or a SQL string that defines such a query. Access projects allow stored procedures and views to be specified as record sources. Whatever the record source, when you bind a form to data by setting a form's RecordSource property, you navigate through the records in the user interface while Access navigates the underlying recordset. Each bound control on a bound form has a control source that binds it to a field in the recordset. If the recordset is updatable and if the form's properties and the user's security rights permit updating, bound controls on the form can be used to make changes to the data in the recordset. The recordset acts as a conduit for passing these changes to the database as each record in the form is committed.

The `RecordsetClone` Property

Bound forms also have a `RecordsetClone` property. When you create a recordset using the `RecordsetClone` property of a form, you're working with the exact same data that's displayed on the form. No extra work is done to retrieve the data from the database. The data that has already been retrieved for the form is available through the recordset clone. Changes to that recordset appear immediately on the form, including added records, and any changes made on the form are immediately evident in the recordset.

The recordset clone has its own separate header structure for maintaining which record is current. The form could be positioned on one customer while the recordset clone is positioned on another. Fortunately, both the form and the recordset clone expose a `Bookmark` property that determines which record is current, and the two can be synchronized by setting their bookmarks to be equal. A common technique for navigating to or searching for a particular record on a form is to open a recordset clone, find the desired record there, and then set the bookmark of the form to equal the bookmark of the recordset clone.

However, when you work with Access projects as opposed to Access databases, things are a little different. A form's native `Recordset` property in an Access project is an ADO 2.1 recordset. If you work with the `RecordsetClone` property, that too is an ADO recordset. You could set a form's `Recordset` property to a DAO 3.6 recordset object in an Access project, but there would be no point to it—an ADO recordset is going to be faster and more efficient because it's the native data access method for connecting to SQL Server in an Access project. The reverse also applies—in an Access database, DAO is going to be faster and more efficient because it's the native data access method for Jet data. Whichever recordset type you choose, the recordset clone of the form will be of that type.

Using the `RecordsetClone` Property in an Access Project

When working in an Access project, every time you retrieve the `RecordsetClone` property of a form, you'll be given a new instance of a cloned recordset. This is different from the way the recordset clone works in an Access database. In an Access database, each recordset clone is just a pointer to the same recordset. The way it works in an Access database is that you can navigate around in the recordset clone of a form, which is not visible to the user, and then set the form's `Bookmark` property equal to the recordset clone's `Bookmark` property to navigate to the record in the user interface. The following code snippet will locate an order by searching the recordset clone of the form for the order ID that matches the value from a combo box. Setting the form's bookmark to the recordset clone's will move to the selected order. Here's the code:

```
Me.RecordsetClone.FindFirst "OrderID=" & Me!cboSearch.Value
Me.Bookmark = Me.RecordsetClone.Bookmark
```

This code won't work in an Access project because each call to the `RecordsetClone` property returns a new recordset. The second line of code will create a completely new recordset, rather than using the recordset that was created in the first line. If, however, you declare a recordset variable first and set it to the recordset clone, you can use that variable to work with the same recordset. Also, because Access projects natively use ADO recordsets rather than DAO recordsets, you cannot use the FindFirst method, which is specific to DAO. Instead, use the ADO Find method. In an Access project, the correct syntax looks like this:

```
Dim rst As ADODB.Recordset
Set rst = Me.RecordsetClone
rst.Find "OrderID=" & Me!cboSearch.Value
Me.Bookmark = rst.Bookmark
```

Therefore, although on the surface the two recordset clones look alike, underneath they are subtly different, with slightly different syntax, properties and methods.

Another possibility here would be to dispense with creating a second recordset using RecordsetClone, and to create a pointer directly to the form's recordset using the new Recordset property. That way there is no need to use bookmarks to coordinate two recordsets. By changing the current record using the Find method with the recordset variable, you are automatically changing the current record in the form, because that variable is pointing directly to the form's recordset, not to a clone of it. Here's a version of the code that uses the form's Recordset property rather than RecordsetClone:

```
Dim rst As ADODB.Recordset
Set rst = Me.Recordset
rst.Find "OrderID=" & Me!cboSearch.Value
```

Unfortunately, the Find method in ADO is not as versatile as the DAO FindFirst method. Find supports the use of only one field in your criteria string.

Managing Your SQL Server Through an Access Project

Access projects provide a bare minimum of tools for developing and managing SQL Server databases from Access. These are provided mainly for managing MSDE databases. If you are building a SQL Server database application from scratch, you'll most likely find that these tools fall short when it comes to performing all the tasks necessary to create, debug, optimize, and deploy a SQL Server database application. The following list details the SQL Server management features present in an Access project:

- *Backing up and restoring databases*. However, you cannot access other management tools, such as creating database maintenance plans, monitoring user activity, and setting up jobs and alerts.

- *Creating and deleting databases.* However, you cannot configure database properties, work with file groups, or set other server and database options. You are limited to setting properties of the Access project or its connection.

- *Creating and managing SQL Server logins, fixed server roles, database users, and database roles.* However, you cannot assign permissions on database objects.

- *Working with SQL Server replication.* However, other advanced SQL Server features, such as creating Web publishing jobs, using DTS (Data Transformation Services), implementing full-text indexing, and monitoring the server are unavailable.

To get the most out of developing SQL Server databases, you'll want to work with the tools available in the Enterprise Manager, the Query Analyzer, the SQL Server Profiler, and the Performance Monitor in SQL Server to supplement the basic tool set that Access provides.

The administrative features of SQL Server are also available through the SQL-DMO (SQL Distributed Management Objects) or SQL-NS (SQL Namespace) object libraries. You can write VBA code using these libraries by setting a reference to them in your VBA project. SQL-DMO provides an object model that serves as a wrapper for the stored procedures that SQL Server uses to perform its administrative tasks. SQL-NS allows you to invoke the Enterprise Manager dialog boxes from your application to run almost any task available in the Enterprise Manager user interface, and it allows you to programmatically run any of the SQL Server wizards. If you wanted to, you could code your own front end to SQL Server using these object libraries, and that is essentially what the Access team did for Access projects.

You can get more information on SQL-DMO and SQL-NS from SQL Books Online or the MSDN Web site (`http://msdn.microsoft.com/library`).

Summary

There are pros and cons to using Access projects. On the one hand, you have a direct connection to SQL Server. On the other hand, you do not have local storage for tables or queries. Access projects do not store any database objects themselves—only Access forms, reports, macros, data access pages, and modules. However, Access projects provide a user interface, allowing you to work directly with SQL Server objects by creating new tables, database diagrams, views, and stored procedures. Access projects have project-specific form properties to make your application more efficient by limiting the amount of data returned from SQL Server. The form's underlying `Recordset` and `RecordsetClone` properties also have subtle differences from their DAO counterparts in Access MDB's. Although Access projects provide a significant part of the functionality needed to develop a SQL Server/Access database application, you'll still need the tools that a full installation of SQL Server provides in order to build a complete client/server solution.

4

INTRODUCTION TO
ACCESS PROJECTS
(ADPs)

Linking to SQL Server Using Access Databases (MDBs)

IN THIS CHAPTER

Advantages of Using a Jet Database (MDB) Front End

When upsizing your Access database to SQL Server, the Upsizing Wizard allows you to link the newly created SQL Server tables to your Access database. When you choose this option, all your original Access tables are copied and renamed with the "_local" suffix, and new table objects are created as links to your new upsized SQL Server tables. This process doesn't modify any of your queries, forms, reports, macros, data access pages, or modules. These Access objects will continue to function pretty much as they did when the data was located in Access instead of SQL Server. The only difference is that the tables are linked SQL Server tables, not Jet tables. A linked-table Access/SQL Server application is considered to be a "bound" application because all objects are directly tied to their data source.

Bound applications using Access front ends with SQL Server back ends have been around for a while now, and this technique offers the quickest way to get up and running with an Access/SQL Server application because very little has to change in the Access front end. The Access front end handles all the translation and conversion issues through the Jet database engine and ODBC, meaning you can use Access queries, forms, and reports without having to learn to write Transact-SQL or having to create additional SQL Server objects. The advantage is that you can get up and running quickly with a SQL Server database application while still using the same familiar tools that Access provides. The disadvantage is that performance and scalability does not necessarily improve—in some situations, it may even degrade. Although using linked tables requires little effort, it may not be the best solution. A linked-table, bound application is going to have limitations in terms of the number of users it can support and is also going to consume more resources on the network and the server.

This chapter discusses ODBC and the mechanics behind linked tables, and it describes how to make bound Access SQL Server applications more efficient.

How Jet Uses ODBC

The Jet database engine used by Access databases is able to communicate with SQL Server (or other database engines) by using Open Database Connectivity (ODBC). You can create Access queries using the usual query design grid, and the Jet engine translates your queries into function calls to the ODBC application programming interface (API). These function calls include Structured Query Language (SQL) statements that Jet formats into an ODBC-compliant dialect of SQL, and the function calls also include information that ODBC needs to find and connect to the SQL Server database.

ODBC Components

ODBC consists of several related pieces that interact to enable applications to communicate with databases. Here's a summary of these ODBC components, which are shown in Figure 5.1.

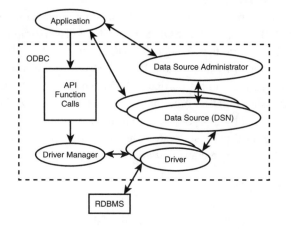

FIGURE 5.1
ODBC components.

ODBC API

The ODBC API isn't a piece of software. It's a document that outlines a specification that any application can follow to communicate with ODBC in any programming language. This specification is based on an international standard named Call Level Interface (CLI), which is published by the standards organizations X/Open and ISO/CAE.

Here are some of the tasks that the ODBC API specifies:

- Selecting a data source and connecting to it
- Submitting a SQL statement for execution
- Retrieving results (if any)
- Processing errors
- Beginning, committing, and rolling back transactions
- Disconnecting from the data source

The ODBC API specification is used by applications such as Access/Jet to properly format their communication with ODBC. Also, database vendors such as Microsoft and Oracle follow the specification to create drivers that support ODBC communication with their products.

Overview of ODBC Drivers

ODBC drivers are the software components that handle communication with specific database management systems (DBMSs), such as SQL Server. These drivers implement the specifications in the ODBC API to ensure that standard ODBC function calls will cause the specified tasks to be performed correctly by a particular DBMS. Drivers act as translators between the generalized language of ODBC and the particular language of a specific DBMS. The SQL Server ODBC driver translates ODBC function calls into calls that SQL Server can understand, and it processes data returned by SQL Server into a standard ODBC format. In addition to the DBMS vendors, there are third-party software companies, such as Merant (formerly Intersolve), that independently create and sell ODBC drivers.

ODBC Driver Manager

When you link a table or execute a query against SQL Server in an Access database, the Jet database engine communicates with the ODBC Driver Manager. As part of that communication, Jet provides the Driver Manager with the information it needs to load the appropriate ODBC driver and pass along the appropriate instructions.

The ODBC Driver Manager is roughly analogous to the Windows Printer Manager, which allows applications to send in printing instructions without having to worry about the specific requirements of each printer. The printer manager takes care of using the appropriate print driver to send the right instructions to the desired printer, much like the ODBC Driver Manager acts as an intermediary between applications and databases.

ODBC Driver

The ODBC driver's job is to take the request passed along by the Driver Manager and translate it into the syntax the DBMS expects. ODBC drivers are available to support communication with all the major relational databases, including Oracle, Informix, Sybase, and DB2. There's also an ODBC driver for the Jet database engine that supports communication with MDB files, Excel workbooks, text files, and older dBase, FoxPro, and Paradox files. However, there is really never a need to make use of ODBC to communicate with Jet when working in Access.

ODBC Data Source Administrator

To process a request from an application, the ODBC Driver Manager needs to know what kind of driver to load, and for each type of driver it also needs additional information required by each type of database. Each application can take care of sending all this information in a properly formatted text string, but to make the process easier, ODBC allows this data to be saved and given a name. These saved packages of connection settings are called *data sources* or *data source names*, and they are commonly referred to as *DSNs*.

The ODBC Data Source Administrator is a tool that provides a friendly user interface for defining and managing DSNs. In addition, it allows you to work with advanced ODBC options, such as connection pooling and the creation of traces. Connection pooling can add efficiency to your application by reusing ODBC connections rather than closing and reopening them, and traces allow you to record and examine detailed records of ODBC activity.

ODBC Data Source

Occasionally, you'll see the term *data source* used to refer to the actual DBMS, such as SQL Server or Oracle, that holds your data. But when used in ODBC, this term and the abbreviation *DSN* (data source name) refer not to the actual source of the data but rather to packages of information used to locate and access that data. ODBC uses this information to load the appropriate driver and to pass it the information needed to connect to the database. This may include the name of the database server, the name of a particular database, a login account and password, or an instruction to use the current Windows security account.

The following section discusses the different kinds of DSNs you can create and the steps you take to create them.

Setting Up a DSN with the ODBC Data Source Administrator

Creating a DSN simplifies the process of linking to SQL Server. The DSN identifies the driver to use as well as other information, such as the server and database that contains the tables to which you want to link.

To create a new ODBC DSN, follow these steps:

1. Double-click the Data Sources (ODBC) icon located in the Control Panel. This loads the ODBC Data Source Administrator's main window, as shown in Figure 5.2. If you are running Windows 2000, choose Programs, Administrative Tools, Data Sources from the Windows Start menu.

   To link to your SQL Server tables, you can use a User DSN, a System DSN, or a File DSN. A User DSN is specific to the logged-on user—if you log onto the same computer as a different user, you won't be able to use it to access the data source. A System DSN is the best choice if you want the DSN to be available to all users. A File DSN stores connection information in a disk file instead of the Windows Registry. Use a File DSN when external users need to be able to connect (for example, over the Internet).

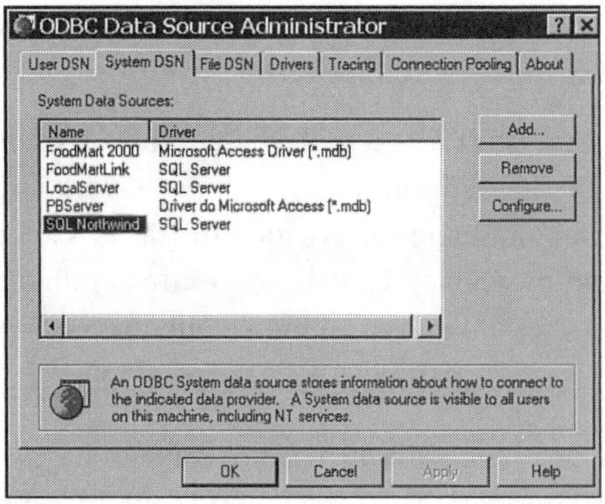

FIGURE 5.2

The ODBC Data Source Administrator with the System DSN tab displayed.

2. Click the Add button to create a new DSN. The ODBC Administrator lists all the ODBC drivers you have installed on your computer on the Drivers tab. Select the SQL Server driver, and click the Finish button.

3. You then need to supply a unique name for the new DSN and an optional description, as shown in Figure 5.3. You can specify the SQL Server by name or by using the string "(local)" if you're connecting to a SQL Server located on the same machine. Click Next when done.

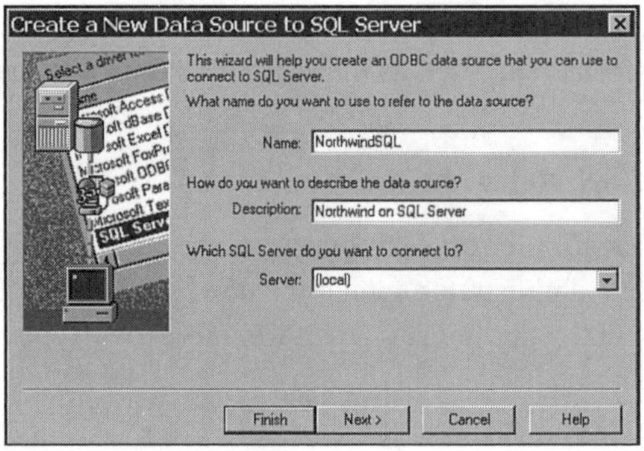

FIGURE 5.3

Naming and creating a new DSN.

4. The wizard dialog box shown in Figure 5.4 lets you specify the authentication mode to be used for the connection. You can also optionally change client configuration options. If you select the check box to connect to SQL Server to obtain default setting for the

additional configuration options, the wizard will connect to SQL Server. If you clear this check box, you can create a DSN without having the server available because the wizard will make no effort to create a connection yet.

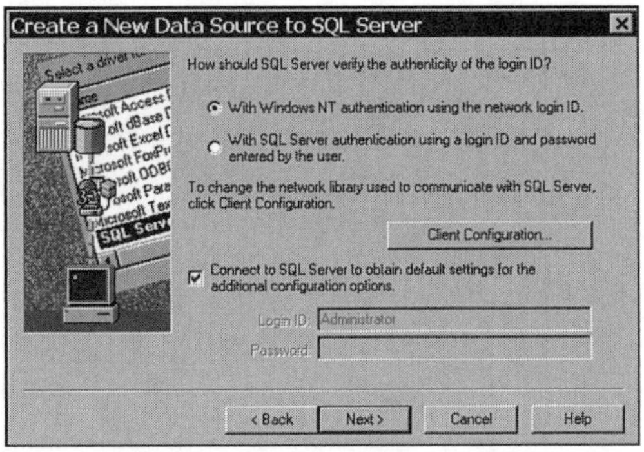

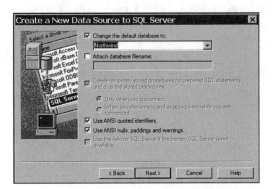

FIGURE 5.4
Setting the authentication level and client configuration options.

5. The wizard dialog box shown in Figure 5.5 lets you change the default database. If you're going to use the DSN to link to tables, change the default database to the database where the linked tables are located. It's not necessary to attach the database file-name. You can leave the ANSI quoted identifiers, ANSI nulls, paddings, and warnings options set to their default values.

FIGURE 5.5
Setting the default database.

6. On the next wizard dialog box, you can accept the default selections and click the Finish button. This will load the dialog box shown in Figure 5.6, which displays all the options

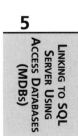

for the DSN. Click the Test Data Source button at the bottom of the dialog box to connect to the server and verify that the connection options you've selected will work with your data source. Click OK, and then click OK again. Your DSN will be created and ready to use.

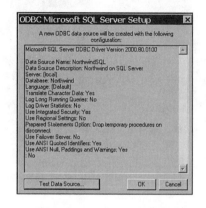

FIGURE 5.6
You can test the DSN before it is created to make sure it works.

The DSN can be reconfigured at any time using the ODBC Data Source Administrator. Simply select it and click the Configure button instead of the Add button shown previously in Figure 5.2.

Working Efficiently with Linked Tables

You can link or relink tables using the Access user interface or through writing VBA code. Besides the mechanics of linking tables, there are other things to consider, such as the size of the linked table. This section looks at how to link tables, and it covers some of the other options available to you.

Linking Tables

You can link to your SQL Server tables by choosing File, Get External Data, Link Tables and selecting ODBC Databases from the drop-down list of available file types. This will load the dialog box to select an ODBC data source. Select the DSN previously defined for the SQL Server database and click OK. This will display a list of tables and views, as shown in Figure 5.7. Select the tables or views you want to link, and click OK. The linked tables will then show up in your database. Linking to views is discussed later in this chapter.

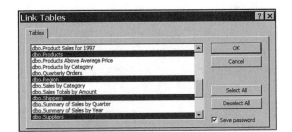

FIGURE 5.7
Selecting the SQL Server tables to be linked.

Linking through the menus is fairly straightforward, except for the fact that Access prepends "dbo_" to the linked table name. In the case of the Northwind database, dbo is the owner of the table. Ownership of objects in SQL Server is discussed in Chapter 3, "Understanding SQL Server Security." You can rename the tables after they've been linked, as shown in Figure 5.8.

FIGURE 5.8
Renaming tables after they have been linked.

Relinking an Access Database to SQL Server Tables in Code

An alternative to linking tables through the Access user interface is to link them in code. You have two object libraries you can choose from that are each capable of linking tables:

- ADOX (Microsoft ADO Ext. 2.5 for DDL and Security)
- DAO (Microsoft DAO 3.6 Object Library)

However, there's a bug with ADOX in Access 2000—you can link the tables, but they are read-only. Hopefully this omission will be remedied in future versions of Access. The code for linking tables using DAO and ADO is shown in this section.

Using DAO to Link Tables

To use DAO to relink your tables, set a reference to the DAO object library first. Open a module and select Tools, References from the menu. Select the listing for the Microsoft DAO 3.6 Object Library, as shown in Figure 5.9. If you are working with Access 97, set a reference to the DAO 3.51 Object Library instead.

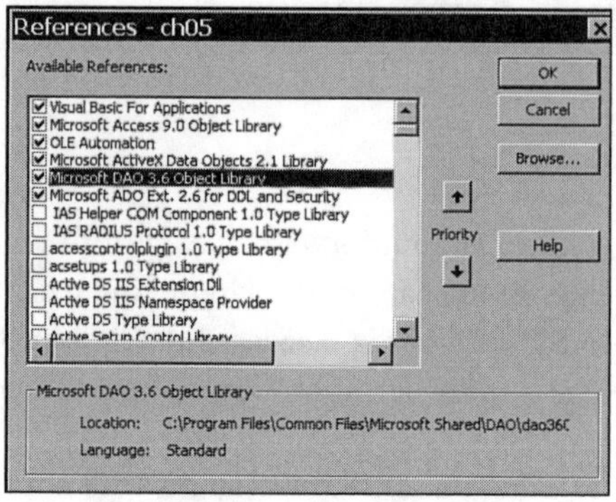

FIGURE 5.9

Setting a reference to the DAO 3.6 Object Library.

Here are the DAO objects used to link the SQL Server tables:

- `Database`. This sets a reference to the current Access database and is used to create the `TableDef` object for the link.
- `TableDef`. A `TableDef` object is used to establish the link to a SQL Server table through its `Connect` and `SourceTable` properties.

Listing 5.1 shows the `LinkTableDAO` function, which takes the following parameters:

- `strLinkName`. Name of the linked table as you want it to appear in the Access database
- `strDBName`. Name of the SQL Server database
- `strTableName`. Name of the SQL Server table or view
- `strDSNname`. Name of the ODBC DSN used for the link

Because the `TableDef` object may already exist in the Access database, the `LinkTableDAO` function first checks for this and deletes it if it does already exist. A new `TableDef` object is then created using the same name, and the `Connect` and `SourceTable` properties are set. The `TableDef` object is then appended to the database's `TableDefs` collection.

LISTING 5.1   Relinking a Table Using DAO

```
Public Function LinkTableDAO( _
    strLinkName As String, _
    strDBName As String, _
    strTableName As String, _
    strDSNname As String) As Boolean

    ' Links or re-links a single table.
    ' Returns True or False based on Err value.

    Dim db As DAO.Database
    Dim tdf As DAO.TableDef

 On Error Resume Next
    Set db = CurrentDb
    ' if the link already exists, delete it
    Set tdf = db.TableDefs(strLinkName)
    If Err.Number = 0 Then
        ' Found an existing tabledef.
        db.TableDefs.Delete strLinkName
        db.TableDefs.Refresh

    Else
        ' No existing tabledef.
        ' Ignore error and reset.
        Err.Clear
    End If
    ' Create a new TableDef object
    Set tdf = db.CreateTableDef(strLinkName)
    ' Set the Connect and SourceTableName
    ' properties to establish the link
    tdf.Connect = _
        "ODBC;Database=" & strDBName _
        & ";DSN=" & strDSNname _
        & ";Integrated Security=True"
    tdf.SourceTableName = strTableName
    ' Append to the database's TableDefs collection
    db.TableDefs.Append tdf

    LinkTableDAO = (Err = 0)
End Function
```

The `LinkTableDAO` function only links a single table. If you have multiple tables that are already linked, use the `RelinkAllTables` function to relink them, as shown in Listing 5.2. The `RelinkAllTables` function examines all the tables in the current database, looking for ODBC tables to relink by testing each `TableDef` object's `Attributes` property. Only `TableDef` objects

with an attributes value that includes `dbAttachedODBC` are relinked by calling the
`LinkTableDAO` procedure (shown previously in Listing 5.1). The `RelinkAllTables` function
takes the following parameters:

- `StrSQLDB`. Name of the SQL Server database
- `strDSN`. Name of the DSN used for the link

LISTING 5.2   Relinking All Tables

```
Function RelinkAllTables( _
    strSQLDB As String, _
    strDSN As String) As Boolean
    'Relinks existing ODBC linked tables

    Dim tdf As TableDef
    Dim fLink As Boolean

    On Error GoTo HandleErr
    RelinkAllTables = False
    For Each tdf In CurrentDb.TableDefs
        With tdf
        ' Only process linked ODBC tables
            If .Attributes And dbAttachedODBC _
                = dbAttachedODBC Then
                    fLink = LinkTableDAO( _
                        strLinkName:=.Name, _
                        strDBName:=strSQLDB, _
                        strTableName:=.SourceTableName, _
                        strDSNname:=strDSN)
                    ' If there's a problem with one table,
                    ' don't bother processing the rest.
                    If Not fLink Then GoTo ExitHere
            End If
        End With
    Next tdf
    RelinkAllTables = fLink

ExitHere:
    Exit Function

HandleErr:
    RelinkAllTables = False
    MsgBox _
        Prompt:=Err & ": " & Err.Description, _
        Title:="Error in RelinkAllTables"
    Resume ExitHere
End Function
```

Although it doesn't work well in ADOX version 2.5 with Access 2000, Listing 5.3 shows the code needed to link tables using ADOX. Hopefully the bug that renders the tables read-only will be fixed in some future version of Access.

LISTING 5.3   Linking Tables Using ADOX

```
Public Function LinkTableADOX( _
    strLinkName As String, _
    strTableName As String, _
    strDSNname As String) As Boolean

    Dim cat As New ADOX.Catalog
    Dim tbl As New ADOX.Table

On Error Resume Next
    ' Point the catalog to the current database
    cat.ActiveConnection = CurrentProject.Connection

    ' If the link already exists, delete it
    Set tbl = cat.Tables(strLinkName)
    If Err = 0 Then
        cat.Tables.Delete strLinkName
    Else
        Err = 0
    End If

    ' Set the name and parent catalog for the link
    tbl.Name = strLinkName
    Set tbl.ParentCatalog = cat

    ' Set the properties to create the link
    tbl.Properties("Jet OLEDB:Create Link") = True
    tbl.Properties("Jet OLEDB:Link Provider String") = _
        "ODBC;DSN=" & strDSNname
    tbl.Properties("Jet OLEDB:Remote Table Name") = _
        strTableName
    ' Append the table to the collection
    cat.Tables.Append tbl

    Set cat = Nothing

    LinkTableADOX = (Err = 0)
End Function
```

LISTING 5.3   Continued

```
Function RelinkAllTablesADOX( _
    strSQLDB As String, _
    strDSN As String) As Boolean
    'Relinks existing ODBC linked tables

    Dim cat As ADOX.Catalog
    Dim tbl As ADOX.Table
    Dim fLink As Boolean

    On Error GoTo HandleErr
    ' Open the catalog
    Set cat = New ADOX.Catalog
    cat.ActiveConnection = CurrentProject.Connection

    For Each tbl In cat.Tables
        With tbl
        ' Only process linked ODBC tables
            If .Type = "PASS-THROUGH" Then
                fLink = LinkTableADOX( _
                    strLinkName:=.Name, _
                    strTableName:=.Properties("Jet OLEDB:Remote Table Name"), _
                    strDSNname:=strDSN)
                ' If there's a problem linking one table, then
                ' don't bother processing the rest.
                If Not fLink Then GoTo ExitHere
            End If
        End With
    Next tbl
    RelinkAllTablesADOX = fLink

ExitHere:
    Set cat = Nothing
    Exit Function

HandleErr:
    RelinkAllTablesADOX = False
    MsgBox _
        Prompt:=Err & ": " & Err.Description, _
        Title:="Error in RelinkAllTablesADOX"
    Resume ExitHere
End Function
```

Using ODBC Connect Strings

The preceding examples use NT authentication with the DSN, which does not require specifying a user ID and password as part of the connection string. If you're using SQL Server authentication, use a variation on the following string, supplying valid values for the DSN, user, and password:

```
"ODBC;DSN=MyDSN;UID=MyUID;PWD=MyPwd;"
```

If you want the password saved as part of the connection string, use the Jet OLEDB:Cache Link Name/Password property to indicate that the password should be cached. If you're using DAO, the equivalent property is the `TableDef.Attributes` value, `dbAttachSavePWD`.

DSN-Less ODBC Connections

You can supply connection information that does not include a DSN. The following example shows the syntax used for NT authentication. Instead of a DSN name, the driver `{SQL Server}` is specified and `Trusted_Connection` is set to `Yes`:

```
"ODBC;Driver={SQL  Server};Server=(local);Database=MyDB;Trusted_Connection=Yes"
```

The alternate syntax using SQL Server authentication requires a user ID and password:

```
"ODBC;Driver={SQL Server};Server=(local);Database=MyDB;UID=sa;PWD="
```

Being able to specify a DSN-less connection is handy when you need to establish ODBC links in code and you can't be sure that a particular DSN actually exists.

Size Matters

Once you've linked your tables, you need to think about how to use them effectively. With SQL Server–linked tables, each request for data must travel across the network and be processed by SQL Server. Therefore, you must be careful about the burden that your use of linked tables will place on the server. If there's one golden rule that applies to all Access/SQL Server applications, it is this: Fetch less data!

You can have only so many people selecting all rows and all columns from large linked tables before your server and your network will become bogged down. Also, if your application is being used to update data, bear in mind that only one row of data can be modified at a time. There is no need to fetch 10,000 rows in order to edit a single row.

One way to optimize data retrieval is to take advantage of the fact that SQL Server allows you to link to views.

Linking to Views

You can use SQL Server views in your Access application just as if they were tables. Linking to views instead of tables provide the following advantages:

- It reduces the number of columns returned. Fetching all columns when only a few of them are going to be used is a waste of processing.

- It enforces security considerations. For example, use one view for managers, who are able to view a Salary column, and another view for data-entry people, who are not allowed to view the Salary column.

- It preaggregates data to speed computations and reporting. Because views are created on the server, selecting rows from a view that has complex calculations will be more efficient than selecting rows from the base tables and performing those calculations in Access.

- It simplifies ad hoc querying. Views can consist of joins between multiple tables, which can be difficult for users to create on their own. If table names are complex, creating a view with the real column names aliased to more user-friendly columns can aid users in creating their own queries.

- It creates a layer of abstraction between the Access application and the SQL Server tables. Linking to SQL Server views is exactly the same as linking to tables, and to users the views look and behave exactly like tables. Views can be used for updating data as long as the rules for updating data in views are observed.

- It reduces the number of rows returned. By including criteria in your views, you can work with a subset of the full data in your tables. Parameters, however, are not permitted in views.

For more information on building and working with views in SQL Server, see Chapter 9, "Creating and Optimizing Views."

Creating Queries Against Linked Tables and Views

When you create Access queries against linked tables and views in the Access query designer, the Jet engine gets involved, and that involvement can often be very helpful. Here are the advantages of writing local Access queries against linked tables and views:

- You don't have to learn Transact-SQL syntax. Jet and ODBC will take care of the translation for you.

- You can use Access-specific functionality, such as user-defined functions and Access-specific queries (such as crosstab queries).

- Access queries can be used as the basis for forms, reports, and updating data.

- You can make use of parameters in your Access queries.

However, if you're working with large tables or many users, these advantages can turn to disadvantages and cause your application to have performance problems, depending on how you build your queries.

Optimizing Access Queries

To provide the best performance and scalability, do as much processing as possible on SQL Server and use Access queries only when necessary. If you do use Access queries, try to avoid forcing Jet to bring more data across the wire than you need.

There's a common misconception that the Jet engine always retrieves all the data in linked SQL Server tables and then processes the data locally. This is not usually true. Jet is perfectly capable of sending efficient queries to SQL Server over ODBC and retrieving only the rows required. However, in some cases, Jet will in fact be forced to fetch all the data in certain tables first and then process it. You should be aware of when you are forcing Jet to do this and be sure that it is justified. The following are some general guidelines to follow when creating your Access queries:

- Using expressions that can't be evaluated by the server will cause Jet to retrieve all the data required to evaluate those expressions locally. The impact of using Access-specific expressions, such as domain aggregate functions, Access financial functions, or custom VBA functions, will vary depending on where in your query the expressions are used. Using such an expression in the SELECT clause will usually not cause a problem because no extra data will be returned. However, if the expression is in the WHERE clause, that criterion cannot be applied on the server, and all the data evaluated by the expression will have to be returned.

- With multiple criteria, as many as possible will be processed on the server. This means that even if you use criteria that you know include functions that will need to be processed by Jet, adding other criteria that can be handled by the server will reduce the number of records that Jet has to process. Adding criteria on indexed columns is especially helpful.

- Query syntax that includes an Access-specific extension to SQL, not supported by the ODBC driver, may force processing to be done on the client by Access. For example, even though SELECT TOP 5 PERCENT is now supported by SQL Server, it is not supported by the ODBC driver. If you use that syntax in an Access query, Jet will need to retrieve all the records and calculate which ones are in the top five percent. On the other hand, even though crosstab queries are specific to Access, Jet will translate them into simple GROUP BY queries and fetch just the required data in one trip to the server unless problematic criteria is used.

- Heterogeneous joins between local and remote tables or between remote tables that are in different data sources will, of course, have to be processed by Jet after the source data is retrieved. However, if the remote join field is indexed and the table is large, Jet will often use the index to retrieve only the required rows by making multiple calls to the remote table, one for each row required.

- Jet allows you to mix data types within columns of UNION queries and within expressions, but SQL Server doesn't. Such mixing of data types will force processing to be done locally.

- Multiple outer joins in one query will be processed locally.

- The most important factor is reducing the total number of records being fetched. Jet will retrieve multiple batches of records in the background until the result set is complete, so even though you may seem to get results back immediately, a continuing load is being placed on the server for large result sets.

Creating Efficient Bound Forms

When creating forms for working with linked SQL Server data, keep in mind the same rules outlined previously for queries. Base forms on the bare minimum of data needed to get the job done. Retrieve only the columns and rows that the users actually need to work with at each point in the flow of your application.

Form Properties

There are several form properties that can help you work efficiently with your SQL Server data:

- *Record Source*. A form's Record Source property determines the data source for the form. Loading a form unbound, without a predetermined record source, and assigning the Record Source property as part of the form's Load event can give you great flexibility in prefiltering data. Choose record sources that minimize the data being returned and maximize the processing on the server.

- *Recordset Type*. The Recordset Type property can be set to Snapshot if the form is not being used to edit data. A snapshot is read-only, and no locks will be held on SQL Server. Use a snapshot when you don't need to modify data on the form. Dynaset recordsets are updatable and consume more resources on the server. Consider displaying data in read-only form and opening dynasets only for individual records that the user chooses to edit. If your data includes memo fields or binary objects, a dynaset recordset may be more efficient than a snapshot, even if you don't need the recordset to be updatable, because dynasets retrieve those large objects only as needed.

- *Recordset Locks*. The Recordset Locks property defaults to No Locks, or *optimistic locking*. To minimize problems, you should use optimistic locking when working with SQL Server data in linked tables. If a user attempts to modify a record that was changed by another user after the first user started editing it, a Write Conflict error message will allow the user to see the other user's changes.

- *Data Entry*. The Data Entry property is handy if you have a form that's being used for adding new records only. When this property is set to Yes, no records are retrieved when the form is opened, and only the new row will show up on the form. This cuts down on network traffic and on locks being held by SQL Server.

Techniques for optimizing forms by prefiltering data and loading only the data you need will be covered in the following sections.

Restricting Data with Prefiltering

Although Access forms have a Filter property, it isn't very efficient when used with SQL Server data. For example, if your bound form selects all rows from the Orders table and then applies a filter to show only the rows a user is interested in, a lot of data has been fetched for no reason, thus taking up network bandwidth and server resources. It is analogous to needing a cup of water but fetching an entire bucket from the well and then throwing the rest away. If you only fetch the cup of water you need to begin with, you save both the water and the effort it takes to get it from the well.

One technique you can use to prefilter data is to open a form that is not initially bound to a recordset. Figure 5.10 shows an unbound form with only the Header section displayed. The Detail and Footer sections are hidden, and the Record Source property is blank. Each letter of the alphabet displayed is a toggle button inside of an option group (or frame) control. When the user clicks a button, the form's Record Source property is defined, and only customer records where the first letter of the company name matches the letter selected are loaded.

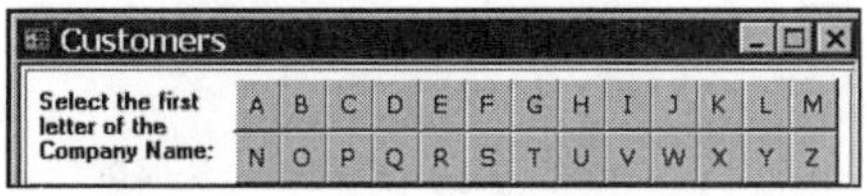

FIGURE 5.10

An unbound form with only the Header section displayed.

In this example, each button's Option Value property is set to the ASCII value of the letter it represents. For example, A is 65, B is 66, and so on throughout the alphabet. When the user selects a letter of the alphabet, the AfterUpdate event procedure for the option group executes. The first operation of the event procedure is changing the form's Record Source property, selecting from the linked Customers table only those records where the company name matches the letter selected. The Chr$() function retrieves the letter value of the ASCII value encoded in the toggle button. Here's the code:

```
Private Sub grpAlphabet_AfterUpdate()
    ' Change record source to match selected letter
    Me.RecordSource = "SELECT * FROM Customers " & _
        "WHERE CompanyName LIKE '" & _
        Chr$(Me!grpAlphabet) & "*';"
```

When the form is first opened, the Detail section, form footer, and navigation buttons are hidden, so the next step is to display them. However, you don't need to continually run code to display them for subsequent selections, so the code conditionally runs only if the Detail section is hidden, which it is when the form is first opened. Here's the code:

```
    ' First time through, the detail section
    ' will be hidden
    If Not Me.Detail.Visible Then
        ' Display form sections
        Me.Detail.Visible = True
        Me.FormFooter.Visible = True
        Me.NavigationButtons = True
        DoCmd.RunCommand acCmdSizeToFitForm
    End If
End Sub
```

The form is then unfurled and all the sections displayed. The user can navigate through the selected records and edit them, as shown in Figure 5.11.

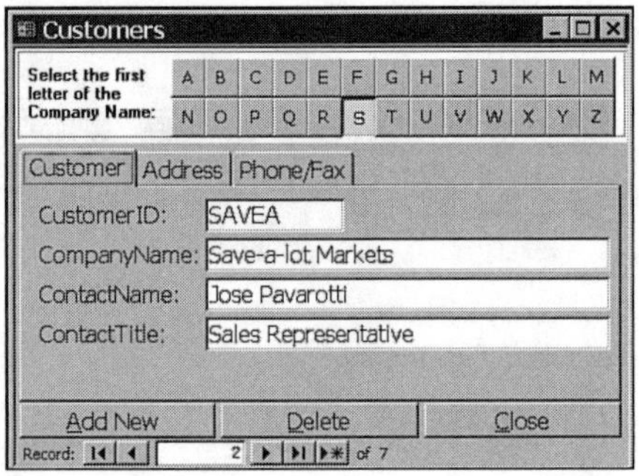

FIGURE 5.11
The Customers form opened with prefiltered data.

The goal is to limit the number of records that a form's recordset contains at any one time. Users really can't work with many hundreds of records at once anyway, and you'll find that if you can limit your recordsets to under a couple hundred records at once, your application will perform snappily and scale to handle potentially thousands of users. This example uses an alphabetical sort. In your application, you may want the user to first select a territory or a combination of product characteristics before you load and display the form's recordset.

Also try to keep the number of fields displayed at any one time to a minimum. Again, the users can't really work with dozens of fields at once anyway. You may want to display only a limited number of fields at first and allow the users to bring up a separate form if they need to see more fields for a particular record. This will be vastly more efficient than retrieving all those fields for every record in the recordset.

Loading a Single Record from an Unbound Form

Another alternative for data-entry forms is loading just a single record after letting users select options to narrow down the data being retrieved. In this example, the user selects a single order from the Form Header section by first selecting the customer and then selecting from a list of orders for the selected customer. The combo box that lists the orders isn't filled until a customer is selected.

Filling List Boxes and Combo Boxes on Demand

Filling a list box or combo box on demand can help your form load faster. Each bound list box and combo box on a form runs a separate query. If you create initially unbound list boxes and combo boxes instead, no query runs automatically. This is a useful technique in situations where the user may elect not to use the combo/list box at all.

This example displays orders for the selected customer, not all the orders in the database. Listing 5.4 shows the code that selects only the orders for the selected customer.

LISTING 5.4   Filling the Customer Orders Combo Box in the Enter Event

```
Private Sub cboOrders_Enter()
    ' Set the RowSource property to
    ' display only orders for the
    ' selected customer.
    Dim strSQL As String
    Dim fOK As Boolean

On Error GoTo HandleErr
    ' Make sure a customer is selected
    If Len(Me!cboCustomer & "") = 0 Then
        MsgBox "Please select a customer.", , _
            "Can't display order list"
        Me!cboCustomer.SetFocus
        GoTo ExitHere
    End If
```

LISTING 5.4   Continued

```
    strSQL = "SELECT OrderID, OrderDate " & _
        "FROM Orders " & _
        "WHERE CustomerID = '" & Me!cboCustomer & _
        "' ORDER BY OrderDate DESC"
    ' Set the RowSource and requery
    Me!cboOrders.RowSource = strSQL
    Me!cboOrders.Requery

ExitHere:
    Exit Sub

HandleErr:
    MsgBox Err & ": " & Err.Description, , _
        "Error in cboOrders_Enter"
    Resume ExitHere
End Sub
```

If the user already knows the order ID of the order he wants to enter, he can bypass the combo boxes and enter it directly into a text box, as shown in Figure 5.12. If the user does use the combo boxes, the text box gets filled in automatically. Providing a way for users to enter data directly into text boxes instead of forcing them to select from a variety of combo boxes can significantly speed data entry when users already know exactly what they want, and it means that the combo boxes may never need to be populated.

FIGURE 5.12
Selecting a single order to load.

When the user clicks the Go button, the Detail and Form Footer sections are displayed, and the order can be edited, as shown in Figure 5.13.

The code in the Click event of the Go button is shown in Listing 5.5. The order is selected, and the Detail section is unhidden by calling the DisplayDetail procedure, which sets the Visible property of the form's Detail and Footer sections. Because the form is bound, any bound controls will display "!Error" if the form is opened without the Record Source property being set, which is why it is hidden when the form is first opened.

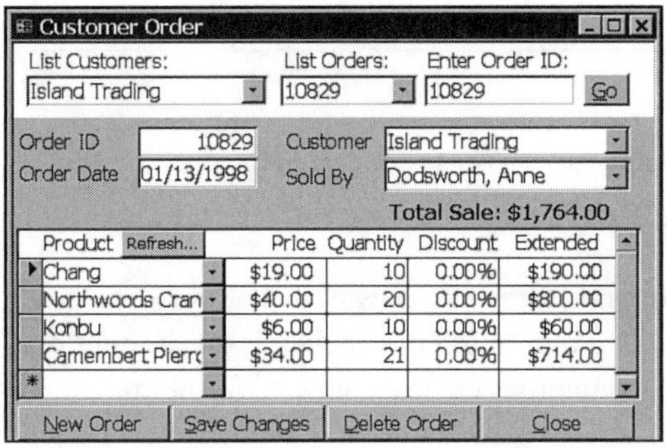

Figure 5.13
Displaying the entire form for editing.

Listing 5.5   Loading a Single Record

```
Private Sub cmdGo_Click()
    Dim strMsg As String
    Dim strSQL As String

    If Len(Me!txtOrderID) > 0 Then
        If IsNumeric(Me!txtOrderID) Then
            strSQL = "SELECT * FROM Orders " & _
              "WHERE OrderID = " & Me!txtOrderID
            ' Assign RecordSource and
            ' display Detail section
            Me.RecordSource = strSQL
            Call DisplayDetail(True)
        Else
            strMsg = "Please select a valid OrderID"
            ' Hide Detail section
            Call DisplayDetail(False)
        End If
    Else
        strMsg = "Please select a valid OrderID"
        ' Hide Detail section
        Call DisplayDetail(False)
    End If
    If Len(strMsg) > 0 Then
        MsgBox strMsg, , "Can't Display Order"
        Me!cboCustomer.SetFocus
        Call DisplayDetail(False)
```

LISTING 5.5   Continued

```
    End If
    ' resize form
    DoCmd.RunCommand acCmdSizeToFitForm
End Sub
```

The advantage of using bound forms in this way is that only one order, along with its related order detail records, is loaded at a time, thus reducing the amount of data that must travel over the network. Later in this chapter you'll learn how to further reduce data loading by caching static data in local tables.

Minimizing the Number of Recordsets Open

You have already seen how to avoid opening unnecessary recordsets by waiting to fill combo boxes until the user needs them. Another factor to consider is the way that recordsets can multiply on forms that contain many subforms. For example, if you have a tab control with several pages and a subform on each page, all those recordsets will be loaded even if the user never visits all the pages, and they will all be refreshed throughout the life of the form. An alternative strategy would be to save the form with the Source Object property of the hidden subforms blank. When the user tabs to a page, you can set the source object for that page. This is especially important if each subform needs to contain a large number of records. In the Change event of the tab control, you can check the tab control's Value property to determine which page the user is on. The value of the tab control will match the page index of the current page.

By controlling the size of your recordsets through well-planned filtering and the number of recordsets open at once, you can build an Access application that scales successfully as the number of users grows.

Using Pass-Through Queries

Pass-through queries allow you to send Transact-SQL statements directly to SQL Server without involving the Jet database engine in any way—the SQL statement is "passed through" to SQL Server via ODBC without being parsed for correct syntax or otherwise tampered with in any way. Pass-through queries allow you to run stored procedures, work with data, and perform other actions quickly and efficiently. There are two types of pass-through queries: those that return data, and those that don't return data.

One thing to bear in mind is that pass-through queries that return data do so in a read-only recordset. You can use the result set of a pass-through query as the record source for a form as long as you don't intend to use that form for updating data. Pass-through queries are excellent record sources for reports and row sources for combo and list boxes, where the data is always read-only. All other things being equal, running a stored procedure will always be the most efficient way to retrieve data from SQL Server, but your pass-through query isn't limited to running stored procedures. Any valid Transact-SQL statement can be sent to SQL Server in a pass-through query.

Creating a Pass-Through Query

To create a pass-through query, create a query that is not based on any tables. Choose Query, SQL-Specific, Pass-Through from the Query menu. This will open the SQL window of the query designer—you can't use the QBE grid for a SQL-specific query. You then need to type the Transact-SQL statements for your query.

You must use valid Transact-SQL syntax in the pass-through query, not Access SQL syntax. The usual rules apply—no user-defined functions or other Access-specific features are allowed. The syntax is not checked or parsed on the Access side—it is processed only at runtime when it is executed and the statements sent to SQL Server.

> **TIP**
>
> Use the SQL Server Query Analyzer to build your pass-through queries. You can use the tools available in the Query Analyzer to build a query and parse the syntax. When you're done, copy and paste your Transact-SQL statements into the pass-through query's SQL window.

In addition to typing in the Transact-SQL statements for your pass-through query, you must also specify two query properties:

- *ODBC Connect Str.* The connection information that the query uses to connect to SQL Server. This can be a DSN, or you can use DSN-less connection information, as shown earlier in this chapter.
- *Returns Records.* Whether or not the query returns records. Set this property to Yes for a SELECT query. If this property is set to No, the query will run, but Access won't be able to use the records returned. Bear in mind that Access can only process one recordset at a time—if the pass-through query returns multiple recordsets, all recordsets after the first one returned will be ignored.

Figure 5.14 shows the properties of a pass-through query that selects the customer ID and company name from the Customers table and sorts by company name. Note that you can also set other query properties, such as the ODBC Timeout, which is the maximum amount of time Access will wait for the query to return records, and Max Records, which will put a cap on the number of rows returned.

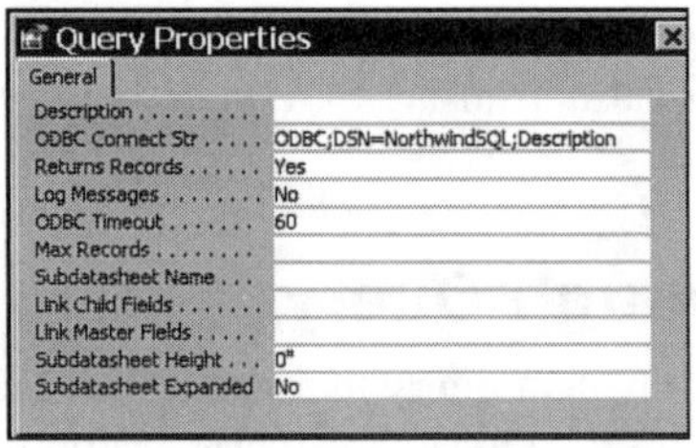

FIGURE 5.14
Creating a pass-through query and setting query properties.

Once you've created the pass-through query to select the customer ID and company name, you can use it anywhere in your application where you need to list customers.

Running a Stored Procedure from a Pass-Through Query

You can execute a stored procedure from a pass-through query the same way you would execute a stored procedure from the Query Analyzer—by invoking its name or using the Transact-SQL EXEC or EXECUTE keyword in front of it. For example, any of the following three statements will execute the Ten Most Expensive Products stored procedure in the Northwind database:

```
[Ten Most Expensive Products]
Exec [Ten Most Expensive Products]
Execute [Ten Most Expensive Products]
```

Note that the stored procedure name is surrounded by square brackets—this is required if the object name has spaces in it. Running this stored procedure will return the result set shown in Figure 5.15.

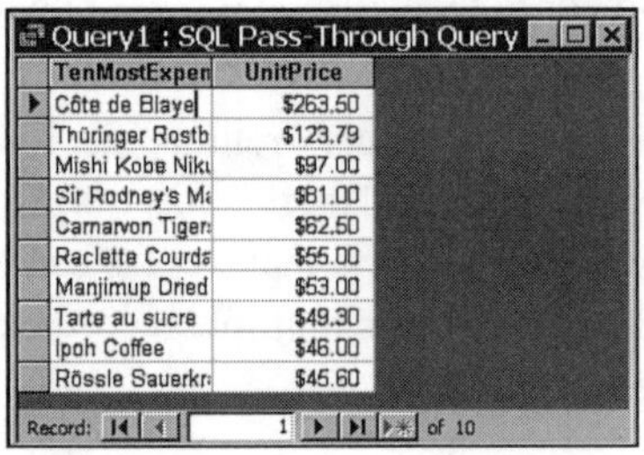

FIGURE 5.15
The Datasheet view from executing a stored procedure.

You can run either user-defined or system stored procedures from a pass-through query. For example, to find out information about the Northwind database, type the following statement in the SQL pane in the query designer, and set the ODBC Connect Str and Returns Records properties:

```
sp_helpdb 'Northwind'
```

How to Pass Parameters to a Pass-Through Query

Access pass-through queries do not handle parameters in the same way regular Access queries do—you must evaluate the parameters first and pass the values that the parameters are expecting. For example, in an Access query you can set the criteria to point to an Access object, such as a combo box, using the following syntax:

```
Forms!frmMyForm!cboMyCombo
```

However, because SQL Server, not Access, processes pass-through queries, this syntax will simply give you a runtime error. SQL Server will have no idea what the expression means. Instead, you need to get the value from the combo box and send a pass-through query that looks like this:

```
procOrdersForProductID 10
```

One way to pass parameters to a pass-through query is to modify the QueryDef object's SQL property in code before running it, concatenating in the parameter values you want to send.

A Generic Procedure for Modifying Pass-Through Queries

Because each parameterized pass-through query needs to set various properties as well as have its parameters set, writing a function to take care of everything in one shot is best. Listing 5.6 shows the PassThroughFixup procedure, which takes the name of the query to modify as well as a string argument that will contain the Transact-SQL statements. The optional varConnect parameter will default to the current connection settings, and the fRetRecords parameter defaults to returning records. Because a pass-through query is a native Access object, DAO is the most efficient object library to use to modify the SQL property of the query. However, Listing 5.7 also shows how to accomplish the same task using ADO and ADOX, if that's your preference.

LISTING 5.6   Changing the Text and Other Pass-Through Query Properties Using DAO

```
Public Sub PassThroughFixupDAO( _
  ByVal strQdfName As String, _
  ByVal strSQL As String, _
  Optional varConnect As Variant, _
  Optional fRetRecords As Boolean = True)
    ' Modifies pass-through query properties
    ' Inputs:
    '   strQdfName  Name of the query
```

LISTING 5.6   Continued

```
'     strSQL       New SQL string
'     varConnect  Optional connection string
'     fRetRecords Optional returns records--
'                 defaults to True (Yes)

Dim db As DAO.Database
Dim qdf As DAO.QueryDef
Dim strConnect As String

Set db = CurrentDb
Set qdf = db.QueryDefs(strQdfName)
If IsMissing(varConnect) Then
    strConnect = qdf.Connect
Else
    strConnect = CStr(varConnect)
End If
qdf.Connect = strConnect
qdf.ReturnsRecords = fRetRecords
qdf.SQL = strSQL
End Sub
```

LISTING 5.7   Changing the Text and Other Pass-Through Query Properties Using ADO

```
Public Sub PassThroughFixupADO( _
  ByVal strQdfName As String, _
  ByVal strSQL As String, _
  Optional varConnect As Variant, _
  Optional fRetRecords As Boolean = True)

    ' Modifies pass-through query properties
    ' Inputs:
    '   strQdfName  Name of the query
    '   strSQL      New SQL string
    '   varConnect  Optional connection string
    '   fRetRecords Optional returns records--
    '               defaults to True (Yes)

    Dim cat As ADOX.Catalog
    Dim cmd As ADODB.Command

    ' Open the catalog
    Set cat = New ADOX.Catalog
    Set cat.ActiveConnection = CurrentProject.Connection
```

LISTING 5.7 Continued

```
    ' Get the command
    Set cmd = cat.Procedures(strQdfName).Command
    ' Be sure it's a pass-through query
    cmd.Properties( _
       "Jet OLEDB:ODBC Pass-Through Statement") = True
    ' Update the SQL
    cmd.CommandText = strSQL
    ' Update the Connect string
    If Not IsMissing(varConnect) Then
       cmd.Properties( _
          "Jet OLEDB:Pass Through Query Connect String") = CStr(varConnect)
    End If
    ' Update the ReturnsRecords property
    cmd.Properties( _
       "Jet OLEDB:Pass Through Query Bulk-Op") = Not fRetRecords

    ' Save the changes
    Set cat.Procedures(strQdfName).Command = cmd

    'Clean up.
    Set cmd = Nothing
    Set cat = Nothing

End Sub
```

Here's how the DAO example works with a simple stored procedure that takes a parameter for the order ID. The `procOrderSelect` stored procedure in Listing 5.8 has a single input parameter: `@OrderID`.

LISTING 5.8 A Simple Parameterized Stored Procedure

```
CREATE PROC procOrderSelect
  @OrderID int = NULL
AS
SELECT OrderID, CustomerID, EmployeeID, OrderDate
FROM Orders
WHERE OrderID = @OrderID
```

The stored procedure, `procOrderSelect`, can be executed from a pass-through query named `qrysptOrderSelect`, whose SQL pane contains the following:

```
EXEC procOrderSelect
```

The `PassThroughFixup` procedure can be used to supply the parameter, as shown in Listing 5.9.

LISTING 5.9   Calling the `PassThroughFixup` Procedure

```
Public Sub TestPassthrough(lngParam As Long)
    Dim strSQL As String
    Dim strSPT As String

    strSPT = "qrysptOrderSelect"
    strSQL = "EXEC procOrderSelect " & lngParam
    Call PassThroughFixupDAO( _
      strQdfName:=strSPT, _
      strSQL:=strSQL)

    DoCmd.OpenQuery strSPT
End Sub
```

Figure 5.16 shows the datasheet view of the pass-through query when the `TestPassthrough` procedure is called from the Immediate window with the following syntax:

```
TestPassthrough 10835
```

After this procedure runs, the SQL of the pass-through query will have been changed to this:

```
EXEC procOrderSelect 10835
```

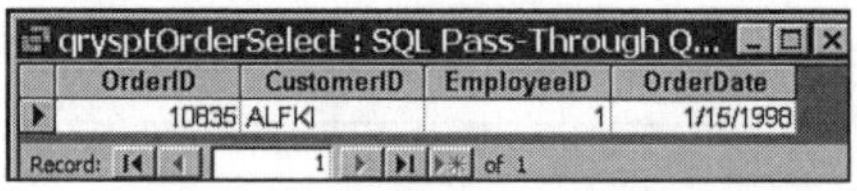

FIGURE 5.16
The result set from opening a pass-through query after modifying its SQL property.

Caching Data in Local Tables

If some of your SQL Server tables contain data that doesn't change much, consider caching the data in local Access tables. Although you can link all tables in your SQL Server database, there may be lookup tables that are static enough to be transferred to local tables instead. For example, lists of departments, states, and other lookup data used to fill list boxes and combo boxes often don't change enough to warrant fetching them from the server every time a user runs your application. Loading data from local lookup tables cuts down on network processing and on resources consumed on the server. Remember that each time a form loads, it must run the query it is based on as well as any queries needed to fill list boxes and combo boxes. Separate ODBC connections are created for each of those queries. Storing data in local tables and querying the local tables instead of the SQL Server tables can speed up your forms while saving on network roundtrips and server resources.

Data in local tables can be refreshed on demand or when your application loads, or at any time of your choosing. It's up to you to determine the needs of your application and to determine when it would be appropriate for the local tables to be refreshed either by an automatic process or by the user.

Creating Local Tables

The Products table in the Northwind database is a good candidate for local caching because it's used in the Order Details form for selecting a product for each order details item. The assumption here is that the product list is not updated frequently and can be refreshed by the user as needed. Follow these steps to create a local table to hold the product information:

1. Create a new query based on the linked SQL Server Products table. Choose Query, Make Table from the menu, and type **Products_local** as the new name for the table, as shown in Figure 5.17.

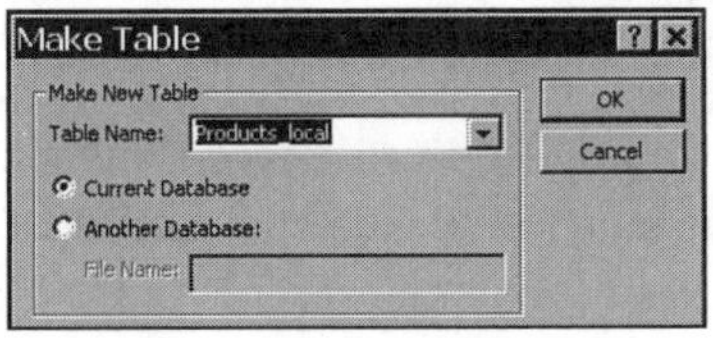

FIGURE 5.17
Creating the Products_local table.

2. Select all the columns from the original Products table, and execute the query. This will create the table. You don't need to save the query, so close it without saving.

3. Open Products_local and set the primary key on the ProductID column. This will prevent duplicates from being entered in the local version of the Products table, and it will allow Jet to work with the table more efficiently. You should also index the ProductName field because it's used for sorting. Set the Indexed property for ProductName to Yes (Duplicates OK) or to Yes (No Duplicates) if you are confident that all product names should be unique. Save the table and close it.

4. Products_local is now a mirror of the Products table, containing the same data as the Products table in SQL Server. If the Access application is not editing the Products table, the link to the SQL Server table can even be deleted. All forms and controls that use the Products table as a record source or row source need to be changed to refer to the Products_local table instead of the Products table. For example, the Row Source property of the Products combo box on the Order Details subform can now be based on the local version of the Products table:

5

LINKING TO SQL SERVER USING ACCESS DATABASES (MDBs)

```
SELECT Products_local.ProductID, Products_local.ProductName
FROM Products_local ORDER BY Products_local.ProductName;
```

Refreshing Data in Local Tables

To refresh the data in your local tables, follow these steps:

1. Create a new pass-through query named *qrysptProducts* with the following SQL property:

   ```
   SELECT * FROM Products
   ```

2. Save and close the pass-through query.

3. Create an append query named *qryappProductsLocal* that's based on the qrysptProducts query and appends records to the Products_local table. This query is not a pass-through query but rather a normal Access query. Save and close the query.

4. You can't run the qryappProductsLocal append query without first deleting all the rows in the Products_local table. This is best handled by writing some VBA code that will delete the old local data and run the append query to insert the fresh data.

Listing 5.10 shows the RefreshLocalTable procedure, which takes as parameters the name of the table being refreshed and the name of the append query that adds records from the SQL Server table. The code first deletes the existing records in the local table and then executes the append query.

LISTING 5.10   The RefreshLocalTable Procedure

```
Public Sub RefreshLocalTable( _
  ByVal strTable As String, _
  ByVal strQuery As String)

    ' Deletes and reinserts data in local table.
    ' Inputs:
    '    strTable    Name of the local table
    '    strQuery    Name of the Append query

    Dim db As DAO.Database
    Dim qdf As DAO.QueryDef
    Dim strConnect As String

    Set db = CurrentDb

    ' Delete data from local table
    db.Execute "DELETE * FROM " & strTable

    ' Run append query
```

LISTING 5.10   Continued

```
    Set qdf = db.QueryDefs(strQuery)
    qdf.Execute
    qdf.Close
End Sub
```

The `RefreshLocalTable` procedure can be called from the `Click` event of a button or when the application starts up:

```
If MsgBox("Do you want to refresh the product list?", _
    vbYesNo + vbQuestion, "Refresh Products") = vbYes Then
      Call RefreshLocalTable( _
        strTable:="Products_local", _
        strQuery:="qryaProductsLocal")
End If
```

Whenever you routinely delete and append data to an Access database, the space that was occupied by the old deleted data is not automatically reused. It is necessary to compact the database regularly to recover this space and avoid bloating of your MDB file.

Tweaking ODBC Settings to Tune Performance

The Jet database engine works efficiently with ODBC to manage communication with your SQL Server data when you use linked tables. In general, the default settings Jet uses are just fine. However, there may be times when you'll want to adjust these defaults to tailor Jets behavior to meet the needs of a particular application. This can be done by changing an option on the Advanced tab of the Tools, Options dialog box, by creating and editing entries in the Windows Registry, and also by creating a special table on SQL Server that Jet will consult to modify its default behavior.

Using the Options Dialog Box

Most of the multiuser settings on the Advanced tab of the Tools, Option dialog box, shown in Figure 5.18, pertain only to data stored in Jet MDB files. One of the settings, however, specifically affects data linked using ODBC. The ODBC refresh interval determines how often Access will check back with SQL Server to update data in the record source of any open forms or datasheets. The default is every 1,500 seconds, or 25 minutes. This can be changed to anything between 1 and 32,766 seconds (about nine hours).

If you have been successful in creating forms that limit the size of recordsets, and if your data changes frequently, you may want to reduce this refresh interval. On the other hand, if your goal is to keep network traffic to a bare minimum, you could bump this setting up.

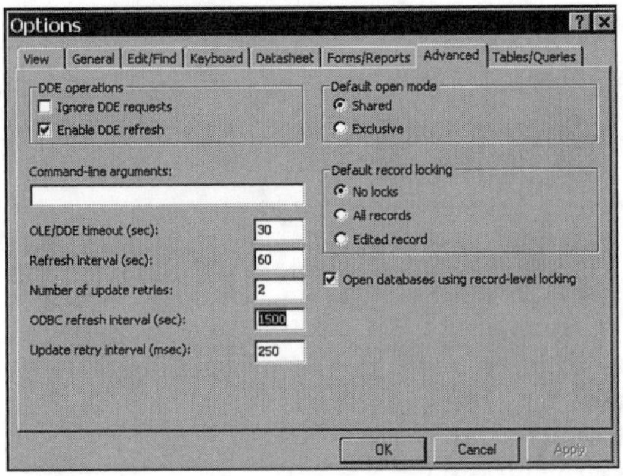

FIGURE 5.18
The Advanced tab of the Options dialog box is where you can specify ODBC settings.

One reason to increase the ODBC refresh interval would be to avoid reactivating connections that have been closed for forms with no activity. Connections can be valuable server resources, and one potential drawback of using forms based on linked ODBC data is that connections can proliferate quickly.

If your form's recordset has over 100 records (you'll see how to change this default value soon), at least two connections will be opened. One connection will be used to open a recordset with just the primary keys of the main table, and a second recordset will be used to load batches of records in the background until all the data has been loaded. With fewer than 100 records, just one connection is used to retrieve all the data. In addition, combo and list box row sources can spawn additional connections, not to mention subforms and their combo boxes.

Even if a user is idle or away from the computer, these connections will be reactivated or maintained every time that refresh interval expires.

Using the Windows Registry

In addition to modifying the ODBC refresh interval to prevent connections from being reactivated, you can also control the length of time it will take an idle connection to time out and be closed automatically due to inactivity. Unfortunately, this ConnectionTimeout setting is not exposed in the Options dialog box. Instead, you need to work with the Windows Registry, where you can control this and several other ODBC parameters.

To adjust these settings, open Regedit.exe or another utility for editing the Registry and navigate to the following subkey:

HKEY_LOCAL_MACHINE\SOFTWARE\Microsoft\Jet\4.0\Engines\ODBC

> **CAUTION**
>
> Creating incorrect Registry settings can have unintended consequences and might even leave your computer in a nonoperational state! Consider these techniques to be advanced-level recommendations for experienced administrators only.

The default value for ODBC connection timeouts is 600 seconds (10 minutes). You can increase or decrease this by right-clicking ConnectionTimeout in the right pane of the RegEdit window and choosing Modify. You'll then get a dialog box like the one shown in Figure 5.19. Select the Decimal option button in the Base frame, and in the Value Data text box enter the desired number of seconds. This setting will take effect the next time you open Access (or run any other software that uses the Jet database engine to make an ODBC connection).

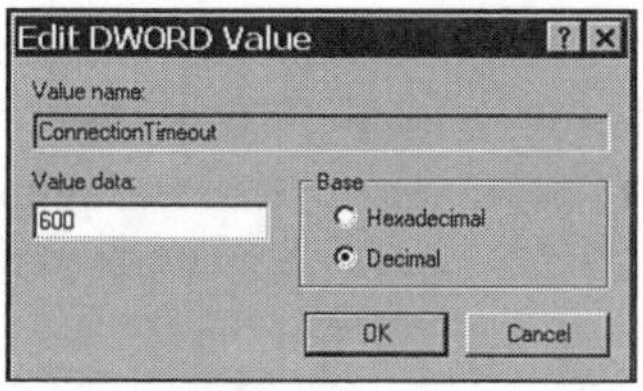

FIGURE 5.19
Modifying the ODBC ConnectionTimeout *value in the Windows Registry.*

You may be familiar with the DBEngine.SetOption method, which can be used to modify temporarily certain Jet engine settings without writing to the Registry. Unfortunately, this method does not allow you to modify settings that affect ODBC. The only way to do this is by making changes to the Registry. Table 5.1 summarizes the other settings that can be modified. Some of these are rather obscure, but several of them can be quite useful. For example, QueryTimeout may need to be increased if you are running any queries that take a long time to return data— perhaps for a complex report. The TracesSQLMode setting can be used to create a log of the SQL statements sent over ODBC. It is also interesting to note that the TryJetAuth setting, which defaults to True, causes Jet to attempt to log onto SQL Server using the current Access username and password.

TABLE 5.1 Registry Settings for Modifying Jet's ODBC Behavior

Name	Default	Description
AsyncRetryInterval	500	Number of milliseconds to wait between retries on an asynchronous connection.
AttachableObjects	TABLE	The list of objects that Microsoft Jet will allow attachments to.
AttachCaseSensitive	0	If False (0), this will attach to the first name matching the specified string in a match that isn't case sensitive. If True (1), it requires a case-sensitive match of the name.
ConnectionTimeout	600	Number of seconds to wait before closing an idle connection.
DisableAsync	0	Forces synchronous query execution. Values are 0 (use asynchronous query execution if possible) and 1 (force synchronous query execution).
FastRequery	0	Uses a prepared SELECT statement for parameterized queries. Values are 0 (False) and 1 (True).
LoginTimeout	20	Number of seconds to wait for a login attempt to succeed.
PreparedInsert	0	Uses a prepared INSERT statement that inserts data in all columns. Values are 0 (use a custom INSERT statement that inserts only non-NULL values) and 1 (use a prepared INSERT statement). Using prepared INSERT statements can cause NULL values to overwrite server defaults and can cause triggers to execute on columns that weren't inserted explicitly.
PreparedUpdate	0	Uses a prepared UPDATE statement that updates data in all columns. Values are 0 (use a custom UPDATE statement that sets only columns that have changed) and 1 (use a prepared UPDATE statement). Using prepared UPDATE statements can cause triggers to execute on columns that weren't changed explicitly.
QueryTimeout	60	Number of seconds to wait for a query to execute before failing.

TABLE 5.1   Continued

Name	Default	Description
SnapshotOnly	0	If False (0), you'll get index information on attachments to allow dynasets if possible. If True (1), Microsoft Jet will ignore index information and thereby force snapshots on all attachments.
TraceODBCAPI	0	Initiates sending a trace of ODBC API calls to the file Odbcapi.txt. Values are 0 (False) and 1 (True).
TraceSQLMode	0	Initiates sending a trace of SQL statements sent to an ODBC data source to the file Sqlout.txt. Values are 0 (False) and 1 (True). This setting is interchangeable with SQLTracemode.
TryJetAuth	1	Uses the Microsoft Access username and password to log onto the server before prompting. Values are 0 (False) and 1 (True).

Using an MSysConf Table

To improve the user experience, Jet cleverly retrieves just enough data to populate the first records displayed in a form, and it then retrieves the balance in batches asynchronously. This allows the user to begin working with a form before all the data has been fetched. It also, however, has the effect of lengthening the amount of time it takes to populate the form fully, possibly increasing the lifetime of the connection and the lifetime of read locks that are placed on the data. The documented default behavior is for Access to retrieve 100 records every 10 seconds, although you may find that certain queries occasionally result in different patterns.

You can control this background data-fetching behavior by creating a special table called *MSysConf* in your SQL Server database. Access looks for this table every time it connects to SQL Server. If it finds this table, it uses the values in the table to determine how many rows to fetch at a time and how long to wait between fetches. You may want to speed up the data retrieval to free up the connection and the server faster, or you may want to slow it down to attenuate the impact on server and network performance. The MSysConf table can also be used to disable the default Access behavior of allowing users to store a username and password with a linked table or pass-through query.

The MSysConf table must have exactly the structure shown in Table 5.2. Otherwise, you will not be able to connect to the SQL Server database from Access.

5

LINKING TO SQL
SERVER USING
ACCESS DATABASES
(MDBs)

TABLE 5.2 Structure of the MSysConf Table

Column Name	Data Type	Allow Nulls
Config	smallint	No
ChValue	varchar(255)	Yes
NValue	int	Yes
Comments	varchar(255)	Yes

All users must have select permissions on the table. You'll probably only want administrators to be able to insert, update, or delete.

At this time, only the Config and NValue columns are used by Jet. Any values in the other columns are ignored, but they must be present. There are only three valid records that you can enter in this table—one to specify whether storage of usernames and passwords should be allowed, one to specify the number of records to be retrieved at a time when populating a recordset, and one to specify the interval between data retrievals. Table 5.3 shows the allowed values.

TABLE 5.3 Values Allowed in the Config and nValue Columns

Config	nValue	Meaning
101	0 or 1	Allow local storage of the logon ID and password only if the value is 1.
102	Any integer	The delay in seconds between each retrieval.
103	Any integer	The number of rows retrieved each time.

Summary

Access MDBs allow you to create linked tables that use ODBC to connect to SQL Server. Although linked tables offer an Access-SQL Server solution that appears to require little work, significant improvements can be made in performance and scalability by reworking your Access application to use linked tables efficiently. The golden rule of client/server development is to fetch only needed data—avoid basing forms on entire tables or large result sets and only retrieve the necessary columns. Prefilter data before it is fetched from the server, and base forms on limited result sets. Fill bound list boxes and combo boxes on demand, and populate subforms only as needed. Use pass-through queries to take advantage of SQL Server to process data instead of having Jet process data locally. Pass-through queries can be set to return data and to execute stored procedures. The easiest way to modify a parameterized pass-through query is through code, by modifying its SQL. Caching data in local tables helps reduce roundtrips to the server for filling list boxes and combo boxes—local data can be refreshed on demand. Finally, the Jet engine's default ODBC behavior can be modified through the Tools, Options dialog box, by making changes to the Windows Registry, or by creating a special MSysConf table on SQL Server.

ActiveX Data Objects (ADO) Fundamentals

IN THIS CHAPTER

A Short History of Data Access Technologies

In the beginning was the void, and data was accessed with great difficulty. Then Microsoft said, "Let there be data access, where data be not divided between platforms!" And Microsoft created Open Database Connectivity, which it called *ODBC*, and it was so. ODBC saw that the data was gathered together unto one place, and multiplied. Henceforth, ODBC begat DAO, which begat RDO, which begat OLE DB, which begat ADO, which begat ADOX, ADOMD, ADOR, and JRO. At least, that's what it seems like on the surface. Here's the way it really happened.

ODBC (Open Database Connectivity)

Microsoft's first data access technology, developed in the early 1990s, was *Open Database Connectivity* (ODBC), which is still in wide use today. ODBC allows programmers to write software that communicates with just about any relational database by using a standard set of interfaces. Database vendors and third parties supply ODBC drivers for each type of database, and you set up named data sources (DSNs) that hold all the information required to connect to a particular database. However, the functions that are used to perform this communication are rather primitive, completely *not* object oriented, and difficult to work with.

DAO (Data Access Objects)

When Microsoft introduced the Jet database engine as part of Microsoft Access, it also began work on an object-based way programmers could communicate with the database. When Access 2.0 was released, it included this revolutionary new data access object model, called *Data Access Objects* (DAO). Rather than forcing programmers to call low-level functions, DAO presented a hierarchical model and allowed programmers to design and manipulate databases by working with the properties and methods of the DAO objects.

Remote Data Objects (RDO)

DAO was great for working with Jet databases, but a lot of important data was still stored in other server-based relational databases. To bring the ease of use that existed in DAO to the world of ODBC, Microsoft introduced *Remote Data Objects* (RDO). RDO used an object model very similar to DAO, but behind the scenes it translated property setting and methods into ODBC function calls.

RDO became very popular with Visual Basic programmers who wanted to access data on server databases but didn't want the overhead of invoking the Jet database engine with DAO. To make it easier for DAO programmers to take advantage of the technology in RDO, Microsoft then introduced a variation on DAO, called *ODBC Direct*. ODBC Direct used the familiar DAO objects but also incorporated RDO's ability to use ODBC directly rather than going through the Jet engine to get to remote databases.

OLE DB

In the middle of all this, Microsoft began working on a project to replace the aging ODBC technology with something that would be object based and that also would not be limited to working only with data stored in relational databases. This new technology was eventually called *OLE DB*. Unlike ODBC, OLE DB can be used to provide programmatic access to all kinds of data, including disk file directories, email message stores, and streaming multimedia data, not just the relational data that ODBC supports.

OLE DB is Microsoft's newest and most powerful data access paradigm, and ADO is its application-level interface. OLE DB provides high-performance access to any data source that has an OLE DB provider. Because OLE DB providers are easier to write than ODBC providers, you'll probably see one eventually for just about every data source imaginable. OLE DB is a specification, not an actual product or library—it consists of a set of COM interfaces that provide access to data.

ADO (ActiveX Data Objects)

Although OLE DB is an object-based technology, it is not possible for VBA programmers to work directly with the properties and methods of OLE DB objects. Instead, Microsoft has provided a VBA-friendly object model for OLE DB; this object model is called *ActiveX Data Objects* (ADO). You can think of ADO as the bridge between VBA and OLE DB, providing access to the COM interfaces in OLE DB. ADO attempts to supply all the capabilities of RDO and DAO while adding a few new tricks of its own, along with the expanded access to nonrelational data that OLE DB makes possible. Because ADO is built on top of OLE DB, it benefits from the rich universal data access infrastructure that OLE DB provides.

Unlike DAO and RDO, which are each implemented in a single object library, ADO is actually a collection of object libraries, each one providing a different area of functionality. The most commonly used library, ADODB, contains objects for retrieving and manipulating data. The ADODB object model defines a set of programmable objects you can use in Visual Basic, Visual C++, various scripting languages, and on any platform that supports both COM and Automation. An overview of several more advanced ADO features, some of which depend on the use of other object libraries, appears at the end of this chapter.

Getting Started with ADO

In Chapter 11, "Scaling Up with Unbound Access Applications," and in Chapter 14, "Architecting Distributed *n*-Tier Applications," we present several examples of how to use ADO in Access applications to retrieve and update SQL Server data. If you've worked with DAO, then ADO may look familiar. However, many of the underlying technologies in ADO are really very different from those in DAO, and the way the object model operates is also quite a departure. So, this chapter gives you the foundation you need to understand ADO and work with it effectively.

Setting a Reference to the ADODB Object Library

As with any object model, the first step in using ADO from your VBA code is to make sure that your project has a reference to the ADODB object library. In Microsoft Access 2000, this reference is provided automatically in new databases and projects. But in Access 97, or in Access 2000 databases that were converted from a prior version, you need to set the reference yourself using the References dialog box available under the Tools menu (see Figure 6.1). Try not to be confused by the fact that all versions of the ADODB library since version 1.5 have retained the same filename—msado15.dll.

If you have an existing reference to an earlier version, you can clear its check box before selecting the ADODB 2.5 library. The version that was originally shipped with Access 2000 was 2.1. At the time of this writing, version 2.5 is current, and because it is the version that ships with SQL 2000 and seems to be quite solid, it's used in these examples. However, the features described in this chapter were almost all available in version 2.1. The only new objects in version 2.5 are the Record and Stream objects.

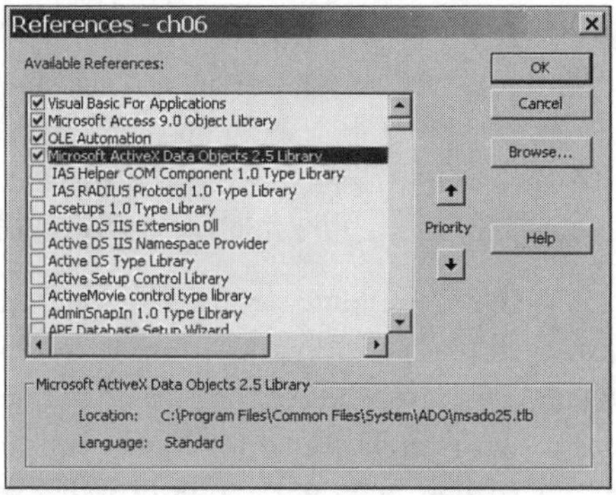

FIGURE 6.1
Setting a reference to the ADODB 2.5 object library.

TIP

We recommend that you always use the latest version of ADO available. ADO is a work in progress—you should expect enhancements in both performance and functionality as Microsoft continues to improve ADO. Up through ADO version 2.1, which shipped with Access 2000, ADO has been available from www.microsoft.com/data, as

ActiveX Data Objects (ADO) Fundamentals

CHAPTER 6

223

6

ACTIVEX DATA
OBJECTS (ADO)
FUNDAMENTALS

part of a collection of components called the *Microsoft Data Access Components* (MDAC). Beginning with version 2.5, which shipped with Windows 2000 and SQL Server 2000, ADO has also become a part of the operating system in Windows 2000, and upgrades are made available as part of operating system service packs. If you're still on a Windows NT or Windows 95/98/ME platform, MDAC updates will to be available on Microsoft's Web site.

The ADO Object Model

Unlike DAO and RDO, the ADODB object model, shown in Figure 6.2, is not a hierarchical system. For example, to create an ADO Recordset object, you do not have to drill down through a complex object hierarchy; you can jump right in and create a new recordset. You then set its properties and invoke its methods to connect it to a data source and retrieve records.

Each of the major ADO objects can be created independently, and the objects cooperate with each other as equals, providing services as needed. For example, you can open a Recordset object without explicitly opening a Connection object first. You can provide connection specifications as properties of the recordset, and the recordset will create its own Connection object behind the scenes, as needed.

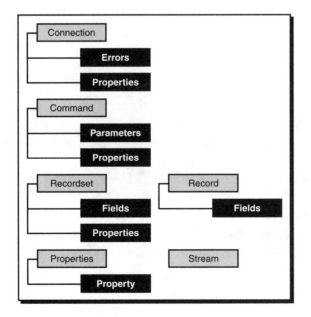

FIGURE 6.2
The ADO 2.5 object model.

Using the Object Browser

Once you've set a reference to the ADODB object library, you can then use the Object Browser to obtain more information at any time. Simply press F2 on your keyboard or right-click anywhere in a module and choose Object Browser from the list. Select ADODB from the top combo box, and all the objects and collections will be displayed. Figure 6.3 shows the Object Browser with the Field object selected in the left pane, and its properties and methods displayed in the right pane.

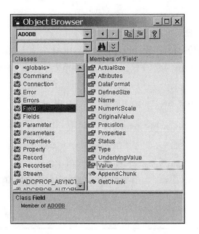

FIGURE 6.3
The Object Browser with the Field object selected.

TIP

ADO help is easy to obtain in the Object Browser by clicking the yellow question mark button in the upper-right corner or by pressing the F1 key after you've selected the object you're interested in. You can also type into the lower combo box and click the binoculars button to find items in the library you have selected.

Introducing the Three Main Objects

Here are the three main objects you'll be working with:

- The Connection object
- The Recordset object
- The Command object

They can work together with each other, or you can invoke them separately, depending on what you're trying to achieve. All three objects are extremely flexible, and there's a lot of overlapping functionality. In ADO you have many choices about how to perform a particular task, which can sometimes make it more confusing than if there were only one single correct way to do something. For example, you can execute a stored procedure using a Connection object, a Recordset object, or a Command object. Each handles the execution of the stored procedure a little differently, but they all work. Which one do you choose? The following is a brief discussion of each object and its intended purpose.

The Connection Object

You can think of a Connection object as specifying the information needed to find and access a particular source of data. It incorporates aspects of both the Workspace and Database objects in DAO. You can use the properties of the connection object, including its ConnectionString property, to define the source of your data and how to find it. The Open method is used to establish the actual connection, and parameters of the Open method can also be used to define the type of connection or to supply a username and password. Connection objects can be opened independently of other ADO objects, or they can be opened in the background when you supply connection information to another object.

The Recordset Object

A Recordset object represents the records (or result set) retrieved from a table, a query, or any command you send to a data source that returns records. You can also create disconnected recordsets that are not bound to any data source at all and populate them with data yourself. When you create a Recordset object to work with SQL Server data, you can base it on an existing Connection object or specify connection information by setting its ConnectionString property prior to invoking the Recordset object's Open method. You can also supply a connection string as a parameter of the Open method. In addition to using Connection objects to access data sources, recordsets also use Command object to define the data that will be retrieved.

The Command Object

Command objects can be used on their own to execute SQL commands and stored procedures, using information you supply to create a Connection behind the scenes, or in conjunction with a previously created Connection object. Command objects can also be used to return records in a Recordset object. Unless a Recordset object is just returning all the records in a particular table or is not based on any data source at all, it will always create a Command object behind the scenes to help it retrieve the records it needs. Command objects have a Parameters collection, which is used for executing parameterized queries and stored procedures. As with recordsets, you can base a Command object on an existing Connection object, or you can provide connection information to the ConnectionString property.

All this versatility can make these objects confusing, but don't despair. The following sections will cover how to use each of these three main objects, with plenty of examples.

Creating an ADO Connection Object

This section will cover creating Connection objects and setting their properties.

Declaring and Creating a Connection Object

To retrieve or manipulate data using ADO, you must provide the information needed to locate and connect with the data. This information and the state of your connection are encapsulated within the Connection object. To work with a Connection object, as with any other kind of object, you create a variable of the appropriate type and then instantiate the object by setting that variable. This creates a Connection object that doesn't yet point to any particular data source:

```
Dim cnn As ADODB.Connection
Set cnn = New ADODB.Connection
```

Opening the Connection Object

There are several different ways to establish the connection to your database using the Connection object's Open method.

The ConnectionString Property

The first option is to specify the ConnectionString in the Open method:

```
Dim cnn As ADODB.Connection
Set cnn = New ADODB.Connection

cnn.Open _
  "Provider=SQLOLEDB.1;" & _
  "Data Source=MyServer;Initial Catalog=MyDatabase;" & _
  "User ID=Dudley;Password=password"
```

Using VBA's syntax for naming arguments, this can also be written as:

```
cnn.Open _
  ConnectionString:="Provider=SQLOLEDB.1;" & _
  "Data Source=MyServer;Initial Catalog=MyDatabase;" & _
  "User ID=Dudley;Password=password"
```

As you can see, the ConnectionString argument is composed of a series of name/value pairs separated by semicolons. Most ConnectionString values begin by specifying the provider. Providers, which are discussed further in the next section, allow you to connect to specific kinds of data. The remaining attributes in the ConnectionString will vary depending on the provider being used.

To work with SQL Server, use the SQLOLEDB.1 provider or the latest SQL Server provider version available. The Data Source attribute in a SQL Server connection string is the name of your SQL Server, and the Initial Catalog attribute is the database you are primarily interested in connecting to. This doesn't, however, limit you to working with only one database per connection. The optional User ID and Password attributes allow you supply the user authentication. If you are using NT authentication, in place of the User ID and Password, use this:

```
"Integrated Security=SSPI"
```

SSPI stands for *Security Support Provider Interface*, which is the interface to NT security for authentication. This tells the Connection object to look to NT to authenticate the user. You can also omit security information from the connection string completely and provide a user ID and password as additional separate parameters to the Open method:

```
cnn.Open _
  ConnectionString:="Provider=SQLOLEDB.1;" & _
  "Data Source=MyServer;Initial Catalog=MyDatabase", _
  UserID:="Dudley", Password:="password"
```

If you specify a user ID and password in both the ConnectionString argument and in the optional UserID and Password arguments, ADO will ignore the values in the ConnectionString argument and will use the ones in the UserID and Password arguments.

Another way of opening a Connection object is to set the ConnectionString property first and then invoke the Open method:

```
Set cnn = New ADODB.Connection
cnn.ConnectionString = _
  "Provider=SQLOLEDB.1;" & _
  "Data Source=MyServer;Initial Catalog=MyDatabase;" & _
  "User ID=Dudley;Password=password"
cnn.Mode = adModeReadWrite
cnn.Open
```

This flexibility—being able to supply individual properties or roll them into a connection string—is typical of ADO. You can pick the one that best suits your immediate needs or programming style. This example also sets the optional Mode property of the Connection object, which can be used to define read-only or read/write connections.

Sometimes, you'll already have a Connection object available to you, and you can set your variable to reference that existing connection. This is the case in Access 2000, where you can reference the connection that Access has already opened:

```
Set cnn = CurrentProject.Connection
```

Open Method Options

In addition to the ConnectionString, UserID, and Password parameters that you can supply values for when you call a Connection object's Open method, there's also a parameter called Options. If you don't specify a value for the Options parameter, ADO will use its default value of adConnectUnspecified, which opens the connection synchronously. This means that your code will not continue until the connection has been completed.

Alternatively, you can supply a value of adAsyncConnect for this parameter, and your code will continue without waiting for the connection to open. You can then use the ConnectComplete event of your Connection object to determine when the connection has actually finished being opened. This is just one example of how ADO objects, unlike the objects in DAO, have events that can be used to monitor and respond to changes in their status.

OLE DB Providers

ADO uses OLE DB technology to connect to data. The OLE DB components that enable connections are called *providers*, and providers are available that allow you to connect to a wide variety of data sources. When ADO was first introduced, Microsoft recognized that ODBC was the most common technology in use for connecting to data, so the first OLE DB provider available allowed you to use ODBC. This OLE DB provider for ODBC, called *MSDASQL*, is still the default provider used automatically if no other provider is specified. Since then, however, many other OLE DB providers have been developed that allow you to connect directly to many data sources without going through ODBC.

When connecting to SQL Server data, you'll get the best results if you use the native OLE DB provider for SQL Server, called *SQLOLEDB*, as shown in the previous code fragments. The following sections, however, provide some examples of how you can use other providers in ADO.

Connecting Using an ODBC DSN

To use an ODBC data source name (DSN) from ADO, you can use the following simple syntax:

```
cnn.Open "DSN=MySource", "Dudley", "password"
```

Notice that, in addition to specifying the name of the DSN, you can also separately pass in arguments for a user name and password, if necessary. This is true no matter what type of provider you use. If you are using ODBC to connect to a SQL Server database, you can save a user ID and password as part of the DSN, or you can specify in the DSN that you want to use NT authentication.

To create ODBC DSNs, use the ODBC applet found in the Windows Control Panel. You can create System DSNs (which can be used by all users), User DSNs (which are specific to a particular user profile), or File DSNs (which are stored in separate files rather than in the

Windows Registry). To create a DSN for a particular type of database, you need to have installed an ODBC driver for that database.

ODBC DSN-less Connections

You can also make use of ODBC without specifying a saved DSN by providing all the information that ODBC needs to make your connection. This is referred to as a *DSN-less connection*, and the "name=value" syntax is quite similar to the ADO ConnectionString syntax that can be used to create OLE DB connections:

```
cnn.Open _
 "Driver=SQL Server;" & _
 "Server=MyServer;" & _
 "Database=Pubs;UID=sa;PWD="
```

In this example, because the provider is not specified, ADO will assume you want to use the ODBC provider. The string looks like an OLE DB connection string, but actually it is an ODBC connect string. The OLE DB provider for ODBC passes this string right along to be used by ODBC. This can be confusing and can lead to errors, because the attributes that are valid in this ODBC connect string would not be correct if the native OLE DB provider for SQL Server were being used. For example, in the ODBC string, you use, "Server=MyServer," but for the native OLE DB SQL Server provider, you must use, "Data Source=MyServer." The ODBC syntax uses "Database," whereas the OLE DB syntax uses, "Initial Catalog." And in the ODBC string, you specify a "Driver," whereas in the OLE DB string, you specify a "Provider." You could be explicit about the fact that you are using the ODBC provider and therefore using ODBC attributes:

```
cnn.Open _
 "Provider= MSDASQL;Driver=SQL Server;" & _
 "Server=MyServer;" & _
 "Database=Pubs;UID=sa;PWD="
```

A username and password can be included within the ODBC connect string, as shown in this example, or as separate arguments to the Open method. If you are using NT authentication, you can also specify that in your ODBC connect string:

```
cnn.Open _
 "Driver=SQL Server;" & _
 "Server=MyServer;" & _
 "Database=Pubs;" & _
 "Trusted_Connection=Yes"
```

Creating a Jet Connection

Instead of using ODBC, you can now probably find a native OLE DB provider that enables you to connect directly to your data. Providers are available for Jet, SQL Server, Oracle, and a growing list of other data sources. In fact, one of the principal advantages of OLE DB is that it has providers for types of data, such as email messages and file directories, that are not available using ODBC.

Here's an example of using the native Jet OLE DB provider to connect to an Access database:

```
cnn.Open _
  "Provider=Microsoft.Jet.OLEDB.4.0;" & _
  "Data Source=C:\YourPath\YourData.MDB"
```

Connecting Using a Data Link File (UDL)

A Data Link file, or *UDL*, is similar to an ODBC File DSN in that it lets you store connection information in a file. Here's how to create one:

1. Open a Windows Explorer window and choose File, New, Microsoft Data Link. If you don't see this option on your Windows Explorer menu, simply create a Notepad file, replacing the .TXT filename extension with .UDL.

2. This will create a new file located in the folder in which you issue the menu command. Rename it to something meaningful, but leave the .UDL extension alone.

3. Double-click the new file. This will open a dialog box in which you can set connection properties. The Provider tab shown in Figure 6.4 lets you specify which OLE DB provider to use.

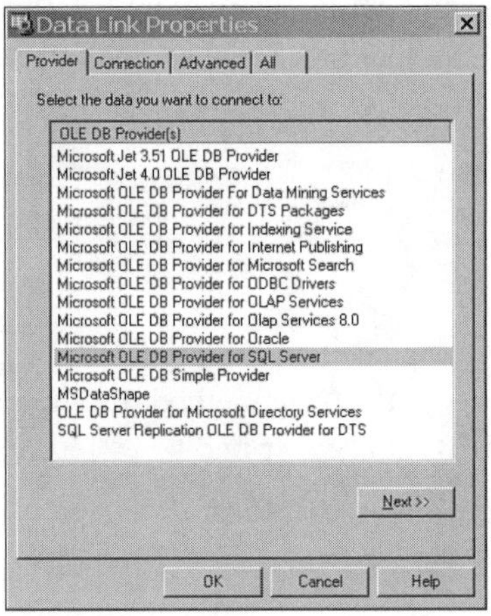

FIGURE 6.4

Selecting the provider in a Data Link file.

4. You can then click the Next button or click directly on the Connection tab. The Connection tab lets you set the connection properties to use in your data link. Figure 6.5 shows connecting to the Northwind database on MABEL using integrated security.

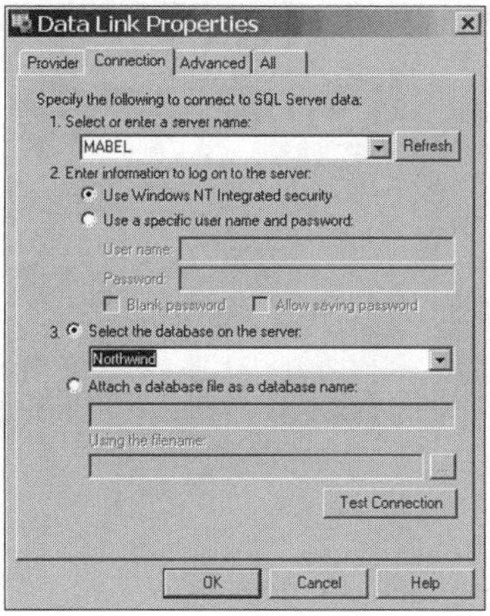

ActiveX Data Objects (ADO) Fundamentals

CHAPTER 6

231

6

ACTIVEX DATA
OBJECTS (ADO)
FUNDAMENTALS

FIGURE 6.5

Setting the Connection properties for the data link.

This is generally all the information you need to connect to SQL Server. Other providers may require setting additional options. Click Test Connection to verify that your settings are correct; then click OK to save the data link.

The All tab on the Data Link Properties dialog box is a good place to look for the names of all the properties that are supported by a particular provider. For example, it is there that you would be able to find and edit the attribute for Access (Jet) databases called "Jet OLEDB:System database," which allows you to specify the path to a security workgroup file.

TIP

The Data link Properties dialog box is very useful, and you'll see it pop up in many different places where a program is asking you to define an ADO connection. In fact, you can make it pop up yourself in your own application, and you can retrieve the ConnectionString value that's generated by the selections that the user makes. To do this, you would set a reference to the object library called the "Microsoft OLE DB Service Component." Once you've set this reference in your VBA project, you can use code like this to pop up the dialog box shown previously in Figure 6.2 and retrieve a valid connect string:

```
Public Function GetConnectionString() As String
    Dim objDialog As MSDASC.DataLinks
    Dim cnn As ADODB.Connection
```

```
        Set objDialog = New MSDASC.DataLinks
        Set cnn = objDialog.PromptNew
        If Not cnn Is Nothing Then
            GetConnectionString = cnn.ConnectionString
        End If
    End Function
```

As you can see from this sample function, the PromptNew method actually returns an ADO connection object, not just a string. But be aware that if the user clicks Cancel, your ADO object is set to Nothing, and any attempt to retrieve its properties or call its methods will result in an error.

Data link files are not secure. You can open them using Notepad (or any other text editor) and view the information saved in them. Therefore, they are not recommended for caching sensitive information, such as usernames and passwords. Instead, use the UserID and Password parameters of the Connection object's Open method. Because they are just text files, you can easily create or edit your own data link files, which take this form:

```
[oledb]
; Everything after this line is an OLE DB initstring
Provider=SQLOLEDB.1;Integrated Security=SSPI;Persist Security Info=

False;Initial Catalog=Northwind;Data Source=MABEL
```

Contrary to what you might expect, the comment in the second line is not optional—if you leave it out or modify it, the UDL won't work! Everything after that comment should be on a single line in your UDL text file.

Once you've created your data link, you can specify it in a connection string. You need to pass the fully qualified path and filename of the UDL. In the following code fragment, the UDL is located in the same folder as the Access database:

```
cnn.ConnectionString = _
    "File Name=" & _
    CurrentProject.Path & "\MyUDL.UDL"
cnn.Open
```

The biggest advantage of using a data link is that you can easily change or replace it without having to touch your code.

> **TIP**
>
> If you're writing code to create a connection string and you're unsure what properties to include in the connection string, create a new data link file and connect it to your intended data source. Then just open the data link file in Notepad or any other text editor and copy the connection string it contains into your procedure.

More About Setting the Connection String

Instead of including the OLE DB provider specification inside the connection string, you can first set the provider, using a property of the Connection object:

```
With cnn
  .Provider = "Microsoft.Jet.OLEDB.4.0"
  .ConnectionString = _
    "Data Source=C:\YourPath\YourData.MDB"
  .Open
End With
```

You may wonder why you couldn't also use a `DataSource` property rather than specifying the data source as part of the connection string. The reason is that not all types of connections have a "data source," but they all have providers. The all-purpose `ConnectionString` property allows you to include any attribute that may be needed for any type of provider.

The following list of sample connection strings gives you an idea of the variety available.

Using a File DSN:

```
"FILEDSN=C:\somepath\mydb.dsn;UID=Admin;PWD=;"
```

Specifying an Access security workgroup file:

```
"Provider=Microsoft.Jet.OLEDB.4.0;Data Source=C:\somepath\mydb.mdb;
```

```
Jet OLEDB:System Database=C:\somepath\system.mdw;"
```

Specifying an Access database password:

```
"Provider=Microsoft.Jet.OLEDB.4.0;Data Source=C:\somepath\mydb.mdb;
```

```
Jet OLEDB:Database Password=MyDbPassword;"
```

Using Jet to get to Excel:

```
"Provider=Microsoft.Jet.OLEDB.4.0;Data Source=Expenses.xls;
```

```
Extended Properties=""Excel 8.0;HDR=Yes;"";"
```

Using a UDL file:

```
"File Name=pubs.udl;"
```

Using the OLE DB provider for Oracle:

```
"Provider=msdaora;Data Source=OracleServer.world;User Id=sa;Password=;"
```

TIP

Once a Connection object's Provider has been set, ADO dynamically fills the object's Properties collection with the properties that are appropriate to that provider. You can use the properties collection to refer to properties that aren't found in the standard type library of an object and therefore aren't visible in the Visual Basic Editor's Object Browser. For each attribute in a valid ConnectionString setting, there is a corresponding property in the Properties collection. You can use these dynamic properties either to set or get values for those attributes once the provider has been set.

For example, in the connection string for an OLE DB connection to SQL Server, you identify the name of the server using the Data Source attribute:

```
cnn.ConnectionString = _
  "Provider=SQLOLEDB.1;" & _
  "Data Source=MyServer;Initial Catalog=MyDatabase;" & _
  "User ID=Dudley;Password=password"
```

To retrieve the name of the server later, use the following syntax:

```
strServerName = cnn.Properties("Data Source")
```

Most objects in ADO have a Properties collection that you can use to work with provider-specific dynamic properties.

Connection Properties and Methods

Certainly, the most comprehensive property of a Connection object is its `ConnectionString` property. As you have seen, you can use the `ConnectionString` property to give ADO all the information it needs to open a connection. This also is the default property of the Connection object, so if you refer to a Connection object without specifying any property, you will retrieve the value of its connection string.

In addition to the `ConnectionString` property, the Connection object supports a number of other properties you can use to refine your definition of a connection that will be opened or to provide information about a connection that has already been opened. Also, the Connection object supports several methods in addition to the `Open` method. There's also an Errors collection you can use to track any problems that might arise with your connections. This section gives you an overview of these additional interfaces of the Connection object.

ActiveX Data Objects (ADO) Fundamentals

CHAPTER 6

235

6

ACTIVEX DATA
OBJECTS (ADO)
FUNDAMENTALS

The `State` Property

Once the connection is open, you can use the `State` property to determine whether the connection succeeded and whether any activity is occurring. Here's an example:

```
Debug.Print cnn.State
```

It will return one of the values shown in Table 6.1.

TABLE 6.1 Intrinsic Constants for the `State` Property of a Connection Object

Constant	Value	Description
adStateClosed	0	Default (closed)
adStateOpen	1	Open
adStateConnecting	2	Connecting
adStateExecuting	4	Executing a command
adStateFetching	8	Rows of a Recordset object are being fetched

The `ConnectionTimeout` and `Mode` Properties

The `ConnectionTimeout` property lets you configure the connection to time out after a specified number of seconds. This property defaults to a timeout period of 15 seconds. Unless you change this value before opening your connection, after 15 seconds without successfully connecting, the attempt to connect will be canceled and an error will be raised. If you set this property to 0, ADO will wait indefinitely for a connection to be completed.

The `Mode` property lets you set or return the access permissions in use by the provider on the current connection. You have to set the mode prior to opening the connection because it is read-only once the connection is open. You can create read-only, write-only, or read-write connections, and you can prevent other users from being able to open read-enabled and/or write-enabled connections while your connection is open.

These properties will only work if the provider you're using to open the connection supports them.

The `CursorLocation` Property

This property specifies the default `CursorLocation` setting that will be applied to recordsets opened using this connection. The `CursorLocation` property of recordsets is discussed later in the chapter, but, briefly, this property determines whether ADO or the server database engine will provide the cursor library used to open a recordset. Some ADO recordset features can only be used if you let ADO provide the cursor by specifying a value of `adUseClient` for the `CursorLocation`.

The `DefaultDatabase` Property

If the provider allows you to work with multiple databases using a single connection, this property lets you set a default database by specifying its name. You then don't have to fully qualify references to objects in that default database.

The `IsolationLevel` Property

You use the `IsolationLevel` property to control the behavior of transactions that you run within the connection. Transactions are discussed in Chapter 10, "Programming Effective Stored Procedures."

The `Provider` Property

Specifies an OLE DB provider, which can also be specified within the `ConnectionString` property.

The `Close` Method

The `Close` method closes the physical connection to the data source. Once a connection has been closed, you can change its properties and open it again. To completely release any resources being consumed by a Connection object, you should first close it and then set it to `Nothing`. Here's an example:

```
cnn.close
Set cnn = Nothing
```

The `Execute` Method and `CommandTimeout` Property

The `Execute` method can be used to run a command or statement. The `CommandTimeout` property lets you configure the number of seconds ADO will wait when it tries to execute a command. Unlike the `ConnectionTimeout` property, which has a default value of only 15 seconds, the default for `CommandTimeout` is 30 seconds. If you think your command may take longer than that, use this property to give it more time.

Here's a simple example of how you can use the `Execute` method of a Connection object in Access to update data, without explicitly creating a Command object:

```
Dim cnn As ADODB.Connection
Set cnn = CurrentProject.Connection
cnn.Execute "Update Employees " & _
    "Set LastName = 'Jones' Where EmployeeID = 4;"
```

Behind the scenes, ADO creates a Command object that's used to perform this update. The `Execute` method has a couple optional parameters, `RecordsAffected` and `Options`, which are covered later when this method is discussed again in relation to the Command object. You'll see then that the `Execute` method of a Command object can also be used to open a recordset, and this can be done using the `Execute` method of a Connection object as well.

ActiveX Data Objects (ADO) Fundamentals

CHAPTER 6

237

6

ACTIVEX DATA
OBJECTS (ADO)
FUNDAMENTALS

The `BeginTrans`, `CommitTrans`, and `RollbackTrans` Methods and the `Attributes` Property

The `BeginTrans`, `CommitTrans`, and `RollbackTrans` methods and the `Attributes` property are all used in ADO to manage transactions, including nested transactions if the provider supports them. Transactions allow you to run a series of operations and ensure that they will only affect your data if they can all be completed successfully. If any one of the operations is unsuccessful, you can roll back the entire transaction.

Using Access with the Jet database engine, you are really forced to use your VBA code to manage transactions. When working with SQL Server, however, you can create transactions within a stored procedure, making ADO's ability to handle transactions less important. The use of stored procedures to manage transactions is discussed in Chapter 10.

The Errors Collection

Unlike the VBA Err object, the ADO Errors collection of a Connection object can handle more than one error at a time. The Errors collection is needed to capture errors that originate in an OLE DB provider. Providers can generate multiple errors on a single operation, which are then placed in the Errors collection. The collection is cleared when another ADO operation generates new errors.

Errors caused by ADO objects themselves are exposed through the VBA Err object. The Error objects in the Errors collection represent only provider errors related to your data connection. You can walk through ADO errors in your error-handling routine by declaring an object variable as `ADODB.Error` and then walking through the Connection object's Errors collection. This code fragment shows the properties of the Error object that are available:

```
Dim cnn As ADODB.Connection
Dim errADO As ADODB.Error
'...
' In your error handling routine:

For Each errADO In cnn.Errors
    Debug.Print "Number: " & errADO.Number
    Debug.Print "Description: " & errADO.Description
    Debug.Print "Source: " & errADO.Source
    Debug.Print "NativeError: " & errADO.NativeError
    Debug.Print "SQLState: " & errADO.SQLState
Next
```

The `NativeError` property allows you to retrieve the error number that was generated within the source database itself, which may be different from the provider error number you get from `errADO.Number`. For example, if you're using an ODBC provider to connect to a SQL Server database, `errADO.Number` will give you an ODBC error code, but `errADO.NativeError` will give you the SQL Server error code.

The `SQLState` property gives you the standard five-character ANSI SQL error code that corresponds to the error that occurred. Particular database engines or providers may use their own parochial error codes, which could differ from these standard ANSI codes.

Creating an ADO Recordset Object

The Recordset object is used to work with rows (or *records*) of data, organized into multiple columns (or *fields*). When you create a bound form in Access, behind the scenes Access creates a recordset, or several recordsets, to manage any data retrieval and updating that can be done with the form.

ADO recordsets are extremely flexible and powerful. They can be based on data from tables, queries, the results of stored procedures or views, or based on data that you add to the recordset yourself. When you create a recordset, you set its properties in order to connect to a data source and manipulate the data. Some recordset properties may not be available, depending on the provider and the type of recordset you open.

Although ADO makes it possible to open a recordset and populate it with data without ever using a connection, the ADO recordset object usually represents the records returned by executing a request for data over a connection. To open one, you need to specify the source of the data, how to connect to that data, and what kind of a recordset you want.

Unlike other data access object models that you may have used, including DAO and RDO, you can create an ADO recordset object before you actually open it. Here's an example:

```
Dim rst As ADODB.Recordset
Set rst = New ADODB.Recordset
```

The Recordset's `Open` Method

As with Connection objects, you can provide all the information needed to open a recordset by first setting properties and then calling the recordset's `Open` method, or you can use parameters of the `Open` method to pass in all the required information.

Here are the possible parameters you can use when opening an ADO recordset:

```
MyRecordset.Open
    [Source], [ActiveConnection], [CursorType], [LockType], [Options]
```

Except for the `Options` parameter, each of these parameters is used to set a corresponding recordset property of the same name. The following sections discuss each one in turn.

The `Source` Parameter

The source can be a SQL string, a table, a query, a stored procedure, a view, a saved file, or a Command object. That's right—it can be a string that holds the name of a source or a valid

ActiveX Data Objects (ADO) Fundamentals

CHAPTER 6

239

6

ACTIVEX DATA
OBJECTS (ADO)
FUNDAMENTALS

SQL string, but it can also be a reference to a Command object that encapsulates all the necessary information within its properties.

The `ActiveConnection` Parameter

The `ActiveConnection` parameter is also capable of handling either a string or an object reference. The string would be a valid `ConnectionString` value, and the object would be a Connection object. If you use the right kind of cursor, you can later disconnect your Recordset object by setting its `ActiveConnection` property to `Nothing` and still work with the data it contains, or you can create and populate a recordset without ever setting its `ActiveConnection` property.

The `CursorType` Parameter

A *cursor* is a memory structure, somewhat similar to an array, that can be used for working with data. Recordsets make use of cursors, and several different kinds of cursors are available in ADO.

The `CursorType` property specifies the way your recordset interacts with the data source and the types of behavior it supports. Will changes made by other users after you have opened your recordset be visible? Can you scroll forward and backward through the records in your recordset? These are the kinds of things that are determined by the `CursorType` property, which you can specify when opening a recordset by supplying a value for the CursorType parameter. Table 6.2 shows the available choices.

TABLE 6.2 Intrinsic Constants for the `CursorType` Property of a Recordset Object

Value	Description
adOpenForwardOnly (0)	A forward-only cursor doesn't allow you to scroll freely forward and backward through the recordset and doesn't allow you to retrieve the record count (the record count value will always be −1). Once a row of data is retrieved, any subsequent changes to the data made by other users are not seen. This is the default type of cursor you get unless you specify another type, and it is the most efficient.
adOpenKeyset (1)	The full data is not retrieved when you open the recordset. Data is retrieved as needed, using a set of key values and indexes if possible. Edits made to the data by other users after the recordset is open are picked up as the data for a row is retrieved. The membership of the recordset remains fixed after you open it, unless records are added or deleted within the recordset. Additions made by other users are not seen, and deletions made by other users result in blank records that are not removed.

TABLE 6.2 Continued

Value	Description
adOpenDynamic (2)	Similar to keyset cursors, but additions and deletions made by other users will change the membership of the recordset. This is the most resource-intensive type of cursor, and all data providers do not support its full functionality. SQL Server supports dynamic cursors, but Access does not.
adOpenStatic (3)	A static recordset can be updatable (it's not the same as a DAO snapshot), but you won't see changes made by other users. You can scroll backward and forward within the recordset and retrieve an accurate record count.

The LockType Parameter

LockType defines the updatability of a recordset and the timing of any locks placed on the data.

Unlike in DAO, where selecting a recordset type determines both the cursor type and the updatability, ADO separates these characteristics into two different properties. You can create a static cursor that's updatable or a keyset cursor that is not, depending on how you set the LockType property.

In addition to updatability, LockType also determines when locks are placed and released. You can lock a record against being changed by another user as soon as you begin editing the record, or you can wait until you are ready to save changes before placing any locks. With client-side cursors (see CursorLocation, later), you can also set the locking to allow changes to be made offline and then sent back to the database in a batch.

Table 6.3 shows your choices for selecting the lock type of a recordset.

TABLE 6.3 Intrinsic Constants for the LockType Property of a Recordset Object

Value	Description
adLockReadOnly (1)	No updates, additions, or deletions are possible. This is the default lock type and the most efficient if data changes are not required.
adLockPessimistic (2)	The data is updatable. Locks are placed on the data as soon soon as you begin editing a record and are not released until your edit is committed or canceled.
adLockOptimistic (3)	The data is updatable, but no locks are placed until you attempt to save a row. The locks are released as soon as the save is completed.

ActiveX Data Objects (ADO) Fundamentals

CHAPTER 6

241

6

ACTIVEX DATA
OBJECTS (ADO)
FUNDAMENTALS

TABLE 6.3   Continued

Value	Description
adLockBatchOptimistic (4)	Updates made to the recordset are cached locally until the UpdateBatch method is called, and then all pending updates are committed at once. No locks are placed until the UpdateBatch method is called. The recordset can periodically be resynchronized with the data source, retrieving the latest values, without having to perform any updates. When a batch update is executed, detailed information on the success or failure of the update is available on a row-by-row basis.

The CursorLocation Parameter

CursorLocation determines whether the recordset cursor will be created and managed by the data source or by ADO itself. Most database engines, including Jet and SQL Server, are capable of creating cursors. Recordsets that use cursors managed by the database engine are referred to as *server-side cursors*.

One of the reasons recordsets have sometimes been considered an inefficient method of manipulating data is that managing them places a burden on the database engine and forces you to keep open an active connection. ADO allows you to circumvent these shortcomings of recordsets by creating recordsets where the cursor is created and managed by ADO itself. Such recordsets are referred to as using *client-side cursors*. All the data is fetched from the data source in one operation and placed in a static cursor. The connection to the database can then be closed while you work with the data and reopened only when necessary.

The values you can use when setting the CursorLocation property are summarized in Table 6.4.

TABLE 6.4   Intrinsic Constants for the CursorLocation Property of a Recordset Object

Value	Description
adUseServer (2)	The cursor will be created and managed by the data source. This option will only take effect if the data source you are using is capable of creating and managing a recordset cursor, as most relational database engines are. This is the default CursorLocation value.
adUseClient (3)	ADO will create and manage the cursor itself. This makes available to you several advanced capabilities that the ADO cursor engine is capable of, including the possibility of using a disconnected recordset.
adUseNone (1)	This option is documented as being obsolete and included only for backward compatibility. It was at one time informally recommended by the Jet team for use with Jet databases. Because that recommendation is undocumented, it is also unsupported, so use it at your own risk.

The `Options` Parameter

Finally, the `Options` parameter of the Recordset object's `Open` method identifies the kind of source that's being used. `Options` is the only parameter of the `Open` method that doesn't have a corresponding Recordset property of the same name. This parameter corresponds to the `CommandText` property of the Command object that's used to open the recordset. That command object may be one that's created behind the scenes by ADO rather than one that you explicitly create. The permissible values are shown in Table 6.5.

TABLE 6.5   Intrinsic Constants for the `Options` Parameter of the Recordset Object's `Open` Method

Value	Description
adCmdText (1)	This tells ADO that you are using a SQL statement to open the recordset.
adCmdTable (2)	Indicates that the source you are using includes all the fields and rows from a table or view.
adCmdStoredProc (4)	A stored procedure or parameterized query is the source of the recordset.
adCmdFile (256)	This option tells ADO that the source you are specifying is a path and filename. ADO is able to save recordsets to several file formats, including XML, and it can open recordsets based on files in these formats.
adCmdTableDirect (512)	This tells ADO that the source is a table. This is the only option that doesn't require ADO to use a Command object to retrieve the recordset. (When a command object is needed, ADO will create one for you behind the scenes, if you haven't supplied one.)
adCmdUnknown (8)	This is the default that's used if you don't specify any other option. You might use this explicitly if you don't know what type of information the `Source` parameter will contain. This option forces ADO to use an extra roundtrip to the server to determine the type of source, so it will negatively impact performance.

For the sake of completeness, note that in addition to the `Options` values shown in Table 6.5, you can also specify `adAsyncExecute`, `adAsyncFetch`, and `adAsyncFetchNonBlocking`, which determine whether ADO will wait while all the records are being retrieved or will continue on asynchronously. These options are described in Table 6.7 later in this chapter.

ActiveX Data Objects (ADO) Fundamentals

CHAPTER 6

243

6

ActiveX Data
Objects (ADO)
Fundamentals

Other Recordset Properties

There are many other properties of a recordset that can affect its behavior:

- The MarshalOptions property of a batch-optimistic recordset can be set to adMarshalModifiedOnly or to adMarshalAll to determine how much information is sent back to the server when you perform the batch update.

- The BOF, EOF, AbsolutePosition, AbsolutePage, RecordCount, and PageCount properties can be useful when navigating through your recordset.

- Each record has a unique bookmark value that you can store in a variant variable. The Bookmark property of the recordset can be used to retrieve the value of the current record's bookmark or to move to a particular record with a known bookmark value.

- The CacheSize and MaxRecords properties can be used to help control the resources that your recordset will consume. The CacheSize property, which defaults to a value of 1, determines how many records will be held in local memory at once. You can change the CacheSize property before or after you open a recordset. MaxRecords defaults to 0, which means ADO will get all the records defined by your data source. The MaxRecords property becomes read-only after you open a recordset.

- The Filter and Sort properties, which are explained later, can be used to affect the composition and order of your recordset, even after it has been opened.

> **TIP**
>
> The AbsolutePosition property of the first record in the recordset is 1, not 0. This is a change from DAO and RDO, where the AbsolutePosition property was zero-based. Also in contrast to DAO, retrieving a value for the RecordCount property in a scrollable cursor will cause ADO to move automatically to the end of the recordset so that it can give you an accurate count, which can also impact performance.

Opening a Recordset

The Source, ActiveConnection, CursorType, and LockType, and CursorLocation properties of a recordset can all be specified either as parameters to the Open method or by setting the values of properties with the same names. The Options value, however, can only be specified as a parameter. So, for example, you could use a syntax like the following, where the strSQL variable contains a SELECT statement, and the strConnectInfo variable contains the connection string:

```
With rst
  .Source = strSQL
  .ActiveConnection = strConnectInfo
  .CursorType = adOpenStatic
  .LockType = adLockOptimistic
```

```
    .CursorLocation = adUseClient
    .Open Options:=adCmdText
End With
```

Updating Data Using Recordsets

In general, using recordsets to update data is the slowest and most resource-intensive way of updating data. Executing stored procedures or SQL statements is usually preferred. However, occasionally you may want to use a recordset for modifying data. The advantage you have when working with a recordset is that you have the full capabilities of VBA available to you while you are moving through the data.

To be able to make changes to data using a recordset, you must not use the default values for CursorType and LockType, because the defaults result in a read-only recordset. You need to explicitly specify values that support updatability:

```
rst.CursorType = adOpenStatic
rst.LockType = adLockOptimistic
```

Editing Data

If the data source and lock type of your recordset permit updating, you can use the following syntax to change the values of the fields in a row of your recordset:

```
rst.Fields("AreaCode") = "561"
rst.Fields("PhoneNumber") = "848-7147"
rst.Update
```

Alternatively, you can use this:

```
Rst!AreaCode = "561"
Rst!PhoneNumber = "848-7147"
rst.Update
```

The Update method is optional in ADO. The update will be performed automatically if you navigate to another record. It's recommended that you always explicitly use the Update method to commit data changes. You'll generate an error if you try to close a recordset that contains a pending update that has not yet been committed or canceled.

To cancel an update to the current row, you can use this:

```
rst.CancelUpdate
```

If you want to update more than one record at a time, you can put the update in a For...Next loop, testing for the EOF property. When you hit EOF, the loop will end. Here's an example:

```
Do Until rst.EOF
    If rst!City = "NYC" Then
        rst!City = "New York"
```

```
        rst.Update
    End If
    rst.MoveNext
Loop
```

This code will visit every row in the table, so it's not the most efficient way of updating data. A SQL UPDATE statement with a WHERE clause would be more efficient. One reason you might use a recordset loop for making data changes would be if you needed to implement complex logic within the loop and couldn't express that logic in Transact-SQL.

Adding New Records

To add new records, you use a similar syntax. The only difference is that you must begin by using the AddNew method and finish with the Update method. If you only use AddNew, the record will never be inserted into the table. Here's an example:

```
rst.AddNew
  rst.Fields("FirstName") = "Ed"
  rst.Fields("LastName") = "Rosman"
rst.Update
```

If you want to position yourself on the new row, you can use the MoveLast method because new records are always appended at the end of a recordset. Here's an example:

```
rst.MoveLast
```

This technique for finding a new row may not be completely reliable in a recordset with a CursorType property of adOpenDynamic, however, because that recordset could also be picking up new records added by other users.

Using Arrays to Edit or Add Records

Instead of setting field values individually, you can use two arrays to specify the field names and values when you edit or add a record, like this:

```
rstCustomer.Update _
 Array("AreaCode", "PhoneNumber") _
 Array("561", "848-7147")

rstCustomer.AddNew _
 Array("FirstName", "LastName") _
 Array("Ed", "Rosman")
```

If you only have one field to update, you can dispense with arrays entirely, passing the field name and the value separated by a comma:

```
rst.Update " PhoneNumber", "848-7147"
```

Deleting Records

Deleting a record couldn't be any simpler. Just navigate to the correct record and call the recordset's `Delete` method:

```
rst.Delete
```

Navigating, Searching, Filtering, and Sorting

The ADO Recordset object is very full-featured, providing parity with most recordset capabilities that exist in previous data access object models, plus a number of distinctive and very useful new properties and methods. ADO gives you several ways to navigate within a recordset and to search for particular records. You can even use ADO to filter and sort the rows of a recordset.

Moving Around

If you open a recordset using a `CursorType` argument of `adOpenForwardOnly` or if you don't specify a cursor type and get that value by default, only two methods of moving are supported. The first is easy:

```
rst.MoveNext
```

Using the `CacheSize` Property

The second possibility for moving within a forward-only recordset will only work if you have set the recordset's `CacheSize` property to a value greater than 1, which is the default in this kind of recordset. `CacheSize` determines the number of records that ADO will hold in local memory. To conserve resources in a forward-only recordset, this property defaults to a value of 1—only one record at a time is held in memory. However, if you set this property to a higher number, you can move around within the local cache of records using the ADO `Move` method, which allows you to specify a starting place and the number of records from that starting place that you want to move to. You can specify a positive or a negative number, so paradoxically you can even move backward in a forward-only recordset. The code that follows opens a default forward-only recordset, but it can successfully move back one record in the cache:

```
With rst
    Set .ActiveConnection = CurrentProject.Connection
    .Source = "Select * From Products"
    .CacheSize = 5
    .Open
    .MoveNext
    ' the next line moves back to the first record
    .Move -1
End With
```

ActiveX Data Objects (ADO) Fundamentals

CHAPTER 6

247

6

ACTIVEX DATA
OBJECTS (ADO)
FUNDAMENTALS

The `Move` Method's Parameters

The `Move` method had two parameters. The first one, `NumRecords`, which is required, specifies the positive or negative number of records you want to move. The second parameter, `Start`, is optional and has a default value of `adBookmarkCurrent`, which causes the move to start at the current record. You can also choose to start at the beginning or end of the recordset by using `adBookmarkFirst` or `adBookmarkLast`. Alternatively, you can use a variant variable to store the `Bookmark` property value of any record in the recordset and supply that bookmark value as the starting point of your move. If your move uses a `NumRecords` value that would move you beyond the beginning or end of the recordset, then `BOF` or `EOF` will become `True`, but you won't get an error.

Using the `Move` Methods

With any of the cursor types besides `adOpenForwardOnly`, you can use all the `Move` methods:

```
With rst
  .MoveFirst
  .MoveNext
  .MoveLast
  .MovePrevious
  .Move 3, adBookmarkFirst
End With
```

Finding Records

ADO supports two methods, `Find` and `Seek`, for locating data in a recordset. Sometimes, the most efficient way to locate a particular record is to use a SQL statement or a parameterized stored procedure to open a recordset that contains just the record you are looking for. But there may be times when you want to open a recordset that contains multiple records and then find certain ones.

Using `Find`

The `Find` method has only one required parameter, `Criteria`, which is a string that allows you to specify a value for one field in your recordset:

```
rst.Find "LastName='Smith'"
```

The optional parameters—`SkipRows`, `SearchDirection`, and `Start`—let you refine the search by specifying a number of rows to skip, the direction to search, and the bookmark of a row to start on. If your search fails, either `EOF` or `BOF` will become `True`, depending on the direction of the search.

Using `Seek`

The `Seek` method is similar to `Find`, but it additionally allows you to specify an index to use when you conduct your search. This method can only be used with providers that support it, and although it is supported by the Jet 4.0 provider, it is not supported at this time by the provider for SQL Server.

Using String and Date Delimiters in ADO

If you have a WHERE clause that has string or date values, you need to use a single quote (') delimiter. If you have an apostrophe or single quote in a string variable, you can use the VBA Replace function to replace any single quote characters (') with two single quotes (' '). This will cause any strings that have single quotes or apostrophes to be processed correctly. Here's an example:

```
Replace(strWithQuote, "'", "''")
```

Unfortunately, this technique can only be used with a single apostrophe inside a quoted string. Doubling up two different apostrophes in the same string won't work. In this case you can simply use pound signs (#) to delimit the string. But beware—this is an undocumented technique and may not always be supported. Here's an example:

```
rst.Find "CompanyName = #Eddy's And Jane's Place#"
```

Filtering Recordsets

The ADO Find method is severely limited by the fact that it only allows you to work with one column when defining your criteria. Fortunately, the Filter method is not hampered by this limitation. You can use as many instances of AND and OR as you need when filtering a recordset. However, syntax like the following is not allowed:

```
rst.Filter = "(State = 'NY' OR State = 'NJ')" _
            & " AND Department = 'Sales'"
```

Instead, you would need to use this syntax:

```
rst.Filter = "(State = 'NY' AND Department = 'Sales')" _
          & " OR (State = 'NJ' AND Department = 'Sales')"
```

Rather than using the Filter property to specify criteria, you can instead specify an array of bookmark values that correspond to the bookmarks of records in the recordset.

Also, you can use an intrinsic constant to create a filter that automatically includes only certain kinds of records, mostly related to batch updates. For example, you can use a filter to show only those records that have been edited but have not yet been updated to the server:

```
rst.Filter = adFilterPendingRecords
```

Table 6.6 displays the values and descriptions of these filter constants.

ActiveX Data Objects (ADO) Fundamentals

CHAPTER 6

249

6

ActiveX Data
Objects (ADO)
Fundamentals

TABLE 6.6 Intrinsic Constants for the `Filter` Property of a Recordset Object

Value	Description
adFilterNone (0)	Restores all records to view.
adFilterPendingRecords (1)	In a recordset with a `LockType` property of `adBatchOptimistic`, this allows you to view only records that have changed but have not yet been sent to the server.
adFilterAffectedRecords (2)	Allows you to view only records affected by the last `Delete`, `Resync`, `UpdateBatch`, or `CancelBatch` method call.
adFilterFetchedRecords (3)	Filters out all but the last records that were retrieved into the recordset cache.
adFilterConflictingRecords (5)	After performing a batch update, this allows you to view only those records that weren't successfully updated to the server. (You can inspect the `Status` property of each record to find out why the update failed.)

NOTE

When you apply a filter to a recordset, you don't actually lose any of the original records. By applying a new filter or by removing all filters, you can always retrieve any of the original records in the recordset, unless they have been deleted.

Sorting Recordsets

You can use a Recordset object's `Sort` property to override any sort that may have been defined in the recordset's original source query or stored procedure. You can also use the property to apply a sort to a source such as a table or view that has no intrinsic order.

To define the sort, you simply list the fields to sort by and optionally specify the order by adding `ASC` or `DESC`:

```
rst.Sort = "OrderDate DESC, LastName, FirstName"
```

If you don't specify a sort order, then ascending order is assumed. With a client-side cursor, specifying a sort will actually create a temporary index. If you set the `Sort` property to an empty string (`""`), any sorts you had previously set will be removed and any temporary indexes will be deleted.

Creating an ADO Command Object

The ADO Command object encapsulates the functionality of a query, SQL statement, view, or stored procedure. You can use a Command object to return a recordset or to execute data changes.

Command Object Properties and Methods

Here's a quick overview of the properties and methods of the Command object.

The `Parameters` Property

The `Parameters` property of a Command object holds a collection of Parameter objects. You use parameters to pass values into a query or stored procedure, or in some cases to get values back. The `CreateParameter` method of a Command object allows you to add parameters to the Command object. You'll see examples of working with Command object parameters later in this chapter.

The `ActiveConnection` Property

Like recordsets, Command objects also have an `ActiveConnection` property. This property holds a reference to a Connection object, but you can set a value for the property either by passing it a reference to an existing Connection object or by passing it a `ConnectionString` value that ADO can use to create a Connection object in the background.

The `CommandText` Property

The `CommandText` property of a Command object is used to retrieve or set the SQL statement or the name of the Database object that defines the behavior of the command.

The `CommandType` Property

The `CommandType` property is similar to the `Options` parameter that you use when opening a recordset—it identifies the type of source contained in the `CommandText` property. The Recordset object's `Options` values shown in Table 6.5 are the same values you can use for the `CommandType` property.

The `CommandTimeout` Property

Like Connection objects, Command objects have a `CommandTimeout` property, with a default value of 30 seconds, which specifies how long ADO should wait for a response before aborting the command.

The `Execute` Method and the `RecordsAffected` Parameter

The `Execute` method of a Command object can be used to invoke an action query or stored procedure that makes changes to the database, or it can be used to open a recordset. When executing a command that changes data, you can use the RecordsAffected parameter of the Execute method to find out how many records in the database were modified.

The Prepared Property

Use the Prepared property to have the provider save a prepared (compiled) version of the command prior to execution. This is useful if your command is based on a SQL statement, not a stored procedure, and you are going to execute the same command multiple times. Subsequent executions happen slightly faster if you set the Prepared property before the first execution.

The Execute Method

There are two different types of syntax for executing a command, depending on whether the Command object is going to return records. Here's the syntax for using the Execute method to return rows into a recordset:

```
Set recordset = command.Execute([RecordsAffected], [Parameters], [Options])
```

If you use the Execute method to open a recordset in this way, you do not ever have to call the Open method of the recordset. But beware! Using the Execute method of a Command object to open a recordset will always give you a read-only, forward-only recordset. If that is all you need, this is a perfectly good way to open your recordset.

Here's the syntax for using Execute with a command that does not return rows:

```
command.Execute [RecordsAffected], [Parameters], [Options]
```

All the parameters of the Execute method are optional.

The RecordsAffected Parameter

You can pass a Long Integer variable into this parameter and the provider will return the number of records that the operation affected. You can get the number by simply inspecting the value of the variable after you have executed the command. This applies only for action queries or stored procedures without the SET NOCOUNT ON statement. RecordsAffected does not give you the number of records returned by a result-returning query or stored procedure. Although it is legal to use this parameter when opening a recordset, there is really little reason to do so.

The Parameters Parameter

This parameter of the Execute method allows you to pass in an array of variant values that will be assigned to the parameters of the command you are executing. You can use the VBA Array function to create an array of parameters from a simple list of values:

```
cmd.Execute Parameters:=Array("Bob", "Jones", 43)
```

You cannot name the values in this array, so you need to ensure that their order exactly matches the order of the parameters in the stored procedure or query that you are executing. If there is only one parameter, you can pass in a single value:

```
cmd.Execute Parameters:="Bob"
```

The `Options` Parameter

The `Options` parameter can be used to pass three different kinds of information to ADO. You can use the values shown in Table 6.5, which tell ADO how to evaluate the `CommandText` property of this Command object. In addition, you can include two values that give ADO added instructions on how to execute the command. These execution options are summarized in Table 6.7 and can be divided into two categories. The first three values in Table 6.7 are used to specify whether ADO should wait for the command to finish executing or continue and let the command execute asynchronously. These three values can also be used with the `Options` parameter of a Recordset object's `Open` method. The last value in the table, `adExecuteNoRecords`, tells ADO not to expect any records to be returned from the execution of this command. Because these three kinds of options contain nonoverlapping numbers, you can supply a number that combines multiple values, and ADO will parse out the various pieces of information from the one number that it receives. Here's an example:

```
cmd.Execute _
  Options:=adCmdStoredProc _
        + adAsyncExecute + adExecuteNoRecords
```

TABLE 6.7 Additional Intrinsic Constants for the `Options` Parameter of a Command Object's `Execute` Method

Value	Description
adAsyncExecute (16)	Executes the command asynchronously.
adAsyncFetch (32)	Fetches the remaining rows asynchronously after the initial quantity is specified in the `CacheSize` property.
adAsyncFetchNonBlocking (64)	Similar to `adAsyncFetch`, but this option further specifies that ADO should never wait for a row to be fetched. Instead, if a recordset row that hasn't been fetched is still required, the `EOF` property of the recordset will become `True`.
adExecuteNoRecords (128)	The command will not return any records. Of course, this option cannot be used when opening a recordset.

ActiveX Data Objects (ADO) Fundamentals

CHAPTER 6

253

6

ACTIVEX DATA
OBJECTS (ADO)
FUNDAMENTALS

Executing a Simple Command

When you create a Command object, it is usually with the intention of running an action query or a stored procedure. You can also declare a Long Integer variable to return the number of records modified:

```
Dim cmd As ADODB.Command
Dim lngRecs as Long
Set cmd = New ADODB.Command
```

You can set the `ActiveConnection` property to a connection string, or you can use an already active Connection object:

```
Set cmd.ActiveConnection = CurrentProject.Connection
```

The `CommandText` property specifies the name of a database object or, in this case, a valid SQL statement. The `CommandType` property tells ADO how to evaluate the command (in this case, as a SQL string). The `Execute` method returns the number of rows affected in its `RecordsAffected` parameter, which here is holding a reference to the Long Integer variable, `lngRecs`:

```
cmd.CommandText = "INSERT INTO Category (CategoryName) " & _
    "VALUES ('Widgets')"
cmd.CommandType = adCmdText
cmd.Execute _
  RecordsAffected:=lngRecs
MsgBox "You updated " & lngRecs & " rows."
```

Executing a SQL Statement with Parameters

The Command object comes in most handy when you need to pass parameters to an action query or a stored procedure. If you are using a SQL statement, you define the query with question marks (?) as placeholders for the parameters:

```
strSQL = "INSERT INTO Categories (CategoryName) " & _
"VALUES (?)"
```

When you execute the stored procedure, you supply the values for any parameters:

```
Set cmd = New ADODB.Command
With cmd
    .ActiveConnection = CurrentProject.Connection
    .CommandText = strSQL
    .CommandType = adCmdText
    .Execute _
        Parameters:="Widgets", _
        RecordsAffected:=lngRecs
End With
MsgBox "You updated " & lngRecs & " rows."
```

If you have more than one parameter, you can also use the built-in VBA `Array()` function to pass in the parameters. You need to pass them in the same order they were defined in the query. Here's an example:

```
cmd.Execute _
    Parameters:=Array(Param1, Param2)
```

Executing a Stored Procedure

Your ADO Command objects can execute stored procedures in two ways.

The first is by using a `CommandType` property of `adCmdText`; the second by using a `CommandType` property of `adCmdStoredProc`.

The first method—executing by setting `CommandType` to `adCmdText`—is the same as the examples shown earlier that use direct SQL. The server will execute the stored procedure. Here's an example:

```
Set cmd = New ADODB.Command
With cmd
    .ActiveConnection = cnn
    .CommandText = "EXEC MyStoredProcedure"
    .CommandType = adCmdText
    .Execute
End With
```

You can also execute the stored procedure by setting `CommandType` to `adCmdStoredProc`:

```
Set cmd = New ADODB.Command
With cmd
    .ActiveConnection = cnn
    .CommandText = "MyStoredProcedure"
    .CommandType = adCmdStoredProc
    .Execute
End With
```

You can't use `EXECUTE` (`EXEC`) if you use a `CommandType` property of `adCmdStoredProc` because the server is expecting just the name of a stored procedure to execute. Here's an example:

```
Set cmd = New ADODB.Command
With cmd
    .ActiveConnection = cnn
    .CommandText = "EXEC MyStoredProcedure"
    .CommandType = adCmdText
    .Execute
End With
```

ActiveX Data Objects (ADO) Fundamentals

CHAPTER 6

255

6

ACTIVEX DATA
OBJECTS (ADO)
FUNDAMENTALS

Executing a Stored Procedure with Parameters

As you might expect, you have several ways of executing stored procedures with parameters as
well. You can have the stored procedure evaluated as a text string, using the command type
`adCmdText`, and passing the parameters in the order in which they were defined in the stored
procedure:

```
Set cmd = New ADODB.Command
With cmd
    .ActiveConnection = cnn
    .CommandText = "EXEC MyStoredProc 100, 200"
    .CommandType = adCmdText
    .Execute
End With
```

You can also execute a stored procedure using VBA's `Array()` function:

```
With cmd
    .ActiveConnection = cnn
    .CommandText = "MyStoredProc"
    .CommandType = adCmdStoredProc
    .Execute Parameters:=Array(100, 200)
End With
```

Another option is to use the Parameters collection of the Command object. This method is a
little more work, but if you need to reuse the Command object with different parameters, they
will already be prepared and ready to go. Here's an example:

```
Dim prm as ADODB.Parameter
'...
With cmd
    .ActiveConnection = cnn
    .CommandText = "procMyProc"
    .CommandType = adCmdStoredProc
    Set prm = cmd.CreateParameter(Name:="Param1", _
      Type:=adVarChar, _
      Direction:=adParamInput, _
      Size:=15)
    cmd.Parameters.Append prm
    prm.Value = "Widgets"
    .Execute
End With
```

You can also use the `Refresh` method of the Parameters collection to populate your Parameters
collection with Parameter objects that have their `Name`, `Type`, and `Size` properties already set
appropriately. However, this is not recommended, because it causes an extra roundtrip to the
server to retrieve each parameter's existence and properties. If you decide that you can afford
to sacrifice performance for convenience, here's the syntax:

```
With cmd
    .ActiveConnection = cnn
    .CommandText = "procMyProc"
    .CommandType = adCmdStoredProc
    .Parameters.Refresh
    .Parameters("Param1").Value = "Widgets"
    .Execute
End With
```

Mixing and Matching the Three Objects

ADO is extremely flexible; you can use all three of the main objects—Connection, Recordset, and Command—together in various combinations. As shown earlier in the chapter, you can use a Connection object for opening Recordset objects and executing Command objects. You also took a brief look at opening Recordset objects by executing Command objects. Here, you'll explore a few more options available to you.

Opening Recordsets with Command Objects

You can use the Execute method of a Command object to open a recordset:

```
cmd.CommandText = "byroyalty"
Set rst = cmd.Execute(Parameters:=100, _
 Options:=adCmdStoredProc)
```

But, beware! Opening a recordset in this way guarantees that you will create a forward-only, read-only recordset, with a cache size of only one record. If you need your recordset to be updatable, or if you want more freedom to move around in the recordset, you can still use a Command object, but you must use it as the Source parameter of a Recordset object's Open method. Here's an example:

```
cmd.CommandText = "byroyalty"
cmd.Execute(Parameters:=100, _
 Options:=adCmdStoredProc)
rst.LockType = adLockOptimistic
rst.Open cmd
```

Reusing Command Objects with Recordsets

You can also reuse the same Command object to do double duty by first executing an action query and then executing a SELECT query into a Recordset object.

The following example uses the Execute method of a single Command object to delete records and then to display the remaining records using a Recordset object:

ActiveX Data Objects (ADO) Fundamentals

CHAPTER 6

257

6

ACTIVEX DATA
OBJECTS (ADO)
FUNDAMENTALS

```
Dim cmd As ADODB.Command
Dim rst As ADODB.Recordset
Dim strSQL As String
```

The first SQL statement deletes records in a table:

```
strSQL = "DELETE MyTable " & _
    "WHERE PK = 3"
```

The Command object then executes the SQL DELETE statement:

```
Set cmd = New ADODB.Command
With cmd
    .ActiveConnection = gcnn
    .CommandText = strSQL
    .CommandType = adCmdText
    .Execute
End With
```

You can reuse the same Command object by specifying a new SQL statement in the CommandText property. You can then execute the command into a Recordset object. Here's an example:

```
cmd.CommandText = "SELECT * FROM MyTable"
cmd.CommandType = adCmdText
Set rst = New ADODB.Recordset
Set rst = cmd.Execute()
```

Going Solo with the Connection Object

The Connection object also has an Execute method. In situations where you have a Connection object already open, you may want it to perform simple tasks without incurring the overhead of instantiating other objects. For example, if you want to quickly delete all the rows in a table, you can execute the TRUNCATE TABLE stored procedure on a Connection object:

```
cnn.Execute "TRUNCATE TABLE MyTable"
```

You can also use the Connection object's Execute method to execute a query into a read-only, forward-only recordset, as shown earlier with the Command object.

Returning Multiple Recordsets

ADO allows you to process multiple recordsets using only one Recordset object. When you set up the Recordset object, you specify the CommandText property to include multiple SELECT statements, delimited by a semicolon:

```
rst.ActiveConnection = cnn
rst.Source = _
```

```
"SELECT * FROM Table1;" & _
"SELECT * FROM Table2"
```

The `CursorType` property is set to `adOpenStatic`, and the `CursorLocation` property is then set to `adUseClient`. The default forward-only cursor won't work here. Here's an example:

```
rst.CursorType = adOpenStatic
rst.CursorLocation = adUseClient
rst.LockType = adLockReadOnly
rst.Open Options:=adCmdText
```

Once the recordset is open, use the `NextRecordset` method to retrieve the second recordset from the server:

```
Set rst = rst.NextRecordset
```

You may not use this ability of ADO's to run multiple `SELECT` statements in a single roundtrip to the server—each time you use the `NextRecordset` method, a new set of records is fetched. However, it's extremely useful when you're executing a stored procedure that returns multiple result sets. This is covered in more detail in Chapter 10, when the topic of stored procedures is discussed.

Advanced ADO

ADO offers a number of useful features that go beyond the basics of retrieving and updating data. Here is a brief overview of a few of these advanced features.

Creatable Recordsets

The ADO cursor engine, which you can use when you work with client-side cursors, allows you to build your own recordsets without having to connect to a data source. You can create a recordset, add fields to it, and populate it with data. Then you can use your recordset as you might otherwise use an array—as a memory structure for manipulating and transferring data from within your VBA code.

Listing 6.1 shows code for creating a Recordset object from scratch. It then walks through the files on the C drive and adds their names and file sizes to the recordset. Note that the code never sets a connection for the recordset.

When you create the fields for a recordset, you need to define their data types and sizes. The `CursorLocation` property must be set to `adUseClient`—after all, there is no server. One advantage of using this technique over arrays is that it's very easy to sort or filter the results. Also, you can use your recordset as a data source for any object capable of binding to an ADO recordset, such as the forms in an Access project.

LISTING 6.1   Creating a Recordset Object with No Data Source

```
Public Sub CreateARecordset()
    Dim strName As String
    Dim rst As ADODB.Recordset
    Set rst = New ADODB.Recordset

    ' Add the fields to the recordset.
    With rst
        With .Fields
            .Append "FileName", adVarChar, 255
            .Append "Size", adUnsignedInt
        End With
        .CursorLocation = adUseClient
        .CursorType = adOpenStatic
        .Open
    End With

    ' Get the files in C:\
    strName = Dir("C:\*.*")
    Do While Len(strName) > 0
        rst.AddNew _
         Array("FileName", "Size"), _
         Array(strName, FileLen("C:\" & strName))
        strName = Dir
    Loop

    ' Sort the recordset
    rst.Sort = "FileName"

    ' Debug.Print the results
    Do Until rst.EOF
        Debug.Print rst!FileName, rst!Size
        rst.MoveNext
    Loop
    rst.Close
    Set rst = Nothing
End Sub
```

Persistent Recordsets

The ADO cursor engine also allows you to save the schema and data contained in a recordset to various file formats as well as to open recordsets by loading in schema and data from these files. This has become an especially important feature because it allows you to use ADO to work with Extensible Markup Language (XML).

You need to set the recordset's `CursorLocation` property to `adUseClient`, which means that the `CursorType` property must be `asOpenStatic`. When you use the `Save` method, you specify a filename and format. Here are two `Save` options:

- `adPersistADTG`
- `adPersistXML`

The first save option, `adPersistADTG`, is a Microsoft proprietary "tablegram" format. The second uses an XML format that can be understood by any XML parser and that can easily be transformed into a formatted HTML table. In Chapter 11, we show how XML files created from ADO recordsets can be used to store lookup data locally for an Access project (ADP), where local Jet tables aren't available.

Listing 6.2 shows how you can create a recordset based on a server table and save it to a file. This example uses a `LockType` value of `adLockBatchOptimistic`, but any lock type would work for saving a recordset. The batch optimistic lock type will allow you to open the recordset later, make changes to the data, and then send those changes back to the server.

In this example, the connection used is one that was previously opened and stored in the Public variable gnn. In an Access 2000 project (ADP), you could use `CurrentProject.Connection` to get a reference to the ADO connection to SQL Server or MSDE that your Access project was using.

LISTING 6.2   Creating a Recordset and Saving It to a File

```
Public Sub SaveRecordsetToDisk( _
  ByVal strFileName As String)
     ' Need to pass in the fully-qualified
     ' path and filename to save the recordset

  Dim rst As ADODB.Recordset

     ' Create the Recordset on the Customers
     ' table using batch optimistic locking
  Set rst = New ADODB.Recordset
  Set rst.ActiveConnection = gcnn
  rst.CursorLocation = adUseClient
  rst.LockType = adLockBatchOptimistic
  rst.CursorType = adOpenStatic
  rst.Source = "Customers"
  rst.Open Options:=adCmdTable

     ' Save the current recordset, and then close it.
  rst.Save _
    FileName:=strFileName, _
```

ActiveX Data Objects (ADO) Fundamentals

CHAPTER 6

261

6

ACTIVEX DATA
OBJECTS (ADO)
FUNDAMENTALS

LISTING 6.2   Continued

```
        PersistFormat:=adPersistXML
    rst.Close
End Sub
```

It's also easy to open the recordset back up again once you've saved it. You just need to use the file path and name as the source and specify adCmdFile in the Option parameter of the Open method. You can edit the recordset offline, as shown in Listing 6.3. Because the recordset was originally opened in batch optimistic mode, changes can be saved temporarily and then updated to the server at any time.

LISTING 6.3   Creating a Recordset Based on a File

```
Public Sub ReadRecordsetFromDisk( _
  ByVal strFileName As String)
    ' Read the recordset from disk using
    ' the fully-qualified path and filename

    Dim rst As Recordset
    Set rst = New ADODB.Recordset

    ' Create the Recordset from the disk
    ' file using batch optimistic locking
    rst.CursorLocation = adUseClient
    rst.LockType = adLockBatchOptimistic
    rst.Source = strFileName
    rst.CursorType = adOpenStatic
    rst.Open Options:=adCmdFile

    ' Update the first record
    rst.Update "ContactName", "Dudley Folsom"
    rst.Save strFileName, adPersistXML
    rst.Close
End Sub
```

The next step would be to synchronize the changes you made offline back to the server database. Listing 6.4 shows opening the recordset from the saved file and then opening a connection to the database on the server.

Before updating to the server, you can set the MarshalOptions property of the recordset, as shown in Listing 6.4. Setting this property of adMarshalModifiedOnly saves network bandwidth by sending only changed values back to the server. The default value for this property is adMarshalAll, which causes all records to be sent, even if they were not edited.

The UpdateBatch method with the adAffectAll parameter updates all of the records that have been changed, even if some are currently hidden by a filter. You can also use adAffectGroup to update only the records exposed through the current filter, or you can use adAffectCurrent to update only the current record.

LISTING 6.4   Updating the Server Database with Your Changes

```
Public Sub SyncChangesFromFile( _
  ByVal strFileName As String)
    ' Open the recordset from the file,
    ' and then synchronize it with the data on the
    ' server by setting the connection to the server
    ' and using the UpdateBatch method.
    Dim rst As ADODB.Recordset

    Set rst = New ADODB.Recordset
    rst.CursorLocation = adUseClient
    rst.LockType = adLockBatchOptimistic
    rst.Source = strFileName
    rst.CursorType = adOpenStatic
    rst.MarshalOptions = adMarshalModifiedOnly
    rst.Open Options:=adCmdFile

    ' Set the connection to the server
    Set rst.ActiveConnection = gcnn
    ' Update all of the records
    rst.UpdateBatch adAffectAll
    rst.Close
    Set rst = Nothing
End Sub
```

This is only half the story—what if other users have made changes to the recordset? You need to filter the records using the Recordset object's Filter property set to adFilterAffectedRecords and then walk through and find where there have been any conflicts by inspecting the Status property for each record. In general, this technique is most useful when there are not likely to be any conflicts. In case of any conflict, the record on the server will prevail.

ADO Events

The ADO objects support events that can be used to provide notification to your VBA code concerning changes made to data in your recordsets or concerning the status of asynchronous operations. For example, you could fire off a command and then use events to track the progress and completion of your command's execution. Figure 6.6 shows the Object Browser

ActiveX Data Objects (ADO) Fundamentals

CHAPTER 6

263

6

ACTIVEX DATA
OBJECTS (ADO)
FUNDAMENTALS

with the Connection object and the `ConnectComplete` event highlighted. You can use this event to find out when a connection has opened successfully.

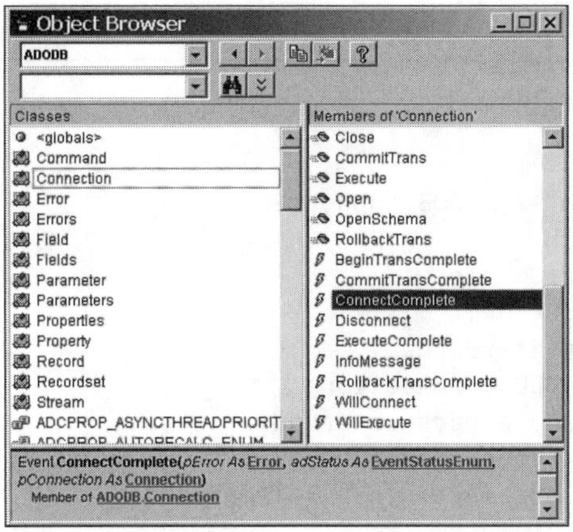

FIGURE 6.6
The Connection *events.*

You can only trap events in a class module (you can use an Access form or report's class module for this). When you want to react to an event, you must use the `WithEvents` keyword when you declare your variable in the Declarations section of your class module. Once declared in this fashion, the events for that ADO object show up in the right side of the event list as though the ADO object were a control on a form, as shown in Figure 6.7.

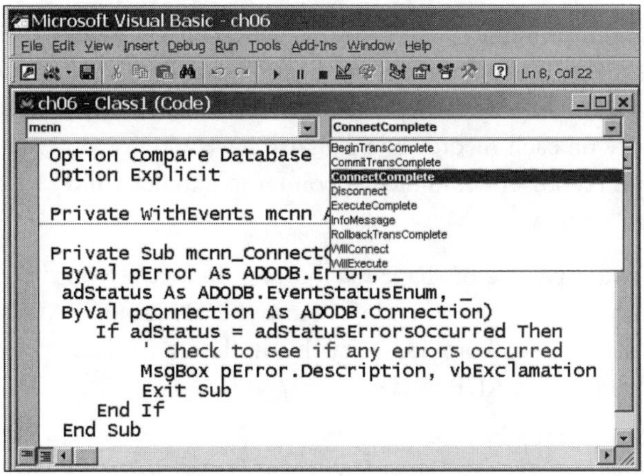

FIGURE 6.7
The available event procedures for a Connection object declared WithEvents.

You can then write code to react to the event, as shown in Listing 6.5, where a message box is called if any connection errors occur.

LISTING 6.5   Reacting to ADO Events

```
Option Compare Database
Option Explicit

Private WithEvents mcnn As ADODB.Connection

Private Sub mcnn_ConnectComplete( _
 ByVal pError As ADODB.Error, _
 adStatus As ADODB.EventStatusEnum, _
 ByVal pConnection As ADODB.Connection)
     ' check to see if any errors occurred
     If adStatus = adStatusErrorsOccurred Then
         MsgBox pError.Description, vbExclamation
     End If
End Sub
```

SHAPE: Creating Hierarchical Recordsets

Microsoft has developed a variation on SQL that allows you to create "shaped" recordsets that contain special fields called *chapters*, which are pointers to other recordsets. So, for example, you could have a customer recordset that contains a field holding a recordset with all the orders for each customer. A shaped recordset is an efficient way of handling hierarchies of information. The subdatasheets that you can use in Access 2000 display hierarchical recordsets.

Listing 6.6 shows building a hierarchical recordset based on the Categories and Products tables in the Northwind database. When the recordset is created using the SHAPE statement, it has three fields: CategoryID, CategoryName, and Chapter1. Chapter1 points to the filtered rows that match the category on each record. You can also have additional nesting levels to any desired depth—a child recordset could have a pointer to another child recordset, which would be a grandchild of the original.

Access 2000 makes extensive use of shaped recordsets. In fact, if you check the Provider property of CurrentProject.Connection in an Access 2000 project (ADP), you'll find that the connection uses the MSDataShape provider: Try this in the Immediate window of the Visual Basic Editor when you have an ADP loaded:

```
?CurrentProject.Connection
Provider=MSDataShape.1;Persist Security Info=True;
Locale Identifier=1033;Data Source=(local);
User ID=sa;Password="";Initial Catalog=Northwind;Data Provider=SQLOLEDB.1
```

This connection string is a bit different from most. It includes both a Provider attribute (MSDataShape) and a Data Provider (SQLOLEDB.1). This is because the Data Shape provider is an OLE DB Service Provider. It uses the Data Provider (in this case the one for SQL Server) to fetch the data and any other information that it needs from the server. It then adds its own capabilities on top of those provided by the native data provider.

The reason that Access makes use of the Data Shape provider when building its own recordsets is not because it needs those recordsets to be hierarchical. Access uses this provider because it supplies extra meta-data (data about the structure of data) that isn't available from the standard SQL Server provider. Access uses this meta-data when performing updates to SQL Server tables in ADP forms. The recordsets behind Access project (ADP) forms are client-side ADO recordsets.

LISTING 6.6   Building a Hierarchical Recordset with the SHAPE Statement

```
Public Sub CreateShapedRecordset()
    Dim cnn As ADODB.Connection
    Dim rst As ADODB.Recordset
    Set cnn = New ADODB.Connection
    Set rst = New ADODB.Recordset

    ' Set the Provider to MSDataShape and the
    ' Data Provider to SQLOLEDB.1
    cnn.Open _
      ConnectionString:="Provider=MSDataShape;" & _
      "Data Provider=SQLOLEDB.1;" & _
      "Data Source=MABEL;" & _
      "Initial Catalog=Northwind;" & _
      "Integrated Security=SSPI"

    ' Keeps the hierarchies in sync
    rst.StayInSync = True

    ' Open the Recordset using the SHAPE syntax with
    ' APPEND to append the chapter and RELATE to tie
    ' the linking fields together
    rst.Open _
      "SHAPE {SELECT CategoryID, CategoryName " & _
      "FROM Categories} " & _
      "APPEND ({SELECT * FROM Products} " & _
      "RELATE CategoryID TO CategoryID)", cnn

    ' Get the first CategoryName
    Debug.Print rst!CategoryName
```

LISTING 6.6   Continued

```
    ' Get the first ProductName from Chapter1
    Debug.Print rst!Chapter1!ProductName

    ' Clean up
    rst.Close
    Set rst = Nothing
    cnn.Close
    Set cnn = Nothing
End Sub
```

> **TIP**
>
> You can avoid typing in the unfamiliar SHAPE syntax yourself by using the Data Environment Designer available in the Microsoft Office Developer Edition of Office 2000 (also available in Visual Basic 6.0). It provides a graphical user interface for generating SHAPE statements that you can paste into your code.

Streams and Records

One of the important promises of OLE DB and ADO was that it would allow programmatic access to nonrelational data, such as the binary data contained in hierarchical file systems and email folders. In version 2.5 of ADODB, which shipped with Windows 2000 as part of the operating system, Microsoft added two new kinds of objects: Records and Streams. Although you won't need to use these objects when working with the standard relational data in a SQL Server database, they can be used to work with binary, semistructured data. Microsoft developed an OLE DB provider for working with Microsoft Active Directory Service Interfaces (ADSI), which can be used in conjunction with Record and Stream objects to bring file system and email data to your recordsets. The new support for binary data also allows XML to be fetched from a Web server over HTTP and placed in a recordset, without first having to be saved to a file. XML is covered in Chapter 13, "Internet Features in Access and SQL Server."

Other ADO Libraries

ADO supports a number of features that go beyond the scope of the objects in the ADODB library. Other ADO object models have been developed by Microsoft to handle these specialized tasks. Here's a brief overview of a few things you can do with these other libraries. Not much time will be spent on them because they are not really necessary for the tasks covered in this book, but you may want to investigate them further on your own.

ActiveX Data Objects (ADO) Fundamentals

CHAPTER 6

267

6

ACTIVEX DATA
OBJECTS (ADO)
FUNDAMENTALS

Microsoft ADO Extensions for DDL and Security (ADOX)

The Microsoft ADO Extensions for DDL and Security (ADOX) library provides objects that allow you to modify the structure of a database and to manipulate its security settings. For example, you could use ADOX to add a new table, add fields and indexes to your table, and to grant permissions to update the table to only a particular group of users.

Because ADOX was designed for the Jet database engine, it's recommended that you work with SQL Server's system stored procedures or create SQL statements of your own for implementing security or schema changes to your databases rather than working with ADOX, which has proved rather incomplete and unreliable even with Jet.

Figure 6.8 shows setting a reference to the ADOX library.

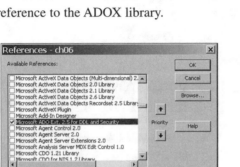

FIGURE 6.8
Setting a reference to the ADOX library.

Microsoft Jet and Replication Objects 2.1 (JRO)

The Microsoft Jet and Replication Objects library provides capabilities that are specific to the Jet database engine, including the ability to compact and repair a database and the ability to work with Jet replication. Figure 6.9 shows setting a reference to the JRO object library.

Microsoft ActiveX Data Objects Recordset (ADOR)

The Microsoft ActiveX Data Objects Recordset library is a stripped-down version of the ADODB object library that doesn't include Command and Connection objects. It's mainly used for Internet and Active Server Page applications where the full functionality of ADODB is not needed. Figure 6.10 shows setting a reference to the ADOR object library.

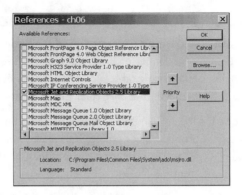

FIGURE 6.9

Setting a reference to the JRO object library.

FIGURE 6.10

Setting a reference to the ADOR object library.

Microsoft ActiveX Data Objects (Multidimensional) (ADOMD)

Beginning with version 7.0, Microsoft SQL Server has shipped with a very powerful engine for performing Online Analytical Processing (OLAP). In SQL Server 2000 it's called Analysis Services. The Microsoft ActiveX Data Objects (Multidimensional) library supports operations using the "cubes" of multidimensional summary data that are produced by OLAP engines. Other OLAP vendors besides Microsoft have also begun supporting ADOMD as a method of performing data analysis. In conjunction with this object library, Microsoft has also developed a successful variation on SQL, called *MDX (Multidimensional Expressions)*, which can be used for building queries against multidimensional data. Access includes minimal native support for

ActiveX Data Objects (ADO) Fundamentals

CHAPTER 6

269

6

**ACTIVEX DATA
OBJECTS (ADO)
FUNDAMENTALS**

working with OLAP data, but that will probably change in future versions. Therefore, this is a technology to start learning about.

FIGURE 6.11
Setting a reference to the ADOMD object library.

ADO.NET

As this book goes to press, Microsoft has just begun previewing a new flavor of ADO that it is currently calling ADO.NET (pronounced, *ADO dot net*). This is a completely new data access technology that is slated to ship with Visual Studio.NET, the next version of Visual Studio after Visual Studio 6.0.

Unlike current versions of ADO, which have only limited ability to save data as XML files or streams, ADO.NET uses XML for its own internal data storage, and therefore can easily bind directly to XML data sources.

ADO.NET offers a brand new set of objects, which are only loosely correlated to the objects previously found in ADO. The DataSet object, for example, provides a strongly typed, client-side, in-memory cache for multiple related "tables" of data. Strongly typed, in this context, means that to refer to a field you will be able to use the field name as a property of table in a dataset, with full Intellisense support when writing code, not just as a member of a collection. The ADODataSetCommand object allows you to specify four different commands for retrieving, updating, adding, and deleting data. The DataView object is used to extract a particular set of fields from a DataSet, providing similar functionality to ADO recordsets. DataReader objects are used for quickly retrieving read-only data from data sources.

ADO.NET is not as closely tied to OLEDB as ADO has been. In addition to continuing to support data access using OLE DB, ADO.NET adds the ability to work with low-level providers that do not go through the generalized OLE DB layer. These providers can work directly with the native communication protocols of individual database engines, allowing faster data access.

For example, a set of ADO.NET objects is specifically tailored to work only with SQL Server, communicating over the same wire-level protocol that SQL Server uses internally.

ADO.NET, as well as the entire .NET framework that is it part of, will introduce many new data access possibilities as Microsoft releases products to support them.

Choosing the Best Tool for the Job at Hand

Many Access developers already have a lot of experience working with DAO and a lot of working DAO code in production. So, you may be asking yourself whether you need to make a total switch to using ADO and convert all your old code.

Microsoft clearly isn't devoting any resources to adding new DAO features. The product may continue to be slightly updated to keep pace with changes in other applications, but even that level of attention may not last long. So, the writing is on the wall: If you want to move forward and take advantage of new developments in data access technology, you really have no choice but to learn and get comfortable with ADO.

The good news is that ADO is really a great product that in a short time has evolved an impressive mix of features and performance. However, there are still several situations where DAO remains the best choice.

When DAO Is the Best Choice

DAO and the Jet database engine have evolved together, and DAO is still the most efficient way to perform just about any data chore that involves Jet. In the area of security and data definition, DAO is still clearly superior to ADOX, and even data retrieval and manipulation using recordsets or query execution will usually run faster with DAO than with ADO.

If you have working code that uses DAO, you probably don't need to change it to use ADO instead. There is no problem mixing both DAO and ADO in the same project or even in the same procedure. Just be sure to prefix any object names that appear in both models with the name of the library when you declare your variables. For example, you should fully qualify such object references, like this:

```
Dim rsDAO As DAO.Recordset
Dim rsADO As ADODB.Recordset
```

These are the objects that ADODB and DAO have in common:

Recordset

Connection

Parameters

ActiveX Data Objects (ADO) Fundamentals

CHAPTER 6

271

6

ACTIVE X DATA
OBJECTS (ADO)
FUNDAMENTALS

Parameter

Fields

Field

Errors

Error

Properties

Property

That covers almost the entire ADODB object library, so to be safe we recommend that you fully qualify all your ADO references, if you are also still using DAO.

When ADO Is the Best Choice

Once you leave the world of Jet, DAO really loses most of its advantages. For working with SQL Server databases, it's recommended that you rely on ADO. When it comes to data retrieval and data manipulation, ADO has achieved almost full parity not just with DAO, but also with RDO and ODBCDirect as well, when it comes to taking advantage of the capabilities of database servers.

Sure, the ADOX objects for performing data definition and security tasks are weak, but that really is not a problem. SQL Server has system stored procedures that you can work with using ADO command objects, and SQL Server even offers its own object models, SQL-DMO and SQL-Namespace, which can provide a programmatic interface to these system stored procedures. However, you should learn to work with the stored procedures directly and use ADO to run them.

Even with the Jet engine, there are several areas where new SQL grammar was added that can only be run from ADO. For example, you can't use DAO to execute a SQL string that uses @@IDENTITY to retrieve the last autonumber value inserted or that uses ALTER COLUMN to change the data type of a field.

Another compelling reason to switch to ADO is to take advantage of the new recordset capabilities that ADO client cursors make possible. Especially when you start working with a server database such as SQL Server, it is great to be able to fetch data into a recordset and then disconnect from the database. The success of the Internet has put pressure on all developers to make their applications scalable and to lessen dependence on having a persistent connection. As tools such as Access and Visual Basic continue to add support for building distributed applications, ADO's great support for offline data manipulation and batch updates will continue to grow in importance.

ADO is also the only alternative for working with the growing list of data sources that are available through OLE DB providers. Microsoft has stopped developing new ISAM drivers for Jet (the drivers that allow Jet to link to and import from foreign data sources), and ODBC can only be used with relational databases. To take advantage of ADSI for working with Microsoft's directory services or to run MDX queries against OLAP data stores, you really must use ADO.

Summary

Microsoft's OLE DB technology adds significantly to the data access options that were previously available to VBA programmers. It provides access to nonrelational data and uses an object-based programming technology that integrates well with other applications. The ADO family of object libraries provides the interfaces that VBA programmers use to interact with OLE DB. The most commonly used ADO object model, ADODB, includes Connection, Recordset, and Command objects for retrieving and manipulating data. ADODB also includes a full-featured cursor engine that supports a range of advanced capabilities, and the new Record and Stream objects can be used to access binary data. Other libraries in the ADO family, including ADOX for data design and security and ADOMD for multidimensional data, are used to supplement the capabilities of ADODB. OLE DB and ADO comprise a very extensible framework that can evolve as new data access requirements and capabilities emerge, and right now they are your best choice for programmatically working with SQL Server data. Microsoft's new XML-based ADO+ technology will emerge as a valuable addition to your data access arsenal as products are released to support it.

Designing and Creating a SQL Server Database

IN THIS CHAPTER

Designing a Relational Database

The most important step in the development of a database application happens before you launch Access or SQL Server. It is the process of defining a set of requirements and modeling how those requirements will be met using a relational database.

You may think about the user interfaces—the forms, reports and, perhaps, Web pages—that will be used for input and output. Showing mockups of user interfaces to users is often an effective way to test your understanding of the requirements. But before you begin actually creating those user interfaces, you must figure out what pieces of data you need to store, what kinds of constraints you need to place on each of those pieces, how the pieces relate to each other, and how you are going to arrange those pieces in database tables.

Because this book assumes that you're already an intermediate to advanced Access developer interested in learning more about SQL Server, it also assumes that you're already familiar with the process of designing a normalized relational database. If not, you really ought to take the time to get up to speed on those concepts. One good introductory book is *Database Design for Mere Mortals*, by Michael J. Hernandez (published by Addison Wesley Longman).

The next section offers a quick review of the principles of relational database design, and the remainder of the chapter goes into detail on how to implement a design in SQL Server. The most essential ingredient for successful database design and implementation, however, is not derived from relational theory or knowledge of database systems, but from knowledge of the business. To build a successful database application, you must have a clear and complete understanding of the process that is being modeled in the database. There is no substitute for industry knowledge, the ability to listen and watch carefully, and the courage to ask lots of questions. This chapter's discussion starts here, at the point where that all-important process has ended—you know which pieces of data need to be stored, and you're ready to build an efficient and safe structure to hold them.

Review of Relational Database Design Principles

The relational model, developed by E. F. Codd just 30 years ago, makes use of mathematical set theory to define a set of rules that can be applied to database systems. The purpose of these rules is to facilitate the creation of databases that can efficiently maintain the consistency of the data and can efficiently answer questions about the data.

Relations, Tuples, Attributes, and Keys

In relational theory, tables are referred to as *relations* (hence the name), columns are called *attributes*, and rows are called *tuples*. Actually, tables containing columns and rows are just the most common representation of the abstract logical construct of relations as sets of tuples, each with the same set of attributes.

The tuples (rows) in a relation (table) must be unique. To do anything with a row of data, you need to be able to find it, which means you need a way to identify it uniquely based on one or more of its attributes. Any attribute or combination of attributes that's guaranteed to be unique is a candidate key.

To make implementation convenient, one of the candidate keys is selected as the primary key.

Also for convenience, if all candidate keys are very long, or composed of many attributes, or subject to frequent changes, then a surrogate key is created that's not only unique to each tuple but also compact and relatively constant. Access AutoNumber fields and SQL Server identity columns are examples of surrogate keys.

It can be argued that surrogate keys should never be necessary, because every tuple should have some other unique attribute or set of attributes reflecting attributes of that entity in the "real world," which is called the *problem set* (also sometimes referred to as the *problem domain* or simply the *problem space*). If database engines were perfect, autonumbers and identity columns wouldn't be needed, because, for example, all customers could be uniquely identified by their name, address, and the date, time, and location of their first order. Even if two people at the same address had the same name, they presumably couldn't both place an order at the same location at the same exact date and time. However, using all that data each time you needed to identify a customer and maintaining changes to all that data every place it is used would place an unacceptable burden on the system. Therefore, surrogate keys are often employed as a concession to the imperfection of database systems, to help them perform in the most efficient way possible.

Normalization

Ensuring that each tuple in a relation is unique by defining a primary key is an important first step, but it still leaves a lot of room for problems. Therefore, Dr. Codd defined a series of progressively more stringent standards, called *normal forms*. Databases containing relations that meet these standards are called *normalized* and are thereby optimized for efficient data storage and retrieval.

First Normal Form

First normal form pertains to the attributes of a relation. Each attribute should contain only one piece of information that you care about, and each piece of information that you care about in a database should be held in only one attribute.

For example, the ContactName column in the Northwind database's Customers table holds the full name of each contact, including the family name, or *last name*, and the given name, or *first name*. Now you can see why the definition of first normal form contained the somewhat awkward phrase, "piece of information that you care about." If all you ever cared about was the customer contact's full name, the Customers table would be in first normal form. But, if you cared about the last name by itself, perhaps to sort a list of contacts by last name, then this table would be in violation of first normal form. To fix it, you would need to break the column up into separate columns, one for each piece of the name that you cared about. If you didn't create separate columns, you would need to create a way to parse out just the last name and then perform the sort, but to do that reliably with all the names would be complex and extremely inefficient. Anytime you find yourself parsing an attribute to retrieve a piece of it, there's a good chance that piece should really be split off as a separate attribute. Relational databases make it very easy to join these pieces later for presentation to the users.

Another way to violate first normal form is to have to look to multiple attributes to find one piece of data. The most common example of this is a pattern that is often seen in spreadsheets—repeating groups.

Suppose you know that Northwind orders always contain up to four items and no more. You could structure the Orders table to contain four groups of columns for each order: ProductID1, UnitPrice1, Quantity1, Discount1, ProductID2, UnitPrice2, Quantity2, Discount2, and so on. All 16 of these columns would be in every record, regardless of whether they were used, thus consuming excessive storage space. Plus, there is always the problem of needing to restructure the database if Northwind decides to accept an order containing five items. However, the most serious problem with repeating groups like this is that to find out how many units of a certain item were sold this week, you'd need to look in four different places, which requires a complex query that would perform slowly.

Second Normal Form

Although second normal form also looks at the attributes of a relation, it is really about the relation as a whole. Just as first normal form ensures that each attribute describes just one "piece of information that you care about," second normal form ensures that each relation models just one entity or event in the problem set. At the technical level, second normal form states that in addition to conforming to first normal form, every attribute of a relation must be functionally dependent on the entire primary key. This means that each primary key value, including all attributes in the key if there are more than one, should uniquely determine the value of every other attribute in each tuple (record).

The primary key in the Northwind OrderDetails table is a composite key comprised of OrderID and ProductID columns. Each of the other columns in the table—UnitPrice, Quantity, and Discount—are dependent on the combination of both of those primary key values. The unit price could be different for that product on different orders, and certainly the unit price could be different for different products on a given order, but knowing both the Order ID and the Product ID uniquely determines a particular unit price.

So, would it be a violation of second normal form to add a ProductName column to the OrderDetails table? This depends on how things are done at Northwind. Does Northwind ever change product names and keep the same Product ID? If it changed the name of Tofu to Fresh Tofu, would Northwind want to be able to look up an old order and know that the name used on that order was Tofu? If the new ProductName column in OrderDetails were truly adding a new piece of information to the database (the name the product had when that order was placed), it wouldn't be a violation of second normal form, because it would be functionally dependent on both OrderID and ProductID. But, if ProductName depended only on ProductID, it would belong in the Products table, where ProductID is the primary key.

Third Normal Form

Third normal form builds on second normal form by ensuring that all attributes that aren't in the primary key not only are functionally dependent on the full key but also are *not* functionally dependent on each other.

If you take another look at the contact information in the Northwind Customers table, you'll find that in addition to putting the full contact name in one column, the designers also added a column for contact title. For example, the customer Alfreds Futterkiste has a contact name of "Maria Anders" and contact title of "Sales Representative." The only way this could be in third normal form would be if the intention was to tell us, "At this company, Alfreds Futterkiste, our contact, no matter who it is, will have the title, Sales Representative." But that is probably not the case. The true message is probably that "Maria Anders is our contact at Alfreds Futterkiste, and her title happens to be Sales Representative." Therefore, ContactTitle isn't functionally dependent on CustomerID; it is really functionally dependent on ContactName. To comply with third normal form, the Northwind database would need a separate table for contacts with Title as a column in that table.

Another common violation of third normal form is having a calculated attribute that must change when other attributes change. For example, you might be tempted to add a LineTotal column to OrderDetails that would hold the calculated total for each row based on the quantity, unit price, and discount. Even though you could write a trigger in SQL Server to ensure that this total would be kept accurate (unless you used a bulk copy operation to add data that bypassed triggers), storing this redundant data would still be considered a violation of third normal form. The correct approach is to store just the "raw ingredients" for any calculation and to use SQL to perform the calculation in queries, views, or stored procedures whenever you need the calculated value.

Third normal form is the most frequently violated normal form, for the sake of convenience or performance. Technically, once you know an address's postal code you can derive the city and state, but few databases go to the trouble of maintaining the postal lookup table that would be needed to implement this. Likewise, few inventory database designers are willing to calculate an on-hand value based on all previous transactions whenever it is needed. Note that the performance argument for violating third normal form is less convincing in SQL Server 2000, which now supports indexed views that allow calculated values to be maintained by the storage engine and retrieved very quickly, without storing the calculated value in a table column. For a discussion of indexed views, see Chapter 9, "Creating and Optimizing Views."

And Beyond

Since Codd formulated his original three normal forms, other database scientists have presented well-accepted arguments for three additional normal forms. Boyce/Codd is a variation on third normal form that addresses fairly uncommon cases where there are at least two composite candidate keys with overlapping values. Fourth normal form deals with separating multivalued dependencies into separate relations, and fifth normal form deals with a rare kind of three-table circular dependency. You can safely ignore these advanced forms and stick to the first three, but if you would like to dig into these and other technical subtleties of the relational model, we recommend the latest edition of *An Introduction to Database Systems*, by C. J. Date (published by Addison Wesley) and *Database Modeling & Design*, by Tobey J. Teorey (published by Morgan Kaufmann).

Relationships

The normalization process results in the partitioning of logically related data across multiple relations (tables). To maintain consistent data, the database must enforce the referential integrity of these logical relationships. For example, if customer data is stored in one table and orders are stored in another table, the database needs a way to know which orders belong to which customers, and it needs to ensure that every order has a corresponding customer.

A relationship between two relations is defined by creating an attribute or set of attributes in one relation, called a *foreign key*, that matches the primary key of the other relation. For example, each row in the Orders table has a foreign key CustomerID column containing a value that can also be found in the primary key CustomerID column in the Customers table.

One-to-Many Relationships

Most relationships match one tuple (record) in the relation (table) with the primary key to many tuples in the relation with the foreign key. For example, one customer has many orders. This is quite logically called a *one-to-many relationship*.

The customer/orders relationship is a master/child or "has a" type of one-to-many relationship. One customer "has" some number of orders. A customer might exist with zero orders, or one, or more, but every order has exactly one customer.

Another type of one-to-many relationship is a lookup or "is a" relationship. For example, perhaps a particular order "is a" COD order, to be paid for on delivery. The one record in the PaymentTerms table with the value "COD" matches any number of records in the Orders table. But each order matches up with exactly one payment term.

Many-to-Many Relationships

Suppose, however, that an order could be paid for partially COD and partially after 30 days (or *Net 30*). In that case, there would be a *many-to-many relationship* between Orders and PaymentTerms. A third table would be required to record the pairings of Orders and PaymentTerms, perhaps also recording the percentage of each order that needed to be paid according to each term of payment. The table might have two records showing this:

OrderID	PaymentTerms	Percent
3456	COD	50
3456	Net 30	50

The primary key in this table would be a composite key composed of unique combinations of OrderID and PaymentTerms, and each of those columns would also be a foreign key to the Orders and PaymentTerms tables, respectively. That is typical of the junction table (also called the *resolver table*) used to form many-to-many relationships from two one-to-many relationships.

One-to-One Relationships

Sometimes a foreign key can also be the entire primary key. This is called a *one-to-one relationship*, because there can only be one matching record in each of the two relations. The most common usage of one-to-one relationships is to define attributes that only apply to a subset of the tuples (records) in a relation (table). For example, you might have one table that holds information about all people in the database and another table that holds extra information that only applies to company employees. Both tables would have the same primary key, perhaps PersonID. Each record in the People table might or might not have one matching record in the Employees table, but each record in the Employees table would have exactly one matching record in the People table, holding all the generic information about that employee. PersonID in the Employees table would be both a primary key and a foreign key.

Enforced Referential Integrity

All database relationships depend on the fact that every foreign key value must have a matching primary key value in the related table. There can be no "orphan" orders with a customer ID that doesn't match up with any of the CustomerID values in the Customers table. This means that a customer record can't be deleted while any related orders are left in the database, and a customer ID can't be changed without making the same change to the CustomerID values in related orders. Also, of course, no orders can be added for customers that haven't first been added to the Customers table. Ensuring that these rules are followed is called *enforcing referential integrity*.

Cascading Updates and Deletes

Some database systems allow you to enforce referential integrity by cascading updates and/or deletes to related tables. So, for example, if you tried to change a CustomerID value in the Customers table that was also used as a foreign key in the Orders table, instead of disallowing the change, the database could permit the change and ensure that all the corresponding values in the Orders table were updated to match the new value in the Customers table. This is a cascading update. Similarly, if an order had related order details, the database could allow the order to be deleted and avoid leaving the details as orphans by automatically deleting them as well, which would be an example of a cascading deletion. Access has supported cascading updates and deletes all along, as does SQL Server 2000. But earlier versions of SQL Server do not.

Data Integrity

Even with fully normalized tables and well-enforced referential integrity, there are plenty of ways that garbage can creep into your database. You can't prevent all data-entry errors, but you can do a lot at the database level to increase the chances that invalid data will be rejected.

Relational theorists have formulated distinct categories of integrity. For example, the uniqueness of each tuple in a relation is generally considered to be a form of entity integrity. The restriction that a particular attribute can contain only dates is one way of enforcing domain integrity, and the creation of relationships between primary and foreign keys enforces relational integrity.

However, these distinctions between different types of data integrity are not as simple as they appear, because entity integrity and relational integrity could be seen as forms of domain integrity. *Domain integrity* is the restriction of attributes to a defined "domain" of valid values. When you select a data type for a column, you are restricting the domain of values that can be stored in that column. When you select whether null s will be permitted, you're refining the definition of the domain. Designating a primary key or a unique index could also be seen as restricting the domain to values that would not result in duplicate key values. Even the creation of relationships can be seen as restricting the domain of non-null foreign key values to values that exist in the corresponding primary key in the related table. So, in a sense, all forms of data integrity are variations on the basic concept of domain integrity.

Business Rules

Some types of data integrity are referred to as *business rules*. For example, you may want to restrict the domain of shipping dates to include only dates that are greater than the order date of that entity. Perhaps you may need to run a procedural test to determine the domain of acceptable order amounts for a customer based on credit rating, payment history, and current outstanding invoices. Although SQL Server includes a rich set of tools for defining and enforcing such business rules, which are discussed later in this chapter, some programmers prefer to define only the most basic forms of data integrity within the database itself and to enforce the more complex and changeable business rules in code that lives outside the database. To ensure that these rules are enforced, that code must always be used to make changes to the affected objects in the database. Business rules that are applied within the database itself have the advantage of being automatically enforced no matter what external method is used to manipulate data.

Implementing Your Design in SQL Server 2000

The relational model is completely independent of the actual physical system used to implement it. Relational database management systems are free to use whatever physical implementation the designers think will be most efficient. It will be easier to work with SQL Server, however, if you know just a bit about the choices that the SQL Server designers made when developing the database engine. SQL Server uses the underlying physical storage concepts of pages, extents, and files to manage storage of databases on computer drives.

How Databases Are Stored in Files

Databases are stored directly in operating system files, which can be configured to grow automatically as data is added to them. You can specify the growth increment and an optional maximum size when you create the database. This is a big improvement over versions prior to SQL Server 7.0, which stored data in devices and stored devices in files, thus adding an additional level of complexity to physical storage operations. Databases can be stored in multiple files, but a single file can contain data from only one database. SQL Server uses the following three file extensions for its data files, one for each of the three types of files it creates—primary data files, secondary data files, and the log file:

- `.MDF`. The primary data file for each database.
- `.NDF`. Secondary data files, which hold additional data for a database. SQL Server allows you to locate tables and indexes in separate files. The advantage of using multiple files is that you can locate them on different devices, targeting file I/O to a specific processor.
- `.LDF`. The log file, which contains the transaction log. It is recommended that you locate the log file on a separate disk from the data files to enable data recovery in case of mechanical failure. You learn how to use the transaction log to recover from a failure in Chapter 15, "Deployment, Tuning, and Maintenance."

How Filegroups Work

When you create a database, a single, primary filegroup is created that contains all the files for your database. SQL Server allows multiple filegroups per database, which improves performance for larger databases by allowing a single database to be located on multiple hardware devices simultaneously. If different drive controllers are servicing different files, data updates can be completed more quickly. When you create tables and indexes, you can also specify that they be located on a filegroup other than the primary filegroup. You can safely ignore these options and just go with the defaults, but if your database grows large, you will do well to devote more time to optimizing the configuration.

Files are further broken down into pages and extents.

Pages

A *page* is the smallest unit of SQL Server storage, at 8,192 bytes (or 8KB). This is also the maximum size of a row in a SQL Server table, not counting large text and image columns, which are stored in separate pages. A page can only contain data from a single object, although an object can occupy multiple pages. For example, the rows from a table can occupy many pages, but a page can only contain data from a single table.

Extents

An *extent* is eight contiguous pages, or 64KB of data. When you create a new table or index, it is given a single page in an existing extent that may contain pages belonging to other objects. When the new object grows to the point where it occupies eight pages in mixed extents, it gets moved to its own uniform extent. SQL Server then creates additional extents as needed, until you run out of disk space.

How the Transaction Log Works

The transaction log is a special file that records all activity in the database. When you create a database, SQL Server automatically creates a transaction log for that database. The transaction log provides an extra layer of protection for your SQL Server data because SQL Server uses a write-ahead strategy to maintain the log. When a user modifies data, SQL Server takes these actions:

1. The change is recorded in the transaction log.
2. The modified data pages are read into the in-memory storage cache.
3. The changes are made in the cached pages.
4. The checkpoint process saves the changes to disk.

This write-ahead strategy of recording changes to the log prior to saving them to disk is valuable in case of system failure. If your database goes down, you can restore the database from a backup and then apply the transactions from the transaction log to the backup copy of the database. Restoring the transaction log allows you to recover data that was recorded after the last backup and that would otherwise have been lost.

TIP

The SQL Server checkpoint process automatically executes at frequent intervals so that data is written from the cache back to the physical drive the data is stored on. You can force the checkpoint process manually by issuing the CHECKPOINT statement in Transact-SQL, which immediately writes any cached pages to disk.

CAUTION

Do not use a write-caching disk controller on any drives storing SQL Server databases. A write-caching disk controller interferes with the internal logic SQL Server uses during the checkpoint process. SQL Server ensures that data can be recovered from the transaction log at the time of any failure by storing disk writes internally and committing them when the CPU is less busy. Because SQL Server depends on knowing when the checkpoint process actually wrote to the physical drive, a write-caching disk controller could make your transaction log unrecoverable.

Creating Databases Using the Enterprise Manager

The SQL Server Enterprise Manager has all the tools necessary for you to implement your database design in SQL Server, from building the database to implementing your business rules. You can also use Transact-SQL statements to perform these tasks, but using the Enterprise Manager provides a graphical user interface and several wizards to make the process easier. To create a new database, right-click the Databases folder and choose New Database. This will bring up the New Database dialog box, displaying the following three tabs:

- *General*. Use this tab to specify the database name and collation name (the default is the server default specified when you installed SQL Server).

- *Data Files*. Use this tab to specify the filenames, filegroups, and the location of the physical database files, which have an .MDF extension. Figure 7.1 shows the dialog box for naming and locating the database files. Use this dialog box to specify the file properties for automatically growing the file and setting the maximum size.

- *Transaction Log*. Use this tab to specify the filename, filegroups, and location of the log files, which have an .LDF extension. Figure 7.2 shows the dialog box for naming, locating, and controlling the growth of the log.

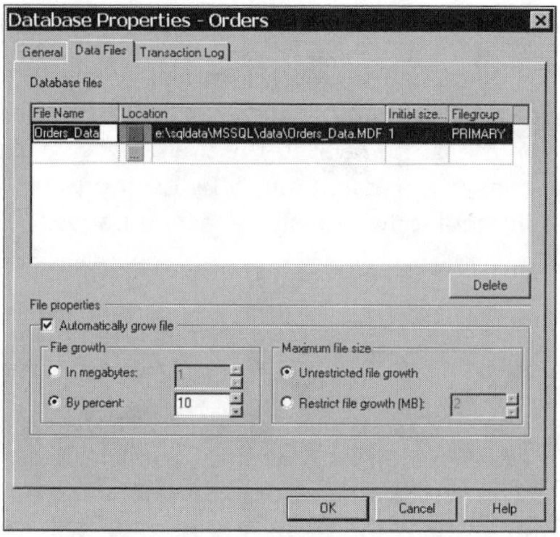

FIGURE 7.1

Specifying the filename and location when creating a new database.

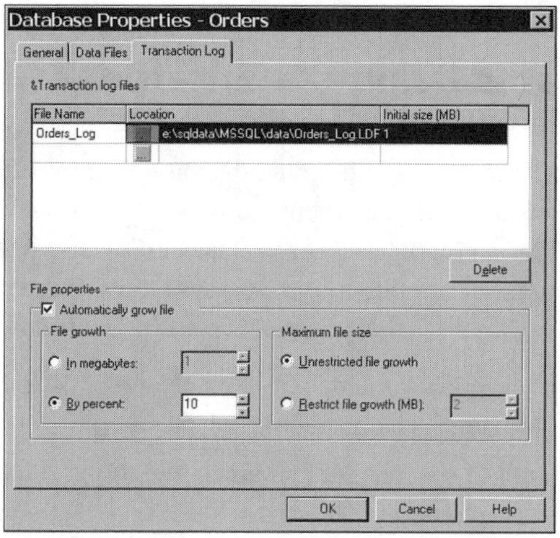

FIGURE 7.2

Specifying the name and location of the log file.

> **TIP**
>
> The transaction log should be kept on a different physical device from the device that holds the main database files. The backup files for the database should also be located on a different device than the main database files. If you locate everything on the same physical device, you won't be able to recover in case of disk failure. Backing up the database regularly keeps the transaction log from growing too large, because the log gets truncated automatically when you do a full database backup. Backups are discussed in Chapter 15.

Once you click the OK button, the database will be created with the options you've specified. To set additional database properties, select your new database in the Databases folder, right-click, and choose Properties. This will bring up the Properties dialog box, which has six tabs:

- *General.* Displays the name and general properties of the database. You can't modify any of the properties on this tab.

- *Data Files.* Displays the name, properties, and location of your data files, as shown previously in Figure 7.1.

- *Transaction Log.* Displays the name, properties, and location of your transaction log, as shown previously in Figure 7.2.

- *Filegroups.* Displays the name of the primary filegroup and any other filegroups you may have created. Use this dialog box to add new filegroups.

- *Options.* Allows you to set additional database options, which are discussed later in this section.

- *Permissions.* Allows you to set permissions for database users and roles, as shown in Figure 7.3. If you haven't created any roles or users in your database, you'll see only the public role listed. SQL Server security is covered in Chapter 3, "Understanding SQL Server Security."

Database Options

The Options tab, shown in Figure 7.4, displays the default options that are automatically selected when the database is created. If you find yourself unsure as to which options to pick, you will generally be safe going with the defaults. However, each of those options are all there for a good reason, so it's important to become familiar with what is available and to understand what each one means. The Options tab is divided into four sections. The top section has two options:

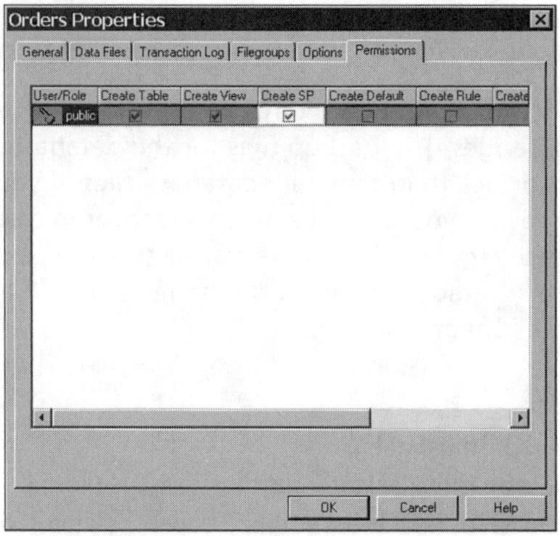

FIGURE 7.3

Setting database permissions for the public role.

- *Restrict Access.* There are two choices for restricting access: to members of the db_owner, dbcreator or sysadmin roles; or to a single user. The single user option is similar to the "Open Exclusive" option that Access uses. If you set this option while the database is in use, current users will not be shut out, but no new users will able to connect to the database.

- *Read-only.* The database will be read-only. Use this setting if the database will be used exclusively for reporting because this will speed up data-access operations. SQL Server will not need to manage any locks on data retrieved from a read-only database.

The second section allows you to specify the recovery model for backing up and restoring the database. Backups are covered in Chapter 15.

The third section, Settings, has the following options:

- *ANSI NULL default.* Columns in tables allow null values unless explicitly defined with NOT NULL. Nulls are discussed in detail later in this chapter.

- *Recursive triggers.* Allows triggers in a table to make changes that cause the same trigger to be fired again. Recursive triggers are not recommended for performance reasons. They can also be difficult to maintain because they overly complicate data operations.

- *Auto update statistics.* Instructs SQL Server to automatically update any out-of-date statistics.

- *Torn page detection.* Causes SQL Server to check for incomplete data pages.

- *Auto close.* Shuts down the database cleanly when the last user exits.

- *Auto shrink*. Instructs SQL Server to periodically shrink the database if necessary.

- *Auto create statistics*. Instructs SQL Server to automatically create any missing statistics needed by a query during the optimization process. Valid statistics help the query processor determine the most efficient execution plan for data access.

- *Use quoted identifiers*. Allows double quotation marks to delimit identifiers (names of objects). If this is turned off, double quotation marks delimit literal strings.

The bottom section allows you to set the database compatibility level. This is useful if you're converting a database from an earlier version of SQL Server because you can force SQL Server to work in 70, 65, or 60 compatibility, as shown in Figure 7.4. However, features introduced subsequent to the selected compatibility level will be unavailable if you select an earlier version. For example, if you choose to work in database compatibility level 60 or 65, you won't be able to employ the TOP keyword in a SELECT query. Search SQL Server Books Online on "Backward Compatibility Details" for the complete list of backward-compatibility issues. Because SQL Server was rebuilt from the ground up between versions 6.5 and 7.0, this topic is quite extensive when dealing with compatibility prior to SQL Server 7.0. For issues involving differences between SQL Server 7.0 and SQL Server 2000, see the topic "SQL Server 2000 and SQL Server version 7.0" in Books Online.

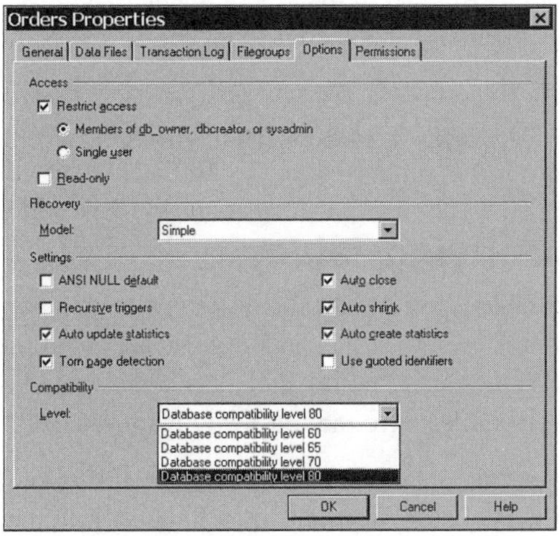

7

DESIGNING AND
CREATING A SQL
SERVER DATABASE

FIGURE 7.4
Setting database options.

> **TIP**
>
> To set default options automatically for every database you create, set them on the system database named *model*. This model system database acts as a template for all databases you create, and options set on model will automatically be applied to each new database.

Setting Other Database Options Using `sp_dboption`

The Enterprise Manager only displays a partial list of all the configurable database options. All these options plus several others can be set using the system stored procedure `sp_dboption`. A complete list of database options and the necessary syntax to change them can be found in SQL Server Books Online under the `sp_dboption` topic. For example, to take the Orders database offline (an option not exposed in Enterprise Manager), run the following statements from the Query Analyzer:

```
USE master
EXEC sp_dboption 'Orders', 'offline', 'TRUE'
```

Note that the context must be switched to the system database before using `sp_dboption` to take one of your databases offline. If that step is skipped, the call will fail. Most options don't require this extra step.

Database options can also be changed using the Transact-SQL syntax, ALTER DATABASE. In SQL Server 2000, `sp_dboption` is supported mainly for backwards compatibility.

Creating and Modifying Tables

When you create a new database, it will contain system tables but no user tables. These system tables, which all start with the prefix "sys," contain metadata about the structure and security settings of your database. You will add tables, called *user tables*, to hold the data that you need to record in the database. All tables have the following features:

- Each table has a name that is unique in the database. Tables can have the same name if they have different owners, and they must then be used with the *ownername.tablename* syntax. Table names must follow the rules for identifiers listed in the following section.

- Tables consist of columns (called *fields* in Access) and rows (or *records*).

- Each column describes a single characteristic of a set and must have a unique name within that table.

- Each row must be unique and describe one set of related information about the subject of the table. The primary key ensures the uniqueness of each row.

- The order of the rows or columns should not be significant or meaningful in any way.

Rules for Identifiers

Identifiers are simply the names of objects, and SQL Server has the same rules governing identifiers for all its objects, including databases, tables, columns, views, and stored procedures:

- Identifiers must be between 1 and 128 characters in length.

- Identifiers must start with a letter or the symbol @, _, or #. This can be any Unicode character, which includes a through z, A through Z, and most foreign characters.

- Identifiers starting with @ can only be local variables.

- Identifiers starting with # can only be local temporary objects.

- Identifiers starting with ## can only be global temporary objects.

- Characters after the first character can be letters, decimal numbers, or the symbols #, $, or _.

- Spaces and other special characters can only be used if the identifier is always delimited with double quotation marks or square brackets. Square brackets are always supported; double quotation marks are only allowed if the Use Quoted Identifiers database option has been set.

- Identifiers must not be a reserved word. The Books Online topic "Reserved Keywords (T-SQL)" lists all reserved words for Transact-SQL and ODBC.

Creating Tables and Columns

When you create a new table in SQL Server, you create the columns at the same time. A new table cannot be saved unless it contains at least one column. Both table names and column names must follow the rules for identifiers listed previously. Columns should consist of atomic, nondecomposable information that cannot be divided into smaller columns. For example, a column should not combine values such as first name and last name in a single column. If this is the case, create two columns—one for the first name and one for the last name. In a relational database, it's infinitely easier to join columns than it is to parse out multiple pieces of information contained inside a single column.

To create a table and define columns in a database, right-click the Tables folder and choose New Table from the list. This will load the New Table dialog box shown in Figure 7.5, allowing you to specify the column names, data types, and other column properties.

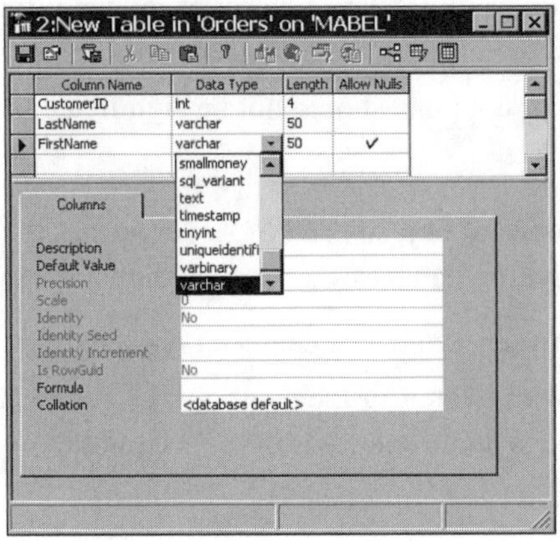

FIGURE 7.5

Setting column properties.

The Columns tab at the bottom of the table designer lets you specify the following properties:

- The Description property is an optional setting that allows you to type descriptive text.

- The Default Value property allows you to specify a default value for a column.

- The Precision and Scale properties can be adjusted only for decimal (numeric) data types; they are read-only for the other data types. Precision controls the maximum number of digits in a number, and scale is the maximum number of digits to the right of the decimal point.

- The Identity, Identity Seed, and Identity Increment properties allow you to set up an auto-incrementing value. This is similar to the AutoNumber data type in Access.

- IsRowGuid applies only if the data type is uniqueidentifier. It creates a globally unique identifier column for that table. The newid() function generates unique values for uniqueidentifier columns. Although you can create multiple uniqueidentifier columns, only one per table can have the IsRowGuid property set to True. This column is used to identify the row for SQL Server replication.

- The Formula property is new in SQL Server 2000 and displays the formula for a computed column.

- The Collation property is new in SQL Server 2000 and applies only to char, varchar, text, nchar, nvarchar, and ntext data types, displaying the collating sequence that SQL Server applies to the column when it's used for sorting. You can specify collations for each character string column that differs from the default collation. Choose <database default> to use the default collating sequence for the database.

SQL Server Data Types

Defining a specific data type for a column guarantees that only values of that data type will be stored in the column. For example, if you define a column as int, and a user tries to enter "Smith," the entry will be rejected. Data types are the first step in protecting your database from "garbage in." You'll investigate the other ways you can restrict data by creating rules, defaults, and triggers later in this chapter.

Figure 7.5 shows the drop-down list of system data types that are available for you to choose from when defining your columns.

System Data Types

When you define a data type for each column in your table, you can either use the system data types supplied by SQL Server or define your own named data types, which are based on the system data types. Table 7.1 describes the system data types and how they are used. The n, p, and s parameters shown with some of the data types in the table are used only when defining columns in Transact-SQL; when you're working in Enterprise Manager, these are represented by the Length, Precision, and Scale properties.

TABLE 7.1   System Data Types in SQL Server

Data Type	Description
binary*[(n)]*	The binary data type holds from 1 to 8,000 bytes of fixed-length binary data, where *n* is a value between 1 and 8,000. The storage size includes whatever is stored in the column, plus four additional bytes. Binary is a fixed-length data type, so if you define a column as binary(5), it will always use five bytes of disk space plus the additional four. Using a fixed-length data type is efficient when data in the column is close to the same size, because fixed-length storage allows SQL Server to retrieve data more efficiently.
varbinary*[(n)]*	The varbinary data type is the same as binary, except that it is a variable-length data type. Only the actual length of the data is stored, and the *(n)* parameter merely specifies the maximum length of the data. Use varbinary when the length of the binary data is unknown or varies in length.
text	The text data type consists of literal non-Unicode string data up to 2,147,483,647 characters. The text data type is managed internally as linked data pages that only appear to be stored in a table. The text data type in SQL Server maps to the memo data type in Access.

TABLE 7.1 Continued

Data Type	Description
ntext	The ntext data type can hold data up to 1,073,741,823 Unicode characters, occupying twice the number of bytes as characters entered, because Unicode characters each use two bytes of storage. Use ntext only if you need to support languages that require Unicode, because it has twice the overhead of the text data type.
image	The image data type is similar to the text data type in that it consists of linked data pages consisting of binary data. It can contain up to 2,147,483,647 bytes of binary data. The image data type maps to the OLE Object data type in Access.
char*[(n)]*	The char data type is fixed width and can contain from 1 to 8,000 non-Unicode characters. The storage size is *(n)* regardless of the actual length of the data. Unused storage is padded with trailing spaces. Use the char data type when data entered in a column is the same length, such as a column that contains state abbreviations (NY, CA, and so on).
varchar*[(n)]*	The varchar data type is similar to char, except that it is a variable-length data type. It can contain from 1 to 8,000 non-Unicode characters. The *(n)* parameter defines the maximum length of the string, and only the data actually contained in the column is stored. Use varchar when you have column lengths that vary.
nchar*[(n)]*	The nchar data type is a fixed-length data type that can contain from 1 to 4,000 Unicode characters. It is similar to char but with twice the storage requirements. Use char when you need to store strings that require Unicode character sets.
nvarchar*[(n)]*	The nvarchar data type is similar to nchar, except it is a variable-length data type that can contain from 1 to 4,000 Unicode characters. Any data that is too long to fit will be truncated at the *n*th character.
datetime	The datetime data type consists of two four-byte segments: four bytes for the number of days before or after the base date of 1/1/1900, and four bytes for the number of milliseconds after midnight, rounded to increments of .000, .003, or .007 seconds. The datetime data type encompasses dates between January 1, 1753 and December 31, 9999. Note that the range of dates SQL Server supports is much more limited than the range of dates supported by Access (which ranges from the year 100 to 9999) and that the internal numeric storage is different. Date and time data is alphanumeric and is entered by enclosing the values with single quotes ('). The date and time parts are processed separately, so you can enter either the time or the date part first. However, when entering time values, you must enter the elements, hours,

Table 7.1 Continued

Data Type	Description
	minutes, seconds, milliseconds, and then AM/PM, in that order, with a colon separator or an AM/PM signifier. The default value for the date part is 1/1/1900, and for the time part it's 12:00:00:000AM.
smalldatetime	The smalldatetime data type consists of two two-byte integers: two bytes for the number of days after 1/1/1900, and two bytes for the number of minutes past midnight. The range of values is much smaller than datetime, with valid dates between 1/1/1900 and 6/6/2079 and with time accuracy only to the minute. Use smalldatetime if you don't need to store dates outside that range or time values with granularity more than a minute.
decimal*[(p[, s])]* and numeric *[(p[, s])]*	The decimal and numeric data types are just two names for the same thing. The decimal/numeric data types are used for numbers with fixed precision and scale, indicated by the (*p, s*) parameters. When maximum precision is used, valid values are from $-10^{38} - 1$ through $10^{38} - 1$. The scale (*s*) is the maximum number of digits that can be stored to the right of the decimal point, and it must be less than or equal to the precision. When specifying the precision, use a value of 1 through a maximum of 28 (this has been increased to 38 in SQL Server 2000). If you don't specify a scale or precision, the default precision is 18, and the default scale is 0. The storage for exact numeric data depends on the precision (*p*) required, precision being the maximum total number of digits that can be stored on both sides of the decimal point. One thing to bear in mind is that SQL Server considers each specific combination of precision and scale as a different data type. For example, decimal(5,5) and decimal(5,0) are considered different data types.
float*[(n)]*	A double precision, or *float*, uses eight bytes of storage and can hold either a positive or negative number from $-1.79E + 308$ through $1.79E + 308$, with a binary precision up to 15 digits. Floats can also include an exponent. The SQL-92 synonym for float is *double precision*, and this data type is comparable to the Access Double data type.
real	The real data type is a smaller version of float that contains floating-point number data with a value range from $-3.40E + 38$ through $3.40E + 38$, with a storage size of four bytes. This is comparable to the Access Single data type.
int	The int data type uses four bytes of storage and can store whole numbers from -2^{31} ($-2,147,483,648$) through $2^{31} - 1$ ($2,147,483,647$). The SQL-92 synonym is *integer*. The int data type maps to the Access Long Integer data type.

TABLE 7.1 Continued

Data Type	Description
smallint	The smallint data type is a smaller version of int, consuming two bytes of storage and storing a range of whole numbers from -2^{15} ($-32,768$) through $2^{15} -1$ ($32,767$). The smallint data type maps to the Access Integer data type.
tinyint	The tinyint data type consumes only one byte of storage and stores whole numbers from 0 through 255. This maps to the Access byte data type.
bigint	The bigint data type is new in SQL Server 2000. It can hold numbers in a range from -2^{63} to $2^{63} -1$, and it uses eight bytes of storage. Use bigint when you need a larger version of int.
money	The money data type can store decimal data scaled to four digits of precision. Values range from -2^{63} ($-922,337,203,685,477.5808$) through $2^{63} -1$ ($+922,337,203,685,477.5807$), with accuracy to a ten-thousandth of a monetary unit. Storage is eight bytes. The money data type maps to the Access currency data type. The money data type is useful when you don't need more than four decimal places of precision because values are preserved exactly, with no rounding beyond the four digits.
smallmoney	The smallmoney data type is a smaller version of money, consuming four bytes of storage and with values ranging from $-214,748.3648$ through $+214,748.3647$ (with accuracy to a ten-thousandth of a monetary unit). Use smallmoney when you don't need to store a large range of money values.
bit	The bit data type can hold a value of either 1 or 0. Null values are not allowed. SQL Server stores bit fields efficiently by collecting multiple bit fields and storing up to eight in a single byte. Use the bit data type for true/false and yes/no types of data where you don't need to store a null value. The bit data type is comparable to the Yes/No Access data type, but note that the value stored for True in Access is -1, not 1.
identity	An identity column isn't really a data type per se; it's a SQL Server–specific column that provides an auto-incrementing int value. This is similar to the Access AutoNumber data type.
timestamp	A column defined as a timestamp generates a database-wide unique number that is generated automatically when a row is inserted, and it's updated every time the row is edited. A table is allowed only one time-stamp column, and it consumes eight bytes of storage. A timestamp column is a monotonically increasing counter whose values are guaranteed to always be unique within a database. It has nothing to do with

TABLE 7.1 Continued

Data Type	Description
	the datetime data type or the actual time on your computer clock. SQL Server uses the timestamp column to indicate the sequence of activity on that row and to speed up certain operations. Timestamps are incompatible with replication.
sql_variant	The sql_variant data type is new in SQL Server 2000. It is used similarly to the Variant data type in VBA to store data values of different types. The sql_variant data type can store int, binary, and char values, but not text, ntext, image, and timestamp, and it cannot hold object references the way VBA variants can. Like VBA variants, sql_variant is the least-efficient data type and should be used only when no other option seems practical.
uniqueidentifier	A uniqueidentifier data type consists of a 16-byte value that is often represented as a 32-digit hexadecimal number, or *GUID* (globally unique identification number). This is analogous to the Access ReplicationID data type. New values can be generated automatically for uniqueidentifier by specifying the NEWID() function as a default value. A table can have multiple uniqueidentifier columns, and if it does not automatically generate unique values it may contain multiple occurrences of an individual uniqueidentifier value, unless the unique or primary key constraint is also specified. The uniqueidentifier data type has a substantial amount of overhead at 16 bytes of storage, which means that indexes built using uniqueidentifier keys will likely be slower than implementing the indexes using an int column, which occupies only four bytes.

User-Defined Data Types

SQL Server allows you to "roll your own" data types when you want to fine-tune restrictions on data that can be entered into a column. A user-defined data type lets you store the data type, length, and nullability of a column definition. Using user-defined data types helps you maintain consistency across a database where multiple columns having the same characteristics may be defined in different tables.

For example, to ensure that all local phone numbers are entered consistently, you can define a data type named LocalPhone. To do this, right-click the User Defined Data Types folder in the database and select New User Defined Data Type. This will allow you to specify the properties of the new data type, as shown in Figure 7.6. The example specifies a base data type of varchar with a maximum length of 7, and it does not allow null values.

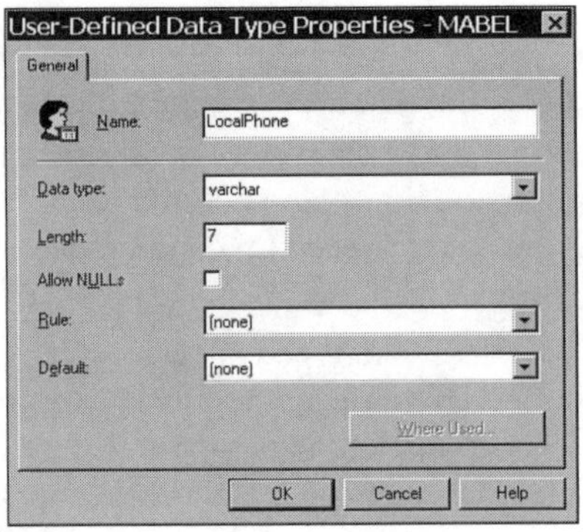

FIGURE 7.6
Creating a user-defined data type.

Once you've created and saved your user-defined data type, it will show up at the end of the list of system data, as shown in Figure 7.7. You won't be able to delete a user-defined data type as long as any table in the database is using it.

TIP

User-defined data types added to the model database will be automatically added to all new databases.

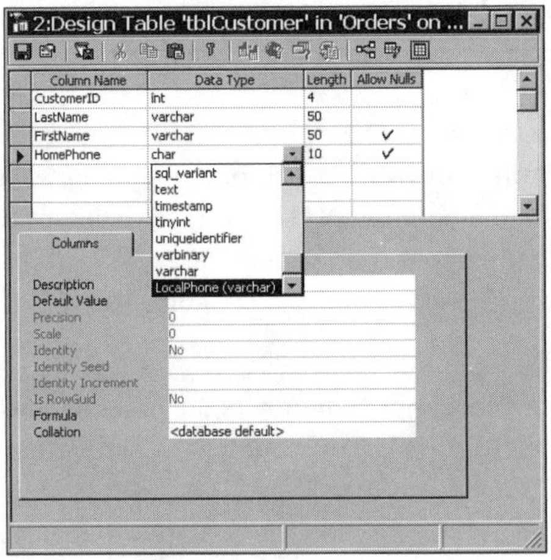

FIGURE 7.7
Selecting a user-defined data type.

Designing and Creating a SQL Server Database

CHAPTER 7

297

7

DESIGNING AND
CREATING A SQL
SERVER DATABASE

Another way of creating a user-defined data type is through using the system stored procedure `sp_addtype`. The following statements will add the LocalPhone user-defined data type to the Orders database:

```
USE Orders
EXEC sp_addtype LocalPhone, 'VARCHAR(7)', 'NOT NULL'
```

Setting Other Column Restrictions

Besides specifying a data type, you can also restrict values entered into a column by setting various constraints.

Constraints

You can restrict the data entered in columns by setting restrictions, or *constraints*, on the types of values allowed. Restrictions can be placed on columns as part of creating tables, or they can be added later. There are five types of constraints you can set on columns, as shown in Table 7.2.

TABLE 7.2   Setting Column Constraints

Constraint	Meaning
Primary key	This constraint is set on a column (or set of columns) to uniquely identify a row in a table. A table can have only one primary key.
Foreign key	This constraint is set on a column (or set of columns) participating in a relationship between tables and referencing only primary key or unique constraints in the related table. Tables can have multiple foreign keys, corresponding to relationships with up to 63 other tables in the same database. Foreign key constraints can also reference the primary key in the same table.
Not null	null (or unknown) values are not allowed. This is equivalent to making the field required.
Default	Default constraints provide default values and can contain constants, functions, ANSI-standard niladic functions (*niladic* is a fancy word for functions that don't take parameters), or null. You can't refer to other columns, tables, views, or stored procedures, and you can't create default constraints on identity or timestamp columns.
Check	This constraint limits the range values that can be entered in a column based on a Boolean expression. If the expression return a True value or a null, the entry is accepted. Multiple check constraints can be entered for a column, and they are evaluated in the order they were entered. You can also create check constraints that refer to multiple columns.
Unique	This constraint requires that each entry in a column (or combination of columns) be unique. A table can have up to 249 unique constraints defined.

You'll soon learn how to use each of these, but first, a word about nulls.

To Null or Not to Null

Several complex issues in SQL Server are related to whether you should allow null values in a column. Here's a brief synopsis of the main concerns:

- *Server issues.* When you allow null values, SQL Server keeps a special bitmap in every row to indicate which nullable columns actually contain null values. SQL Server must then decode this bitmap for each row accessed, which adds additional overhead to data operations.

- *Application logic issues.* Allowing null values in columns introduces three-state logic into your application. In other words, a comparison can evaluate to one of three conditions: true, false, or unknown. Because null is considered to be unknown, two null values are not considered to be equal. The ANSI SQL-92 standard does not support the WHERE *colname* = NULL clause, although earlier versions of SQL Server do. The ANSI_NULLS option controls both database default nullability and comparisons against null values. If ANSI_NULLS is turned on, you must use the IS NULL operator when testing for null values. There's a Transact-SQL extension that allows you to use the WHERE *colname* = NULL clause, but it's dependent on turning off ANSI_NULLS. Because both the ODBC driver and the OLE DB provider can, and do, set these options on, using the equality operator when testing for null values is not guaranteed to work.

- *Untangling various null options.* Whether or not you can use the = NULL syntax depends on the ANSI_NULLS and ANSI_DEFAULTS options being turned off and the database ANSI NULLS option set to False. However, SQL Server 7.0 introduced new options in order to become ANSI SQL-92 compliant and kept the old ones around for backward compatibility. You can enable all ANSI SQL-92 options as a group by setting SET ANSI_DEFAULTS ON, but you can't prevent different connections from setting null options for that connection. The safest course of action is to use IS NULL whenever you're testing for a null value, because this will always work.

SQL Server developers have come up with various strategies for working around the problem of null values in columns. In many cases, simply not allowing null values and providing a default value for a column is a good solution. If the value is contained in a lookup table, often a dummy row with a value such as <None> can serve. However, there are cases in which allowing a null value is the best solution—for example, in a date/time column, where it is often logically impossible to specify a meaningful default value. Keeping null s to a minimum will simplify your application logic.

Creating Default Constraints

A default constraint provides for a value to be automatically entered into a table when no data is explicitly entered. You can define one default constraint per column.

For example, an Orders table might have a default constraint for the order date, where the computer's date and time is inserted into the column if a data entry operator does not specifically enter an order date. Figure 7.8 shows setting a default value using the built-in system function GETDATE(). This will automatically insert the current date and time in the OrderDate column.

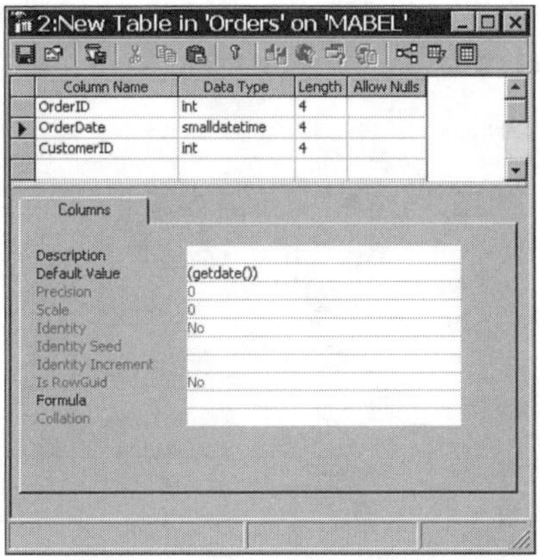

FIGURE 7.8

Creating a default constraint.

The value supplied for a default constraint can be a constant, a function, null, or a niladic function. Niladic functions are functions such as GETDATE() that are supplied by SQL Server and do not take arguments. You can't implement a default constraint on a column that's defined with a user-defined data type that itself has a default constraint already defined.

Creating Check Constraints

A *check constraint* checks the data before the record is saved. If the incoming data does not conform to the constraint, the record won't be saved. Check constraints are similar to validation rules in Access, although they don't allow you to specify an error message the way the validation text property in Access does (that's why the Access Upsizing Wizard translates validation rules into triggers, not check constraints). They are useful for setting limits on acceptable data to enforce domain integrity as well as for enforcing more complex user-defined integrity rules. The expression used in a check constraint must return a Boolean value. If the return value is False, the constraint has been violated and the command that caused the violation will be terminated. If the expression contains null values, it could return a null value, which is not treated as a violation of the rule.

To create a check constraint, right-click in the table designer and choose Constraints. Click New and type in the expression for your constraint. You don't have to live with the default name suggested; you can change it once you've typed in the expression. Figure 7.9 shows creation of a check constraint named DiscountPercent, which will prevent a discount rate of less than zero or greater than 20. This implements a business rule that says that the maximum discount allowed to any customer cannot exceed 20. When you close the Properties dialog box and save the table, this constraint will be enabled, and any values that do not fall in that range will not be allowed. The check boxes at the bottom of the dialog box allow you to specify whether the constraint should retroactively be applied to existing data, whether it should be applied to new data inserts and updates, and whether it should be applied if the table is replicated.

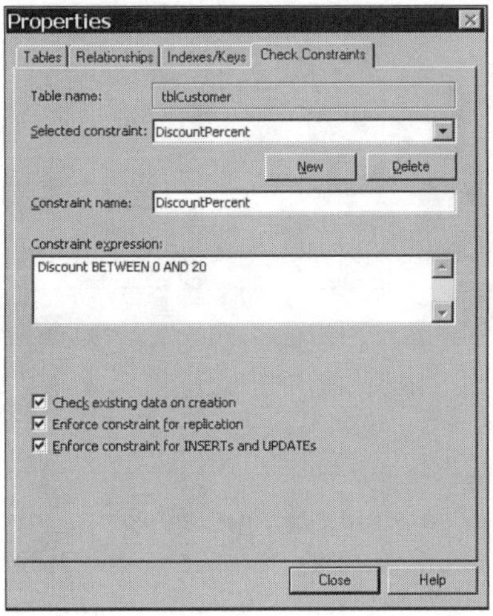

FIGURE 7.9

Creating a check constraint.

You can also use check constraints to serve a similar purpose to input masks in Access. For example, suppose the CustCode column is defined as varchar(5) and requires input consisting of two letters followed by three numbers. To ensure that all data is entered correctly, create a check constraint using the following expression:

```
CustCode LIKE '[a-z][a-z][0-9][0-9][0-9]'
```

Users would be able to enter bb100, but not 100bb.

NOTE

Access makes a distinction between field-level validation rules and table-level validation rules, allowing only one field-level rule per column and one table-level rule per table. SQL Server, on the other hand, does not really make this distinction. All check constraints are at the table level and can refer to multiple columns in the table. For example, you could create a constraint for the Orders table in the Northwind database based on the expression ([RequiredDate] > [OrderDate]), and then you could create a second constraint that enforced the rule ([ShippedDate] > [OrderDate]).

SQL Server constraints don't allow you to reference columns in other tables, but perhaps someday it will. The SQL-92 standard for check constraints actually allows for constraints that span tables. For now, any constraints that involve columns in multiple tables need to be enforced using triggers or by limiting updates to stored procedures.

Creating Unique Constraints

A unique constraint guarantees that all values in a given column or combination of columns will be unique. To create a unique constraint on a column, choose the Indexes/Keys tab of the Properties dialog box in the table designer. Figure 7.10 displays the Indexes/Keys dialog box, where a unique constraint has been created on the first name and last name columns in the customers table. Creating a unique constraint based on two columns will prevent duplicate names from being entered. For example, you won't be allowed to have two employees named Joe Smith. However, you will be able to enter a Joe Jones or a Sam Smith with no problems.

Creating a unique constraint also automatically creates a corresponding unique index. SQL Server indexes are discussed later in this chapter.

Unlike primary keys, unique constraints can be placed on columns that allow null values. However, only one row can have a null value in that column. Multiple null values are considered to be duplicates.

Foreign key constraints do not have to point to primary keys in SQL Server—they can also point to non–primary key columns that have unique constraints.

TIP

If you use an identity column in a table and you don't designate it as the primary key, SQL Server will allow you to insert duplicate values into the column. Create a unique constraint or designate the identity column as a primary key if you need identity column values to be unique in a table.

7

DESIGNING AND CREATING A SQL SERVER DATABASE

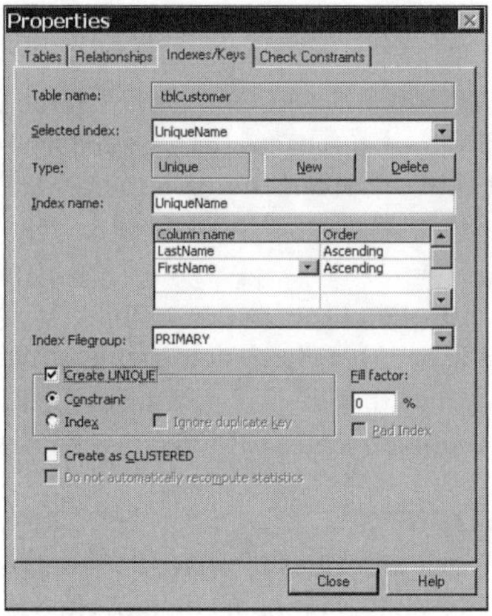

Figure 7.10

Creating a unique constraint.

Creating Reusable Rules

If you have the same constraints that you use over and over again for different columns in different tables, you could create a rule. The advantage of using a rule is that you only need to define it once and then can bind it to as many columns in the database as you like. To create a rule, right-click the Rules node and select New Rule. This will load the Rule Properties dialog box. Type a name for the rule and an expression that defines the rule. You won't be able to bind the rule to any columns until after you save it. For example, to create a rule that limits a percent to values between 0 and 100, name it "PercentRange" and type the following expression:

```
@percent BETWEEN 0 AND 100
```

The variable, @percent, represents the column name, which can vary because you bind rules to many different columns. Once you've saved the rule, you can then bind it to columns by right-clicking the rule and choosing Properties. Select the tables and add the columns you want to apply the rule to, as shown in Figure 7.11.

Once you've bound the rule to a column, you won't be able to delete the rule unless you unbind it from any columns that use it. If you ever need to view the tables and columns that are dependent on the rule, right-click the rule and choose All Tasks, Display Dependencies. This will bring up the dialog box shown in Figure 7.12.

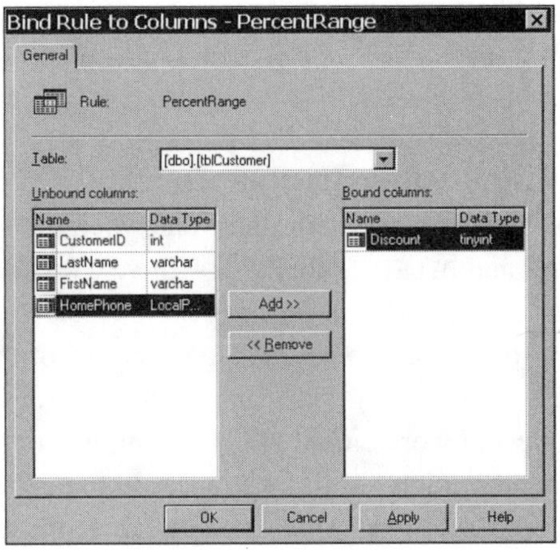

FIGURE 7.11
Binding a rule to a column.

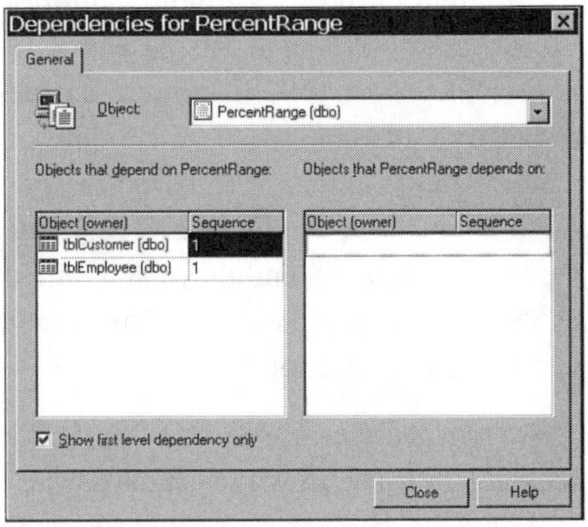

FIGURE 7.12
Displaying dependencies for a rule.

Rules may seem appealing because they can be defined once and then applied to many columns, but rules also have limitations compared to check constraints. You can only apply one rule to a column, whereas you can define multiple check constraints. Rules cannot refer to other multiple columns in a table the way constraints can, and rules cannot call system functions. Using constraints rather than rules is also more consistent with standard SQL practices, because check constraints and not rules are part of the ANSI-92 standard. Books Online describes rules as being present in the product only to provide backward compatibility, and it recommends using constraints instead. But if you find rules more convenient, you can be assured that they will certainly do the job, and they offer similar performance to check constraints.

Enforcing Business Rules with Triggers

You can think of a trigger as an event procedure that runs when data changes. Triggers are fired only on INSERT, UPDATE, and DELETE statements—there's no such thing as a trigger for a SELECT statement. There's also no equivalent for triggers in Access tables because Access only supports event procedures in forms and reports. A trigger is part of the statement or transaction that fires it, and a rollback issued in a trigger cancels the whole transaction. This works the same way the BeforeUpdate event works in an Access form, where setting the Cancel parameter to True causes the data modification not to take place. In the case of a trigger, a ROLLBACK TRANSACTION statement can be conditionally executed to cancel the INSERT, UPDATE, or DELETE operation. As in a form's BeforeUpdate procedure, you can also use triggers to modify other values in the database.

When to Use Triggers

Triggers can be used for many different purposes, including enforcing business rules, updating aggregate fields, enforcing referential integrity, and raising alerts. Generally speaking, you'll want to use constraints or rules whenever possible to enforce business rules. Triggers tend to slow down data modifications because they add more processing to a transaction. However, constraints and rules are limited to simple expressions based on the single row being modified (and in the case of rules, based on that single column). Triggers can reference values from other columns, other tables, or other databases, and they can contain more complex logic. There are some business rules that are too complex to be implemented as constraints or rules and for which triggers are the appropriate solution.

As handy as triggers can be, however, there are many SQL Server developers who avoid them at all costs. You'll learn the reasons for this and why you may want to use triggers anyway in the section "The Trouble with Triggers." But before getting too deep into that debate, take a look at what triggers can do.

How Triggers Work

When SQL Server fires a trigger, it copies both the new values and the old values to two virtual tables named "inserted" and "deleted." The inserted table is used for INSERT and UPDATE statements to hold the new values. The deleted table holds deleted rows for a DELETE statement and the old value for an UPDATE statement. Triggers can also reference other objects, working with other tables or joining other tables to the inserted and deleted tables in the trigger Transact-SQL code. For example, if you wanted to create an audit trail that saved deleted records to another table, you could simply insert the values contained in the deleted table into a backup table. Because the trigger fires each time a row is deleted, no further action is necessary. You can perform almost any Transact-SQL operation in a trigger except creating or modifying the design of objects and performing system administration tasks.

Creating Triggers

Triggers tend to be buried pretty deep within a table and can be difficult to find unless you know where to look. To view existing triggers or create a new trigger, right-click a table in the table designer and choose Task, Manage Triggers, or you can click the Triggers toolbar button. This will load the Trigger Properties dialog box, as shown in Figure 7.13. The Name drop-down list box will display all the triggers currently defined in a table. You can type your trigger code directly into the Text window and click the Check Syntax button when you're ready to save it. The Query Analyzer is also a good tool to use for creating triggers, and it will also parse your trigger syntax for you before you save the trigger. You won't be able to save a trigger that has syntax errors.

FIGURE 7.13
Creating triggers in the Enterprise Manager.

Triggers use the following syntax, which is very similar to that for stored procedures:

```
CREATE TRIGGER NameofTrigger
ON NameofTable
FOR [INSERT], [UPDATE], [DELETE]
AS
--Your code here
```

Implementing Business Rules with Triggers

To implement a business rule that prevents most but not all users from either raising or lowering a product's list price, create the trigger shown in Listing 7.1, which runs whenever an order detail item is inserted or updated. First, the IS_MEMBER function is checked—only users mapped to dbo (or sysadmin) are allowed to change prices. If the user isn't a dbo, the inserted table is joined to the Product table to check to see whether the price about to be entered is the same as the list price. If it's not, the transaction is rolled back, and an error is raised. This particular business rule would be impossible to implement as a constraint or a rule because you're not allowed to reference other tables to look up the list price.

LISTING 7.1 Creating a Trigger to Validate Price Changes

```
CREATE TRIGGER trigValidatePrice
ON [Order Details] FOR INSERT, UPDATE
AS
  --Only dbo can adjust prices.
  IF IS_MEMBER ('dbo') = 0
  BEGIN
  /* Join the inserted table with Products to check price.
     If the price isn't the same as the list price, rollback
     the transaction.
  */
    If (SELECT COUNT(*)
      FROM Inserted INNER JOIN Products
      ON Inserted.ProductID = Products.ProductID
      WHERE Inserted.UnitPrice <> Products.UnitPrice) > 0
    BEGIN
      ROLLBACK TRAN
      RAISERROR ('User not allowed to change price',16,1)
      RETURN
    END
  END
```

New Trigger Types in SQL Server 2000

SQL Server 2000 introduces two new types of triggers: INSTEAD OF and AFTER triggers. INSTEAD OF triggers are executed instead of the action that raised the trigger. They can also be used on views. AFTER triggers are executed after any declarative referential actions. AFTER is synonymous with FOR, which has always been available when specifying triggers. AFTER/FOR triggers are only available for tables, not views. An AFTER trigger fires after the INSERT, UPDATE, or DELETE triggering action and after any constraints and referential actions have been processed.

Creating an INSTEAD OF Trigger

An INSTEAD OF trigger fires in place of the triggering action. For example, if you create an INSTEAD OF trigger on a table or view using the following syntax, the INSTEAD OF trigger code will execute instead of an insert to the table:

```
CREATE TRIGGER trigInsertInstead ON MyTable
INSTEAD OF INSERT
AS
--This code will execute instead of data being
--inserted into MyTable
```

An INSTEAD OF trigger is executed after the inserted and deleted tables are created but before any other actions are taken. Unlike AFTER/FOR triggers, they are executed before any constraints are applied. This allows you to perform preprocessing to supplement existing constraints or to implement more complex business rules than a mere constraint would allow.

Unlike AFTER/FOR triggers, INSTEAD OF triggers do not fire recursively. If an INSTEAD OF trigger does something that would normally cause the INSTEAD OF trigger to fire a second time, the second INSTEAD OF trigger is ignored, and any constraints and then AFTER/FOR triggers fire. For example, if you define an INSTEAD OF INSERT trigger that executes an INSERT on the same table, the INSERT statement executed by the trigger will bypass the INSTEAD OF trigger and will process any constraints and AFTER/FOR triggers defined for the table.

INSTEAD OF Triggers and Views

INSTEAD OF triggers defined on views also do not fire recursively. Instead, the statement is resolved as modifications against the base tables underlying the view. An UPDATE executed by an INSTEAD OF trigger is processed against the view as if the view did not have an INSTEAD OF trigger. Any constraints and AFTER/FOR triggers defined on the underlying table will fire. See Chapter 9 for more information on creating views.

Creating an AFTER (or FOR) Trigger

You can use either the AFTER or FOR keywords to create an AFTER trigger:

```
CREATE TRIGGER trigAfterInsert ON MyTable
AFTER INSERT
AS
-- or:
CREATE TRIGGER trigForInsert ON MyTable
FOR INSERT
AS
```

The FOR syntax is compatible with earlier versions of SQL Server. Triggers using the FOR and AFTER syntax behave exactly the same. For each triggering action (UPDATE, DELETE, and INSERT), you can have multiple FOR/AFTER triggers but only one INSTEAD OF trigger. If you have implemented a REFERENCES clause that specifies a CASCADING option (covered later in this chapter), any INSTEAD OF triggers are not fired for any modifications resulting from cascading referential actions. In other words, the referential integrity cascading constraint takes precedence. An AFTER trigger is never executed if any constraint violation occurs.

Specifying AFTER Trigger Firing Order

You can specify that one of the AFTER triggers associated with a table be either the first AFTER trigger or the last AFTER trigger executed for each triggering action. This feature is new in SQL Server 2000. You can't specify the order of any triggers firing in between the first and last trigger specified. Use the sp_settriggerorder stored procedure to set the order to either 'first' or 'last':

```
sp_settriggerorder @triggername = 'trigFirst', @order = 'first'
```

```
sp_settriggerorder @triggername = 'trigLast', @order = 'last'
```

The Trouble with Triggers

In earlier versions of SQL Server, triggers were used to enforce referential integrity. SQL Server 7.0 introduced Declarative Referential Integrity (DRI) with the Database Diagram feature, which will be covered later in this chapter. However, when you implemented DRI in SQL Server 7.0, you couldn't cascade updates or deletes using triggers, because any referential integrity constraint fired before the trigger got a chance to update data. SQL Server 2000 now supports cascading updates and deletes with foreign key constraints, allowing you to have DRI, cascading update and delete actions, plus additional triggers. However, cascading is still an issue in earlier versions of SQL Server, where you can't have both declarative referential integrity and cascading update/delete triggers.

So, in SQL Server 7, the only way to use DRI and still support cascading updates or deletes is to force all updates and deletes to be done using stored procedures. For example, if you want to delete an order that has order details, use a stored procedure that first deletes any order details and then deletes the order.

Because triggers consist of additional Transact-SQL code, they add overhead to data operations and negatively impact performance. In addition, triggers' code is buried deep within a table definition. Other than designating a first and last AFTER trigger, you have no control over the firing of triggers. Complex business rules implemented in stored procedures instead of triggers will improve performance and simplify code maintenance. Stored procedures are covered in detail in Chapter 10, "Programming Effective Stored Procedures."

Since triggers execute code which extends a transaction, they can potentially extend the duration of a transaction for a longer period of time, especially when they access other tables. This performance penalty has the potential to lower multi-user concurrency to unacceptable levels.

Another issue to consider is whether your business rules should even be handled within the database. An alternative is to create middle-tier components that enforce business rules before any instructions are sent to the database. Chapter 14, "Architecting Distributed *n*-Tier Applications," discusses this alternative strategy.

Understanding and Creating Indexes

The only relational constraint that makes use of an index for its implementation in SQL Server is uniqueness. Apart from that, indexes don't really serve the relational integrity of the database. However, index creation is a very important part of defining the columns and tables in your database because of the impact that indexes have on the speed of data retrieval.

How Indexes Work

Like the index in a book, database indexes make it much faster to find data meeting certain criteria or sorted in a certain order. A book index groups all the words starting with a certain letter together, allowing you to drill down and find the words or phrases you are interested in. Database indexes are similar, using a hierarchical structure called a *B-tree* (or *balanced tree*), organized across multiple data pages in the physical storage of the database.

Unlike a book index, a database index can require several hops to get from the most general index entry to the one with the data being sought. Imagine a book so big that it had a multi-level index, where if you wanted to find the word *Access*, you would first look up what page the index of words starting with "A" was on, then what page the index of words starting with "Ac" was on, and so on until you finally found a list of the location or locations of "Access."

The database engine drills down from more general entries on the root pages of the index, to more specific entries on pages at intermediary levels, until the leaf page is located that contains the exact value being sought. What makes the tree balanced is that the database engine is constantly regrouping entries so that the size of the groupings is close to equal. This means that no matter which value the engine is seeking, it will have to hop across roughly the same number of index pages to find it.

SQL Server supports two types of indexes: clustered and nonclustered.

Clustered Indexes

You can think of the page numbers in a book as a clustered index. When you thumb through a book and find a page number, you find with it all the "data" as well (that is, the words on that page). Similarly, when the database engine gets to the leaf node of a clustered index, what it finds is the actual row containing the data it was seeking. In other words, the leaf node pages of a clustered index are in fact the data pages, and the data is physically stored according to the order defined by the clustered index, just as the pages of a book are ordered by page number.

You can only have one clustered index per table, because the data can only be stored in one physical order. Although the primary key is often a good choice for a clustered index, you don't have to use the primary key. In fact, you don't even have to use an index that contains unique values—if necessary, SQL Server will add a four-byte value called a *uniqueifier* to each entry, thus ensuring that it points to one unique row of data.

When SQL Server is able to use a clustered index to satisfy a query, performance is very fast, especially if the query is retrieving a contiguous set of values.

It is generally a good idea to add a clustered index to each of your tables if the speed of data retrieval is important to you. If you are uncertain which column to use, the primary key is usually a safe choice. Here are some additional guidelines:

- Choose columns with a high percentage of unique values.
- Choose columns that are frequently used in joins.
- Avoid columns that get edited often.
- Favor columns used in queries that return a range of values using BETWEEN or any of the comparison operators.
- Avoid large character-based columns. With numeric columns, favor integers over floating-point numbers. The larger the values are in your index, the more page hops will be required to get to the leaf nodes.

Nonclustered Indexes

A *nonclustered index* is much like the alphabetical index found in the back of a book. You look up a word and find one or more page numbers that take you to the data. If a clustered index, like the book page numbers in the analogy, exists for a table, when the database engine gets to the leaf nodes of any nonclustered index on that table, what it finds is the value of the corresponding key in the clustered index, like the page numbers in a book index. The database engine then goes through the clustered index to its leaf node to find the actual row containing the data it was seeking.

Because nonclustered indexes aren't directly related to the order of the physical data storage, you can have many different nonclustered indexes for each table. SQL Server allows up to 249 nonclustered indexes per table.

Because the leaf nodes of nonclustered indexes will contain key values from the clustered index (if there is one), always create your clustered index before creating nonclustered indexes if there is already data in the table. If there is no clustered index defined, SQL Server will use its own internal pointer to the data and then substitute the clustered index value later if one is created. If you create an index and don't specify whether it is clustered or nonclustered, it will default to nonclustered.

You can create covering indexes consisting of two or more columns, up to a maximum of 16 columns, for a combined size of 900 bytes. These are effective when you use more than one column as a unit in a query, but indexes that contain combinations resulting in large values may not be efficient enough to get used much.

Consider the following additional guidelines when creating nonclustered indexes:

- Pick columns that contain a high number of distinct values.
- Pick columns that are used in joins.
- Pick columns used in ORDER BY, GROUP BY, or WHERE clauses that return few duplicates.
- Don't use nonclustered indexes for range selections that are different from the physical data order, unless the range reflects a small percentage of the values in the table.

When to Create an Index

Although indexes can speed up data retrieval, they will also slow down data manipulation, because every change that affects an indexed column must also cause that index to be altered. So, unless you have a read-only database, you should exercise some restraint when deciding which columns to index.

Just because you create an index doesn't mean it will be used. SQL Server uses statistical sampling and sophisticated optimization algorithms to decide which indexes to use and when. However, even unused indexes will be updated, so be judicious about creating them, and test whether they are giving you the performance benefits you hoped for.

Consider creating indexes on columns that are used in WHERE, ORDER BY, and GROUP BY clauses as well as any columns used in joins. Indexes are effective on columns with a high degree of selectivity, meaning that only a few rows would be returned that meet the criteria. For example, a column that stores "M" for male and "F" for female would not be a good candidate for an index because there are only two possible values, reflecting a low degree of selectivity. The time it would take to use the index wouldn't help narrow the search enough to be worthwhile. This would be like using a book index to find the word *the*—it would take longer than just looking at every page. However, an index on OrderDate in the Orders table makes sense if you're looking up orders by date or sorting by order date.

If you're not sure which columns you need to index when you create your tables, you can wait until you're further along in the development cycle and have loaded some data. The Index Tuning Wizard in the Query Analyzer will assist you in making the right choices based on the distribution of values in your tables. Using the Query Analyzer to tune queries is covered in Chapter 9, and the Index Tuning Wizard is covered in Chapter 15.

Creating an Index

To create an index in the table designer, right-click and choose Indexes/Keys from the list. Click the New button and fill in the columns and name for the new index. Figure 7.14 shows creating a nonclustered index on the order date for the orders table.

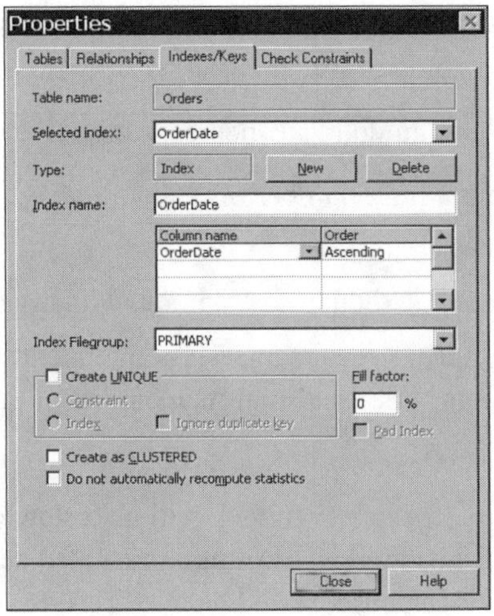

FIGURE 7.14
Creating a nonclustered index.

Setting Index Options

When you're creating an index, setting its properties determines how it behaves. Here's a rundown of the properties and the impact each one has on the index:

- *Create UNIQUE.* Unique indexes are extremely efficient and SQL Server will generally favor them over nonunique indexes given a choice. So, if you have a column that you know will always contain unique data, check the Create UNIQUE checkbox when creating the index. Unique constraints are discussed earlier in this chapter in the section on constraints. When you create a unique constraint, a unique index is always created to support it. Nulls are allowed in columns with unique indexes, but as with any other value, only one null value is allowed.

- *Ignore duplicate key.* The Ignore Duplicate Key check box for unique indexes allows you to specify that if multiple rows are inserted into the table and some are duplicates, only the duplicates will be rejected. Otherwise, all the rows, including those with acceptably unique values, would be rejected if any were duplicates.

- *Fill factor.* The Fill Factor option determines how densely the index is packed when it is created. If the table is going to have many updates and inserts, create an index with a low fill factor to leave room for the future keys to be inserted. However, if the table is read-only or will otherwise not change much, a high fill factor will reduce the physical size of the index, thus lowering the number of disk reads needed. The fill factor only applies when you create the index—indexes stabilize at a certain density over time as keys are inserted and deleted. The Fill Factor option also only applies if there is already data in the table. If the table is empty at the time you create the index, you can ignore this setting.

- *Create as CLUSTERED*. Clustered indexes are discussed earlier in this chapter. Only one index per table can be clustered, and generally it should be a unique index.

- *Don't automatically recompute statistics*. SQL Server automatically recomputes statistics on a table when its optimization algorithms conclude that enough changes have occurred to justify the work. You can override this by checking the Don't Automatically Recompute Statistics check box, which is rarely a good idea unless you plan to create the statistics yourself as needed. You can create statistics manually using Transact-SQL (see CREATE STATISTICS in Books Online) or by right-clicking and choosing Create Missing Statistics in the Execution Plan view in Query Analyzer.

Setting Relationships Between Tables

Declarative Referential Integrity, or *DRI*, is implemented in SQL Server using constraints on the tables involved in the referential relationship. Here are the two constraints used:

- *Primary key*. A table can only have one primary key constraint. SQL Server automatically creates a unique index on the primary key and defaults that index to being clustered unless another clustered index already exists.

- *Foreign key*. A table can have multiple foreign key constraints. Unlike Access, SQL Server does not automatically create indexes for foreign keys.

7

DESIGNING AND
CREATING A SQL
SERVER DATABASE

NOTE

In SQL Server, all columns that define the primary key must be defined as NOT NULL. Access does not have this restriction—primary key fields are not marked Required even though in fact they are required; therefore, you'll need to modify any tables you upsize. Null values are allowed in foreign keys in both Access and SQL Server. Foreign keys can only reference tables in the same database.

You can define primary and foreign keys in the table designer by opening the Properties dialog box and clicking the Relationships tab. However, the Database Diagram designer not only allows you to create relationships, it also provides a graphical user environment that gives you a bird's-eye view of all the relationships in your database at once. Diagrams also allow you to drill down to the detail level to create new tables and modify the design of existing tables and columns. You'll find SQL Server diagrams much more useful than the familiar Access Relationships window.

Database diagrams are a part of the Microsoft Visual Data Tools. These tools are also hosted by both Microsoft Visual Studio and Microsoft Office 2000, and they're readily available in an Access project (ADP).

Creating a Database Diagram

To create a database diagram, right-click the Diagrams node in the Enterprise Manager and choose New Database Diagram. This will load the Create Database Diagram Wizard. The wizard always runs when you create a new database diagram, but you can edit an existing database diagram by double-clicking it in the Diagrams node without the wizard being launched. The introductory dialog box tells you what the Database Diagram Wizard does—that it creates the diagram as well as adds tables and rearranges them on the diagram. The next wizard pane displays a list of the tables in the database and lets you add them to the diagram by clicking the Add button, as shown in Figure 7.15. Because you can have multiple database diagrams in the same database, you only need to select closely related tables to add to the diagram. Additional diagrams can be created for different groups of tables.

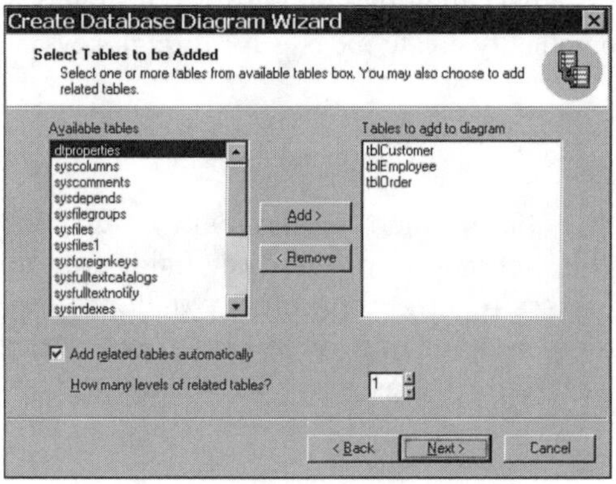

FIGURE 7.15

Adding tables to the database diagram.

The final wizard dialog box has a Finish button and will create the database diagram and arrange the tables for you. Note that there are no menu commands—all actions in the database diagram are performed from the toolbar, from the right-click menu, or by dragging and dropping columns from one table to the other. Figure 7.16 shows the database diagram created by the wizard, with the right-click menu for the database diagram activated.

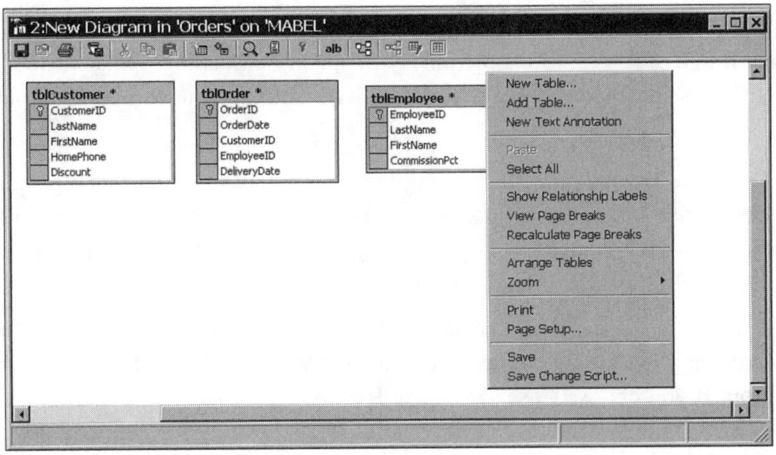

FIGURE 7.16
The database diagram after the wizard has added the tables and before any relationships have been created.

Creating Relationships Using a Database Diagram

To create a relationship using a database diagram, select the primary key column on the one side of the relationship and drag it to the related table and drop it. This will display the Create Relationship dialog box, as shown in Figure 7.17. You can name the relationship and specify its properties. Click OK when finished.

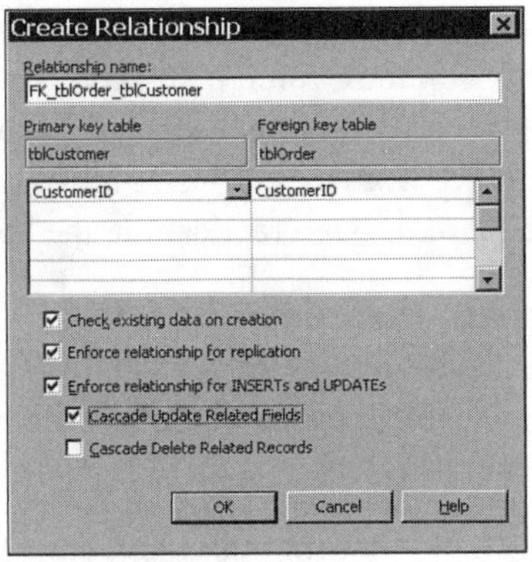

FIGURE 7.17
Creating a relationship between the Customers table and the Orders table.

Cascading Updates and Deletes

A new feature in SQL Server 2000 is the ability to specify cascading updates and cascading deletes, which Access has had all along. There are two options you can set to implement cascading:

- *Cascade update related fields.* Checking this option will cause changed primary key values to be cascaded to the corresponding foreign key fields in related tables. For example, if your CustomerID changes in the Customer table, the CustomerID foreign key in the Orders table will be automatically updated to reflect the new value.

- *Cascade delete related fields.* Checking this option will cause deletion of records on the one side of the join to delete related records on the many side. Be careful when choosing this option. If you choose Cascade Delete Related Records when creating the relationship between the Customers and the Orders tables and a customer is deleted, then all the orders for that customer will also be deleted. This could cause you to lose your history should a customer be inadvertently or maliciously deleted from the database. If you do not choose the Cascade Delete option, a customer cannot be deleted who has outstanding orders. The attempted deletion will fail, and neither the customer nor the orders will be deleted. On the other hand, setting cascade deletes between the Orders and the Order Details tables makes sense—when an order is deleted, all related order details are automatically deleted. It would be painful for users of your database to have to delete each order detail's item before deleting the order itself.

Integrity and Replication

If you are implementing replication, SQL Server allows you to use the option NOT FOR REPLICATION in identity columns, foreign key constraints, and check constraints. NOT FOR REPLICATION enforces the constraint on users but not on data changes that result from the replication process. In other words, the constraint won't let users violate it, but if a row is inserted from another database through replication, the constraint won't be applied.

Modifying Tables in a Database Diagram

The default view displayed in a database diagram is Column Names. However, other view options are available for a selected table by right-clicking a table and choosing Table View and following the arrow, as shown in Figure 7.18.

If you choose Standard from the Table View options, certain table properties will be displayed, as shown in Figure 7.19. You can modify any of the properties displayed. When you save the diagram, any changes you've made to the tables are also saved.

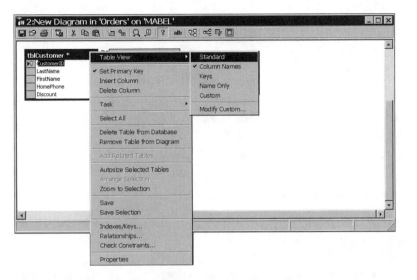

FIGURE 7.18

The options for displaying tables in a database diagram.

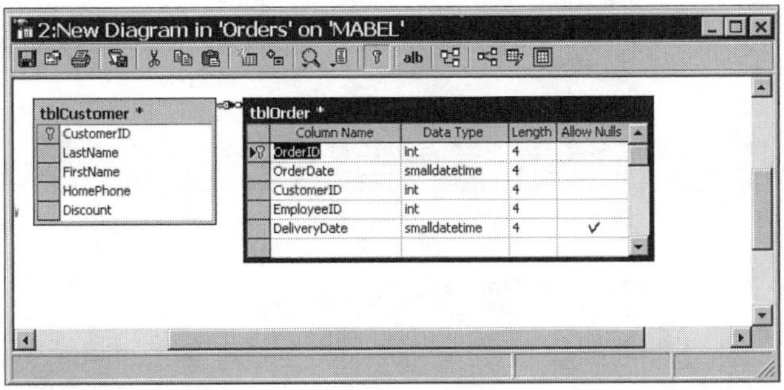

FIGURE 7.19

Standard view lets you modify table properties and add new columns.

However, not all column properties are displayed in the standard view. You can choose to create a custom view of the table, as shown in Figure 7.20. The columns listed in the Selected Columns list will be displayed. Only columns that are displayed in the database diagram can be modified.

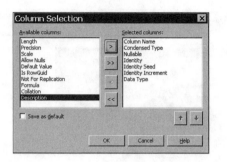

FIGURE 7.20
Defining your own custom view in a database diagram.

When you display the custom view, you can then edit any of the properties defined in the view, as shown in Figure 7.21.

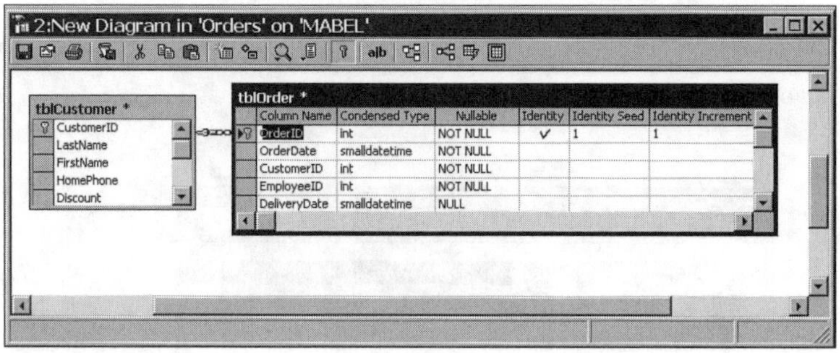

FIGURE 7.21
Custom views allow you to edit the properties displayed.

All the options available in the table designer are also available in the database diagram. You can create, modify, and delete tables from the database, and you can modify table and column properties. You can also modify constraints and indexes by choosing any of the options on the right-click menu, as shown previously in Figure 7.18. The database diagram provides true one-stop shopping when it comes to defining your tables, not just a way to work with relationships.

Summary

A solid database design is essential to the success of your SQL Server database application. Taking time at the outset to properly design and specify your database will save you countless hours during the implementation phase. A well-designed database is amenable to change and can be modified easily to conform to new requirements. The Enterprise Manager provides a robust and easy-to-use graphical user interface for creating your tables and defining columns. Database diagrams allow you to build relationships between your tables and to work with table and column properties.

Introduction to Transact-SQL (T-SQL)

IN THIS CHAPTER

Defining Transact-SQL

Entire books have been written about Transact-SQL (T-SQL), and nothing close to a definitive treatment is attempted here. This chapter reviews the history of Transact-SQL and explains the major areas of Transact-SQL syntax. It also points out some of the important differences between Transact-SQL and the Access SQL dialect that you may have already come to know well. Much of Transact-SQL will be familiar to you if you're already familiar with Access SQL, especially when it comes to basic querying syntax. Just as learning VBA opens up whole vistas of possibilities that are beyond the reach of Access macros, Transact-SQL allows you to solve problems that Access SQL alone could never handle. You'll learn how to convert your Access query expressions to their Transact-SQL equivalents. Chapter 10, "Programming Effective Stored Procedures," explains how to assemble the building blocks presented here into useful stored procedures. Chapter 11, "Scaling Up with Unbound Access Applications," and Chapter 12, "Building Access Reports from SQL Server Data," both show some advanced Transact-SQL techniques.

A Brief History of the SQL Standard

Transact-SQL is an implementation of a well-defined standard called SQL-92, which was codified by a committee of the American National Standards Institute (ANSI) and was also adopted by the International Organization for Standardization (ISO). No vendor has fully implemented every part of the ANSI/ISO standard, and each vendor has added its own proprietary extensions to the language. But Transact-SQL is as good as any at following the recommendations contained in SQL-92.

The drive to develop an easy but effective structured query language began soon after Dr. E. F. Codd first presented his Relational Database Model, which itself contained no specific query language syntax. The pioneering work was done at IBM's Santa Teresa Research Laboratory in San Jose, California, where a major research project on relational database development, called System/R, was undertaken in the early 1970s. In 1974, the first formal query language developed by this team was presented. It was called Structured English Query Language and became known as SEQUEL. The first actual database system to implement the language was called SEQUEL-XRM. The language was completely rewritten between 1976 and 1977, and although the new version was at first called SEQUEL/2, the name was eventually shortened to just SQL because it turned out that the acronym SEQUEL had already been patented. The original "sequel" pronunciation has stuck to this day—SQL Server is still widely referred to as *sequel server*, although some purists insist that the language name should now properly be pronounced *ess-que-ell*.

Many experts agree that the true origins of the modern SQL language are not actually to be found in the IBM SEQUEL language at all, despite the success of that name, but rather in a language called SQUARE (Specifying Queries as Relational Expressions), which was presented in CACM (*Communications of the Association for Computing Machinery*) in 1975, in a paper authored by Boyce, R. F Chamberlin, D. D. King, and W. F. III.

It wasn't long before other companies, in addition to IBM, realized the power of this nascent technology and began developing their own relational database products. One of the first was a company aptly named Relational Software, Inc., formed in Menlo Park, California by a group of engineers. It was formed in 1977, and in 1979 it shipped the first commercial relational database system, which ran on the Digital VAX minicomputer platform, rather than on expensive IBM mainframes. This company continues to this day to be the dominant figure in the relational database market, although it changed its name to match the name of that first product—Oracle.

Another pioneering relational database was INGRES, developed by a group of Berkeley professors who formed Relational Technology, Inc., and released their first product in 1981. That product has also survived and is now owned by Computer Associates International, Inc. IBM came out with its first commercial relational database in 1982, called SQL/Data System (SQL/DS). Soon thereafter IBM announced a new database product, called DB2, which it finally shipped in 1985. DB2 has continued to evolve, and it has been adapted to run on IBM's full line of computer platforms, rather than just on the mainframes for which it was first developed.

Amid all the excitement about this promising new technology, the application developers, IT managers, and the database vendors themselves, realized that a common standard language would help ensure their success. This was not very different from the recent efforts to standardize the HTML language, which occurred as the importance of the Internet became apparent. The task was assigned to an ANSI technical committee, called X3H2, in 1982. The committee labored for several years to come up with an adequately complete and consistent recommendation, while still attempting to keep it as compatible as possible with what was being used out in the real world. Finally, in 1986, ANSI ratified a specification formally called ANSI X3.135-1986 Database Language SQL, which become commonly known as SQL/86. The ISO soon thereafter endorsed SQL/86 as an international standard.

As could be expected, after the SQL/86 standard was published, it was widely criticized. The criticisms focused on confusing redundancies in the language—in an effort to avoid incompatibilities, SQL/86 supported multiple ways of accomplishing certain tasks—and on the lack of support for declaring referential integrity. A revised version that came to be known as SQL-89 and that addressed many of these concerns was eventually endorsed, first by the ISO this time and then by ANSI. The most notable change was the addition of support for referential integrity. Without concurrence from the ISO, ANSI also released a version geared toward embedding SQL within programming languages.

There were still several important holes in the language, mostly in areas where the dominant vendors had gone off in wildly different directions and couldn't agree on a standard. The most important of these was the inability within pure SQL-89 to alter the structure of database objects once they had been created. This need for syntax to alter objects, plus the need for standard ways to manipulate strings and dates, as well as a desire to add support for security operations were all driving factors in the development of the next standard, SQL-92, which addressed them all. SQL-92, which was endorsed by both ANSI and ISO, was relatively well received and remains the most widely supported standard to this day.

Unlike the previous SQL specifications, SQL-92 included three levels of conformance: Entry, Intermediate, and Full. Almost all current SQL dialects conform to the Entry level; most conform to Intermediate; and not one comes very close to Full conformance.

Because SQL-92, especially the Intermediate level, was so widely accepted, progress toward a new standard slowed markedly. The ANSI H3 committee was renamed as the National Committee for Information Technology Standards (NCITS), and it is the same committee that's also responsible for the MPEG/JPEG, SCSII, and C++ standards.

The latest ANSI/ISO SQL standard, called SQL3, contains many separate parts. The additions to SQL-92 are mostly related to support for objects and object-relational database systems. In fact, one of the parts is related strictly to using SQL within the Java language.

As with other computer languages and protocols that are implemented by multiple vendors, SQL has been tossed and turned by the shifting winds of various competing interests. However, a quite extensive set of core features has by now become well accepted and is supported by almost all vendors of relational database systems. It is really quite amazing that a technology that has so thoroughly permeated and so profoundly influenced modern society is really only about 25 years old. Relational theory and the database technologies that implemented it—including SQL—comprise a great, largely unsung, scientific and technological marvel of the late twentieth century. Every time you make a purchase on the Internet, check out your groceries at a supermarket, pay a speeding ticket, purchase shares of stock, or write a check, you are indirectly running SQL queries.

For a more complete and very accessible account of the history of SQL, plus a great introduction to the basics of the language itself, see *SQL Queries for Mere Mortals—A Hands-on Guide to Data Manipulation in SQL*, by Michael J. Hernandez and John Viescas, published by Addison Wesley Longman.

The Evolution of SQL Server

Transact-SQL (T-SQL) is a query language that was first developed by Sybase, Inc., the original developer of SQL Server. Back in 1987, Sybase was a startup company with a promising new relational database management system, named DataServer, designed to run under the

UNIX and VMS operating systems. In an era when the database world was still dominated by software built for mainframes that were accessed over dumb terminals, Sybase was part of an emerging trend toward distributed client/server systems that used powerful workstations to do some of the application processing. DataServer also supported innovative features such as triggers and stored procedures, and its query language, called Transact SQL, contained significant extensions to the SQL standard.

Microsoft procured an exclusive license from Sybase to distribute versions of DataServer that would run on OS/2, the network operating system that Microsoft was still developing with IBM, and on any other Microsoft operating systems. Sybase retained control over all the development work, and, in addition to royalties on copies sold by Microsoft, it expected that by keeping its UNIX and VMS products compatible with the PC version, it would pick up customers who outgrew the capabilities of PC systems.

Microsoft had no database products of its own at that time. The dominant force in PC file-server databases was dBASE, from Ashton-Tate. Microsoft made a deal with Ashton-Tate to cooperate on marketing and distribution, and Ashton-Tate planned to support the new product, called Ashton-Tate/Microsoft SQL Server, as a back end for future client/server versions of dBASE.

Version 1.0 of Ashton-Tate/Microsoft SQL Server shipped in May of 1989. However, the OS/2 platform wasn't catching on as hoped, and Ashton-Tate's client/server version of dBASE hadn't materialized, so sales were slow. The relationship between Microsoft and Ashton-Tate ended, and version 1.1 shipped during the summer of 1990 as simply *Microsoft SQL Server*. Few new features had been added, but one important capability of the new version was its support for applications running under Microsoft's newest operating system: Windows 3.0. As new Windows applications started to take advantage of SQL Server's support for Windows dynamic link libraries (DLLs), the product started to attract interest.

Sybase still controlled all the source code, although Microsoft managed to get read-only access to it for support purposes in 1991. A core group of Microsoft engineers began getting familiar with the internals of the product, and they were eventually able to program their own bug fixes and submit them to Sybase for final approval.

In May 1991, Microsoft's development agreement with IBM for mutual work on OS/2 ended, and Microsoft began devoting almost all its resources to the Windows operating system and software to run on it. Although Microsoft SQL Server supported Windows APIs, it still ran on OS/2 only, as did the next version, released in March 1992, which was called version 4.2 to coordinate with Sybase's version numbering. Microsoft was much more involved in the development of this version, and it turned out to be the last version of SQL Server that Sybase and Microsoft worked on together.

8

INTRODUCTION TO
TRANSACT-SQL
(T-SQL)

The SQL Server team at Microsoft then made the brave decision to shift the bulk of its resources toward work on a version that would run under Microsoft's new network operating system, Windows NT, which at that time was still under development and had exactly zero users. Maintenance work continued on the OS/2 version, and those customers weren't abandoned, but the future was clearly with NT, and most customers eventually supported the shift.

The new emphasis on NT did, however, cause a rift between Microsoft and Sybase. NT was seen as eventually becoming more competitive with Sybase's core UNIX market, and the development work required to support NT fully was not as important to Sybase as it was to Microsoft.

Instead of working together on Sybase's next version, called System 10, the companies agreed that Microsoft's engineers would focus on porting the current version, 4.2, to Windows NT. The SQL Server group at Microsoft worked very hard at this and managed to take advantage of many of the valuable new core features in NT. Without damaging compatibility by reworking the core database engine, the SQL Server group made significant changes to the networking kernel in SQL Server and also built in support for much greater extensibility through dynamic linking to Windows DLLs. SQL Server was redesigned to run as an NT service, with full support for NT's event model and with its performance statistics integrated into NT's performance monitor. A lot of work was also done to make it easy to migrate from the old OS/2 version.

The first beta of SQL Server for Windows NT shipped in October 1992, and it was extremely well received. The integration between the database engine and the operating system was impressive, and performance was much improved over the OS/2 version, despite no changes at all to the core query engine. Sales were ahead of projections, and customers were migrating from OS/2 to NT in droves. By late 1993, it was clear that there was little reason to continue with the plans to port Sybase's System 10 to OS/2.

Sybase had already begun work on a version of System 10 for Windows NT, but it wasn't nearly as tightly integrated with the operating system as Microsoft's version 4.2 implementation had been, because Sybase had to maintain portability among the various operating systems it was supporting. In the meantime, the SQL Server team at Microsoft had grown to include a technical staff of more than 50 people, in addition to the marketing and support personnel, and they wanted to build their own next version.

In April 1994, the companies agreed to sever their relationship and to follow their own divergent paths with the product. Microsoft gave up its exclusive right to distribute versions that ran on its operating systems and essentially became a competitor to Sybase rather than a partner. Microsoft continued, however, to support Sybase's effort to port System 10 to NT, as a way of promoting the viability of NT as a database platform.

Sybase has continued to grow and to innovate since then, and its latest version of SQL Server is now called Adaptive Server. Microsoft, of course, has also added significant enhancements to the product. SQL Server versions 6.0 and 6.5 were built on the core engine that Microsoft inherited from Sybase.

While work was going on in versions 6.0 and 6.5, however, Microsoft reached into its deepening pockets and hired several of the top database scientists in the world to work on a completely new database engine. The intention was that it would integrate well with Microsoft's new OLE DB database technologies (discussed in Chapter 6) and that it would scale significantly beyond the performance range supported by older versions of SQL Server. Originally code-named Sphinx, this completely rewritten product was released in 1998 as SQL Server 7.0. With version 7.0 and then the release of SQL Server 2000, Microsoft has admirably achieved its goal of developing a database engine that can scale down for use on the desktop, scale up to handle high-performance tasks on high-memory multiprocessor systems, and scale out to offer added stability and growth by supporting clusters of networked computer systems cooperating as a unified database server. In addition to its scalability, the new technology in SQL Server 7.0 also added a much more sophisticated lock manager, with support for row-level locking. By incorporating OLE DB, the new version additionally provided innovative support for queries against heterogeneous data sources.

For a more comprehensive look at the history of SQL Server, see *Inside Microsoft SQL Server 7.0*, by Ron Soukup and Kalen Delaney, published by Microsoft Press. This book (and editions that cover newer versions of SQL Server) is strongly recommended to readers looking for an advanced, highly technical drill-down into the capabilities of SQL Server.

SQL Server and Transact-SQL

Both Sybase and Microsoft have continued to refer to their implementations of the SQL standard as Transact-SQL (or T-SQL; usually pronounced *tee-sequel*). Microsoft has extended the language somewhat since taking it over from Sybase, but the vast majority of the syntax in Transact-SQL remains from the days when the companies were working together, and in fact from the days before Microsoft even became involved.

Transact-SQL has been certified to be compliant with the ANSI/ISO SQL-92 standard, but it is a superset of that standard and includes some very useful extensions to the language. Most of these extensions add procedural capabilities that allow Transact-SQL to perform the kinds of tasks that are usually performed by a programming language such as VBA.

For example, Transact-SQL includes an IF...ELSE syntax that adds branching to query execution based on evaluation of conditions. It also includes looping capabilities using the WHILE keyword, similar to Do...While loops in VBA. In Access databases, queries follow a fixed path and contain a single query execution, but using Transact-SQL you can create queries that process multiple statements, and you can use branching and looping to control the flow of execution, much the way you would in VBA code.

Another extension to the SQL standard that enhances your ability to program with Transact-SQL is its support for variables. All implementations of SQL support parameters that can be fed values when a query is called, but variables in Transact-SQL allow you to assign and inspect their values while the query is running.

Like other programming environments, Transact-SQL also supports complex manipulation of strings, dates and times, as well as complex mathematical calculations such as square roots, which go beyond the capabilities specified in the SQL standard.

In Chapter 10, you learn how to use Transact-SQL to build stored procedures that are much more similar to programming code than to the kinds of queries possible in Access. Access, however, has also introduced some innovative extensions to the SQL standard. One of them—the use of TOP to return just a portion of an ordered result set—has been adopted into Transact-SQL, although, as you'll see later in this chapter, Transact-SQL adds extra control over how tied values are handled.

Apart from differences between the SQL syntax that's supported in Access and in SQL Server, there are also differences in the role that SQL plays within the products. Unlike Access, which uses low-level proprietary APIs to communicate with the Jet database engine, the SQL Server user interface, including Enterprise Manager and all its wizards, is mainly just a wrapper around a set of system stored procedures written in Transact-SQL. Although SQL Server does make use of extended stored procedures, which call DLLs for performing tasks such as reading the Windows Registry, just about anything you can do with Enterprise Manager can also be done by typing the right Transact-SQL into the Query Analyzer and executing it there. In many cases, it's just a matter of calling the right system stored procedures and passing in the right parameters, as shown in Chapter 3, "Understanding SQL Server Security," in the context of programming security.

One good aid to learning how to program in Transact-SQL is to examine the system stored procedures found in the master database. Listing 8.1 shows the text that defines the sp_addapprole stored procedure, which creates an application role. Like most of the system stored procedures, sp_addapprole is fully commented, making it easy to figure out what's going on. By the time you finish this chapter and Chapter 10, you should have no trouble following how it works.

LISTING 8.1 The sp_addapprole Stored Procedure

```
create procedure sp_addapprole
    @rolename   sysname,   -- name of new app role
    @password   sysname    -- password for app role
as
    -- SETUP RUNTIME OPTIONS / DECLARE VARIABLES --
  set nocount on
```

LISTING 8.1 Continued

```
declare @ret int,      -- return value of sp call
        @uid smallint

-- CHECK FOR NULL PASSWORD
if (@password is null)
begin
  raiserror(15034,-1,-1)
  return (1)
end

  -- CHECK PERMISSIONS --
  if (not is_member('db_securityadmin') = 1) and
     (not is_member('db_owner') = 1)
begin
  raiserror(15000,-1,-1)
  return (1)
end

  -- DISALLOW USER TRANSACTION --
set implicit_transactions off
if (@@trancount > 0)
begin
  raiserror(15002,-1,-1,'sp_addapprole')
  return (1)
end

  -- VALIDATE APPROLE NAME --
execute @ret = sp_validname @rolename
if @ret <> 0
  return (1)
if (charindex('\', @rolename) > 0)
  begin
      raiserror(15006,-1,-1,@rolename)
      return (1)
  end

  -- ERROR IF SYSUSERS NAME ALREADY EXISTS --
  if user_id(@rolename) is not null OR
  @rolename IN ('system_function_schema','INFORMATION_SCHEMA')
  begin
      raiserror(15363,-1,-1,@rolename)
      return (1)
  end

  -- OBTAIN NEW APPROLE UID (RESERVE 1-4) --
```

LISTING 8.1   Continued

```
    if user_name(5) IS NULL
        select @uid = 5
    else
    select @uid = min(uid)+1 from sysusers
      where uid >= 5 and uid < (16384 - 1)--stay in users range
      and user_name(uid+1) is null -- uid not in use
    if @uid is null
  begin
    raiserror(15065,-1,-1)
    return (1)
  end

    -- INSERT THE ROW INTO SYSUSERS --
    insert into sysusers values
        (@uid, 32, @rolename, NULL, 0x00, getdate(),
                    getdate(), 1, convert(varbinary(256),
pwdencrypt(@password)))

    -- FINALIZATION: PRINT/RETURN SUCCESS --
    if @@error <> 0
        return (1)
    raiserror(15425,-1,-1)
    return (0) -- sp_addapprole
```

What You Can Do with Transact-SQL

Transact-SQL lets you declare variables and global variables, work with temporary objects, and declare cursors, which are analogous to recordsets. Transact-SQL also contains its own specialized functions, which you can use to aggregate data, to work with numbers, strings, and dates, and to retrieve information from the system.

It's a Programming Language (Sort Of)

You would never use Transact-SQL as a complete substitute for a programming language such as VBA, Java, or C++, but Transact-SQL does have many features of a programming language. It would be pretty hard to build an application using Transact-SQL alone because it has no ability to provide a user interface and its programming constructs are very limited, as you'll see in later sections in this chapter. However, it does allow you to execute complex tasks with branching, looping, error-handling, variables, and other programming language features.

The main advantage to programming in Transact-SQL is that your routines execute on the server. Transact-SQL provides the building blocks for all your views, stored procedures, and triggers. Doing as much work as possible in Transact-SQL, rather than in VBA code, improves performance because less data has to traverse the network for processing at the client. It also allows you to know that the rules you implement will be applied no matter what application or what method is used to work with your SQL Server data. The negative side to this is that your business rules become inextricably intertwined with your SQL Server data, making it much harder to apply them to other data sources if you ever need to.

You can break down Transact-SQL into two main categories:

- Data Definition Language (DDL)
- Data Manipulation Language (DML)

Data Definition Language (DDL)

Data Definition Language lets you create and modify objects in your database. The main commands used are CREATE, ALTER, and DROP. The SQL Server Enterprise Manager uses DDL behind the scenes to create and modify objects.

Data Manipulation Language (DML)

Data Manipulation Language lets you work with your data. SELECT, INSERT, UPDATE, DELETE, and TRUNCATE are all part of DML. The remaining sections of this chapter focus on using Transact-SQL for data manipulation.

In most situations, you'll be creating your data structures using a graphical user interface such as Enterprise Manager or the data tools in ADPs and in Visual Studio. The majority of your Transact-SQL programming will be working with data manipulation.

Differences Between Transact-SQL and Access

One thing that makes it difficult for Access developers to migrate their queries to SQL Server is that Access is much looser about what it will allow you to do. For example, you can call VBA functions, including your own custom functions, from within your queries, and the Access expression service will process them for you. Those same expressions will not be processed in Transact-SQL because the VBA-based expression service that Access uses is no longer present.

Translating Delimiters, Constants, and Operators

Transact-SQL and Access also don't see eye to eye on delimiters, constants, and operators. Table 8.1 shows the SQL Server equivalents for Access delimiters, constants, and operators. Notice, for example, that the commonly used & operator for string concatenation in Access has a completely different usage in SQL Server, where it is the equivalent of the Access bitwise AND operator. The other differences that commonly trip up Access developers moving to SQL Server are the wildcards and the delimiters for dates and strings.

TABLE 8.1 Comparing Access and SQL Server Delimiters, Constants, and Operators

Access	SQL Server	Description
#	'	Date delimiter
"	'	String delimiter
&	+	Concatenation operator
?	_	Single-character wildcard
*	%	Multiple-character wildcard
Mod	%	Modulus operator
Yes, On, True, (-1)	1	Constants for True or Yes
No, Off, False	0	Constants for False or No
AND	&	Bitwise AND
OR	|	Bitwise OR
XOR	^	Bitwise exclusive OR
<>	!=	Not equal to*
=>	!<	Not less than*
<=	!>	Not greater than*

This syntax is not SQL-92 standard. It is provided in SQL Server for backward compatibility with earlier versions of SQL Server. SQL Server supports the <>, =>, and <= operators as part of the ANSI SQL-92 standard.

The following operators work the same way in both Access and SQL Server:

+	Addition
-	Subtraction
*	Multiplication
/	Division
=	Equals
>	Greater than
<	Less than
>=	Greater than or equal to
<=	Less than or equal to
<>	Not equal to

Transact-SQL also supports the logical operators shown in Table 8.2. These are supported in Access as well.

TABLE 8.2 Transact-SQL Logical Operators

Operator	Meaning
ALL	TRUE if all of a set of comparisons are TRUE.
AND	TRUE if both Boolean expressions are TRUE.
ANY	TRUE if any one of a set of comparisons are TRUE.
BETWEEN	TRUE if the operand is within a range.
EXISTS	TRUE if a subquery contains any rows.
IN	TRUE if the operand is equal to one of a list of expressions.
LIKE	TRUE if the operand matches a pattern.
NOT	Reverses the value of any other Boolean operator.
OR	TRUE if either Boolean expression is TRUE.
SOME	TRUE if some of a set of comparisons are TRUE.

You'll see examples of using most of these operators later in this chapter.

Any Access queries that you want to move to SQL Server need to be cleaned up so that they will convert successfully. In addition to delimiters, operators, and constants, you also need to rewrite any VBA functions to their Transact-SQL equivalents, which will also be covered later in this chapter.

Translating Data Types Using CAST and CONVERT

Access queries are quite tolerant in terms of data typing and will perform implicit conversion for you behind the scenes if your data types don't exactly match up. Transact-SQL requires you to use the CAST or CONVERT functions to do your own explicit type conversions where necessary.

If you do perform any explicit data type conversions in your Access queries, you'll need to replace your existing code with the Transact-SQL CAST or CONVERT functions. CAST is the ANSI synonym for CONVERT, so either one will work. Table 8.3 shows the Access conversion functions and their Transact-SQL equivalents using CONVERT.

TABLE 8.3 Converting Data Types

Access Data Type	Conversion Function	SQL Server
Integer	Cint(x)	CONVERT(smallint, x)
Long Integer	Clng(x)	CONVERT(int, x)
Single	Csng(x)	CONVERT(real, x)

TABLE 8.3 Continued

Access Data Type	Conversion Function	SQL Server
Double	`Cdbl(x)`	`CONVERT(float, x)`
String	`Cstr(x)`	`CONVERT(varchar, x)`
Currency	`Ccur(x)`	`CONVERT(money, x)`
Date/Time	`CVDate(x)`, `CDate(x)`	`CONVERT(datetime, x)`

Note that the new SQL Server data type, bigint, is not covered here because there is no Access equivalent. If you use bigint in a SQL Server table as a primary key, you won't be able to read data when you link tables through ODBC from an Access MDB. If the bigint column is not part of the primary key, then just the column value will not be visible, and values from other columns will be displayed. In Access projects (ADPs) and in ADO recordsets, you won't have this problem, because OLE DB is able to handle bingint values.

Working with Transact-SQL

When you write Transact-SQL code, it will generally be because you want to create a view, trigger, or stored procedure. Typing in Transact-SQL code by hand can be a laborious process that's prone to error. There are several graphical tools that can help ease the process and improve your accuracy.

The Query Analyzer

The Query Analyzer is one of the most important tools you have in SQL Server. It not only helps you write Transact-SQL code, but it also runs the code interactively. Use the Query Analyzer to test whether your code runs successfully. You can even open multiple connections from the Query Analyzer, as shown in Figure 8.1, with the same query running on two different connections. The top pane shows that the Administrator is logged on and has executed the query. The bottom pane shows that Dudley, who does not have SELECT permissions on the Customers table, has received an error message to that effect. You set specific connection configuration options for each execution and test your queries, emulating the users who will be running your application.

The Query Analyzer in SQL Server 2000 is a good candidate for "most improved component" from version 7.0. Its many new features make it so much easier to work with that once you get familiar with it, you probably won't want to use any other tool for writing and testing Transact-SQL.

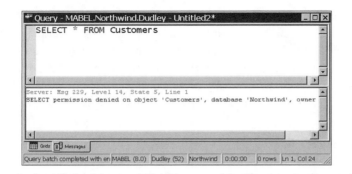

FIGURE 8.1

Test your queries in the Query Analyzer using different security accounts.

The Object Browser

One powerful new feature in the SQL Server 2000 Query Analyzer is its Object Browser, which you can load with the familiar F2 keyboard shortcut or from the Tools, Object Browser menu item. It has drag-and-drop functionality for both the left and right mouse buttons. If you drag with the left mouse button, you can drag and drop object names. Figure 8.2 shows how the Query Analyzer looks after dragging and dropping a table and several of its columns from the Object Browser, thereby creating a SELECT query. You could then modify the query to create a stored procedure or a view.

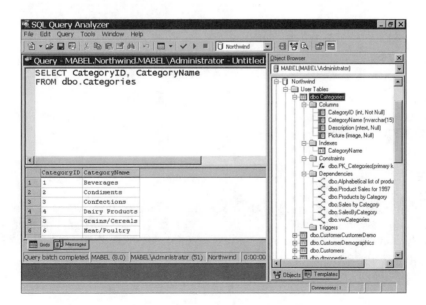

FIGURE 8.2

Using the left mouse button to drag and drop lets you select names of objects and drop them to create queries.

If you drag with the right mouse button, you can select from a list of menu options. Figure 8.3 shows the results of a right mouse button drag-and-drop operation, with the available menu choices and the Create option having been selected. This option creates a script for duplicating the structure of the Categories table. If you choose Select, Insert, Update, or Delete from the list, a query of that type will automatically be generated at your cursor insertion point. If you choose an action query, it will add a WHERE clause in angle brackets, much like the Expression Builder in Access:

```
WHERE <Search conditions>
```

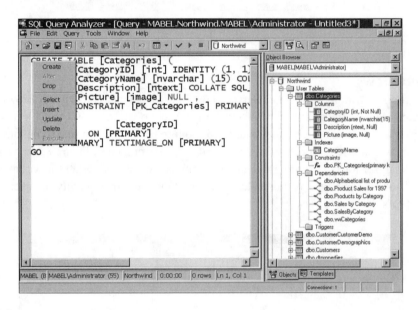

FIGURE 8.3

Using the right mouse button to drag and drop will present you with a menu, where you can select the type of Transact-SQL you want generated.

NOTE

You can also use drag and drop in the query pane to move lines, words, and blocks of text around. It works the same way it does in VBA or Word, which means that you probably don't want to drag and drop text very far. After scrolling for a short distance, things speed up and you lose control over the drop location.

Templates

The Object Browser in the Query Analyzer also comes with built-in templates, which you can find on its Templates tab. Templates are a new concept in SQL Server 2000 that did not exist in SQL Server 7.0. They are simply script files with a .tsq filename extension. These templates are a great tool for learning Transact-SQL because they include boilerplate Transact-SQL syntax for many commonly performed tasks. Templates supplied with the Object Browser create databases, tables, views, indexes, stored procedures, triggers, statistics, and functions. In addition, there are templates to help you manage extended properties, linked servers, logins, roles, and users; and to help you declare and use cursors. Click on the Templates tab in the Object Browser to display the different template categories. Expand the category you are interested in, and either double-click or left-mouse drag the item to the Query Analyzer, which then displays the Transact-SQL statements for that template. Note that you have to replace text in chevrons (<>) with actual object names. Figure 8.4 shows the template for creating a table with computed columns before the replacements have been made.

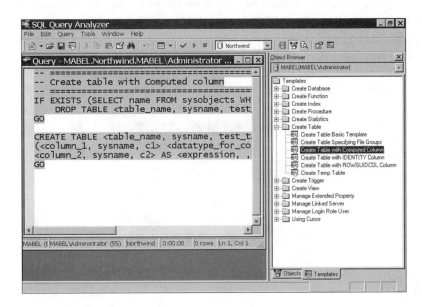

FIGURE 8.4

Using a template to load syntax for creating a table.

If you want to use a dialog box to replace template parameters instead of typing them in by hand, choose Edit, Insert Template from the menu and then choose Edit, Replace Template parameters. This will bring up the dialog box shown in Figure 8.5. The Replace Template Parameters dialog box is not available if you drag and drop the template from the Object Browser.

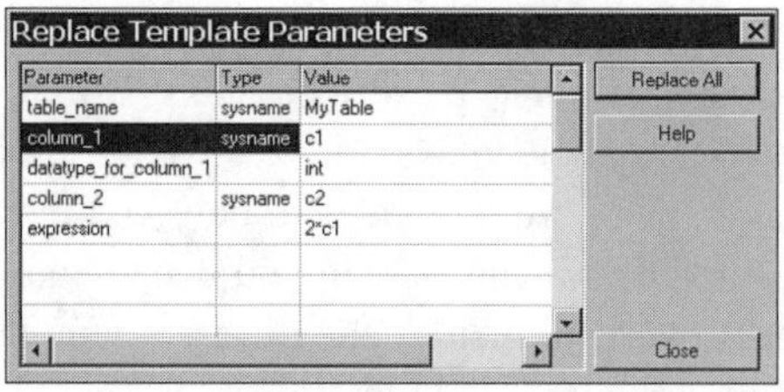

FIGURE 8.5
Using a template to load syntax for creating a table.

You are not limited to the templates supplied with SQL Server 2000. Create your own templates from reusable pieces of Transact-SQL code by saving a script as a template. Choose File, Save As and select Template SQL Files (*.tql) from the Save As Type dialog box. Specify a path and filename and click Save. Figure 8.6 shows saving a template in the Templates folder located in \Program Files\Microsoft SQL Server\80\Tools\Templates\SQL Server Query Analyzer. The next time you load the Object Browser, your template will show up, along with the built-in templates.

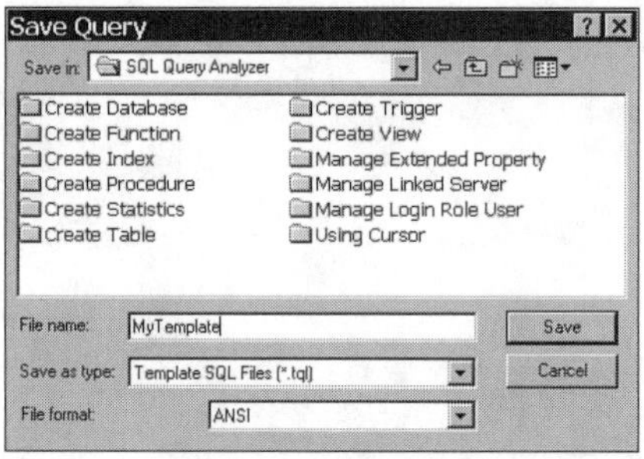

FIGURE 8.6
Create your own templates by saving them to the directory where the built-in templates are located.

Object Search

There's also a new object search functionality that lets you locate specific objects on your server. It can be activated from the Tools, Object Search menu option, the F4 key, or from the Object Search toolbar button. Figure 8.7 shows searching for a stored procedure whose name starts with "proc" in all databases on the server.

Query Analyzer Menu Items

One easy way to explore the Query Analyzer is to examine the top-level menu items. Many of the menu items are also on the toolbar, but not all of them.

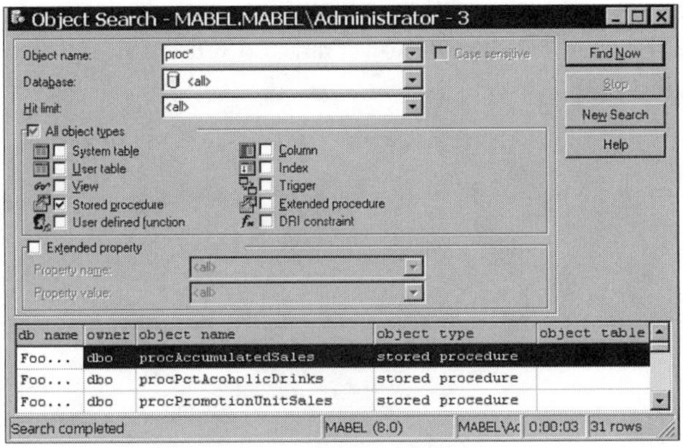

FIGURE 8.7
Searching for a stored procedure using the Object Search dialog box.

The File Menu

The File menu, shown in Figure 8.8, allows you to manage connections, create new files, open existing scripts, and save scripts or templates. To save the top pane as a script, click in the top pane and choose File, Save As and type in the path and file name for your script. To save the results of a query, click in the bottom pane and choose File, Save As. You will see "Save Grid Results" in the Save As dialog box, so you know you're saving the results, and not the script. If you choose Print from the File menu, you will only be able to print the top pane, not the result pane.

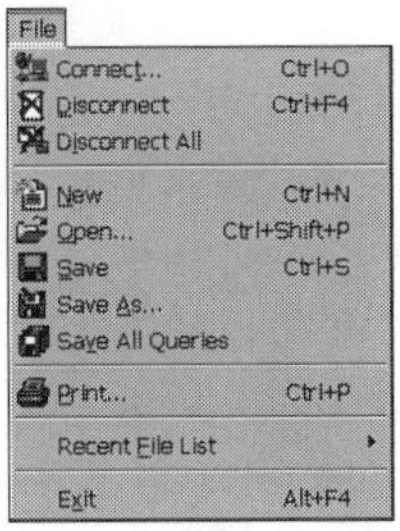

FIGURE 8.8
The File Menu.

The Edit Menu

The Edit menu, shown in Figure 8.9, gives you the standard editing commands, as well as search and replace. The Go to Line option will prompt you for a line number. The Bookmarks menu item allows you to set and remove bookmarks in your Transact-SQL code. The Advanced options allow you to change the case of a selection, increase or decrease indents, or comment out blocks of code. You'll learn how Transact-SQL allows you to include comments in your code later in the chapter.

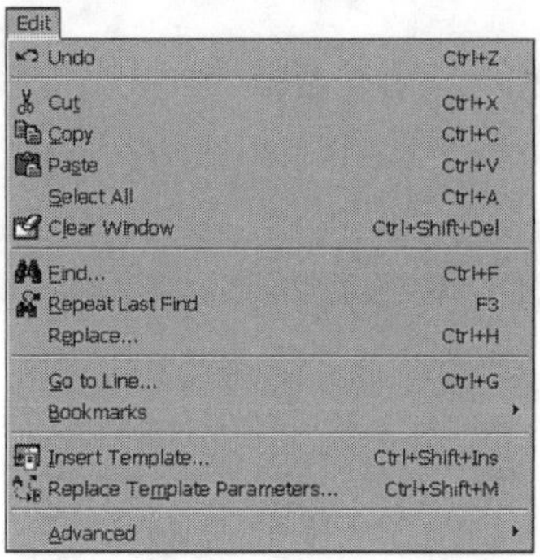

FIGURE 8.9
The Edit menu.

The Query Menu

The Query menu, shown in Figure 8.10, exposes some of the Query Analyzer's most powerful functionality:

- Change Database lets you select another database to query.
- Parse will check the syntax of your query before you execute it.
- Execute will run the query.
- Cancel Executing Query will stop execution.
- Display Estimated Execution Plan will give you a graphical showplan displaying the statistics for your query. Using execution plans to tune your queries is discussed in Chapter 9, "Creating and Optimizing Views."
- Index Tuning Wizard will load the Index Tuning Wizard, which will help you analyze the query, suggest indexes to improve performance, and optionally create the suggested indexes.

- You can elect to see the results of your query displayed in text, in a grid, or saved to a file. You will be prompted for a path and file name when the query executes.

- Show Execution Plan will create an additional results pane to show you the plan used when the query executes.

- Show Server Trace automatically creates a trace on the fly and adds another results pane to show the results. Traces are used by the Index Tuning Wizard and the SQL Profiler.

- Show Client Statistics will give you a results pane displaying statistics for the application, the connection, the network, and the processing time.

- Current Connection Properties lets you configure various settings that are applied to the current connection. You will rarely need to change these from the default settings.

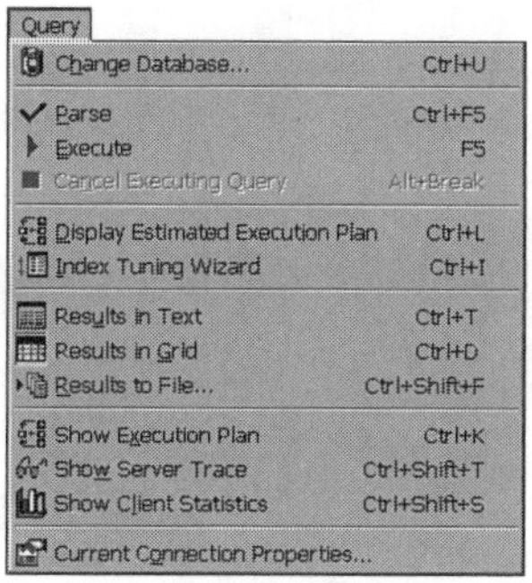

FIGURE 8.10
The Query menu.

The Tools Menu

The Tools menu, shown in Figure 8.11, lets you kick off the Object Browser and the Object Search. It also allows you to perform other tasks:

- Manage Indexes will display all the indexes for the selected database and allow you to edit them.

- Manage Statistics lets you create, update, and delete statistics for your tables. Having up-to-date statistics is important for SQL Server to be able to generate an efficient query plan. Unlike the Jet database engine, SQL Server exposes and fully documents the statistics used to determine a query execution plan, as well as the plans themselves.

- Options lets you set options for the Query Analyzer itself, including file locations, fonts, connection properties, and results pane options.

- Customize allows you to set up keyboard shortcuts and to customize the Query Analyzer menu.

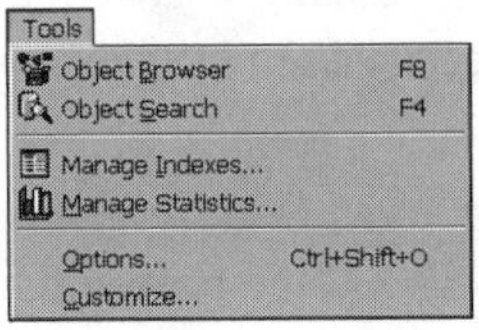

FIGURE 8.11
The Tools menu.

The Window Menu

Use the Window menu, shown in Figure 8.12, to manipulate the windows in the Query Analyzer and switch between connections.

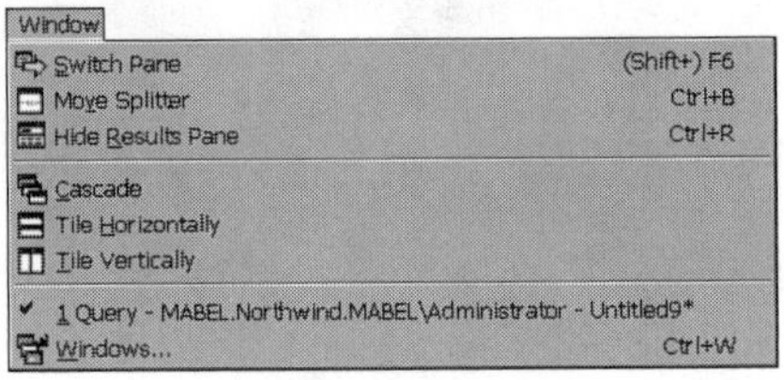

FIGURE 8.12
The Window Menu.

The Help Menu

The Help menu, shown in Figure 8.13, may be the most important menu of all. It lets you perform the following actions:

- Contents and Index loads Books Online with the Overview of SQL Query Analyzer topic selected.

- Using Help loads Books Online with the Using SQL Server Books Online topic selected.

- Transact-SQL Help loads Books Online with the Transact-SQL Overview Books Online topic selected. Transact-SQL help is also context sensitive. Simply press the Shift+F1 key on any Transact-SQL keyword. This loads Books Online with the selected keyword topic.

- Database Object Information displays a list of all the objects in the selected database.

The Query Analyzer is a powerful tool that helps you create and manage the Transact-SQL in your databases. Although it may at first appear to be no more than a passive window for typing SQL text, like the SQL view window in Access, the Query Analyzer is in fact a programming environment and an analysis tool that you can use to improve the effectiveness of your queries. The Query Analyzer optimization tools are covered in more detail in Chapter 9.

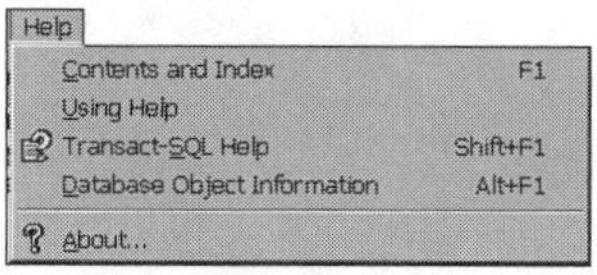

FIGURE 8.13
The Help menu.

The Enterprise Manager Create View

In addition to the Query Analyzer, the Enterprise Manager's Create View data tools can also help you create Transact-SQL (see Figure 8.14). This graphical interface comes in handy when you have joins and criteria to define. You can create the query and then paste it into the Query Analyzer or the design view of a stored procedure. Alternatively, you can always just save the view directly.

An Access Project Create View

You can also use an Access project (ADP) to create a view and copy the Transact-SQL statement from the SQL pane or save it to the server, as shown in Figure 8.15. This is similar to Enterprise Manager's Create View window; however, there are some subtle differences. For example, there is no results pane, and you must save the view to a SQL Server database before you can see the results in an Access datasheet grid.

The Access Query Grid

You can also use the Access Query Grid in an Access database (MDB) to create a query and copy the SQL statements from the SQL pane. However, you'd have all the problems of incorrect syntax, delimiters, and expressions to worry about. Therefore, you'd be better off using the tools that ship with SQL Server or using an ADP. The query design grid in an Access database (MDB) really won't help you much in writing Transact-SQL. The best choice is to do your query design in the SQL Server 2000 Query Analyzer, making full use of the new tools and drag-and-drop features that it includes.

8

INTRODUCTION TO
TRANSACT-SQL
(T-SQL)

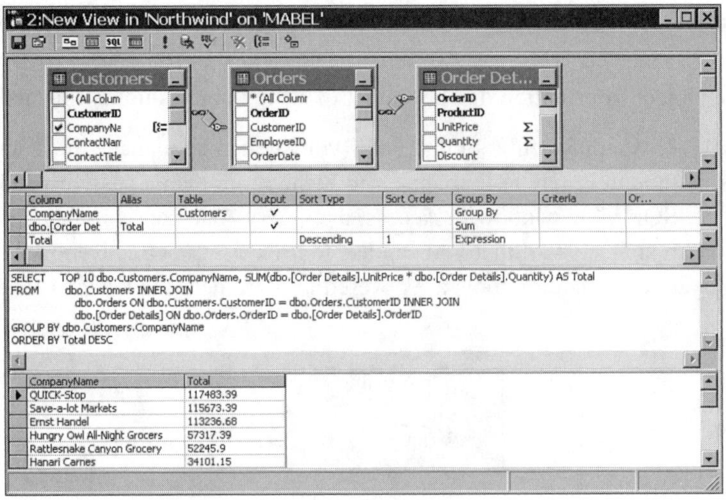

FIGURE 8.14

Creating a view in the Enterprise Manager.

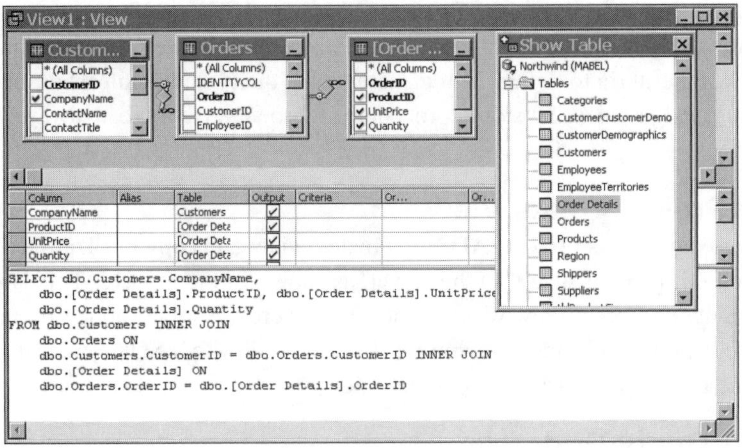

FIGURE 8.15

Creating a view from an Access project (ADP).

Referring to Objects

Here's the full syntax for referring to objects in SQL Server:

```
Server.Database.OwnerName.ObjectName
```

You do not always need to specify every portion of the object reference. Just as you can use commas as placeholders for default values when listing arguments to a VBA function, you can use dots with nothing between them as placeholders for the different parts of a SQL Server object reference. Unlike VBA arguments, here you can leave leading dots out altogether:

```
Server.Database..ObjectName
Server..OwnerName.ObjectName
Server...ObjectName
Database.OwnerName.ObjectName
Database..ObjectName
OwnerName.ObjectName
ObjectName
```

Much of the time, just specifying the object name is adequate. However, unlike in a Jet database, SQL Server allows multiple objects of a particular type that have the same name in one database, as long as they have different owners. If that's the case, and you have objects with the same base name but with different owners, you need to specify the owner name in front of the object name. Also, if the object is owned by anyone other than the dbo, you must use the owner name, as shown here, where Dudley is the owner of CustomersView:

```
SELECT * FROM Dudley.CustomersView
```

To refer to objects in different databases, preface the object name with the database name and the owner name:

```
SELECT * FROM pubs.dbo.authors
SELECT * FROM Northwind.dbo.Customers
```

You can also use the USE keyword to specify a different database:

```
USE Northwind
SELECT * FROM Customers
```

You can leave out the owner name in a remote reference if dbo owns the object:

```
SELECT * FROM pubs..authors
SELECT * FROM Northwind..Customers
```

To refer to objects located on a different server, you must use the full, four-part syntax with the server name. For a remote server, you must supply the owner name even if it's dbo:

```
SELECT * FROM Manta.Northwind.dbo.Customers
```

If you are using an Access project (ADP), then you must also specify the owner name along with the object name. This is required to allow users to run your application if they are not logged on the SQL Server as a member of the sysadmin role. For example, if you create forms and reports where you specify the record source as a SQL Server object, and you are logged on as a member of the sysadmin role, then you won't need to specify "dbo.tablename"—just "tablename" will work. However, users of your ADP who are not members of sysadmin will need to use "dbo.tablename." So it's a good practice to get to get in the habit of always specifying the owner name as well as the object name. Ownership, dbo, and the sysadmin role are explained in Chapter 3.

In the final section of this chapter, you'll learn how to create queries that pull together data from multiple servers by creating what are called *linked servers*. With linked servers, you can even perform heterogeneous queries that use information from non–SQL Server data sources.

Selecting Data

To retrieve data from SQL Server, you use a SELECT statement. Here's the basic syntax:

```
SELECT <field1, field2, ...> FROM <Table>
```

There can be a lot more to it than that, as this section will show.

> **NOTE**
>
> The terms "column" and "field" are used interchangeably in this chapter. SQL Server Books Online generally refers to "selecting columns," whereas Access developers are more familiar with "selecting fields." Whichever term is used, they both refer to the same thing.

The SELECT Statement

To select a single column in a table, write a query that looks like the following, which selects the au_lname column from the authors table in the pubs sample database:

```
Use pubs

SELECT au_lname FROM authors
```

Here are the first few rows returned from the query.

```
au_lname
----------------------------------------
Bennet
```

```
Blotchet-Halls
Carson
DeFrance
del Castillo
Dull
Green
Greene
Gringlesby
Hunter
```

To select all the fields in the table, you use an asterisk (*). This will return all the rows and all the columns in the authors table in the order they were specified with the CREATE TABLE col1, col2 statement:

```
SELECT * FROM titleauthor
```

Here are the first few rows of the result set:

```
au_id         title_id au_ord royaltyper
-----------   -------- ------ ----------
172-32-1176   PS3333   1      100
213-46-8915   BU1032   2      40
213-46-8915   BU2075   1      100
238-95-7766   PC1035   1      100
267-41-2394   BU1111   2      40
```

Concatenating Columns

To display columns that combine data from multiple fields in an expression, use the plus sign (+) as the concatenation operator:

```
SELECT au_lname + ', ' + au_fname
FROM authors
```

Here are the first few rows of the result set:

```
------------------------------------------------------------
Bennet, Abraham
Blotchet-Halls, Reginald
Carson, Cheryl
DeFrance, Michel
del Castillo, Innes
Dull, Ann
Green, Marjorie
Greene, Morningstar
```

Aliasing Column Names with AS

Note that the preceding result set is displayed without a column name. To have a column name displayed, use the AS keyword to alias it. Note that the column name that follows has spaces in it—in SQL Server versions 7.0 and later you can have spaces in object names as long as you use square brackets around the name. Here's an example:

```
SELECT au_lname + ', ' + au_fname AS [Full Name]
FROM authors
```

Here are the first few rows of the result set:

```
Full Name
-------------------------------------------------------------
Bennet, Abraham
Blotchet-Halls, Reginald
Carson, Cheryl
DeFrance, Michel
del Castillo, Innes
Dull, Ann
Green, Marjorie
Greene, Morningstar
```

The AS keyword is optional, but it makes your query easier to read. You could also use this syntax to achieve the same result:

```
SELECT LastName + ', ' + FirstName FullName
FROM Employees
```

This looks like FullName could be another column name with a comma missing in front of it. The following, which also works, looks like some sort of formula until you realize it's just another way of concatenating string values and another way of doing column aliasing:

```
SELECT FullName = LastName + ', ' + FirstName
FROM Employees
```

These forms of syntax are supported in SQL Server mainly for backward compatibility. They're included here because you may see them in someone else's code. In your own Transact-SQL, it's recommended that you always use AS because it is the clearest way to alias a column.

Selecting Unique Values with the DISTINCT Keyword

To select only unique values from a table that may contain duplicates in the field or combination of fields that you are selecting, use the DISTINCT keyword. For example, suppose you select just the state column from the authors table, like this:

```
SELECT state FROM authors
```

In this case, you'll get a state listed for every row, including many duplicates. If you use the DISTINCT keyword, you'll see each state listed only once. Here's an example:

```
SELECT DISTINCT state FROM authors
```

The WHERE Clause

Another way to limit the number of rows returned is to restrict them using a WHERE clause. You rarely need all the rows in a table, and selecting all rows and all columns can cause network bottlenecks and slow down your application. In Access, this might not have been such big concern, but in SQL Server you should plan for growth and develop habits that will work even with very large tables and very many users. When writing queries in SQL Server, return only the rows and columns that are absolutely necessary by using criteria in a WHERE clause and by including only the columns you need in the SELECT clause. The following query will return the names of authors in the pubs database who live in Oakland:

```
SELECT au_lname, au_fname
FROM authors
WHERE City = 'Oakland'
```

The LIKE Operator

The LIKE operator lets you use wildcard characters to match values. Note that the Transact-SQL wildcard character, %, is not the same as the Access wildcard character, *. If you try to use * in a Transact-SQL query, you won't get the results you expect. For example, to find every author whose last name starts with *S*, write the following query:

```
SELECT au_lname, au_fname
FROM authors
WHERE au_lname LIKE 'S%'
```

If, instead, you get trapped by your Access habits and use LIKE 'S*', then you'll get a match only if some particularly creative author has the actual last name of S*.

To return authors with an *s* anywhere in the last name, you'd write it this way:

```
SELECT au_lname, au_fname
FROM authors
WHERE au_lname LIKE '%S%'
```

Note that *s* and *S* are considered the same thing as long as your server is not configured to be case sensitive. If it is, forcing the comparison to uppercase would solve the problem and find all of the matches for *s* and *S*. Here's an example:

```
SELECT au_lname, au_fname
FROM authors
WHERE UPPER(au_lname) LIKE '%S%'
```

8

However, a SELECT query with a WHERE clause that has a conversion function in it is not recommended. It can never be optimized properly, and on large tables will likely cause performance problems, because SQL Server will be forced to use a table scan and run the function for every row returned. To avoid this inefficiency, use a WHERE clause like this, instead:

```
SELECT au_lname, au_fname
FROM authors
WHERE (au_lname LIKE '%S%') OR (au_lname LIKE '%s%')
```

Use the underscore character as a wildcard that matches any single character. The following example will return authors named O'Leary as well as any other combination of *O* and *Leary* that has a single character separating them:

```
SELECT au_lname, au_fname
FROM authors
WHERE au_lname LIKE 'O_Leary'
```

The wildcard characters in SQL Server behave the same way wildcard characters do in Access. You just have to remember to use a percent sign instead of an asterisk as well as an underscore in place of a question mark.

Another option for wildcard querying is to use square brackets to delimit a list of values to match. The following query returns Carson and Karsen.

```
SELECT au_lname
FROM authors
WHERE au_lname LIKE '[CK]ars[eo]n'
```

The BETWEEN Operator

Use BETWEEN to test for values that fall within a particular range. The following query will find all the titles in the roysched table, where the royalty is between 22 and 24. BETWEEN is inclusive, so any royalties that equal 22 or 24 will also be included in the output. Here's the query:

```
SELECT title_id, royalty FROM roysched
WHERE royalty BETWEEN 22 AND 24
```

Here are the first few rows of the output:

```
title_id royalty
-------- -----------
BU2075   22
BU2075   24
MC3021   22
MC3021   24
TC3218   22
```

Testing for Nulls

To test for a null value, use the IS NULL or IS NOT NULL syntax. The following query of the titles table finds books that have no royalties defined:

```
SELECT pub_id, title
FROM titles
WHERE royalty IS NULL
```

You can also reverse the condition to show books that do have a royalty defined. This would return all the rows that have a royalty:

```
SELECT pub_id, title
FROM titles
WHERE royalty IS NOT NULL
```

> **TIP**
>
> When testing for nulls, always use IS NULL or IS NOT NULL. Attempting to test for nulls using the equality operator (=) may or may not work, depending on your database settings for ANSI NULLS. With ANSI NULLS set to Yes, the comparison operators equal (=) and not equal (!= or <>) will always return null if you test for null. With ANSI NULLS set to No, these operators will return True or False, depending on whether the values you are testing are null. If you just always test for nulls using IS NULL or IS NOT NULL, you won't have to worry about this distinction. Also note that the session level setting overrides the database setting, and the default for ODBC and OLE DB connections is SET ANSI NULLS True.

Testing Multiple Conditions

You have several ways to test multiple conditions in Transact-SQL.

The AND, OR, and NOT Operators

Use the Boolean AND operator to check for multiple conditions that all must be true for a row to be returned. The following query returns all authors with a last name starting with *S* who also live in California:

```
SELECT au_fname, au_lname
FROM authors
WHERE au_lname LIKE 'S%'
AND state = 'CA'
```

The OR operator allows you to fetch rows that meet any of several conditions. To search for all authors who either have a last name starting with *S* or who live in California, use the following query:

```
SELECT au_fname, au_lname, state
FROM authors
WHERE au_lname LIKE 'S%'
OR state = 'CA'
```

The NOT operator reverses the logic in your criteria. To find all authors from California whose last name begins with any letter but *S*, use this syntax:

```
SELECT au_fname, au_lname
FROM authors
WHERE au_lname NOT LIKE 'S%'
AND state = 'CA'
```

When combining multiple criteria, use these operators. The precedence of the operators determines which conditions get evaluated first, which can affect your results. Here's the order of precedence:

- NOT

- AND

- OR

An operator that's higher in this list will be evaluated before an operator that's lower in the list.

For example, the following query will return all authors from California, regardless of their names, plus any whose name fits the specified pattern regardless of where they're from. Here's the query:

```
SELECT au_fname, au_lname, state
FROM authors
WHERE au_lname LIKE 'S%'
AND au_fname LIKE 'M%'
```

Here is the result set:

```
au_fname               au_lname                                         state
------------------     ----------------------------------------         -----
Meander                Smith
```

The AND operator gets evaluated first, creating a condition that is true if the last name and first name are both right. The OR operator comes next, evaluating whether authors meet that first name-based condition *or* are from California.

To clarify the order of precedence or to override the default order, you can use parentheses. An expression nested in parentheses is evaluated before an expression that's less deeply nested. The following query is equivalent to the preceding one:

```
SELECT au_fname, au_lname, state
FROM authors
```

```
WHERE ((au_lname LIKE 'S%'
AND au_fname LIKE 'M%')
OR (state = 'CA'))
```

To instead fetch authors whose last name starts with *S* and who also either have a first name starting with *M* or who live in California, use parentheses to override the default order of precedence. Here's the query:

```
SELECT au_fname, au_lname, state
FROM authors
WHERE (au_lname LIKE 'S%'
AND (au_fname LIKE 'M%'
OR state = 'CA'))
```

Here's the result set:

```
au_fname             au_lname                                 state
-----------------    -----------------------------------      -----
Meander              Smith                                    KS
Dean                 Straight                                 CA
Dirk                 Stringer                                 CA
```

By combining the logical operators—AND, OR, and NOT—and by using parentheses to enforce or clarify your desired order of applying them, you can create very specific and complex criteria.

The IN Operator

One way to check for any of several values in a column is to use the OR operator:

```
SELECT au_lname, state
FROM authors
WHERE state = 'CA'
OR state = 'NY'
OR state = 'KS'
```

A much simpler way of expressing this, however, would be to use the IN operator:

```
SELECT au_lname, state
FROM authors
WHERE state IN ('CA','NY','KS')
```

You could also look for authors who live anywhere except California, New York, or Kansas by using NOT IN. Here's an example:

```
SELECT au_lname, state
FROM authors
WHERE state NOT IN ('CA','NY','KS')
```

SQL Server and Case Sensitivity

Whether or not text comparisons in SQL Server are case sensitive depends on the options you chose when SQL Server was installed. If you installed SQL Server to be case sensitive, your queries must be written with the correct case. This includes specifying object names in the correct case as well as criteria values. If you installed SQL Server to be case insensitive, you can use either uppercase or lowercase for both object names and criteria values.

If you do have a case-sensitive database, one way to create case-insensitive criteria is to use the UPPER function:

```
SELECT au_lname
FROM authors
WHERE UPPER(state) = "CA"
```

The ORDER BY Clause

Use an ORDER BY clause if you want to sort the results of a query. If you do not use ORDER BY, there's no way of telling in what order SQL Server will return the rows. In Access, you could count on the rows being returned in primary key order, but in SQL Server there is no way to guarantee any order for the return of rows without an ORDER BY clause. Different algorithms for query optimization can yield results that are sorted differently, unless you use ORDER BY. The following query concatenates the first and last names and sorts by the last name. Here's the query:

```
SELECT au_fname + ' ' + au_lname AS FullName
FROM authors
ORDER BY au_lname
```

Here are the first few rows of the result set:

```
FullName
-------------------------------------------------------------
Abraham Bennet
Reginald Blotchet-Halls
Cheryl Carson
Michel DeFrance
Innes del Castillo
Ann Dull
```

To sort in descending order, use the keyword DESC. You can also sort by multiple columns. In the following query, the store ID, order date, and quantity are selected from the sales table. The result set is sorted by quantity in descending order and then by order date in ascending order for rows with the same quantity. Here's the query:

```
SELECT stor_id, ord_date, qty
FROM sales
ORDER BY qty DESC, ord_date
```

Here are the first few rows of the result set:

```
stor_id ord_date                   qty
------- -------------------------- ------
7066    1994-09-13 00:00:00.000    75
7066    1993-05-24 00:00:00.000    50
7067    1992-06-15 00:00:00.000    40
7896    1993-02-21 00:00:00.000    35
8042    1993-05-22 00:00:00.000    30
```

Sorting can also be based on an expression, but just remember that this can impose a performance penalty if you are working with a lot of data. The following query selects the titles from the titles table and sorts them by the length of their name. Here's the query:

```
SELECT title
FROM titles
ORDER BY LEN(title)
```

Here are the first few rows of the result set:

```
title
-------------------------------------------------------------------------------
Net Etiquette
Sushi, Anyone?
Life Without Fear
Is Anger the Enemy?
The Gourmet Microwave
But Is It User Friendly?
```

Summarizing and Aggregating Data

You can think of select queries as answering questions, and many of those questions will be looking for summary calculations performed on groups of rows. For example, you might want to know the total number of units sold or count the number of orders taken since a certain date. Transact-SQL supports the aggregate functions shown in Table 8.4.

TABLE 8.4 Aggregate Transact-SQL Functions

Function	Description
AVG	Averages numeric column values
COUNT	Counts the number of rows
MAX	Returns the largest value

TABLE 8.4 Continued

Function	Description
MIN	Returns the smallest value
STDEV	Returns the statistical standard deviation of all values in the given expression
STDEVP	Returns the statistical standard deviation for the population for all values in the given expression
SUM	Sums numeric column values
VAR	Returns the statistical variance of all values in the given expression
VARP	Returns the statistical variance for the population for all values in the given expression

You use these aggregate functions to return summary data. For example, if you want to know the number of authors in your database, you could use the following query:

```
SELECT COUNT(*) as NumAuthors
FROM authors
```

Here's the result set:

```
NumAuthors
-----------
23
```

When you use an aggregate function with a column, null values are excluded. The following query counts the title_id (which is the primary key of the table) and the royalty. Here's the query:

```
SELECT COUNT(title_id) AS TitleCount,
  COUNT(royalty) AS RoyaltyCount
FROM titles
```

The result set shows that there are 18 titles, but RoyaltyCount is only 16 because two rows have a null in the royalty column.

```
TitleCount  RoyaltyCount
----------- ------------
18          16
```

You can also aggregate data that has first been filtered with a WHERE clause, as shown in the following query that averages sales on titles with a price greater than $10:

```
SELECT AVG(ytd_sales) AS AvgOver10
FROM titles
WHERE price > 10
```

Here's the result set:

```
AvgOver10
----------
4419
```

If you wanted to get the average sales per type of title, you might think that the following query would work:

```
SELECT type, AVG(ytd_sales) AS AvgByType
FROM titles
```

However, you'll instead get the following error message:

```
Server: Msg 8118, Level 16, State 1, Line 1
Column 'titles.type' is invalid in the select list because it is not contained
in an aggregate function and there is no GROUP BY clause.
```

As the error message indicates, you need a GROUP BY clause to achieve the desired result.

The GROUP BY Clause

Grouping allows you to aggregate over groups of data, so you can, for example, easily obtain the average sales per type of title. The following query gives you the average sales by type for all titles with a price greater than $10, sorted in descending order:

```
SELECT type, AVG(ytd_sales) AS AvgByType
FROM titles
WHERE price > 10
GROUP BY type
ORDER BY AvgByType DESC
```

The HAVING Clause

When you use a WHERE clause in an aggregate query, the WHERE clause excludes rows before the grouping takes place. To limit the result set using criteria applied after an aggregate value has been calculated, use a HAVING clause. This allows your criteria to be based on the results of the aggregation. The following query returns types of titles that have average year-to-date sales greater than $5,000. The grouping by type takes place for all rows, the averages are computed, and the HAVING criterion is then applied. Here's the query:

```
SELECT type, AVG(ytd_sales) AS AvgByType
FROM titles
GROUP BY type
HAVING AVG(ytd_sales) > 5000
ORDER BY AvgByType DESC
```

Here's the result set:

```
type          AvgByType
------------  -----------
mod_cook      12139
business      7697
trad_cook     6522
popular_comp  6437
```

Joins

One of the basic principles of relational databases is joining tables based on fields that have values in common. These could be key fields, such as CustomerID and OrderID, that are used to enforce referential integrity between tables (referential integrity is discussed in Chapter 7, "Designing and Creating a SQL Server Database)," but query joins are not limited to key fields. For example, you might want to join the SaleDate field in a sales table to dates in a table of legal holidays to track the impact of holidays on sales.

To understand the different kinds of joins that Transact-SQL supports, consider the two tables shown in Figure 8.16. Each has a single column (Col1 and Col2, respectively), and each table has three rows.

Table1
Col1
1
2
3

Table2
Col2
2
3
4

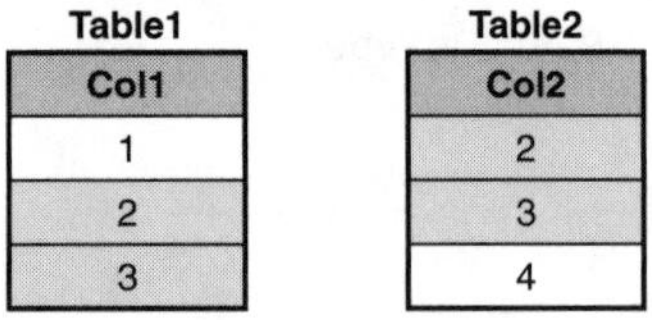

FIGURE 8.16
Two tables without a join.

If you write a query to select the rows from both tables, without defining a join between them, you will get the results shown in Figure 8.17. This is known as a *Cartesian product*, named after the French mathematician Rene Descartes who developed the concept. All possible combinations of the rows in Table1 and Table2 are returned, totaling nine rows. Because each table has three rows, there are 3*3, or 9, possible combinations. Here's the syntax:

```
SELECT Col1, Col2
FROM Table1, Table2
```

Col1	Col2
1	2
2	2
3	2
1	3
2	3
3	3
1	4
2	4
3	4

FIGURE 8.17
The results of a Cartesian product.

To return just the rows that have matching values, you could add criteria such as this:

```
WHERE Col1 = Col2
```

However, it would be more efficient to create an inner join.

Inner Joins

An *inner join* returns the intersecting values between two tables—those rows where the two tables have values in common. The syntax looks like this:

```
SELECT Col1, Col2
FROM Table1
  INNER JOIN Table2
  ON Table1.Col1 = Table2.Col2
```

Figure 8.18 shows the values in each table that will be returned when the columns are joined with an inner join. Only matching values qualify, so only the two rows with values 2 and 3 will be in the result set. Although this example is isolating just the columns that are being compared, a real-world query would probably also select other columns from those rows in the tables that had matching values in the joined columns.

Table1

Col1
1
2
3

Table2

Col2
2
3
4

Result Set

Col1	Col2
2	2
3	3

FIGURE 8.18
An inner join returns only rows with matching values.

Outer Joins

In addition to inner joins, there are two types of outer joins: LEFT JOIN and RIGHT JOIN. A left join includes all rows of the first table and only those rows from the right table that match. Figure 8.19 shows all values being returned from Table1 and only matching values from Table2. The result set includes three rows, one for each row in Table1. For rows that do not have a matching value in Table2, the query returns a null value in Col2. Here's the syntax:

```
SELECT Col1, Col2
FROM Table1
  LEFT JOIN Table2
  ON Table1.Col1 = Table2.Col2
```

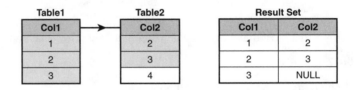

FIGURE 8.19

A left join returns all rows from the first table and only rows with matching values from the second table.

Figure 8.20 illustrates a right outer join that returns all rows from the second table, Table2. Only rows with matching values from Table1 are included, and on rows where there are no matching values, Col1 from Table1 has a null value. If more columns from Table1 had been included in the query, they would all have null values in those unmatched rows. Here's the syntax:

```
SELECT Col1, Col2
FROM Table1
  RIGHT JOIN Table2
  ON Table1.Col1 = Table2.Col2
```

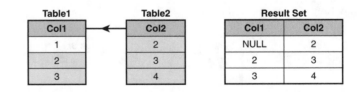

FIGURE 8.20

A right join returns all rows from the second table and only rows with matching from the first table.

So, when do you use an outer join? Suppose you have an orders table that includes a code for the shipping company that delivered each order. You create a query that returns order information and gets the full name of the shipping company from tblShippers:

```
SELECT tblOrders.OrderID, tblOrders.OrderAmount,
  tblShippers.ShipperName
FROM tblOrders
INNER JOIN tblShippers
  ON tblOrders.ShipperID = tblShippers.ShipperID
```

But what if some orders are picked up by the customer and don't get shipped? If these order records have a null value in the ShipperID field, they won't have a matching value in tblShippers, and they therefore won't be returned by this query. If you wanted to see all the orders and the shippers' names of those orders that were sent, you'd use an outer join:

```
SELECT tblOrders.OrderID, tblOrders.OrderAmount,
  tblShippers.ShipperName
FROM tblOrders
LEFT JOIN tblShippers
  ON tblOrders.ShipperID = tblShippers.ShipperID
```

Another way to use an outer join with these sample tables is to find all the shippers who haven't yet delivered any orders. To do that, you would run the outer join from the shippers table to the orders table and limit it to show only those rows where OrderID is null. Because OrderID would only be null in those rows where no match for ShipperID was found in the orders table, this would give you the answer you want—all shippers who haven't yet shipped orders. Here's the query:

```
SELECT tblShippers.ShipperID, tblShippers.ShipperName
FROM tblShippers
LEFT JOIN tblOrders
  ON tblShippers.ShipperID = tblOrders.ShipperID
WHERE tblOrders.OrderID IS NULL
```

This could also be written as a right outer join by reversing the order of the tables, like this:

```
SELECT tblShippers.ShipperID, tblShippers.ShipperName
FROM tblOrders
RIGHT JOIN tblShippers
  ON tblOrders.ShipperID = tblShippers.ShipperID
WHERE tblOrders.OrderID IS NULL
```

Although both versions will work, the first one is slightly better because it is customary when dealing with a one-to-many relationship to put the primary table (the "one" table) on the left side and the foreign table (the "many" table) on the right side. In this example, tblShippers is the *primary table* and tblOrders is the *foreign table*. An EXISTS subquery could actually be the best choice in terms of performance, which will be covered later in this chapter.

Full Joins

A *full join* combines a left and right outer join to return all the matching values. It's not the same thing as a Cartesian product because there is a joining key involved. A Cartesian product returns all the rows in the left table multiplied by all of the rows in the right table. A full join returns all rows that match (inner join), all rows from the first table that did not match (the left join), and all rows from the second table that did not match (the right join).

Using a full join would find of the shippers who had shipped orders, all the shippers who hadn't shipped any orders, and all of the orders that did not have a shipper. Here's the query:

```
SELECT tblShippers.ShipperID, tblShippers.ShipperName
FROM tblOrders
FULL JOIN tblShippers
  ON tblOrders.ShipperID = tblShippers.ShipperID
```

Self-Joins

Use a self-join when the data you are interested in joining exists in two different fields in a single table. The Northwind sample database has a good example of this in the Employees table. There is a ReportsTo column that contains the employee ID of each person's boss. Because this ReportsTo field contains the ID of another employee in the same table, you need to join Employees to Employees using an alias for the second copy of the Employees table. The following query aliases the second copy of the Employees table as Bosses and joins the ReportsTo column from the Employees table to the EmployeeID field in the Bosses table:

```
SELECT Employees.LastName, Bosses.LastName AS Boss
FROM Employees
INNER JOIN Employees AS Bosses
  ON Employees.ReportsTo = Bosses.EmployeeID
```

The results shown here display the eight-row result. However, there are nine rows in the Employees table.

```
LastName              Boss
-------------------   -------------------
Davolio               Fuller
Leverling             Fuller
```

```
Peacock          Fuller
Buchanan         Fuller
Suyama           Buchanan
King             Buchanan
Callahan         Fuller
Dodsworth        Buchanan
```

In order to list all employees and show the boss for each where there is one, combine the self join with an outer join. Here's the query:

```
SELECT Employees.LastName, Bosses.LastName AS Boss
FROM Employees
LEFT JOIN Employees AS Bosses
  ON Employees.Reportsto = Bosses.EmployeeID
```

The result set shows that Fuller, with a NULL in the Boss column, must be the big boss.

```
LastName             Boss
-------------------- --------------------
Davolio              Fuller
Fuller               NULL
Leverling            Fuller
Peacock              Fuller
Buchanan             Fuller
Suyama               Buchanan
King                 Buchanan
Callahan             Fuller
Dodsworth            Buchanan
```

Using Subqueries

A subquery is used to ask more complex questions about your data than could be accomplished using a simple query. A simple subquery is evaluated before the main query it is contained in. A subquery can be contained in the SELECT clause, FROM clause, or WHERE clause. A subquery in the FROM clause is also known as a derived table and is discussed in Chapter 9.

A correlated subquery can be used in the SELECT clause to list author names and their maximum royalties from the titleauthor table:

```
SELECT authors.au_id, authors.au_lname,
 (SELECT MAX(titleauthor.royaltyper)
 FROM titleauthor
 WHERE authors.au_id = titleauthor.au_id)
AS MaxRoyalty
FROM authors
```

A correlated subquery runs once for each row returned in the result set. It is called "correlated" because values from the results of the outer query are used by the subquery. Correlated subqueries are covered further in the next section.

Use a subquery in the WHERE clause to find out which authors have a royalty percentage that's above average. In this example, the subquery gets evaluated only once when it computes the average royalty from the titleauthor table, and that value is then used in the outer query where the rows are selected based on the computed value:

```
SELECT au_id, royaltyper FROM titleauthor
WHERE royaltyper >
  (SELECT AVG(royaltyper) FROM titleauthor)
```

Correlated Subqueries

A more complex example would be finding the names of publishers who have books on psychology. The type column (type of book) exists in the titles table, not the publishers table, so the query needs to extract the psychology titles first and then find their publishers. This subquery runs once for every row in the main query since it is looking for a specific pub_id in the subquery. The outer query passes each publisher's pub_id as an argument to the subquery, which then checks to see if the pub_id and type columns for that title match the publisher's pub_id and the string 'psychology', respectively:

```
SELECT pub_id, pub_name
FROM publishers
WHERE EXISTS
  (SELECT DISTINCT pub_id
   FROM titles
   WHERE type = 'psychology' AND
   pub_id = publishers.pub_id)
```

This example is known as a *correlated subquery* because the subquery depends on a value in the outer query in order to do its work. Correlated subqueries can be very inefficient, and in this case, using a join would be a better choice. The following query uses an inner join to return the same results:

```
SELECT DISTINCT publishers.pub_id, publishers.pub_name
FROM publishers
INNER JOIN titles
  ON publishers.pub_id = titles.pub_id
WHERE titles.type = 'psychology'
```

The DISTINCT keyword is necessary to avoid listing each publisher repeatedly for every one of its psychology titles.

Using a correlated subquery does not have to be inefficient. If you restrict the number of rows in the main query so that the subquery only runs a few times, it can be more efficient than a join when the tables being joined are quite large. The following query has a further restriction on the WHERE clause, limiting the outer query to publishers in the state of Massachusetts. In the pubs database, this only returns one row. Your mileage will vary depending on the amount of data in your tables. Here's the query:

```
SELECT pub_name
FROM publishers
WHERE state = 'MA' AND EXISTS
  (SELECT DISTINCT pub_id
   FROM titles
   WHERE type = 'psychology' AND
   pub_id = publishers.pub_id)
```

Other examples of subqueries and derived tables are shown in Chapter 9.

Union Queries

Union queries provide a way to combine tables without joins and without producing a Cartesian product. With a union query, you can combine the results of multiple select statements into one big result set that contains all the rows returned by each of the component selections. Here's the basic syntax:

```
SELECT col1, col2 FROM table1
UNION
SELECT col1, col2 FROM table2
UNION
SELECT col1, col2 FROM table3
```

Here are some sample uses for union queries:

- You want to combine tables from multiple databases that store similar data, such as orders from different locations.

- You want to join archive tables to tables in active use to create summary reports.

- You want to create a mailing list that includes people from different tables, such as employees, suppliers, and customers.

Here are some rules you must observe:

- Each SELECT statement in the union query must have the same number of columns.

- The columns must be of the same data type (which isn't the case in Access), but they don't have to have the same name. For example, you can use EmployeeID in one SELECT statement and CustomerID in another, as long as both are the same data type. If you need to combine columns of different data types, you can use conversion functions to achieve a unified type.

- If you want to sort the results, you must use column names from the first SELECT statement. Here's an example:

```
SELECT au_lname, au_fname
FROM authors
UNION
SELECT lname, fname
FROM employee
ORDER BY au_lname
```

Here are the first few rows of the results, combining records from both tables in alphabetical order:

```
au_lname                                        au_fname
--------------------------------------------    --------------------
Accorti                                         Paolo
Afonso                                          Pedro
Ashworth                                        Victoria
Bennet                                          Abraham
Bennett                                         Helen
Blotchet-Halls                                  Reginald
Brown                                           Lesley
Carson                                          Cheryl
```

TIP

A union query will eliminate duplicates automatically, so if you have authors who were also employees, they'd show up only once. To return all records, including duplicates, use UNION ALL. Eliminating duplicates is expensive, however. To make your query execute more quickly, use UNION ALL if you know there are no duplicates to worry about. A UNION ALL is more efficient than a plain UNION because the query processor doesn't have to take the time to figure out whether a row is a duplicate.

Updating Data with Action Queries

Action queries modify data with an INSERT, UPDATE, or DELETE statement, and they don't return a result set as SELECT queries do. Action queries are the fastest and most efficient way to modify data.

When editing data using bound forms in Access databases (MDBs), you are working with updatable recordsets, which are based on SELECT statements. In SQL Server, you can do the same thing, because SQL Server allows you to create an editable recordset by using a SELECT statement based on a table or a view. However, using a SELECT statement to modify data requires SQL Server to create a cursor, which is a memory structure for managing records of data. SQL Server also applies intent locks in preparation for the exclusive locks that would be necessary during an actual update. This all means that cursors consume significant resources on the server. Using client-side, read-only, or batch update cursors (client-side cursors are discussed in Chapter 6, "ActiveX Data Objects (ADO) Fundamentals"), unbound forms, and action queries to modify data is by far a more efficient use of SQL Server than updatable server-side cursors. Unbound applications have been proven to be capable of supporting thousands of simultaneous users on SQL Server, updating millions of rows of data per day. Chapter 11 discusses several strategies for building Access applications that don't rely on server-side cursors. To perform efficient manipulation of data, you need to understand how to construct INSERT, UPDATE, and DELETE statements.

Using the INSERT Statement to Add Rows to a Table

The INSERT statement adds new rows to a table. The following example will add a new store with a stor_id of 9153 named "Books 2 Go" to the stores table:

```
INSERT INTO stores (stor_id, stor_name)
  VALUES ('9153', 'Books 2 Go')
```

When writing INSERT statements, you must follow the rules and constraints defined in the underlying table. For example, if the store name is required (nulls are not allowed) and you fail to supply a value, you will get an error and the row will not be inserted. Also, you must use the single-quote delimiter (') for any values added to columns with nonnumeric data types.

You can combine an INSERT statement with a SELECT statement to insert more than one row of data into a table at a time. The following INSERT statement will select data from the RegionalStores table for all Palm Beach stores and add it to the stores table:

```
INSERT INTO stores (stor_id, stor_name)
  SELECT stor_id, stor_name
  FROM RegionalStores
  WHERE City = 'Palm Beach'
```

If you have any duplicate primary key values in the RegionalStores table (in this case, stor_id), the duplicate would not be inserted.

TIP

If the primary key of a table you are inserting rows into is an identity column, you do not need to supply the value. If you want to insert a value in an identity column, you need to set the database option SET IDENTITY_INSERT *tablename* ON prior to executing the INSERT statement.

Using SELECT INTO to Create a Temp Table

SELECT INTO is the syntax used in an Access make-table query, which allows you to create a new table from the result set of a query. In SQL Server, you probably won't want to be creating permanent new tables in the database this way, but you may find it useful to create temporary tables, commonly referred to as, *temp tables*. Temp tables have the following features:

- Temp tables are local to the connection that creates them, so they come in handy for doing processing that might otherwise require an array or a cursor. Each connection maintains its own set of temp tables, even if they have the same names as temp tables created by other connections.
- Temp tables are automatically destroyed when the connection ends.
- Temp table names always start with a pound sign (#).
- Once created, you can work with a temp table and its data the same way you work with regular tables.

CAUTION

If you want to use SELECT...INTO to create a persistent table, you need to set the SELECT INTO/BULKCOPY database options to TRUE. However, you should not do this lightly—it will create a break in the transaction log because this is considered a non-logged operation. Any break in the log means you must do a full database backup immediately afterward, because you will be unable to restore from a backup set with breaks in the log. Transaction logs and backups are covered in Chapter 15, "Deployment, Tuning, and Maintenance."

The following SELECT INTO statement creates a temp table named #stores and inserts the data from the stor_id and the stor_name columns. Note that you can still use the base table named stores without ambiguity. The name of the temp table is actually different from that of the base table. '#stores' has seven characters in its name, while 'stores' contains only six characters. In addition, a temp table is created in the tempdb system database, so there's no namespace conflict even without the '#' prefix. A semicolon can be used to delimit the first Transact-SQL statement from the second SELECT statement, which retrieves the values from the temp table. This semicolon is optional and has no effect on performance, but it improves readability. Here's the query:

```
SELECT stor_id, stor_name INTO #stores
  FROM stores;
SELECT * FROM #stores
```

NOTE

You can create a global temp table by prefacing the name with two pound signs (##). Global temp tables are visible to all connections and are destroyed when the last connection terminates.

See Chapter 12 for an example that builds a cross-tab report using a temp table.

Using the UPDATE Statement to Modify Data

To modify existing data, you use the UPDATE statement. The following UPDATE statement will set the discount to 9.5 only where discounttype is "Initial Customer":

```
UPDATE discounts
  SET discount = 9.5
WHERE discounttype = 'Initial Customer'
```

The UPDATE clause specifies the table; the SET clause lists all the column-level changes to be made, and the WHERE clause restricts the rows being modified.

CAUTION

If you omit the WHERE clause, every row in the discounts table will be updated to 9.5, regardless of the discount type. When creating queries that modify data, it's always best to create them as SELECT queries first and test the results to ensure that only the rows you want changed actually get changed.

You can also use UPDATE in conjunction with another table. In the following example, a join is created between Table1 and Table2; then the SET statement updates the Description column in Table1 with the contents of the Description column from Table2:

```
UPDATE Table1
  INNER JOIN Table2
```

```
ON Table1.Col1 = Table2.Col2
SET Table1.Description = Table2.Description
```

Using the DELETE and TRUNCATE Statements to Delete Data

The DELETE statement deletes entire rows. It's usually combined with a WHERE clause to restrict the number of rows deleted. One difference in syntax between Transact-SQL and Access is that in Access you would write DELETE * FROM *tablename*. If you use the asterisk in Transact-SQL, you'll get a runtime error. The following DELETE statement will delete all records from the sales table with dates earlier than 1/1/1993:

```
DELETE FROM sales
WHERE ord_date < '1/1/1993'
```

If you omit the WHERE clause, all rows will be deleted from the table. If this is your intention, using TRUNCATE TABLE is more efficient. It's faster and uses fewer system and transaction log resources than DELETE. The following TRUNCATE TABLE statement will delete every row in the sales table:

```
TRUNCATE TABLE sales
```

CAUTION

Note that TRUNCATE TABLE is not recommended in a production environment because it causes a break in the transaction log. If your server should crash, you will not be able to restore from the transaction log past any breaks. If you use TRUNCATE TABLE, you should perform a database backup immediately afterwards.

Using Transact-SQL Functions

One challenging aspect of migrating your Access SQL code to Transact-SQL is translating functions that worked well in Access into their Transact-SQL equivalents. This chapter doesn't cover all the Transact-SQL functions available to you—there's a complete listing in SQL Books Online. However, the next few sections will cover some of the functions more commonly used in business applications.

Working with Nulls

In Access, you can use two functions when working with nulls:

- IsNull(*fieldname*) returns True if the contents of field name is null.
- Nz(*Value, ValueIfNull*) is used to replace nulls with another value, such as zero.

In Transact-SQL, you have two functions for working with nulls:

- ISNULL(*check_expression*, *replacement_value*), which you can use in place of the Access Nz() function, not the Access IsNull function.
- NULLIF(*expression1*, *expression2*), which evaluates to null if *expression1* and *expression2* are equal.

Using ISNULL

The following SELECT statement uses ISNULL to display the string "N/A" in place of the null values in the stor_id column:

```
SELECT discounttype, ISNULL(stor_id, 'N/A') AS store, discount
FROM discounts
```

Here is the result set:

```
discounttype                             store discount
---------------------------------------- ----- --------
Initial Customer                         N/A   10.50
Volume Discount                          N/A   6.70
Customer Discount                        8042  5.00
```

It is very easy for Access developers to get confused over the usage of ISNULL in Transact-SQL because the name is the same as the commonly used and completely unrelated VBA function IsNull(). Just try to remember that ISNULL in Transact-SQL is really almost identical to the Access Nz() function. Unlike Access, Transact-SQL also has a function, called NULLIF, for changing certain values *to* nulls.

Using NULLIF

The NULLIF system function is just the opposite of ISNULL. With NULLIF, you replace values with nulls. NULLIF is useful when you want to eliminate values from an aggregate function. For example, if you wanted an average of the lorange column from the table, you would write the following statement, which would give you the result of 9454:

```
SELECT AVG(lorange) FROM roysched
```

However, the zero values are being counted in the average. In order to see an average that excludes the zero values, use NULLIF to convert the zeros to nulls. Because nulls are not included in aggregate functions, the result from the following statement will be 11615:

```
SELECT AVG(NULLIF(lorange, 0)) FROM roysched
```

Using COALESCE

The COALESCE function is used to return the first non-null expression in a series of expressions:

```
COALESCE(expression1, expression2 [,...n])
```

The logic goes something like this: If *expression1* is not null, then return *expression1*. If *expression1* is null and *expression2* is not null, then return *expression2*, and so on.

COALESCE is useful if you have data stored in any one of a set of fields. For example, you might have different wage fields for hourly wages, annual salaries, and commissions, with each record containing only one of the three. The following expression could be used to compute wages:

```
COALESCE(hourly_wage * 40 * 52,
         salary,
         commission * annualsales)
```

Date Functions

There are three date functions that work the same way in SQL Server as they do in Access:

- DATEPART(*datepart, date*), where the first argument specifies the part of the date to return
- DATEADD(*datepart, number, date*), where the first argument is the interval you want to add to the date, and the second is the increment
- DATEDIFF(*datepart, startdate, enddate*), where *datepart* is the interval you want to count between *startdate* and *enddate*
- ISDATE(*expression*), which returns 1 if the expression is a date, and 0 if it's not a date

However, converting other Access date functions isn't as straightforward because Access has several date-processing functions that are all replaced by the Transact-SQL DATEPART function, with different parameters. Several Access date functions and their Transact-SQL equivalents are listed in Table 8.5.

TABLE 8.5   Access and Transact-SQL Date Functions

Access	Transact-SQL	Usage	Returns
Now()	GETDATE()	SELECT GETDATE()	Current date/time
Date()	CONVERT(varchar, GETDATE(),101)	SELECT CONVERT (varchar, GETDATE(),101)	Date part of current date/ time
Year()	DATEPART(yy, *date*)	SELECT DATEPART (yy, GETDATE())	Year of current date/time

TABLE 8.5 Continued

Access	Transact-SQL	Usage	Returns
Month()	DATEPART(mm, *date*)	SELECT DATEPART(mm, GETDATE())	Month number of current date/time
Day()	DATEPART(dd, *date*)	SELECT DATEPART (dd, GETDATE())	Day of current date/time
Weekday()	DATEPART(dw, *date*)	SELECT DATEPART (dw, GETDATE())	Day of week of current date/time
Hour()	DATEPART(hh, *date*)	SELECT DATEPART (hh, GETDATE())	Hour of current date/time
Minute()	DATEPART(mi, *date*)	SELECT DATEPART (mi, GETDATE())	Minute of current date/time
Second()	DATEPART(ss, *date*)	SELECT DATEPART (ss, GETDATE())	Second of current date/time

String Functions

If you always worked with perfectly normalized and consistently entered data, you would rarely need to use any string functions in Transact-SQL, but in the real world of messy data, good string manipulation functions are a necessity. There are six string functions whose syntax is unchanged from Access to SQL Server:

- SPACE(*integer_expression*), which returns a string consisting of the number of spaces specified in *integer_expression*.

- STR(*float_expression*[, *length*[, *decimal*]]), where a string is returned from *float_expression*. The length and decimal optional parameters for the length and decimal places in the Transact-SQL version don't exist in the Access version. STR offers more flexibility than CAST or CONVERT when converting decimal data types to characters because it gives you explicit control over formatting.

- LEFT(*character_expression*, *integer_expression*), which returns the leftmost characters indicated by *integer_expression*.

- RIGHT(*character_expression*, *integer_expression*), which returns the rightmost characters indicated by *integer_expression*.

- LTRIM(*character_expression*), which returns a string after removing all trailing blanks.

- RTRIM(*character_expression*), which returns a string after removing all leading blanks.

There is no Transact-SQL equivalent for Trim()—you need to use LTRIM or RTRIM (or both).

Table 8.6 shows the rest of the Access string functions and their Transact-SQL equivalents.

TABLE 8.6 Access and Transact-SQL String Functions

Access	Transact-SQL	Usage	Returns
Chr(x)	CHAR(integer_expression)	SELECT CHAR(88)	X
Asc(x)	ASCII(character_expression)	SELECT ASCII('X')	88
LCase	LOWER(character_expression)	SELECT LOWER('X')	x
UCase	UPPER(character_expression)	SELECT UPPER('x')	X
Len(x)	LEN(expression)	SELECT LEN('XYZ')	3
	DATALENGTH(expression)	SELECT DATALENGTH('XYZ')	3
Mid(x)	SUBSTRING(expr, start, length)	SELECT SUBSTRING ('ABCDEFG', 3, 3)	CDE

Functions to Return Information

Transact-SQL also has many built-in functions that return information that haven't been explicitly covered so far. These functions all won't be covered in detail here because they are documented in SQL Books Online. However, here are a few functions that you may find handy, several of which will seem familiar:

- ISNUMERIC(expression) is used just like in VBA to test whether an expression contains valid numeric data. If you use it on the Northwind database Employees.PostalCode column, it will return 1 for all postal codes that can be translated into numeric data, and it will return 0 for those that can't (such as Canadian postal codes, which have letters in them). Here's an example:

```
USE Northwind
SELECT ISNUMERIC(PostalCode), PostalCode
FROM Employees
```

- RAND([seed]) is similar to the VBA Rnd function, used to generate seemingly random numbers with a value between 0 and 1. The optional seed gives Transact-SQL a starting point for generating the resulting number. If you use the same seed multiple times, you'll get the same "random" number each time. To base the random number on the current date/time, which will presumably always give a different result, you could use this:

```
SELECT RAND( (DATEPART(mm, GETDATE()) * 100000 )
+ (DATEPART(ss, GETDATE()) * 1000 )
+ DATEPART(ms, GETDATE()) )
```

- ROUND(*expression*, *length*[, *function*]) is used to round the expression to the specified length. The optional function argument is used to specify the type of operation. If you specify 0 (the default), the expression is rounded. Any other value causes the expression to be truncated.

- ASCII(*expression*) is used to return the ASCII code of the leftmost character specified in the expression argument. The following two statements both return 70, which is the ASCII value for F:

```
SELECT ASCII('Fred')
SELECT ASCII('F')
```

- REPLACE('*expression1*', '*expression2*', '*expression3*') is used to replace all occurrences of *expression2* that occur in *expression1* with *expression3*. The following statement will return "Hewwo":

```
SELECT REPLACE('Hello', 'll', 'ww')
```

- REVERSE(expression) is used to reverse a string. This seemingly useless function seems to occur in just about every programming language, including the most recent versions of VBA. The following statement will return "olleH":

```
SELECT REVERSE('Hello')
```

- STUFF(*expression*, *start*, *length*, *expression2*) is used to delete *length* characters from *expression* at *start* and insert *expression2* at *start*. The following statement will return "Now is the place":

```
SELECT STUFF('Now is the time', 12, 4, 'place')
```

- DATALENGTH(expression) is used to return the number of bytes used. Both statements shown return 4. This function can be useful with data types such as varchar that are capable of storing variable length data. Here are the statements:

```
SELECT DATALENGTH('help')
SELECT DATALENGTH(3333)
```

- OBJECT_ID('*object*') is used to retrieve an object's identifier from the systems tables. This saves having to query the systems tables directly. SQL Server uses object ID's internally when processing queries. Here's an example:

```
USE master
SELECT OBJECT_ID('pubs.dbo.authors')
```

- SUSER_SID([*'login'*]) is used to return a user's SID (security identification number) for a login name. The login can be either a SQL Server login or an NT login. If the login isn't supplied, the SID of the current user will be returned. Here's an example:

```
SELECT SUSER_SID()
```

8

INTRODUCTION TO
TRANSACT-SQL
(T-SQL)

- `SUSER_SNAME()` is used to return a user's name. The following statement will return your login name (this is similar to the `CurrentUser()` function in Access):

```
SELECT SUSER_SNAME()
```

The @@ Functions

There are a group of built-in niladic functions used to return information about SQL Server. *Niladic* is just a five-dollar word referring to a function that doesn't have any parameters. These niladic functions are often referred to as *global variables* because their names all start with @ the way variables do, but their only resemblance to variables is their names. They aren't variables, because you can't declare them or set their value, and many of them also aren't really global, because they return values that pertain only to the current connection. You'll see more about how to use these functions in Chapter 10.

@@ERROR

@@ERROR is set to 0 after the execution of every Transact-SQL statement if the statement executes successfully. If an error occurs, @@ERROR returns the number of the error message. The following example inserts a row into the jobs table and captures any error messages into a local variable, @errNum:

```
DECLARE @errNum int
INSERT INTO jobs (job_id, job_desc, min_lvl, max_lvl)
VALUES (15, 'Gofer', 5, 75)
SELECT @errNum = @@ERROR
SELECT @errNum as ErrorReturned
```

@@IDENTITY

After you insert a value into an identity column, @@IDENTITY is used to retrieve the new value. The `SELECT` statement in this example will retrieve the new job_id once the new Gofer position is added to the jobs table:

```
INSERT INTO jobs (job_desc, min_lvl, max_lvl)
VALUES ('Gofer', 5, 75)
SELECT @@IDENTITY AS 'New job_id'
```

If the insert had caused a trigger to also insert a row in another table, the value of @@IDENTITY would be the identity value from that other table.

@@ROWCOUNT

@@ROWCOUNT returns the number of rows returned or affected by a statement that selects or modifies data. If no values are returned by a `SELECT` statement or affected by an action query, it returns 0.

@@TRANCOUNT

When you start a transaction with a BEGIN TRAN statement, @@TRANCOUNT is set to 1. The ROLLBACK TRAN statement sets @@TRANCOUNT to 0. The COMMIT TRAN statement decrements @@TRANCOUNT by 1, allowing you to keep track of how many transactions are still pending. Transactions are covered in Chapter 10. The following example uses the @@ROWCOUNT function to determine whether the transaction should be committed (if @@TRANCOUNT is greater than zero after the COMMIT TRAN statement, something went wrong and the transaction is rolled back):

```
BEGIN TRAN
UPDATE authors SET au_lname = 'Witte'
WHERE au_lname = 'White'
IF @@ROWCOUNT = 2
    COMMIT TRAN
IF @@TRANCOUNT > 0
    ROLLBACK TRAN
```

New! User-Defined Functions

New in SQL Server 2000 is the ability to create your own Transact-SQL functions. Functions can consist of Transact-SQL statements, and they make it easier to encapsulate code for reuse. There are three different kinds of user-defined functions:

- Scalar functions return a single data value of the type defined in a RETURNS clause. The body of the function, defined in a BEGIN-END block, contains the series of Transact-SQL statements that return the value. The return type can be any data type except text, ntext, image, cursor, or timestamp.

- Inline table-valued functions return a table. There is no function body; the return table is the result set of a single SELECT statement.

- Multi-statement table-valued functions also return a table, but the function body is defined in a BEGIN-END block, which contains multiple TRANSACT-SQL statements that build and insert rows into the return table.

Scalar functions are useful in places where you need to perform the same calculations in multiple places. Functions can also be nested, allowing complex processes to be broken down into simpler functions. Table-valued functions can be looked at as hybrids of views and stored procedures. They return a table (a result set), and thus you select from them like you do a view, yet they can also accept parameters and can contain complex logic like a stored procedure. In addition, user-defined functions possess many of the performance benefits of stored procedures.

User-defined functions can be called from views, stored procedures, other user-defined functions, batches, scripts, and from external applications. The following sub-sections show how to create simple scalar and table-valued functions. See Chapter 12 for more advanced examples of user-defined, multi-statement, table-valued functions.

Create a Simple Scalar Function

To create a simple scalar function to calculate the average price of the Products in the Northwind Products table, you need to specify the return data type (money) and place all statements within a BEGIN...END statement block. Variables are allowed in a function as long as you declare them within the BEGIN-END block. Here's an example:

```
CREATE FUNCTION fnAvgPrice()
  RETURNS money
AS
BEGIN
  DECLARE @AvgPrice money
  SELECT @AvgPrice = (SELECT AVG(UnitPrice) FROM Products)
  RETURN @AvgPrice
END
```

The following SELECT statement calls the function. You must use the owner name of the function in order to call it—table-valued functions can't be called by using a single-part name. Also note that you can't ORDER BY a column that uses a function. Here's the statement:

```
SELECT ProductName, UnitPrice, dbo.fnAvgPrice() AS AvgPrice
from Products
```

The user-defined function can also be used in a WHERE clause:

```
SELECT ProductName, UnitPrice
FROM Products
WHERE UnitPrice > dbo.fnAvgPrice()
```

Create a Scalar Function with Parameters

The same function could be rewritten to take a parameter for the CategoryID, where the average price for a specific category is returned:

```
CREATE FUNCTION fnAvgPriceParam
  (@CategoryID int)
  RETURNS money
AS
BEGIN
  DECLARE @AvgPrice money
  SELECT @AvgPrice =
    (SELECT AVG(UnitPrice)
```

```
    FROM Products
    WHERE CategoryID = @CategoryId)

  RETURN @AvgPrice
END
```

The following example queries the Products table to display all products with a CategoryID of
5 and a price greater than the average price for that category.

```
SELECT ProductName, UnitPrice
FROM Products
WHERE CategoryID = 5 AND
  UnitPrice > dbo.fnAvgPriceParam(5)
```

Create an Inline Table-Valued Function

An inline table-valued function is defined as having a RETURN argument comprised of a single SELECT statement, without a BEGIN...END block. The following example accepts a parameter for the CategoryID and selects products whose price is greater than the average for that
category, calling the inline scalar function fnAvgPriceParam. This example takes advantage of
a feature that makes user-defined functions extremely flexible; you're allowed to nest functions
inside of other functions:

```
CREATE FUNCTION fnAvgPriceTable
  (@CategoryID int)
  RETURNS table
AS
  RETURN (
    SELECT ProductName, UnitPrice
    FROM Products
    WHERE CategoryID = @CategoryID AND
    UnitPrice > dbo.fnAvgPriceParam(@CategoryID)
    )
```

Calling a function that returns a table requires different syntax from calling scalar functions.
To invoke the function, use a SELECT statement, passing the parameter value inside the
parenthesis:

```
SELECT * FROM dbo.fnAvgPriceTable(5)
```

The result set will look like this:

```
ProductName                              UnitPrice
---------------------------------------- --------------------
Gustaf's Knäckebröd                      21.0000
Gnocchi di nonna Alice                   38.0000
Wimmers gute Semmelknödel                33.2500
```

Programming in Transact-SQL

Programming concepts like batches, variables, flow control, and conditional logic become most important when you are writing stored procedures, which are covered in detail in Chapter 10. However, here are a few basic concepts to get you started.

Batches

A *batch* is nothing more than a collection of SQL statements that are sent in one unit to be processed. Each batch is compiled into a single execution plan, where all the optimized steps needed to perform the statements are built into the plan. If there is a compile error in one of the statements, none of the statements will be executed. However, not all runtime errors prevent subsequent execution of batch statements. Batches are covered in more detail in Chapter 10 when stored procedures are covered.

You can create ad hoc batches in the Query Analyzer, separating statements with the GO statement. The GO causes any statements before it to be treated as a single batch separate from any statements following it. Here's an example that creates two separate batches. The Query Analyzer can display multiple result sets, as shown in Figure 8.21.

```
SELECT au_id, au_lname FROM authors
GO
SELECT * FROM titleauthor
GO
```

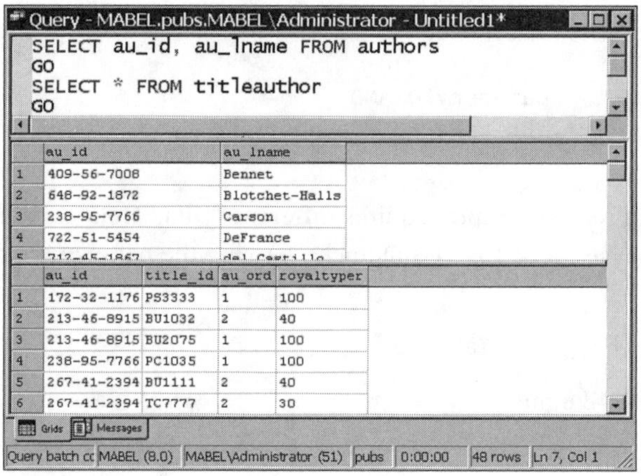

FIGURE 8.21
The Query Analyzer can display multiple result sets.

Variables

Variables in Transact-SQL work the same way they do in any programming language—you declare them and assign values to them. In Transact-SQL you use the DECLARE keyword to declare the variable name and data type. Variables are always preceded by the at (@) symbol. The SET statement assigns a value to the variable. You can then use it in your Transact-SQL code. The following statements declare and set a variable and then concatenate it to a column value:

```
DECLARE @home varchar(12)
SET @home = 'Home State: '

SELECT au_lname, au_fname, @home + state AS State
FROM authors
```

Here's the result set:

au_lname	au_fname	State
White	Johnson	Home State: CA
Green	Marjorie	Home State: CA
Carson	Cheryl	Home State: CA
O'Leary	Michael	Home State: CA
Straight	Dean	Home State: CA

Chapter 10 covers variables in more detail.

Control of Flow Syntax

Control of flow syntax is primarily used within stored procedures to branch and loop as necessary.

IF...ELSE

Use IF to test for a condition. All statements to be executed when the IF condition is true must be enclosed in a BEGIN...END block, because Transact-SQL has no End If. Here's the syntax:

```
IF (SomeCondition)
  BEGIN
    --Execute multiple statements
    --Execute multiple statements
  END
```

You can follow IF with ELSE. The ELSE part contains the statements you want to execute if the condition evaluates to False. Here, too, you must enclose all statements that are part of the ELSE block within a BEGIN...END. If you omitted either of the BEGIN...END structures, only one line after IF and one line after ELSE would be affected by the condition being evaluated, and all other lines would execute regardless of whether the condition were true or false. Here's the syntax:

```
IF (SomeCondition)
  BEGIN
    --Execute multiple statements
    --Execute multiple statements
  END
ELSE
  BEGIN
    --Execute multiple statements
    --Execute multiple statements
  END
```

GOTO

You can use GOTO in Transact-SQL much the same way you do in VBA. It will jump to the specified label. Here's the syntax:

```
IF (SomeCondition)
  GOTO MyLabel
...

MyLabel:
--Processing continues here
```

Looping with WHILE

You can set up a loop using the WHILE statement. The BREAK statement is used to break out of the loop and then CONTINUE continues looping. Here's the full syntax:

```
WHILE Boolean_expression
    {sql_statement | statement_block}
    [BREAK]
    {sql_statement | statement_block}
    [CONTINUE]
```

The following example of a WHILE loop keeps doubling prices until the maximum price is greater than $50 or the average price is greater than $30:

```
WHILE (SELECT AVG(price) FROM titles) <= $30
BEGIN
    UPDATE titles
```

```
        SET price = price * 2
    IF (SELECT MAX(price) FROM titles) > $50
        BREAK
    ELSE
        CONTINUE
END
```

RETURN

The RETURN statement unconditionally terminates execution of a batch or stored procedure. It's the equivalent to Exit Sub or Exit Function in VBA. Here's the syntax:

```
IF (SomeCondition)
  RETURN
--Following statements never execute
```

CASE

Technically speaking, CASE is not a control of flow statement in Transact-SQL the way Select Case is in VBA. It doesn't really affect the order of execution. You can think of CASE as providing control of flow for data output rather than control of flow for commands. A simple use of CASE is where an input expression is evaluated, and then you have any number of WHEN...THEN statements for the return values of the input expression. As you can see, the syntax is quite different from the VBA Select Case control structure. Here's the syntax:

```
CASE input_expression
    WHEN when_expression THEN result_expression
        [...n]
    [
        ELSE else_result_expression
    ]
END
```

A searched CASE function does not have an initial input expression. Instead, it evaluates multiple WHEN...THEN statements. Here's the syntax:

```
CASE
    WHEN Boolean_expression THEN result_expression
        [...n]
    [
        ELSE else_result_expression
    ]
END
```

You can use CASE to replace values in the category column in the title table with more descriptive text. The CASE function is inserted in the SELECT statement:

```
SELECT category =
  CASE type
    WHEN 'popular_comp' THEN 'Popular Computing'
    WHEN 'mod_cook' THEN 'Modern Cooking'
    WHEN 'business' THEN 'Business'
    WHEN 'psychology' THEN 'Psychology'
    WHEN 'trad_cook' THEN 'Traditional Cooking'
    ELSE 'N/A'
  END,
  title, price
FROM titles
```

Here's the first few rows of the result set:

category	title	price
Business	The Busy Executive's Database Guide	19.9900
Business	Cooking with Computers: Surreptitious Balance Sheets	11.9500
Business	You Can Combat Computer Stress!	2.9900
Business	Straight Talk About Computers	19.9900
Modern Cooking	Silicon Valley Gastronomic Treats	19.9900
Modern Cooking	The Gourmet Microwave	2.9900
N/A	The Psychology of Computer Cooking	NULL
Popular Computing	But Is It User Friendly?	22.9500

Using CASE to Replace the Iif() Function

An immediately useful example of the CASE function is to replace the VBA immediate if function (Iif). The Iif() function has this syntax:

```
Iif(Expression, TruePart, FalsePart)
```

The expression is evaluated, and if true, TruePart is returned. If the expression is false, FalsePart is returned. The CASE function can be used as follows:

```
CASE
WHEN Expression THEN TruePart
ELSE FalsePart
END
```

The following SELECT statement uses CASE to print out whether the quantity of books ordered by a store is above the average quantity or below the average quantity:

```
SELECT stor_id, qty, qtyavg =
  CASE
```

```
   WHEN qty > 23
   THEN 'above average'
   ELSE 'below average'
  END
FROM sales
```

Here are the first few rows of the result set:

```
stor_id qty     qtyavg
------- ------  -------------
6380    5       below average
6380    3       below average
7066    50      above average
7066    75      above average
7067    10      below average
```

WAITFOR

The WAITFOR statement pauses Transact-SQL until either the specified amount of time has passed or until a specific time has been reached. Here's how to pause Transact-SQL for 10 seconds:

```
WAITFOR DELAY '000:00:10'
```

Here's how to wait until noon:

```
WAITFOR TIME '12:00:00'
```

Your connection will be blocked from any activity during the WAITFOR period.

Commenting Your Code

Commenting your code is a good thing—Transact-SQL supports two different ways to comment code. You can use either a double-dash (- -) for commenting a single line or slash star (/*) and star slash (*/) for comments that need to span multiple lines. Here's an example:

```
--This is a single-line comment

/* This
    is
    a multiple
    line comment
*/
```

Other Querying Techniques

In addition to the basics covered so far in this chapter, SQL Server supports some very useful advanced techniques that are not part of standard SQL but that may seem like old hat to experienced Access developers.

Top Values Queries

If you've worked with top values queries in Access, the good news is that they also work in SQL Server. However, the syntax and behavior isn't exactly the same, as you'll see in this section.

TOP Syntax

The TOP operator is actually part of the SELECT statement syntax:

```
SELECT [ ALL | DISTINCT ]
    [ TOP n [PERCENT] [ WITH TIES] ]
    <select_list>
```

You can specify either a top percent or a number.

Creating a TOP Query

To write a query to show the top three authors in terms of quantity of books sold, you need to join the sales table to the titleauthor table. The grouping is by author ID, and the aggregate function is summing the quantity sold. It is very important to have the right ORDER BY clause in descending order because that determines which rows will qualify as top values. If the ORDER BY were in ascending order, you'd be showing the authors with the fewest number of books sold:

```
SELECT TOP 3
  titleauthor.au_id,
  SUM(sales.qty) AS TotalQuantity
FROM titleauthor INNER JOIN sales
  ON titleauthor.title_id = sales.title_id
GROUP BY titleauthor.au_id
ORDER BY SUM(sales.qty) DESC
```

Here's the result set:

```
au_id        TotalQuantity
-----------  -------------
899-46-2035  148
998-72-3567  133
213-46-8915  50
```

Using WITH TIES

So far, the top values syntax in SQL Server looks the same as what you may be used to in Access. But here's an important difference: Imagine a scenario where two authors are tied for third place. SQL Server automatically truncates the output at three rows in a top values query, even if there's a tie for third place and more rows actually qualify. Access will show all the rows that are tied for last place. You aren't getting the top *x* number of rows; you are getting the top *x* number of values, appearing in an indeterminate number of rows. If you want SQL Server to behave like Access and show you all the ties, you need to use the keywords WITH TIES after the TOP operator. Here's the query:

```
SELECT TOP 3 WITH TIES
  titleauthor.au_id,
  SUM(sales.qty) AS TotalQuantity
FROM titleauthor INNER JOIN sales
  ON titleauthor.title_id = sales.title_id
GROUP BY titleauthor.au_id
ORDER BY SUM(sales.qty) DESC
```

Here's the result set, which returns five rows instead of the original three rows that were returned without the WITH TIES modifier:

```
au_id        TotalQuantity
-----------  -------------
899-46-2035  148
998-72-3567  133
846-92-7186  50
213-46-8915  50
427-17-2319  50
```

8

Creating Distributed Queries with Linked Servers

One of the big advantages of working with Access is its ability to link to data in other file formats and to run queries against that foreign data without having to import it. SQL Server 7.0 introduced the ability to create linked servers, which provides similar functionality.

How Linked Servers Work

Linked servers in SQL Server are implemented using OLE DB, which means you can access data from any source that has an OLE DB provider, including all ODBC data sources. OLE DB providers return data in rowsets, which you can reference directly in Transact-SQL as though the rowsets were SQL Server tables. OLE DB providers are discussed in Chapter 6.

There are two steps to setting up a linked server:

1. Set up the link using the Enterprise Manager or run the `sp_addlinkedserver` system stored procedure.

2. Define a login for the linked server to provide authentication. You can handle this in the Enterprise Manager when you set up the linked server or by running the `sp_addlinked-serverlogin` system stored procedure.

Once you've got your linked server set up, there are two different ways to query it:

- Using Transact-SQL statements. You need to refer to linked server objects with a special four-part syntax, but otherwise it is the same as querying native SQL Server tables. This is similar to the way Access handles linked tables—you can use the Access Query Designer to create a query against a linked table without having to know anything about the native syntax of the data source. That same capability now exists in SQL Server using linked servers.

- Using `OPENQUERY`. `OPENQUERY` lets you write the query in the syntax of the provider, much the same way Access lets you write pass-through queries when you work with external data in Access. `OPENQUERY` isn't parsed by SQL Server; it's simply passed along to the data source.

See Chapter 12 for examples of using linked servers and `OPENQUERY` to work with OLAP data, by using the OLE DB provider for Analysis Services, the OLAP and data warehousing server that ships with SQL Server.

Setting Up a Linked Server

You can easily set up a linked server to the Northwind database in Access by using the Enterprise Manager. Right-click the Linked Servers icon in the Security folder on your server and choose Linked Servers, New Linked Server. This will load the dialog box shown in Figure 8.22. Name the linked server and specify the OLE DB provider in the drop-down list box. The only other option you need to fill in is the path and filename in the Data Source field—leave the other text boxes blank. You don't need to bother with the Security or the Server Options tab for an Access database.

Providing Login Information

For linked servers that require user authentication, you must click the Security tab and provide login information to the linked server. Choose the **Be made using this security context** option and type the user name in as the **Remote login.** This is shown in Figure 8.23, where the Admin user is specified. The Northwind database is not secured, thus all users are silently logged in as the Admin user with no password. As noted earlier, for Access this option is irrelevant—the linked server will work just fine if you choose the default **Be made without using a security context** option.

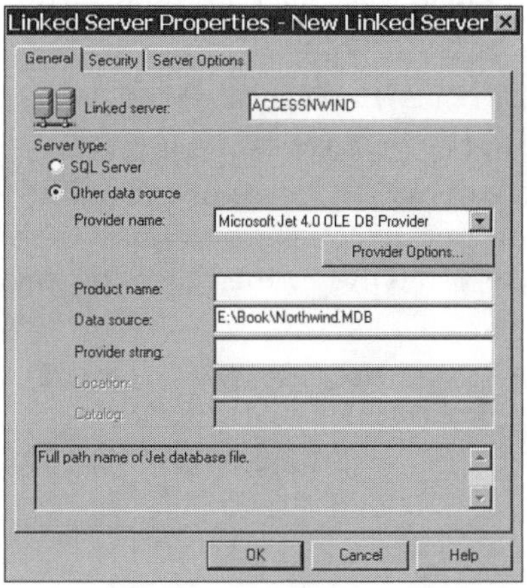

Figure 8.22
Setting up a linked server using the Enterprise Manager.

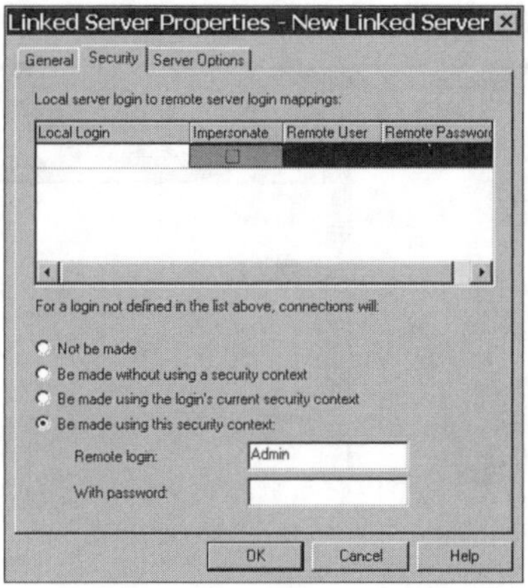

Figure 8.23
Setting the security context of a linked server using the Enterprise Manager.

Displaying a Table List

When you click OK, the linked server (and its associated login) will be created. To see a list of tables on the linked server, expand the plus sign to the left of the linked server name and double-click the Tables icon. This displays the tables available in the Northwind database, as shown in Figure 8.24.

FIGURE 8.24

Viewing the linked tables in the Enterprise Manager.

Setting Up a Linked Server Using Stored Procedures

You can also run the `sp_addlinkedserver` and `sp_addlinkedsrvlogin` stored procedures to create a linked server. When you run the stored procedure, you need to supply the parameters values, which correspond exactly to the dialog box entries in Enterprise Manager. All Enterprise Manager is doing is running this system stored procedure behind the scenes:

```
sp_addlinkedserver
    @server = 'AccessNwind',
    @provider = 'Microsoft.Jet.OLEDB.4.0',
    @srvproduct = '',
    @datasrc = 'E:\Book\Northwind.mdb'
```

Once you've created the linked server, a login must still be added using `sp_addlinkedsrvlogin`, which corresponds to the Security tab of the Add Linked Server dialog box in the Enterprise Manager:

```
sp_addlinkedsrvlogin
  @rmtsrvname='AccessNwind',
  @useself='False',
  @rmtuser='Admin'
```

As noted earlier in this section, running the `sp_addlinkedsrvlogin` stored procedure to create a login is not required for Access.

Querying the Linked Server

Once the linked server is set up and configured, you can write queries against it.

Getting a Table List Using `sp_tables_ex`

To see a list of tables in the Query Analyzer, run the `sp_tables_ex` system stored procedure. A partial result set is shown in Figure 8.25. Note that the system tables are listed and that there are null values displayed in the TABLE_CAT (the database name) and TABLE_SCHEM columns (the table owner) because those columns don't have any meaning for an Access database. TABLE_NAME corresponds to the table name as it's defined in Access. The Remarks column corresponds to the Comments database property in Access. Here's the query:

```
sp_tables_ex 'AccessNwind'
```

Writing Transact-SQL Against a Linked Server

When you query the linked server, you need to use a special, four-part syntax:

```
ServerName.[table_catalog].[table_schema].TableName
```

The optional `[table_catalog]` and `[table_schema]` identifiers map to the TABLE_CAT and TABLE_SCHEM columns, which are null in an Access database. So when you write a query against Access, you just leave the place in between the dots empty when you specify the linked server name and the table you're interested in. It looks like an ellipsis (...), but each dot is a placeholder for the null category and schema identifiers. Figure 8.26 shows the result set of the following query:

```
SELECT CustomerId, CompanyName, ContactName
FROM AccessNwind...Customers
```

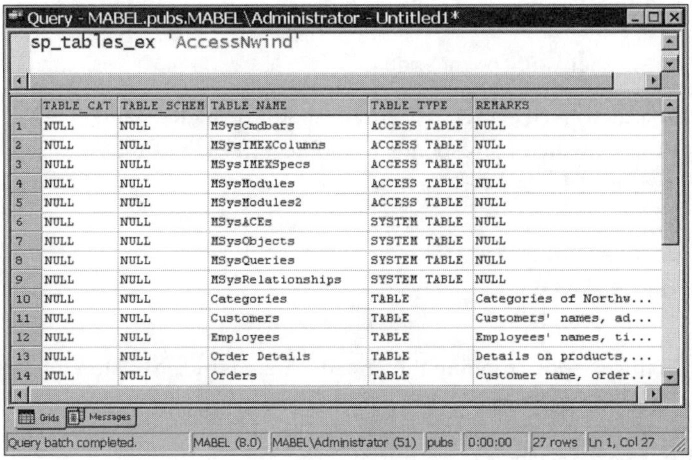

FIGURE 8.25

Viewing the linked tables using sp_tables_ex *in the Query Analyzer.*

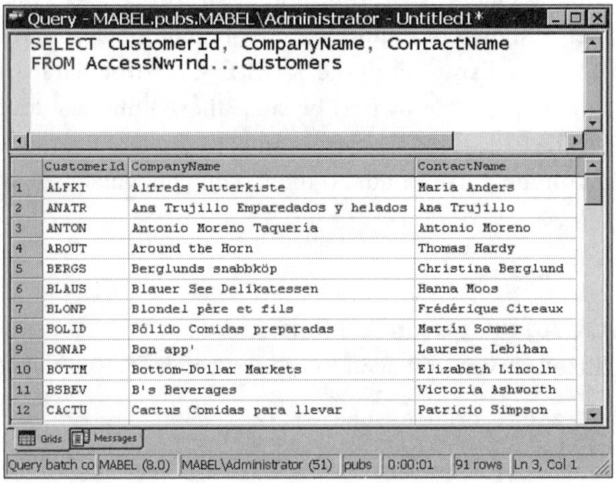

FIGURE 8.26

Viewing the results of the linked server query in the Query Analyzer.

If you need to prepend the table name to field names in a linked server query because you have more than one table, you can't use the four-part syntax because you will get a compile error. For column references in the SELECT column list, the syntax is reduced to three parts: the linked server name, the table name, and the column name. You still need the four-part syntax for the FROM clause table reference. Here's an example:

```
SELECT AccessNwind.Customers.CustomerId,
  AccessNwind.Customers.CompanyName,
  AccessNwind.Customers.ContactName
FROM AccessNwind...Customers
```

Other than the multipart syntax for referring to linked server object names, writing queries against linked servers is exactly the same as writing queries against native SQL Server tables. You can perform heterogeneous joins between linked tables and native SQL Server tables or between linked tables in different linked servers.

Using OPENQUERY with a Linked Server

OPENQUERY works with a linked server to allow you to process a query on the linked server. This allows you to use SQL syntax that's not supported in Transact-SQL. For example, if you have data that's still in Access and you want to create an Access crosstab query, you can do so using OPENQUERY. OPENQUERY simply passes a string to Access for processing in Access. Note that the string used here also contains the Access-VBA Format() function in addition to the non–Transact-SQL TRANSFORM and PIVOT statements. Any Access-VBA function or user-defined function that is legal in Access can be used with OPENQUERY, because the Jet database engine is doing all the processing, not SQL Server. Note that the SQL statement being sent to Jet is surrounded by single quotes, yet the query itself contains invalid Transact-SQL syntax. Here's the example:

```
SELECT * FROM OPENQUERY(AccessNwind,
  'TRANSFORM Count(Orders.OrderID) AS NumOrd
  SELECT [CompanyName] & ", " & [ContactName] AS Name
  FROM Customers INNER JOIN Orders
    ON Customers.CustomerID = Orders.CustomerID
  WHERE (((Orders.OrderDate) Between #1/1/1995# And #12/31/1995#))
  GROUP BY [CompanyName] & ", " & [ContactName]
  PIVOT Format([OrderDate],"mm/yyyy")')
```

OPENQUERY only works with linked servers and exists solely to provide extended functionality that exists on your linked server but that isn't available in SQL Server.

Cleanup: Removing Linked Servers

If you want to delete a linked server from the Enterprise Manager, all you need to do is select it in the Linked Servers folder and press the Delete key. You'll get prompted to confirm, and once you click OK, both the linked server and its associated logins are dropped.

To delete the linked server using Transact-SQL, run the `sp_dropserver` stored procedure, supplying the linked server name to the `@Server` parameter and the literal string `'droplogins'` to the `@DropLogins` parameter. That achieves the same result as deleting the linked server in the Enterprise Manager, without the dialog box prompting you to confirm. Here's an example:

```
sp_dropserver
  @Server='AccessNwind',
  @DropLogins='droplogins'
```

An Alternative to Linked Servers: OPENROWSET

To query a remote server, you aren't forced to set up a linked server every time. Instead, you can use OPENROWSET. The arguments you pass to OPENROWSET provide the same information that the linked server uses—the OLE DB provider, data source, login information, and so on. Here's an example:

```
OPENROWSET('provider_name'
    {
        'datasource';'user_id';'password'
        | 'provider_string'
    },
    {
        [catalog.][schema.]object
        | 'query'
    })
```

The advantage of OPENROWSET is that it can be used dynamically at runtime to query a remote server without establishing a linked server. The disadvantage is that there is overhead involved in locating the remote server and establishing the connection, so the query will run more slowly than a query against a linked server.

Using OPENROWSET to Query an Access Database

To use OPENROWSET to query the Access Northwind Categories table, you supply all the connection information to OPENROWSET as well as the SQL statement you want processed:

```
SELECT Nw.*
FROM OPENROWSET(
  'Microsoft.Jet.OLEDB.4.0',
  'E:\Book\Northwind.mdb';'admin';'',
  'SELECT CategoryName, Description
  FROM Categories'
  ) AS Nw
```

Here's the result set:

```
CategoryName    Description
--------------  --------------------------------------------------------
Beverages       Soft drinks, coffees, teas, beers, and ales
Condiments      Sweet and savory sauces, relishes, spreads, and seasonings
Confections     Desserts, candies, and sweet breads
Dairy Products  Cheeses
Grains/Cereals  Breads, crackers, pasta, and cereal
Meat/Poultry    Prepared meats
Produce         Dried fruit and bean curd
Seafood         Seaweed and fish
```

Summary

In this chapter you've learned a bit about the history of Transact-SQL and seen a small part of what you can accomplish using it. This is only scratching the surface—one chapter couldn't possibly cover all there is to know about Transact-SQL when there are whole books devoted solely to this subject. However, if you haven't had much previous experience with Transact-SQL or with any dialect of SQL, then you're now off to a good start. A solid Transact-SQL grounding will help you get up to speed quickly in your transformation from Access developer to SQL Server developer. When you're ready to explore Transact-SQL in more detail, you'll find that it is very well documented in SQL Server Books Online and that there are other excellent third-party books on the topic.

Creating and Optimizing Views

IN THIS CHAPTER

Defining Views

Views are often puzzling to Access developers. It can take a while to understand exactly what views can and cannot do. Think of views as saved SELECT statements, with just a couple of limitations. The biggest problem is that just when you get used to accepting a limitation, Microsoft comes up with an amazing, new feature that overcomes it! It's great to get the extra features, but it makes it harder to nail down exactly what you can and cannot do with views.

Views have never in the past been able to contain parameters; however, as shown later in the chapter, user-defined functions can now be used like views, effectively allowing you to create parameterized views that return different results depending on the parameter values that get passed in each time the function is run. Unlike stored procedures (which also support parameters), these parameterized functions can be updateable, as you'll see later in this chapter.

The SQL-92 standard also mandates that views cannot be sorted with an ORDER BY clause. Like tables in a relational database, the order of the records in a view is undefined. However, Transact-SQL includes an extension to the language that allows you to select TOP values with a view; to support that, it also supports sorting. To return the top 10 customers or the top 10% of customers, based on sales over the past year, SQL Server needs to sort customers by sales. So, a view that returns the top 100% by sales would essentially be a sorted view. The TOP syntax is covered in Chapter 8, "Introduction to Transact-SQL (T-SQL)."

Views have also never been able to contain triggers. In SQL Server 2000, however, a view can contain one INSTEAD OF trigger for each triggering action (INSERT, UPDATE, and DELETE). If any of these actions is performed on a view, SQL Server calls the INSTEAD OF trigger "instead of" making any direct changes to the data. INSTEAD OF triggers in views are covered later in this chapter.

Another limitation of views that you may be familiar with is that a view cannot be indexed. Guess what? In SQL Server 2000, you can indeed create indexed views, as shown later in this chapter.

Views still, however, don't allow you to perform any of the other major SQL actions besides selecting—views can't contain INSERT, UPDATE, or DELETE statements or DDL (Data Definition Language).

View Syntax

View syntax is very simple—it's nothing more than a SELECT statement with a CREATE VIEW...AS wrapper that causes the statement to be saved as a view. Listing 9.1 shows a simple view that selects certain columns from the Customers table in the Northwind database.

LISTING 9.1   A Simple View

```
CREATE VIEW vwCustomerAddressList
AS
SELECT CompanyName, ContactName, Address,
  City, Region, PostalCode, Country
FROM Customers
```

Later in the chapter, the special options WITH ENCRYPTION and WITH CHECK OPTION are discussed. These can be added to the basic SELECT syntax when defining a view.

What Views Are Good For

The primary use of views is to present data to users of an application. Views can be used in place of tables in your Access front-end application, whether you're using an Access database or an Access project. Views can also reference functions and other views.

Join Tables

A user can query a single view instead of having to learn complex join syntax and understand the structure of your database. As far as the user is concerned, the view looks just like a table. The following Transact-SQL statement selects all the data for the view shown in Listing 9.1, sorting the result set on the CompanyName column:

```
SELECT * from vwCustomerAddressList
ORDER BY CompanyName
```

In this case, the underlying view didn't contain any joins. But even if it had, the SELECT statement wouldn't have to change. The information about where the data in a view comes from and how it is pulled together from various tables is all encapsulated inside the view.

Customize Data

Tables can be customized and tailored to the needs of the users by way of views. For example, you could create a view for a salesperson that only displays her own orders, or you might create a view for the manager, who is only interested in seeing the total sales for each salesperson. Views give you a mechanism for presenting the same data to different users in different ways.

Restricting Columns and Rows

Columns and rows can be restricted, allowing users to focus on specific data that interests them. Unnecessary data is left out. This also helps network performance because less data is traveling over the wire to client applications. Using a view to filter data on the server is much more efficient than fetching an entire table and then applying a filter on the client. To restrict the rows in a view, you use the same kinds of criteria in a WHERE clause that you are already familiar with. To restrict the columns, you simply leave certain columns out of the SELECT clause. For example, the following view limits the result set by selecting only the employee first name, last name, and hire date columns from the Employees table, and it limits the rows returned to employees hired this year:

```
CREATE VIEW vwEmployeesHiredThisYear
AS
   SELECT LastName, FirstName, HireDate
   FROM Employees
   WHERE Year(HireDate) = Year(Getdate())
```

Preaggregate Data

One of the most powerful uses of views is for reporting. A view can be used to wrap up complex queries containing subqueries, outer joins, and aggregation. This simplifies access to the data because the underlying query does not have to be written on the client and then submitted each time a report is run.

You may already have discovered that you can often greatly speed up Access reports by first saving the results of a complex record source query into a temporary table and then basing the report on that table rather than on the query. Similar performance benefits can be gained with SQL Server by basing your reports on views. For example, the following view selects a customer's total orders and contains joins between the Customers table, the Orders table, and the Order Details table. When a user selects data from the view, only the result set is passed over the network—all of the joins and aggregations are performed on the server, not on the client.

```
CREATE VIEW vwCustomerOrders
AS
SELECT dbo.Customers.CompanyName,
   SUM(dbo.[Order Details].UnitPrice *
   dbo.[Order Details].Quantity) AS Total
FROM dbo.Customers
   INNER JOIN
     dbo.Orders
     ON
     dbo.Customers.CustomerID = dbo.Orders.CustomerID
   INNER JOIN
     dbo.[Order Details]
     ON
     dbo.Orders.OrderID = dbo.[Order Details].OrderID
GROUP BY dbo.Customers.CompanyName
```

Rules for Creating and Using Views

Views are created inside individual databases, however, views can reference tables and views in other databases or even on other servers (if the view is defined using distributed queries). Here are some general guidelines for creating views:

- Names of views must follow the same rules for identifiers, discussed in Chapter 7, "Designing and Creating a SQL Server Database," and they must be unique for each owner in the database. However, your best bet is to make sure that all objects are owned by dbo so that there are no breaks in the ownership chain. Later in this chapter, views, security, and ownership chains are discussed.

- Views can be built on other views and can be nested up to 32 levels deep.

- To create a view, you must be granted permission to do so by the database owner, and you must have appropriate permissions on any tables or views referenced in the view definition.

Things You Can't Do in Views

Views are much more restricted in their capabilities than Access queries. Here's a list of the things you can't do in a view:

- Rules, defaults, and triggers cannot be associated with views. An exception to this is INSTEAD OF triggers, which are new to SQL Server 2000 and are discussed later in this chapter.

- ORDER BY, COMPUTE, and COMPUTE BY clauses or the INTO keyword can't be used in views. An exception to this is the ORDER BY clause, which is allowed only in conjunction with the TOP keyword. ORDER BY and TOP are covered later in this chapter.

- Full-text indexes can't be defined on views. However, other types of indexes can be defined on views in SQL Server 2000. (This feature is not available in SQL Server 7.0.)

- Views cannot be based on temporary tables.

- You cannot issue full-text queries against a view, although a view definition can include a full-text query if the query references a table that has been configured for full-text indexing.

- You can't pass parameters to views, although you'll learn later in the chapter how user-defined functions in SQL Server 2000 enable you to skirt this restriction.

Views and Security

Views are frequently used as security mechanisms to prevent users from having direct access to tables while still allowing them to work with data. All permissions can be removed from the underlying tables, and as long as the owner of the table is the same as the owner of the view, the user will be able to interact with the data based on the permissions granted to the view. Figure 9.1 shows the Permissions dialog box for vwCustomeraddressList. As long as both the view and the Customers table are owned by dbo, the permissions granted on the view will take precedence over permissions removed from the Customers table.

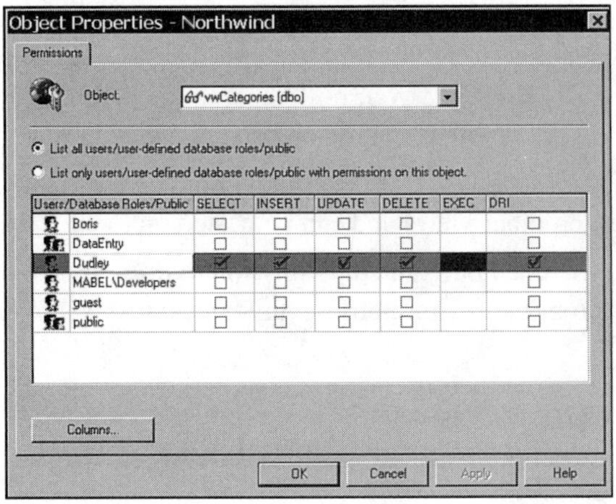

FIGURE 9.1
Setting permissions on a view.

Because views allow you to restrict the rows and columns that are available, using them as a security tool is very convenient. For example, you could create two views on an Employees table, one with a sensitive salary column included that only managers had permissions on, and a second view with that column omitted for everyone else.

Chain of Ownership Issues

One reason it's recommended that the dbo own all objects in a database is that problems arise when the chain of ownership is broken. This happens when the view and the underlying table do not have the same owner. When the chain of ownership is broken, you need to grant users the same permissions on the underlying tables as you want them to have on the view, which nullifies the effectiveness of views as security mechanisms. Another problem you'll encounter with Access projects (ADPs) is that if you want users to be able to update data using a view, you also have to grant them permissions on the underlying tables.

Using Views to Implement Column-Level or Row-Level Security

Although you can set column-level security in SQL Server, it is tricky to maintain because it's pretty well buried in the table properties. Row-level security must be defined at runtime because it's impossible to know what values a table will contain until then. A simple solution to the issue of implementing row-level and column-level security is to revoke all permissions to the underlying tables. Instead, define views with only selected columns to implement column-level security and define views with a WHERE clause to implement row-level security. Then grant appropriate permissions on the views for the users and roles you want to be able to access the data.

Hiding Underlying Table or Column Names

Views can also be used to hide the real column names or underlying schema of your tables. This can be implemented using the AS keyword to alias columns in your SELECT statements:

```
CREATE VIEW vwObscure
AS
SELECT CompanyName AS C, ContactName AS CN
FROM Customers
```

Anyone using the view would query it using the following syntax and would never know which actual tables or columns were being used:

```
SELECT C, CN
FROM vwObscure
```

A second technique is to use a column list:

```
CREATE VIEW vwObscure (C, CN)
AS
SELECT CompanyName, ContactName
FROM Customers
```

The following query will also work with either view:

```
SELECT * FROM vwObscure
```

Encrypting Views

The definition of a sensitive view can be encrypted to ensure that its definition cannot be obtained by anyone, including the owner of the view, by using the WITH ENCRYPTION option when the view is created. Listing 9.2 shows the syntax for creating an encrypted view.

LISTING 9.2   Creating an Encrypted View

```
CREATE VIEW vwEncrypted
WITH ENCRYPTION
AS
   SELECT CompanyName AS C, ContactName AS CN
   FROM Customers AS CL
```

9

CREATING AND OPTIMIZING VIEWS

Once the view is created, its definition will be unreadable, as shown in Figure 9.2. Therefore, make sure that you save your view definition in a script file in case you ever need to modify it.

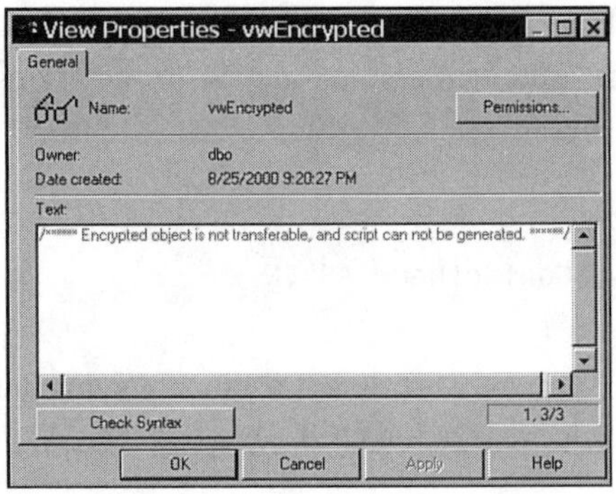

FIGURE 9.2
The definition of an encrypted view.

Creating and Modifying Views

You can create views using the Enterprise Manager, the Query Analyzer, or an Access project. In addition, the Enterprise Manager has the Create View Wizard, which walks you through the process of creating a simple view.

Creating Views Using the Create View Wizard

To create a view using the Enterprise Manager, select Tools, Wizards, Database, Create View Wizard. The introductory dialog box on the wizard informs you that the wizard can perform the following actions:

- Select the database referenced by the view
- Select one or more tables referenced by the view
- Select one or more columns that you want the view to display
- Name the view and define restrictions

The second wizard dialog box then lets you select the database. The one after that lets you select the tables involved in the view, as shown in Figure 9.3, where the Employees, Order Details, Orders, Products, and Customers tables are selected from the Northwind database.

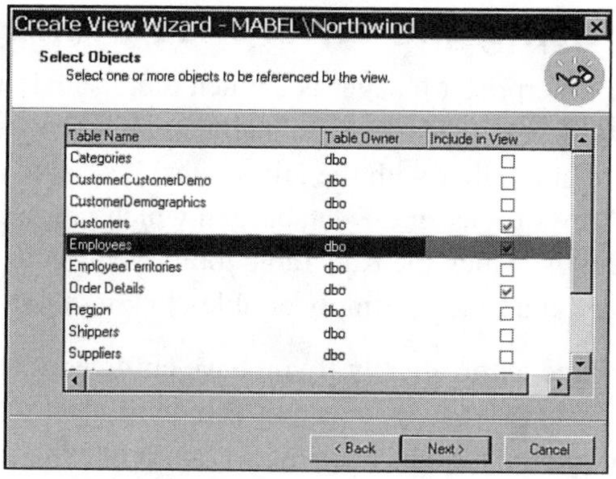

FIGURE 9.3

Selecting tables using the Create View Wizard.

Figure 9.4 shows the dialog box for selecting the columns to be displayed in the view.

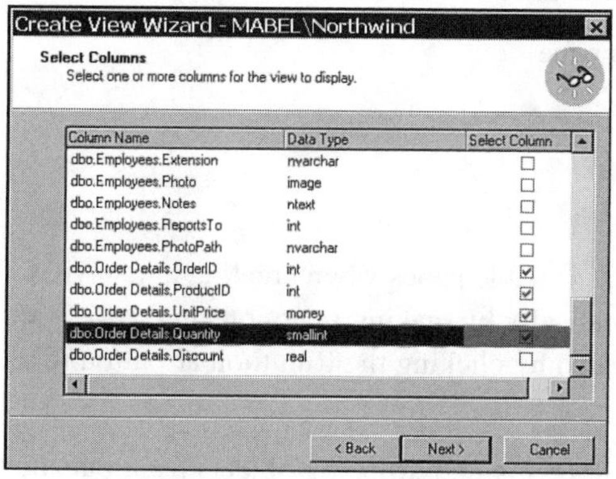

FIGURE 9.4

Selecting the columns to be displayed in the view.

The next wizard dialog box lets you type in a WHERE clause, thus limiting the rows in the view. The following one lets you name the view. The final wizard dialog box summarizes your options and lets you view the SELECT statement that will be created.

The main problem with using the Create View Wizard is that it does not create the join syntax between tables if you select multiple tables. This limitation results in a Cartesian product query if you do not go in and modify the view by typing in the join syntax yourself. Also, it doesn't help at all in building criteria into a WHERE clause. For these reasons, using the Create View Wizard is pretty much a waste of time if you need anything other than a simple view on a single table.

Creating Views Using the Enterprise Manager

Creating a view using the Enterprise Manager is a much more satisfying experience than running the Create View Wizard. It will also automatically create join syntax for you, which is extremely useful if you are unfamiliar with the join syntax. To create a view in the Enterprise Manager, right-click the Views folder in the database in which you want to create the view and choose New View from the list. Click the Add Table toolbar button to add tables to the view. You can add multiple tables at a time by simply double-clicking them in the table list.

This time the joins are created automatically if you have enforced referential integrity in your SQL Server database. You can delete any joins that you don't want included in your view by selecting the join line and pressing the Delete key, without affecting the underlying referential integrity join that it was modeled on. You can also create ad hoc joins by dragging and dropping from one field to another. Select the columns to be displayed in the view by checking their associated check boxes.

The data tools have a four-pane window, the display of which is controlled by the toolbar buttons or the right-click menu. Here are the panes:

- Show/hide diagram pane
- Show/hide grid pane
- Show/hide SQL pane
- Show/hide results pane

Figure 9.5 shows the four available panes when creating a new view. The contents of the SQL pane are generated automatically by making selections in the diagram pane and the grid pane. The results pane is generated by clicking the Run toolbar button (or right-clicking and choosing Run from the list).

There are no options for dragging and dropping objects from outside the New View window when you create a view using the Enterprise Manager. Unfortunately, the New View window is opened modally, so you can't do anything else in the Enterprise Manager until you close the window. However, you can copy and paste from this window to other applications, which makes it useful even if you create views using the Query Analyzer, as discussed later in this chapter.

Creating Views Using an Access Project

To create a new view in an Access project, select Views from the object list and click New. The visual data tools are very similar to the ones in the Enterprise Manager, but there are a few differences in the toolbar buttons and the panes available. The display of results in a datasheet works only after the view has been saved. (You can display the results of a view in the Enterprise Manager without having to save it first.)

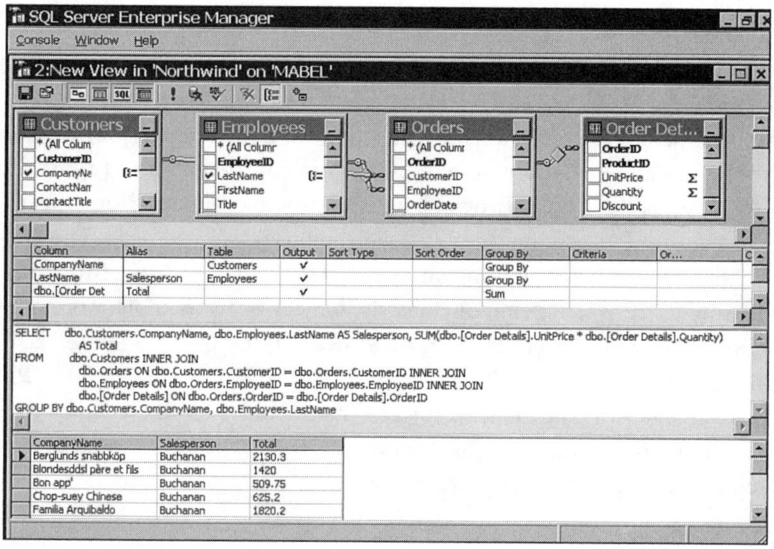

FIGURE 9.5
The new view in the Enterprise Manager displays four sections.

The main advantage of using Access to create views is that the designer window isn't modal. In fact, you can drag and drop tables and views from the main object list to the diagram pane. Figure 9.6 shows the design of a view in an Access project.

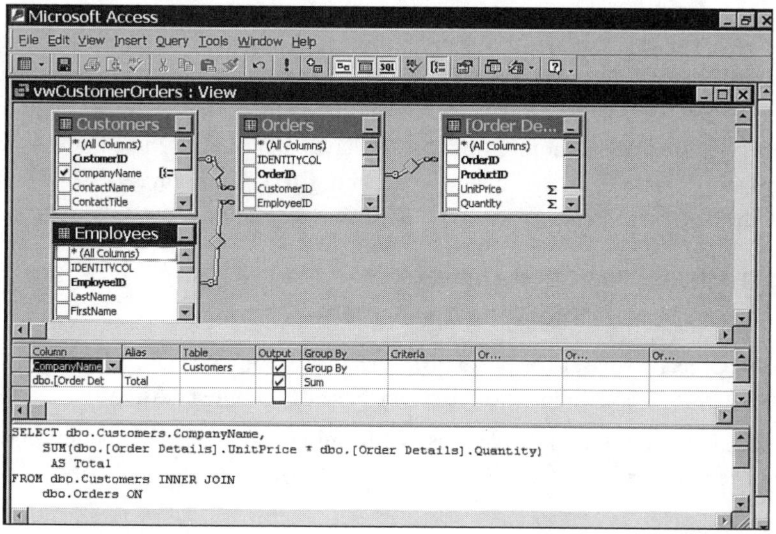

FIGURE 9.6
Creating a view using an Access project.

9

CREATING AND OPTIMIZING VIEWS

Creating Views Using the Query Analyzer

The Query Analyzer in SQL Server 2000 makes it much easier to create views than it was in past versions of the Query Analyzer. However, unlike using the visual data tools found in the Enterprise Manager and an Access project, you still have to do some typing (or some copying/pasting) because there's no tool that will create joins for you. A new feature in SQL Server 2000 Query Analyzer is the Object Browser, which lets you drag-and-drop objects and will automatically create SELECT statements with a right-mouse drag and drop. The Object Browser also contains three templates for creating simple views. Load the Object Browser by choosing View, Object Browser from the menu, clicking the Object Browser toolbar button, or pressing the F2 key. If you drag a table from the Object Browser to the Query Analyzer using the right mouse button instead of the left, you'll get a list of menu items to choose from. Pick SELECT, and a SELECT statement will be generated for you that includes all the columns in the selected table. However, if you have multiple tables and joins in your view, you need to type the join syntax yourself or paste it in from another source.

> **TIP**
>
> Because typing in join syntax is prone to errors, you can create joins using the visual data tools in the Enterprise Manager or an Access project and paste them into the Query Analyzer. This can be a great timesaver if you're not a good typist, or you're a little weak on join syntax.

You can test your SELECT statement prior to executing the CREATE VIEW by highlighting just the SELECT statement, leaving out the CREATE VIEW...AS header, and then clicking the Execute Query button or pressing the F5 key. This will run the SELECT statement, and you can view the result set in the results pane. Another option is to have your syntax parsed before executing it by choosing Query, Parse from the menu (or clicking Ctrl+F5). Figure 9.7 shows the definition of a view, with the Object Browser loaded, just after executing the CREATE VIEW statement.

Creating a View from a Template

There are two ways to create a view from a template:

- Load the Object Browser (or press F8), select the Templates tab, and drag a template from the Create View node onto the query pane of the Query Analyzer.
- Choose Edit, Insert Template (or press Ctrl+Shift+Ins) and select the template from the Create View folder.

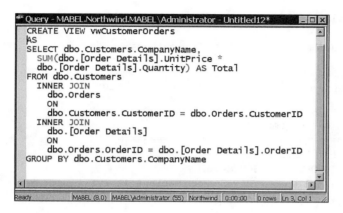

FIGURE 9.7

Creating a view using the Query Analyzer.

The three available templates are

- *Create View Basic Template.* Choose this to create a simple view.
- *Create View* WITH CHECK OPTION. Choose this to create a view that contains the WITH CHECK OPTION clause. This option prevents saving data to the underlying tables that does not match the view definition.
- *Create View* WITH SCHEMA BINDING. Choose this to create a view that contains the WITH SCHEMA BINDING clause. This option does not allow changes to the underlying tables unless the view is dropped first. However, views without this clause might not work properly if the schema of an underlying table is changed after the view is created.

The Query Analyzer will help you fill in the template parameters if you Choose Edit, Replace Template Parameters (or press Ctrl+Shift+M), by displaying a dialog box for you to fill in the template parameters. Click the Replace All button to have all the template parameters filled in automatically. The following output displays the view created by using the basic template before the parameters are replaced:

```
-- =============================================
-- Create view basic template
-- =============================================
IF EXISTS (SELECT TABLE_NAME
      FROM   INFORMATION_SCHEMA.VIEWS
      WHERE  TABLE_NAME = N'<view_name, sysname, view_test>')
   DROP VIEW <view_name, sysname, view_test>
GO
```

9

CREATING AND OPTIMIZING VIEWS

```
CREATE VIEW <view_name, sysname, view_test>
AS
    <select_statement, , SELECT * FROM authors>
GO
```

And here's the view after the parameters have been replaced:

```
-- ===============================================
-- Create view basic template
-- ===============================================
IF EXISTS (SELECT TABLE_NAME
      FROM   INFORMATION_SCHEMA.VIEWS
      WHERE  TABLE_NAME = N'vwProductsSelect')
    DROP VIEW vwProductsSelect
GO

CREATE VIEW vwProductsSelect
AS
    SELECT * FROM Products
GO
```

Note that all the text inside the chevrons in the template has been replaced. You can also add your own custom templates by following the instructions for creating new templates outlined in Chapter 8.

Using ALTER VIEW to Modify a View

If you try to use the CREATE VIEW syntax on a view that has already been saved, you'll get an error. SQL Server allows you to alter the definition of a view using the ALTER VIEW syntax, which is almost identical to the CREATE VIEW syntax (with the substitution of the word ALTER for the word CREATE). Listing 9.3 modifies an existing view by adding a WHERE clause to show only products that are not discontinued.

LISTING 9.3 Modifying a View That Already Exists

```
ALTER VIEW vwProductByCategory
AS
  SELECT CategoryName, ProductName, UnitPrice
    FROM Products
  INNER JOIN Categories
    ON Products.CategoryID = Categories.CategoryID
  WHERE Discontinued = 0
```

The ALTER VIEW syntax was introduced in SQL Server 7.0. In prior versions of SQL Server, you had to drop a view and then re-create it. The advantage of ALTER VIEW is that only the definition of the view is changed. If the view was dropped and re-created, a new object ID would be generated, and all internal references to the view would be invalidated. All permissions on the view would be lost, and any stored procedures using the view would need to be recompiled.

> **NOTE**
>
> If you use an Access project to modify an existing view, only the SELECT statement defining the view is shown. Access takes care of using the ALTER VIEW syntax behind the scenes.

Views, Subqueries, and Outer Joins

Another use of views is to encapsulate complex joins and subqueries. For example, here are a couple of ways to find out if there are any orders without corresponding order detail line items.

The following view uses NOT EXISTS to determine if there are any orders that do not have any line items:

```
CREATE VIEW vwNoOrderDetails
AS
  SELECT OrderID
  FROM Orders
  WHERE NOT EXISTS
    (SELECT OD.OrderID
      FROM [Order Details] OD
      WHERE Orders.OrderID = OD.OrderID)
```

A user simply has to write the following query to find empty orders:

```
SELECT * FROM vwNoOrderDetails
```

Another way to write the same query would be to use a LEFT JOIN instead of a subquery:

```
CREATE VIEW vwNoOrderDetailsJoin
AS
  SELECT Orders.OrderID
  FROM Orders
    LEFT JOIN [Order Details] OD
    ON Orders.OrderID = OD.OrderID
    WHERE OD.OrderID IS NULL
```

The second technique, using a LEFT JOIN, will be more efficient in most cases. However, performance will also depend on the amount of data in your tables and the indexes you have defined.

Sorting and Top Values in Views

If you look back to Figure 9.5, you'll see that the syntax used in the SELECT statement reads like this:

```
SELECT TOP 100 PERCENT ...
```

This apparently superfluous statement is needed because an ORDER BY clause appears at the end of the view definition. Here's a brief history of how SQL Server 2000 came to support sorting in views.

The TOP syntax was introduced in SQL Server 7.0 to provide the equivalent of an Access "top values" query, although there are some subtle differences—TOP is discussed in more detail in Chapter 8. To get top values, you need a sort order, so an ORDER BY clause is required in order for TOP to work properly.

The TOP syntax with its associated ORDER BY clause are Transact-SQL extensions and are not part of the ANSI SQL-92 standard. As far as the ANSI SQL-92 standard is concerned, the definition of a view is unordered. If you want an ordered view, you're supposed to use the ORDER BY clause in a SQL statement querying the view, the same way you would with a table. Here's an example:

```
SELECT * FROM MyView ORDER BY SomeColumn
```

However, enterprising developers working with SQL Server 7.0 soon discovered by reading the error message returned from SQL Server that they could use SELECT TOP 100 PERCENT to work around the ANSI SQL-92 restriction of not sorting in view definitions. If you try to use the ORDER BY clause in a view without the TOP syntax, you'll get an error message that tells you to use TOP. In SQL Server 2000, when you create a view in Enterprise Manager, TOP 100 PERCENT is inserted by default, and sorting options are provided. This new sorting capability in views might offend some SQL purists, but developers, who have long found it frustrating not to be able to sort in views, welcome it wholeheartedly. The complete view syntax is shown in Listing 9.4.

LISTING 9.4 Creating a Sorted View

```
CREATE VIEW dbo.vwCustomerOrderTotals
AS
  SELECT TOP 100 PERCENT Customers.CompanyName,
    Orders.OrderID, Orders.OrderDate,
    Employees.LastName AS SoldBy,
    SUM([Order Details].UnitPrice *
    [Order Details].Quantity) AS Total
```

LISTING 9.4   Continued

```
FROM  Customers
  INNER JOIN Orders
    ON Customers.CustomerID = Orders.CustomerID
  INNER JOIN Employees
    ON Orders.EmployeeID = Employees.EmployeeID
  INNER JOIN [Order Details]
    ON Orders.OrderID = [Order Details].OrderID
GROUP BY Customers.CompanyName, Orders.OrderID,
  Orders.OrderDate, Employees.LastName
ORDER BY Customers.CompanyName, Orders.OrderDate DESC
```

Views with Functions

Aside from the inability to sort in views, the other major limitation has traditionally been that views cannot contain parameters. This, too, is now no longer a problem. SQL Server 2000 allows you to work with user-defined, table-valued functions as though they were views and to pass parameters to the functions as though they were stored procedures. Before switching over to user-defined functions, however, consider the advantages of using standard aggregate and system functions in views.

Using Aggregate Functions

Listing 9.5 shows a view that's used to calculate the total value sold by each employee. The SUM() function is used in the SELECT clause, and the GROUP BY clause groups by employee.

LISTING 9.5   Using an Aggregate Function in a View

```
CREATE VIEW vwOrderTotalsByEmployee
AS
  SELECT Employees.LastName, SUM([Order Details].UnitPrice *
    [Order Details].Quantity) AS Total
  FROM  Employees INNER JOIN Orders
    ON Employees.EmployeeID = Orders.EmployeeID
  INNER JOIN [Order Details]
    ON Orders.OrderID = [Order Details].OrderID
  GROUP BY Employees.LastName
```

Using System Functions

Listing 9.6 shows using a view employing the SUSER_SNAME() system function to query the Orders table. The SUSER_SNAME() system function returns the name of the current user. This would restrict the current user to viewing only orders in which that user was the recorded salesperson.

LISTING 9.6 Using a System Function in a View

```
CREATE View vwOrdersByUser
AS
SELECT * FROM Orders
WHERE SalesPerson = SUSER_SNAME()
```

In order for this view to work, you need to create a new column in the Orders table named "SalesPerson" with a data type of nvarchar. You also need to ensure that all rows have the correct values for each user. For example, each INSERT statement would need to place the username in the table so that views based on the table would return the correct results:

```
INSERT INTO Orders (CustomerID, SalesPerson)
VALUES ('BONAP', SUSER_SNAME())
```

An even better option would be to create a default value of SUSER_SNAME() for the SalesPerson column. That way you wouldn't have to explicitly insert the username each time. Setting up the table and view this way gives you a dynamic view, where users would see only their own orders.

The SUSER_SNAME() system function is similar to the CurrentUser() function in Access. You may be wondering why it isn't just called USER_NAME. Well, there's already a function by that name, but it returns the database username, not necessarily the login name of the user. For example, if you are logged on to SQL Server as user Bart, who is mapped to the sysadmin role, USER_NAME will return "dbo," but SUSER_SNAME() will return "Bart." SUSER_SNAME() will also return the Windows NT/Windows 2000 login name if you're using integrated security.

Using Views with User-Defined Functions

The three types of user-defined functions are

- Scalar functions, which return a single value. Here's an example of a simple scalar function that computes the average price of all products:

```
CREATE FUNCTION fnAvgProductPriceScalar()
RETURNS money
AS
BEGIN
  Declare @Average money
  SELECT @Average = (SELECT AVG(UnitPrice)FROM Products)
  RETURN @Average
END
```

- Inline table-valued functions, which contain a single SELECT statement that returns a set of rows, referred to as a *table*. Here's an example of an inline table-valued function that returns a table consisting of the ProductID, ProductName, and UnitPrice from the Products table:

```
CREATE FUNCTION fnProductSelectInline()
RETURNS TABLE
AS
  RETURN
  (SELECT ProductID, ProductName, UnitPrice
  FROM Products)
```

- Multi-statement table-valued functions, which can contain more complex statements contained within a BEGIN...END block. Like inline table-valued functions, multi-statement table-valued functions also return a table as the result set. Here's an example of a multi-statement table-valued function that has an optional input parameter. (All the function types support input parameters.) If the parameter is supplied, then only products matching a CategoryID are returned. If the parameter value is not supplied, all rows are returned:

```
CREATE  FUNCTION fnProductSelectTableMulti
  (@CategoryID int = NULL)
RETURNS @retProducts TABLE
  (ProductID int primary key,
  ProductName nvarchar(50) NOT NULL,
  UnitPrice money)
AS
BEGIN
-- Declare local table variable
DECLARE @temp TABLE (
  ProductID int primary key,
  ProductName nvarchar(50) NOT NULL,
  UnitPrice money)

IF @CategoryID IS NULL -- insert all records into variable
  BEGIN
    INSERT @temp
    SELECT Products.ProductID,
      Products.ProductName,
      Products.UnitPrice
    FROM Products
  END
ELSE   -- insert records matching parameter into variable
  BEGIN
    INSERT @temp
    SELECT Products.ProductID,
      Products.ProductName,
      Products.UnitPrice
    FROM Products
    WHERE CategoryID = @CategoryID
  END
```

9

CREATING AND OPTIMIZING VIEWS

```
  --Insert local table variable into Return table
  INSERT @retProducts
    SELECT ProductID, ProductName, UnitPrice
    FROM @temp
  RETURN
END
```

Each type of user-defined function can be used with views (or in place of views) in different ways.

Using Scalar Functions in Views

Scalar functions can be used in the SELECT clause of a query. The following view uses the fnAvgProductPriceScalar in the SELECT list.

```
CREATE VIEW vwUseScalarSELECT
AS
  SELECT ProductName,
    dbo.fnAvgProductPriceScalar() as AvgPrice,
    UnitPrice
  FROM Products
```

Here are the first few rows of the result set created by selecting all the rows from the view:

ProductName	AvgPrice	UnitPrice
Geitost	28.8923	2.5000
Guaraná Fantástica	28.8923	4.5000
Konbu	28.8923	6.0000

The scalar function can also be used in the WHERE clause. The following view selects only products whose prices are greater than the average computed by fnAvgProductPriceScalar:

```
CREATE VIEW vwUseScalarWHERE
AS
  SELECT ProductName, UnitPrice
  FROM Products
  WHERE UnitPrice > dbo.fnAvgProductPriceScalar()
```

Here are the first few rows of the result set from selecting all the rows from this view, which returns only products with prices that are above average:

ProductName	UnitPrice
Uncle Bob's Organic Dried Pears	30.0000
Ikura	31.0000
Gumbär Gummibärchen	31.2300

You can also use a function in both the SELECT and the WHERE clause. The following view uses the function in the SELECT clause to display the amount over average for any product whose UnitPrice is greater than average:

```
CREATE VIEW vwUseScalarBoth
AS
  SELECT ProductName, UnitPrice,
    (UnitPrice -dbo.fnAvgProductPriceScalar()) as AmtOverAverage
  FROM Products
  WHERE UnitPrice > dbo.fnAvgProductPriceScalar()
```

Here are the first few rows of the result set created by selecting all the rows from that view:

```
ProductName                             UnitPrice            AmtOverAverage
--------------------------------------- -------------------- ----------------
Uncle Bob's Organic Dried Pears         30.0000              1.1077
Ikura                                   31.0000              2.1077
Gumbär Gummibärchen                     31.2300              2.3377
```

Using Inline Functions in Views

Since inline functions return a table, they can be used in the FROM clause of a SELECT statement, as shown in the following view, which acts as a wrapper around the fnProductSelectInline() function:

```
CREATE VIEW vwInlineSelect
AS
  SELECT * FROM dbo.fnProductSelectInline()
```

Users could select columns from the view instead of using the more complicated function syntax:

```
SELECT ProductID, ProductName, UnitPrice
FROM vwInlineSelect
ORDER BY UnitPrice DESC
```

Another way to use an inline function in a view is as a subquery. The following view scans the Order Details table for ProductIDs that don't exist in the Products table by using the fnProductSelectInline() in a subquery.

```
CREATE VIEW vwInlineSelectFROM
AS
  SELECT ProductID, UnitPrice
  FROM [Order Details]
  WHERE NOT EXISTS
    (SELECT ProductID
    FROM dbo.fnProductSelectInline())
```

You can also use a view as the source for an inline function. For example, the following view joins the Customers, Orders, and Order Details tables to provide the total sales for each customer:

```
CREATE VIEW vwCustomerOrderTotals
AS
  SELECT dbo.Customers.CustomerID, dbo.Customers.CompanyName,
    SUM(dbo.[Order Details].UnitPrice *
    dbo.[Order Details].Quantity) AS Total
  FROM dbo.Customers
    INNER JOIN
      dbo.Orders
      ON
      dbo.Customers.CustomerID = dbo.Orders.CustomerID
    INNER JOIN
      dbo.[Order Details]
      ON
      dbo.Orders.OrderID = dbo.[Order Details].OrderID
  GROUP BY dbo.Customers.CustomerID, dbo.Customers.CompanyName
```

The following parameterized function selects data from the view that matches a particular CustomerID:

```
CREATE FUNCTION fnCustomerOrderTotalsView
    (@CustomerID char(5))
RETURNS TABLE
AS
    RETURN
    SELECT CompanyName, Total
    FROM vwCustomerOrderTotals
    WHERE CustomerID = @CustomerID
```

Note that the RETURN statement has a completely different meaning in functions than it does in stored procedures. In a stored procedure, RETURN causes the procedure to terminate, but in a function it just introduces the definition of the return set. Here's how you would query the function and supply a value for the parameter:

```
SELECT * FROM fnCustomerOrderTotalsView('ALFKI')
```

Although user-defined functions are useful in views, in some circumstances you may want to use them to replace views entirely. Their capability to support input parameters makes them more versatile than views. Plus, multi-statement table-valued functions give you all of the processing power of stored procedures.

Replacing Views with Table-Valued Functions

Multi-statement table-valued functions combine the best of both views and stored procedures. You can select from one like a view, and have parameters as with a stored procedure. The `fnProductSelectTableMulti()` function listed earlier in this section is flexible enough to be called with a parameter value or without one. Here's the syntax for calling it with specifying the default value for the `@CategoryID` input parameter:

```
SELECT * FROM dbo.fnProductSelectTableMulti(default)
```

Note that the keyword `default` is used inside the parentheses. This behavior is different from parameters with default values in stored procedures in which omitting the parameter implies the default value. If you omit both the parameter and the default keyword, you'll get the "An insufficient number of arguments were supplied for the procedure or function..." error.

The function will return all of the products in the Products table. If you call it with a parameter, then only the products matching the `@CategoryID` value will be returned. Here's the syntax for calling it with a parameter value:

```
SELECT * FROM dbo.fnProductSelectTableMulti(5)
```

Here's the first few rows of the result set, showing products from the one specified category:

```
ProductID   ProductName                                  UnitPrice
----------  -------------------------------------------  ----------
22          Gustaf's Knäckebröd                            21.0000
23          Tunnbröd                                        9.0000
42          Singaporean Hokkien Fried Mee                  14.0000
```

Note that you can also use an `ORDER BY` clause when selecting rows from a function. This query will sort the result set by `UnitPrice` in ascending order:

```
SELECT * FROM dbo.fnProductSelectTableMulti(5)ORDER BY UnitPrice
```

Multi-statement table-valued functions are a very useful hybrid, combining features of both views and stored procedures. Just like stored procedures, however, multi-statement table-value functions cannot be used in queries that update, insert, or delete data. To be updateable, a function must be based on a single `SELECT` statement. Inline functions (ones with a single `SELECT` statement) can both be updateable and take parameters—a feature not available in views or in stored procedures. Updating inline functions is covered later in this chapter.

Choosing Between Views and Functions

Once you've learned about SQL Server 2000's new user-defined functions, it's natural to wonder whether you ever really need to use the old-fashioned views. Here are some guidelines to follow when choosing between views and table-returning functions:

- As covered in this chapter, functions offer greater flexibility than views. Parameters are supported, and multi-statement functions can support stored-procedure-like Transact–SQL logic and flow control. If you need these features, then functions are a clear choice over views.

- Microsoft has stated that its intention was for there to be no performance penalty for using functions rather than comparable views. If you find a performance difference, it's a bug. But only time and experience will bear out whether Microsoft succeeded in meeting this goal. Initial tests indicate that it has.

- Views do offer the performance benefit of supporting indexing, a new feature in SQL Server 2000 that is discussed later in this chapter. You cannot create indexes for functions. You could, however, wrap an indexed view in an inline function.

- Views can be created with graphical tools, such as the New View dialog in the Enterprise Manager, or the Visual Data Tools in Access ADPs or in Visual Basic. There are no comparable tools for creating functions. Of course, you could create a view and copy and paste the T-SQL into a function.

Overall, you'll probably find that as you become more familiar with user-defined functions, you'll be using them more than views. Even stored procedures will start losing ground to functions, because of the way that you can SELECT from the table-type result set of a function but not from the static results of running a stored procedure.

Horizontally Partitioned Views

If you have very large tables, SQL Server can take a while to run a query. For example, if all your sales data is in one very large table, but you typically only need to work with a subset of rows, then partitioning the table makes a lot of sense. If you have 100,000,000 rows in the table, SQL Server might have to look through the entire table, or at least the entire index, to fetch the few hundred rows you're interested in. The solution to this is to create a horizontal partition by splitting the table into separate, smaller tables. You design the member tables so that each table stores a horizontal slice of the original table based on a range of key values. Figure 9.8 diagrams what this would look like if you split a sales table holding data for a single year into quarters. However, it's not enough to just split the table into separate tables; you also need to create constraints to make sure the data in each of the new tables falls between certain values. In this case, each table has data only for one quarter of the calendar year. This is enforced by creating CHECK constraints on each table, limiting the range of dates entered to those occurring in a particular quarter. Without these CHECK constraints, the partitioned view won't work.

Once you've partitioned the table and it's now many separate tables, you need an efficient way to query all the separate tables. This is where a partitioned view comes in. Listing 9.8 shows the view created using the UNION ALL statement to combine the tables. Users can issue a single query against the view without having to worry about the fact that there are actually four separate tables involved. The view appears to the user as a single table.

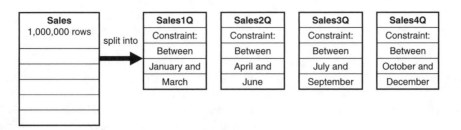

FIGURE 9.8
Creating a horizontal partition involves breaking a large table into smaller tables.

LISTING 9.8 Creating a Partitioned View

```
CREATE View vwSales
AS
  SELECT OrderID, OrderDate, OrderTotal FROM Sales1Q
  UNION ALL
  SELECT OrderID, OrderDate, OrderTotal FROM Sales2Q
  UNION ALL
  SELECT OrderID, OrderDate, OrderTotal FROM Sales3Q
  UNION ALL
  SELECT OrderID, OrderDate, OrderTotal FROM Sales4Q
```

The beauty of using a partitioned view is that SQL Server won't waste time looking through all the tables to fulfill a query that works with a particular customer. It examines all four tables in the view and determines which table is likely to have the data based on the constraint, and it ignores the other tables. It doesn't attempt to select data from any of the other tables where the constraint would rule out the possibility of the data being present. The following SELECT statement will have SQL Server look in the Sales1 table to satisfy the query since the WHERE clause limits the search to that range of data:

```
SELECT * FROM vwSales
WHERE OrderDate BETWEEN '1/1/2000' AND '1/22/2000'
```

Unlike normal UNION queries, a partitioned view is updateable if it meets the following conditions:

- The view is a set of SELECT statements, whose individual result sets are combined into one using the UNION ALL statement.

- Each individual SELECT statement references one SQL Server base table. The table can be either a local table or a linked table referenced using a four-part name, the OPEN-ROWSET function, or the OPENDATASOURCE function.

9

CREATING AND OPTIMIZING VIEWS

> **Tip**
>
> Always use UNION ALL in any union query if you want all the data to be included, even when you know there are no duplicate records. UNION ALL is faster because SQL Server does not have to worry about eliminating duplicates from the result set. You may recall that in Access, union queries are not updateable, but SQL Server overcomes this limitation for the union queries used in partitioned views, allowing them to be used in queries that modify, insert, or delete data.

Distributed Partitioned Views

Partitioned views can be based on data from multiple heterogeneous sources, such as remote servers, not just tables in the same database. To combine data from different remote servers, create distributed queries that retrieve data from each data source and then create a view based on those distributed queries.

When you partition data across multiple tables or multiple servers, queries accessing only a fraction of the data can run faster because there's less data to scan. If the tables are located on different servers or on a computer with multiple processors, each table involved in the query can also be scanned in parallel, thereby improving query performance. Additionally, maintenance tasks, such as rebuilding indexes or backing up a table, can execute more quickly.

By using a partitioned view, the data still appears as a single table and can be queried as such without having to reference the correct underlying table manually.

Here are the steps for setting up distributed partitioned views:

- Add each member server as a linked server. The view needs direct access to data located on all of the other servers.

- Use the sp_serveroption system stored procedure on each server to set the lazy schema validation option. This prevents the query processor from requesting metadata for the linked tables until it actually needs the data, thus boosting performance.

- Create a distributed partitioned view on each server. Here's what it would look like if the linked server names were LinkedServer2, 3, and 4:

```
CREATE VIEW vwDistributedPartitionedView
AS
 SELECT * FROM ThisDatabase.Owner.Sales1Q
UNION ALL
 SELECT * FROM LinkedServer2.Database2.Owner.Sales2Q
UNION ALL
 SELECT * FROM LinkedServer3.Database3.Owner.Sales3Q
```

```
UNION ALL
   SELECT * FROM LinkedServer4.Database4.Owner.Sales4Q
```

Each of the linked servers needs its own copy of the distributed partitioned view that references the other servers, so that all of the servers "talk" to each other.

To a user selecting data from the view, it appears as though the data is being fetched from a single table in a single database on a single server. Distributed partitioned views allow you to scale out your database in a very transparent way. This is similar to the way you might have worked with linked tables in your Access database, where you could link to tables from multiple MDB files. However, the implementation in SQL Server is designed for high-end OLTP (Online Transaction Processing) and Web site databases with individual SQL statements retrieving minimal data from enormous tables. Distributed partitioned views can also be used to implement a federation of database servers. Each server is administered independently, but they cooperate to share the processing load. This allows you to scale out a set of servers to support the processing requirements of extremely large and/or high-transaction-rate databases. See the Books Online topic "Designing Federated Database Servers" for more information. If you are building a decision-support application that needs to fetch summary information from large amounts of data, then consider Analysis Services (formerly known as OLAP Services) instead.

Using Derived Tables and Nested Views

A *derived table* is nothing more than another SELECT statement in the FROM clause of a SELECT query. In Access, this would be a query that's based on another nested query because Access SQL doesn't allow you to embed SELECT statements in the FROM clause of a query. Derived tables and views are very similar—the main difference is that a derived table is not a saved object; it's dynamic and only exists at runtime.

The example shown in Listing 9.9 uses a derived table to put together a product list, with the product name, price, and average price for each product's category. The derived table is the SELECT statement inside the parentheses that calculates the average price per category and then is joined to the product list.

LISTING 9.9   Using a Derived Table to Calculate an Average Price Per Category for a Product Price List

```
SELECT Products.ProductName, Products.UnitPrice, DerivedTable.CatAvg,
   Categories.CategoryName
FROM   Products
INNER JOIN
   (SELECT Products.CategoryID, AVG(Products.UnitPrice) AS CatAvg
    FROM Products
```

LISTING 9.9   Continued

```
  GROUP BY Products.CategoryID)
  AS DerivedTable ON DerivedTable.CategoryID = Products.CategoryID
INNER JOIN
  Categories ON Products.CategoryID = Categories.CategoryID
ORDER BY ProductName
```

The first few rows of the output are shown in Figure 9.9.

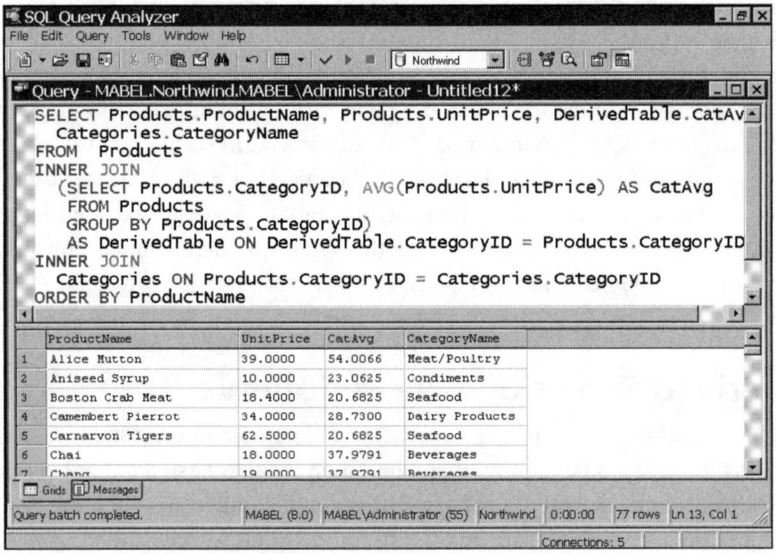

FIGURE 9.9
The output from using a derived table.

To write the same query using views, you'd need two of them. The first view would create the average, as shown in Listing 9.10.

LISTING 9.10   Creating the Inner View to Calculate the Average Price Per Category

```
CREATE VIEW vwAvgPricePerCategory
AS
  SELECT Products.CategoryID, AVG(Products.UnitPrice) AS CatAvg
  FROM Products
  GROUP BY Products.CategoryID
```

The next step is to create the outer view and join it to the inner view, as shown in Listing 9.11.

LISTING 9.11 Creating a Nested View

```
CREATE VIEW vwPriceListWithAvg
AS
  SELECT Products.ProductName, Products.UnitPrice,
vwAvgPricePerCategory.CatAvg,
    Categories.CategoryName
  FROM   Products
  INNER JOIN
    vwAvgPricePerCategory
    ON vwAvgPricePerCategory.CategoryID = Products.CategoryID
  INNER JOIN
    Categories ON Products.CategoryID = Categories.CategoryID
```

To query the view, use the following syntax:

```
SELECT * FROM vwPriceListWithAvg
ORDER BY ProductName
```

This produces the same result set shown in Figure 9.9. Derived tables and nested views can be used to do pretty much the same thing. The advantages of derived tables is that you have fewer database objects to maintain, and you can dynamically build up complex, nested Transact-SQL queries and execute them without having to create and save a view for each nested SELECT. Another way to approach solving this problem would be to populate temp tables and select from them, but in many cases derived tables will be faster or more convenient.

Using Views to Update Data

A view can be used in a query that updates data, subject to a few restrictions. Bear in mind that a view is not a table and contains no data—the actual modification always takes place at the table level. Views cannot be used as a mechanism to override any constraints, rules, or referential integrity defined in the base tables.

Restrictions on Updating Data Through Views

You can insert, update, and delete rows in a view, subject to the following limitations:

- If the view contains joins between multiple tables, you can only insert and update one table in the view, and you can't delete rows.
- You can't directly modify data in views based on union queries.
- You can't modify data in views that use GROUP BY or DISTINCT statements.
- All columns being modified are subject to the same restrictions as if the statements were being executed directly against the base table.

- Text and image columns can't be modified through views.
- There is no checking of view criteria. For example, if the view selects all customers who live in Paris, and data is modified to either add or edit a row that does not have City = 'Paris', the data will be modified in the base table but not shown in the view, unless WITH CHECK OPTION is used when defining the view.

Using WITH CHECK OPTION

The WITH CHECK OPTION clause forces all data-modification statements executed against the view to adhere to the criteria set within the WHERE clause of the SELECT statement defining the view. Rows cannot be modified in a way that causes them to vanish from the view. Listing 9.12 creates a view showing customers from Paris using the WITH CHECK OPTION statement.

LISTING 9.12   Creating a View Using WITH CHECK OPTION

```
CREATE VIEW vwCustomersParis
AS
  SELECT CompanyName, ContactName, Phone, City
  FROM Customers
  WHERE City = 'Paris'
WITH CHECK OPTION
```

The following Transact-SQL statement attempting to update data by moving everyone from Paris to Lyons will fail because Lyons does not meet the criteria defined in the view. If you did not have WITH CHECK OPTION defined, the UPDATE statement would succeed, and a requery of the view would return no rows. Here's the statement:

```
UPDATE vwCustomersParis
SET City = 'Lyons'
```

You may have noticed in Access that placing criteria on the RecordSource query of a form limits the records that are displayed in the form when you open it, but it doesn't limit what records can be added in the form. Using an Access project or an Access database with a form bound to a view that contains WITH CHECK OPTION would allow you to automatically have the criteria enforced for new or updated records.

Updating Views with Joins

A view that contains a join will only be updateable on one side of the join, unless an INSTEAD OF trigger is created on the view. INSTEAD OF triggers are discussed in the next section. For example, the view shown in Listing 9.13 is based on a join between the Categories and Products tables.

LISTING 9.13   A View with a Join

```
CREATE VIEW vwCategoriesProducts
AS
```

```
SELECT Categories.CategoryName,
  Products.ProductID, Products.ProductName
FROM Products INNER JOIN
  Categories ON
  Products.CategoryID = Categories.CategoryID
```

The first few rows of the output for this view are shown in Figure 9.10.

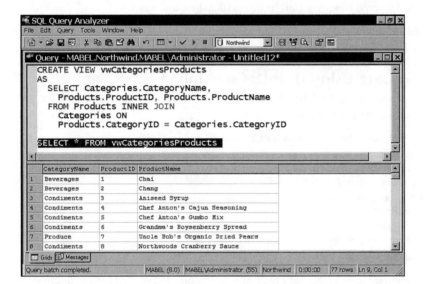

FIGURE 9.10

A view selecting data from both the Categories and Products tables.

The following UPDATE statement will work because it's only affecting the Products table's side of the join:

```
UPDATE vwCategoriesProducts
  SET ProductName = 'Chay'
  WHERE ProductID = 1
```

This UPDATE statement will also work because only affects the Categories table's side of the join:

```
UPDATE vwCategoriesProducts
  SET CategoryName = 'Drinks'
  WHERE ProductID = 1
```

However, the following UPDATE statement attempting to modify columns in both the Products and Categories tables won't work (you'll get the error "View or function 'vwCategoriesProducts' is not updateable because the FROM clause names multiple tables"):

9

CREATING AND OPTIMIZING VIEWS

```
UPDATE vwCategoriesProducts
  SET ProductName = 'Chay', CategoryName = 'Drinks'
  WHERE ProductID = 1
```

The Trouble with Updateable Views

In general, you'll want to make views that use joins read-only. Allowing updates in views with joins is likely to confuse users because it's not intuitive that they can't update different columns on the same row. After all, it looks like the same table to them.

If you want users to be able to use views to update data, base the view on a single table, or use a stored procedure to perform the update.

Updating Data Using User-Defined Inline Functions

The rules for updating user-defined inline functions are the same as they are for views. Consider these three statements:

```
SELECT * FROM dbo.fnProductSelectInline()
WHERE ProductID = 1

UPDATE dbo.fnProductSelectInline()
SET UnitPrice = 20
WHERE ProductID = 1

SELECT * FROM dbo.fnProductSelectInline()
WHERE ProductID = 1
```

The first statement selects the data from the fnProductSelectInline() function, the second statement updates it, and the third statement selects the new value. Here's the output for the two SELECT statements demonstrating that the function worked:

ProductID	ProductName	UnitPrice
1	Chai	19.0000

ProductID	ProductName	UnitPrice
1	Chai	20.0000

An inline function that has a parameter can also be used to update data, with the parameter limiting the scope of the update. Here is a function where a parameter is used to return a single row from the Products table:

```
CREATE FUNCTION fnProductInlineParam
  (@ProductID int)
  RETURNS TABLE
```

```
AS
    RETURN
    (SELECT ProductID, ProductName, UnitPrice
    FROM Products
    WHERE ProductID = @ProductID)
```

Call the function as follows to update the price of ProductID 5 to 29.95:

```
UPDATE dbo.fnProductInlineParam(5)
SET UnitPrice = 29.95
```

Only the one product with the ProductID of 5 will have its price changed.

Using INSTEAD OF Triggers to Update Non-Updateable Views

An INSTEAD OF trigger on a view allows you to get around many of the restrictions on updating views. For example, only one table in a view with multiple joined tables can be updated. An INSTEAD OF trigger can support inserts, updates, and deletes that reference data in more than one table. INSTEAD OF triggers also allow you to code more complex logic than is normally supported in views; and they let you work with time stamp data, computed columns, and identity columns.

The following view selects the CompanyName values in a UNION query between the Customers and Suppliers tables:

```
CREATE VIEW vwUnionCustomerSupplier
AS
    SELECT CompanyName, 'Customer' AS Type
    FROM Customers

    UNION ALL

    SELECT CompanyName, 'Supplier' AS Type
    FROM Suppliers
```

Normally a UNION query is not updateable. However, an INSTEAD OF trigger lets you update the tables involved because it can execute code instead of the default action (UPDATE). The trigger makes use of the inserted table, which contains the new value, to insert data into the appropriate table based on the Type value. It also makes use of the deleted table, which contains the old value, to find the correct record in the base table.

```
CREATE TRIGGER trigUnion ON vwUnionCustomerSupplier
    INSTEAD OF UPDATE
AS
BEGIN
SET NOCOUNT ON
    DECLARE @DelName nvarchar(50)
```

```
    IF (SELECT inserted.Type FROM inserted) Is Null
      RETURN

    SELECT @DelName =  deleted.CompanyName FROM deleted

    IF (SELECT inserted.Type FROM inserted) = 'Company'
      UPDATE Customers
      SET CompanyName =
        (SELECT CompanyName
        FROM inserted)
        WHERE Customers.CompanyName =
          @DelName
    ELSE
      UPDATE Suppliers
      SET CompanyName =
        (SELECT CompanyName
        FROM inserted)
        WHERE Suppliers.CompanyName =
          @DelName
END
```

This allows the following UPDATE statement to update the Customers table with a new company name:

```
UPDATE vwUnionCustomerSupplier
SET CompanyName = 'Around the Block'
WHERE CompanyName = 'Around the Horn'
```

As you can see, INSTEAD OF triggers on views can make them very powerful indeed, allowing actions that would not normally be permitted. You could also use INSTEAD OF triggers to call stored procedures to perform the requested data modification.

Indexed Views

This is an important new feature in SQL Server 2000. You can significantly improve performance by creating a unique clustered index on a view that involves complex processing of large quantities of data, such as aggregating or joining many rows. Calculated values can be indexed, effectively storing the calculation in the database and dynamically maintaining it. Another benefit of creating an index on a view is that the optimizer starts using the view index, even in queries that do not directly name the view in the FROM clause. Existing queries can benefit from the improved efficiency of retrieving data from the indexed view without having to be rewritten.

Indexed views have been available for some time in other relational database management systems, like Oracle, where they are referred to as *materialized views*. Their inclusion in SQL

Server 2000 represents one more area where Microsoft is catching up in features and performance with its more expensive competitors.

How the Query Optimizer Considers Indexed Views

One interesting feature in SQL Server 2000 is that if you have a view with indexes, and the underlying table does not have indexes, the query optimizer might use the view even if the view is not specifically referenced by the query. The query optimizer considers any and all indexes defined in the database when executing a query, regardless of whether the index was defined on a view or on a base table. If the optimizer estimates that using the indexed view provides the lowest-cost access mechanism, the optimizer chooses the indexed view, similarly to the way it chooses base table indexes even when they are not directly referenced in a query. The optimizer might choose the view when it contains columns that are not referenced by the query, if the view offers the lowest cost option for covering one or more of the columns specified in the query.

When to Use Indexed Views

Because indexed views are more complex to maintain than indexes on base tables, you should use them only when the improved speed in retrieving the results outweighs the increased overhead of data modifications. In other words, indexing views is not a good idea in a high-volume OLTP system. Indexed views work best when the data is relatively static, and you need to process many rows or the view will be referenced by many queries.

When Not to Use Indexed Views

Do not index views without careful consideration. Remember that indexed views work best when the underlying data is infrequently updated, or when a performance penalty for updates is acceptable. Because the structure of an indexed view is more complex than the structure of an index on a base table, the cost of maintaining an indexed view is higher than the cost of maintaining an index on a base table. Do not use indexed views in the following situations:

- An OLTP (Online Transaction Processing) system with many writes
- Frequently updated databases
- Queries that do not involve aggregations or joins
- Aggregate queries where the result set has almost as many rows as the base table
- A view with expanding joins in which the result set is larger than the original data stored in the base tables

Requirements for Indexed Views

A view must meet the following requirements before you can create a clustered index on it:

- Set the ANSI_NULLS option to ON when you create the tables referenced by the view.
- Set the ANSI_NULLS and QUOTED_IDENTIFIER options to ON prior to creating the view.
- The view must only reference base tables, not any other views.
- Base tables referenced by the view must be in the same database as the view and must have the same owner.
- Create the view and any user-defined functions referenced in the view with the SCHEMABINDING option. This means that the underlying tables or other database objects cannot be altered or dropped as long as the view or function exists. In other words, don't create indexed views until your table design is finalized since you'll just have to drop the view to make schema changes to the table.
- Reference all table names and user-defined functions with two-part names only—for example, "dbo.Customers" for the Customers table.
- Any functions used by the view must be deterministic, meaning that the function must always return the same result anytime it's called with the same set of input values.

The following Transact-SQL syntax elements are illegal in an indexed view:

- The * syntax to specify all columns. Column names must be explicitly stated.
- Repeated columns—for example, SELECT Col1, Col2, Col1 AS Col. However, you can re-use a column if it's part of a different expression—for example, SELECT Col1, AVG(Col1), Col1 + Col2 AS Total.
- Derived tables and subqueries.
- ROWSET.
- UNION.
- Outer joins or self joins.
- TOP and ORDER BY.
- DISTINCT.
- COUNT(*). Use COUNT_BIG(*) instead, which returns a bigint data type and is allowed.
- The following aggregate functions: AVG, MAX, MIN, STDEV, STDEVP, VAR, and VARP.

Indexed Views and Inline Functions

Inline functions can also be used to increase the power and flexibility of indexed views. An indexed view does not support parameters—it stores the complete set of data. However, you can define an inline function with parameters that references the view. Your user-defined function can then apply the parameter values to filter the result set generated by the indexed view. The complex aggregations and joins are done once, at CREATE INDEX time, and all subsequent queries referencing the inline function filter rows from this prebuilt result set.

Optimizing Views and Queries

Before getting into the details of optimizing views and queries, consider how SQL Server processes commands that are sent to it.

How SQL Server Processes Commands

When a command is sent to SQL Server for execution, SQL Server performs five steps to execute that command:

1. The command is parsed.
2. The Transact-SQL is standardized. Names are converted into codes that SQL Server can work with internally (such as table names being turned into object IDs, column names into column IDs, and so on).
3. The query is optimized, and an execution plan is generated.
4. The query is compiled.
5. The query is executed.

When you create and save a view or a stored procedure, SQL Server goes through the first two steps only. However, there's a catch where views are concerned. Because you use views as though they were virtual tables, any command that uses a view (SELECT * FROM MyView) has to go through the first two steps a second time, so you really don't gain anything. Nevertheless, there's no real performance hit either, because once SQL Server gets through the first two steps on the command using the view, it can ignore the view itself. Then the command and the view go through optimization, compilation, and execution.

Any command sent to SQL Server benefits from the way SQL Server caches ad hoc statements. If the command is executed a second time in more or less the same form, SQL Server will reuse the cached plan. The performance advantage can be significant if you reuse the same view because the view portion is exactly the same each time.

This is where indexing becomes important—one of the things you can do to improve the performance of your queries, views, and stored procedures is to utilize efficient index design. The SQL Server query optimizer will automatically select the most efficient index for any given query, but that index has to exist in order for it to be used. To get optimal performance out of your queries, you need to create the necessary indexes. However, creating indexes incorrectly can cause worse performance problems than if you had no indexes, so the query optimizer

9

CREATING AND OPTIMIZING VIEWS

might not use an index if using that index would result in a worse plan than it could achieve otherwise.

Indexing Guidelines

The following are some useful guidelines to observe when you're creating indexes:

- Create indexes on columns that are used for searching or sorting. Index columns in WHERE and GROUP BY clauses that either return an exact match or have a high proportion of distinct values.

- Don't create indexes on columns with few unique values. For example, do not create an index on the Country column if the only values it ever contains are the United States, Canada, and Mexico, even though you sort or search by country all the time.

- Index columns used in joins. In Access, when you create a foreign key, Jet creates a hidden index on the column automatically. SQL Server does not do this, even if you have enforced Declarative Referential Integrity (DRI) by creating a foreign key. In SQL Server, you need to explicitly create indexes on any columns used in joins, unless the values are highly duplicated. Again, don't index Country even though it may be a foreign key if the data only contains a small number of distinct Country values.

- You can't create indexes on columns defined with the text, ntext, image, or bit data types.

- Let the Query Analyzer help you out, as discussed in the next section.

Using the Query Analyzer to Tune Performance

Whether your query is implemented in a view or in a stored procedure, using the Query Analyzer's tools can be a big help in optimizing it to run as quickly as possible.

Displaying the Plan

The Query Analyzer's options for helping you understand how a given query is going to execute are all on the Query menu, shown in Figure 9.11. You can display the estimated execution plan for the query, perform index analysis, show the execution plan when the query executes, show a server trace, and show client statistics.

The Display Estimated Execution Plan Option

To display the estimated execution plan for a query, highlight the text of the query and press Ctrl+L or select Display Estimated Execution Plan from the Query menu. The execution plan is a graphical display of the data-retrieval methods the SQL Server query optimizer uses. Figure 9.12 shows the estimated execution plan for a query that totals the amount sold by an employee. The icons shown represent the execution of specific statements and queries. If you hover your mouse above each icon, a pop-up box appears listing the statistics for that specific statement. This can alert you to potential problems before you roll out your queries, as shown in Figure 9.12, which displays a warning box that statistics are missing for a table used in the query. The importance of updating statistics will be discussed later in this section.

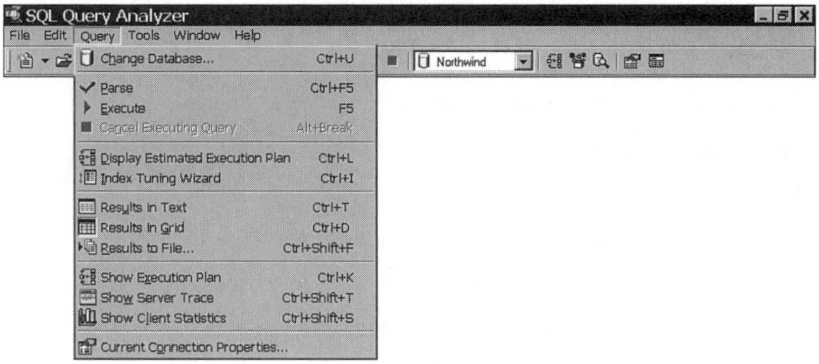

FIGURE 9.11

Options available on the Query menu.

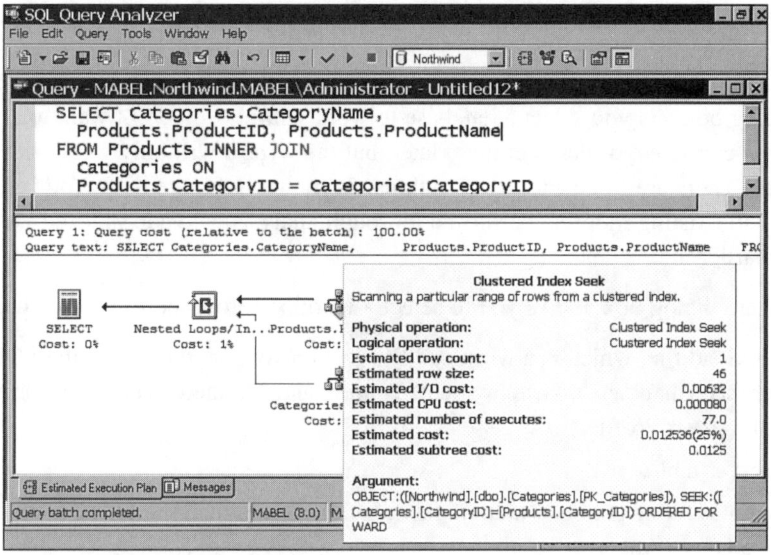

FIGURE 9.12

Displaying the estimated execution plan for a query.

Displaying Index Analysis with the Index Tuning Wizard

In SQL Server 2000, choosing Display Index Analysis from the Query menu runs the Index Tuning Wizard, which analyzes the workload and the database and then recommends an index configuration that will improve the performance of the workload. The introductory dialog box the Index Tuning Wizard displays after launching informs you that it can perform the following tasks:

- Identify the server and databases to tune
- Identify the workload to analyze
- Select the tables to tune
- Analyze the data and make index recommendations
- Implement the index recommendations

> **NOTE**
>
> In SQL Server 7.0, the option in the Query Analyzer for performing index analysis simply analyzes the current query and displays its results and recommendations in the Messages pane. It will also offer to create any indexes it thinks might help.

The next dialog box lets you select a database to work with. If you don't want to analyze all the tables, you can select or deselect them later, but the wizard will only work with one database at a time. There are three additional options, as shown in Figure 9.13. You can elect to keep or drop all existing indexes, perform a thorough analysis, and add indexed views, which are covered earlier in this chapter.

The next wizard dialog box allows you to select a workload from the following three options:

- My workload file, which is a workload file previously generated with the SQL Server Profiler (see Chapter 15, "Deployment, Tuning, and Maintenance," for information on the SQL Server Profiler).
- SQL Server table.
- Query Analyzer selection, which is the default if you launch the Index Tuning Wizard from the Query Analyzer.

You can also use the Advanced Options tab to limit the number of queries that are sampled, to set a limit on the space used for any recommended indexes, and to limit the maximum number of columns per index.

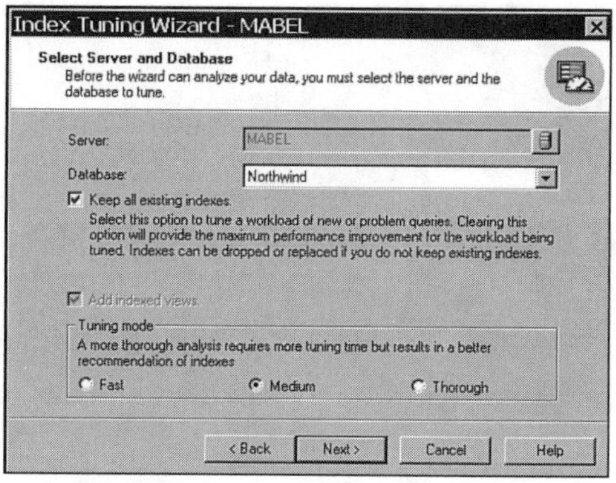

FIGURE 9.13

Selecting the database to tune and setting options for the Index Tuning Wizard.

The next wizard dialog box allows you to select the tables to tune, as shown in Figure 9.14.

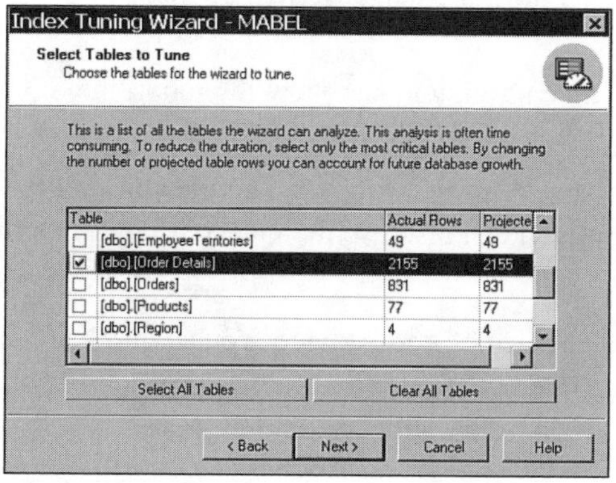

FIGURE 9.14

Selecting the tables to tune.

The following dialog box in the wizard displays recommendations, if any. Running the Index Tuning Wizard on the Northwind database is not very productive because the indexes are already in place.

You can then elect to implement the recommendations on the final wizard dialog box, as shown in Figure 9.15.

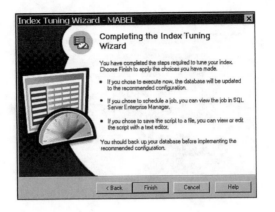

FIGURE 9.15
Applying the recommended changes.

The final wizard dialog box displays the following information:

- If you chose to execute now, the database will be updated to the recommended configuration.
- If you chose to schedule a job, you can view the job in the SQL Server Enterprise Manager.
- If you chose to save the script to a file, you can view or edit the script with a text editor. (It doesn't say so, but you can also use the Query Analyzer or the Profiler for this editing job.)

The wizard then gives you a piece of good advice: You should back up your database before implementing the recommended configuration. Once you click Finish, the job will be processed (or not, depending on the options you've chosen).

The Show Execution Plan Option

The Show Execution Plan (Ctrl+K) option is different from the Display Estimated Execution Plan option discussed earlier. This option can be toggled on or off. When it's turned on, an additional tab is added to the results pane that displays the execution plan for the query, as shown in Figure 9.16. You won't see anything before the query is executed.

The Show Server Trace Option

The Show Server Trace option, which is new in SQL Server 2000, also adds an additional tab to the results pane to display the trace results, as shown in Figure 9.17. A server trace provides information about the event class, subclass, integer data, text data, database ID, duration, start time, reads and writes, and CPU usage.

In earlier versions, you had to use the Profiler to see this information. Now it is available right in Query Analyzer.

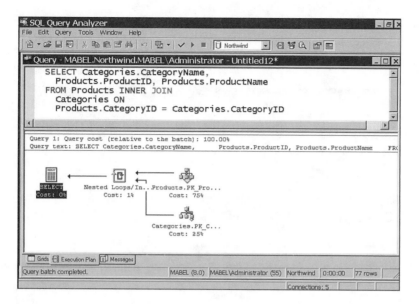

FIGURE 9.16

Show Execution Plan adds two tabs to the results pane for the execution plan and the statistics.

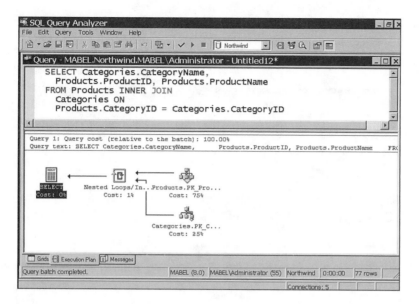

FIGURE 9.17

Displaying server trace information for a query.

The Show Client Statistics Option

The Show Client Statistics option is also new in SQL Server 2000. It adds one more tab to the results pane to display statistics, as shown in Figure 9.18.

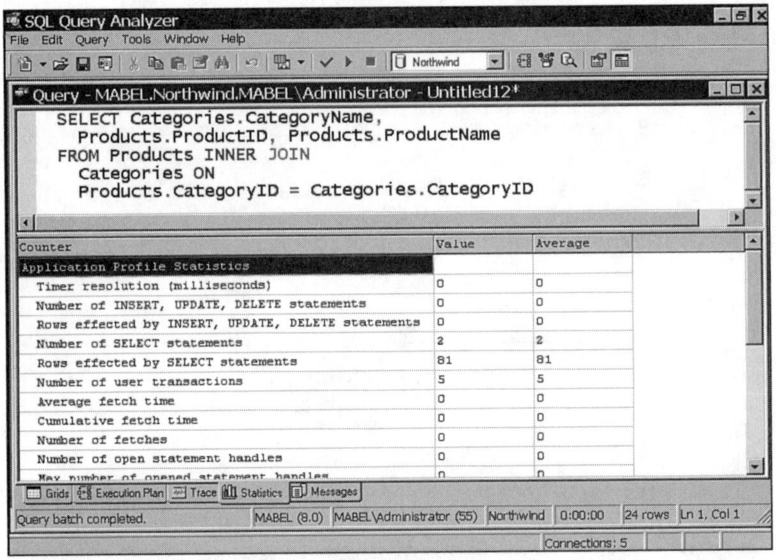

FIGURE 9.18
Displaying client statistics.

Statistics and Indexes

Statistics are very important to the query optimizer—if it does not have good statistical information, it can't make useful recommendations or process queries efficiently. All indexes have distribution statistics that describe the selectivity and distribution of the key values in the index. The selectivity of an index relates to how many rows are identified by each key value. For example, a unique key has high selectivity, whereas a key that is found in many rows has poor selectivity. Fields with a small set of values, like gender for employees, benefit little from indexes, because those indexes will have poor selectivity and will therefore usually be ignored by the optimizer. Distribution statistics measure how the values are spread out among your records. You might have customers in 50 different countries, but if 90% of your customers are in one country, then country isn't a very useful index. The selectivity and distribution statistics are used by SQL Server when processing Transact-SQL statements and are crucial for estimating how efficient an index would be when retrieving data associated with a key value or a range specified in the query. The query optimizer can even compile and use statistics on non-indexed fields. It's very important that your statistics be updated if the composition of your data changes significantly. You can set statistics to be created and updated automatically by going into the Options tab in the Database Properties dialog box, as shown in Figure 9.19.

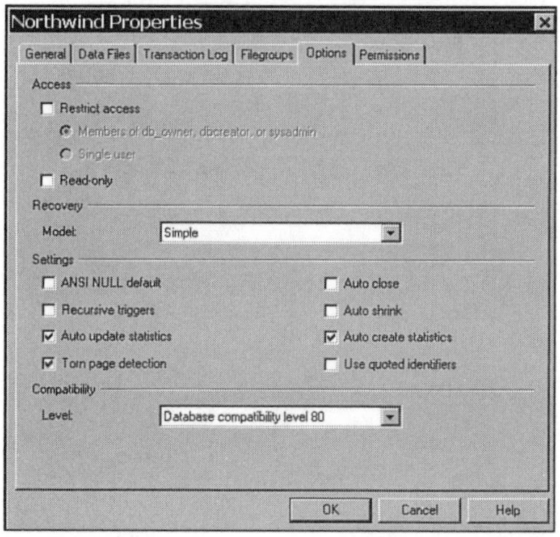

FIGURE 9.19
Setting Auto Create Statistics and Auto Update Statistics in the database's Properties dialog box.

Updating Statistics (New)

You can update statistics in the Query Analyzer by choosing Tools, Manage Statistics from the menu bar. This will bring up the dialog box shown in Figure 9.20.

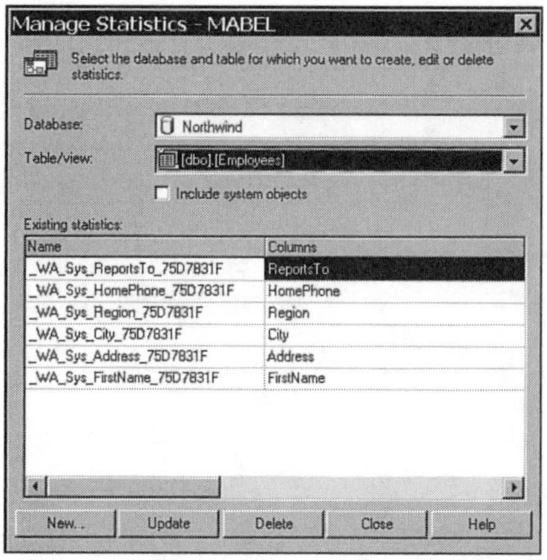

FIGURE 9.20
The Manage Statistics dialog box lets you update statistics.

Click the New button to create statistics for columns not listed. This will bring up the dialog box where you can create additional statistics, as shown in Figure 9.21.

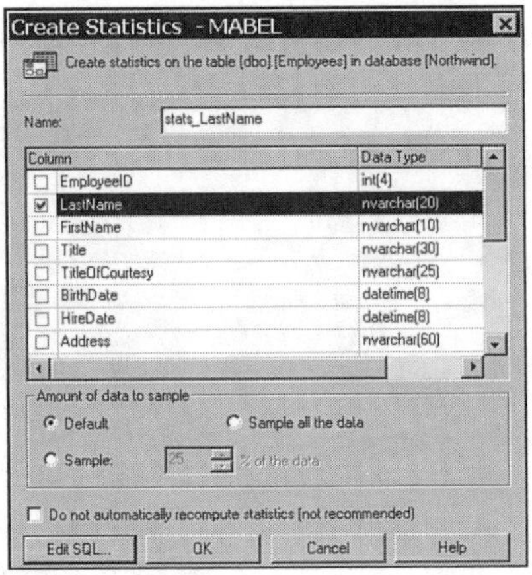

FIGURE 9.21
Creating missing statistics.

Managing Indexes

A new feature in SQL Server 2000 is the way you can use the Query Analyzer to manage indexes without having to use the Enterprise Manager or another tool. Choose Tools, Manage Indexes from the menu bar. This will load the dialog box shown in Figure 9.22. You can create a new index or edit an existing one.

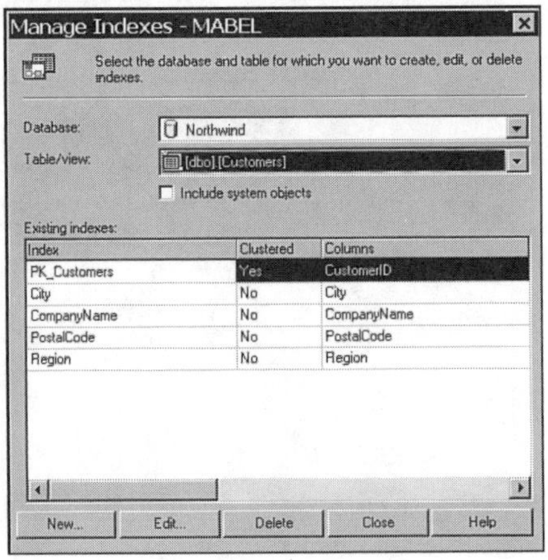

FIGURE 9.22
The Manage Indexes dialog box lets you add a new index or edit an existing one.

If you choose the Edit option, you'll get the Edit Existing Index dialog box, as shown in Figure 9.23.

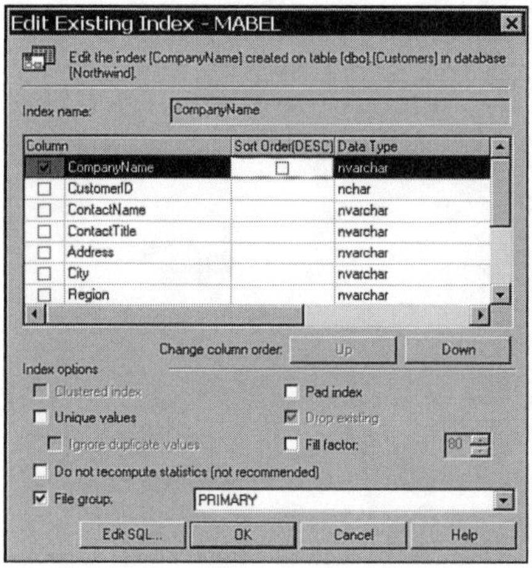

FIGURE 9.23
Editing an existing index.

As you can see, the Query Analyzer offers a powerful set of tools for tuning and optimizing your queries. Performance tuning is also covered in Chapter 15.

Summary

Views are saved SELECT statements that allow you to operate on the results returned from them. Views can be used to provide row- or column-level access to data, to wrap up complex joins, to perform complex aggregate queries, and to otherwise customize the display of data. Views are a powerful security tool because users can be granted permission to access limited data in views and denied access to the underlying tables. Views can be updateable, but if a join is involved, only one table at a time is updateable. You can create views using the Enterprise Manager, the Query Analyzer, or an Access project. In SQL Server 2000, there are new view features, such as the capability to index and partition views, and to work with user-defined functions in views or in place of views. The SQL Server 2000 Query Analyzer also has enhanced tools to help you perform index analysis and to optimize performance.

Programming Effective Stored Procedures

Stored Procedure Fundamentals

You need to be comfortable both using and creating stored procedures in order to get the most out of SQL Server. This chapter starts by discussing batches and scripts and then defines precisely what a stored procedure is and what makes it different from a batch or a script.

Understanding Batches, Scripts, and Stored Procedures

The most granular unit of work in Transact-SQL is the statement. Each statement performs some kind of action in the SQL Server environment. Sometimes statements can act alone, such as a statement that selects data from a table. For some tasks, however, statements need to be executed together. The simplest way to do so is to group them in a batch.

Grouping Statements in Batches

A *batch* is set of Transact-SQL statements submitted together as a group. Batches are delimited in the Query Analyzer with a GO statement at the end, and each batch is run as a single block of code. The GO statement itself is not part of Transact-SQL; it is a marker that tells the parser to begin processing the statements that preceded it. The only time you'll use GO is when you're working in the Query Analyzer. GO is recognized only by the Query Analyzer and the osql and isql command-line utilities. Each batch has a single unified execution plan, instead of the separate plans that would otherwise be generated for each individual statement. Batches are executed more efficiently than individual separate statements, and certain tasks require that you group statements into a batch. You'll see examples of such tasks later in this chapter. Stored procedures and triggers are themselves considered to be batches in which all statements are grouped together to create a single execution plan.

The improved efficiency that comes from using batches is easy to understand. Just as it is more efficient for a baker to make a batch of ten dozen cookies than to make each one from scratch, SQL Server can be more efficient about performing a series of tasks if it knows ahead of time what all those tasks are.

There are some limitations on what statements can run together within one batch. Any execution of a stored procedure after the first statement in a batch must include the EXECUTE keyword (covered later in this chapter), and the scope of local variables cannot span multiple batches. In addition, you can't combine CREATE DEFAULT, CREATE PROCEDURE, CREATE RULE, CREATE TRIGGER, and CREATE VIEW statements with other statements in a batch, or use ALTER TABLE and then reference the new columns within that same batch.

When executing a group of statements in Query Analyzer, you'll occasionally be required to use GO in order to avoid errors. The Transact-SQL statements shown in Listing 10.1 need to be executed in several batches in order to conform to batch rules (CREATE VIEW needs to be in its own batch). The first batch creates the TestTbl table and populates it with data. The second batch creates the vwTest view. The third batch selects from the view, and the last batch deletes the objects. The GO command packages up each set of commands separately and passes it to the server for execution.

LISTING 10.1   Creating a Batch to Execute Multiple Statements

```
CREATE TABLE TestTbl
  (test_id int NOT NULL,
  test_name varchar(50) NOT NULL)

INSERT INTO TestTbl (test_id, test_Name)
  VALUES (1000, 'Testing')
INSERT INTO TestTbl (test_id, test_Name)
  VALUES (2000, 'Testing2')
INSERT INTO TestTbl (test_id, test_Name)
  VALUES (3000, 'Testing3')
GO

CREATE VIEW vwTest
AS
SELECT * FROM TestTbl
GO

SELECT * FROM vwTest
GO

DROP VIEW vwTest
DROP TABLE TestTbl
GO
```

You can use Query Analyzer to create ad hoc batches and run them, and you can save your batches as scripts files.

Saving Statements in Scripts

A *script* is a text file containing one or more batches, with each batch in the script separated by a GO statement. You can open a script in Query Analyzer and execute the batches contained in the script. To create a script, simply choose File, Save or press Ctrl+S. You'll then be prompted to provide the path and filename where you want your script stored. The default filename extension is .sql, but you can change that default extension in the Tools, Options dialog box or from the File Save dialog.

The Query Analyzer saves scripts in the following file formats:

- *ANSI*. Use ANSI if the script will be run again in Query Analyzer or another Windows application.

10

PROGRAMMING
EFFECTIVE STORED
PROCEDURES

- *OEM*. Use OEM if you will execute the script from the command line of a console application or if you need to preserve characters not preserved in the ANSI character set. OEM uses the current Windows code page formatting. In other words, it adjusts to the locale settings in the current system.

- *Unicode*. Some characters—including those in most Asian languages, for example—cannot be handled with ANSI or even OEM formats. Use Unicode if the script requires special international characters that are supported only in the Unicode character set. Unicode requires two times the disk space of either ANSI or OEM because two bytes of storage are used for each character.

Generating Scripts from the Enterprise Manager

Scripts are a great way to document and back up your SQL Server database. Because scripts are just text files, they don't take up much disk space, and you can load and run them to rebuild your database (or parts of your database). You can generate scripts in several places in the Enterprise Manager:

- From the main console, choose Tools, Generate Scripts. This gives you the option of scripting all your database objects.

- Right-click any table, view, or stored procedure listed in the Enterprise Manager and choose All Tasks, Generate SQL Script.

- From a database diagram, click the Save Change Script toolbar button or right-click and choose Save Change Script.

- From the Table Designer, click the Save change script toolbar button or choose All Tasks, Generate SQL Scripts from the right-click menu.

Figure 10.1 shows the General tab of the Generate SQL Scripts dialog box, where you select the objects you want to script. Click the Show All button to enable the lists where you can select individual objects to script. The Formatting tab lets you choose formatting options for the script file. The Options tab lets you specify further options for scripting your objects.

Clicking the Preview button on the General tab shows you the completed script, as displayed in Figure 10.2, so you can preview what it will look like before it actually gets saved to a file.

When you click the OK button on the General tab, the script is saved into the folder you specify. You can run the script in the Query Analyzer to re-create the objects you've scripted.

You might think of scripts as macros that you can save and run to re-create objects you've defined in your database. Rather than sending someone a copy of a database, you could send a script that would build and populate the database. However, scripts are not limited to creating objects—they can also be used to save ways of manipulating objects that already exit. Any Transact-SQL code you write can be saved as a script to be retrieved and run later. But scripts are not themselves SQL Server objects.

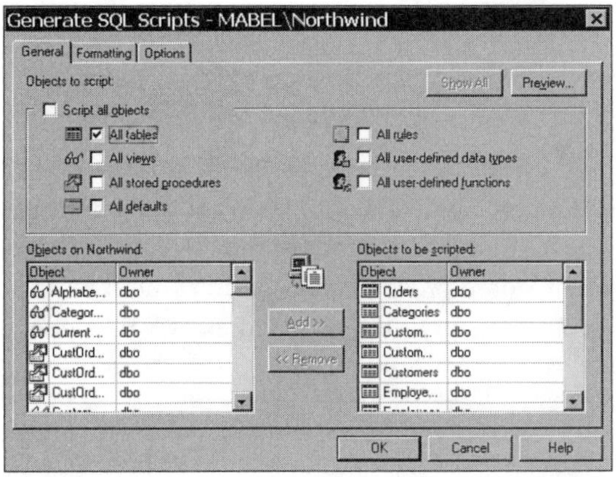

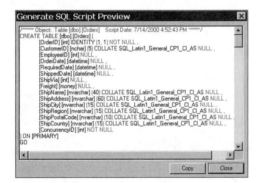

FIGURE 10.1
Scripting all tables from the Enterprise Manager.

FIGURE 10.2
Previewing the script.

Compiling Statements into Stored Procedures

Unlike scripts, which are saved outside of your database as text files, *stored procedures* are saved as objects inside your database. Stored procedures can be executed from applications, batches, or other stored procedures. They are parsed and syntax-checked when they are created and compiled when they are first executed. The execution plan is then cached, and subsequent calls to the stored procedure can reuse the cached plan, even if different users call the stored procedure. This compilation and caching of the execution plan gives stored procedures a significant performance advantage over running raw Transact-SQL.

Unlike views, which are also saved as database objects, stored procedures support the full capabilities of Transact-SQL. Although user-defined functions, introduced in SQL Server 2000, do allow views to work with input parameters, stored procedures can make use of parameters without requiring you to use functions. Views and stored procedures both can return resultsets, but a stored procedure can return more than one and can also return data in the form of output parameters and a return value, as shown in Figure 10.3.

To take full advantage of the procedural capabilities of Transact-SQL, including flow control and variables, you really need to use stored procedures. Because of these advanced procedural capabilities, you can think of stored procedures as giving you in SQL Server the capabilities of Access saved queries as well as many of the capabilities of VBA code.

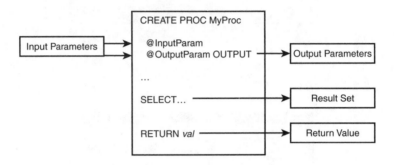

FIGURE 10.3

A stored procedure can take input parameters and return information through output parameters, resultsets, and a return value.

Basic Stored Procedure Syntax

Here is the basic syntax for creating a stored procedure. Optional parts of the syntax are in square brackets ([ ]), and elements you name are italicized. Everything in between the optional BEGIN...END statement block consists of your Transact-SQL statements. The RETURN statement at the end of the stored procedure is optional, but including it is good programming practice because RETURN unconditionally exits a stored procedure:

```
CREATE PROCEDURE StoredProcedureName
   [@ParameterName datatype (length)],
   [@ParameterName datatype (length)],...n
AS
   [BEGIN]
     [DECLARE @VariableName datatype (length)],
     [DECLARE @VariableName datatype (length)],...n

     --Your Transact-SQL code goes here

   [END]
[RETURN]
```

Using Comments in Your Transact-SQL Code

Commenting your stored procedures and scripts is just as good an idea in Transact-SQL as it is in any programming language. Transact-SQL supports two different ways to comment your code, depending on whether you want a single-line comment or multiple lines. To comment a single line, use a double hyphen:

```
--This is a comment on a single line
--This is another comment on a single line
```

These single-line comments can even be tacked on to the end of lines that contain Transact-SQL:

```
SELECT CompanyName --This is a comment
```

This is exactly analogous to the way an apostrophe is used to create a comment in VBA. Unlike VBA, however, Transact-SQL also supports blocks of comments that span multiple lines. For multiline comments, instead of putting hyphens at the start of each line, use a slash-star, star-slash pair to delimit the start and end of the comment:

```
/* This is a comment block that spans
   multiple lines. You can type as many
   lines as you want, as long as you end
   with a star-slash.
*/
```

The query processor will ignore all comments when compiling the code, with one strange exception. If you embed the word GO inside of a /*...*/ comment block, you will get a compile error. The GO word doesn't cause the same problem inside of a single-line comment using the double-hyphen syntax (--).

Figure 10.4 shows the empty stored procedure shell the Enterprise Manager creates for you when you right-click the Procedures folder and choose New Stored Procedure. Replace the [OWNER].[PROCEDURE NAME] text with the name of your stored procedure and type in the Transact-SQL statements after the AS keyword. Click the Check Syntax button to examine your stored procedure for syntax errors. Clicking the OK button will also cause the syntax to be checked prior to saving it. If there are any syntax errors, you won't be able to save the stored procedure and you will have to either fix the errors or cancel the creation of the stored procedure.

Stored procedures are specific to individual databases (except for system stored procedures, which can be run in any database and are covered later in this chapter). Once saved, a stored procedure shows up in the Enterprise Manager in the Stored Procedures folder of the database you created it in.

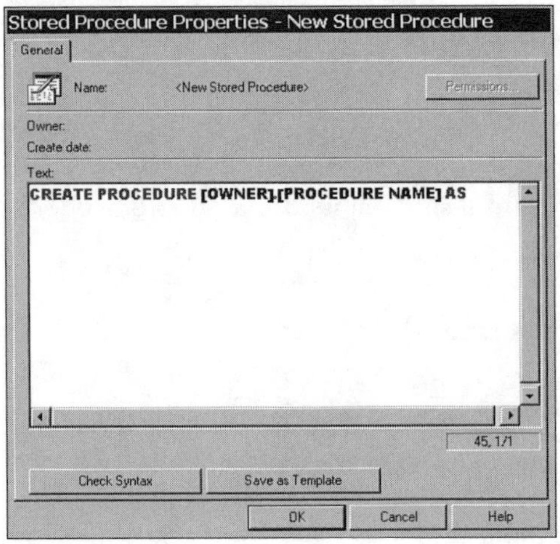

FIGURE 10.4
The dialog box for creating a new stored procedure in the Enterprise Manager.

To create a simple stored procedure that selects data from the Customers table in the Northwind database, your stored procedure code would look like this:

```
CREATE PROCEDURE dbo.procCustSelect
AS
SELECT CustomerID, CompanyName, ContactName
FROM
Customers
```

Stored Procedures and Security

Stored procedures provide an excellent way to limit access to your data. The EXECUTE permission on a stored procedure takes precedence over any permissions on the base tables that the procedure works with, as long as both the stored procedure and the tables have the same owner. In this case, SQL Server simply ignores the base table permissions if the user has EXECUTE permissions on the stored procedure. This works even if all permissions on the underlying tables have been revoked or denied. This way, you have complete control over what actions the users can perform on the data. When it comes to modifying data, the advantages of this technique are readily apparent—a stored procedure provides a wrapper around INSERT, UPDATE, and DELETE actions that might otherwise harm data. You can place validation and conditional processing statements in the body of a stored procedure before allowing transactions that modify or delete data. The advantages of stored procedures for retrieving data might not be so apparent until you consider the cost in terms of network load of retrieving tens of thousands of rows in a SELECT * FROM ... statement.

Using stored procedures in SQL Server is roughly comparable to the way Access programmers usually like to force users to work only through forms to make changes to data, rather than being able to open tables directly in datasheet view. Stored procedures give you a lot of power to determine exactly what your users can and cannot do with your data, and they allow you to apply the same kinds of conditional logic, transactions, and error handling that you are probably using VBA code for in Access.

Tools for Creating Stored Procedures

Stored procedures can be created in the Enterprise Manager by right-clicking the Stored Procedures tab and selecting New Stored Procedure from the list, as shown in Figure 10.4.

Your alternative for creating stored procedures using the Enterprise Manager is the Create Stored Procedure Wizard, which you can activate from the Tools, Wizards, Database, Create Stored Procedure Wizard menu option. This wizard will assist you in creating a stored procedure that inserts, updates, or deletes data only. Because the wizard is somewhat limited, you'll probably want to learn how to write stored procedures on your own. The Query Analyzer provides the best user interface for creating stored procedures.

Using the Query Analyzer to Create Stored Procedures

The Query Analyzer in SQL Server 2000 gained important new functionality that did not exist in previous incarnations of SQL Server and that makes it easy to create stored procedures. In older versions of the Query Analyzer, you had to type in Transact-SQL statements yourself, or copy them from another source. The introduction of the Object Browser and templates eliminates the need for a lot of typing.

There are two ways to create a new stored procedure from a template:

- Load the Object Browser (or press F8), select the Templates tab, and drag a template from the Create Procedure node onto the query pane of the Query Analyzer.

- Choose Edit, Insert Template (or press Ctrl+Shift+Ins) and select the template from the Create Procedures folder.

This will load the following template into the SQL pane:

```
-- ================================================
-- Create procedure basic template
-- ================================================
-- creating the store procedure
IF EXISTS (SELECT name
      FROM    sysobjects
      WHERE   name = N'<procedure_name, sysname, proc_test>'
      AND     type = 'P')
   DROP PROCEDURE <procedure_name, sysname, proc_test>
GO
```

```
CREATE PROCEDURE <procedure_name, sysname, proc_test>
    <@param1, sysname, @p1> <datatype_for_param1, , int> =
<default_value_for_param1, , 0>,
    <@param2, sysname, @p2> <datatype_for_param2, , int> =
<default_value_for_param2, , 0>
AS
    SELECT @p1, @p2
GO


-- ==============================================
-- example to execute the store procedure
-- ==============================================
EXECUTE <procedure_name, sysname, proc_test>
<value_for_param1, , 1>, <value_for_param2, , 2>
GO
```

The Query Analyzer will help you fill in the template parameters if you choose Edit, Replace Template Parameters (or press Ctrl+Shift+M). Figure 10.5 displays the dialog box for you to fill in the template parameters. Click the Replace All button to have all of the template parameters filled in automatically.

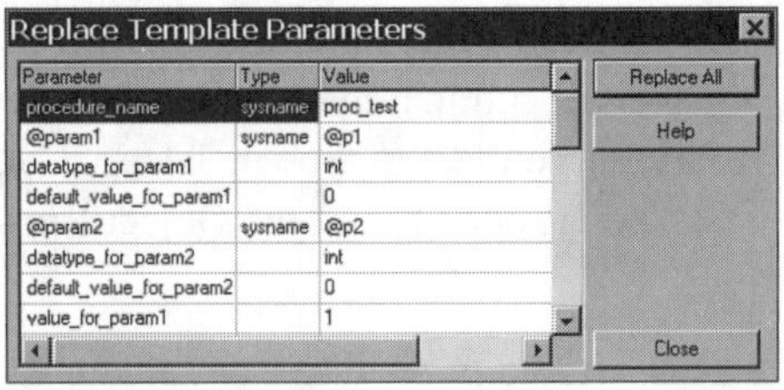

Figure 10.5

The Query Analyzer will help you fill in template parameters with values from your tables.

There are three stored procedure templates that ship with SQL Server 2000: the Create Procedure Basic Template, the Create Procedure with CURSOR OUTPUT Parameter, and the Create Procedure with OUTPUT Parameter. You can also add your own custom templates by following the instructions outlined in Chapter 8, "Introduction to Transact SQL (T-SQL)."

When working with stored procedures in SQL Server, you never actually see just the Transact-SQL contained within the procedure. What you create and execute is Transact-SQL that creates the stored procedure or modifies it. So, when adding or editing a stored procedure your code will always start with CREATE PROCEDURE or ALTER PROCEDURE. When using CREATE, it is also a good idea to include Transact-SQL code that first deletes any existing procedure that has the same name, as the template-generated code does.

When you execute a `CREATE PROCEDURE` ... statement from the Query Analyzer, your stored procedure statements will be parsed prior to saving the procedure. If there are any syntax errors, the procedure won't be saved. You'll receive an error message in the Messages pane that gives you the reason the stored procedure couldn't be saved, along with the line number of the offending statement. Here's an example:

```
Server: Msg 170, Level 15, State 1, Procedure procTest, Line 5
Line 5: Incorrect syntax near 'NO'.
```

It's up to you to figure out what's going on and fix the error. Fortunately, the Query Analyzer's online Transact-SQL help and the excellent new user interface make this a lot easier than in previous versions.

TIP

The line number of the current line displays on the status bar pane at the bottom of the Query Analyzer window.

The Query Analyzer is a better tool than the Enterprise Manager or even the Stored Procedure Wizard for creating stored procedures, because, unlike the Enterprise Manager or the Stored Procedure Wizard, it's not a modal dialog box. That makes it easier to copy and paste syntax from other locations. Plus, the addition of the Object Browser makes the creation of queries with complex joins much easier. The Query Analyzer is discussed in more detail in Chapter 8.

Using an Access 2000 Project to Create Stored Procedures

You can create and edit stored procedures in an Access project in a nonmodal window (meaning you can copy and paste from other windows), but you're on your own as far as tools are concerned. Access provides a simple template form with comment blocks indicating where you should type in your Transact-SQL commands, but it doesn't provide any other help, other than checking the syntax when you click the Save button. You're also forced to save before switching to datasheet view if your stored procedures returns rows. SQL Server 2000 provides a much richer tool set with the Query Analyzer, as well as superior help with Books Online. This is the format of the template that Access provides for new stored procedures:

```
Create Procedure "StoredProcedure1"
/*
    (
        @parameter1 datatype = default value,
        @parameter2 datatype OUTPUT
    )
*/
As
```

```
/* set nocount on */
return
```

We strongly recommend that you get comfortable with the Query Analyzer in SQL Server 2000, and use it whenever you need to create a stored procedure.

Executing a Stored Procedure

When you execute a stored procedure from an application, only the single command to execute the stored procedure travels over the network, rather than the full SQL, thus reducing network traffic. All the work is done on the server where the execution plan is cached, and only the resultsets, output parameters, and return value, if any exist, are passed back to the client application. Stored procedures let you encapsulate your logic in one place and call it from many applications instead of having to maintain logic in multiple places. As long as the interface to your stored procedure, comprised of its name and parameters, doesn't change, you can change the internal logic of the procedure or tune its performance without affecting your applications.

To execute the new stored procedure from the Query Analyzer, use any of the following syntax choices:

```
procCreateTest
EXECUTE procCreateTest
EXEC procCreateTest
```

Bear in mind that if you are executing the stored procedure as part of another batch, then the first choice, calling the stored procedure by name alone, will work only if the stored procedure call is the first statement in the batch.

NOTE

It's perfectly legal in Transact-SQL to shorten the EXECUTE statement to just plain EXEC. Other examples of allowed abbreviations are using TRAN for TRANSACTION and PROC for PROCEDURE. Later in this chapter we'll examine the difference between the EXEC statement and the EXEC() function.

Executing Stored Procedures from an Access Project

To execute a stored procedure from an Access project, you can simply double-click it in the object list for stored procedures. You can also use stored procedures as the record source for a form or report, or in the row source of a combo or list box. The InputParameters property allows you to pass in parameters to record sources. For row sources, use VBA code to concatenate parameter values:

```
Me.MyCombo.RowSource = "Exec MyStoredProc " & MyNumericParamValue
'or:
Me.MyCombo.RowSource = "Exec MyStoredProc '" & MyStringOrDateParamValue & "'"
```

Executing Stored Procedures from an Access Database

To execute a stored procedure from an Access database, use any form of the EXEC syntax with the stored procedure name in the SQL property of a pass-through query, as shown in Figure 10.6. You also have to fill in the ODBC Connect property to provide connection information for the pass-through query. The Returns Records property is set to No for a query that does not return a recordset. Chapter 5, "Linking to SQL Server Using Access Databases (MDBs)," and Chapter 11, "Scaling Up with Unbound Access Applications," include examples of how to programmatically change the SQL and Connect properties of pass-through queries at runtime.

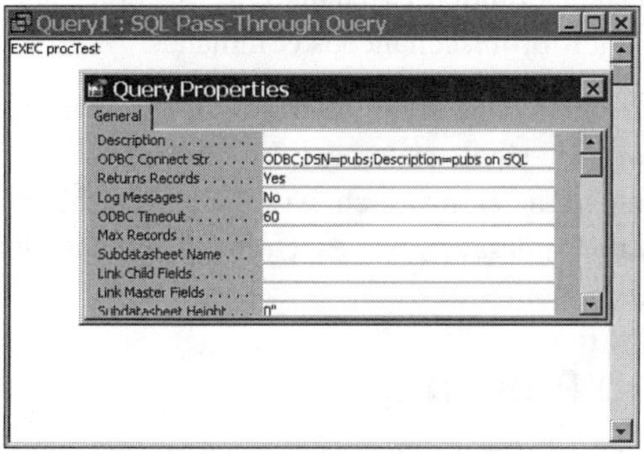

Figure 10.6
Executing a pass-through query from an Access database.

Executing Stored Procedures from ADO

You can execute stored procedures from ADO Connection and Command objects by using the Execute method, or from Recordset objects by using the Open method. Here are examples:

```
cnn.Execute "procCreateTest"
...
cmd.CommandText = "procCreateTest"
cmd.CommandType = adCmdStoredProc
cmd.Execute
rst.Open cmd
```

For a detailed discussion of using Connection, Command and Recordset objects in ADO, see Chapter 6, "ActiveX Data Objects (ADO) Fundamentals."

What's Under the Hood

When you submit any command for SQL Server to execute, it goes through the following stages:

1. The syntax gets checked by the command parser and translated into an internal format known as a *sequence tree* or *query tree*. Sometimes step 1 is considered to be two separate steps: the parsing and then the conversion into an internal format.

2. An optimization and execution plan is generated from the sequence tree that contains all the necessary steps to check constraints and carry out the commands.

3. Each step of the execution plan is dispatched to an internal "manager" responsible for carrying out that command type. There are separate managers for DDL (Data Definition Language), DML (Data Definition Language), transactions, and stored procedures, and there's a utility manager for miscellaneous commands.

If you send direct SQL statements one at a time from your application, then each statement requires all three stages for each single statement. If you send a batch, then stages 1 and 2 can be run for all the statements in the entire batch, wrapping everything up in a single plan. As you can imagine, this is a real timesaver over executing statements one at a time. The process is even more efficient when it comes to stored procedures.

Compiling Stored Procedures

For a stored procedure, stage 1 happens only once, when you save the stored procedure. Contrary to common belief, the execution plan is *not* saved with the stored procedure. It is created and cached in memory the first time a stored procedure is executed. This allows the optimization of stored procedures to be much more dynamic than if the plans were saved when stored procedures are first created. The plan would become obsolete if the database statistics changed significantly. So, the first time a stored procedure is executed, it passes through stages 2 and 3. However, subsequent calls to the stored procedure that are made soon after the first one only pass through stage 3 (execution) because they can reuse the plan that was cached the first time the stored procedure was run. If the stored procedure is not used for a while, the plan is flushed from the cache, and the next time the stored procedure is called, a fresh plan is created based on the latest statistics. Several factors can cause a fresh execution plan to be generated.

Execution Plans

Stored procedure execution plans are held in a memory cache and are shared among multiple connections. However, there are certain conditions when SQL Server needs to compile a new execution plan:

- If a copy of the plan isn't in memory yet
- If an index on one of the tables is dropped

- If statistics on one of the tables are updated
- If a table has been modified with an ALTER TABLE statement
- If the sp_recompile system stored procedure is run on one of the tables
- If the stored procedure was created using the WITH RECOMPILE option

SQL Server's ability to recompile the plan is valuable, because the last thing you need is for your stored procedure to run using an obsolete and inefficient plan.

Using WITH RECOMPILE to Force Recompiling

In certain situations, you won't want to use the same plan for every execution of a stored procedure. This can happen when a stored procedure parameter is used in the WHERE clause of a query where there can be different distributions of values, depending on the actual value passed in. Consider a scenario in which the WHERE clause is specifying a city in the Customers table. Fifty percent of your customers live in London, and the other 50% are distributed among the other cities. The first time the stored procedure is run, the WHERE clause specifies San Francisco, which has maybe 2% of your customers. A plan is compiled that uses a nonclustered index on City as the most efficient way to execute the stored procedure. On the next execution, London is selected. In this case, using a table scan would most likely be a better plan because half the rows in the table match the criteria, but the plan using the nonclustered index is already cached in memory, so it is used regardless. Using a nonclustered index on highly duplicated data is not efficient, because the index does little to narrow down the search, and checking the index takes time.

In the case where you have a wide variance in the distribution of values, you have two choices:

- Use the WITH RECOMPILE statement when you execute the stored procedure. This will selectively force recompiling at execution time. If you do not execute the stored procedure with the WITH RECOMPILE option, the existing cached plan will be used if there is one. Here's an example:

```
EXEC procCustomerSelect 'London' WITH RECOMPILE
```

- Use the WITH RECOMPILE statement when you create your stored procedure. This will force recompiling a new execution plan each time the stored procedure is run. Here's an example:

```
CREATE PROC procCustomerSelect
  @City nvarchar(15)
  WITH RECOMPILE
AS
SELECT CompanyName, City
FROM Customers
WHERE City = @City
```

Although forcing a new plan to be compiled each time can itself hurt performance, there are cases where this is outweighed by the advantages of generating a fresh plan based on the latest statistics, because a fresh plan will give better performance than a previously compiled plan that is all wrong for the data being selected.

How Jet Queries Are Compiled

The way Jet and SQL Server handle compiling execution plans for queries is quite different. When you first run a saved query in Access, a plan is computed based on the data distributions and statistics that are current at that time. Compacting your Access database generates fresh statistics and puts all your queries in an uncompiled state. It flags them to be compiled on the next run. With a split database architecture, where your tables are in one database and your queries are in another, you would need to compact the back end to update the statistics and also compact the front end to decompile the queries. The first time a query is run after the database has been compacted, a new plan is generated based on the new statistics, and the plan is saved to disk (in SQL Server, plans are stored in memory only). Subsequent executions of the query will use that plan until the next time the database is compacted. Making a design change to a query causes it to be decompiled, but it doesn't mean that the statistics needed to create a good new plan will have been updated. This is one area where SQL Server offers significant advantages over Jet, especially in databases that change their statistics markedly.

Where Stored Procedures Live

When you create a stored procedure, the text defining the stored procedure is saved in plain text in the syscomments table, in the text column. However, you don't need to directly query syscomments to see the stored procedure text—the sp_helptext stored procedure will do the trick for you. Figure 10.7 shows the output from the following sp_helptext stored procedure in the Query Analyzer results pane:

```
sp_helptext procSp_executesql
```

Encrypting Your Stored Procedure

This exposure of your stored procedure text in plain text might not be desirable if you want to hide your source code from prying eyes. You can use the WITH ENCRYPTION modifier when you create your stored procedure. If the stored procedure is already in existence, use the ALTER PROCEDURE syntax to modify the existing text. Here's an example:

```
ALTER PROC procSp_executesql
   @col varchar(20),
   @table varchar(20)
   WITH ENCRYPTION
```

```
AS
 DECLARE @SQL nvarchar(100)

 SET @SQL = N'SELECT ' + @col + ' FROM ' + @table

EXEC sp_executesql @SQL
```

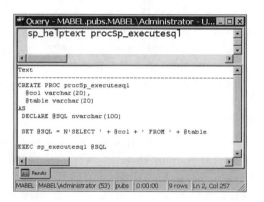

FIGURE 10.7
The output from the sp_helptext *stored procedure.*

If you run sp_helptext on the encrypted stored procedure, you'll simply see the message "The object comments have been encrypted" in the Query Analyzer results pane. Figure 10.8 shows what the encrypted stored procedure looks like when you attempt to edit or view it from the Enterprise Manager.

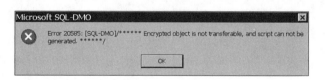

FIGURE 10.8
Once a stored procedure has been encrypted, you can no longer view its definition.

TIP

If you encrypt your stored procedures, you'll want to save them as scripts first so that you have a backup in case you need to modify the stored procedure at some later time. Even though the stored procedure is encrypted, you can still edit it using the ALTER PROCEDURE syntax from the Query Analyzer as long as you have the original text for the stored procedure in a script file. If you don't, you'll have to type it in from scratch.

10

PROGRAMMING
EFFECTIVE STORED
PROCEDURES

Temporary Stored Procedures

There are two types of temporary stored procedures:

- *Local temporary stored procedures.* This type of stored procedure is visible only to the connection that created it. Only the user who created it can use it. A local temporary stored procedure's name is preceded with a pound sign (#).

- *Global temporary stored procedures.* This type of stored procedure is visible to all connections. A global temporary stored procedure's name is preceded with two pound signs (##). All users can use global temporary stored procedures without having to have explicit permissions granted to them. A global temporary stored procedure is dropped after the connection that created it is closed and after any other connections have stopped using it. This means that if the connection that created it closes, no other connections that are not already using the object can use it.

All temporary objects are created and live in tempdb. You can also create stored procedures in tempdb without using the pound sign in the name by using the CREATE PROC syntax shown earlier. Temporary stored procedures created explicitly in tempdb can have permissions assigned and revoked from them. Note that all temporary objects are dropped when the SQL Server service is stopped since tempdb itself is dropped. It is re-created from the model database when the SQL Server service restarts.

TIP

If you have too many temporary objects in tempdb, tempdb can get bogged down and adversely affect performance on the server. To get the flexibility of temporary stored procedures without the problems of heavy use in tempdb, use the sq_executesql statement discussed earlier in this chapter instead, because it does not use tempdb to do its work.

Understanding Transactions

A *transaction* is a set of tasks performed as a single unit of work. Either all the tasks in the transaction are committed or, if any single task fails, all the tasks are rolled back. The most commonly used example of a transaction is a banking transfer of money from one account to another. If money is debited from one account, it must be credited to the other account at the same time. If either part of the transaction fails, both the debit and the credit must be rolled back. You wouldn't want one to succeed without the other.

If you've worked with transactions in Access, you most likely used the DAO BeginTrans, CommitTrans, and Rollback methods of a Workspace object using VBA. You might be tempted to convert your DAO transaction code to ADO, but this would probably be a mistake. Unlike the Jet engine, SQL Server lets you work with transactions within your queries by using Transact-SQL. Creating stored procedures to implement transactions gives you the benefits of performance, security, and scalability.

Transactions in SQL Server are guaranteed to pass to the ACID test.

The ACID Test

The ACID test here isn't something to do with chemistry—it's an acronym for Atomicity, Consistency, Isolation, Durability. If a transaction passes the ACID test, it does not violate the integrity or consistency of the data, and its effects are permanent in the database. Here's a breakdown of each component of the test:

- *Atomicity* means that the entire transaction must fully commit as a single unit or else fully roll back when complete.

- *Consistency* means that all data is left in a consistent state, regardless of whether the transaction is committed or rolled back. All data integrity rules must be enforced, and all internal storage mechanisms must be correct, even in the event of a system failure.

- *Isolation* means that each transaction is completely independent of any other transaction. The default isolation level ensures that concurrent transactions can only see data before other transactions are completed or after other transactions are completed. This means that in the banking example, another transaction can't see the debit or the credit operations while the transaction is still in progress. SQL Server will hold the necessary locks to ensure transactional consistency.

- *Durability* means that the effects of the transaction are permanent, even in the event of a system failure. It also means that if a system failure occurs in the middle of a transaction, the entire transaction will be completely rolled back. SQL Server uses write-ahead logging and automatic rollback and rollforward during the recovery process to ensure transactional durability.

Using Transactions in Transact-SQL

Because each transaction needs to conform to the ACID test, you need to make sure that transactions commit as quickly as possible in order to minimize resource use and locking on the server. The longer each transaction runs, the more likely it's going to block other transactions and limit the number of concurrent users your server can support.

The two kinds of transactions in SQL Server are implicit transactions and explicit transactions.

Implicit Transactions

Every Transact-SQL statement is treated as a transaction. This is the default mode of operation in SQL Server when working with INSERT, UPDATE, or DELETE Transact-SQL statements. Each statement that changes data is a separate implicit transaction. The following statements would each be executed as separate transactions. If statement 1 fails, it would have no impact whatsoever on statement 2, and vice versa:

```
--Statement 1
INSERT INTO Transactions (Account, Amt)
  VALUES (123, 23.95)

--Statement 2
INSERT INTO Transactions (Account, Amt)
  VALUES (321, -23.95)
```

Explicit Transactions

You can package up multiple statements within a BEGIN TRANSACTION, COMMIT TRANSACTION, or ROLLBACK TRANSACTION statement. You need to test for errors after every statement by writing the error value into a local variable. Error handling is covered later in the chapter, but for now, the @@ERROR function returns an error number for any errors occurring on the preceding line. Statement 1 and statement 2 in the example that follows will either both be committed or both be rolled back based on the value in the local @Err variable. If the server fails before the COMMIT TRAN or ROLLBACK TRAN statements, the incomplete transaction would be rolled back when the server comes back online. Here's the example:

```
DECLARE @Err int
SET @Err = 0
BEGIN TRAN
  --Statement 1
  INSERT INTO Transactions (Account, Amt)
    VALUES (123, 23.95)
--If an error occurs, @Err will be non-zero
SET @Err = @@Error

  --Statement 2
  INSERT INTO Transactions (Account, Amt)
    VALUES (321, -23.95)
--Test to see if an error occurred on the second statement
SET @Err = @@Error

--Test for errors on either statement before committing
IF @Err = 0
  COMMIT TRAN
ELSE
  ROLLBACK TRAN
```

Using stored procedures is the best way to implement explicit transactions because you also get the benefits of having a compiled query plan.

How SQL Server Uses Locks

In order to ensure the ACID properties of transactions, SQL Server must apply locks. The different lock types and lock modes are described in Books Online in the topic "Understanding Locking in SQL Server," so all that information won't be repeated here. SQL Server manages locks for you by figuring out which locks would be appropriate for a given query. Several locking modes are supported, including exclusive, update, and shared locks. The type of lock determines how restrictive the lock is and what other actions are possible while the lock is being held.

For example, if you have a SELECT * FROM mytable query, SQL Server will probably not lock individual rows of data but instead employ shared page or table locking. Shared locks are used for read-only operations such as SELECT statements. Even in read-only operations, locks are needed to prevent changes to the data just during the bit of time it takes to retrieve the data. You wouldn't want to read half a row before a change was made and the other half after the change was made.

If you are modifying data with an INSERT, UPDATE, or DELETE statement, SQL Server will need to acquire an exclusive lock on the data being modified. Exclusive locks are held for the duration of a transaction and only one process at a time can obtain one. Once a transaction places an exclusive lock, other transactions cannot update or even read the data until the lock has been released.

The type of locking used is also tied into the isolation level of the transaction, which is discussed in the next section.

Setting Lock Hints

If you don't want to let SQL Server decide on a locking scheme, you can specify a lock hint. Lock hints are set on a per-query basis. For example, suppose you want to prevent other users from reading or updating data from a table because you're running a summary report. Setting a lock hint overrides the default locking scheme that would otherwise have been applied. The following query uses the TABLOCKX lock hint to exclusively lock the Orders table from the BEGIN TRAN statement until all the records have been read (the COMMIT TRAN statement). The TABLOCKX lock hint specifies that an exclusive lock is held until the end of the transaction. With a small table and few users, this probably won't cause a problem. However, if your table has thousands of rows and many concurrent users, other processes will be blocked while the table is being read. Here's the query:

```
BEGIN TRAN
SELECT * FROM Orders (TABLOCKX)
COMMIT TRAN
```

You can easily test the effects of lock hints yourself. Open two connections to the Northwind database in the Query Analyzer. In the first connection, execute the first two lines of the statement by highlighting them and pressing the F5 key:

```
BEGIN TRAN
SELECT * FROM Orders (TABLOCKX)
```

In the second connection, execute this statement:

```
SELECT * FROM Orders
```

The second connection will be blocked until you execute the third statement (COMMIT TRAN) or cancel the query.

If the lock manager can't acquire exclusive locks on the Orders table right away, the request will go into a queue until all the exclusive locks can be acquired. Subsequent requests for locks on the Orders table will queue behind it. Once the exclusive locks are acquired, all other processes are blocked until the transaction completes.

Probably 99.9% of the time you'll want SQL Server to decide which type of locking is appropriate. Whenever you do use lock hints, make sure to test your application fully to make sure you understand the impact on the server and the application. If you have too many processes holding onto exclusive table locks, you're probably going to have big problems with blocking issues, which are discussed shortly. Locking hints are documented fully in SQL Books Online.

Setting Isolation Levels in Transactions

The default isolation level of all transactions in SQL Server is READ COMMITTED. This guarantees that all rows of data being read actually exist and prevents what are known as *dirty reads*. A dirty read is when you read a value that is in the middle of a transaction and has not yet been either committed or rolled back, so the value may not actually exist when the transaction ends up being committed. If you don't explicitly set an isolation level in your transactions, SQL Server will execute the transaction using the READ COMMITTED isolation level. However, you can set the isolation level for a transaction manually to override READ COMMITTED. The SQL/92 standard specifies four isolation levels, all of which are supported by SQL Server:

- READ UNCOMMITTED
- READ COMMITTED
- REPEATABLE READ
- SERIALIZABLE

Setting the READ UNCOMMITTED and READ COMMITTED Isolation Levels

You can test how READ UNCOMMITTED handles a dirty read by opening two different connections to SQL Server in the Query Analyzer, using the Northwind database. In the first connection, run the following statements by highlighting all except for the very last statement (ROLLBACK TRAN):

```
USE Northwind
BEGIN TRAN
 UPDATE Categories
 SET CategoryName = 'Widgets'

--Don't execute the next line yet:
ROLLBACK TRAN
```

In the second connection, run these statements:

```
USE Northwind
SET TRANSACTION ISOLATION LEVEL READ UNCOMMITTED
SELECT CategoryName FROM Categories
```

The second connection's result set will show "Widgets" for every CategoryName row, as shown in Figure 10.9. This is a dirty read—you're looking at data that hasn't been committed yet.

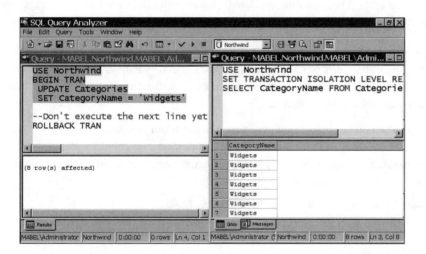

FIGURE 10.9

READ UNCOMMITTED *allows dirty reads.*

In the first connection, execute the following statement:

```
ROLLBACK TRAN
```

Now run the second connection's query again. You'll see that the changes have been rolled back and each category name is restored to its original value.

Of course, in real life you won't be updating every row in a table this way. Allowing dirty reads with READ UNCOMMITTED uses no locks whatsoever on the data, and it's very fast. You might use READ UNCOMMITTED in a situation where you want to create a report in which accuracy isn't as important as speed. For example, you want to quickly compute average sales over a vast time period. Chances are that the averages will come out pretty much the same even if individual rows of data are being modified. Another example in which READ UNCOMMITTED is safe is when you are working with historical data that you know won't change during your operation. However, you definitely don't want to use READ UNCOMMITTED where data consistency is important and there's a chance that the data may be modified during your query operation.

If you run the two Widgets queries a second time, but with the READ COMMITTED transaction isolation level specified by connection 2, you'll be blocked. You won't be able to read data from the table until you roll back or commit connection 1's transaction.

Once you specify an isolation level, all SELECT statements run in that session will be executed at the specified level. That isolation level will continue in effect until the session is terminated or until another isolation level is specified.

Setting the REPEATABLE READ Isolation Level

REPEATABLE READ prevents other transactions from updating data, but not from inserting data. New rows inserted are known as *phantom rows*, because they are not seen by any transactions that were begun prior to their insertion.

REPEATABLE READ prevents lost updates, which occur when two separate transactions try to commit updates to data on the same row. Lost updates are prevented by stopping other transactions from making any updates. Using the Query Analyzer, execute the following statements except for the very last statement in connection 1:

```
SET TRANSACTION ISOLATION LEVEL REPEATABLE READ
BEGIN TRAN
 SELECT * FROM Categories
 WHERE CategoryID = 3

--Don't execute the next line yet:
COMMIT TRAN
```

Open a second connection, and execute these statements:

```
UPDATE Categories
 SET CategoryName = 'Sweets'
 WHERE CategoryID = 3
```

Connection 2 will be blocked until you roll back or commit the transaction in connection 1.

However, with REPEATABLE READ there's nothing to stop you from inserting a new row without it being blocked. Execute the following statements in connection 1, except for the last statement:

```
SET TRANSACTION ISOLATION LEVEL
  REPEATABLE READ
BEGIN TRAN
 SELECT CategoryName
 FROM Categories

--Don't execute the next line yet:
COMMIT TRAN
```

In connection 2, type the following statements:

```
INSERT INTO Categories
  (CategoryName)
 Values('Junk Food')

SELECT CategoryName
FROM Categories
```

If you select the data from connection 2, you'll see the phantom row, as shown in the right-hand window in Figure 10.10. However, connection 1 won't pick it up.

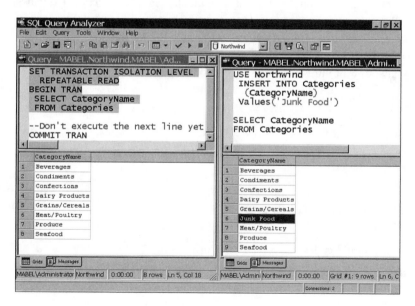

FIGURE 10.10

REPEATABLE READ *allows the insertion of phantom rows.*

Using REPEATABLE READ prevents data from being updated (or deleted). However, it does not prevent a new row from being inserted. You should use REPEATABLE READ in situations where users need to be protected from simultaneously updating the same data but should be allowed to simultaneously add new data. For example, you might need to produce a report showing sales up to the moment, and then do a modification using that data while ensuring that it does not change during the course of the transaction. You don't want to stop ongoing sales by preventing the entry of new orders, but you don't want the data used to produce the report to be changed, either.

Setting the SERIALIZABLE Isolation Level

The SERIALIZABLE isolation level is the most restrictive isolation level of all. It ensures that if a query is reissued inside of the same transaction, existing rows won't look any different and new rows won't suddenly appear. It employs a range of locks to prevent the editing or insertion of data until the transaction is completed. The name *serializable* comes from the fact that running concurrent serializable transactions is the same as running them serially—one at a time, one after another.

Phantom rows are never inserted when the SERIALIZABLE isolation level is in effect. Once a transaction has begun, it is as if no other users are in the tables, as far as the data affected by that transaction is concerned. If you run the examples shown for REPEATABLE READ and substitute SERIALIZABLE, connection 2 will always be blocked until connection 1 finishes, which won't be until you issue the ROLLBACK TRAN or COMMIT TRAN statement. For example, you may need to produce a closing report summarizing transactions for the day, while preventing both inserts and modifications. By reading with SERIALIZABLE, inserts can be forced to tomorrow's date or will have to wait until the COMMIT TRAN statement.

Here's the connection 1 code:

```
SET TRANSACTION ISOLATION LEVEL
 SERIALIZABLE
BEGIN TRAN
 SELECT CategoryName
 FROM Categories

--Don't execute the next line yet:
COMMIT TRAN
```

Here's the connection 2 code:

```
 INSERT INTO Categories
  (CategoryName)
 Values('Junk Food')

SELECT CategoryName
FROM Categories
Serializable
```

Avoiding Deadlocks and Blocking

If you do not specify any lock hints and operate under the default isolation mode using implicit transactions, SQL Server will lock data for only the fraction of a second that it takes to make the necessary changes. However, you can still create situations where users are blocked. Here are some simple rules to follow to avoid deadlocking and blocking situations:

- *Keep transactions as short as possible.* The longer the transaction, the more likely that other processes will be in contention for the same resources. Stored procedures are good for this—your transactions can all go in one batch and be optimized to execute as quickly as possible.

- *Avoid user intervention in transactions.* If a transaction is open and the user goes out to lunch, other users are blocked from using those resources until the transaction either commits or rolls back.

- *Use as low an isolation level as possible.* This includes situations where you access data from an application. If you use any kind of pessimistic locking, which causes locks to be placed as soon as editing begins, you are forcing SQL Server to tie up resources, and the more locks, the more blocking. The other side effect of pessimistic locking is reducing scalability.

- *Avoid recursive and nested triggers.* Triggers that fire other triggers cause cascading transactions that lengthen the duration of locks.

Dealing with Deadlocks

Deadlocking occurs when two processes vie for the same resources at the same time. Each is trying to escalate a shared lock already being held to an exclusive lock, and neither is able to acquire the lock it requires. For example, process A has a lock on Table1 and is trying to get a lock on Table2, while process B has a lock on Table2 and is trying to lock Table1. This kind of a standoff would last forever if SQL Server didn't step in to declare a winner. The database engine detects the problem and simply chooses a deadlock victim. A trappable error—in this case, error code 1205—is returned to the loser (this and other error codes are fully documented in Books Online). This error is not fatal, and when you detect it, you can simply try your transaction again. Error handling is discussed later in this chapter.

Many deadlocks can be prevented if you develop rules about accessing resources in a specific order. If the developer of process A and the developer of process B get together, they can agree to always access Table1 first, then Table2. That way, locks are always acquired in the same order, and the chances of deadlocking are eliminated. If process A beats process B to an exclusive lock on Table1, process B simply goes into the wait queue while process A acquires the needed locks in Table2. Eventually both transactions complete successfully with no errors raised.

Creating Parameterized Stored Procedures

Now that you understand some of how transactions work, you can get down to creating more complex stored procedures. Most stored procedures you write will require some input at runtime, and many will return information after the procedure has completed. Parameters give you a way of supplying values to your stored procedure at runtime as well as a way of passing return values back to the calling process. In addition to parameters, you can also declare and use variables in your stored procedures.

Declaring and Using Variables in Stored Procedures

A variable in a stored procedure serves the same purpose as a variable in any programming language—it's simply a named location in memory that temporarily holds a value. A variable declared in a stored procedure is automatically discarded when the stored procedure ends. It is private to the stored procedure in which it is declared. When you declare a variable, you must preface the variable name with the @ symbol and also define a data type. The following Transact-SQL statement declares a variable named @ID with an int data type:

```
DECLARE @ID int
```

When the variable is declared, its initial value is Null, regardless of the data type. You have two ways of assigning a value to the variable: by using the SET keyword and as part of a SELECT statement. Either of the two following statements will assign a value to the @ID variable:

```
SET @ID = 123
```

```
SELECT @ID = 123
```

More examples of using variables appear later in this chapter.

Input and Output Parameters

You can declare parameters as input parameters or input/output parameters. Input parameters let you supply values for your stored procedure, and input/output parameters let you return values to a calling program. In SQL Server, any output parameter can always also be used as an input parameter. There's no way to specify that a parameter can never receive an input value; all you can do is specify whether it can also be used to return an output value.

Using Input and Output Parameters for an INSERT Stored Procedure

A good example of when you would want to have both input and output parameters is when you add a record to a table that has an identity column and you want the stored procedure to let you know the new identity column value. If you add a new shipper to the Shippers table in the Northwind database, you don't need to supply an ID because the identity column will generate one for you. You just supply the CompanyName value and, optionally, a phone number. However, to then use that new shipper on an order, you'll need to know its new ShipperID value. You could write your stored procedure to look like the following:

```
CREATE PROCEDURE procShipperInsert
  @CompanyName nvarchar(40),
  @Phone nvarchar(24),
  @ShipperID int OUTPUT
AS

INSERT INTO Shippers (CompanyName, Phone)
VALUES(@CompanyName, @Phone)

SELECT @ShipperID = @@IDENTITY
```

The @CompanyName and @Phone input parameters are declared using the data types of the corresponding fields in the Shippers table. The INSERT statement adds the values to the table and uses a SELECT statement with the @ShipperID output parameter to return the new identity column value. @@IDENTITY is a system function that gives you the last identity value created in that connection.

Executing the Stored Procedure

To execute the stored procedure in Transact-SQL, pass the input parameter values in by position or by name. To see the output parameter value, you must supply a variable to be passed to the procedure. The following Transact-SQL example calls the stored procedure, passing values to the input parameters by name, and it declares and passes a variable to the output parameter. At the end, a SELECT statement is used to return a record containing the new shipper ID. You must use the OUTPUT keyword after your local variable in order to retrieve the output parameter value from the stored procedure. Without the word OUTPUT, you won't get an error, but you also won't get back any value from the output parameter. Here's the example:

```
DECLARE @id int
EXEC procShipperInsert
  @CompanyName='Shippit',
  @Phone='561-345-2345',
  @ShipperID=@id OUTPUT
SELECT @id AS NewShipID
```

You can also pass values to the parameters by position. You must supply the values in the order in which the parameters were declared in the stored procedure that you are calling. Here's an example:

```
DECLARE @id int
EXEC procShipperInsert 'Shippit',
  '561-345-2345', @id OUTPUT
SELECT @id AS NewShipID
```

Chapter 6 discusses how to work with the parameters of a stored procedure when you call the procedure from VBA code, using the parameters collection of an ADO Command object.

The Difference Between EXECUTE and EXECUTE()

The EXEC (or EXECUTE) statement lets you execute a stored procedure from an external application or from within another stored procedure. However, you can also execute statements using EXECUTE(*character_string*), or EXEC(*character_string*), to execute a character string that contains a command. The character string must be less than 8,000 bytes (8KB). Even if the EXEC() function is located in a stored procedure, it is not compiled until runtime and the plan generated is not cached and reused. EXEC() comes in handy when you want to assemble a dynamic SQL statement to be executed from variables or parameters in your stored procedure. The following example has input parameters for a column name and a table name. The parameters are then concatenated inside of the EXEC() function into a SELECT statement that selects any column from any table:

```
CREATE PROC procDynamicSQL
   @col varchar(20),
   @table varchar(20)
AS

EXEC('SELECT ' + @col + ' FROM ' + @table)
```

Execute the stored procedure using EXEC, passing in a column and table name from the database the stored procedure was created in (in this case, pubs):

```
EXEC procDynamicSQL 'au_lname', 'authors'
```

All of the author last names will be returned from the authors table. Note that the character string inside the EXEC() statement isn't parsed or compiled until runtime, so any syntax errors will surface then.

Using sp_executesql

An alternative to the EXEC() statement is sp_executesql. Unlike EXEC(), sp_executesql generates an execution plan, which can then be reused by SQL Server during subsequent executions of the stored procedure. Also unlike EXEC(), sp_executesql requires that you pass in a string constant. This means you can't build it on-the-fly while executing sp_executesql, as you could in the previous example using EXEC(). This limitation is easy enough to circumvent by declaring a variable and then assembling the string inside the variable. The following stored procedure builds on the example used previously for EXEC(). It has the same input parameters, but the variable @SQL has been declared in the body of the stored procedure. Concatenating the pieces of the SQL statement together at runtime is not acceptable as a parameter to sp_executesql, but the @SQL variable is fine, as long as you declare it as nvarchar:

```
CREATE PROC procSp_executesql
  @col varchar(20),
  @table varchar(20)
AS
 DECLARE @SQL nvarchar(100)

 SET @SQL = N'SELECT ' + @col + ' FROM ' + @table

EXEC sp_executesql @SQL
```

> **NOTE**
>
> The N before the literal string in this example is a part of Transact-SQL syntax that signals that the literal string that follows it is a Unicode string. In most cases, this is optional, because an ANSI string can be implicitly converted to Unicode by the parser, but it is technically correct and safer to use. The SQL Server documentation will indicate where Unicode strings are expected by including the N when presenting syntax specifications. Unicode strings are used internally by SQL Server in its own systems tables and stored procedures that require strings.

Security Issues with EXEC() and sp_executesql

One limitation of both EXEC() and sp_executesql is that both of these dynamic statements do not run within the security context of the stored procedure. For example, you revoke all permissions on the underlying tables since you wish to prevent users from ad hoc querying or modifying data directly. To that end, you write stored procedures, relying on the fact that granting Execute permissions on the stored procedure enables users to work with data they wouldn't be able to select or modify. However, any stored procedures utilizing EXEC() or sp_executesql will fail since these dynamic statements are not run within the context of the stored procedure, but within the context of the permissions granted the user.

Using SET NOCOUNT ON

When you're writing stored procedures, it's often a good idea to have the first line of your stored procedure code be the statement SET NOCOUNT ON. This suppresses the "done in proc" message sent back to a client application for each statement executed. When you're calling stored procedures from your application, it prevents an extra roundtrip to the server, thus providing a performance boost due to reduced network traffic.

When you use SET NOCOUNT ON, you won't be able to take advantage of the RecordsAffected property in ADO. However, SET NOCOUNT ON has no effect whatsoever on @@ROWCOUNT. You can always return the number of rows affected in an output parameter or a recordset if you need to. In the case of a stored procedure that inserts a single record, as the previous shipper example does, the count of records affected is not useful information anyway.

To add this line suppressing the return of a count to the stored procedure already written, use the ALTER PROCEDURE syntax:

```
ALTER PROCEDURE procShipperInsert
  @CompanyName nvarchar(40),
  @Phone nvarchar(24),
  @ShipperID int OUTPUT
AS
SET NOCOUNT ON
INSERT INTO Shippers (CompanyName, Phone)
VALUES(@CompanyName, @Phone)

SELECT @ShipperID = @@IDENTITY
```

Setting Parameter Defaults

The stored procedure created so far does what it's supposed to do, but what happens if you don't supply values for all the parameters? For example, calling the procedure using the following syntax will cause a runtime error because the value for the phone number is not supplied, even though null values are allowed in the Phone column in the Shippers table:

```
EXEC procShipperInsert 'Shippit'

Server: Msg 201, Level 16, State 1, Procedure procShipperInsert, Line 0
Procedure 'procShipperInsert' expects parameter '@Phone', which was not
supplied.
```

The way around this is to supply a default null value (or some other default value, if you prefer) for any parameter that you want to be optional. The next time the procedure is called, the CompanyName value will be inserted and the default null value will be supplied for the Phone column. In the following example, it's optional to supply the output parameter, @ShipperID:

```
ALTER PROCEDURE procShipperInsert
  @CompanyName nvarchar(40),
  @Phone nvarchar(24) = NULL,
  @ShipperID int = NULL OUTPUT
AS
SET NOCOUNT ON
INSERT INTO Shippers (CompanyName, Phone)
VALUES(@CompanyName, @Phone)

SELECT @ShipperID = @@IDENTITY
```

Now, just to make this interesting, suppose you have a column in a table that has a default value defined. What if you want that default value, rather than null, to be inserted in that column if no parameter value is specified? Here is a case where the procedural capabilities of Transact-SQL come in handy. You can conditionally leave out that column from your insert, thus allowing the defined default value to be inserted automatically. For example, if you had defined a default value for the Phone field in Shippers, you could alter the procedure to use that default value if the Phone parameter is not specified:

```
ALTER PROCEDURE procShipperInsert
  @CompanyName nvarchar(40),
  @Phone nvarchar(24) = NULL,
  @ShipperID int  = NULL OUTPUT
AS
SET NOCOUNT ON
IF @Phone IS NULL
    INSERT INTO Shippers (CompanyName)
    VALUES(@CompanyName)
ELSE
    INSERT INTO Shippers (CompanyName, Phone)
    VALUES(@CompanyName, @Phone)

SELECT @ShipperID = @@IDENTITY
```

Error Handling in Stored Procedures

Error handling in Transact-SQL may seem cumbersome if you're used to error handling in VBA. There's no such thing as an "On Error Goto" statement that allows you to have an error-handling section in your code that processes all runtime errors. In Transact-SQL, errors are handled inline as they occur, on a statement-by-statement basis. One reason for this is that, unlike in VBA, most runtime errors are not fatal and do not prevent subsequent statements from executing. If you don't check for errors after every statement, your code just barrels merrily along executing statement after statement and possibly piling up quite a few errors along the way. So whatever you can do at the outset to prevent runtime errors from occurring will simplify the process of handling them when they occur in your Transact-SQL code.

Preventive Error Handling

In the example of inserting data into the Shippers table, setting default values for all the optional parameters helped minimize errors. But what about CompanyName? A default null value wasn't defined for that field because it's a required field. This means, however, that if no value is supplied for that parameter, an error will be raised. Even if a default null value was provided for CompanyName, there still would be an error if you tried to insert a null in CompanyName, because CompanyName is a required (non-nullable) field. If the stored procedure were called with no value specified for the CompanyName parameter, you'd receive the following runtime error:

```
Server: Msg 515, Level 16, State 2, Procedure procShipperInsert, Line 7
Cannot insert the value NULL into column 'CompanyName', table
'Northwind.dbo.Shippers';
column does not allow nulls. INSERT fails.
The statement has been terminated.
```

This sort of scary error message is probably the last thing you want the user to see coming from your SQL Server. The stored procedure can be rewritten to test to see whether the required CompanyName value is supplied, and if it isn't, it could exit the procedure gracefully. Having set the CompanyName default value to NULL allows you to test it to see if it's still null when the procedure is executing. The RETURN statement will unconditionally terminate execution of the stored procedure before the INSERT statement is attempted. Here's an example:

```
ALTER PROCEDURE procShipperInsert
  @CompanyName nvarchar(40) = NULL,
  @Phone nvarchar(24) = NULL,
  @ShipperID int = NULL OUTPUT
AS
SET NOCOUNT ON

-- Bail if company name is NULL
IF @CompanyName IS NULL
  RETURN

-- If we got this far, insert the record
INSERT INTO Shippers (CompanyName, Phone)
VALUES(@CompanyName, @Phone)

SELECT @ShipperID = @@IDENTITY
```

This is a start—no more runtime errors for missing parameters. However, there's no message to the calling application that there was a problem and that the new record was not inserted. As far as the user can tell, the record was successfully inserted.

Returning Success/Failure Information

Every stored procedure you write should return information to the caller as to whether it succeeded or failed. Usually this consists of a success/failure code and some kind of message. This way, the client application is fully aware of whether the stored procedure succeeded and can take action based on the results. If you are used to programming in VBA, you might want to use -1 (the VBA value of True) for the success code and 0 (False) for failure. Because VBA will evaluate any nonzero number as True, you could also use 1 for success, as is done in the examples that follow. Another good approach would be to return 0 for success and an error code if the procedure fails to complete the insert. Regardless of what value you use as a success/failure code, you should also return a message, which should be a varchar data type to hold a variable-length string.

You can then rewrite the stored procedure, supplying the appropriate error code and error message when a value for CompanyName isn't supplied. After the INSERT statement, you can check @@ROWCOUNT to see whether the record got inserted correctly. If it didn't, you can return the appropriate code and message there as well. Here's an example:

```
ALTER PROCEDURE procShipperInsert
  @CompanyName nvarchar(40) = NULL,
  @Phone nvarchar(24) = NULL,
  @ShipperID int = NULL OUTPUT,
  @RetCode int = NULL OUTPUT,
  @RetMsg varchar(150) = NULL OUTPUT
AS
SET NOCOUNT ON

IF @CompanyName IS NULL
BEGIN
  SELECT @RetCode = 0, -- Zero is used for failure
  @RetMsg = 'Company Name required.'
  RETURN
END

INSERT INTO Shippers (CompanyName, Phone)
VALUES(@CompanyName, @Phone)
IF @@ROWCOUNT > 0
  SELECT @ShipperID = @@IDENTITY,
    @RetCode = 1, -- Success
    @RetMsg = 'New Shipper Inserted'
ELSE
  SELECT @ShipperID = 0,
    @RetCode = 0, -- Failure
    @RetMsg = 'New Shipper Not Inserted'
```

The only problem with the stored procedure so far is that it can't handle any runtime errors.

Handling Runtime Errors

The errors you need to handle in your stored procedures can arise from constraint violations, data errors (such as illegal values for a specific data type or duplicates encountered where none are allowed), deadlocks, and NOT NULL violations. The previous section discussed preventive measures for NOT NULL violations, the following sections will tackle handling other types of errors.

Few Errors Are Fatal

As mentioned earlier, if you have multiple statements in your stored procedure—perhaps executing multiple inserts within a single transaction—and you hit a nonfatal runtime error, execution simply proceeds on to the next statement. A fatal runtime error for SQL Server would be system wide, like running out of disk space or memory. In that situation, all bets are off and none of your procedures are going to execute anyway. But inside a transaction, you can hit a constraint error or a data type error, and unless you specifically check for an error condition *on the next line*, SQL Server will just march on and continue execution. All the statements without errors will be committed. Using VBA as an analogy, it is as if every stored procedure begins with the line On Error Resume Next. This causes VBA to ignore any and all errors in much the same way that stored procedures ignore errors, unless the severity of the error is such that it crashes the application.

Using @@ERROR to Capture Runtime Errors

The following version of the procShipperInsert example checks the @@ERROR function immediately after the INSERT statement. Because @@ROWCOUNT is also being used, the procedure captures both in local variables immediately after the INSERT statement. If there's a runtime error, the GOTO statement will branch to the label at the end of the procedure, and appropriate return values will be sent back to the calling procedure:

```
ALTER PROCEDURE procShipperInsert
  @CompanyName nvarchar(40) = NULL,
  @Phone nvarchar(24) = NULL,
  @ShipperID int = NULL OUTPUT,
  @RetCode int = NULL OUTPUT,
  @RetMsg varchar(150) = NULL OUTPUT
AS
  DECLARE @Err int
  DECLARE @Rows int

SET NOCOUNT ON

IF @CompanyName IS NULL
BEGIN
  SELECT @RetCode = 0,
  @RetMsg = 'Company Name required.'
  RETURN
END

INSERT INTO Shippers (CompanyName, Phone)
VALUES(@CompanyName, @Phone)

  SELECT @Err = @@ERROR, @Rows = @@ROWCOUNT
```

```
IF (@Err <> 0) GOTO HandleErr

IF @Rows > 0
  SELECT @ShipperID = @@IDENTITY,
    @RetCode = 1,
    @RetMsg = 'New Shipper Inserted'
ELSE
  SELECT @ShipperID = 0,
    @RetCode = 0,
    @RetMsg = 'New Shipper Not Inserted'
RETURN

HandleErr:
  SELECT @ShipperID = 0,
    @RetCode = 0,
    @RetMsg = 'Runtime Error: ' + CONVERT(VarChar, @Err)
  RETURN
```

Note that you must explicitly convert the numeric error code into a varchar string before concatenating it onto the message text.

VBA developers have complained for years about how cumbersome error handling is in the language (and Microsoft has promised some interesting changes in Visual Studio 7). However, as you can see, error handling in SQL Server makes VBA's implementation look elegant. Maybe future versions will have better error handling capabilities, but so far this is all you've got, and you really need to consider adding error handling code every time you write a stored procedure.

Using PRINT to Return Information

One handy tool you can use in your stored procedures is the PRINT statement. Use PRINT in the Query Analyzer to display variable values, to execute functions, and to display the values of expressions. Think of PRINT as a Transact-SQL substitute for the Debug.Print method in VBA, and you'll not be far off. The following statement executed in the Query Analyzer will return the current date and time:

```
PRINT GETDATE()
```

This will display the current date and time in the results pane of the Query Analyzer:

```
Apr  2 2000  5:19PM
```

Use PRINT to help in troubleshooting Transact-SQL code, to check the values of data, or to produce reports in the results pane of Query Analyzer.

Using RAISERROR to Return Errors

The RAISERROR function returns a user-defined error message and sets a system flag to record that an error has occurred. These error messages are stored in the sysmessages system table.

Using RAISERROR allows you to generate your own errors and pass them back to the client, which are also optionally written to the Windows NT event log. Here's the syntax:

```
RAISERROR ({msg_id | msg_str}{, severity, state}
    [, argument
        [,...n]] )
    [WITH option[,...n]]
```

When you call RAISERROR, @@ERROR returns the error number passed as msg_id. Error numbers for user-defined error messages should be greater than 50,000. Ad hoc messages, which are simply user-defined error messages, raise an error of 50,000. The maximum value for msg_id is 2,147,483,647 (2 (31) −1). The state parameter can be any arbitrary number you assign, with values ranging from 1 to 127. As far as SQL Server is concerned, the state parameter has no meaning. However, the severity level determines how SQL Server handles the error. You can set any severity level for your own custom ad hoc error messages:

- Set a severity level of 0 or 10 for informational messages.
- Severity level 15 messages are warnings.
- Severity 16 and higher messages are errors.
- Severity 20 or higher errors are fatal and can only be set by a system administrator. In this case, no message is sent to the client, and the connection will be severed. Errors with a severity level greater than 19 are automatically written to the SQL Server error log and the Windows NT event log.

A system administrator (the sa user or any member of the sysadmin fixed server role) can cause an error of any severity to be written to the log using the WITH LOG option.

Raising Ad Hoc Error Messages

The following statements will raise an ad hoc error message. Because the msg_id parameter isn't specified, it will have the default user-defined error number of 50,000. The severity level is set to 10 (informational). If you want to escalate it to a warning or an error, you could use 15 or 16 instead, like this:

```
IF NOT EXISTS (SELECT * FROM Shippers)
  RAISERROR ('The shippers have been deleted!', 10, 1)
ELSE
  PRINT 'All is Well'
```

Creating UPDATE, DELETE, and SELECT Stored Procedures

So far you've seen how to build one simple stored procedure for inserting a shipper. What about other operations, such as UPDATE, DELETE, and SELECT? The next few sections will briefly explore how to construct these other kinds of stored procedures.

Creating an UPDATE Stored Procedure

When you write a stored procedure to update data, you usually need an input parameter corresponding to each column in the table. Although you don't update identity columns, you'll need parameters corresponding to those columns in order to locate the records you want to modify. In addition, you also need variables to keep track of errors, for flags, or for constructing dynamic SQL statements. Here's the declarations section for a stored procedure to update data in the Shippers table:

```
CREATE PROCEDURE procShipperUpdate
  @ShipperID int = NULL,
  @CompanyName nvarchar(40) = NULL,
  @Phone nvarchar(24) = NULL,
  @RetCode int = NULL OUTPUT,
  @RetMsg varchar(150) = NULL OUTPUT
AS
  DECLARE @Err int
  DECLARE @Exists bit
  DECLARE @strSQL nvarchar(200)
SET NOCOUNT ON
```

The first thing you need to do after verifying that there's an input parameter for ShipperID is to check to see whether the record actually exists, because you don't want to trigger a runtime error by sending an UPDATE statement to a nonexistent record.

```
IF @ShipperID IS NULL
BEGIN
  SELECT @RetCode = 0,
  @RetMsg = 'Shipper ID required.'
  RETURN
END

--Bail if record does not exist
IF
  (SELECT COUNT(*) FROM Shippers
   WHERE ShipperID = @ShipperID) = 0
BEGIN
  SELECT @RetCode = 0,
```

10

PROGRAMMING
EFFECTIVE STORED
PROCEDURES

```
   @RetMsg = 'Shipper does not exist.'
   RETURN
END
```

Make your UPDATE stored procedure flexible enough to accept some or all parameters by supplying default null values and dynamically building a SQL statement to modify only columns that have non-null parameter values. Along the way you need to test to make sure that at least one parameter value is supplied. Note that the variable for the dynamic SQL statement is declared as nvarchar, because SQL Server uses Unicode strings internally.

```
--Start building the UPDATE statement
SELECT @strSQL = N'UPDATE Shippers SET '

IF @CompanyName IS NOT NULL
  BEGIN
    SELECT @strSQL = @strSQL +
    'CompanyName = ''' + @CompanyName + ''', '
    --Flag indicating that CompanyName exists
    SELECT @Exists = 1
  END
ELSE
    --Set flag indicating no CompanyName
  SELECT @Exists = 0

IF @Phone IS NOT NULL
  BEGIN
    SELECT @strSQL = @strSQL +
    'Phone = ''' + @Phone + ''', '
    --Flag that we had a phone number
    SELECT @Exists = 1
  END

--Bail if nothing to update
IF @Exists = 0
  BEGIN
    SELECT @RetCode = 0,
    @RetMsg = 'Nothing to do.'
    RETURN
  END
```

The sp_executesql stored procedure is then called on the completed string, which executes the INSERT statement.

```
--Strip the trailing comma
SELECT @strSQL=LEFT(@strSQL,LEN(@strSQL)-1)
```

```
--Add the WHERE clause
SELECT @strSQL = @strSQL +
 ' WHERE ShipperID = ' + CAST(@ShipperID AS varchar(7))

--Generate a plan
EXECUTE sp_executesql @strSQL
```

If there is an error triggered by the EXECUTE sp_executesql statement, then the GOTO statement branches to the error handler, which then sets the return code and return message, and ends the procedure with the RETURN statement.

```
--If error, branch to error handler
SELECT @Err = @@ERROR
IF (@Err <> 0) GOTO HandleErr

--If we got this far, then no error
  SELECT @RetCode = 1,
  @RetMsg = 'Record Edited'
RETURN

HandleErr:
  SELECT @ShipperID = 0,
    @RetCode = 0,
    @RetMsg = 'Runtime Error: ' + CAST(@Err AS varchar(10))
  RETURN
```

There will be times when you'll want to allow an update stored procedure to receive a null value and actually set the value of a field to NULL, rather than just ignoring that field. Naturally, in those cases, you wouldn't want to use the preceding technique, which ignores nulls for that field. You would either need to use a different default value—something that you knew would never be in the domain of the field—or force a value to be supplied to that parameter by the calling procedure by checking for nulls and using the RETURN statement if no valid value is supplied.

Creating a DELETE Stored Procedure

A stored procedure to delete records takes a single parameter for the WHERE clause in order to locate the record (or multiple parameters if you need to create criteria based on multiple fields). Here's the declaration for a stored procedure to delete a shipper.

```
CREATE PROCEDURE procShipperDelete
  @ShipperID int = NULL,
  @RetCode int = NULL OUTPUT,
  @RetMsg varchar(150) = NULL OUTPUT
AS
SET NOCOUNT ON
```

10

After testing to see whether a valid shipper ID was passed, the record is deleted.

```
--Bail if ShipperID not suppied
IF @ShipperID IS NULL
BEGIN
  SELECT @RetCode = 0,
  @RetMsg = 'Shipper ID required.'
  RETURN
END

--Go ahead and delete the record
DELETE FROM Shippers
WHERE ShipperID = @ShipperID
```

The @@ROWCOUNT system function is then used to make sure that the delete actually occurred. If it didn't, a test is run to see whether the record actually exists. The appropriate message is then returned.

```
IF @@ROWCOUNT = 1
  BEGIN
    SELECT @RetCode = 1,
      @RetMsg = 'Record Deleted'
    RETURN
  END
ELSE
  BEGIN
  IF (SELECT COUNT(*) FROM Shippers
   WHERE ShipperID = @ShipperID) = 0
    SELECT @RetCode = 1, @RetMsg = 'Record does not exist.'
  ELSE
    SELECT @RetCode = 0, @RetMsg = 'Delete failed'
  END
```

You can probably think of ways to improve this example by adding more return codes that give more information on why the delete failed. That way, the calling procedure could decide whether to keep trying or to give up and raise an error or provide feedback to the user. Designing robust stored procedures is very similar to designing robust VBA code—you try to think of everything that can go wrong and provide a useful response for each possibility.

Creating a SELECT Stored Procedure

A SELECT stored procedure is pretty straightforward. This one simply selects all the rows and columns and sorts them by company name. Because no data is being modified, error handling isn't used. Here's an example:

```
CREATE PROCEDURE procShipperSelect
  @ShipperID int = NULL
```

```
AS
  SET NOCOUNT ON
  IF @ShipperID IS NULL
    SELECT ShipperID, CompanyName, Phone
      FROM Shippers
      ORDER BY CompanyName
  ELSE
    SELECT ShipperID, CompanyName, Phone
      FROM Shippers
      WHERE ShipperID = @ShipperID
```

Some General Guidelines for Writing Stored Procedures

Design stored procedures to accomplish a single task. As with VBA code, keep your procedures modular and single purpose—if you need a procedure to do many things, have it call out to separate procedures for each separate task. This makes your stored procedures easier to read and maintain.

Create, test, and debug your stored procedure on the server before testing it on the client. SQL Server 2000 introduces great debugging tools, which are discussed in the next section. Unfortunately, these tools are not available in Access 2000, although similar debugging capabilities are available in Visual Studio 6.0 and later. But even if you need to debug without the benefit of these new tools because you're working with Access 2000 and SQL Server 7.0, you'll most likely find that you can be much more productive working in the SQL Server Query Analyzer than in any of the tools provided by Access.

Use a naming convention, but avoid using "sp_" as a prefix so that your stored procedures can be distinguished from the system stored procedures. As with VBA variables and Access objects, a naming convention can make it much easier to know what you are dealing with. Unfortunately, naming conventions in SQL Server have not received the same kind of acceptance and consensus that exists in Access and VBA, so you'll be more likely to be fending for yourself. Hopefully, standards will emerge as more developers who have become accustomed to working with naming conventions start working with SQL Server.

Use white space, indentation, and comments in your stored procedures to make them easier to read and maintain. You'll be glad you did when you have to go back and try to figure out what you were thinking six months earlier, and any developer who comes in after you will be eternally grateful.

Supply default values for your parameters. The runtime error you'll get if a parameter that hasn't been given a default value is missing leaves you few options and makes your procedures very unforgiving. Use default values to allow parameters to be optional. You can always provide your own error codes and/or messages if a missing parameter value is required, but you can often accomplish the task at hand without needing the calling procedure to provide values for every single parameter.

Always have a return code and a return value for stored procedures that modify data. The opportunity is there to provide useful return information, and there's almost always going to be useful information to return, so be creative and give some thought to how you can make your stored procedures easier to work with by providing feedback to the calling procedure or application.

Debugging Stored Procedures

In SQL Server 2000, the Query Analyzer comes equipped with a new Transact-SQL Debugger. The debugger allows you to set breakpoints, define watch expressions, and single step through your stored procedures.

If you browse the user interface of the Query Analyzer, it's not that apparent how to start the debugger. Before you start, you need to have the target procedure already created and saved. Once launched, the debugger will open in its own window.

There are two ways to start the debugger, one using the Object Browser, the other using the Object Search tool.

Starting the Transact-SQL Debugger

1. Choose Tools, Object Browser or press the F8 key to bring up the Object Browser.
2. Click the Objects tab and then double-click to open the database for the stored procedure you want to debug.
3. In the Stored Procedures folder, right-click the stored procedure and select Debug from the menu. This will bring up a dialog box where you can input parameter values, as shown in Figure 10.11. If you also check the Auto roll back option, then any changes you make during the session will automatically be rolled back.

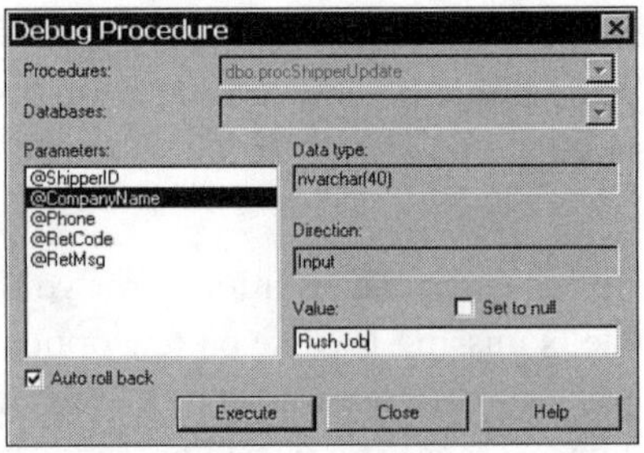

FIGURE 10.11

Specifying parameter values for a debugging session.

4. When you're finished, click the Execute button. This launches the debugger in its own window, based on the current connection, as shown in Figure 10.12.

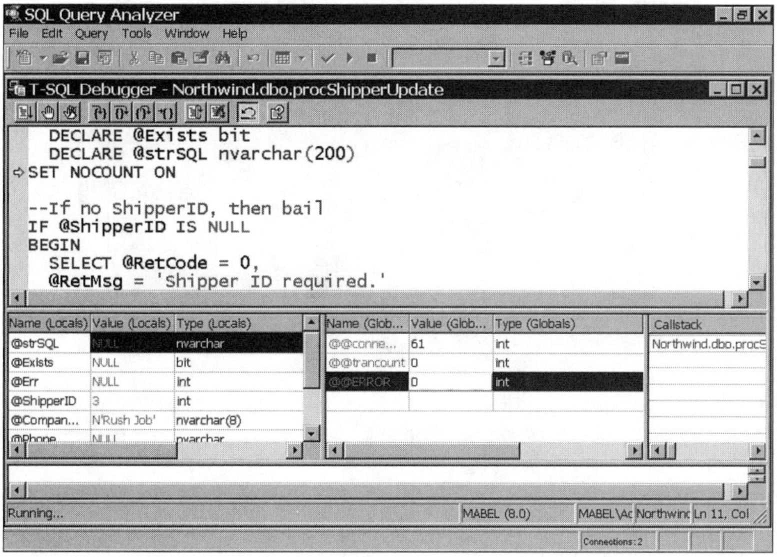

FIGURE 10.12
The T-SQL Debugger window in debug mode.

The top pane displays the text of the stored procedure to be debugged, with a yellow arrow in the margin indicating the statement about to be executed. The toolbar buttons allow you to step through the stored procedure (and any nested stored procedures), set and clear breakpoints, and restart debugging. The three resizable panes at the bottom of the debugger window under the stored procedure text allow you to view and set local and global variables and to view the call stack. If you don't see a global variable listed, such as @@ERROR, simply type it in and its value will appear.

To start the debugger from Object Search:

1. Choose Tools, Object Search and enter the appropriate search parameters required to locate the procedure you are looking for in the Object Search dialog box.

2. Click Find Now to display a list of matches, and then right-click the name of the stored procedure and select Debug, as shown in Figure 10.13.

3. You will then see the context menu, as shown in Figure 10.13. It is not required that you set the input parameters here; you can leave them blank if you want to and set the input parameters in the locals pane in the main debugging window after the stored procedure is loaded.

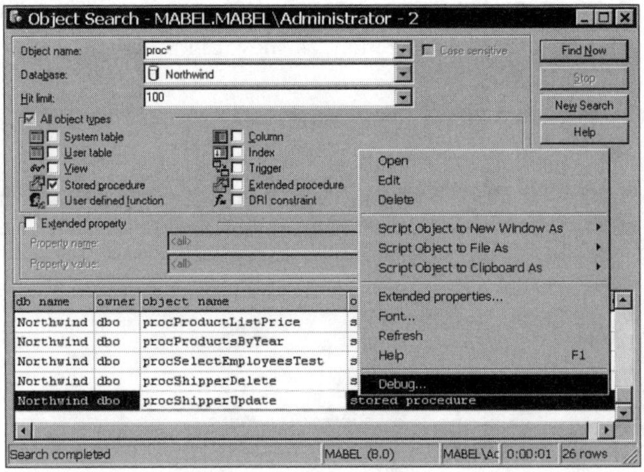

FIGURE 10.13
Launching the T-SQL Debugger from the Object Search menu.

Whichever method you choose to load it, the Transact-SQL Debugger is a welcome addition to the Query Analyzer. It lets you do all of your debugging without launching a client application or having to rely on primitive PRINT statements.

Advanced Stored Procedure Topics

This section discusses a couple of advanced techniques that can come in handy when creating stored procedures, such as using temp tables and using cursors.

Using Temp Tables

Temporary (or *temp*) tables are created in a system database called tempdb that's automatically re-created every time SQL Server is started up. Temporary tables are created and destroyed constantly by SQL Server itself for its own work, and creating them yourself can be extremely useful for sharing information between different stored procedures or for performing complex tasks.

Private temp tables are created by prefixing the table name with a single pound sign (#) and are visible only to a single connection. When the connection terminates, the temp table is destroyed. Global temp tables, created by starting the name with a double pound sign (##), are visible to all connections and follow the same rules as for global temporary stored procedures, listed earlier in this chapter. One way to ensure that global temp tables are always available is to simply create the table directly in tempdb using the CREATE TABLE syntax without the pound signs. You then need to grant permissions for users to use it. Tables created in this special way will persist for the lifetime of tempdb and will be available to all users who have been granted the appropriate permissions.

Temp tables created inside stored procedures behave differently from temp tables created outside a stored procedure. They are visible to child procedures called by the procedure in which the temp table was created, and they exist only for the duration of the stored procedure in which they were created.

Temp tables are useful for performing operations that can't easily be done (if at all) using simple Transact-SQL statements. For example, a common need is to clean up non-normalized data after it has been imported. The following example uses a table named tblTestAddress with the definition shown in Table 10.1. The idea is to take the contents of Address1, split it into two parts (one for the base address and one for the apartment/suite number) and update the table, writing just the base address into Address1 and the apartment/suite number into Address2.

TABLE 10.1   The tblTestAddress Definition

Column Name	Data Type and Description
ID	int (identity column, primary key).
Address1	varchar(50). Contains address information with the street number combined with the apartment or suite number.
Address2	varchar(50). The new destination column to receive apartment/suite number information.

This simple example assumes that the two parts of the address will always be delimited with a comma (wouldn't it be nice if real life were that simple!). The procAddressClean stored procedure uses the SELECT INTO Transact-SQL syntax to create a temp table containing the data from Address1, split at the comma into two columns in #tmpAddress. Rows from tblTestAddress where Address2 already has data are ignored. Column A1 in #tmpAddress has the base address with a comma at the end, and column A2 has a comma and a space at the beginning, with the apartment or suite number. Once the temp table has been created, tblTestAddress is updated with the contents of #tmpAddress, with the data in #tmpAddress.A1 having its trailing comma stripped off and the data in #tmpAddress.A2 having the leading comma and space stripped off. The stored procedure then returns the cleaned-up data from tblTestAddress with a SELECT statement, as shown in Listing 10.2.

10

PROGRAMMING EFFECTIVE STORED PROCEDURES

LISTING 10.2   procAddressClean Is Used to Clean Up Address Data

```
CREATE PROC procAddressClean
AS
/*  Parse the Address1 Column at the comma and
      insert into the temp table. Only take addresses
      with no Address2 data previously entered.
*/
SELECT ID,
  SUBSTRING(Address1, 1, CHARINDEX(',',Address1))
    AS A1,
  SUBSTRING(Address1, CHARINDEX(',',Address1),
    LEN(Address1))
    AS A2
INTO #tmpAddress
FROM tbltestaddress
WHERE Address2 IS NULL OR LEN(Address2) = 0

/*  Update the Address table with the data
      from the temp table, stripping off the
      extra commas and spaces
*/
UPDATE tblTestAddress
SET Address1 = LEFT(#tmpAddress.A1, LEN(#tmpAddress.A1)-1),
  Address2 = RIGHT(#tmpAddress.A2, LEN(#tmpAddress.A2)-2)
FROM tblTestAddress, #tmpAddress
WHERE tblTestAddress.ID = #tmpAddress.ID
  AND #tmpAddress.A2 IS NOT NULL
  AND LEN(#tmpAddress.A1) > 0
--Display the results
SELECT * FROM tblTestAddress
```

This relatively simple example could have avoided the use of the temp table and performed the updates in place. The benefits of using temp tables become more apparent as your data manipulation tasks become increasingly complex, perhaps requiring several iterative passes through the data. By using temp tables, you also can avoid having to place locks on the real data, which might otherwise be necessary should you have to roll back your changes before they were completed. The temp table can simply be discarded if the task is not completed successfully.

See Chapter 12, "Building Access Reports from SQL Server Data," for an example that builds a cross-tab report using a stored procedure with a temp table.

Using Cursors

A Transact-SQL cursor allows you to navigate through and manipulate individual rows of a result set. In other words, it acts just like a recordset, except instead of being opened by your

VBA code to run on the client, it's opened using Transact-SQL and runs on the server. It also has completely different syntax, so cursors can be confusing at first. But the concept is the same, and you use cursors for many of the same reasons you use recordsets. However, cursors are expensive, and they should be used only when a more efficient alternative isn't available.

Unlike temp tables, a cursor is global by default (this option is controlled by the default to local cursor database option), and it can be referenced outside of the stored procedure it was declared in. It can also be explicitly declared using either the GLOBAL or LOCAL keywords to define the scope of the cursor name. GLOBAL specifies that the cursor name is global to the connection. LOCAL specifies that the cursor name is local to the stored procedure, trigger, or batch creating it. If you create a cursor in a stored procedure, it isn't automatically closed and de-allocated when the stored procedure ends, as a temp table is. You must explicitly de-allocate the cursor when you're finished with it to release the memory it's consuming in the procedure cache.

You have several options when opening cursors in a stored procedure, as shown in Table 10.2. These options are not part of the ANSI SQL-92 standard. They are SQL Server–specific extensions that can only be used in Transact-SQL, although they will look familiar to any developer who has worked with ADO recordsets.

TABLE 10.2 Options when Declaring a Cursor

Option	Description
LOCAL	The scope is limited to the stored procedure it was declared in.
GLOBAL	The default. The cursor is available outside the stored procedure it was declared in.
FORWARD_ONLY	The default. Allows forward-only scrolling from the first to the last row only. FETCH NEXT is the only fetch option allowed. If the STATIC, KEYSET, or DYNAMIC argument is specified, the default value for the cursor will be Scroll.
STATIC	The default. The entire contents of the rows in the cursors are stored in tempdb. The cursor is read-only, and changes made by other users are not visible.
KEYSET	Membership is fixed, and only key values are stored in tempdb. Changes made to rows in the cursor by other users are visible to the cursor, but insertions are not. Keyset cursors are updatable.
DYNAMIC	A fully updatable cursor. All changes made by other users, including insertions, are visible. The ABSOLUTE fetch option is not available.
FAST_FORWARD	A FORWARD_ONLY, READ_ONLY cursor with performance optimizations enabled. FAST_FORWARD and FORWARD_ONLY are mutually exclusive.

TABLE 10.2 Continued

Option	Description
READ_ONLY	No updates can be made through the cursor.
SCROLL_LOCKS	Positioned updates or deletes made are guaranteed to succeed because SQL Server locks the rows as they are read into the cursor. SCROLL_LOCKS and FAST_FORWARD are mutually exclusive.
OPTIMISTIC	Positioned updates or deletes made through the cursor do not succeed if the row has been updated since it was read into the cursor.
TYPE_WARNING	A warning message is raised if the cursor is implicitly converted from the requested type.

The following example shows the steps for creating a cursor. The same problem shown in the previous examples, which was solved with temp tables by splitting an address into two columns, can also be solved by using a cursor instead:

1. The first step is to declare the cursor using a local, fast-forward cursor. All you need to do is walk through the cursor once, from beginning to end, reading data from tblTestAddress, manipulating the variables, and updating the table. It's always a good idea to use the most efficient cursor possible, and this procedure doesn't need to do anything more than read a single row at a time.

2. The next step is to open the cursor and fetch the data from the first row into the variables.

3. Then, the procedure uses a WHILE loop to update the table.

4. The final step is to close and deallocate the cursor, releasing all the locks and memory it consumes. Here's an example:

```
CREATE PROC procAddressCursor

AS
--Declare some variables for local processing
DECLARE @ID int
DECLARE @Adr1 varchar(50)
DECLARE @Adr2 varchar(50)

--Declare and set up the cursor
DECLARE curAddress CURSOR LOCAL FAST_FORWARD
FOR
SELECT ID,
  SUBSTRING(Address1, 1, CHARINDEX(',',Address1))
    AS A1,
  SUBSTRING(Address1, CHARINDEX(',',Address1),
```

```
        LEN(Address1))
        AS A2
FROM tbltestaddress
WHERE Address2 IS NULL OR LEN(Address2) = 0

--Open the cursor
OPEN curAddress

--Fetch the data into the variables
FETCH NEXT FROM curAddress
INTO @ID, @Adr1, @Adr2

--Set up a loop and update the table
  WHILE @@FETCH_STATUS = 0
  BEGIN
    UPDATE tblTestAddress
      SET Address1 = LEFT(@Adr1, LEN(@Adr1)-1),
        Address2 = RIGHT(@Adr2, LEN(@Adr2)-2)
      WHERE tblTestAddress.ID = @ID
        AND @Adr2 IS NOT NULL
        AND LEN(@Adr1) > 1
    FETCH NEXT FROM curAddress
    INTO @ID, @Adr1, @Adr2
  END

--Close and de-allocate the cursor
CLOSE curAddress
DEALLOCATE curAddress

--Display the results
SELECT * FROM tblTestAddress
```

In the WHILE loop, the procedure checks the value of @@FETCH_STATUS. This system function lets you know the results of the last FETCH statement that was executed within that connection. It returns a value of 0 if the FETCH was successful. Two failure codes are supported: -1 indicates that the statement failed or that the row was beyond the cursor result set, and -2 indicates that the row is missing. As with many system functions, be very careful to call @@FETCH_STATUS immediately after the operation you're checking.

Stored Procedures and User-Defined Functions

User-defined functions combine some of the best elements of stored procedures and views. Instead of having both a parameterized stored procedure and a view, you can combine both in one object. Unlike stored procedures, user-defined functions allow you to do a SELECT on the result set, which is impossible with stored procedures.

10

PROGRAMMING
EFFECTIVE STORED
PROCEDURES

You might want to consider writing many of your stored procedures as multi-statement table-valued functions. For example, the table-type variables used in functions are not the same as temp tables, which are actually stored in tempdb. These table-type variables are in memory, like all variables, and therefore can have an advantage over creating temp tables, if your server has plenty of RAM.

However, you shouldn't blindly convert all of your stored procedures to user-defined functions. In most cases you will see some improvements, but you need to test the conversion thoroughly to confirm the expectations and check for any unwanted side effects.

The System Stored Procedures

SQL Server uses system stored procedures for administrative and informational purposes. These stored procedures are the "under-the-hood" components that the Enterprise Manager and SQL-DMO (Distributed Management Objects) call to do their work. Most are also written purely in Transact-SQL.

The system stored procedures usually start with the prefix "sp_" and most are stored in the master database. Naming a procedure with an "sp_" prefix and storing it in the master database is somewhat magical—the stored procedure can be called from any other database without having to use the full reference syntax, *databasename.objectname*. Another quality of system stored procedures that have the "sp_" prefix is that when they are called from a database, they can automatically reference the tables in that database, not those in the master database.

System stored procedures are most commonly used to return information saved in the system tables. Microsoft discourages direct querying of the systems tables, because they change from version to version. However, the stored procedures will always be rewritten to take any changes to the system tables into account. Therefore, you can reliably call system stored procedures without worrying about whether the structure of the underlying system tables has changed.

The system stored procedures are fully documented in Books Online. However, there are some that you won't find—those that are called by other system stored procedures and are not intended for independent usage.

Extended Stored Procedures

Extended stored procedures are Windows dynamic link libraries (DLLs) that SQL Server can dynamically load and execute. They usually have names that begin with the "xp_" prefix, but some of them are named "sp_" so they can be easily called from any database. However, extended stored procedures are not written in Transact-SQL—they are external components written in C or C++ that are dynamically loaded and run in the same address space as SQL

Server. This makes them very fast and efficient, because they are running "in process" within the thread that calls them.

One useful extended stored procedure, `xp_sendmail`, allows you to send an email message from your stored procedures, triggers, or user-defined functions. The email message can be one of the following:

- A message string
- The result set of a query
- A Transact-SQL statement or batch to execute
- A page for an electronic pager

The following example sends an email message to AndyB alerting him that inventory is running low and cc'ing BossMan:

```
EXEC xp_sendmail @recipients = 'AndyB',
    @message = 'Inventory running low.',
    @copy_recipients = 'BossMan',
    @subject = 'Low Inventory Alert'
```

You can write your own extended stored procedures to expand on the capabilities of SQL Server, but you cannot use Visual Basic as your programming tool—these are not the same kind of ActiveX DLLs that VB allows you to create. They are the old-fashioned function library kind of DLLs, which must be created in C or C++. If you do create your own extended stored procedures, you must be sure to thoroughly test and debug them. If a system stored procedure crashes, it could possibly bring down SQL Server with it.

Summary

Much of the power available to you in SQL Server will only be tapped if you invest the time in becoming comfortable writing stored procedures. Transact-SQL combines the standard SQL commands for designing, retrieving and manipulating data with procedural extensions that make real programming possible. If you are an Access developer who has come to rely on VBA to implement much of the logic in your applications, you'll find that stored procedures allow you to transfer a lot of that processing from your client applications to the server, where it can be performed much more reliably and efficiently.

The next chapter shows how you can incorporate stored procedures into Access applications that are capable of scaling to serve hundreds or even thousands of simultaneous users.

Scaling Up with Unbound Access Applications

IN THIS CHAPTER

What Is an Unbound Application and Why Build One?

In its simplest form, an unbound Access application is one where none of the forms has a record source. Instead of "binding" forms to data by giving them tables or queries as record sources and then selecting control sources from the fields in the record source, you create "unbound" forms by leaving the record source and all the control sources blank. It is then up to you to use VBA code to populate the controls with data that you somehow fetch from the database, and it's up to you to take care of editing, adding, or deleting data by using code to issue commands to the database.

That sounds like a lot of work, and it can be, so why bother? The reason is that the convenience that Access bound forms give the developer comes at a price, and that price becomes harder and harder to afford as the number of users grows.

Access was originally developed as a single-tier, desktop database, using the Jet database engine. Even when multiple users share an Access/Jet database, the database engine runs on each user's computer. As far as the Access application is concerned, the only thing running on the server where the data is stored is the operating system. Jet uses network operating systems such as Microsoft Windows and Novell NetWare to read and write to the data file, and Jet also updates a locking file (the LDB file) with information that is used to prevent users from colliding if they try to work on the same block of data. Jet instructs the operating system to place locks on virtual addresses beyond the actual physical bounds of the LDB file. Because the operating system itself is generally not considered a separate tier in an *n*-tiered model, this traditional Access architecture would be considered a one-tiered system. (For more on the meaning of "*n*-tier," see Chapter 14, "Architecting Distributed *n*-Tier Applications.")

In a traditional one-tiered Access application, bound forms perform beautifully. Each bound form, each bound subform, and each combo or list box causes Jet to open and maintain a `Recordset` to manage the data. That doesn't cause a problem, however, because each user has the full attention of the instance of the Jet engine that is running on the local machine, and Jet is quite capable of handling all the `Recordsets` needed for even very complex applications. The strains that develop in multiuser Access applications as more than a couple dozen users become active have to do with the operating system–based locking scheme.

When SQL Server (or any other database server) is used as the database engine, the picture changes. Now, the database engine handles all users' requests on the server and manages all their locks and connections. Whether using OLE DB in an ADP or ODBC in an MDB, maintaining all those active `Recordsets` and connections places a burden on the database server, and that burden increases proportionately to the increase in the number of users. You can do many things to minimize this burden, which are discussed in Chapter 4, "Introduction to Access

Scaling Up with Unbound Access Applications

CHAPTER 11

499

11

SCALING UP WITH
UNBOUND ACCESS
APPLICATIONS

Projects (ADPs)," and Chapter 5, "Linking to SQL Server Using Access Databases (MDBs)." However, you are still paying for the convenience of using bound forms by tying up resources on the server.

To achieve the greatest possible scalability in an Access application, you'll need, instead, to consume as few server resources as possible. Instead of creating active open connections for the lifetime of each Recordset created by each user, connect only for a moment to grab the data needed or to execute an action query, and then free up the connection immediately. This takes a bit more planning and programming, but the results will be worth it if you need to support many users or are concerned with network/server overload.

This chapter presents a range of techniques—some tailored for use in MDBs and some for ADPs. Some techniques follow the classic unbound model of using only code to fetch data into unbound controls and to send updates back to the server. Other techniques stretch the definition of *unbound*—for example, binding to downloaded data stored in local tables in an MDB. In all cases, however, the emphasis is on using whatever tools are available to minimize the resources being held on the server. One strategy that many of these techniques share is a reliance on the use of SQL Server stored procedures. Stored procedures are covered in detail in Chapter 10, "Programming Effective Stored Procedures." This chapter, however, presents some general principles and then specific examples of how to integrate stored procedures into your Access applications.

Using Stored Procedures

The backbone of your Access/SQL Server application should be stored procedures. This gives you not only the best performance but also the best data security. Stored procedures protect data by preventing users from directly reading or writing to the database. All permissions can be removed from tables and selectively granted only to stored procedures.

Stored Procedures and Business Rules

The benefits of using stored procedures for enforcing business rules are that performance is optimized and you can be assured that your rules will be enforced for all applications using the database.

However, the downside to this is that the rules have to be coded in Transact-SQL, which isn't the most elegant or user friendly of languages, and your business logic becomes inextricably tied to SQL Server. If you need to work with data in other databases or (Heaven forbid!) decide to switch to another product, such as Oracle, then you are forced to rewrite your code (or to go through SQL Server and use linked servers, which can be inefficient). In general, the use of complex business logic in stored procedures doesn't lend itself to an object-oriented approach to modeling and code reuse. The alternative is to use a middle tier of business objects that encapsulate your business rules and that communicate with the data tier to perform reads, updates, inserts, and deletes.

In the real world, some combination of the two often emerges as the optimum solution. In Chapter 14, you learn how to build that middle tier using Visual Basic and COM+. Perhaps future versions of SQL Server will ease some of these conundrums by allowing modern, object-oriented programming to be integrated directly into stored procedures; the SQL Server team has expressed its intention to move in that direction.

Coding Conventions for Stored Procedures

Just like your VBA code, stored procedures should also follow naming and coding conventions. One convention we like for naming stored procedures is using the prefix proc, then the primary data entity the stored procedure is working with, and finally the action the procedure is performing. The following hypothetical list shows some examples:

```
procCustomerDelete
procCustomerInsert
procCustomerList
procCustomerUpdate
procOrderDelete
procOrderInsert
procOrderList
procOrderUpdate
```

This type of naming convention makes it easy to locate the stored procedure you're interested in and to understand quickly what each one does.

Coding Action Stored Procedures

Any stored procedure that modifies data needs to return information on whether it has succeeded or failed. Output parameters provide one efficient method of returning success/failure information. Here are two output parameters that we've found useful:

- A parameter that returns a long integer value. This can be set to 1 (True) for success or 0 (False) for failure. An alternative is to return 0 for success and an error number (a nonzero value) on any failure. Whichever approach you choose, make sure to use it consistently.

- A parameter that returns a string. This can contain an error message or other supplemental information.

All input parameters should have a default value of NULL, even if they are required. If a required parameter is not passed in, your Transact-SQL code can evaluate the situation and pass back the appropriate failure information to the application rather than suffering a runtime error.

Scaling Up with Unbound Access Applications

CHAPTER 11

501

11

SCALING UP WITH
UNBOUND ACCESS
APPLICATIONS

Every UPDATE stored procedure should have input parameters for each column in the table to be updated. Required input parameter values can be checked in your code and the appropriate return value and message sent. (You also can perform validation in the client application to avoid ever sending bad data to the server.) Here is what the declarations area of an UPDATE stored procedure might look like:

```
CREATE PROCEDURE procCategoryUpdate
  @CategoryName nvarchar(15) = NULL
  @CategoryDescription ntext = NULL
  @RetCode int = NULL OUTPUT
  @RetMsg varchar(100) = NULL OUTPUT
AS
-- Stored procedure code here
```

INSERT stored procedures often also need to have an additional output parameter to return an identity column value from the new record. The identity value can be retrieved by using the @@IDENTITY function in your code. Here is what the declarations area of an INSERT stored procedure might look like:

```
CREATE PROCEDURE procCategoryInsert
  @CategoryName nvarchar(15) = NULL
  @CategoryDescription ntext = NULL
  @CategoryID int = NULL OUTPUT
  @RetCode int = NULL OUTPUT
  @RetMsg varchar(100) = NULL OUTPUT
AS
-- Stored procedure code here
```

Every DELETE stored procedure should have an input parameter to be used in the WHERE clause to limit the number of rows being deleted. The stored procedure will conditionally delete records based on the validated input parameter value. Here is what the declarations area of a DELETE stored procedure might look like:

```
CREATE PROCEDURE procCategoryDelete
  @CategoryID int = NULL
  @RetCode int = NULL OUTPUT
  @RetMsg varchar(100) = NULL OUTPUT
AS
-- Stored procedure code here
```

At the end of each stored procedure, set the return code and return message to let the calling application know what happened. The following stored procedure snippet checks the @@ROWCOUNT function to see whether deleting a category succeeded. The integer output parameter, @RetCode, is used to denote success (1) or failure (0), and the string output parameter, @RetMsg, returns a message that can be passed along to the user. The @@ROWCOUNT function measures the results of the statement that directly precedes it. Here's the procedure:

```
IF @@ROWCOUNT = 1
  --Return success
  SELECT @RetCode = 1,
   @RetMsg = 'Category ' +
   CONVERT(VarChar, @CategoryID) + ' Deleted!'
ELSE
  SELECT  @RetCode = 0,
  @RetMsg = 'Delete Failed.'
END
```

Coding your stored procedures in this way allows the client application code to branch according to the success or failure of every data operation. Because stored procedures can fail silently in many different ways without triggering a fatal error, it's necessary to check for the success or failure of every single statement that performs a data operation.

Deciding Between Access Databases and Access Projects

When deciding on an Access front end for your SQL Server database, you have two choices:

- Access project (ADP)
- Access database (MDB)

At first blush, you might think that an Access project would be the best choice, because it can connect to SQL Server using a single OLE DB connection instead of multiple ODBC connections. And, after all, it is the new kid on the block, so it must be better, right? There is, however, one important limitation that comes into play: No native local database objects are allowed. You can't create local tables, and you can't create local queries unless you install a version of SQL Server on each user's machine and use linked servers to get at the shared data, thus adding an extra layer that can degrade efficiency and complicate administration.

Local storage can be an important factor when building an unbound client/server application, especially if you want the user to be able to view multiple records at once and select items from combo or list boxes. Local tables can be used as temporary holding pens for record source or row source data. For example, the order detail rows of an order can be stored in a local table while they are being viewed and edited, and a product combo box could draw its list from another local table. Inserting and deleting limited amounts of data into a local Access table is fast and reliable. Even larger tables make sense for data that doesn't change frequently. Local queries can be created to work directly with the local tables. Forms, reports, and controls can be bound to those local queries, saving unnecessary network roundtrips.

If you anticipate needing to use local tables, an Access database (MDB) is a better choice than an Access project (ADP). Later, this chapter covers some workarounds for the lack of local storage in Access projects, but the bottom line is that an unbound Access database (MDB) application gives you more options and flexibility in creating your front-end application. An Access project has no native local storage, so you'll need to write a lot more code than if you choose the Access database format, where you can work with local tables. On the other hand, even bound ADPs offer some of the advantages usually associated with unbound applications, as is discussed later in this chapter. The remainder of the chapter is divided into two sections that cover techniques you can use to build unbound applications in Access databases and in Access projects. Many of these techniques apply to both kinds of applications, and for the most part, those are covered in the first section (on MDBs).

Unbound MDBs

An unbound Access front-end MDB doesn't have *any* linked tables. You need to do all the work yourself—loading data into the forms, displaying data in list boxes, combo boxes, and subforms, and inserting, updating, and deleting data as needed.

The most efficient way to work with your SQL Server database is to use ADO, which is introduced in Chapter 6, "ActiveX Data Objects (ADO) Fundamentals," or to use pass-through queries, which are described in Chapter 5. Both are fast, efficient, and very flexible. The sample database for this chapter uses an ADO connection object to connect to SQL Server, various ADO command objects to run parameterized stored procedures, and ADO Recordsets to retrieve and work with data. This example also shows how to combine local Jet append queries with pass-through queries that fetch data from the server in order to populate a local cache of data stored in Jet tables. In addition, a dynamically modified pass-through query fetches records that meet search criteria specified by the user.

You'll also want to work programmatically with your local Jet tables, in which case DAO is generally the best choice, because it is optimized to work with Jet. There is no problem including references to both ADO and DAO in the same VBA project, using each library where it performs best. Just be sure that any object names that exist in both ADO and DAO are fully qualified when you work with the objects in code. Here are two examples:

```
Dim rstLocal as DAO.Recordset
Dim rstServer as ADO.Recordset
```

The Sample Application

The sample application used to demonstrate these techniques is a very simple order-entry Access database that connects to the Northwind SQL Server database. The user logs onto SQL Server using an Access login form, selects a record to edit, and then can edit, add, or delete a single order at a time. The user selects an order by either typing in its order number or by selecting from a list of customers and then a list of orders for that particular customer. A separate search form allows the user to retrieve batches of order records that meet more complex criteria and to select a particular record to view in the order form. All of an order's details are displayed with the order and can be edited, added, or deleted. The user can make multiple changes to an order and its details and then can save or cancel all those changes in one command. Each of these features will be covered in the following sections, starting with the login form, which is used by the application for defining both ADO and ODBC connections to SQL Server.

ADO Connections: Using a Global Connection Object

One downside of bound Access applications is that you have no control over the connections Access is using. A complex form with subforms and multiple combo boxes could possibly be maintaining quite a few connections. With an unbound Access application, you have complete control over those connections. Instead of using a separate connection for each command and `Recordset` object, you create a single, global connection object.

The advantage of a global connection object is that it can be reused at any time for creating `Recordsets` or executing stored procedures. In a bound, linked-table application, Access might employ multiple ODBC connections to open a single form, depending on the number of queries it needs to run to populate the form, subform, and combo/list boxes. By using a single connection object, you can cut down on the number of concurrent connections to SQL Server, and you can ensure that the connection becomes active only when you activate it.

A global connection object gives you the option of holding a single connection open for an entire session or opening and closing the connection as needed. In a two-tier application, with your Access database as the front-end tier and SQL Server on the back end, holding a single connection object open for the duration of the session is often more efficient than having Access open and close multiple connections behind the scenes.

This works well in a two-tier implementation, but it still limits scalability because each concurrent user would add a connection even if they weren't all active. The ideal solution in terms of scalability would be to implement an *n*-tier structure using an ActiveX DLL in the middle tier for data access, managed under Microsoft Transaction Server (MTS) in NT 4, or the Windows 2000 version, COM+ Component Services. These services provide connection pooling and object brokering, allowing many users to share a small pool of connections. The examples in this chapter make use of a global connection object that remains open. In Chapter 14, you learn how to use middle-tier objects and COM+ to pool connections. With pooled connections, your code would look like you were opening and closing connections, but the "closed" connections would actually remain open a while longer and be available to be used by the next request.

Even in a two-tier system, you might choose to open and close connections each time, absorbing the performance hit for the sake of conserving connections. This would involve only minor changes to the ADO code in this chapter. If your licensing allows you to keep a connection for each user open, however, that is usually the best choice in a two-tier system, and it's the one shown here.

In addition to the global ADO connection, the MDB example for this chapter also makes use of several pass-through queries that use ODBC. Later in this section, you'll see how to programmatically create the connection settings for those queries.

Creating a Global Connection Object

To create a global (or `Public`) connection object, declare it in the declarations section of a standard module. Here's an example:

```
Option Compare Database
Option Explicit

' For ADO, use a global connection object
'    visible to all forms.
Public gcnn As ADODB.Connection
```

Once the connection object is declared, create a public function to instantiate it. Listing 11.1 shows the `OpenConnection` function, which returns `True` if the connection succeeds or `False` if it fails. If the connection object hasn't been instantiated yet or was destroyed, then a new `gcnn` object is created. Once the object is verified to exist, it's tested to see whether it's already open. If not, the connection is opened using the information gathered from the user in frmLogin, shown in Figure 11.1. If that form isn't open, the code opens it. For more coverage of opening OLE DB connection objects, see Chapter 6.

This connection-checking code will run over and over again for each `Command` and `Recordset` object in the application that needs to connect. If the connection object is already up and running, there's no need to do any more processing, and the function simply returns `True`. If the connection isn't open, then an attempt is made to open it by passing the connection string information retrieved from the form. The function returns `True` if it succeeds and `False` if it doesn't. This efficient function can be run prior to executing any task that needs to communicate with SQL Server.

LISTING 11.1   Connecting to the SQL Server Database Using a Global ADO Connection Object

```
Public Function OpenConnection() As Boolean
    ' Opens Global ADO Connection,
    '    if it isn't already open.
    ' Returns True if connected.
    ' Passes any errors back to the procedure
```

LISTING 11.1 Continued

```
    ' that called this one.
    On Error GoTo HandleError
    Dim boolState As Boolean

    If gcnn Is Nothing Then
        Set gcnn = New ADODB.Connection
    End If

    If gcnn.State = adStateOpen Then
        boolState = True
    Else
        If Not IsFormOpen("frmLogin") Then
            DoCmd.OpenForm "frmLogin", WindowMode:=acDialog
        End If
        gcnn.ConnectionString = Forms!frmlogin.OLEDBConnect
        gcnn.Open
        If gcnn.State = adStateOpen Then
            boolState = True
        Else
            boolState = False
        End If
    End If

    OpenConnection = boolState

ExitHere:
    Exit Function
HandleError:
    OpenConnection = False
    Err.Raise Err.Number, Err.Source, _
      Err.Description, Err.HelpFile, Err.HelpContext
    Resume ExitHere
End Function
```

Using a Global Connection Object

After a global connection object is opened, every procedure that uses ADO to interact with SQL Server data uses that object. Here's a typical section of code that ensures that the connection is open:

```
If Not OpenConnection() Then
    MsgBox "Unable to connect to the database.", , "Login Required"
    Forms!frmlogin.Visible = True
    GoTo ExitHere
End If
```

If a procedure that needs to work with SQL Server data can't connect, it exits gracefully and gives the user another chance to enter valid connection information. If the procedure succeeds in validating the connection, it uses the global connection object to set the active connection of ADO objects, like this:

```
Dim cmd As ADODB.Command
Set cmd = New ADODB.Command
Set cmd.ActiveConnection = gcnn
```

Be careful not to use the following code, which will also work:

```
Dim cmd As ADODB.Command
Set cmd = New ADODB.Command
cmd.ActiveConnection = gcnn
```

In the second example, because the `Set` keyword isn't used, VBA doesn't actually point the `ActiveConnection` property of the command at the global connection object. Instead, it works with the default property of the two connections, which is `ConnectionString`, assigning the `ConnectionString` value from `gcnn` to be the connection string of the command object's active connection. This has the effect of causing a second connection object to be opened based on that `ConnectionString` value. This works fine, but it creates needless extra connections.

The User Authentication form, frmLogin, shown in Figure 11.1, lets the user select whether to use NT authentication or SQL Server authentication. These two authentication alternatives are discussed in Chapter 3, "Understanding SQL Server Security." Another possibility would be to let the user browse to a Data Link file, which is covered in Chapter 6, or to select an ODBC DSN, which is explained in Chapter 5. The text boxes on the right side of the form allow input of the server and database names needed to construct the connection string. If SQL Server authentication is selected, the text boxes for entering a username and password become visible.

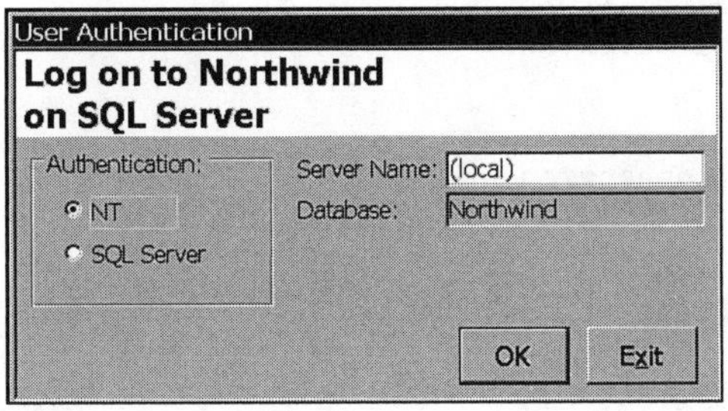

FIGURE 11.1

Gathering connection information from the user.

When the user clicks the OK button, the cmdOK_Click() event procedure, shown in Listing 11.2, runs. The option group is evaluated, and the appropriate connection string is created based on the authentication choice that the user has selected.

LISTING 11.2 Choosing an Authentication Mode and Connecting to SQL Server

```
Private Sub cmdOK_Click()
    ' Log on to SQL Server and open Order Form
    On Error GoTo HandleErr
    Dim fOK As Boolean

    Select Case Me!optAuthentication
        Case 1        ' NT authentication
            mstrOLEDBConnect = "Provider=SQLOLEDB.1;" & _
              "Data Source=" & Me!txtServer & ";" & _
              "Initial Catalog=" & Me.txtDatabase & ";" & _
              "Integrated Security=SSPI"
            mstrODBCConnect = "ODBC;Driver={SQL Server};" & _
              "Server=" & Me!txtServer & ";" & _
              "Database=" & Me.txtDatabase & ";" & _
              "Trusted_Connection=Yes"
        Case 2        ' SQL server authentication
            mstrOLEDBConnect = "Provider=SQLOLEDB.1;" & _
              "Data Source=(local);" & _
              "Initial Catalog=" & Me.txtDatabase & ";" & _
              "User ID=" & Me!txtUser & _
              ";Password=" & Me!txtPwd
            mstrODBCConnect = "ODBC;Driver={SQL Server};" & _
              "Server=" & Me!txtServer & ";" & _
              "Database=" & Me.txtDatabase & ";" & _
              "UID=" & Me!txtUser & _
              ";PWD=" & Me!txtPwd
    End Select

    ' Open global ADO Connection
    fOK = OpenConnection()
    If fOK Then
        Me.Visible = False
    Else
        ' Connection failed.
        ' User can try again or
        '   close the form (and possibly exit).
        If MsgBox( _
          "Connection attempt failed." _
          & vbCrLf & vbCrLf _
          & "Do you want to try again?", _
```

Scaling Up with Unbound Access Applications

CHAPTER 11

509

11

SCALING UP WITH
UNBOUND ACCESS
APPLICATIONS

LISTING 11.2   Continued

```
            vbQuestion + vbYesNo, _
            "Unsuccessful. Try again?") _
            = vbNo Then
               DoCmd.Close acForm, Me.Name
         End If
      End If

ExitHere:
    Exit Sub
HandleErr:
    Select Case Err.Number
        Case -2147217843   'OLE DB error. Failed to connect
           Resume Next
        Case Else
           MsgBox Err.Number & ": " & Err.Description, _
               Title:="Error Connecting"
    End Select
    Resume ExitHere
    Resume
End Sub
```

The cmdOK_Click() code in Listing 11.2 builds two different connection strings based on the
selections and entries the user makes in frmLogin. One is formatted for ADO, and the other is
in the form of an ODBC connect string. Both strings are stored in private module-level variables that are accessible to other code in the project through the custom read-only properties of
the form. Here's the code that creates those properties:

```
Private mstrOLEDBConnect As String
Private mstrODBCConnect As String

Public Property Get OLEDBConnect() As String
    OLEDBConnect = mstrOLEDBConnect
End Property

Public Property Get ODBCConnect() As String
    ODBCConnect = mstrODBCConnect
End Property
```

You've seen how the OLEDBConnect property is used to open a global ADO connection object
that's used by all the ADO code in the application. The next section discusses how the
ODBCConnect property is used to determine the connection settings of pass-through queries.

Working with ODBC Connections in Pass-Through Queries

Although linked tables are generally not the most efficient way to connect to SQL Server data
from Access MDBs, pass-through queries, which also use ODBC, are quite efficient. Chapter 5
covers the use of both linked tables (and linked views) and pass-through queries, as well as

how to use them effectively. In an unbound application, you'll avoid the use of linked tables to avoid the overhead created by their persistent connection to the database. Pass-through queries are an effective alternative because they go in, do their work, and then get out, without creating a lingering burden on the server. They are especially effective when used to execute stored procedures rather than direct Transact-SQL statements. As a result of this efficient get-in-and-get-out behavior, however, the result sets retrieved by pass-through queries are not updatable. They are ideal for retrieving read-only data or for executing action queries.

You need to provide two pieces of information to a pass-through query to make it work: the Transact-SQL text to be sent to the server, and an ODBC connect string. A third property, ReturnsRecords, is optional; setting this to False makes the query run more efficiently if you are executing an action query that doesn't return any data. The Access user interface allows you to set the Connect property of a pass-through query by selecting an ODBC DSN (Data Source Name), but a DSN is not required. ODBC connect strings can be used without a DSN as long as they include all the information that would normally be fetched from the DSN, formatted using the pattern that ODBC expects. A properly formatted ODBC connect string is what frmLogin stores in its ODBCConnect property, and the application uses it to dynamically modify pass-through queries.

Because of their ability to efficiently retrieve read-only data, pass-through queries are especially well suited to populating combo and list boxes. However, doing this repeatedly to retrieve the same data can place unnecessary demands on the server. In the sample application, local Jet tables are used to store lookup data that doesn't change often, such as lists of products or employees. The pass-through query is called only when the list needs to be refreshed. Later in the chapter you'll learn how pass-through queries are combined with Jet append queries to cache data in local tables.

A generic procedure, called PassThroughFixup (shown in Listing 11.3), is used to adjust either the connection information or the SQL text of a pass-through query. A version of this code is also presented in Chapter 5, where a version that works with ADO rather than DAO is included as well. The SQL text in pass-through queries is often static, but sometimes you may want to dynamically add parameter values to calls to stored procedures or even build custom Transact-SQL code. An example of this appears later in the chapter when discussing the search form frmOrderLocate.

LISTING 11.3   Dynamically Changing the SQL and Connect Properties of a Pass-Through Query

```
Public Sub PassThroughFixup( _
  strQdfName As String, _
  Optional strSQL As String, _
  Optional strConnect As String, _
  Optional fRetRecords As Boolean = True)
```

Scaling Up with Unbound Access Applications

CHAPTER 11

511

11

SCALING UP WITH
UNBOUND ACCESS
APPLICATIONS

LISTING 11.3   Continued

```
    ' Modifies pass-through query properties
    ' Inputs:
    '   strQdfName: Name of the query
    '   strSQL: Optional new SQL string
    '   strConnect: Optional new connect string
    '   fRetRecords: Optional setting for ReturnsRecords--
    '                defaults to True (Yes)

    Dim db As DAO.Database
    Dim qdf As DAO.QueryDef

    Set db = CurrentDb
    Set qdf = db.QueryDefs(strQdfName)
    If Len(strSQL) > 0 Then
        qdf.SQL = strSQL
    End If
    If Len(strConnect) > 0 Then
        qdf.Connect = strConnect
    End If
    qdf.ReturnsRecords = fRetRecords
    qdf.Close
    Set qdf = Nothing
End Sub
```

The connect properties of pass-through queries can hold user names and passwords, if SQL Server authentication is being used. To protect that data, the sample application includes code, shown in Listing 11.4, that runs every time frmLogin is closed. Normally this only happens when the user exits, because the form is kept open in a hidden state throughout each session. This code also closes the global ADO connection.

LISTING 11.4   Stripping Out All Cached Connection Info When the Application Closes

```
Private Sub Form_Unload(Cancel As Integer)
    ' To avoid exposing user name and password
    '   in pass-through queries,
    '   blank out all connect strings when closing.
    ' This form should usually only close when the app closes,
    '   but the connect info is refreshed anyway if the form
    '   is closed and then re-opened.
    ' The connect string is set when
    '   a pass-through query is used.
    Dim qdf As DAO.QueryDef
```

LISTING 11.4   Continued

```
    Dim db As DAO.Database
    Set db = CurrentDb
    For Each qdf In db.QueryDefs
        If qdf.Type = dbQSQLPassThrough Then
            qdf.Connect = "ODBC;"
        End If
    Next qdf
    If MsgBox( _
      "Do you want to exit the application?", _
      vbQuestion + vbYesNo, _
      "Quit now?") = vbYes Then
            ' Release the global connection object
            If Not gcnn Is Nothing Then
                If gcnn.State = adStateOpen Then gcnn.Close
                Set gcnn = Nothing
            End If
            DoCmd.Quit
    End If
    ' Release the global connection object
    '   when the form is closed,
    '   even if the user doesn't quit
    If Not gcnn Is Nothing Then
        If gcnn.State = adStateOpen Then gcnn.Close
        Set gcnn = Nothing
    End If
End Sub
```

Every time the application runs a pass-through query, it first ensures that the connection information is filled in based on the login data gathered in frmLogin:

```
Call PassThroughFixup( _
    "qrysptEmployeeList", _
    strConnect:=Forms!frmlogin.ODBCConnect)
```

With your connection strategy all worked out, you're ready to start displaying and updating data.

Displaying Data in Unbound Forms

The first issue you need to consider when creating an unbound data-inquiry or data-entry form is how to fetch the data to be displayed on the form.

Fetching Data

The central idea behind unbound forms is that the form itself has no connection to the server. Data is retrieved and loaded into unbound controls on the form or stored in a local cache. The

Scaling Up with Unbound Access Applications

CHAPTER 11

513

11

SCALING UP WITH
UNBOUND ACCESS
APPLICATIONS

user then works independently of the server, with no links to the tables in the underlying database. This technique minimizes network traffic and server resources consumed—no locks or other resources are being held on the server because the data is fetched as read-only. Adding, updating, or deleting data takes place as an independent transaction, with data being explicitly saved back to the server when the user clicks the Save button.

Unbound forms are fairly easy to populate when based on a single record. All you need to do is pour the data into unbound controls on the form. Things get trickier when there are multiple rows to be displayed, such as on the order details subform in the example shown in Figure 11.2. In this example, order details are cached in a local table that the subform can be bound to. We still refer to this as an "unbound" technique because the subform is not bound to server data.

Once you have a global connection object, it's very easy to open additional Command and Recordset objects. Read-only, client-side ADO Recordsets provide the best method for retrieving data to populate an unbound form. These ADO Recordset options are covered in Chapter 6. Once the Recordset is created, data can then be loaded into the unbound controls on the form or into a local cache.

The frmOrder form allows the user to select from a list of customers located in the form's header section. Then the orders for the selected customer are listed in the Select Order (cboOrders) combo box.

When an order is selected, the order ID of the selected order is copied to the Enter Order ID text box in the AfterUpdate() event procedure of the cboOrders combo box. The advantage of having this seemingly redundant text box is that if the user already knows the order number of the order he or she wants to view, the user can just enter it directly in the Enter Order ID text box and click Load.

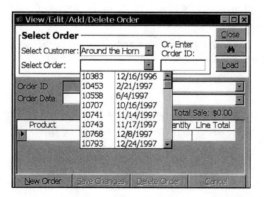

FIGURE 11.2
The Order form, frmOrder, allows the user to select and load a single sales order, along with its order details.

Once the order has been selected (or typed in, as the case may be), the user clicks the Load button. The record is fetched from the server, the local order detail table is populated, and the data is displayed on the form, as shown in Figure 11.3.

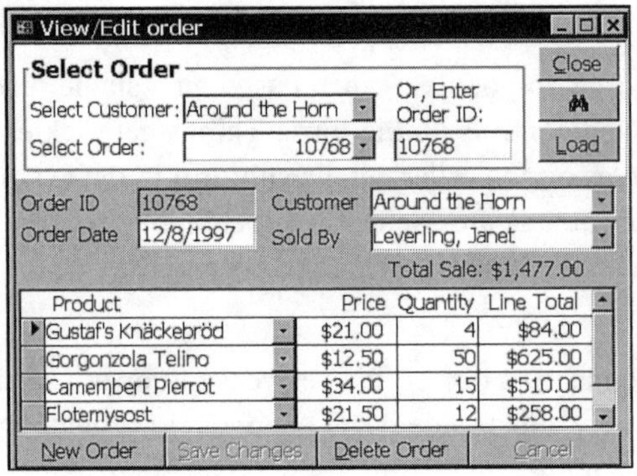

FIGURE 11.3

The Order form, with the entire order displayed for editing.

Here's how it works: The cmdLoad_Click() event procedure validates whether an order has been selected by checking whether the OrderID text box contains numeric data. If the text box is blank or contains nonnumeric data, the IsNumeric function will return False:

```
If IsNumeric(Me.txtOrderID) Then
    lngOrderID = CLng(Me.txtOrderID)
Else
    strMsg = "Please select or enter an OrderID"
End If
```

If it fails the test, the order will not be displayed and the user is notified:

```
If Len(strMsg) > 0 Then
    MsgBox strMsg, , "Can't Display Order"
    Me.cboCustomer.SetFocus
    GoTo ExitHere
End If
```

If the order ID checks out, the connection to the database is verified again by calling the OpenConnection function shown earlier in Listing 11.1. The order data is fetched from SQL Server by creating and opening a new ADO Recordset object. The data source for the Recordset object is the procOrderSelect stored procedure, which takes a single parameter—the order ID. By using a client-side ADO cursor, the code ensures that no resources are held on the server once the Recordset is populated. All client-side cursors are read-only and forward-only (the fastest kind), as far as the server is concerned. Any scrolling or updatability

Scaling Up with Unbound Access Applications

CHAPTER 11

515

11

SCALING UP WITH
UNBOUND ACCESS
APPLICATIONS

is handled thereafter by ADO's cursor engine, not by the server. Because a lock type is not specified for the Recordset, the default adReadOnly lock type is used, which is the most efficient type for ADO but has no effect on the server. Client-side cursors always use a cursor type of adOpenStatic. This example uses a SQL statement to execute the stored procedure and concatenate the parameter value into the SQL (when it comes time to save data, you'll see an example of using a command object and populating its Parameters collection, which is necessary if you want to retrieve the values of output parameters):

```
Set rst = New ADODB.Recordset
rst.CursorLocation = adUseClient
rst.Open Source:="EXEC procOrderSelect " & _
  lngOrderID, _
  ActiveConnection:=gcnn
```

Once the data is fetched, the Recordset is checked to make sure it's not empty. If there's data in the Recordset, the form's unbound text boxes are assigned values. The For Each…Next loop uses the field names of the Recordset to assign values to the form's controls. This simple code loop works because the controls on the form have the same names as the Recordset's field names. Although this departs from common naming conventions for controls, it makes it possible to use generic, efficient code, like the following, for any form:

```
If rst.EOF Then
    MsgBox "Record can't be found.", , _
      "Order does not exist"
    GoTo ExitHere
Else
    For Each fld In rst.Fields
        Me(fld.Name).Value = fld.Value
    Next
End If
```

The error handler for this procedure ignores the errors generated for any fields in the Recordset that do not happen to have a matching control on the form. The full procedure, including the error handler and some parts that haven't been discussed yet, is shown in Listing 11.5. Once the data for the main form has been loaded, it's time to load the order detail line items.

LISTING 11.5   The cmdLoad_Click Event Procedure That Loads Order Data

```
Private Sub cmdLoad_Click()
    Dim rst As ADODB.Recordset
    Dim fld As ADODB.Field
    Dim lngOrderID As Long
    Dim fOK As Boolean
```

LISTING 11.5 Continued

```
    Dim strID As String
    Dim strSQL As String
    Dim strMsg As String

On Error GoTo HandleErr

    ' Check to make sure we have a numeric OrderID
    If IsNumeric(Me.txtOrderID) Then
        lngOrderID = CLng(Me.txtOrderID)
    Else
        strMsg = "Please select or enter an OrderID"
    End If
    ' Bail if invalid OrderID type
    If Len(strMsg) > 0 Then
        MsgBox strMsg, , "Can't Display Order"
        Me!cboCustomer.SetFocus
        GoTo ExitHere
    End If


    ' Connect to Northwind
    fOK = OpenConnection(Me.LoginInfo)
    If fOK = False Then
        MsgBox "Unable to Connect", , _
          "Can't connect to SQL Server"
        GoTo ExitHere
    End If


    ' Get the record data
    Set rst = New ADODB.Recordset
    rst.CursorLocation = adUseClient
    rst.Open Source:="EXEC procOrderSelect " & _
      lngOrderID, _
      ActiveConnection:=gcnn

    ' Display record data in form controls
    If rst.EOF Then
        MsgBox "Record can't be found.", , _
          "Order does not exist"
        GoTo ExitHere
    Else
        For Each fld In rst.Fields
            Me(fld.Name).Value = fld.Value
        Next
    End If
```

Scaling Up with Unbound Access Applications

CHAPTER 11

517

11

SCALING UP WITH
UNBOUND ACCESS
APPLICATIONS

LISTING 11.5 Continued

```
    ' Set ConcurrencyID property
    Me.ConcurrencyID = rst!ConcurrencyID

    ' Clean out OrderDetailsLocal
    CurrentDb.Execute _
      "Delete * From OrderDetailsLocal Where User = '" & CurrentUser & "'"

    ' Get the matching order detail records using
    '   an append query based on a pass-through query.
    strSQL = "EXEC procOrderDetailSelect " & _
      lngOrderID
    Call PassThroughFixup( _
      "qrysptOrderDetailsForOrder", strSQL, _
      Forms!frmlogin.ODBCConnect)
    CurrentDb.Execute "qryaGetOrderDetailsForOrder"

    Me.fsubOrderDetail.Requery
    SaleRecalc

    ' Nothing to save yet
    Me.IsDirty = False
    ' Not on a new record
    Me.IsNew = False

ExitHere:
    Exit Sub

HandleErr:
    Select Case Err
        Case 2465   ' Field does not exist
            Resume Next
        Case Else
            MsgBox Err & ": " & Err.Description, , _
              "cmdLoad_Click() Error"
    End Select
    Resume ExitHere
    Resume
End Sub
```

Taking Advantage of Local Storage

As you've already seen, loading a single record and populating controls on a form is fairly
easy. The hard part comes when you want to display multiple records (such as the "many" side
of a one-to-many join—in this case, the order detail records). There's no way to assign
unbound control values from a Recordset if the form is displayed in continuous or datasheet
view mode. The solution in this case is to take advantage of the local storage that Jet makes

available, by inserting the order detail records into a local table. The subform is then bound to the local data. When users make changes to the order detail line items, those changes are written to the local table, not SQL Server. When it comes time to save the entire order back to SQL Server, the data contained in order detail records in the local table will be written back to the server. Later in this chapter, during the coverage of techniques for creating forms in ADPs, and also in Chapter 14, you'll learn how to bind a form directly to a client-side ADO Recordset. However, updating the form becomes trickier because the form then becomes read-only. Using local Jet tables to create updatable continuous subforms is both efficient and relatively easy to code, while providing a rich user interface.

Allowing Multiple Users to Share a Local Cache

In the early days of Access, it became conventional wisdom that users should be given their own copies of the front-end database, containing forms, reports, queries, and code, and that they should all be linked to a back-end database, containing only tables. The advantage of splitting the front end from the back end was clear when it came time to distribute a new version of the front end, because you could just copy over the old copy without affecting data. However, the advantage of giving each user a separate copy of that front end became less clear as hardware and networks improved. The performance advantage of working off a local drive versus a network share became negligible, and many companies started sharing the front end among multiple users. Also, many companies have adopted solutions such as Terminal Services from Microsoft, based on early work done by Citrix, which allows multiple remote users to dial into a shared application.

The need to support multiple users on your front-end application MDB is not a problem if you are caching static lists of read-only data, such as a product list to populate combo boxes. However, when you use local tables dynamically, as the example does with the order details cache, then each user needs his or her own set of data. One way to solve this is to have the users log into Access with unique usernames, using Jet's user-level security. This is very easy to set up in Access 2000, where the Security Wizard has been much improved. With user-level security in place, you can use the Access CurrentUser() function to get the identity of the logged-in user, and you can add a column to your dynamic local tables to record which user each record belongs to. That technique is used for the dynamic local list of orders displayed in cboOrders when a user selects a customer, as well as for the order detail records that the subform is bound to. Another possibility would be to use a Windows API call to retrieve the local machine name or the user's network identity instead of using Jet security, which requires an extra login. Of course, you can dispense with this concern altogether if you simply give each user a separate copy of the front-end Access database.

Working with Local Tables for Subform Data

When cmdLoad_Click() loads the order form, it populates the main form with the single record for the selected order. A custom form property called ConcurrencyID is set, which is

Scaling Up with Unbound Access Applications

CHAPTER 11

519

11

SCALING UP WITH
UNBOUND ACCESS
APPLICATIONS

discussed later in the chapter when updating data is covered. Then `OrderID` is used to fetch the related order detail records from SQL Server. However, before inserting records into the local table, you need to remove any order details that may have been stored there previously by that user. A single line of DAO code removes all those records in the local table:

```
CurrentDb.Execute _
  "Delete * From OrderDetailsLocal Where User = '" & CurrentUser & "'"
```

An alternative is to use ADO, which also involves a single line of code:

```
CurrentProject.Connection.Execute _
  "Delete * From OrderDetailsLocal Where User = '" & CurrentUser & "'"
```

However, if you are working with versions of Access prior to Access 2000, the `CurrentProject.Connection` syntax is not available. Also, in general, DAO seems to be more efficient when working with Jet data.

Speaking of efficiency, any time you create an application that routinely adds and deletes Access data, be sure to set up regular compacts of the database, because the space consumed by deleted records is not automatically recovered. Access 2000 allows you to automatically have the database compact itself when the last connected user exits. To do this, select Compact on Close from the General tab of the Tools, Options dialog box.

Once the local table has been cleaned out, the next step is to fetch the data for the line items of the selected order from SQL Server. This time, a pass-through query is used in a pattern that is repeated throughout the application. A local append query, `qryaGetOrderDetailsForOrder`, updates the local table, `OrderDetailsLocal`, with data retrieved using the pass-through query `qrysptOrderDetailsForOrder`. The SQL text of the pass-through query is dynamically modified to call the SQL Server stored procedure, `procOrderDetailSelect`, and to pass in the order ID of the selected order as an input parameter:

```
strSQL = "EXEC procOrderDetailSelect " & _
  lngOrderID
Call PassThroughFixup( _
  "qrysptOrderDetailsForOrder", strSQL, _
  Forms!frmlogin.ODBCConnect)
CurrentDb.Execute "qryaGetOrderDetailsForOrder"
```

This technique is illustrated further, later in this chapter, when it is used for populating local tables used to populate combo boxes.

Once you've loaded the data into the local table, requery the `fsubOrderDetail` subform, which is based on the following local query:

```
SELECT OrderDetailsLocal.* FROM OrderDetailsLocal
WHERE [OrderDetailsLocal].[User])= CurrentUser();
```

Guiding the Users Toward Valid Actions

The final step after loading the details is to adjust the appearance of the form by calling a procedure to update the order total that appears on the main form and by setting a couple of custom properties—IsDirty and IsNew—to False. These properties are used to enable and disable buttons on the form and to update captions, based on which actions should be available to the user as the form moves through different states. For example, once data has been edited, the user must save or cancel those changes before selecting to view another order. Some actions are implemented in the Property Let procedures for these properties, but most are handled by a common function, AdjustDisplayBasedOnState, which alters the appearance of the form and limits the user's options based on the states defined by the various combinations of the properties IsDirty (data has been edited but not saved) and IsNew (a new order is being entered). The code appears in Listing 11.6.

LISTING 11.6   The State of the Form Is Maintained Using Two Custom Properties—
IsDirty and IsNew

```
Option Compare Database
Option Explicit

'Private variables for form properties.
Private mblnIsDirty As Boolean
Private mblnIsNew As Boolean

' Private variable used when
'   canceling new records.
Private mlngLastOrderID

'State-dependent form captions
Private Const conCaptionDirtyNew As String = _
  "Enter new order, and Save or Cancel"
Private Const conCaptionDirtyNotNew As String = _
  "Edit order, and Save or Cancel"
Private Const conCaptionNotDirtyNew As String = _
  "Enter new order, or Select and Load existing order"
Private Const conCaptionNotDirtyNotNew As String = _
  "View/Edit order"

'IsDirty and IsNew properties used to
'   enable/disable buttons on the form
'   and adjust the caption.
Public Property Let IsDirty(ByVal NewValue As Boolean)
    mblnIsDirty = NewValue
    AdjustDisplayBasedOnState
End Property
```

LISTING 11.6   Continued

```
Public Property Get IsDirty() As Boolean
    IsDirty = mblnIsDirty
End Property


Public Property Let IsNew(ByVal NewValue As Boolean)
    If NewValue = True Then
        ' Save last OrderID to restore if addition is canceled
        mlngLastOrderID = Me.OrderID
    End If
    mblnIsNew = NewValue
    AdjustDisplayBasedOnState
End Property


Public Property Get IsNew() As Boolean
    IsNew = mblnIsNew
End Property


Public Sub AdjustDisplayBasedOnState()
  Select Case IsDirty
        Case True 'Dirty
            cmdNew.Enabled = False
            cmdSave.Enabled = True
            cmdDelete.Enabled = False
            cmdCancel.Enabled = True
            cmdClose.Enabled = False
            Select Case IsNew
                Case True 'Dirty, New
                    Me.Caption = conCaptionDirtyNew
                Case False 'Dirty, Not New
                    Me.Caption = conCaptionDirtyNotNew
            End Select
        Case False 'Not Dirty
            Select Case IsNew
                Case True 'Not Dirty, New
                    Me.OrderDate.SetFocus
                    cmdNew.Enabled = False
                    cmdSave.Enabled = False
                    cmdDelete.Enabled = False
                    cmdCancel.Enabled = False
                    cmdClose.Enabled = True
                    Me.Caption = conCaptionNotDirtyNew
                Case False 'Not Dirty, Not New
                    Me.OrderDate.SetFocus
                    cmdNew.Enabled = True
                    cmdSave.Enabled = False
```

LISTING 11.6   Continued

```
                cmdDelete.Enabled = True
                cmdCancel.Enabled = False
                cmdClose.Enabled = True
                Me.Caption = conCaptionNotDirtyNotNew
        End Select
    End Select
End Sub
```

The various combinations of settings implemented in `AdjustDisplayBasedOnState` can be bewildering. The easiest ways to understand what's going on is to look at which buttons are being enabled for each combination of property values. Then it starts to make sense. For example, if the form is not dirty and is on a new record, the only thing the user can do is enter data or close the form. If the data is not dirty and also not new, the user can additionally choose to enter a new record or delete the current one. If the record is dirty, the user must choose to either save or cancel the changes.

All the controls on the form set the `IsDirty` property after they've been edited. Conversely, the `IsDirty` property is turned off when a record is saved or when changes are canceled. The `IsNew` property is turned on when there are no records yet to display or when the user chooses to enter a new record and the existing data is cleared.

Coding your form in this way allows for maximum flexibility. If new controls are added to the form, additional statements that enable them appropriately can be added to the existing `AdjustDisplayBasedOnState` procedure.

Using Combo Boxes and List Boxes with Unbound Data

In the MDB example, all the combo boxes are populated using the same technique that is used to import order details when an order is selected. A local append query uses a pass-through query to run a stored procedure on SQL Server and adds the retrieved records to a local table. Unlike the order details table, however, most of these tables contain static data that only gets refreshed when the user requests it. Most of the time, the combo boxes simply load data from the local tables. The server is hit only when those tables are empty or when someone feels he or she is outdated and need to be refreshed. Then, the old data is deleted and a fresh batch is imported. An administrator could drive this process remotely by executing queries to delete the data in users' local databases. The various forms contain code that checks whether the `ListCount` property of a combo box is zero and runs the appropriate append query if it is:

```
If Me.cboCustomer.ListCount = 0 Then
    CurrentDb.Execute "qryaGetCustomers"
    Me.cboCustomer.Requery
End If
```

Scaling Up with Unbound Access Applications

CHAPTER 11

523

11

SCALING UP WITH
UNBOUND ACCESS
APPLICATIONS

There is also a form in the application that allows the user to select tables to be refreshed with new data, which is covered in the next section. You could use ADO to open Recordsets and then append each record individually to the local table, but the Jet database engine is a powerful tool that is loaded anyway when you use an MDB, and a Jet append query will run much faster than walking through a Recordset. The impact on the server of using a pass-through query to execute a stored procedure that returns records versus using an ADO Recordset is roughly comparable, but you can't take advantage of Jet append queries if you use Recordsets.

Using Pass-Through and Append Queries to Refresh Local Tables

Pass-through queries combined with append queries provide a fast and reliable method of repopulating your local tables. The first step is to create the pass-through query to execute a stored procedure that returns the data, as shown in Figure 11.4. The procCustomersList stored procedure, which fetches all the customers, is executed from the qrysptGetCustomers pass-through query.

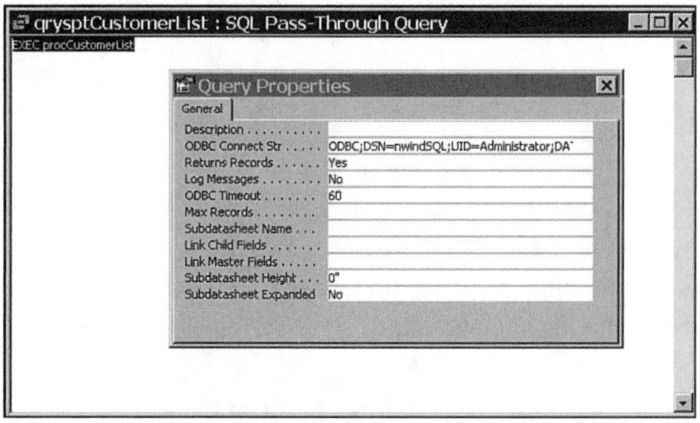

FIGURE 11.4
Setting up the pass-through query to run the procCustomerList *stored procedure to retrieve all the customers.*

Because the qrysptCustomerList pass-through query returns records, it can be used as the domain for an append query. The qryaGetCustomers append query appends the rows returned from the qrysptCustomerList pass-through query to the CustomersLocal table. Figure 11.5 shows the qryaGetGustomers append query in Design view, with the Append dialog box displayed.

Once you've set up these queries, you need a way for the users to run them. That part will vary quite a bit, depending on the application. In the example, the Refresh Local Tables form, shown in Figure 11.6, allows users to select tables to refresh. The only code you need to write is for the Go button—to delete old data and execute the queries.

FIGURE 11.5
The qrysptCustomerList *pass-through query is used as the domain for the* qryaGetCustomers *append query.*

FIGURE 11.6
The Refresh Local Tables form allows users to refresh local data on demand.

Listing 11.7 shows the cmdGo_Click() event procedure. Because executing the append query directly involves Jet, the DAO database object is used instead of ADO (although, as noted earlier, ADO would also work). The procedure deletes all data from the local table and executes the appropriate append query, if the corresponding check box has been checked. A message box at the end confirms what has happened.

LISTING 11.7 The cmdGo_Click Code Deletes Old Data and Retrieves a Fresh Batch for the Selected Local Tables

```
Private Sub cmdGo_Click()
    ' Refreshes the data in the
    '   selected local tables

    Dim strMsg As String

On Error GoTo HandleErr

    If Me!ckCustomer = True Then
        ' Update pass-through query
        '   connect string
        Call PassThroughFixup( _
            "qrysptCustomerList", _
            strConnect:=Forms!frmlogin.ODBCConnect)
        Call RefreshLocalTable("CustomersLocal", "qryaGetCustomers")
        strMsg = strMsg & vbCrLf & "Customers Refreshed"
```

Scaling Up with Unbound Access Applications

CHAPTER 11

525

11

SCALING UP WITH
UNBOUND ACCESS
APPLICATIONS

LISTING 11.7   Continued

```
    End If

    If Me!ckEmployee = True Then
        Call PassThroughFixup( _
            "qrysptEmployeeList", _
            strConnect:=Forms!frmlogin.ODBCConnect)
        Call RefreshLocalTable("EmployeesLocal", "qryaGetEmployees")
        strMsg = strMsg & vbCrLf & "Employees Refreshed"
    End If

    If Me!ckProduct = True Then
        Call PassThroughFixup( _
            "qrysptProductList", _
            strConnect:=Forms!frmlogin.ODBCConnect)
        Call RefreshLocalTable("ProductsLocal", "qryaGetProducts")
        strMsg = strMsg & vbCrLf & "Products Refreshed"
    End If

    If Me!ckCountry = True Then
        Call PassThroughFixup( _
            "qrysptCountryList", _
            strConnect:=Forms!frmlogin.ODBCConnect)
        Call RefreshLocalTable("CountriesLocal", "qryaGetCountries")
        strMsg = strMsg & vbCrLf & "Countries Refreshed"
    End If

    If Len(strMsg) = 0 Then
        MsgBox "No local tables were selected." & _
        vbCrLf & "Select at least one item to refresh.", , _
          "Nothing Selected"
    Else
        MsgBox strMsg, , "Tables Refreshed:"
    End If

ExitHere:
    Exit Sub

HandleErr:
    MsgBox Err & ": " & Err.Description, , _
      "Error in Refreshing Local Tables"
    GoTo ExitHere
End Sub
```

It would be relatively easy to create an automated procedure that repopulates the local lookup table during off hours. Also, the static data lists controlled by this form could be placed in a shared MDB that multiple local users could link to as a way to take pressure off the server. Because the data will be read-only, Jet could comfortably support several dozen concurrent users. There would be more of a problem, however, to have many users share a Jet database containing the frequently updated orders and order details tables, which change every time a user makes a different selection on the order form.

Creating an Efficient Search Form

The sample application includes a search form, frmOrderLocate, that has the ability to search for orders based on several user-supplied criteria values. The form, shown in Figure 11.7, is quite simple, but the techniques employed could easily be extended to support a wider range of choices. If a user doesn't remember the customer who placed a particular order, she can click the binoculars button in the order form header and bring up this form to search for a set of record. The user can then double-click an order in the list, or select it and click the Select Order button, to redisplay the order form with that order loaded.

The most interesting feature of this form is that no matter what criteria the user selects, only 25 records are retrieved from the server at one time. The Transact-SQL that is executed calculates the total number of orders meeting the criteria and where in that result set the current batch lies, and it returns those totals along with the details of the first 25 records in the batch. The form code calculates how many "pages" of 25 records each are in the full return set and allows the user to navigate forward and backward through the data. The stored procedure has input parameters that allow the code to specify a starting order number and the direction—forward or backward—from that order to move when assembling the next batch to be returned. This technique protects the server from having to return huge data sets if the user selects very broad criteria, while at the same time allowing the user complete freedom to explore the data.

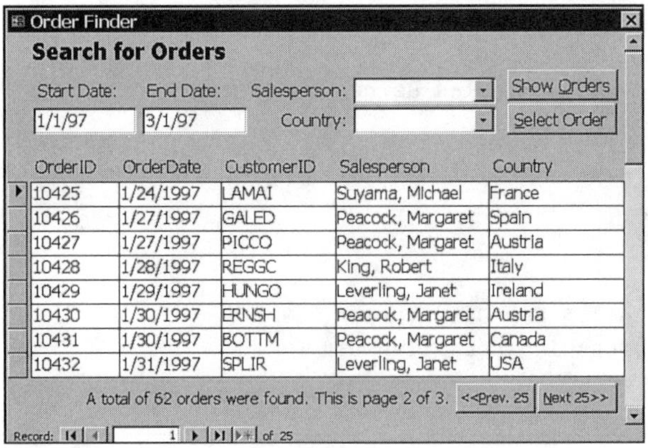

FIGURE 11.7

A search form that retrieves only 25 records at a time.

How It Works

The form is based on a pass-through query that calls one of two stored procedures to return either the next or previous top-25 records meeting the criteria, sorted by the order ID. The order IDs are sequential, and the query used in the stored procedure is sorted in ascending order. The form includes code that submits the first or last order ID as a parameter, depending on which direction the user wants to navigate in the result set.

This technique will work for any data set that has a field or set of fields that can be used to sort the data and that will deterministically set the order of records. In other words, ties would make it impossible to know for sure where one batch of 25 ends and the next should begin. You could always add an identity field to be used as a tiebreaker or just include the primary key of the "most-many" table in the set if multiple related tables are involved. In most cases, coming up with a set of sort fields that meet these requirements isn't a problem.

Aside from supporting navigation through the result set, the stored procedures also allow null parameters to be passed in and then dynamically select the Transact-SQL statement to run based on the values that have been submitted. Another way to code this would be to build a dynamic SQL statement in the stored procedure and use sp_executesql to execute it, but the problem is that sp_executesql requires the user to have SELECT permissions on the underlying tables. Hard-coding a separate Transact-SQL SELECT statement for each combination of criteria takes more typing up front, but it allows you to secure the base tables and give users only permission to execute the stored procedure. The techniques used in this stored procedure are covered in Chapter 10.

The procOrderLocateNext stored procedure is shown in Listing 11.8. The procOrderLocatePrevious procedure is very similar, except that it retrieves the 25 rows before the @OrderID parameter value and returns a count of all previous orders plus the total number of orders. ProcOrderLocateNext returns a count of the subsequent orders remaining in the result set as well as the grand total. By calculating and returning these totals every time a batch is fetched, the stored procedures can give the user accurate figures even if orders are being added or deleted while the search is going on.

LISTING 11.8   procOrderLocateNext and procOrderLocatePrevious (not shown) Support Paging Through Large Sets of Search Results

```
CREATE PROC procOrderLocateNext
  (
  @Start datetime = NULL,
  @End datetime = NULL,
  @EmpID int = NULL,
  @Country nvarchar (15) = NULL,
```

LISTING 11.8   Continued

```
  @OrderID int = 0
  )
/* Retrieves the next 25 rows based on
   OrderID. If no OrderID supplied, then
   starts at lowest OrderID.
*/
WITH RECOMPILE
AS
SET NOCOUNT ON

-- Variable used for getting order counts
Declare @PreviousOrderCount int
Declare @RemainingOrderCount int
Declare @TotalOrderCount int

-- Handle start and end dates
IF @Start IS NULL
  SELECT @Start = MIN(OrderDate) FROM Orders

IF @End IS NULL
  SELECT @End = MAX(OrderDate) FROM Orders

-- Handle Date Only (null EmployeeID and Country)
If @EmpID IS NULL AND @Country IS NULL
BEGIN
  SELECT @PreviousOrderCount =
    (Select Count(*)
     FROM dbo.Orders
     WHERE dbo.Orders.OrderDate BETWEEN @Start AND @End
      AND dbo.Orders.OrderID <= @OrderID)

  SELECT @TotalOrderCount =
    (Select Count(*)
     FROM dbo.Orders
     WHERE dbo.Orders.OrderDate BETWEEN @Start AND @End)

  SELECT @RemainingOrderCount =
    (@TotalOrderCount-@PreviousOrderCount-25)
  If @RemainingOrderCount < 0   -- less than 25 in this batch
    SELECT @RemainingOrderCount = 0

  SELECT TOP 25 dbo.Orders.OrderID, dbo.Orders.CustomerID,
    (dbo.Employees.LastName + ', ' + dbo.Employees.FirstName) As Salesperson,
     dbo.Orders.OrderDate, dbo.Customers.Country,
    @TotalOrderCount As TotalOrderCount,
```

LISTING 11.8   Continued

```
  @RemainingOrderCount As RemainingOrderCount
  FROM dbo.Customers INNER JOIN
   dbo.Orders ON dbo.Customers.CustomerID = dbo.Orders.CustomerID
   INNER JOIN dbo.Employees ON dbo.Orders.EmployeeID=dbo.Employees.EmployeeID
  WHERE dbo.Orders.OrderDate BETWEEN @Start AND @End
   AND dbo.Orders.OrderID > @OrderID
  ORDER BY dbo.Orders.OrderID
  RETURN
END

-- Handle Dates & Country only (Null Employee)
If @EmpID IS NULL
BEGIN
  SELECT @PreviousOrderCount =
   (Select Count(*)
    FROM dbo.Customers INNER JOIN
     dbo.Orders ON dbo.Customers.CustomerID = dbo.Orders.CustomerID
    WHERE dbo.Orders.OrderDate BETWEEN @Start AND @End
     AND dbo.Customers.Country = @Country
     AND dbo.Orders.OrderID <= @OrderID)

  SELECT @TotalOrderCount =
   (Select Count(*)
    FROM dbo.Customers INNER JOIN
     dbo.Orders ON dbo.Customers.CustomerID = dbo.Orders.CustomerID
    WHERE dbo.Orders.OrderDate BETWEEN @Start AND @End
     AND dbo.Customers.Country = @Country)

  SELECT @RemainingOrderCount =
    (@TotalOrderCount-@PreviousOrderCount-25)
  If @RemainingOrderCount < 0  -- less than 25 in this batch
    SELECT @RemainingOrderCount = 0

  SELECT TOP 25 dbo.Orders.OrderID, dbo.Orders.CustomerID,
   (dbo.Employees.LastName + ', ' + dbo.Employees.FirstName) As Salesperson,
    dbo.Orders.OrderDate, dbo.Customers.Country,
   @TotalOrderCount As TotalOrderCount,
   @RemainingOrderCount As RemainingOrderCount
  FROM dbo.Customers INNER JOIN
   dbo.Orders ON dbo.Customers.CustomerID = dbo.Orders.CustomerID
   INNER JOIN dbo.Employees ON dbo.Orders.EmployeeID=dbo.Employees.EmployeeID
  WHERE dbo.Orders.OrderDate BETWEEN @Start AND @End
   AND dbo.Customers.Country = @Country
   AND dbo.Orders.OrderID > @OrderID
```

LISTING 11.8   Continued

```
  ORDER BY dbo.Orders.OrderID
  RETURN
END


-- Handle Dates and Employee only (Null Country)
If @Country IS NULL
BEGIN
  SELECT @PreviousOrderCount =
   (Select Count(*)
    FROM dbo.Orders
    WHERE dbo.Orders.OrderDate BETWEEN @Start AND @End
     AND dbo.Orders.EmployeeID = @EmpID
     AND dbo.Orders.OrderID <= @OrderID)

  SELECT @TotalOrderCount =
   (Select Count(*)
    FROM dbo.Orders
    WHERE dbo.Orders.OrderDate BETWEEN @Start AND @End
     AND dbo.Orders.EmployeeID = @EmpID)

  SELECT @RemainingOrderCount =
   (@TotalOrderCount-@PreviousOrderCount-25)
  If @RemainingOrderCount < 0  -- less than 25 in this batch
   SELECT @RemainingOrderCount = 0

  SELECT TOP 25 dbo.Orders.OrderID, dbo.Orders.CustomerID,
   (dbo.Employees.LastName + ', ' + dbo.Employees.FirstName) As Salesperson,
   dbo.Orders.OrderDate, dbo.Customers.Country,
   @TotalOrderCount As TotalOrderCount,
   @RemainingOrderCount As RemainingOrderCount
  FROM dbo.Customers INNER JOIN
   dbo.Orders ON dbo.Customers.CustomerID = dbo.Orders.CustomerID
   INNER JOIN dbo.Employees ON dbo.Orders.EmployeeID=dbo.Employees.EmployeeID
  WHERE dbo.Orders.OrderDate BETWEEN @Start AND @End
   AND dbo.Orders.EmployeeID = @EmpID
   AND dbo.Orders.OrderID > @OrderID
  ORDER BY dbo.Orders.OrderID
  RETURN
END


-- Handle parameters for everything
-- If we get this far, @EmpID IS NOT NULL AND @Country IS NOT NULL
```

Scaling Up with Unbound Access Applications

CHAPTER 11

531

11

SCALING UP WITH
UNBOUND ACCESS
APPLICATIONS

LISTING 11.8   Continued

```
SELECT @PreviousOrderCount =
 (Select Count(*)
  FROM dbo.Customers INNER JOIN
   dbo.Orders ON dbo.Customers.CustomerID = dbo.Orders.CustomerID
  WHERE dbo.Orders.OrderDate BETWEEN @Start AND @End
   AND dbo.Orders.EmployeeID = @EmpID
   AND dbo.Customers.Country = @Country
   AND dbo.Orders.OrderID <= @OrderID)

SELECT @TotalOrderCount =
 (Select Count(*)
  FROM dbo.Customers INNER JOIN
   dbo.Orders ON dbo.Customers.CustomerID = dbo.Orders.CustomerID
  WHERE dbo.Orders.OrderDate BETWEEN @Start AND @End
   AND dbo.Orders.EmployeeID = @EmpID
   AND dbo.Customers.Country = @Country)

SELECT @RemainingOrderCount =
  (@TotalOrderCount-@PreviousOrderCount-25)
If @RemainingOrderCount < 0  -- less than 25 in this batch
  SELECT @RemainingOrderCount = 0

SELECT TOP 25 dbo.Orders.OrderID, dbo.Orders.CustomerID,
 (dbo.Employees.LastName + ', ' + dbo.Employees.FirstName) As Salesperson,
  dbo.Orders.OrderDate, dbo.Customers.Country,
 @TotalOrderCount As TotalOrderCount,
 @RemainingOrderCount As RemainingOrderCount
FROM dbo.Customers INNER JOIN
 dbo.Orders ON dbo.Customers.CustomerID = dbo.Orders.CustomerID
 INNER JOIN dbo.Employees ON dbo.Orders.EmployeeID=dbo.Employees.EmployeeID
WHERE dbo.Orders.OrderDate BETWEEN @Start AND @End
 AND dbo.Orders.EmployeeID = @EmpID
 AND dbo.Customers.Country = @Country
 AND dbo.Orders.OrderID > @OrderID
ORDER BY dbo.Orders.OrderID
```

In the form, a generic FetchOrders procedure is used to call the appropriate stored procedure
and pass it the starting OrderID value. The order ID that is passed to FetchOrders is either the
first or last order ID in the current batch, depending on which direction the next batch is coming from. The cmdNext and cmdFirst buttons are dynamically disabled when there are no more
records to retrieve in one direction or the other. The caption of a label on the form is updated
to tell the user how many 25-record pages of data are in the set and which page is current. A
complete listing of the code that implements this appears in Listing 11.9.

LISTING 11.9   The Code Behind `frmOrderLocate`

```
Private Sub cmdNext_Click()
    Dim rst As DAO.Recordset
    Dim lngLastOrderID As Long
    Set rst = Me.RecordsetClone
    rst.MoveLast
    lngLastOrderID = rst!OrderID
    Call FetchOrders(lngLastOrderID)
End Sub

Private Sub cmdPrev_Click()
    Dim rst As DAO.Recordset
    Dim lngFirstOrderID As Long
    Set rst = Me.RecordsetClone
    rst.MoveFirst
    lngFirstOrderID = rst!OrderID
    Call FetchOrders(lngFirstOrderID, True)
End Sub

Private Sub cmdShow_Click()
    Call FetchOrders
End Sub

Private Sub FixupButtons( _
  Optional lngCurrentBatch As Long = 0, _
  Optional lngTotalBatches As Long = 0)

    Me.cmdNext.Enabled = lngCurrentBatch < lngTotalBatches
    Me.cmdPrev.Enabled = lngCurrentBatch > 1
    If Len(Me.RecordSource) > 0 Then
      Me.cmdSelect.Enabled = Me.RecordsetClone.RecordCount > 0
    Else
      Me.cmdSelect.Enabled = False
    End If
End Sub

Private Sub FetchOrders( _
      Optional lngOrderID As Long = 0, _
      Optional fPrevious As Boolean = False)

    ' Loads the orders to select from.
    ' Uses lngOrderID as starting point,
    '   and fetches:
    '   next 25 orders after that ID if fPrevious is False,
    '   or previous 25 before that ID, if fPrevious is True.
    ' Retrieves counts of remaining and total orders,
```

LISTING 11.9 Continued

```
    '   and fixes up form display.

    On Error GoTo HandleErr
    Dim strSQL As String
    Dim strMsg As String
    Dim lngTotalBatches As Long
    Dim lngCurrentBatch As Long
    Dim lngRemainingBatches As Long

    strSQL = BuildOrderLocateSQL(lngOrderID, fPrevious, strMsg)
    If Len(strMsg) > 0 Then
        ' Invalid data
        MsgBox strMsg, , "Invalid Parameters Entered"
        GoTo ExitHere
    End If

    ' Modify pass-through query SQL and Connect string
    Call PassThroughFixup("qrysptOrderLocate", strSQL, _
      Forms!frmlogin.ODBCConnect)

    ' Assign recordsource
    Me.RecordSource = "qrysptOrderLocate"

    ' Calculate batch counts
    lngTotalBatches = Nz(Round((Me!TotalOrderCount + 12) / 25), 0)
    lngRemainingBatches = Nz(Round((Me!RemainingOrderCount + 12) / 25), 0)

    ' Reset current batch number
    lngCurrentBatch = lngTotalBatches - lngRemainingBatches

    ' Expand display, if necessary
    Call ExpandFormAsNeeded

    ' Show totals and fix up batch nav buttons
    Me.lblBatch.Caption = "A total of " & _
      Nz(Me!TotalOrderCount, 0) & " orders were found. This is page " & _
      lngCurrentBatch & " of " & lngTotalBatches & "."
    Call FixupButtons(lngCurrentBatch, lngTotalBatches)

ExitHere:
    Exit Sub
HandleErr:
    MsgBox Err.Number & ": " & Err.Description, , "FetchOrders Error"
    Resume ExitHere
    Resume
End Sub
```

LISTING 11.9   Continued

```
Private Sub ExpandFormAsNeeded()
    Dim i As Integer

    If Me.Detail.Visible = False Then
        ' Unhide labels
        For i = 1 To 5
            Me("lbl" & i).Visible = True
        Next i
        Me.NavigationButtons = True
        Me.Detail.Visible = True
        Me.Section(acFooter).Visible = True
        Me.InsideHeight = 5530
    End If
End Sub

Private Function BuildOrderLocateSQL( _
  ByVal lngOrderID As Long, _
  ByVal fPrevious As Boolean, _
  ByRef strMsg As String) As String

    Dim strSQL As String

    If (fPrevious) Then
        strSQL = "EXEC procOrderLocatePrevious "
    Else
        strSQL = "EXEC procOrderLocateNext "
    End If

    ' Check for valid start date, and add parameter
    If IsNull(Me.txtStart) Then
        strSQL = strSQL & "NULL, "
    Else
        If IsDate(Me.txtStart) Then
            strSQL = strSQL & "'" & Me.txtStart & "', "
        Else
            strMsg = strMsg & "Start date must be a valid date." & vbCrLf
        End If
    End If

    ' Check for valid end date, and add parameter
    If IsNull(Me.txtEnd) Then
        strSQL = strSQL & "NULL, "
    Else
        If IsDate(Me.txtEnd) Then
            strSQL = strSQL & "'" & Me.txtEnd & "', "
```

LISTING 11.9   Continued

```
        Else
            strMsg = strMsg & "End date must be a valid date." & vbCrLf
        End If
    End If

    ' Add EmployeeID parameter
    If IsNull(Me.cboEmployee) Then
        strSQL = strSQL & "NULL, "
    Else
        strSQL = strSQL & "'" & Me.cboEmployee & "', "
    End If

    ' Add Country parameter
    If IsNull(Me.cboCountry) Then
        strSQL = strSQL & "NULL, "
    Else
        strSQL = strSQL & "'" & Me.cboCountry & "', "
    End If

    ' Add boundary OrderID parameter
    strSQL = strSQL & lngOrderID

    ' Return the result
    BuildOrderLocateSQL = strSQL
End Function
```

Coding your search form this way protects the server and the network from being burdened by queries that return too many records at once. Yet, it still allows users to see all the records matching their desired criteria.

Saving Changes to the Data

Modifying data in an unbound application requires you to deal with issues that you're sheltered from when working with conventional bound forms. In a bound application, the server takes care of enforcing concurrency issues between multiple users contending for the same records, and Access automatically refreshes the data displayed on your form.

In an unbound application, you need to handle concurrency yourself. What happens if a user retrieves a record and, based on what he sees, attempts to save a change to the record, not knowing that in the meantime another user also saved a change to the same record? The first user's changes may be invalid in view of the changes made by the second user. This is referred to as a *write-after-write* concurrency problem. In a bound form, Access would present the user with a somewhat confusing write conflict message, allowing him to overwrite the record, discard his changes, or copy his changed record to the Clipboard and see the current values. In an unbound application, you need a way to handle all this in code. You'll also want to validate the data first in many cases, to ensure that only valid data makes the trip across the wire.

Several things need to happen when the user clicks the Save button on the form:

1. Validate the data in the controls. You don't want the user to post back bad or incomplete data and have SQL Server return a runtime error. The validation for order details is a little easier because it's bound to the local table, so you get enforcement of data types for free. You could also add required fields, unique indexes, and validation rules to the local table.

2. Determine whether the user is editing an existing record or inserting a new one.

3. Make sure you can establish a connection to the server.

4. If the user is editing, you need to handle any concurrency violations that have occurred if another user has edited or deleted the order the first user is trying to save.

5. If a user is adding a new record, you need to return the new OrderID value, which is generated by SQL Server using an identity column.

The first step is validating the data.

Validating Data

Whether you're inserting a new record or editing an existing one, you should validate the data being sent to SQL Server as well as you can without having all the resources of the server available. You could just send whatever data the user types in and let the stored procedure return any error information, but that could conceivably waste a trip across the network—or several trips. To conserve both network throughput and the burden on the server, it's generally better to validate data in Access first, before calling the stored procedure. Any bad or incomplete data that slips past this validation should, of course, still be checked on the server, and you still need validation on the server if other clients besides your application are used to change data. You may not want to assume the burden of making changes to your Access application anytime a rule on the server changes. But the more validation you can perform before the data is saved, the more efficient your application will become. In an *n*-tiered application, middle-tier objects can perform some of this validation after they've received instructions from the presentation tier (your form) and before they send data changes to the server.

In the sample application, the only validation performed is to check that required fields are filled in and that duplicate products are not entered in one order. Listing 11.10 shows the ValidateControls() function, which is called before adding a new record or editing an existing record. It returns a string indicating which required controls are not filled in. Note that it calls the CheckForNulls() procedure to do the actual processing. Other types of validation besides checking for nulls could be added to the ValidateControls function. You could also add validation code that runs when particular controls are updated, but it is generally

Scaling Up with Unbound Access Applications

CHAPTER 11

537

11

SCALING UP WITH
UNBOUND ACCESS
APPLICATIONS

considered friendlier to allow the user freedom to enter invalid data while working on a form and to wait to validate it all at once. Validation strategies will, of course, vary depending on the needs of each application.

LISTING 11.10   Validating Data in Access

```
Private Function ValidateControls() As String
    ' Call CheckForNulls to get message to return.
    ' CheckForNulls also sets focus
    '    to first required control that is null.
    ' Pass in control names and descriptions.
    ' CheckForNulls uses a ParamArray parameter
    '    that allows a variable number of parameters to be passed in.

    Dim strMsg As String

    strMsg = CheckForNulls(Me, _
      "OrderDate", "Order Date", _
      "CustomerID", "Customer", _
      "EmployeeID", "Sold By", _
      "fsubOrderDetail", "Product/Price/Quantity line item")

    ValidateControls = strMsg

End Function
```

The CheckForNulls procedure is a generic function that can work with any form that needs to check for required entries. You pass it a form object, the names of the controls being validated, and a display label for each one. The controls and display values are handled by the parameter array varListOfControlsAndLabels(), which can handle any number of control names and labels you send it. If any nulls are found in the specified controls, a string is returned listing the display labels, as shown in Figure 11.8, and focus is set to the first one on the form. If no nulls are found, a zero-length string is returned. Subform controls submitted to CheckForNulls are checked to ensure that they contain at least one record, as shown in Listing 11.11. In addition, CheckForNulls is called in the BeforeUpdate event of the subform to validate each record there.

LISTING 11.11   The CheckForNulls Validation Function

```
Public Function CheckForNulls( _
 frm As Form, _
 ParamArray varListOfControlsAndLabels()) As String
```

LISTING 11.11 Continued

```
On Error GoTo HandleErr
' Example calling syntax:
'   strMsg=CheckForNulls(Me, _
'     "cboCustomerID", "Customer", _
'     "fsubOrderDetail", "Line Items")
' If control is a subform, then check for no records.
' Return a string suitable for message box.
' If no nulls are found, return a zero-length string.

Dim intI As Integer
Dim ctl As Access.Control
Dim strMsg As String
Dim strFirstNullControl As String
Dim lngMsgReturn As Long
Dim fNullFound As Boolean
Dim fMultipleNullsFound As Boolean

For intI = LBound(varListOfControlsAndLabels) _
 To UBound(varListOfControlsAndLabels) Step 2

  Set ctl = frm(varListOfControlsAndLabels(intI))
  If ctl.ControlType = acSubform Then
    'Check for any records
    If Len(ctl.SourceObject) > 0 Then
      fNullFound = _
        ctl.Form.RecordsetClone.RecordCount = 0
    Else
      'No source object
      fNullFound = True
    End If
  Else 'not a subform
    fNullFound = IsNull(ctl)
  End If
  If fNullFound Then
    strMsg = strMsg & varListOfControlsAndLabels(intI + 1) & vbCrLf
    'Store the first null Control, to set focus to it later.
    If Len(strFirstNullControl) = 0 Then
      strFirstNullControl = varListOfControlsAndLabels(intI)
    Else
      'More than one null was found
      fMultipleNullsFound = True
    End If
  End If
Next intI
```

Scaling Up with Unbound Access Applications

CHAPTER 11

539

11

SCALING UP WITH
UNBOUND ACCESS
APPLICATIONS

LISTING 11.11   Continued

```
If Len(strMsg) > 0 Then 'at least one null was found
  If Not fMultipleNullsFound Then
    'There was only one null Control found.
    ' Use single case in message.
    'Trim trailing CrLf
    strMsg = Left(strMsg, Len(strMsg) - 2)
    strMsg = """" & strMsg & """" is a required entry. " _
      & "Please fill in a value for this item."
  Else
    'There was more than one null Control found.
    ' Use plural case in message.
    strMsg = "The following required entries were left blank:" _
      & vbCrLf & vbCrLf & strMsg & vbCrLf _
      & "Please fill in values for these items."
  End If

  frm(strFirstNullControl).SetFocus
End If

CheckForNulls = strMsg

ExitHere:
  Exit Function

HandleErr:
  Select Case Err.Number

    Case Else
      MsgBox "Error: " & Err.Number & " " _
        & Err.Description, , "CheckForNulls"
  End Select
  Resume ExitHere
  Resume
End Function
```

The primary key of the Northwind Order Details table is comprised of OrderID and ProductID. A particular product can't appear in more than one order detail per order. Using local tables, this unique index could be enforced by the Jet engine, but instead the code uses a procedure to do it, which allows the application to give a more informative message to the user. Here is the code, which simply checks whether a record with this product ID already exists in the table; if it finds a duplicate, it tells the user how many of those items are already on order:

```
Dim rst As DAO.Recordset
Set rst = CurrentDb.OpenRecordset("OrderDetailsLocal", dbOpenSnapshot)
rst.MoveFirst
```

```
rst.FindFirst "ProductID=" & Me.cboProduct _
    & " And User = '" & CurrentUser & "'"
If Not rst.NoMatch Then
    'Found the entered product in the form
    CheckForDuplicateProducts = vbNewLine & _
        "This product already has been entered on this order" _
        & " with a quantity of " & rst!Quantity & _
        ". Products cannot appear more than once per order."
End If
Set rst = Nothing
```

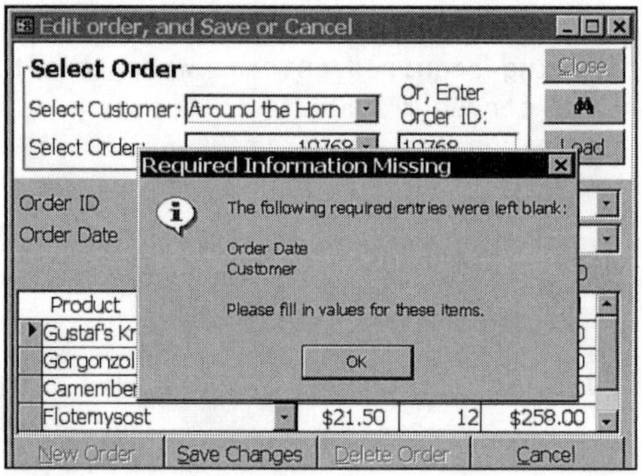

FIGURE 11.8
The CheckForNulls *function creates a message to the user if required data is missing.*

Assuming the data in the order details subform passes muster, it is saved to the local Jet table. At this point, the user can continue editing the form or can click the Save or Cancel button. If the user clicks Cancel, the data from the current order is reloaded as if that order had just been selected. The original values are filled into the unbound controls on the main form, and the local order details table is refreshed with whatever line items are stored in SQL Server for that order. If, on the other hand, the user is satisfied with the modified data and clicks the Save button, the form's code determines whether the order is a new one or an existing one that has been edited by checking for a null order ID—if OrderID is null, the order must be new because the user is not permitted to edit the order ID.

Adding New Records

There are several ways you can add new records in an unbound application:

- *Use a* Recordset. Opening a Recordset on a table to add a new row can be expensive, because the Recordset itself needs to be updatable. If it is a server-side Recordset, that requires holding locks and resources on the server. Even if it is a client-side ADO

Scaling Up with Unbound Access Applications

CHAPTER 11

541

11

SCALING UP WITH
UNBOUND ACCESS
APPLICATIONS

`Recordset` that is going to be reconnected to perform a batch update, this will consume extra resources on the server. Using a `Recordset` also may require the user to have insert permissions on the base table. The exception to that is inserting to a properly secured view, with an unbroken ownership chain to the table. In that case, a user can be denied insert permissions to the table and granted insert permissions to the view.

- *Use an append query.* The Transact-SQL INSERT statement inserts data into a table quickly and efficiently. This is much better than using a `Recordset`, especially if multiple records are being added. To execute an insert SQL statement still may require permissions on the base table unless a view is used, and it requires the server to parse the statement and create an optimized execution plan.

- *Use a stored procedure.* This is the best choice—stored procedures are compiled, optimized, and cached in memory the first time they are run. Also, they can contain conditional processing logic, as well as output parameters indicating success or failure. A stored procedure can also easily return a new identity column value, either in an output parameter or in a `Recordset`. No permissions are needed on the base table—just permission to execute the stored procedure. Whenever possible, use stored procedures to execute your inserts.

Setting Up an Insert Stored Procedure

When you're creating a stored procedure to insert data into a table, create an input parameter for each editable column in the table. Create output parameters to return any identity column values or success/failure information. For example, the following code snippet shows the declaration of input parameters for a stored procedure to insert a new record in the Orders table in the Northwind database. To simplify this presentation, the stored procedure only includes fields that actually appear on the Order form in the application. In "real life," you'd need to include input parameters for all the fields in the table that might receive values. This is not actually the stored procedure code used in the sample application. You'll see why a little later in the chapter. However, it's a good starting point for looking at how an insert stored procedure is structured. Here's the code:

```
CREATE PROCEDURE procOrderInsertX(
  @CustomerID nchar(5) = NULL,
  @EmployeeID int = NULL,
  @OrderDate datetime = NULL, ...
```

An `@OrderID` output parameter is useful to return the new identity column value after the row has been inserted. The SET NOCOUNT ON statement eliminates an unnecessary "done in proc" message:

```
  @OrderID int = NULL OUTPUT,
  @RetCode int = NULL OUTPUT,
```

```
    @RetMsg varchar(100) = NULL OUTPUT)
AS
SET NOCOUNT ON
```

Note that all parameters have null defaults, making them optional—you can evaluate the null values in the body of the stored procedure later to see if values required by the table constraints have been supplied. In the orders table, OrderDate, CustomerID, and EmployeeID are required, so those are checked to see whether they're null, and the return code and return message are set:

```
SELECT  @RetCode = 1,  @RetMsg = ''

IF @OrderDate IS NULL
    SELECT  @RetCode = 0,
      @RetMsg =  @RetMsg +
      'Order Date required.' + CHAR(13) + CHAR(10)

IF @CustomerID IS NULL
    SELECT  @RetCode = 0,
      @RetMsg =  @RetMsg +
      'Customer required.' + CHAR(13) + CHAR(10)

IF @EmployeeID IS NULL
    SELECT  @RetCode = 0,
      @RetMsg =  @RetMsg +
      'Salesperson required.' + CHAR(13) + CHAR(10)
```

If any of the required parameters do not have values supplied, the stored procedure simply ends with the RETURN statement. The @RetMsg output parameter transmits information about the missing values:

```
IF  @RetCode = 0
    RETURN
```

The stored procedure then inserts the data into the Orders table (the use of the ConcurrencyID field is covered later in this chapter):

```
INSERT INTO Orders(
  CustomerID, EmployeeID, OrderDate, RequiredDate,
  ShippedDate, ShipVia, Freight, ShipName, ShipAddress,
  ShipCity, ShipRegion, ShipPostalCode, ShipCountry,
  ConcurrencyID)
VALUES(
  @CustomerID, @EmployeeID, @OrderDate, @RequiredDate,
  @ShippedDate, @ShipVia, @Freight, @ShipName, @ShipAddress,
  @ShipCity, @ShipRegion, @ShipPostalCode, @ShipCountry,
  1)
```

Scaling Up with Unbound Access Applications

CHAPTER 11

543

11

SCALING UP WITH
UNBOUND ACCESS
APPLICATIONS

After inserting the new row, check the value of the @@ROWCOUNT function. If it returns a value of 1, the row was inserted successfully, and you can use the @@IDENTITY function to obtain a value for the @OrderID output parameter. If for some reason the row failed to be inserted, set @RetCode to 0 and return a failure message in the @RetMsg output parameter:

```
IF @@ROWCOUNT = 1
    SELECT @OrderID = @@IDENTITY,
      @RetCode = 1,
      @RetMsg = 'Order Number ' +
      CONVERT(VarChar, @@IDENTITY) + ' Added!'
ELSE
    SELECT @OrderID = 0,
      @RetCode = 0,
      @RetMsg = 'Insert Failed.'
RETURN
```

So, what's wrong with this insert stored procedure? Nothing, it will work great for inserting new records into the Orders table. But what about the order details for this order? You can insert them next, after you know that the order was inserted successfully. However, this means that you are opening up the possibility that an order could be inserted and that something could go wrong with inserting some or all of its accompanying order details. That is the kind of inconsistency that you need to guard your database against at all costs. A lot of attention in this book is focused on optimizing performance, but don't forget that much more important than performance is ensuring that your data can never be left in an inconsistent state. SQL Server will take care of that for you, using its transaction log (even in the event of a disaster that brings down the server), but only if you do your part and enclose all atomic operations in unified transactions. In other words, if A and B should stick together, don't enter them into the database in two separate operations.

To address this problem, the application uses a stored procedure for inserting orders that contains one more input parameter:

```
@OrderDetails varchar(1000) = NULL
```

The size 1000 is arbitrary. The size could be larger if needed. This string is used to send all the order details for an order to the procedure in a delimited format. The string is parsed using Transact-SQL string functions, and the order details are entered as part of the same transaction used to enter the order. That way, there is no chance that only part of the order will make it into the database. There are other ways you could structure a transaction to include the entire order, including the use of the transaction capabilities of Microsoft Transaction Server (MTS) in Windows NT, which became COM+ in Windows 2000. MTS/COM+ is covered in Chapter 14. Transact-SQL transactions are explained in Chapter 10. Listing 11.12 shows the full text of procOrderInsert, which adds an order and all its line items within one transaction. Unless all the data is inserted successfully, the transaction is rolled back.

LISTING 11.12   The procOrderInsert Stored Procedure Inserts Order and Order Detail Records Within a Transaction

```
CREATE PROCEDURE procOrderInsert(
  @CustomerID nchar(5) = NULL,
  @EmployeeID int = NULL,
  @OrderDate datetime = NULL,
  @OrderDetails varchar(1000) = NULL,
  @OrderID int = NULL OUTPUT,
  @RetCode int = NULL OUTPUT,
  @RetMsg varchar(100) = NULL OUTPUT)
AS
SET NOCOUNT ON
  DECLARE @SQLBase varchar(200)
  DECLARE @SQLComplete varchar(200)
  DECLARE @DetailCount int

  /* Validate input parameters.

   Assume success.   */
  SELECT @RetCode = 1, @RetMsg = ''

  IF @OrderDate IS NULL
     SELECT @RetCode = 0,
       @RetMsg = @RetMsg +
       'Order Date required.' + CHAR(13) + CHAR(10)

  IF @CustomerID IS NULL
     SELECT @RetCode = 0,
       @RetMsg = @RetMsg +
       'Customer required.' + CHAR(13) + CHAR(10)

  IF @EmployeeID IS NULL
     SELECT @RetCode = 0,
       @RetMsg = @RetMsg +
       'Salesperson required.' + CHAR(13) + CHAR(10)

  IF @OrderDetails IS NULL
     SELECT @RetCode = 0,
       @RetMsg = @RetMsg +
       'Order line item(s) required.' + CHAR(13) + CHAR(10)

  /* Create a temp table,
     parse out each order detail
     from input parameter string,
     count number of detail records,
     and create SQL statement to
     insert detail records into the temp table. */
```

LISTING 11.12 Continued

```
CREATE TABLE #tmpDetails
  (OrderID int,
  ProductID int,
  UnitPrice money,
  Quantity smallint,
  Discount real DEFAULT 0)

SELECT @SQLBase =
  'INSERT INTO #tmpDetails (OrderID, ProductID,
  UnitPrice, Quantity) VALUES ('
SELECT @DetailCount=0
WHILE LEN( @OrderDetails) > 1
BEGIN
    /* @OrderDetails is a string
       of comma-separated field values.
       Each record is terminated with a semicolon:
       Value1a,Value2a,Value3a;Value1b,Value2b,Value3b;
       First, grab everything before the first semicolon,
       and insert it into the VALUES clause of the SQL. */
    SELECT @SQLComplete = @SQLBase +
      LEFT( @OrderDetails, Charindex(';',  @OrderDetails) -1) + ')'
    /* Insert the OrderDetail record in the temp table. */
    EXEC(@SQLComplete)
    /* Increment the count of detail records. */
    SELECT @DetailCount = @DetailCount + 1
    /* Truncate the string, removing the values that
        were just inserted. */
    SELECT  @OrderDetails =
      RIGHT( @OrderDetails, Len( @OrderDetails)
        -Charindex(';',  @OrderDetails))
    /* The loop repeats until no values are left. */
END

IF (SELECT Count(*) FROM #tmpDetails) <> @DetailCount
  SELECT @RetCode = 0,
    @RetMsg = @RetMsg +
    'Order Details couldn''t be saved.' + CHAR(13) + CHAR(10)

-- If validation failed, exit proc
IF @RetCode = 0
  RETURN
```

LISTING 11.12 Continued

```sql
-- Start transaction by inserting into Orders table
BEGIN TRAN
  INSERT INTO Orders(
    CustomerID, EmployeeID, OrderDate, ConcurrencyID)
  VALUES(
    @CustomerID, @EmployeeID, @OrderDate, 1)

-- Check if insert succeeded. If so, get OrderID.
IF @@ROWCOUNT = 1
  SELECT @OrderID = @@IDENTITY
ELSE
  SELECT @OrderID = 0,
  @RetCode = 0,
  @RetMsg = 'Insertion of new order failed.'

-- If order is not inserted, rollback and exit
IF @RetCode = 0
  BEGIN
    ROLLBACK TRAN
    RETURN
  END

-- Update temp table with new OrderID
UPDATE #tmpDetails
SET OrderID = @OrderID

--   Insert from temp table into Order Details table
INSERT INTO [Order Details]
SELECT OrderID, ProductID, UnitPrice, Quantity, Discount
FROM #tmpDetails

-- Test to see if all details inserted
IF @@ROWCOUNT = @DetailCount AND @@ERROR = 0
  BEGIN
  COMMIT TRAN
    SELECT @RetCode = 1,
      @RetMsg = 'Order number ' +
      CONVERT(VarChar, @OrderID) + ' added successfully.'
  END
ELSE
  BEGIN
  ROLLBACK TRAN
  SELECT @OrderID = 0,
    @RetCode = 0,
    @RetMsg = 'Insertion of new order failed. Order Details couldn't be saved.'
  END
RETURN
```

Inserting a New Record from the Access Application

The `cmdSave_Click()` event procedure handles saving changes when the user adds a new row or edits an existing one. It begins by validating that any required entries were filled in:

```
strOK = ValidateControls
If Len(strOK) > 0 Then
    MsgBox strOK, vbInformation, "Required Information Missing"
    GoTo ExitHere
End If
```

The code then calls the `OpenConnection()` procedure to ensure that a connection to the server is open, and then it takes a few precautionary steps in case the operation takes few moments to complete:

```
DoCmd.Hourglass True
Me.OrderDate.SetFocus
Me.cmdSave.Enabled = False
Me.cmdCancel.Enabled = False
```

The next step is to use the very convenient `GetString` method of an ADO `Recordset` to create a delimited string from the current order detail records, which are stored in a local Jet table:

```
Set rstDetails = New ADODB.Recordset
With rstDetails
    .ActiveConnection = CurrentProject.Connection
    ' Sort by Access autonumber field, to preserve entry order of details.
    .Source = "Select OrderID, ProductID, UnitPrice, Quantity " _
      & "From OrderDetailsLocal " _
      & "Where User = '" & CurrentUser _
      & "' Order By OrderDetailID;"
    ' Open a default read-only, forward-only Recordset
    .Open
    ' Build a string to marshall order details to the stored procedure
    strDetails = .GetString( _
      StringFormat:=adClipString, _
      ColumnDelimeter:=",", _
      RowDelimeter:=";", _
      NullExpr:="NULL")
    .Close
End With
Set rstDetails = Nothing
```

Next, the code checks the status of the OrderID field to see whether the order being saved is a new one or an edited one. There is a custom property, called `IsNew`, that could also be used for this, but checking the OrderID field of the current record is a simpler technique that you may find handy. If it's a new order, the code creates an ADO command object, populates its `Parameters` collection, and uses the command to execute `procOrderInsert`:

```
If Len(Me.OrderID & "") = 0 Then
    ' Add order
    Set cmd = New ADODB.Command
    With cmd
        .ActiveConnection = gcnn
        .CommandText = "procOrderInsert"
        .CommandType = adCmdStoredProc

        .Parameters.Append .CreateParameter( _
          "RETURN_VALUE", adInteger, adParamReturnValue)
        .Parameters.Append .CreateParameter( _
          "@CustomerID", adWChar, adParamInput, 5, Me.CustomerID)
        .Parameters.Append .CreateParameter( _
          "@EmployeeID", adInteger, adParamInput, , Me.EmployeeID)
        .Parameters.Append .CreateParameter( _
          "@OrderDate", adDBTimeStamp, adParamInput, , Me.OrderDate)
        ' The maximum size of 1000 for this parameter is arbitrary.
        '  It needs to match the size used in the stored procedure,
        '    which is limited only by the amount of memory on the server.
        .Parameters.Append .CreateParameter( _
          "@OrderDetails", adVarChar, adParamInput, 1000, strDetails)
        .Parameters.Append .CreateParameter( _
          "@OrderID", adInteger, adParamOutput)
        .Parameters.Append .CreateParameter( _
          "@RetCode", adInteger, adParamOutput)
        .Parameters.Append .CreateParameter( _
          "@RetMsg", adVarChar, adParamOutput, 100)
        .Execute
```

If the stored procedure call is successful, the new order ID is filled in on the form and on each of the records in the local order details table. Also the form's ConcurrencyID custom property is set to 1. The use of ConcurrencyID is covered in the next section of this chapter. Here's the code:

```
fOK = .Parameters("@RetCode")
strMsg = .Parameters("@RetMsg")
If fOK Then
    ' Set the form's OrderID
    Me.OrderID = .Parameters("@OrderID")
    Me.txtOrderID = Me.OrderID
    ' Update order details subform records OrderID
    '   in case user edits these details.
    CurrentDb.Execute _
        "Update OrderDetailsLocal Set OrderID = " _
            & Me.OrderID & " Where User = '" _
            & CurrentUser & "'"
    Me.ConcurrencyID = 1
```

Scaling Up with Unbound Access Applications

CHAPTER 11

549

11

SCALING UP WITH
UNBOUND ACCESS
APPLICATIONS

At the end of the procedure some cleanup occurs, and a message box is displayed for the user, based on the @RetMsg output parameter from the stored procedure:

```
Set cmd = Nothing
If fOK Then
    Me.IsDirty = False
    Me.IsNew = False
Else
    Me.cmdSave.Enabled = True
    Me.cmdCancel.Enabled = True
End If
DoCmd.Hourglass False
MsgBox strMsg, , "Save"
```

The entire cmdSave_Click procedure, which handles both inserts and updates, appears later in Listing 11.13.

Updating Data

Updating data is a little trickier than inserting new records. Because this is an unbound form, you need to check whether the order has been edited by someone else since the user started working on it. If you were using bound data, the server would keep track of that for you by applying the appropriate locks on the data. But because no locks are held with unbound data, write-after-write conflicts can occur.

Write-After-Write Conflicts

Write-after-write conflicts happen when a user tries to save changes to a record that has changed since the user first retrieved it. Here is the sequence of events:

1. User 1 and User 2 both retrieve the same record. Each starts out with the same data. They are using an unbound application with no locking in place, so they are both free to edit the data.

2. User 1 makes a change to the record and saves it. User 2's data is now out of synch with the data on the server.

3. User 2 makes a change to her version of the record and attempts to save the record back to the server.

As far as SQL Server is concerned, this isn't a conflict. Both User 1 and User 2 are ancient history to the server by the time they submit their changes, and each of them is submitting a valid update statement, unrelated to each other. In a bound application using optimistic locking, SQL Server would have notified User 2 that the record had been updated since she started editing it, but this is not the case in an unbound application. Nobody is ever notified that there was a problem and that User 1's changes were unknown to User 2 when she overwrote them. In other words, it's your problem.

The approach taken here is to create a new column in the Orders table named ConcurrencyID. Figure 11.9 shows the design view of the Orders table with the ConcurrencyID definition selected. The data type is int, and a default value of zero is set.

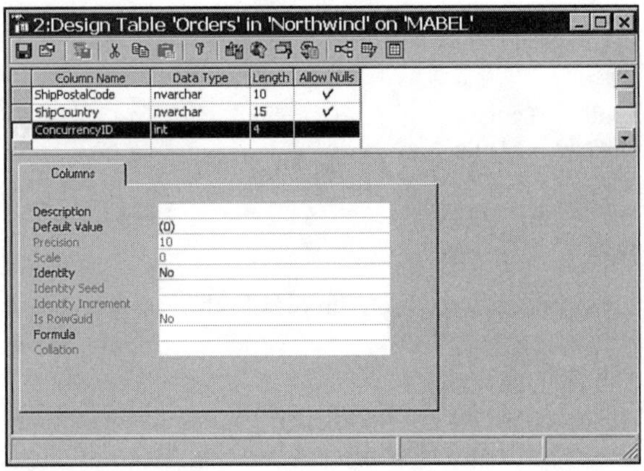

FIGURE 11.9

Creating a ConcurrencyID column in the Orders table.

The ConcurrencyID column is used to keep track of the number of times a record is saved. Each time the record is saved, ConcurrencyID is incremented by one. Prior to the save operation, ConcurrencyID is checked, and the value that exists in the table is compared with the value that was retrieved with the rest of the data. If they match, that means that nobody has edited the record since it was fetched. If they don't match, you can decide how to handle the situation. Here is the sequence of events when ConcurrencyID is used:

1. User 1 and User 2 both retrieve the same record. Each starts out with the same data. They are using an unbound application with no locking in place, so they are both free to edit the data. Each retrieves the same ConcurrencyID value.

2. User 1 makes a change to the record and saves it. The save operation checks the ConcurrencyID value, and because the two match, the save is committed and the ConcurrencyID value in the SQL Server table is incremented by one.

3. User 2 makes a change to her version of the record and attempts to save the record back to the server. User 2's version of ConcurrencyID is not the same as the one currently in the table, so the update fails. User 2 is notified that the data on the server has changed since the record was fetched.

Scaling Up with Unbound Access Applications

CHAPTER 11

551

11

SCALING UP WITH
UNBOUND ACCESS
APPLICATIONS

At this point it's up to you, the developer, to decide on the correct way of handling the situation. Here are some of your options after notifying the user that the data has changed:

- Cancel User 2's changes and fetch the current version of the data.
- Program a custom conflict-resolution function.
- Load the new version of the data alongside the proposed new changes and let the user edit one or the other.
- Allow the user to overwrite User 1's changes.

As you can see, implementing a concurrency ID gives you complete control over the outcome of a write-after-write conflict, and all without holding excessive resources on the SQL Server or taking the hit of comparing every field in the record with a saved copy of its old value. In this case, we've elected to allow the user to overwrite the data after being notified of the conflict or to drop her changes, as shown in Listing 11.13.

Using a Timestamp (or Rowversion) Column for Concurrency Tracking

Using a timestamp column in a table is another option for checking concurrency, and it is often used for this purpose. The timestamp data type started life as a Transact-SQL extension, not part of the ANSI standard. Rowversion is the Microsoft SQL Server 2000 synonym for the timestamp data type. Microsoft changed the name to conform to the ANSI standard for this type of column, and it may change the functionality to more closely match the standard in future versions. There are technical differences between how Transact-SQL timestamps have worked and the way they "should" work according to the ANSI standard. Microsoft has changed the name as a first step toward conforming to the standard. Rowversion is actually a more accurately descriptive name, because the field has nothing to do with the time of day. In any case, a timestamp/rowversion column contains a unique sequentially incrementing binary number. The advantage of a timestamp column is that it automatically increments when data is saved—you don't have to do anything to increment it. However, there are several disadvantages. A timestamp requires eight bytes of storage, making it less efficient than the example (ConcurrencyID), which uses the int data type and requires only four bytes of storage. Another advantage of using ConcurrencyID over a timestamp is that you can use the column to do double-duty and track the number of times a row has been edited. In SQL Server 7.0, the presence of a timestamp column in a table would have prevented the table from being replicated, but that is not the case anymore in SQL Server 2000. Timestamps are also more unwieldy to work with in VBA, where they must be treated as an array of bytes. All in all, we have seen few disadvantages to "rolling your own" int ConcurrencyID, rather than relying on the built-in rowversion/timestamp, and several advantages.

LISTING 11.13 The `cmdSave_Click` Procedure Handles Inserts and Updates to the Orders and Order Details Tables by Calling Stored Procedures

```
Private Sub cmdSave_Click()
    Dim lngConcurrencyID As Long
    Dim fOK As Boolean
    Dim strMsg As String
    Dim strOK As String
    Dim cmd As ADODB.Command
    Dim rstDetails As ADODB.Recordset
    Dim strDetails As String

On Error GoTo HandleErr
    ' Validate controls
    strOK = ValidateControls
    If Len(strOK) > 0 Then
        MsgBox strOK, vbInformation, "Required Information Missing"
        GoTo ExitHere
    End If


    ' Validate the connection
    If Not OpenConnection() Then
        MsgBox "Unable to connect to SQL Server.", , "Login Required"
        Forms!frmlogin.Visible = True
        GoTo ExitHere
    End If
    ' In case this takes a while,
    '     put up an hourglass,
    '     and prevent the user from clicking
    '     save again or cancel while it's running.
    DoCmd.Hourglass True
    Me.OrderDate.SetFocus
    Me.cmdSave.Enabled = False
    Me.cmdCancel.Enabled = False

    ' Build string from Order Details.
    ' Using ADO Recordset.GetString.
    Set rstDetails = New ADODB.Recordset
    With rstDetails
        .ActiveConnection = CurrentProject.Connection
        ' Sort by Access autonumber field, to preserve entry order of details.
        .Source = "Select OrderID, ProductID, UnitPrice, Quantity " _
            & "From OrderDetailsLocal " _
            & "Where User = '" & CurrentUser _
            & "' Order By OrderDetailID;"
        ' Open a default read-only, forward-only Recordset
        .Open
        ' Build a string to marshall order details to the stored procedure
```

Scaling Up with Unbound Access Applications

CHAPTER 11

553

11

SCALING UP WITH
UNBOUND ACCESS
APPLICATIONS

LISTING 11.13   Continued

```
      strDetails = .GetString( _
        StringFormat:=adClipString, _
        ColumnDelimeter:=",", _
        RowDelimeter:=";", _
        NullExpr:="NULL")
      .Close
End With
Set rstDetails = Nothing

' Check to see if adding or editing,
'   and execute appropriate stored procedure.
If Len(Me.OrderID & "") = 0 Then
    ' Add order
    Set cmd = New ADODB.Command
    With cmd
        .ActiveConnection = gcnn
        .CommandText = "procOrderInsert"
        .CommandType = adCmdStoredProc

        .Parameters.Append .CreateParameter( _
          "RETURN_VALUE", adInteger, adParamReturnValue)
        .Parameters.Append .CreateParameter( _
          "@CustomerID", adWChar, adParamInput, 5, Me.CustomerID)
        .Parameters.Append .CreateParameter( _
          "@EmployeeID", adInteger, adParamInput, , Me.EmployeeID)
        .Parameters.Append .CreateParameter( _
          "@OrderDate", adDBTimeStamp, adParamInput, , Me.OrderDate)
        ' The maximum size of 1000 for this parameter is arbitrary.
        '   It needs to match the size used in the stored procedure,
        '     which is limited only by the amount of memory on the server.
        .Parameters.Append .CreateParameter( _
          "@OrderDetails", adVarChar, adParamInput, 1000, strDetails)
        .Parameters.Append .CreateParameter( _
          "@OrderID", adInteger, adParamOutput)
        .Parameters.Append .CreateParameter( _
          "@RetCode", adInteger, adParamOutput)
        .Parameters.Append .CreateParameter( _
          "@RetMsg", adVarChar, adParamOutput, 100)

        .Execute

        fOK = .Parameters("@RetCode")
        strMsg = .Parameters("@RetMsg")
```

LISTING 11.13   Continued

```
              If fOK Then
                  ' Set the form's OrderID
                  Me.OrderID = .Parameters("@OrderID")
                  Me.txtOrderID = Me.OrderID
                  ' Update order details subform records OrderID
                  '   in case user edits these details.
                  CurrentDb.Execute _
                      "Update OrderDetailsLocal Set OrderID = " _
                        & Me.OrderID & " Where User = '" _
                        & CurrentUser & "'"
                  ' Set ConcurrencyId to 1
                  Me.ConcurrencyID = 1
              Else
                  strMsg = "Order was not added." & vbCrLf & strMsg
              End If
          End With
          Set cmd = Nothing
      Else
          ' Edit order
          lngConcurrencyID = Me.ConcurrencyID
          Set cmd = New ADODB.Command
          With cmd
              .ActiveConnection = gcnn
              .CommandText = "procOrderUpdate"
              .CommandType = adCmdStoredProc
              .Parameters.Append .CreateParameter( _
                "RETURN_VALUE", adInteger, adParamReturnValue)
              .Parameters.Append .CreateParameter( _
                "@OrderID", adInteger, adParamInput, , Me.OrderID)
              .Parameters.Append .CreateParameter( _
                "@CustomerID", adWChar, adParamInput, 5, Me.CustomerID)
              .Parameters.Append .CreateParameter( _
                "@EmployeeID", adInteger, adParamInput, , Me.EmployeeID)
              .Parameters.Append .CreateParameter( _
                "@OrderDate", adDBTimeStamp, adParamInput, , Me.OrderDate)
              ' The maximum size of 1000 for this parameter is arbitrary.
              '  It needs to match the size used in the stored procedure,
              '     which is limited only by the amount of memory on the server.
              .Parameters.Append .CreateParameter( _
                "@OrderDetails", adVarChar, adParamInput, 1000, strDetails)
              .Parameters.Append .CreateParameter( _
                "@ConcurrencyID", adInteger, adParamInputOutput, , _
                lngConcurrencyID)
              .Parameters.Append .CreateParameter( _
                "@RetCode", adInteger, adParamOutput)
```

Scaling Up with Unbound Access Applications

CHAPTER 11

555

11

SCALING UP WITH
UNBOUND ACCESS
APPLICATIONS

LISTING 11.13   Continued

```
            .Parameters.Append .CreateParameter( _
              "@RetMsg", adVarChar, adParamOutput, 100)

            .Execute

            fOK = .Parameters("@RetCode")
            strMsg = .Parameters("@RetMsg")
            lngConcurrencyID = .Parameters("@ConcurrencyID")
        End With

        ' Process results
        If lngConcurrencyID <> Me.ConcurrencyID Then
            ' A write-after-write conflict happened here
            strMsg = strMsg & _
            "Order was changed by another user while you were editing it." & _
              vbCrLf & "Your changes will overwrite the " & _
              "other changes if you click Save again. " & _
              "Click Cancel to see the other user's changes."
            fOK = False
            ' Update ConcurrencyID
            Me.ConcurrencyID = lngConcurrencyID
        Else
            ' Update succeeded; increment ConcurrencyID
            Me.ConcurrencyID = lngConcurrencyID + 1
        End If
    End If
    Set cmd = Nothing
    If fOK Then
        Me.IsDirty = False
        Me.IsNew = False
    Else
        Me.cmdSave.Enabled = True
        Me.cmdCancel.Enabled = True
    End If
    DoCmd.Hourglass False
    MsgBox strMsg, , "Save"

ExitHere:
    DoCmd.Hourglass False
    Exit Sub

HandleErr:
    MsgBox Err & ": " & Err.Description, , "cmdSave error"
  Resume ExitHere
    Resume
End Sub
```

Handling Updates

The `cmdSave_Click()` event procedure, shown in Listing 11.13, handles updating data by calling the `procOrderUpdate` stored procedure, passing it the ConcurrencyID value that was retrieved with the data, along with the other input parameter values that contain the proposed changes to the data.

The code for the `procOrderUpdate` stored procedure is shown in Listing 11.14. The required input parameters are validated, and then the Orders table is checked for a write-after-write conflict by comparing the `@ConcurrencyID` parameter with the value currently existing in the table. If they match, an UPDATE statement is constructed based on the values of the input parameters and executed. If the ConcurrencyID values don't match, that information is passed back to the calling procedure. No attempt is made to handle the write-after-write conflict in the stored procedure—that task is handled by the application. If the update to the Orders table succeeds, the order details line items are also reinserted as part of the same transaction.

LISTING 11.14   The `procOrderUpdate` Stored Procedure

```
CREATE PROCEDURE procOrderUpdate(
  @OrderID int,
  @CustomerID nchar(5) = NULL,
  @EmployeeID int = NULL,
  @OrderDate datetime = NULL,
  @OrderDetails varchar(1000) = NULL,
  @ConcurrencyID int OUTPUT,
  @RetCode int = NULL OUTPUT,
  @RetMsg varchar(100) = NULL OUTPUT)
AS
SET NOCOUNT ON
  DECLARE @SQLBase varchar(200)
  DECLARE @SQLComplete varchar(200)
  DECLARE @CheckOrder int
  DECLARE @DetailCount int

  /* Check if order exists. */
  SELECT @CheckOrder=OrderID FROM Orders
  WHERE OrderID = @OrderID

  IF @CheckOrder IS NULL
  BEGIN
      SELECT @RetCode = 0,
        @RetMsg = 'Order ' +
                  CONVERT(VarChar, @OrderID) +
                  ' does not exist.'
      RETURN
  END

  /* Use ConcurrencyID to check
```

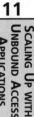

LISTING 11.14   Continued

```
    whether the order has changed
    since it was retrieved. */
SELECT @CheckOrder = ConcurrencyID FROM Orders
WHERE OrderID = @OrderID

IF @CheckOrder <> @ConcurrencyID
BEGIN
    SELECT @ConcurrencyID = @CheckOrder,
      @RetCode = 0,
      @RetMsg = 'Another user updated this order ' +
      'while you were editing it.'
  RETURN
END

/* Validate input parameters.

 Assume success.  */
SELECT @RetCode = 1, @RetMsg = ''

IF @OrderDate IS NULL
    SELECT @RetCode = 0,
      @RetMsg = @RetMsg +
      'Order Date required.' + CHAR(13) + CHAR(10)

IF @CustomerID IS NULL
    SELECT @RetCode = 0,
      @RetMsg = @RetMsg +
      'Customer required.' + CHAR(13) + CHAR(10)

IF @EmployeeID IS NULL
    SELECT @RetCode = 0,
      @RetMsg = @RetMsg +
      'Salesperson required.' + CHAR(13) + CHAR(10)

IF @OrderDetails IS NULL
    SELECT @RetCode = 0,
      @RetMsg = @RetMsg +
      'Order line item(s) required.' + CHAR(13) + CHAR(10)

/* Create a temp table,
   parse out each order detail
   from input parameter string,
   count number of detail records,
```

LISTING 11.14 Continued

```
   and create SQL statement to
   insert detail records into the temp table. */
CREATE TABLE #tmpDetails
(OrderID int,
  ProductID int,
  UnitPrice money,
  Quantity smallint,
  Discount real DEFAULT 0)

SELECT @SQLBase =
  'INSERT INTO #tmpDetails (OrderID, ProductID,
    UnitPrice, Quantity) VALUES ('
SELECT @DetailCount=0
WHILE LEN( @OrderDetails) > 1
  BEGIN
    /* @OrderDetails is a string
        of comma-separated field values.
       Each record is terminated with a semicolon:
        Value1a,Value2a,Value3a;Value1b,Value2b,Value3b;
       First, grab everything before the first semicolon,
        and insert it into the VALUES clause of the SQL. */
    SELECT @SQLComplete = @SQLBase +
      LEFT( @OrderDetails, Charindex(';',  @OrderDetails) -1) + ')'
    /* Insert the OrderDetail record in the temp table. */
    EXEC(@SQLComplete)
    /* Increment the count of detail records. */
    SELECT @DetailCount = @DetailCount + 1
    /* Truncate the string, removing the values that
        were just inserted. */
    SELECT  @OrderDetails =
      RIGHT( @OrderDetails, Len( @OrderDetails)
        -Charindex(';',  @OrderDetails))
    /* The loop repeats until no values are left. */
  END

IF (SELECT Count(*) FROM #tmpDetails) <> @DetailCount
  SELECT @RetCode = 0,
    @RetMsg = @RetMsg +
    'Order Details couldn''t be saved.' + CHAR(13) + CHAR(10)

-- If validation failed, exit proc
IF @RetCode = 0
  RETURN

-- Start transaction by updating Orders table
```

Scaling Up with Unbound Access Applications

CHAPTER 11

559

11

SCALING UP WITH
UNBOUND ACCESS
APPLICATIONS

LISTING 11.14   Continued

```
BEGIN TRAN
  UPDATE Orders SET
      CustomerID = @CustomerID,
      EmployeeID = @EmployeeID,
      OrderDate = @OrderDate,
      ConcurrencyID = @ConcurrencyID + 1
  WHERE
      OrderID = @OrderID AND ConcurrencyID = @ConcurrencyID

-- Check if update succeeded.
SELECT @CheckOrder = ConcurrencyID FROM Orders
  WHERE OrderID = @OrderID

IF @CheckOrder = @ConcurrencyID + 1
  SELECT @RetCode = 1
ELSE
  SELECT @RetCode = 0,
    @RetMsg = 'Update of order failed.'

-- If order update failed, rollback and exit
IF @RetCode = 0
  BEGIN
    ROLLBACK TRAN
    RETURN
  END

/* Delete all existing order details
    for this order. Replace with new values. */
DELETE [Order Details]
  WHERE OrderID = @OrderID

/* Insert from temp table into Order Details table.
   Use @OrderID to allow client flexibility when editing details
     that were added to a new order
     (client doesn't have to fill in new OrderID before editing). */

INSERT INTO [Order Details]
  SELECT @OrderID, ProductID, UnitPrice, Quantity, Discount
  FROM #tmpDetails

-- Test to see if all details were inserted.
IF @@ROWCOUNT = @DetailCount AND @@ERROR = 0
  BEGIN
    COMMIT TRAN
    SELECT @RetCode = 1,
      @RetMsg = 'Order number ' +
```

LISTING 11.14 Continued

```
          CONVERT(VarChar, @OrderID) + ' updated successfully.'
    END
  ELSE
    BEGIN
      ROLLBACK TRAN
      SELECT
        @RetCode = 0,
        @RetMsg = 'Update failed. Order Details couldn''t be saved.'
    END
RETURN
```

The `cmdSave_Click()` event procedure is responsible for dealing with the write-after-write conflict after the stored procedure has been executed. The output parameter values `@RetCode` and `@RetMsg` are stored in local variables along with `@ConcurrencyID`:

```
fOK = .Parameters("@RetCode")
strMsg = .Parameters("@RetMsg")
lngConcurrencyID = .Parameters("@ConcurrencyID")
```

If the ConcurrencyID value returned by the stored procedure doesn't match the value that was passed in, a write-after-write conflict has occurred. The user is notified that the data has changed and is given the chance to overwrite the changes by clicking the Save button again. The form's concurrency ID is then updated with the new value, so the write-after-write conflict won't occur a second time if the user elects to save:

```
If lngConcurrencyID <> Me.ConcurrencyID Then
    ' A write-after-write conflict happened here
    strMsg = strMsg & _
      "Order was changed by another user while you were editing it." & _
      vbCrLf & "Your changes will overwrite the " & _
      "other changes if you click Save again.
        Click Cancel to see the other user's changes."
    fOK = False
    ' Update ConcurrencyID
    Me.ConcurrencyID = lngConcurrencyID
Else
    ' Update succeeded; increment ConcurrencyID
    Me.ConcurrencyID = lngConcurrencyID + 1
End If
```

If the update succeeds without any write-after-write conflicts, then the form's ConcurrencyID value is incremented by 1 to match that in the table:

```
Me.ConcurrencyID = lngConcurrencyID + 1
```

Scaling Up with Unbound Access Applications

CHAPTER 11

561

11

SCALING UP WITH
UNBOUND ACCESS
APPLICATIONS

Deleting Data

Deleting data is handled by the `procOrderDelete` stored procedure, shown in Listing 11.15. The `@OrderID` input parameter is used in the WHERE clause to delete only the row selected. Because SQL Server 2000 supports cascading deletes, there's no need to delete the order detail line items first—they will be handled automatically when the order is deleted. However, make sure that Cascade Delete Related Records is set on the relationship between the Order and Order Details tables in your copy of the Northwind sample database; otherwise, the stored procedure will fail.

LISTING 11.15   The `procOrderDelete` Stored Procedure

```
CREATE PROCEDURE procOrderDelete
(
  @OrderID int,
  @RetCode int = NULL OUTPUT,
  @RetMsg varchar(100) = NULL OUTPUT
)
AS
  SET NOCOUNT ON

  DECLARE @OrderCheck int

BEGIN
    --Check if order exists
    SELECT @OrderCheck = OrderID FROM Orders
    WHERE OrderID = @OrderID
    IF @OrderCheck IS NULL
        BEGIN
        SELECT @RetCode = 1,
         @RetMsg = 'Order does not exist.'
        --Bail
        RETURN
        END
    ELSE
        BEGIN
        /*Delete Order. This depends on cascading deletes
          to whack the order detail line items.*/
        DELETE FROM Orders
        WHERE OrderID = @OrderID

        IF @@ROWCOUNT = 1
          --Return success
          SELECT @RetCode = 1,
          @RetMsg = 'Order Number ' +
```

LISTING 11.15 Continued

```
                CONVERT(VarChar, @OrderID) + ' Deleted!'
        ELSE
          SELECT  @RetCode = 0,
          @RetMsg = 'Delete Failed.'
        END
END
```

The user is then asked to confirm the deletion. If Yes is the answer, the connection to SQL Server is validated and then order is deleted by calling the procOrderDelete stored procedure:

```
strMsg = _
  "Are you sure you want to delete this order?" _
  & vbCrLf & "Click Yes to Delete, No to Cancel."
' Get confirmation
If MsgBox(strMsg, vbYesNo + vbQuestion, _
  "Delete Order?") = vbYes Then
    ' Validate the connection
    If Not OpenConnection() Then
        strMsg = "Can't Connect to Northwind"
        Forms!frmlogin.Visible = True
        MsgBox strMsg, , "Order Deletion"
        GoTo ExitHere
    End If
    ' Delete the order
    Set cmd = New ADODB.Command
    With cmd
        .ActiveConnection = gcnn
        .CommandText = "procOrderDelete"
        .CommandType = adCmdStoredProc

        .Parameters.Append .CreateParameter( _
          "RETURN_VALUE", adInteger, adParamReturnValue)
        .Parameters.Append .CreateParameter( _
          "@OrderID", adInteger, adParamInput, , Me.OrderID)
        .Parameters.Append .CreateParameter( _
          "@RetCode", adInteger, adParamOutput)
        .Parameters.Append .CreateParameter( _
          "@RetMsg", adVarChar, adParamOutput, 100)

        .Execute
```

If the stored procedure is executed successfully, the form is cleaned up and the records are deleted from the OrderDetailsLocal local table:

```
        fOK = .Parameters("@RetCode")
        strMsg = .Parameters("@RetMsg")
```

```
    End With
    If fOK Then
        ' Clear OrderID to
        '  avoid assigning the deleted
        '  order ID to mlngLastOrder.
        Me.OrderID = Null
        ' Clear form
        Call cmdNew_Click
    End If
    MsgBox strMsg, , "Order Deletion"
End If
```

Unbound ADPs

In some respects, all ADP applications are unbound. The previous section of this chapter presented a strategy that employs local tables in an MDB to cache data that has been retrieved from the server. Although the order details subform in that example has a record source, it's considered "unbound" because it is not maintaining an active connection to SQL Server. Instead, it communicates only briefly with the server when it needs to fetch data or execute an update. This is actually very analogous to what happens in an ADP by default, except in an ADP the local cache is not made up of Jet tables.

Instead, ADPs use the ADO client cursor engine to hold data that has been retrieved from the server. As far as SQL Server is concerned, all ADO client-side Recordsets—even updatable and scrollable ones—are just read-only, forward-only Recordsets. ADO gets all the data quickly and efficiently from the server and then holds it in memory on the client. When a new or modified record is saved, the cursor engine also takes care of constructing a SQL statement that inserts or updates records in the base tables. You can set up a trace using the Profiler in SQL Server to see this in action (Profiler is discussed in Chapter 15, " Deployment, Tuning, and Maintenance"). This works even if a form is based on a stored procedure.

The OLE DB provider used by Access when creating a connection to SQL Server in an ADP is not just the SQL Server provider (SQLOLEDB). Access uses a service provider called the *Data Shape provider* (MSDATASHAPE), which acts as a wrapper around the SQL Server provider, adding functionality of its own. This Data Shape provider is generally used to create hierarchical Recordsets, with special fields called *chapters*, which themselves can hold sets of records. However, it is not the hierarchical capabilities of the Data Shape provider that Access needs. Access uses this provider because it fetches and supplies metadata from SQL Server that is not supplied by the SQL Server provider alone. This metadata (data about the structure of data) provides information that Access uses to create SQL statements for adding and updating data. All this extra work is needed because, in a very real sense, ADPs are unbound—they don't rely on server-side cursors the way traditional bound applications have in the past. There are a couple of shortcomings, however, to this quasi-unbound data access strategy in ADPs.

First, all inserts and updates are performed with SQL instructions that use the base tables. Even if you base a form on a stored procedure, that stored procedure can only be used to retrieve the records. The "updatable snapshot" Access uses as the Recordset behind the form is only updatable because Access can make use of metadata to obtain the names of the base tables and run updates and inserts against them. With multitable sources, you can select the "unique table" to be updated. However, your users must have security permissions on the base tables themselves for this approach to work. There is no way to specify stored procedures that should be called to perform inserts, updates, and deletions. Using the truly unbound techniques described in this chapter and in Chapter 14, you can use stored procedures for all data manipulation and give users permissions only to execute those stored procedures.

The second disadvantage of using the default behavior of ADPs is essentially the same problem encountered in bound MDBs. You lose control of the relationship with the server. The convenience of allowing Access to handle things transparently comes at the price of needing to trust Access to handle them efficiently. In an unbound application, you create your own connection and you maintain full control over how and when it is used.

This is not to imply that standard ADPs with bound forms are bad, just as standard bound MDBs are not bad. Chapter 4 presents a range of techniques you can use to take advantage of all the cool features available in ADPs. But in some cases, especially when scalability is a priority, you may want to try the unbound ADP techniques presented in this chapter. As with Access MDBs, the first thing you'll want to do is take control of the connection.

Handling ADP Connections

When you create an Access project, you get prompted for the information needed to connect to SQL Server. In a bound application, the connection stays active for the life of the application. However, under the covers, Access may actually be consuming more connections as needed. You can also open additional connections in code by reusing the existing connection information anywhere in your project by taking advantage of the CurrentProject object's Connection and BaseConnectionString properties.

The CurrentProject object is a child of the Application object. Figure 11.10 shows its location in the Object Browser in the Visual Basic Editor with the CurrentProject and Connection items selected.

The CurrentProject.Connection property in an ADP holds an ADO Connection object that gives you a reference to the OLE DB connection that Access has opened. If you inspect the connection string in the Immediate window of the Visual Basic Editor, you'll see that this connection is based on the Data Shape service provider as well as the data provider for SQL Server:

Scaling Up with Unbound Access Applications

CHAPTER 11

565

11

SCALING UP WITH
UNBOUND ACCESS
APPLICATIONS

```
?CurrentProject.Connection.ConnectionString
Provider=MSDataShape.1;Persist Security Info=False;Data Source=MABEL;Integrated
Security=SSPI;Initial Catalog=Northwind;Data Provider=SQLOLEDB.1
```

FIGURE 11.10

The Object Browser showing the CurrentProject *object.*

A separate property, BaseConnectionString, gives you the string to use if you want to create a connection without the extra overhead of the Data Shape provider:

```
?CurrentProject.BaseConnectionString
PROVIDER=SQLOLEDB.1;INTEGRATED SECURITY=SSPI;PERSIST SECURITY INFO=FALSE;
  INITIAL CATALOG=Northwind;DATA SOURCE=MABEL
```

Even if the connection is explicitly closed with the CurrentProject.CloseConnection method, the BaseConnectionString property will persist and can be retrieved. The BaseConnectionString value can be reused in the CurrentProject object's OpenConnection method, or you can create your own connection object. The following code snippet shows closing the current connection and reusing the CurrentProject.BaseConnectionString property as the ConnectionString value for a new ADO Connection object:

```
' Close current project's connection
CurrentProject.CloseConnection

' Re-use BaseConnectionString for new ADO connection
Set cnn = New ADODB.Connection
cnn.ConnectionString = CurrentProject.BaseConnectionString
cnn.Open
```

You can take advantage of this technique to disconnect an Access project and work unbound with a global ADO Connection object that you open in code. Alternatively, you can simply create an unbound Access project from scratch and open your connection without using `BaseConnectionString`.

Creating an Unbound Access Project

To create an unbound Access project, follow these steps:

1. Choose File, New from the menu bar and select Project (New Database). Click OK.

2. In the File New Database dialog box, specify the name and location of the new project file.

3. This will create a new ADP file and launch the SQL Server Create Database Wizard. Instead of running the wizard, click Cancel. This will create a totally empty project that is not connected to any SQL Server database. This allows you to code the ADO connection yourself and use it as the basis for forms, reports, and other objects.

Displaying Data: Creating Unbound Forms

You can use the same technique for maintaining a code-generated connection to your data that was shown for Access databases in Listing 11.1: Create a global ADO `Connection` object and reuse it for ADO `Command` and `Recordset` objects. An unbound form in an Access project is populated in the same way as a form in an Access database—by creating a `Recordset` and assigning the values from the `Recordset` to the controls on the form. This code is identical to the code used in the `cmdLoad_Click()` event procedure earlier in this chapter in Listing 11.3:

```
' Get the record data
Set rst = New ADODB.Recordset
rst.CursorLocation = adUseClient
rst.Open Source:="EXEC procOrderSelect " & _
    lngOrderID, _
    ActiveConnection:=gcnn

' Display record data in form controls
If rst.EOF Then
    MsgBox "Record can't be found.", , _
      "Order does not exist"
    GoTo ExitHere
Else
    On Error Resume Next
    For Each fld In rst.Fields
        Me(fld.Name).Value = fld.Value
    Next
End If
```

Displaying data on the main form is easy—where things get tricky is with subforms shown in continuous or datasheet view.

Scaling Up with Unbound Access Applications

CHAPTER 11

567

11

SCALING UP WITH
UNBOUND ACCESS
APPLICATIONS

Handling Subform Data

When working with an Access database (MDB), you have the luxury of using local tables to cache subform data. This usually represents the "many" side of a one-to-many relationship—in this case, the order details for a single order. Because Jet is not available in an Access project, other techniques are required. For an ADP, an unbound, disconnected ADO `Recordset` can be used to store and edit the order detail line items. Here's how it works:

1. The `Recordset` is opened on the SQL Server Order Details table for only the order detail line items that are related to the main order.

2. The `Recordset` is then bound to the subform using the subform's `Recordset` property.

3. The connection between the `Recordset` and the server is then severed.

As far as the server is concerned, the `Recordset` no longer exists—no locks or resources are being held on the server. This actually is not different from what happens when you use a conventional record source in an ADP, but it does give you an extra measure of control, especially over how modifications to the data are handled. To achieve the same level of control using a standard record source in an ADP, you would need to make the form read-only. Unfortunately, when binding your form to a disconnected `Recordset` in Access 2000, the form becomes read-only anyway, and you have to get creative about finding ways for the user to modify data. We hope and expect that future versions of Access will provide more options for working with disconnected `Recordset`s in Access forms.

You can make the `Recordset` be updatable and change values in it yourself in code, as you'll see a little later in this chapter, but the form will remain read-only. To allow the user to edit data, you'll need to pop up a separate dialog form showing just one row of data. Changes made in that pop-up form are saved to the local disconnected `Recordset`. The Save button on the main form updates the database using the same technique used in the MDB—calling a stored procedure and passing it all the current values for the order and its details.

Fetching Data

The first step is to fetch the data for the order detail line items. The `LoadLineItems` procedure, located in the subform, is shown in Listing 11.16. The `Recordset` is opened on the `procOrderDetailSelect` stored procedure, which selects the order detail records based on the order ID. The form's `Recordset` property is then set, and the `Recordset`'s `ActiveConnection` property set to `Nothing`. This disconnects the `Recordset` from SQL Server. The `Recordset` variable itself is also set to `Nothing`, because it is no longer needed. The form now has a reference to the `Recordset`, so it is not destroyed by this action.

LISTING 11.16   Loading the Line Items Using an Unbound ADO Recordset

```
Public Sub LoadLineItems()
    On Error GoTo HandleErr
    ' Open a client-side ADO Recordset
    '   based on a stored procedure,
    '   bind form to the Recordset,
    '   and disconnect the Recordset.
    ' Connection is verified before this
    '   routine is called.
    Dim cmd As ADODB.Command
    Dim rst As ADODB.Recordset

    ' Check connection
    If OpenConnection() = False Then
        MsgBox "Unable to Connect", , _
            "Can't connect to the database."
        Forms!frmlogin.Visible = True
        DoCmd.Close acForm, "frmOrder"
        Forms!frmlogin.SetFocus
        GoTo ExitHere
    End If

    Set cmd = New ADODB.Command
    With cmd
        .Parameters.Append .CreateParameter( _
            "@OrderID", _
            adInteger, _
            adParamInput, , _
            Nz(Me.Parent.txtOrderID, 0))
        .CommandText = "procOrderDetailSelect"
        Set .ActiveConnection = gcnn
    End With

    Set rst = New ADODB.Recordset
    With rst
        .CursorLocation = adUseClient
        .LockType = adLockOptimistic
        .Open cmd, Options:=adCmdStoredProc
    End With

    Set Me.Recordset = rst
    Set rst.ActiveConnection = Nothing
    Set cmd = Nothing
    Set rst = Nothing
ExitHere:
    Exit Sub
```

LISTING 11.16   Continued

```
HandleErr:
    Select Case Err
        Case -2147467259 'Error trying to connect
            MsgBox "Unable to Connect", , _
                "Can't connect to the database."
            Forms!frmlogin.Visible = True
            DoCmd.Close acForm, "frmOrder"
            Forms!frmlogin.SetFocus
            Resume ExitHere
        Case Else
            MsgBox Err & ": " & Err.Description, , "LoadLineItems() Error"
    End Select
    Resume ExitHere
    Resume
End Sub
```

The new ADO `Recordset` uses a cursor location of `adUseClient` and a lock type of `adLockOptimistic`. Setting these two properties is important because the `Recordset` needs to be updatable after it is disconnected from the server.

You could have used a lock type of `adLockBatchOptimistic`, if you were planning to reconnect the `Recordset` to the database to perform updates later. But that would really defeat part of the purpose for doing all this work. You want to use stored procedures, not `Recordset` updates, to perform data modifications. So, using `adLockOptimistic` is all that is needed—you only want to be able to perform updates to the local cache, which contains data that is later posted back to SQL Server as part of a transaction consisting of the order item.

Once the `Recordset` is created, attach it to the subform by setting the subform's `Recordset` property. Then disconnect the `Recordset` from the SQL Server database by setting its `ActiveConnection` property to `Nothing`:

```
Set Me.Recordset = grst
Set grst.ActiveConnection = Nothing
```

The order of these operations is important. You'll find that you cannot bind a form to a `Recordset` that is already disconnected. Access seems to need that connection to do some work behind the scenes when you assign a `Recordset` to a form. This is another limitation that we hope and expect will be remedied in future versions. It would be great to be able to get a disconnected `Recordset` from a middle-tier object and assign it to the `Recordset` property of a form.

After setting the `Recordset` property of the form and disconnecting the `Recordset`, the records are displayed in the subform, but they are read-only in the user interface, even though they can be modified in code. Figure 11.11 shows the order form with the order details displayed in the subform.

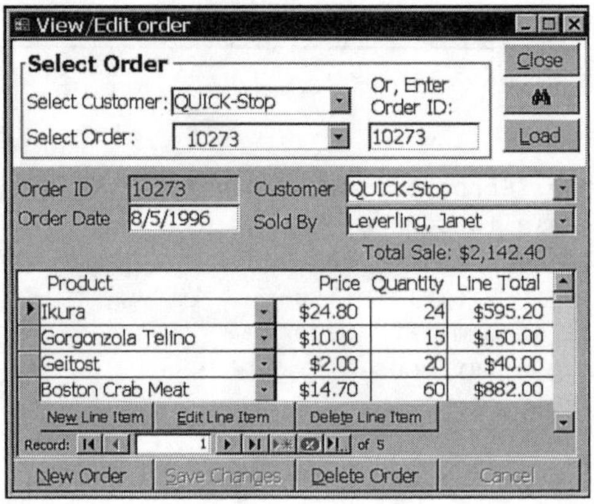

FIGURE 11.11

The Unbound Order/Order Details form.

Modifying Data

Modifying data on the "one" side of the relationship (the order) is the same as it was using an Access database. The user types in new values in the unbound controls, and when the order is saved, the data is validated and written back to the server using a stored procedure. However, because the order detail line items in the subform are bound to a client-side disconnected `Recordset`, you need another mechanism to edit the values in the controls. You can't use the subform itself the same way you could with the Access database because forms bound to disconnected `Recordset`s become read-only. Figure 11.11 shows buttons in the subform that allow for adding and deleting records as well as a label instructing users to double-click a row to edit a line item. The following sections cover the techniques used in this example for adding, editing, and deleting records in the order details subform.

Adding and Editing Records

Because the order details subform is bound to a disconnected `Recordset`, it can't be used to edit data directly—a second subform that is normally hidden is used instead. When the user clicks the New Line Item button, the hidden subform is displayed, as shown in Figure 11.12. The user can select a product from the Product combo box and fill in the price and quantity. The form stays displayed until the user clicks either the Save or Cancel button.

If the user clicks the Cancel button, the following code runs, which redisplays the original subform:

```
Private Sub cmdCancel_Click()
    ' User canceled update. Switch subforms.
    Forms!frmOrder!fsubOrderDetail.Visible = True
    Forms!frmOrder.Section(acFooter).Visible = True
```

Scaling Up with Unbound Access Applications

CHAPTER 11

571

11

SCALING UP WITH
UNBOUND ACCESS
APPLICATIONS

```
    Forms!frmOrder!fsubOrderDetail.SetFocus
    Forms!frmOrder!fsubLineItemAddEdit.Visible = False
End Sub
```

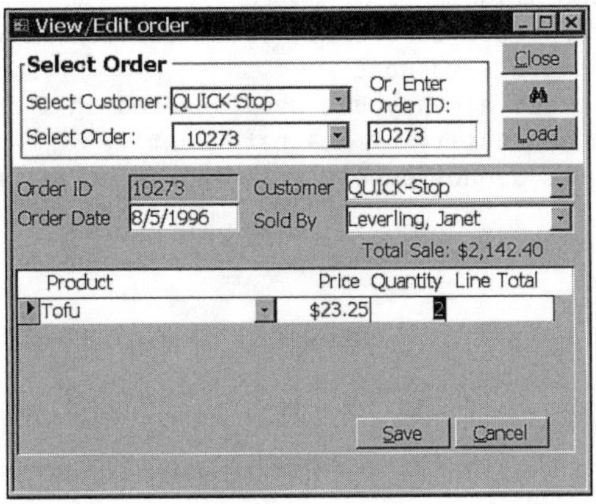

FIGURE 11.12
Editing a line item in the order details subform.

Editing and adding line items in the subform share the same code, which runs from the Save button. The first step in saving the record is to validate the data:

```
' Validate line item controls
strMsg = CheckForNulls(Me, _
  "ProductID", "Product", _
  "UnitPrice", "UnitPrice", _
  "Quantity", "Quantity")

strMsg = strMsg & CheckForDuplicateProducts
```

The CheckForDuplicateProducts procedure, shown in Listing 11.17, checks for duplicate product IDs in the Recordset. If the product ID already exists, the record can't be saved because ProductID and OrderID form the primary key for the order details table.

LISTING 11.17   Validating That There Aren't Duplicate Products

```
Private Function CheckForDuplicateProducts() As String
    On Error GoTo HandleErr
    Dim rst As ADODB.Recordset
    Set rst = Forms!frmOrder!fsubOrderDetail.Form.Recordset.Clone
    rst.MoveFirst
    rst.Find "ProductID=" & Me.ProductID
    If Not rst.EOF Then
        'Found the same product in the form.
```

LISTING 11.17   Continued

```
        ' Check if it's a different record.
        If Me.AddEdit = "Add" Or _
           rst.AbsolutePosition <> _
           Forms!frmOrder!fsubOrderDetail.Form.Recordset.AbsolutePosition Then
              CheckForDuplicateProducts = _
                 "This product already has been entered on this order" _
               & " with a quantity of " & rst!Quantity & _
               ". Products cannot appear more than once per order."
        End If
    End If
ExitHere:
    Exit Function

HandleErr:
    Select Case Err

    Case Else
     MsgBox Err & ": " & Err.Description, , "CheckForDuplicateProducts() Error"
    End Select
    Resume ExitHere
    Resume
End Function
```

If the validation check fails, the user has the chance to click the Cancel button. If so, the original records are displayed:

```
If Len(strMsg) > 0 Then
    If MsgBox(strMsg, _
      vbOKCancel + vbInformation, _
      "Required Information Missing") = vbCancel Then
        ' User canceled update. Switch subforms.
        Forms!frmOrder!fsubOrderDetail.Visible = True
        Forms!frmOrder.Section(acFooter).Visible = True
        Forms!frmOrder!fsubOrderDetail.SetFocus
        Forms!frmOrder!fsubLineItemAddEdit.Visible = False
    Else
        ' Give the use a chance to fix the problem
        '  and to try again.
    End If
```

If the record is being saved, it is added to the Recordset using the AddNew method. If the line is being edited, the value of the field in the Recordset is assigned to the corresponding value on the subform:

```
With Forms!frmOrder!fsubOrderDetail.Form.Recordset
    If AddEdit = "Add" Then
```

Scaling Up with Unbound Access Applications

CHAPTER 11

573

11

SCALING UP WITH
UNBOUND ACCESS
APPLICATIONS

```
        .AddNew
    End If
    For Each fld In .Fields
        ' Subform field names match
        fld.Value = Me(fld.Name)
    Next fld
    Set fld = Nothing
    .Update
End With
```

The last step is to display the form. The main form's `IsDirty` property is set to `True`, the line item totals are recalculated, and all the order details are displayed:

```
Me.Parent.IsDirty = True
Call Me.Parent.SaleRecalc
Forms!frmOrder!fsubOrderDetail.Visible = True
Forms!frmOrder.Section(acFooter).Visible = True
Forms!frmOrder!fsubOrderDetail.SetFocus
Forms!frmOrder!fsubLineItemAddEdit.Visible = False
```

Deleting Subform Records

Deleting a `Recordset` uses the `Delete` method on the current row and sets the main form's `IsDirty` property to `True`. The line item total is recalculated, and an explicit save or cancel is forced by disabling the other buttons:

```
If Me.Recordset.RecordCount > 0 Then
  Me.Recordset.Delete
  Me.Parent.IsDirty = True
  Call Me.Parent.SaleRecalc
  ' Deletions mess up the Recordset,
  '  so force a Save or Cancel
  Me.cmdParkHere.SetFocus
  Me.cmdDelete.Enabled = False
  Me.cmdEdit.Enabled = False
  Me.cmdNew.Enabled = False
End If
```

Saving Changes Back to SQL Server

The logic behind saving the Order and Order Detail records is the same as shown earlier in this chapter when working with Access databases. The user clicks the Save button on the main form, and both the order and order details are written back to SQL Server. The only difference is how the order detail items are handled because they are based on a `Recordset` instead of a local table.

The `GetString` method of an ADO `Recordset` will package up the line items in a delimited string so that they can be passed back to SQL Server in the `@OrderDetails` parameter for the `procOrderInsert` stored procedure:

```
With Me.fsubOrderDetail.Form.Recordset
    ' GetString will fail if BOF or EOF is true
    .MoveFirst
    strDetails = .GetString( _
      StringFormat:=adClipString, _
      ColumnDelimeter:=",", _
      RowDelimeter:=";", _
      NullExpr:="NULL")
End With
```

List Box and Combo Box Techniques for Unbound ADPs

One of the trickier aspects of trying to create a viable unbound Access project is filling list boxes and combo boxes. Unlike forms, list boxes and combo boxes don't have a Recordset property, and you can't set the RowSource property to an unbound ADO Recordset. This leaves you with several choices:

- Set the RowSourceType property to Value List and supply the values for the combo box.
- Don't use Access combo boxes—use Microsoft Forms combo boxes, which have friendlier interfaces than Access combo boxes do for populating the list in code.
- Create local storage using XML and use a callback function to populate the controls.

The following sections examine each of these techniques in turn.

Using Value Lists

You have four choices when setting the RowSourceType property of a combo box:

- *Table/view/stored procedure*. The RowSource property is then set to the name of the table, view, or stored procedure.
- *Value List*. Displays a list of values supplied by you in a semicolon-delimited string for the RowSource property.
- *Field List*. Displays a list of column headings for the RowSource property.
- *Custom Function*. This option isn't listed but it's documented in the Help topic for RowSourceType. You can create a custom function, which must meet some stringent requirements, and have Access call into your function by naming it in the RowSourceType property.

The Value List setting is useful if you don't have a long list of values—it's limited to 2,048 characters. If that limitation is acceptable, it's relatively easy to create the delimited list in code and set the row source at runtime. The Enter event of a combo box is a good place for this code, because it will only fire if the combo box is used. If you only want to fill the list once, not every time the control is entered, use the load event of the form or just check first whether the list already has data:

Scaling Up with Unbound Access Applications

CHAPTER 11

575

11

SCALING UP WITH
UNBOUND ACCESS
APPLICATIONS

```
If Len(Me!cboCustomer.RowSource & "") > 0 Then
    GoTo ExitHere
End If
```

Then set up an ADO `Recordset` object to grab the data with which you want to fill the combo box. In this simple example, the CustomerID values are retrieved using a `SELECT` statement:

```
Set rst = New ADODB.Recordset
With rst
    .ActiveConnection = gcnn
    .CursorLocation = adUseClient
    .Open _
      Source:="SELECT CustomerID FROM Customers", _
      ActiveConnection:=gcnn, _
      CursorType:=adOpenStatic, _
      Options:=adCmdText
```

The ADO `Recordset` object's `GetString` method is then used to format the string. The `adClipString` value is the only one that works for that parameter, and it allows you to specify column and row delimiters. Semicolons are the documented delimiters for Value List row sources:

```
strList = rst.GetString(adClipString, _
    ColumnDelimeter:=";", RowDelimeter:=";")
```

Because the `RowSource` property can only take a maximum string length of 2KB, the `Left` function is used to strip any extra characters off the string and thus avoid a runtime error. The `Recordset` is then closed, and the memory is released:

```
    Me!cboCustomer.RowSource = Left(strList, 2048)
End With
rst.Close
Set rst = Nothing
```

You can also specify the number of columns you want in the combo box's ColumnCount property. For example, if you specify two columns and create a list such as "1;Mary;2;Andy", the numbers will appear in the first column and the names in the second column.

Obviously, this technique has its limitations—it's only going to handle combo or list boxes with a very limited amount of data. For unbound combo boxes that need to hold more data, you'll need to use one of the other techniques. If Microsoft expands the limit on the length of the row source property, as we hope it will in the next version of Access, creating value lists could become a very handy way of easily populating combo box lists.

Using Microsoft Forms

The main problem with trying to fill an Access combo box or list box programmatically is that there are no easy ways to do so. However, the Microsoft Forms package that ships with Office, which provides the forms used in Word and Excel, includes ActiveX controls that you can legally use as long as your users are running Microsoft Office. These ActiveX controls are part of the VBA environment for Office and for Access 2000. Figure 11.13 displays the list of Microsoft Forms ActiveX controls that are available by choosing Insert, ActiveX Control from the menu bar in a form's design view. Once you've inserted the ComboBox ActiveX control on your form, you'll automatically get a reference to the MSForms library, which provides properties, methods, and events for the control.

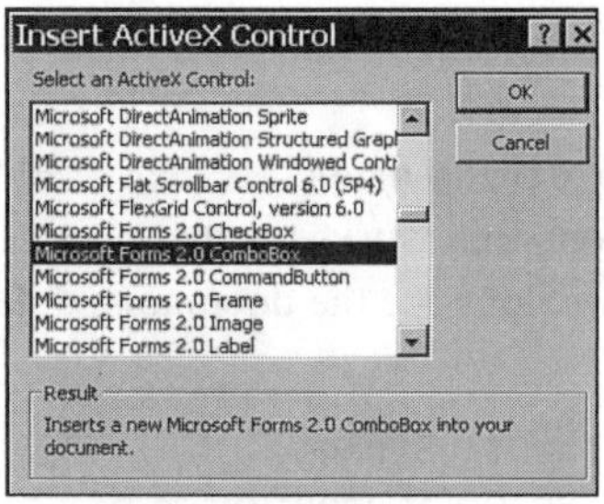

FIGURE 11.13
Listing the Microsoft Forms ActiveX controls.

The advantage of using the Microsoft Forms ComboBox control is that it is easy to add items to it using its AddItem method. The main disadvantage is that it adds additional overhead to your project (as does any ActiveX control). It also does not have the same properties, methods, and events that the Access built-in combo box controls possess, so working with it can be a bit tricky at first until you get familiar with it. In addition, the appearance of the control does not exactly match the look of the native Access combo box, as shown in Figure 11.14. For example, the selected item in the drop-down list is highlighted with the Windows highlight color (blue in a standard Windows setup), whereas Access list items are always highlighted in black.

One of its quirks is that you need to set an object variable to point to the control itself if you want to get early binding and Intellisense in your VBA code. Using Me.MyCombo.property won't work. Instead, you could use late binding with Me.MeCombo.Object.property, but the best way is to create a strongly typed variable and use early binding:

```
Dim cbo as MSForms.ComboBox
Set cbo = Me.cboOrder.Object
```

Then when you type the dot after Me.MyCombo, you'll get a nice drop-down list of properties and methods. There is no way to set many of the properties of the control in form design

Scaling Up with Unbound Access Applications

CHAPTER 11

577

11

SCALING UP WITH
UNBOUND ACCESS
APPLICATIONS

view—the properties just won't show up in the Access properties box and there isn't a custom property page for the control. However, you can examine the properties, methods, and events of the control in the Object Browser in the Visual Basic Editor once you have a reference to the control, and you can easily set the properties in code. For example, cboOrder in the header of frmOrder in the sample ADP is an MSForms combo box, and the following code runs in the Open event of that form:

```
Dim cbo As MSForms.ComboBox

Set cbo = Me.cboOrder.Object
With cbo
    .Font = "Tahoma"
    .Font.Size = 12
    .ColumnCount = 2
    .ColumnWidths = "1.25 in; 1.25 in"
    .ListWidth = "2.5 in"
End With
Set cbo = Nothing
```

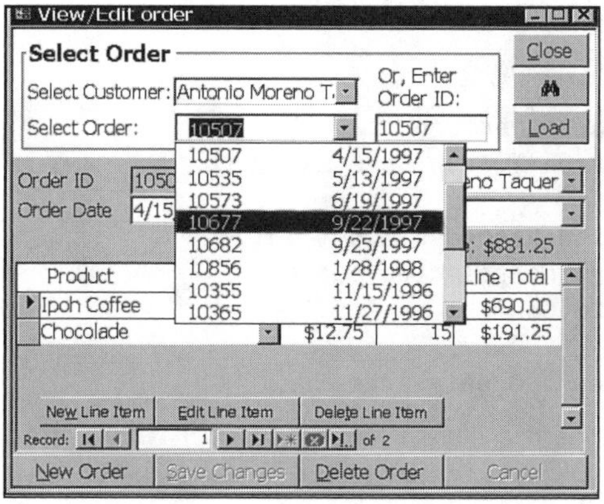

FIGURE 11.14

The Microsoft Forms combo box doesn't look exactly the same as an Access combo box.

To write event procedures for the control, select it from the object list in the upper-left corner of the module editor window and then select an event from the event list on the right.

Populating the combo box with data is the part that justifies all this extra inconvenience. Listing 11.18 shows the code from the cboOrder control's Enter event procedure. This code uses an ADO command object to open a Recordset based on a stored procedure that returns a list of all the order IDs and order dates for a given customer. The code then loops through the

Recordset and uses the AddItem method of the combo box to fill the list. This code runs each time the user enters the combo box after a customer has been selected, dynamically repopulating the list each time.

LISTING 11.18 The cboOrder_Enter Event Procedure Is Used to Populate the MSForms Combo Box Using AddItem

```
Private Sub cboOrder_Enter()
    On Error GoTo HandleErr
    ' Use an object variable
    '    to get intellisense and early binding
    Dim cbo As MSForms.ComboBox
    Dim cmd As ADODB.Command
    Dim rst As ADODB.Recordset

    ' Make sure a customer is selected
    If Len(Me.cboCustomer & "") = 0 Then
        MsgBox "Please select a customer.", , _
          "Can't display order list"
        Me.cboCustomer.SetFocus
        GoTo ExitHere
    End If
    ' Test for a valid connection
    If Not OpenConnection() Then GoTo ExitHere

    ' Open a client-side Recordset containing
    '    order info for the selected customer
    Set cmd = New ADODB.Command
    With cmd
      .Parameters.Append .CreateParameter( _
      "@CustomerID", _
      adWChar, _
      adParamInput, _
      5, _
      Me.cboCustomer)
      .CommandText = "procOrderListForCustomer"
      Set .ActiveConnection = gcnn
    End With
    Set rst = New ADODB.Recordset
    With rst
      .CursorLocation = adUseClient
      .LockType = adLockOptimistic
      .Open cmd, Options:=adCmdStoredProc
      Set .ActiveConnection = Nothing
    End With
    Set cmd = Nothing
```

Scaling Up with Unbound Access Applications

CHAPTER 11

579

11

SCALING UP WITH
UNBOUND ACCESS
APPLICATIONS

```
    ' Set a reference to the combo box
    '    and transfer data from the Recordset
    Set cbo = Me!cboOrder.Object
    If Not rst.EOF Then
        Do Until rst.EOF
            cbo.AddItem rst!OrderID
            ' Add date to the second column of the combo
            cbo.Column(1, cbo.ListCount - 1) = rst!OrderDate
            rst.MoveNext
        Loop
    End If
    rst.Close
    Set rst = Nothing

ExitHere:
    Exit Sub

HandleErr:
    MsgBox Err & ": " & Err.Description, , _
      "Error in cboOrder_Enter"
    Resume ExitHere
    Resume
End Sub
```

There's another, even easier technique you could use to fill the list of orders for the selected customer. Just like Access combo boxes, the MSForms combo box has a column property that allows you to refer to an individual item in the list by specifying an index for the column and, optionally, for the row of the data you want to extract. In Access, the property is read-only, but in the MSForms control it is read-write, allowing you to add items to the list. The code in Listing 11.18 uses this feature to add the date to the second column of each row. But wait, there's more! The column property can also be set to an array, thereby populating the list in one line of code. Fortunately, the ADO Recordset object has a GetRows method that returns an array that exactly matches what the column property of the combo box is looking for. So, once you have your Recordset, only a couple of lines of code are needed to populate the list:

```
Dim varList As Variant

varList = rst.GetRows
cbo.Column = varList
```

Using XML and a Callback Function

There's one important problem in ADPs when it comes to combo boxes: the lack of local Jet tables to use for storage of static lookup values. In the MDB example, the product list was downloaded once and reused every time the application was run, and the list was refreshed only occasionally, as needed. In the case of cboOrders, it wouldn't make much sense to cache the data locally because it probably changes very frequently (or else Northwind would have gone under long ago!). However, the Northwind employee roster and the product list, or even the list of countries used in frmOrderLocate, probably don't change that much. By storing data locally instead of hitting the server every time, a lot of network and server activity could be saved.

This section describes a set of functions and class modules that can be used generically to save data from any combo or list box row source to a local XML file using an ADO Recordset. But that is only half the battle. The other half is how to get the data into the combo boxes. Instead of using MSForms controls, this code takes advantage of a seldom-used option in Access combo boxes—the ability to create a custom callback function that Access will call repeatedly to populate a combo box list. For this to work, the function must meet a very precise set of requirements. Each time Access calls the function, it will be looking for a special kind of information—sometimes the number of rows, sometimes the number of columns, sometimes a unique ID for the control, and sometimes a particular value to place in one of the combo box list's cells. Each piece of data in the combo box is requested in a separate call to your function.

The format for these callback list-filling functions is described in the Access Help file, and many developers have written functions that work for a particular combo box based on a particular row source. The code presented here is intended to be generic enough to work for any type of row source except a value list or a field list—tables, views, stored procedures, and SQL statements all work fine. And one function can manage all the combo and list boxes in your application. The code is a bit complex, but you really don't need to remember how it works to make use of it in your ADP or MDB application. Just import the code from the example and enter the name of the callback function, UseLocalFile, in the Row Source Type property of any Access combo or list box. Before going through the combo box code, here's some more background on how the XML is used for persistent local storage.

Using XML for Local Storage

You're either tired by now of hearing about how XML will save the world or just back from a long vacation in Antarctica. But the fact is, XML does give you something useful that you haven't had before: A standard way to store and transmit data in text files or streams that include not only the data itself but also a specification of its structure and semantics. Chapter 13, "Internet Features in Access and SQL Server," describes the support for XML that was added to SQL Server 2000, and more is sure to come. This example doesn't take advantage of those new features, although it could have. Instead, ADO is used, which makes it very easy to move data back and forth between a text file and a Recordset.

Starting with ADO 2.1 (the version of ADO that ships with Office 2000), it has been possible to save a Recordset to an XML file with just a simple line of code and to open a Recordset based on that file later. ADO 2.5, which ships with Windows 2000, has added support for

Scaling Up with Unbound Access Applications

CHAPTER 11

581

11

SCALING UP WITH
UNBOUND ACCESS
APPLICATIONS

saving Recordsets in XML format to binary streams rather than to text files, which makes the use of XML in ADO much more scalable, because it eliminates the need for constant disk access. In Chapter 14, the code in this example is altered slightly to use ADO streams, created in middle-tier objects, for returning XML efficiently to client applications. In this chapter, the ability to save to disk is what you want because it allows you to create a cache of lookup data that persists between sessions of the application, thus allowing the application to avoid extra trips to the server.

Another file format, called *Advanced Data Tablegram* (ADTG), which was available in ADO 2.0 before support for XML was added, can also be used for saving recordsets to disk. This is an older, proprietary format, but it actually would work fine for this application. I chose XML because it can easily be viewed for debugging in IE 5 by simply double-clicking the file, and it is more likely that the data in XML could be useful elsewhere. Neither format is secure, however, so you may need to consider encryption/decryption or file-level security if the data is sensitive. For extremely sensitive data, you are probably better off just keeping it in SQL Server and absorbing the performance hit.

Generic VBA Code for Populating Controls

The sample application includes the public function UseLocalFile, shown in Listing 11.19, which is used to populate almost all the combo boxes in the application. The only exception is the MSForms combo box, cboOrder, discussed earlier in this chapter. This function can be used with any number of combo and list boxes on any number of forms. You can set all the usual properties to define your controls, including the RowSource property, column widths, and even column headings. Also, you can reset these properties in code if you need to. To make use of local XML storage, all you need to do is set the RowSourceType property of the control to UseLocalFile. This signals Access to use the specified function and its supporting code for populating the control.

LISTING 11.19   The UseLocalFile function is Called by Access to Populate Combo Box or List Box Controls

```
Public Function UseLocalFile( _
  ctl As Control, _
  UniqueID As Variant, _
  row As Variant, _
  col As Variant, _
  Code As Variant) As Variant

  On Error GoTo Handle_Err
  'To use this function, enter the function name
  '  for a control's Row Source Type,
```

LISTING 11.19 Continued

```
'   and enter a table/query/stored proc/view/SQL
'   as the Row Source.
'Uses a local XML file to store lookup data,
'   and loads a combo or list box with that data.
'The XML file name consists of the application file name,
'   an underscore character,
'   and the name of the control, with an extension of .xml.
'The XML file is placed in the same directory as the application.
'If the file isn't found, create it from an ADO Recordset.

'Procedure name used in error handler
Const conProcName As String = "UseLocalFile"

Dim rst As ADODB.Recordset
Dim strFile As String
Static scolControlsToFill As ControlsToFillLocally

Select Case Code
  Case acLBInitialize
    UseLocalFile = True
  Case acLBOpen
    'Open Recordset based on XML file, if found,
    '   or on control's row source.
    'Create XML file if necessary.
    'Use a custom collection of custom objects
    '   to maintain a separate Recordset for each control.
    'Return a unique ID based on
    '   the number of milliseconds since Windows started.
    UseLocalFile = HandleLocalStorage( _
      ctl, scolControlsToFill)
  Case acLBGetRowCount
    'During debugging or if error handlind is inadequate,
    '   the objects and variables could be reset
    '   after UniqueID's were already assigned.
    'Access retains the old UniqueID,
    '   so use it to recreate the objects.
    If scolControlsToFill Is Nothing And UniqueID <> 0 Then
      Call HandleLocalStorage( _
        ctl, scolControlsToFill, UniqueID)
    End If

    'Retrieve the correct custom object, using the UniqueID key.
    'And call its RowCount method,
    '   to get and return the control's row count.
    UseLocalFile = scolControlsToFill.Item( _
      CStr(UniqueID)).RowCount
```

Scaling Up with Unbound Access Applications

CHAPTER 11

583

11

SCALING UP WITH
UNBOUND ACCESS
APPLICATIONS

LISTING 11.19   Continued

```
        Case acLBGetColumnCount
          'Use the control's property setting
          UseLocalFile = ctl.ColumnCount
        Case acLBGetColumnWidth
          'Use the control's property settings
          UseLocalFile = -1
        Case acLBGetValue
          'During debugging or if error handlind is inadequate,
          '  the objects and variables could be reset
          '  after UniqueID's were already assigned.
          'Access retains the old UniqueID,
          '  so use it to recreate the objects.
          If scolControlsToFill Is Nothing And UniqueID <> 0 Then
            Call HandleLocalStorage( _
              ctl, scolControlsToFill, UniqueID)
          End If

          'Retrieve the correct custom object, using the UniqueID key.
          'And call its GetValue method,
          '  using the row and column data that Access passes in.
          UseLocalFile = scolControlsToFill.Item( _
            CStr(UniqueID)).GetValue(CLng(row), CLng(col))
        'acLBEnd doesn't pass in the UniqueID,
        '  but the undocumented acLBClose does.
        Case acLBClose
          'acLBEnd doesn't pass in the UniqueID,
          '  but the undocumented acLBClose does.
          'However, when requerying rather than closing,
          '  the UniqueID is always 0.
          If UniqueID <> 0 Then
              scolControlsToFill.Remove CStr(UniqueID)
          End If
      End Select

Exit_Here:
  Exit Function

Handle_Err:
  Select Case Err.Number
    Case 5, 91 'Invalid Argument, Object not set
      'Occurs when calling scolControlsToFill.Item,
      '  if project has been reset and the custom collection
      '  no longer contains an item with
```

LISTING 11.19   Continued

```
    '   the specified UniqueID key.
    'So, create new objects using the existing UniqueID,
    '   and try again.
    If UniqueID <> 0 Then
      Call HandleLocalStorage( _
        ctl, scolControlsToFill, UniqueID)
      Resume
    Else
      MsgBox Err.Number & ": " & Err.Description, _
        vbInformation, conProcName
    End If
  Case Else
      MsgBox Err.Number & ": " & Err.Description, _
        vbInformation, conProcName
  End Select
  UseLocalFile = 0
  Resume Exit_Here
  Resume
End Function
```

Once you put the name of this function in a combo box's Row Source Type property, Access will call the function repeatedly any time it needs to fill the combo box. Each time Access calls the function, it passes in code that signals what the function needs to do that time. The big Select Case block is used to implement to response to each kind of code that Access passes to the function. Access also passes in a reference to the control that is being populated.

The function first looks to see if an XML file with the data for the control already exists. It checks the directory that contains the application for a file that incorporates the name of the application and the name of the control. For instance, the example for this chapter is called ch11adp.adp, and it includes a combo box called cboCustomer. The XML file holding data for that combo box would be named ch11adp.adp_cboCustomer.XML. This means that all combo boxes in the application named cboCustomer would display the same data. Using this naming convention avoids redundant files for identical lists. If, however, you want to support several different lists for different sets of customers, be sure to give their respective combo boxes different names.

If the XML file is found, a Recordset is opened based on the file. If not, the Recordset is opened based on the RowSource property of the control, and that Recordset is saved to an XML file with the appropriate name. In either case, the Recordset is then used to populate the control. To refresh a list with newly added or modified data, just delete the associated XML file and requery the control, as shown in Listing 11.20. This creates a new XML file. An administrator can delete any of the XML files at any time and be assured that the next time they're needed, a fresh trip to the server will be made and new XML files will be created.

LISTING 11.20 The `RefreshControl` Function Ensures That a Fresh XML File Will Be Created

```
Public Function RefreshControl(ctl As Control)
  'For use with UseLocalFile
  'Call this function to refresh the data
  '  in a combo or list box.
  'Delete the XML file, if one exists.
  'Requerying the control then causes
  '  a new XML file to be created.
  On Error Resume Next
  Kill CurrentProject.Path & "\" _
    & CurrentProject.Name & "_" & ctl.Name & ".xml"
  ctl.Requery
End Function
```

Because Access makes a separate call to the `UseLocalFile` function to populate each cell in each combo or list box, the one generic function must have a way of keeping track of the various `Recordsets` for all the open combo and list boxes that are using the function. This is accomplished by using a pair of class modules.

The first class module, `ControlToFillLocally`, shown in Listing 11.21, can potentially be used to create many objects—one for each control using the `UseLocalFile` function. Each `ControlToFillLocally` object stores the `Recordset` for the associated control and a Boolean flag indicating whether column headings are used in the control. `ControlToFillLocally` objects also have a `RowCount` property that returns a value based on the `RecordCount` property of the `Recordset`, plus one more row if column headings are in use. A `GetValue` method takes two arguments that specify the desired row and column, and it returns the value that belongs in that cell, again adjusting for whether column headings are used in that control.

LISTING 11.21 This Class Module Is Used to Create an Object for Each Control That Uses a Local XML File

```
Private mrst As ADODB.Recordset
Private mfColumnHeads As Boolean

Public Function GetValue( _
  lngRow As Long, lngCol As Long) As Variant
    If lngRow = 0 And mfColumnHeads Then
      'Return field names for column headings.
      GetValue = mrst.Fields(lngCol).Name
    Else
      'row is 0-based, AbsolutePosition is 1-based
      mrst.AbsolutePosition = _
        lngRow + 1 + mfColumnHeads
```

LISTING 11.21 Continued

```
        GetValue = mrst.Fields(lngCol).Value
    End If
End Function

Public Property Set Recordset( _
  rst As ADODB.Recordset)
    Set mrst = rst
End Property

Public Property Let ColumnHeads( _
  fColumnHeads As Boolean)
    mfColumnHeads = fColumnHeads
End Property

Public Property Get RowCount() As Long
    RowCount = mrst.RecordCount - mfColumnHeads
End Property

Private Sub Class_Terminate()
    Set mrst = Nothing
End Sub
```

The second class module, `ControlsToFillLocally`, shown in Listing 11.22, defines a custom collection that's used to hold and retrieve the other objects. When Access opens each combo or list box, it requires the `UseLocalFile` function to provide a unique ID. `UseLocalFile` calls a private function, `HandleLocalStorage`, shown in Listing 11.23, which does the actual work of creating the `Recordsets` and the XML files. `HandleLocalStorage` also assigns each control its unique ID using the `timeGetTime` Windows API call, which returns the number of milliseconds since Windows was started. This unique ID is used as the key for each `ControlToFillLocally` object that is added to the custom collection. The unique ID is also passed back to Access, and, fortunately, Access passes that ID back into the function any subsequent time it needs a piece of data for that combo or list box. Access also passes in a control object that points to the control it is working with.

LISTING 11.22 This Custom Collection Class Is Used to Add, Retrieve, and Remove the `ControlToFill` Objects

```
Private mcolControls As Collection

Public Function Add(ID As String, _
  fColumnHeads As Boolean, _
  rst As ADODB.Recordset)
    On Error GoTo Handle_Error
```

Scaling Up with Unbound Access Applications

CHAPTER 11

587

11

SCALING UP WITH
UNBOUND ACCESS
APPLICATIONS

LISTING 11.22 Continued

```
    Dim ctl As ControlToFillLocally
    Set ctl = New ControlToFillLocally
    ctl.ColumnHeads = fColumnHeads
    Set ctl.Recordset = rst
    mcolControls.Add ctl, ID
Exit_Here:
    Exit Function
Handle_Error:
    Select Case Err.Number
      Case 457    'duplicate key
        'Occasionally, the Add method
        '  can be called twice for the same item.
        'Just ignore the error.
      Case Else
        Err.Raise Err.Number, _
          Err.Source, Err.Description
    End Select
End Function

Private Sub Class_Initialize()
    Set mcolControls = New Collection
End Sub

Public Function Item(ID As String) _
  As ControlToFillLocally
    On Error Resume Next
    Set Item = mcolControls.Item(ID)
End Function

Public Sub Remove(ID As String)
    On Error Resume Next
    mcolControls.Remove ID
End Sub

Private Sub Class_Terminate()
    Set mcolControls = Nothing
End Sub
```

LISTING 11.23 This Private Function Is Called by UseLocalFile to Handle the Creation of Recordsets and XML Files

```
'Timer might give duplicate ID values on a fast computer,
'  so use the more precise timeGetTime
Private Declare Function timeGetTime Lib "winmm.dll" _
  As Long
```

LISTING 11.23   Continued

```
Private Function HandleLocalStorage( _
  ByRef ctl As Control, _
  ByRef colControlsToFill As ControlsToFillLocally, _
  Optional ByVal lngUniqueID As Long) As Long

  On Error GoTo Handle_Err
  Const conProcName As String = _
    "HandleLocalStorage"
  Dim strFile As String
  Dim rst As ADODB.Recordset
  Dim lngID As Long

  'Locate XML file in the application directory,
  '  and name it based on the project name
  '  plus the name of the control.
  strFile = CurrentProject.Path & "\" _
  & CurrentProject.Name & "_" & ctl.Name & ".XML"

  'Create a client-side Recordset.
  Set rst = New ADODB.Recordset
  rst.CursorLocation = adUseClient
  rst.CursorType = adOpenStatic
  rst.LockType = adLockReadOnly
  'Find or create the XML file,
  '  and open the Recordset.
  If Len(Dir(strFile)) > 0 Then
      'File was found. Open Recordset from the file.
      rst.Open Source:=strFile, Options:=adCmdFile
  Else
      'File wasn't found.
      'Open Recordset using the Row Source,
      '  and create the XML file.
      Set rst.ActiveConnection = _
        CurrentProject.Connection
      rst.Open Source:=ctl.RowSource
      rst.Save strFile, adPersistXML
      Set rst.ActiveConnection = Nothing
  End If

  'If the project is reset
  '  (for example, during debugging)
  '  and the objects need to be recreated,
  '   the optional parameter, lngUniqueID,
  '   has a non-zero value. In that case, use it.
  'Otherwise, create a unique ID based on
```

LISTING 11.23 Continued

```
'    the number of milliseconds
'    since Windows started.
If lngUniqueID <> 0 Then
  lngID = lngUniqueID
Else
  lngID = timeGetTime
End If


'Add to the collection of custom objects.
'   These objects hold the Recordsets
'   for controls being populated.
'Store whether control should have
'   column headings. If yes, field names
'   are used as the first row returned.
 If colControlsToFill Is Nothing Then
    Set colControlsToFill = _
      New ControlsToFillLocally
 End If
 Call colControlsToFill.Add( _
   CStr(lngID), ctl.ColumnHeads, rst)


 'Return the unique ID
 HandleLocalStorage = lngID

Exit_Here:
  Exit Function


Handle_Err:
  Select Case Err.Number
    Case Else
        Err.Raise Err.Number, _
          conProcName, Err.Description
  End Select
  Resume Exit_Here
End Function
```

For each control that specifies UseLocalFile in its RowSourceType property, Access first passes a code of acLBInitialize to the UseLocalFile function. All the function has to do then is return a value of True, letting Access know that it is available to process requests.

Next, Access calls the function passing in a code of acLBOpen. This time, Access expects to have the UniqueID parameter assigned a value. The function uses this opportunity to call HandleLocalStorage, which takes care of creating the XML file if necessary, opening the

Recordset, creating or referencing the ControlsToFillLocally collection, and calling the collection's Add method to create a new ControlToFillLocally object with a unique key that is returned to Access as the UniqueID parameter.

When Access calls the function and passes in a code of acLBGetRowCount, it also passes in the UniqueID parameter, which is used to retrieve the correct ControlToFillLocally object from the collection and call its RowCount property's Property Get procedure. This part of the code also includes some defensive programming to allow for the possibility that the VBA project may have been reset through debugging or faulty error handling. If so, a new ControlToFillLocally object is created with the UniqueID parameter that Access is expecting for that control. The HandleLocalStorage function has an optional UniqueID parameter that is used only when such a problem requires an object to be re-created.

Calls to UseLocalFile that pass in the code acLBGetColumnCount are easy to handle, because they also pass a control reference to the ctl parameter. The function can simply return the value of ctl.ColumnCount. It is possible to use a list-filling function to override the property settings for the column count and column widths, but here the settings provided at design time are used. So, when Access passes in acLBGetColumnWidth, the function returns the special value –1. This instructs Access to use the column widths defined in the control's ColumnWidths property.

Access makes repeated calls to the function to retrieve data to be displayed in the control, passing in a code of acLBGetValue each time. If there are many rows in the control, Access may wait to retrieve them until the user scrolls down in the list. Each time the acLBGetValue code is passed in, Access also supplies the row and column numbers identifying the piece of data it is looking for. UseLocalFile passes those values along to the GetValue method of the appropriate ControlToFillLocally object, which it retrieves from the custom collection using the UniqueID parameter value, which is also supplied by Access.

Finally, when Access is ready to close or requery the control, it passes in a code of acLBClose. Unfortunately, the use of this code is not documented in the Help file. Through trial and error, you can discover that a UniqueID value of 0 is passed in when the control is being requeried, and the actual UniqueID value is passed in when the form is actually being unloaded. This is very useful, because that UniqueID value can then be used to remove the ControlToFillLocally object that was created for that control from the custom collection. With no pointers left to that object, it is destroyed. There is also a documented code value of acLBEnd, but I found this useless because a UniqueID value isn't passed in with it, and the function runs fine without handling it at all.

Try It Out

We've tested this code in a couple of projects and found it to be reliable. The internals are a bit complex, but you'll find that it is easy to use without remembering what's going on behind the scenes. Just import the modules—basLocalStorage, ControlsToFillLocally, and `ControlToFillLocally`—into your project and enter `UseLocalFile` for the row source type of any combo or list boxes you want populated using local XML data. The sample application includes several combo boxes that you can inspect. In Chapter 14, a small change is made to the section of the function `HandleLocalStorage` that actually goes out to SQL Server for the data. In that example, instead of opening a connection to the server locally, the code uses a middle-tier object to retrieve a stream of XML data.

Summary

When designing an Access/SQL Server application, you need to plan for growth. The most efficient way to build a scalable, high-performance Access front end to SQL Server is to use stored procedures in SQL Server and unbound forms in Access. A single ADO `Connection` object can be used to keep connections to SQL Server at a minimum. Access databases (MDBs) provide the most built-in functionality—you can take advantage of local tables to hold data for combo and list boxes as well as for subforms, and pass-through queries provide an efficient way of running stored procedures. When editing data using unbound forms, you need to handle concurrency issues yourself. Setting up a ConcurrencyID column in SQL Server is an efficient way of handling the write-after-write conflicts.

Although Access projects do not have the same flexibility as Access databases in terms of local storage, you can work around the problem with disconnected ADO `Recordsets` and XML. Even bound ADPs offer many of the advantages of unbound applications because of the way they make use of the ADO cursor engine to cache data and to manage updates. Perhaps in future versions of Access there will be more support in Access projects for binding disconnected `Recordsets` directly to forms without losing updatablily. In the meantime, Access provides a rich set of options for building highly scalable SQL Server applications.

Building Access Reports from SQL Server Data

IN THIS CHAPTER

The same principal rule applies to reports that applies to reports based on an entire data set. In those situations where fetching less data isn't an option, the goal is to try to do as much of the raw data processing as possible on the server, not on the client, sending only the results across the network. In this chapter you'll learn how to get the most out of Access reports when reporting on SQL Server data, whether you're using an Access project or an Access database. In addition, you'll also see how you can report on multidimensional data from an Online Analytical Processing (OLAP) cube with Access.

General Guidelines for Creating Efficient Reports

You can do several things to speed up reports by optimizing your data storage and by making intelligent choices when you design the reports themselves.

Fetch Less Data

Do not select all the rows and columns from a table or view. Instead, select only the rows and columns needed for the report.

Tune the SQL Server Tables

If the underlying tables do not have indexes, a table scan may be necessary in order to retrieve the data. All fields used for filtering or sorting should be properly indexed.

Preaggregate Data with Views

Preaggregating data can significantly speed up reports because summary data is computed on the server, not the client, and only the aggregated results are sent over the network.

A view is a saved SELECT statement and can be used just like a table. The advantage of creating views is that queries involving complex joins and aggregates can be created on the server. Users can select columns and rows from the view in exactly the same way they select columns and rows from a table, without having to understand Transact-SQL join notation.

Preaggregate Data with Stored Procedures

A stored procedure supports parameters and can return results that can be used as the basis for reports. All data processing in a stored procedure is done on the server, and only the resultset is returned. In addition, a plan is cached that can be reused for subsequent calls to the stored procedure. Complex reports make many calls to the server for data, so the benefit of reusing execution plans with stored procedures is significant. Stored procedures can be used directly as the RecordSource of a report in an Access project (ADP) and indirectly through a pass-through query in an Access database (MDB).

Preaggregate Data with User-Defined Functions

New in SQL Server 2000, user-defined functions can return tables. This lets users combine the performance of a stored procedure with the flexibility of a view. A table-returning function can be queried just like a view and can accept parameters just like a stored procedure. User-defined functions are discussed in Chapter 9, "Creating and Optimizing Views," and later in this chapter.

Using Access Features to Filter Data

In addition to fine-tuning things on the SQL Server side, you can also use the tools available in Access to filter data, following the golden rule of "fetching less data." The following are some techniques you can use that apply to both ADPs and MDBs. Other techniques specific to one or the other will be covered later in this chapter.

Opening a Report Using `DoCmd.OpenReport`

The `DoCmd` object's `OpenReport` method has two parameters that limit the data being returned in the report: `WhereCondition` and `FilterName`. These allow you to use the same report to display many different subsets of records, instead of creating separate reports.

Using `WhereCondition`

Use the `WhereCondition` parameter of `DoCmd.OpenReport` to specify a SQL `WHERE` clause. The `WHERE` clause is incorporated into the query that is sent to SQL Server, and only data that meets the `WhereCondition` criteria is returned to Access. You can collect input from a form with a combo box to select a particular supplier, as shown in Figure 12.1. The bound column of the combo box is SupplierID.

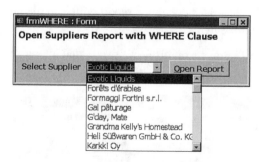

FIGURE 12.1

Collecting the information for the WHERE *clause from a combo box on a form.*

12

BUILDING ACCESS
REPORTS FROM
SQL SERVER DATA

The Open Report button has the following code, which opens the report based on the selected supplier (if one is selected) or simply opens the report displaying all records:

```
If IsNull(Me.cboSupplier) Then
    DoCmd.OpenReport "rptSuppliersList", View:=acViewPreview
Else
    DoCmd.OpenReport "rptSuppliersList", View:=acViewPreview, _
      WhereCondition:="SupplierID=" & Me!cboSupplier
End If
Me.cboSupplier = Null
```

Figure 12.2 shows the report opened with the WHERE clause.

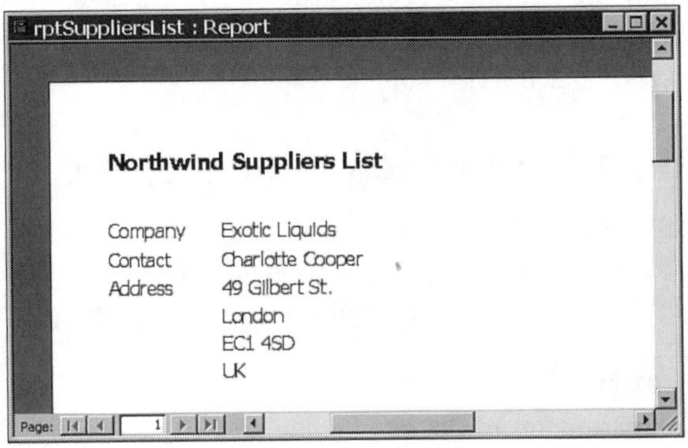

FIGURE 12.2
The report opened with a single record selected.

Selecting Multiple Items Using the SQL IN Clause

The preceding example demonstrates opening a report with a single item selected in the WHERE clause. But what about multiple items?

The form shown in Figure 12.3 has a multiselect list box that allows the user to select several records to print.

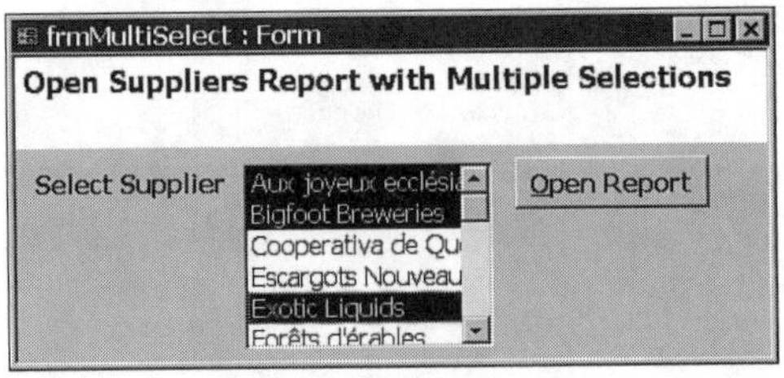

FIGURE 12.3
A form with a multiselect list box.

The OnClick event of the Open Report button opens the report after first calling the BuildWhere() function to construct the WHERE clause by using the SQL IN() clause, as shown in Listing 12.1.

LISTING 12.1   Building the SQL IN Clause to Specify Multiple Items for the Report

```
Public Function BuildWhere( _
  lst As ListBox, _
  strBoundCol As String, _
  Optional strDelimiter As String = "") As String
    Dim varItem As Variant
    Dim strWhere As String

    If lst.MultiSelect = 0 Then
    ' Single-select list box
        If IsNull(lst.Value) Then
            'Show all items by using criterion that is always true
            ' (using "True" won't work on some database engines)
            BuildWhere = "1=1"
        Else
            BuildWhere = _
                strBoundCol & "=" & strDelimiter & lst.Value & strDelimiter
        End If
    Else 'Multi-Select
        If lst.ItemsSelected.Count = 0 Then
            'Return all items if nothing is selected
            BuildWhere = "1=1"
        Else
            'Build In clause.
            'Cycle through the ItemsSelected
            '  and build a comma-delimited list
            '  of the values in the bound column
            With lst
                For Each varItem In .ItemsSelected
                    strWhere = strWhere & ", " & strDelimiter _
                        & .ItemData(varItem) & strDelimiter
                Next varItem
            End With
            'Strip off the leading ", "
            strWhere = Mid(strWhere, 3)
            'Complete the syntax
            strWhere = strBoundCol & " In(" & strWhere & ")"
            BuildWhere = strWhere
        End If
    End If
End Function
```

The `FilterName` parameter of `DoCmd.OpenReport` is similar to the `WhereCondition` parameter. It allows you to specify a saved query that supplies the criteria for the report. Most of the time, it's easier to use a variation of one of the `WhereCondition` techniques shown previously because it's more flexible and doesn't require that a `WHERE` clause always be specified. In other words, using `WhereCondition` gives you the option of opening the report and displaying all the records, whereas using the `FilterName` does not.

Dynamically Changing the `RecordSource`

Another option is to change the `RecordSource` property of the report at runtime. You can create an entire SQL statement to base the report on, not just a `WHERE` clause or filter. Here's an example:

```
Private Sub Report_Open(Cancel As Integer)
    Me.RecordSource = _
      "SELECT ... _
        & " FROM ... "_
        & " WHERE ... "
End Sub
```

If you are using an Access database (MDB), you could also change the SQL of a saved query that a report is based on. This technique is especially useful if you are using pass-through queries, which cannot handle parameters in the same way regular Access queries can. Instead, you can just change the SQL of the pass-through query to include the correct literal parameter values. Changing the SQL that defines a query is easy to do using DAO or ADO code, as shown in the section on pass-through queries in Chapter 5, "Linking to SQL Server Using Access Databases (MDBs)."

Beware of Differences Between MDBs and ADPs

When the report opens, you can use VBA to set the `Filter` and `FilterOn` properties of a report:

```
Private Sub Report_Open(Cancel As Integer)
    Me.Filter = "SupplierID = " & Forms!frmWhere!cboSupplier
    Me.FilterOn = True
End Sub
```

This may seem like a good idea, and in MDBs it works fine. The Jet database engine helps Access create a query sent over ODBC to SQL Server that includes the specified criteria. In ADPs, however, all the data in the `RecordSource` is retrieved and a pretty weak attempt is made to apply the filter on the client. This is covered in more detail later in this chapter.

In an Access database (MDB), you could also use a parameterized query as the RecordSource of the report, with a parameter that references controls on a dialog form. Here's an example:

```
SELECT * FROM Suppliers
WHERE SupplierID = Forms!frmWhere!cboSupplier
```

You can save this in a query in an MDB that has a linked table called Suppliers, or you can just type it into the RecordSource property as a SQL string (in which case Access still saves it as a hidden query). But in an ADP, this won't work. You don't have local queries in an ADP, and if you type this in as a RecordSource, Access will send it unchanged to SQL Server, where Forms!frmWhere!cboSupplier will be meaningless. In ADPs, you need to be sure that any references to controls on forms are resolved on the client before being sent to SQL Server. You learn how later in this chapter.

Apart from being unusable in ADPs, these two techniques share another disadvantage. They tightly couple the report to a particular form. By using the WhereCondition parameter of DoCmd.OpenForm instead, you can use the same generic report in many different ways and open it from many different forms. In general, using WhereCondition is the best way to filter a report, but it won't work if your report is based on a stored procedure. Later in the chapter, you learn how to base reports on stored procedures in both MDBs and ADPs, using different techniques in each case.

Reporting in Access Projects

Reporting in an Access ADP is a little different from reporting in an Access MDB. You must pay attention to the SQL syntax used, if your RecordSource is a SQL statement. For example, Transact-SQL can't process any references to controls on forms the way Access SQL can—it simply doesn't know anything about Forms!MyForm!MyControl. However, you do have some new report properties not found in Access MDBs that allow you to get around this limitation and filter data dynamically:

- The Input Parameters property allows you to send parameter values to a query or stored procedure.
- The ServerFilter property allows you to filter data at the server before it is returned to populate the report.

Using Input Parameters

Use the Input Parameters property to specify parameter values for a SQL statement or for a stored procedure that's the RecordSource of your report. A form is generally the best way to collect the parameter values from the user.

Setting Up the Form

To select a particular customer for a report, create a combo box with a bound column of CustomerID and a Print button to open the report, as on the sample form frmCustomerTotals. The code in the Click event of the Print button simply opens the report:

```
DoCmd.OpenReport "rptCustomerTotals", acViewPreview
```

As you will see in the following section, you design the report to pick up a parameter from this form.

Setting Up the Report

The rptCustomerTotals report has a SELECT statement with a WHERE clause that terminates in a question mark:

```
WHERE Customers.CustomerID = ?
```

Here is what the entire query assigned to the report's RecordSource property looks like:

```
SELECT Customers.CustomerID, Customers.CompanyName, Customers.ContactName,
  SUM(CONVERT (money, [Order Details].UnitPrice * [Order Details].Quantity *
  (1 - [Order Details].Discount) / 100) * 100) AS Total
FROM Customers
INNER JOIN Orders ON Customers.CustomerID = Orders.CustomerID
INNER JOIN [Order Details] ON Orders.OrderID = [Order Details].OrderID
WHERE (Customers.CustomerID = ?)
GROUP BY Customers.CompanyName, Customers.CustomerID, Customers.ContactName
```

You define where the parameter will be resolved by setting the Input Parameters property. Note that you must define the data type of the data being fetched from the form (varchar) and set a reference to the form control:

```
CustomerID varchar=Forms!frmCustomerTotals!cboCustomer
```

When the report opens, the query runs and looks to the form to supply its parameters. This technique tightly couples this report to a certain form. Using the WhereCondition parameter of DoCmd.OpenReport avoids this tight coupling between the form and the report, but the advantage of using the Input Parameters property is that it allows you to work with stored procedures in an ADP. In the example, a SQL statement is used with a question mark to create a parameter.

Another option with Input Parameters is to prompt the user for a parameter value using the standard Access Enter-Parameter-Value dialog box. Just as with Access queries in an MDB, you can enclose a prompt in brackets and Access will use your prompt in the dialog box. For example, you could use the following in the Input Parameters property:

```
CustomerID varchar=[Please enter Customer ID:]
```

When the form opens, the dialog shown in Figure 12.4 will be displayed.

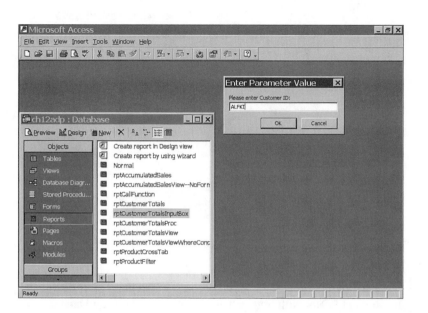

FIGURE 12.4
Entering the CustomerID *parameter in an input box.*

Using Server Filter By Form

The Server Filter By Form property lets a user dynamically filter records on a form by selecting items from combo boxes that Access creates and populates automatically for each text box on the form. The user then can pass the server filter to a report that is based on the same query as the form. One limitation of using Server Filter By Form is that the record source cannot be a stored procedure. If you need to use a stored procedure, use Input Parameters.

Setting Up the Form

The form is bound to the same query as the report. In this example, the query is based on a join between the Products and the Categories tables. When you set the Server Filter By Form property to Yes, the form is automatically put into a Filter By Form view when you open the form. The user is able to select from combo box lists to filter the data, as shown in Figure 12.5. You can control the behavior of the Server Filter By Form combo boxes by setting the Filter Lookup property of the text boxes on the form to Always. This causes the combo boxes on the form to display all the distinct values from the underlying tables instead of the default choices—Is Null and Is Not Null—thus making it easy for the user to enter valid choices.

FIGURE 12.5

Form view of a form with the Server Filter By Form property set to Yes.

Figure 12.6 shows setting up the Filter Lookup property. Selecting Never causes the list to include only Is Null and Is Not Null, rather than actual data. Choosing Database Default uses the setting selected in the Tools, Options dialog box on the Edit/Find tab, under Show List of Values In. This page of the Options dialog box is shown in Figure 12.7. Checking the Records at Server box causes controls that have their Filter Lookup property set to Database Default to get fully populated combo boxes in Server Filter By Form view. That page of the Options dialog box also allows you to set a maximum size for the list. If the complete list would have more items than the maximum allowed, only the two standard choices (Is Null and Is Not Null) are displayed if a control's Filter Lookup property is set to Database Default.

Once the form is set up this way, it will be in Server Filter By Form view when it's opened, showing the last filter that was selected. You can use the following code in the Load event of the form to clear any previously set filters so that the form is blank when opened:

```
Private Sub Form_Load()
    Me.ServerFilter = ""
End Sub
```

The filtered data is then fetched from the server and displayed on the form when the user clicks the Apply Filter button on the toolbar. All command buttons are disabled until the filter is applied—once it is, the user can print a report showing just the filtered data by clicking a button that opens a report that has been designed to pick up the form's server filter:

```
Private Sub cmdReport_Click()
    On Error Resume Next
    DoCmd.OpenReport "rptProductList", acViewPreview
End Sub
```

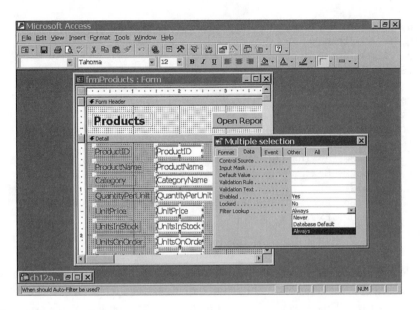

FIGURE 12.6
Setting the Filter Lookup property.

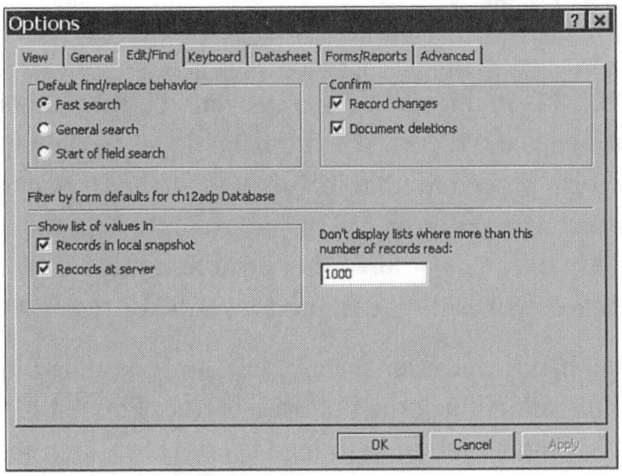

FIGURE 12.7
Setting the Records at Server property.

Setting Up the Report

The report is bound to the same data source as the form. The report's Open event procedure applies the form's ServerFilter to the report:

```
Private Sub Report_Open(Cancel As Integer)
On Error GoTo HandleErr
```

```
    ' Synchronize the report's ServerFilter with the form
    Dim str As String
    str = Forms!frmproducts.ServerFilter
    Me.ServerFilter = str

ExitHere:
    Exit Sub
HandleErr:
    Select Case Err
        Case 2450    ' the report is opened without the form
            Resume Next
        Case Else
            MsgBox Err & ", " & Err.Description, , "rptProductList"
            Resume ExitHere
    End Select
End Sub
```

This code includes an error handler that opens the report with no filter if the form is not open. Another possible cause of errors in the report would be when the user selects a filter that does not return any rows. This is handled by writing code in the report's NoData event:

```
Private Sub Report_NoData(Cancel As Integer)
    Cancel = True
    MsgBox "No data to report."
End Sub
```

Anytime you use code like this in a report's NoData event, be sure to also use error handling in the code in the form that opens the report. If there is no data and the report is canceled by code in the NoData event, the form procedure that included the DoCmd.OpenReport method (probably the Click event of a button) will get error 2501. The example kept the code simple by using On Error Resume Next to skip over this or any other error and just exit the procedure. Figure 12.8 shows the report opened with only the filtered records for the Produce category displayed.

Server Filter By Form is a handy end-user feature, but don't be lulled into thinking that it adds any efficiency to your application—just the opposite is true. Populating all those combo boxes can take more work than would be required to load every record into the form and the report. There is no way around this—if you want values in all those combo boxes, the form has to run extra queries just to populate them in addition to the query that is run when the user applies the server filter. A potentially more efficient way of filtering data for reports is to use the ServerFilter property, setting it before the form opens.

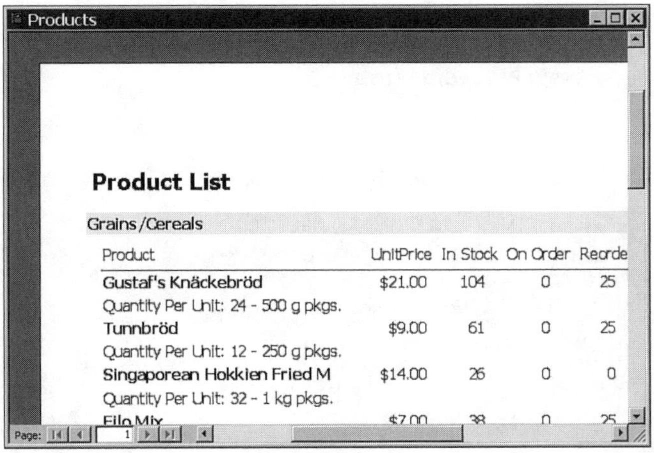

FIGURE 12.8
The Product List report, where only the filtered records are displayed.

Using the `ServerFilter` Property

In the previous example, a report's `ServerFilter` property was set to equal the `ServerFilter` property of a form that had been opened in Server Filter By Form view. This is easy to set up, but using Server Filter By Form can be quite inefficient and gives you limited control over the dialog form being used to build the filter. An alternative is to build your own server filter in the Open event of a report. This gives you complete freedom to use your own dialog form or to base the filter on information drawn from other sources, and it avoids the potential inefficiency of populating all those combo boxes that Access loads in Server Filter By Form view.

Setting Up the Report

This example, rather than using any form at all, prompts the user with a simple input box in the Open event of rptProductServerFilter, as shown in Figure 12.9.

Here's the code from the report's Open event procedure:

```
Private Sub Report_Open(Cancel As Integer)
    Dim strPriceCriteria
    ' Get the price range of products to display
    strPriceCriteria = InputBox( _
      "Enter the price range of products to display.", _
      Title:="Filter Products by Price", _
      Default:="Between $5.00 and $10.00")
```

```
' Set the ServerFilter
Me.ServerFilter = _
    "UnitPrice " & strPriceCriteria
End Sub
```

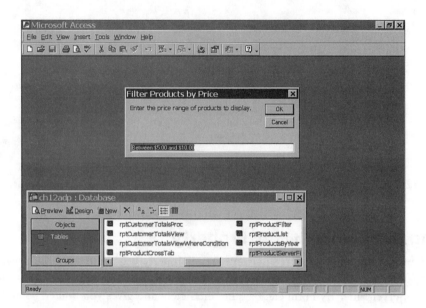

FIGURE 12.9
Prompting the user for a range of values for a server filter.

Rather than using the input box shown in this example (which leaves you vulnerable to the user entering valid syntax), you could open your own unbound form in dialog mode, gather whatever information you need from the user, and then build the appropriate server filter. Access will send a SQL statement to the server that requests only those records that meet your filter criteria.

The `Filter` and `FilterOn` Properties

You may have experience using the `Filter` and `FilterOn` properties in Access forms and reports. You set the `Filter` property to a valid `WHERE` clause and set the `FilterOn` property to `True`. These properties are still available when you are working with SQL Server data in an Access project. However, it is rarely advisable to use these properties instead of `ServerFilter`.

Unlike `ServerFilter`, the `Filter` criteria is applied on the Access client, not on SQL Server. All the data specified in the report's `RecordSource` will be returned over the network, and Access will then apply whatever criteria is contained in the filter if the `FilterOn` property is set to `True`.

There are two important disadvantages to using these properties:

- First, there's the inefficiency of having SQL Server process and return more records than you need.

- The second problem is that some criteria that seem perfectly valid will not be handled properly.

The report, rptProductFilter, runs the following code when it opens:

```
Private Sub Report_Open(Cancel As Integer)
    Dim strPriceCriteria
    ' Get the price range of products to display
    strPriceCriteria = InputBox( _
      "Enter the price range of products to display.", _
      Title:="Filter Products by Price", _
      Default:="Between $5.00 and $10.00")

    ' Set the Filter and turn it on
    Me.Filter = _
      "UnitPrice " & strPriceCriteria
    Me.FilterOn = True
End Sub
```

You'll find that if you run this report and accept the default value in the input box, `"Between $5.00 and $10.00"`, Access will raise the strange error shown in Figure 12.10.

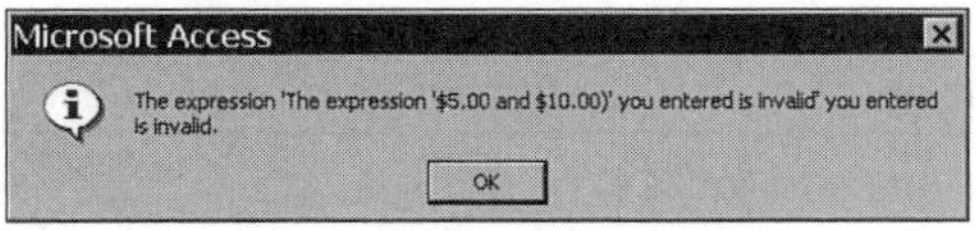

FIGURE 12.10
The bizarre error message raised when using the `Filter` *property.*

Even simplifying the expression to `"> $5.00"` will produce a similar error. But if you enter `"> 5"`, you'll get the expected results. The lesson here is that the filtering capabilities available on the client in an Access project are very limited. You can't assume that the full range of criteria expressions you are used to being able to use in Access will work.

So, why would you ever need to use the `Filter` property rather than `ServerFilter`? Well, it's a stretch to come up with a good reason, but consider the fact that the `Filter` property can be used with RecordSources that are stored procedures. `ServerFilter` cannot be used with stored procedures. In general, it's best to build parameters into your stored procedures and to use the report's Input Parameters property. However, if you want to use a stored procedure that you don't have permission to change and can't create your own, you might want to use `Filter` and `FilterOn`. Just be sure to test thoroughly that Access is able to process your filter expressions!

Basing Reports on Views

You can base a report on a view whether you're using an Access project or an Access database. A view is a saved SELECT statement and can be used just like a table. There are several advantages to using views as the basis for reports:

- Queries involving complex joins and aggregates can be created on the server.
- Users can select data from views the same way they do with tables, selecting columns and rows and using WHERE and ORDER BY clauses.
- Views create another layer of abstraction between the tables and the application. Users don't have to understand Transact-SQL join notation or aggregates in order to work with the data effectively. A view can provide a simplified interface to complex data.

The main limitation of views is that they can't accept parameters. However, there are workarounds, such as using a SQL statement with a WHERE clause when selecting from the view, opening the report using WhereCondition, or using a server filter. All these options have the same result: Access sends a query to SQL Server that selects from the view and applies the criteria on the server.

Creating a Simple View to Aggregate Data

The view shown in Listing 12.2 totals all the orders for all the customers. The query joins the Customers, Orders, and Order Details tables, performs a calculation on the UnitPrice, Quantity, and Discount fields, and aggregates the results into a sum.

LISTING 12.2   The Definition of the vwCustomerOrderTotals View

```
CREATE VIEW dbo.vwCustomerOrderTotals
AS
SELECT dbo.Customers.CustomerID, dbo.Customers.CompanyName,
  SUM(CONVERT(money, dbo.[Order Details].UnitPrice *
  dbo.[Order Details].Quantity * (1 - dbo.[Order Details].Discount))
    ) AS Total
FROM dbo.Customers
INNER JOIN
  dbo.Orders ON dbo.Customers.CustomerID = dbo.Orders.CustomerID
INNER JOIN
  dbo.[Order Details] ON dbo.Orders.OrderID =
  dbo.[Order Details].OrderID
GROUP BY dbo.Customers.CompanyName, dbo.Customers.CustomerID
```

The output for the view is displayed in Figure 12.11. Note that three columns are used: CustomerID, CompanyName, and Total.

FIGURE 12.11
The Datasheet view of the vwCustomerOrderTotals view.

The view can be queried just like a table with a SELECT statement and a WHERE clause. The form shown in Figure 12.12 will print out the results for the selected customer or for all customers if none are selected.

FIGURE 12.12
Selecting a customer (or not) to print the results from a view.

The code that runs when the Print button is clicked simply opens the report.

The On Open event of the report, shown in Listing 12.3, checks the combo box to see whether a customer is selected. If a customer is selected, it prints the report based on the selected customer. If nothing is selected, the report displays all the customers.

LISTING 12.3 Setting the Record Source of a Report to Be a View or to Select Records from a View

```
Private Sub Report_Open(Cancel As Integer)
    Dim varID As Variant
    Dim strSQL As String

On Error GoTo HandleErr
    varID = Forms!frmCustomerTotals!cboCustomer
    If IsNull(varID) Then
        strSQL = "vwCustomerOrderTotals"
    Else
```

LISTING 12.3 Continued

```
        strSQL = "SELECT * FROM vwCustomerOrderTotals " & _
            "WHERE CustomerID = '" & varID & "'"
    End If
    Me.RecordSource = strSQL

ExitHere:
    Exit Sub
HandleErr:
    Select Case Err
        Case 2450   ' the form is not open
            varID = Null
            Resume Next
        Case Else
            MsgBox Err & ", " & Err.Description, , "rptCustomerTotalsView"
            Resume ExitHere
    End Select
End Sub
```

Figure 12.13 shows the report with a single record displayed.

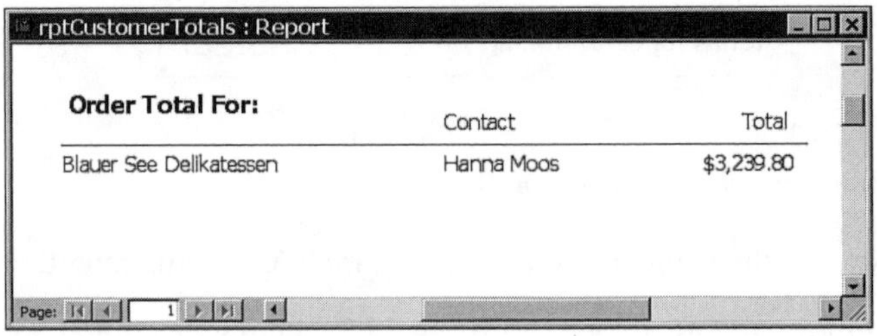

FIGURE 12.13
The report with a single customer's totals displayed.

The same result can be achieved by moving the logic to the code that opens the report, in the
Click event procedure of the button on the form. The following code uses the WhereCondition
parameter of DoCmd.OpenForm to filter the view if necessary:

```
Private Sub cmdPrint_Click()
    Dim strSQL As String
    ' Skip error that occurs if
    '   there are no orders for the selected customer.
    On Error Resume Next
    If IsNull(Me.cboCustomer) Then
        DoCmd.OpenReport "rptCustomerTotalsView", acViewPreview
    Else
```

```
        DoCmd.OpenReport "rptCustomerTotalsView", acViewPreview, _
            WhereCondition:="CustomerID = '" & Me.cboCustomer & "'"
    End If
    Me.cboCustomer = Null
End Sub
```

The advantage of using this technique is that the report remains independent of the form. No code is required in the Open event procedure of the report. The SQL statement that is sent to SQL Server is identical.

Reporting on a View Using WITH CUBE

Transact-SQL has an interesting extension to the GROUP BY clause—WITH CUBE. The CUBE operator produces a resultset above and beyond the original grouping of data, with superaggregate rows for every possible combination of GROUP BY keys. For example, if you sum the number of products sold by year, you end up with an aggregate on the quantity of products sold and a grouping on year and product. What WITH CUBE generates, in addition, is a row for each product showing the total sold for that product for each year of sales, plus a total for all the products for each year, plus a total for all the products for all the years.

Listing 12.4 shows the definition of the vwProductsByYear view.

LISTING 12.4   The vwProductsByYear View Using the WITH CUBE Operator

```
CREATE VIEW vwProductsByYear
AS
SELECT Products.ProductName,
  DATEPART(year, Orders.OrderDate) AS [Year],
  SUM([Order Details].Quantity) AS Quantity
FROM [Order Details]
INNER JOIN
  Products ON [Order Details].ProductID = Products.ProductID
INNER JOIN
  Orders ON [Order Details].OrderID = Orders.OrderID
GROUP BY
  DATEPART(year, Orders.OrderDate), Products.ProductName
WITH CUBE
```

When you select all the rows from vwProductsByYear, the superaggregate values are represented by NULL, as shown in Figure 12.14. You could think of NULL as meaning *all*.

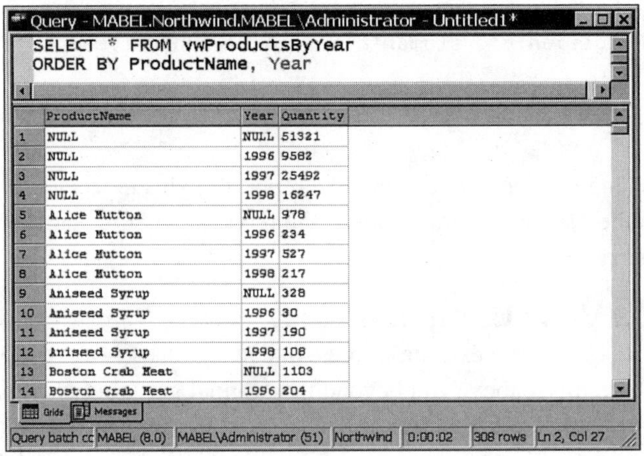

FIGURE 12.14
The resultset from selecting all the rows from vwProductsByYear.

This view can be used as the RecordSource of a report. In the Design view of the report, open the Sorting and Grouping dialog box and enter the following settings:

ProductName	Sort: **Ascending**
	Group Header: **No**
	Group Footer: **Yes**
	Group On: Each **Value**
	Group Interval: **1**
	Keep Together: **Whole Group**
Year	Sort: **Ascending**
	Group Header: **No**
	Group Footer: **No**
	Group On: **Each Value**
	Group Interval: **1**
	Keep Together: **No**

In order to prevent blanks for displaying in the place of the null values, use the Nz() function in the control source for the ProductName and Year text boxes:

```
Control Name: =Nz([ProductName],"ALL")
```

> **NOTE**
>
> The Access Nz() function works the same way as the Transact-SQL ISNULL() function. The first argument for both is an expression or value, and the second is the replacement value if the first argument is NULL. Use the Transact-SQL ISNULL() function when you want NULL values computed as some other value in your Transact-SQL procedures. For example, if you're computing averages and you want NULL values to be included as zeros in the average, ISNULL() is called for. If, on the other hand, you just want to display a zero in place of a NULL in a report, use the Access Nz() function.

Figure 12.15 displays the output of the report. Because all the NULL values sort to the top, the ALL grouping will always be listed first, both for the report overall and for each product grouping. Setting the Hide Duplicates text box property to Yes for each product name causes each product grouping level to display only once, thus eliminating report clutter that would be generated if each product were listed multiple times consecutively.

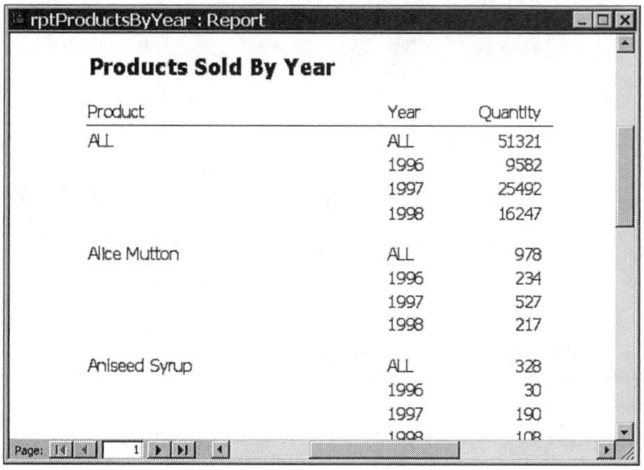

FIGURE 12.15
Viewing the report based on a view with the WITH CUBE operator.

Using the WITH CUBE operator lets you quickly generate data in a cube using Transact-SQL and without having to resort to building a cube using Analysis Services. Later in this chapter, you'll learn how to create an Access report based on an actual Analysis Services (OLAP) cube.

Basing Reports on Stored Procedures

Stored procedures give a performance boost to your reports because all processing is done on the server and a plan is cached the first time the stored procedure is run. Stored procedures can accept parameters and perform complex operations, making them ideal as the basis for reports, as shown in Figure 12.16.

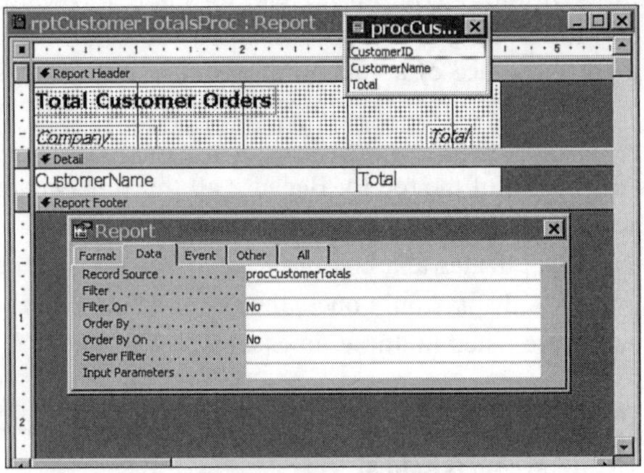

FIGURE 12.16

A report with a stored procedure as the record source.

The stored procedure, procCustomerTotals, appears in Listing 12.5. It has one optional parameter: @CustomerID. If no customer ID is passed to it, all the customer records are returned. If there is a customer ID, the selected customer record is displayed.

LISTING 12.5   The procCustomerTotals Stored Procedure

```
CREATE Procedure procCustomerTotals
    (@CustomerID nchar(5) = NULL)
AS
  IF @CustomerID IS NULL -- return all records
   SELECT
     dbo.Customers.CustomerID,
     dbo.Customers.CompanyName AS CustomerName,
     SUM(CONVERT(money,
      [Order Details].UnitPrice * [Order Details].Quantity *
      (1 - [Order Details].Discount)
        ) AS Total
   FROM dbo.Customers
   INNER JOIN
    dbo.Orders
    ON dbo.Customers.CustomerID = dbo.Orders.CustomerID
```

LISTING 12.5 Continued

```
 INNER JOIN
  dbo.[Order Details]
  ON dbo.Orders.OrderID = dbo.[Order Details].OrderID
 GROUP BY dbo.Customers.CustomerID, dbo.Customers.CompanyName

ELSE  -- return selected record
 SELECT dbo.Customers.CustomerID,
  dbo.Customers.CompanyName AS CustomerName,
   SUM(CONVERT(money,
    [Order Details].UnitPrice * [Order Details].Quantity *
    (1 - [Order Details].Discount))
      ) AS Total
 FROM dbo.Customers
 INNER JOIN
  dbo.Orders
  ON dbo.Customers.CustomerID = dbo.Orders.CustomerID
 INNER JOIN
  dbo.[Order Details]
  ON dbo.Orders.OrderID = dbo.[Order Details].OrderID
 WHERE dbo.Customers.CustomerID = @CustomerID
 GROUP BY dbo.Customers.CustomerID, dbo.Customers.CompanyName
```

Using the Input Parameters Property

You can take advantage of the optional parameter in this stored procedure to use the same report to display either all the records or only the selected record by using the Input Parameters property of the report. To set up the report to retrieve the input parameter from a form, fill in the Input Parameters property, as shown in Figure 12.17.

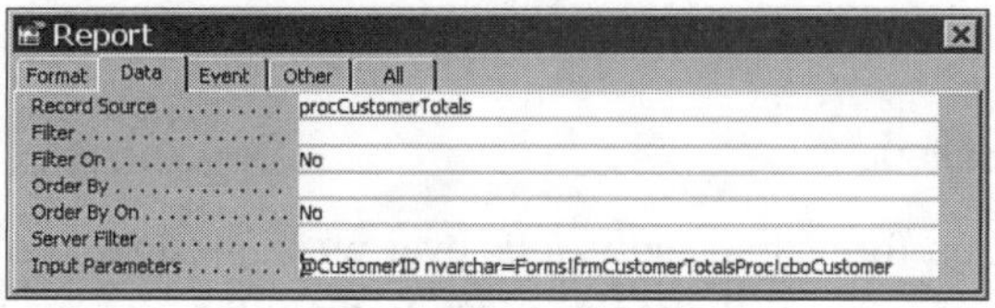

FIGURE 12.17
Setting the Input Parameters property in the property sheet.

Techniques That Don't Work but Should

Hard-wiring the Input Parameters property in the property sheet makes your report very inflexible. If it is opened by itself without the form being opened that supplies the input parameter value, the user is prompted for a value at runtime—a poor user interface design.

Unfortunately, there is no way to set the Input Parameters property in code without opening the report in Design mode first:

```
DoCmd.OpenReport "rptCustomerTotalsProc", _
   View:=acViewDesign
  Reports!rptCustomerTotalsProc.InputParameters = strParam
  DoCmd.RunCommand acCmdPrintPreview
```

Two things are wrong with this approach:

- It won't work if you've compiled your application as an ADE.
- The user is always prompted to save the report.

Even leaving the RecordSource property of the report blank and setting it after you set the InputParameters property won't work. For example, you could try putting something like this in a report's Open event:

```
Me.InputParameters = "@CustomerID nvarchar=" & varCust
Me.RecordSource = "procCustomerTotals"
```

This code looks like it should work, but unfortunately, it doesn't. The InputParameters setting is totally ignored, and the report opens displaying all the records.

These failures might lead you to attempt to assign both the RecordSource and the parameter at runtime, using the Transact-SQL EXECUTE statement. The EXECUTE (or EXEC, for short) Transact-SQL statement can be used to both execute the stored procedure and supply the optional parameter. Here's an example:

```
varID = Forms!frmCustomerTotalsProc!cboCustomer
If IsNull(varID) Then
    strSQL = "EXEC procCustomertotals"
Else
    strSQL = "EXEC procCustomertotals '" & varID & "'"
End If
Me.RecordSource = strSQL
```

This code works great on forms but, sadly, falls over when used in a report. EXEC or EXECUTE either generates a runtime error if the report is run without the form or fails silently if run from the Print button on the form. (The reason it fails silently is that the code in the Print button has an On Error Resume Next statement prior to the DoCmd.OpenReport statement.)

The Technique That Works but Should Be Unnecessary

The easiest way to get the report to work reliably, whether or not the form is initially opened, is to open the form yourself, if necessary. In the Declarations section of the report, declare a private form variable:

```
Option Compare Database
Option Explicit

Private mfrm As Form
```

The On Open event of the report then sets a reference to the form. If the form is opened, all is well. If not, an error is generated. The error handler then opens the form hidden. A Resume statement then branches back to the Set statement, and the report opens with all the records displayed. Listing 12.6 shows the code for the On Open event of the form.

LISTING 12.6   Opening the Report and Setting the Form Reference

```
Private Sub Report_Open(Cancel As Integer)

On Error GoTo HandleErr
    Set mfrm = Forms!frmCustomerTotalsProc

ExitHere:
    Exit Sub
HandleErr:
    Select Case Err
        Case 2450    ' the form is not open
            DoCmd.OpenForm "frmCustomerTotalsProc", _
                WindowMode:=acHidden
            Resume
        Case Else
            MsgBox Err & ", " & Err.Description, , _
                "rptCustomerTotalsProc"
            Resume ExitHere
    End Select
End Sub
```

The report's On Close event then takes care of cleanup:

```
Private Sub Report_Close()
    If Forms!frmCustomerTotalsProc.Visible = False Then
        DoCmd.Close acForm, mfrm.Name
    End If
End Sub
```

If the form is open in hidden mode, it is closed. Nothing happens if the form is visible—the user can continue using the form to run additional reports. Figure 12.18 shows the report displaying all the records.

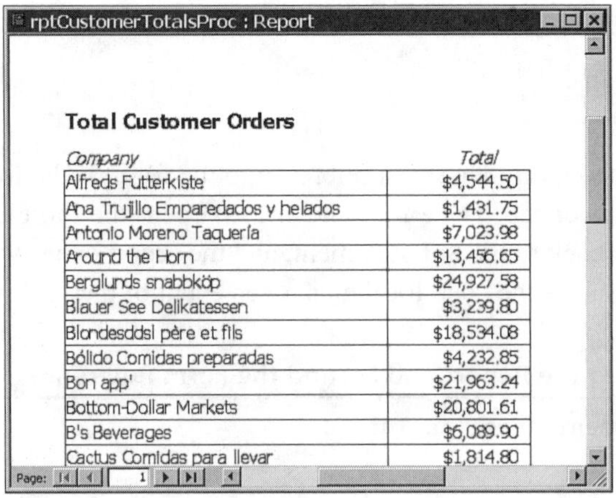

FIGURE 12.18

The report displaying all the records from the stored procedure.

Creating a Crosstab Report

As you probably know by now, Access crosstab queries are not supported in Transact-SQL. The Transform/Pivot syntax used in crosstab queries is something that was invented for Access and hasn't been adopted by SQL Server in any of its Transact-SQL extensions. There are workarounds, which usually involve complex Transact-SQL queries with CASE expressions or using a temp table. The example used in this section creates a stored procedure that selects summary data from a view, inserts it into a temp table in crosstab format, and selects the output from the temp table.

The Setup

Even when working with a Jet database, reporting is difficult when you use a dynamic crosstab query as the RecordSource. The column names are derived from the data, so they cannot be known until runtime. You have two choices:

- *Hard-wire the column names*. This is okay if you don't need flexibility or to ever vary the values being reported on.

- *Dynamically assign the column names at runtime*. This involves writing quite a bit of code, even in an Access crosstab query.

This example uses a hybrid approach, creating a crosstab report where the columns are fixed for only five years of data being reported. In other words, the report displays the number of products sold by year going back five years. This way, both the report and the stored procedure can be set up ahead of time to work backward from today's date. The downside of this arrangement is that both the report and the stored procedure will need to be modified to display data going back beyond five years. Figure 12.19 shows the first few rows of the finished crosstab report, where the total number of products sold is tracked by year. Note that the Northwind sample database does not have current data, so there are no sales for 1999 and 2000.

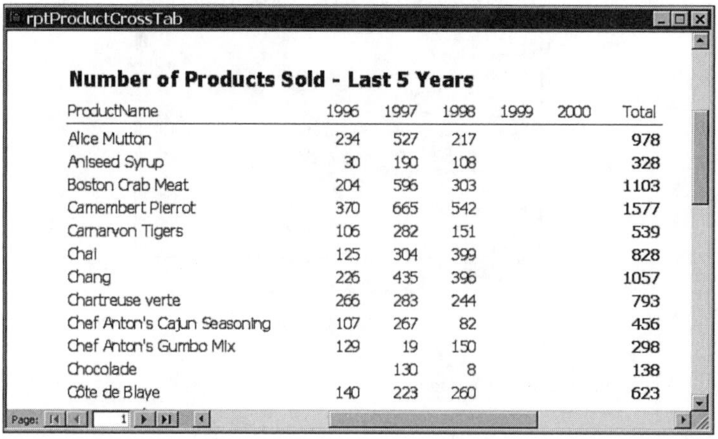

rptProductCrossTab

Number of Products Sold - Last 5 Years

ProductName	1996	1997	1998	1999	2000	Total
Alice Mutton	234	527	217			978
Aniseed Syrup	30	190	108			328
Boston Crab Meat	204	596	303			1103
Camembert Pierrot	370	665	542			1577
Carnarvon Tigers	106	282	151			539
Chai	125	304	399			828
Chang	226	435	396			1057
Chartreuse verte	266	283	244			793
Chef Anton's Cajun Seasoning	107	267	82			456
Chef Anton's Gumbo Mix	129	19	150			298
Chocolade		130	8			138
Côte de Blaye	140	223	260			623

FIGURE 12.19
The finished crosstab report.

Note that the Total column is calculated in the report. The report's grand totals at the bottom of the last page (not visible in Figure 12.19) are also calculated in the report. The ProductName and Year columns come from the stored procedure.

The Stored Procedure

The stored procedure makes use of a temporary table to hold the product name and year data. The data is selected from a view that computes the quantity for each year and product. Figure 12.20 shows the output from the view that will be used to produce the report.

The header of the stored procedure declares the variables that are used to track the year and to construct the `INSERT` statement to add data into the temp table. `SET NOCOUNT ON` reduces overhead by eliminating the done-in-proc messages that would be generated with each insert.

```
CREATE PROC procProductCrossTab
AS
SET NOCOUNT ON
  DECLARE @StartYear int
  DECLARE @SQL nvarchar(255)
  DECLARE @Counter tinyint
```

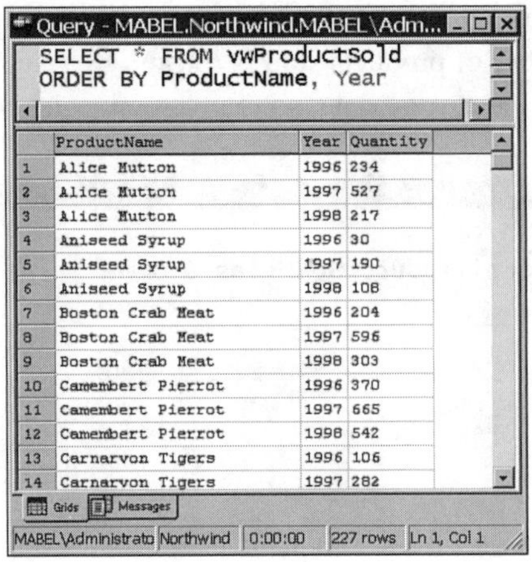

FIGURE 12.20

The raw data that will be inserted into the temp table.

The first step is to create the temp table:

```
CREATE TABLE #Crosstab
(
  ProductName nvarchar(40),
  Y1 int NULL,
  Y2 int NULL,
  Y3 int NULL,
  Y4 int NULL,
  Y5 int NULL
)
```

Once the table is created, data is inserted into the ProductName column by selecting unique product names from the Products table. Then a unique, clustered index is created on the ProductName column. This will help speed up data operations on the temp table. Here's the code:

```
INSERT #Crosstab(ProductName)
  SELECT DISTINCT ProductName
  FROM Products
  ORDER BY ProductName

CREATE UNIQUE CLUSTERED INDEX ixCross
  ON #Crosstab (ProductName)
```

The final step is to loop from the start year to the end year, building a dynamic Transact-SQL statement to update the year data in the temp table. This statement will be executed multiple times:

```
--Initialize start year
  SET @StartYear = DATEPART(year, GETDATE()) -4

--Initialize counter
  SET @Counter = 1

/*Loop through to year 2000
  executing multiple updates to temp table*/

WHILE @Counter <=5
  BEGIN
    SET @SQL = 'UPDATE #Crosstab '
    SET @SQL = @SQL + 'SET [Y' + CAST(@Counter AS char(2))
    SET @SQL = @SQL + '] = (SELECT Quantity FROM vwProductSold o '
    SET @SQL = @SQL + 'WHERE o.ProductName = c.ProductName AND '
    SET @SQL = @SQL + 'o.Year = ' + CAST(@StartYear AS char(4)) + ') '
    SET @SQL = @SQL + 'FROM #Crosstab c'

    --This is here for debugging
    PRINT @SQL

    --Execute the insert
    EXEC sp_executesql @SQL

    --Increment the year by 1
    SET @StartYear = (@StartYear + 1)
    --Increment the counter by 1
    SET @Counter = (@Counter + 1)
  END
```

The last statement in the stored procedure returns the data from the temp table:

```
SELECT * FROM #Crosstab
```

Once the stored procedure ends, SQL Server automatically drops the temp table. Listing 12.7 shows the complete stored procedure.

LISTING 12.7 The procProductCrossTab Stored Procedure

```
CREATE PROC procProductCrossTab
AS
SET NOCOUNT ON
  DECLARE @StartYear int
  DECLARE @SQL nvarchar(255)
  DECLARE @Counter tinyint
```

LISTING 12.7 Continued

```
--Create temp table
CREATE TABLE #Crosstab
(
  ProductName nvarchar(40),
  Y1 int NULL,
  Y2 int NULL,
  Y3 int NULL,
  Y4 int NULL,
  Y5 int NULL
)

--Insert ProductName into temp table
INSERT #Crosstab(ProductName)
  SELECT DISTINCT ProductName
  FROM Products
  ORDER BY ProductName

--Create a unique clustered index
CREATE UNIQUE CLUSTERED INDEX ixCross
  ON #Crosstab (ProductName)

--Initialize start year
  SET @StartYear = DATEPART(year, GETDATE()) -4

--Initialize counter
  SET @Counter = 1

/*Loop through to year 2000
  executing multiple updates to temp table*/

WHILE @Counter <=5
  BEGIN
    SET @SQL = 'UPDATE #Crosstab '
    SET @SQL = @SQL + 'SET [Y' + CAST(@Counter AS char(2))
    SET @SQL = @SQL + '] = (SELECT Quantity FROM vwProductSold o '
    SET @SQL = @SQL + 'WHERE o.ProductName = c.ProductName AND '
    SET @SQL = @SQL + 'o.Year = ' + CAST(@StartYear AS char(4)) + ') '
    SET @SQL = @SQL + 'FROM #Crosstab c'

    --This is here for debugging
    PRINT @SQL

    --Execute the insert
    EXEC sp_executesql @SQL
```

LISTING 12.7   Continued

```
   --Increment the year by 1
   SET @StartYear = (@StartYear + 1)
   --Increment the counter by 1
   SET @Counter = (@Counter + 1)
END


--Return resultset from temp table
SELECT * FROM #Crosstab
```

The Report

Setting up the report in the Access project is a bit tricky. Because the stored procedure returns results from a temp table, Access has a hard time reading the schema information of the result-set. If you try to specify the stored procedure name directly as the RecordSource of the report, you'll receive the error message shown in Figure 12.21.

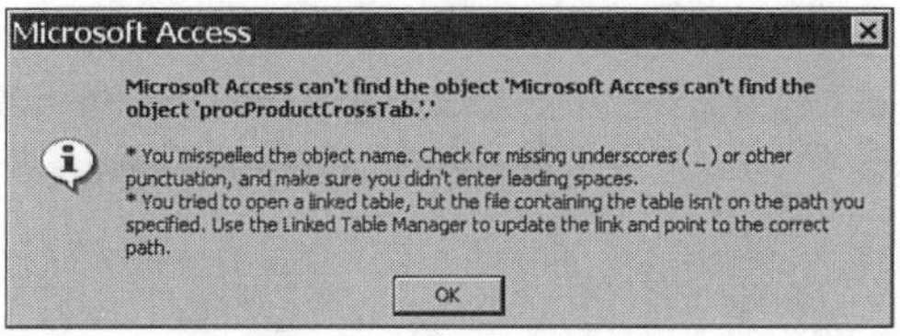

FIGURE 12.21

The error message displayed when you try to base a report on a stored procedure that returns the results from a temp table.

You can go ahead and set up the report anyway—you just won't be able to have the convenience of using the field list to drag and drop fields onto the report. Another alternative is to create the report in an Access MDB basing it on a pass-through query that executes the stored procedure. Access will run very, very slowly as you design the report in the MDB, because Access reexecutes the pass-through query multiple times to retrieve the schema needed to design the report, but it works. Once the report is finished, you can then import it into an Access project and change the RecordSource property to point back to the stored procedure instead of the pass-through query.

The sample report itself is very straightforward—the row-summary columns are computed by adding the years' figures together. The Nz() function is used in the Control Source property of the Totals text box to convert any NULL values to zeros, as shown here for the txtTotal text box, which displays the total for each row:

```
=(Nz([Y1],0))+(Nz([Y2],0))+(Nz([Y3],0))+(Nz([Y4],0))+(Nz([Y5],0))
```

The column totals for each year, located in the report footer, are computed using the Sum aggregate function, as shown here for txt1, which sums the first year of data:

```
=Sum([Y1])
```

The grand total is computed by adding all the footer section controls:

```
=(Nz([txt1],0))+(Nz([txt2],0))+(Nz([txt3],0))+(Nz([txt4],0))+(Nz([txt5],0))
```

Figure 12.22 shows the crosstab report in Design view.

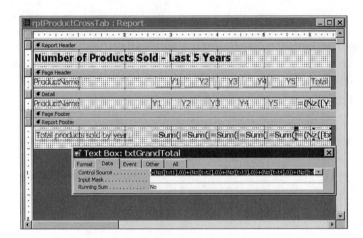

FIGURE 12.22

The crosstab report in Design view.

The only items you can't fix in Design view of the report are the column headings for the years. However, you can write code in the Format event of the Page Header section using the same algorithm used in the stored procedure for calculating the year-summary values:

```
Private Sub PageHeaderSection_Format( _
  Cancel As Integer, FormatCount As Integer)

    Dim i As Integer
    Dim intYear As Integer

    ' Get the start year
    intYear = Year(Date) - 4

    For i = 1 To 5
        Me("lbl" & i).Caption = intYear
```

```
        intYear = intYear + 1
    Next i
End Sub
```

Each label is named lbl1 for the first year, lbl2 for the second year, and so on. Once you figure out the earliest year being reported on, each label can be set to the appropriate year in the For Next loop.

> **NOTE**
>
> If you are using an Access database, of course it is far simpler to create a crosstab report using an Access query. The raw data can be provided by a pass-through query, table, or view.

Basing Reports on Functions

Functions in SQL Server 2000 provide many of the benefits of using stored procedures. They offer good performance and have the ability to accept parameters. Functions can also be created to return tables, making them more like views in their usage. You might think that creating the crosstab stored procedure shown in the previous example would be a good candidate, but unfortunately you can't use temp tables in user-defined functions.

To use a user-defined function that returns a table as the basis for a report, set the report's RecordSource to use the Transact-SQL SELECT statement with the function, passing in any parameter values in parentheses:

```
SELECT * FROM MyFunction(paramValue)
```

The syntax looks a little bit like a hybrid between Transact-SQL and VBA, and it works like a hybrid between a view and a stored procedure. You select data from it like a view, but the function can accept parameters and contain Transact-SQL statements that a view cannot. However, there is no way to base reports directly on functions by specifying the function names (as you would for a view). Furthermore, like user-defined data types, functions don't even show up in the Access object list, but that shouldn't stop you from using them for reporting.

Creating the Function

To demonstrate creating a function that takes an optional parameter and returns a table, this example features a function that returns either the selected customer's total sales or all the customer totals, depending on whether the input parameter is specified.

The function definition includes the parameter declaration plus the RETURNS statement, which defines the output table:

```
CREATE FUNCTION fnCustomerOrderTotals
    (@CustomerID nchar(5) = NULL)
RETURNS @retOrderTotals TABLE
    (CustomerID nchar(5) primary key,
      CustomerName nvarchar(50) NOT NULL,
      Total money NOT NULL)
```

Next comes AS followed by BEGIN, which is required syntax in a function. The body of every function needs to have a BEGIN-END block, with all work being processed in between. You can use variables in a function. In this case, a table variable is declared, which in structure is a mirror of the RETURNS output table. This variable is used internally as a work table; the final records of which will be inserted into the RETURNS table. A work table variable is necessary here—you can't use the output table internally as a work table:

```
AS

BEGIN
  DECLARE @temp TABLE (CustomerID nchar(5) primary key,
      CustomerName nvarchar(50) NOT NULL,
      Total money)
```

The function then branches based on whether a customer ID was passed in. If no customer ID was passed in, all records are inserted into the @temp table variable:

```
  IF @CustomerID IS NULL -- return all records if no parameter
  BEGIN
   INSERT @temp
   SELECT dbo.Customers.CustomerID,
     dbo.Customers.CompanyName AS CustomerName,
     SUM(CONVERT(money,
      [Order Details].UnitPrice * [Order Details].Quantity *
      (1 - [Order Details].Discount)
)) AS Total
   FROM dbo.Customers INNER JOIN
    dbo.Orders ON dbo.Customers.CustomerID = dbo.Orders.CustomerID
   INNER JOIN
    dbo.[Order Details]
    ON dbo.Orders.OrderID = dbo.[Order Details].OrderID
   GROUP BY dbo.Customers.CustomerID, dbo.Customers.CompanyName
  END
```

If there is a customer ID, only the single matching record is inserted into the @temp table variable:

```
ELSE  -- return selected record
BEGIN
 INSERT @temp
 SELECT dbo.Customers.CustomerID,
   dbo.Customers.CompanyName AS CustomerName,
   SUM(CONVERT(money, dbo.[Order Details].UnitPrice * dbo.[Order _
   Details].Quantity *
    (1 - [Order Details].Discount)))
   AS Total
 FROM dbo.Customers
 INNER JOIN
   dbo.Orders
   ON dbo.Customers.CustomerID = dbo.Orders.CustomerID
 INNER JOIN
   dbo.[Order Details]
   ON dbo.Orders.OrderID = dbo.[Order Details].OrderID
 WHERE Customers.CustomerID = @CustomerID
 GROUP BY dbo.Customers.CustomerID, dbo.Customers.CompanyName
END
```

The final statement inserts the contents of the @temp variable into the @retOrderTotals return
table. The RETURN statement causes the table to be returned by the function, and the END statement delimits the function:

```
INSERT @retOrderTotals
SELECT CustomerID, CustomerName, Total
FROM @temp
RETURN
END
```

Listing 12.8 shows the completed function.

LISTING 12.8   The fnCustomerOrderTotals User-Defined Function

```
CREATE FUNCTION fnCustomerOrderTotals
    (@CustomerID nchar(5) = NULL)
RETURNS @retOrderTotals TABLE
    (CustomerID nchar(5) primary key,
      CustomerName nvarchar(50) NOT NULL,
      Total money NOT NULL)
AS
BEGIN
  DECLARE @temp TABLE (CustomerID nchar(5) primary key,
      CustomerName nvarchar(50) NOT NULL,
      Total money)
  IF @CustomerID IS NULL -- return all records if no parameter
```

LISTING 12.8   Continued

```
BEGIN
 INSERT @temp
 SELECT dbo.Customers.CustomerID,
   dbo.Customers.CompanyName AS CustomerName,
   SUM(CONVERT(money,
    [Order Details].UnitPrice * [Order Details].Quantity *
    (1 - [Order Details].Discount)
)) AS Total
  FROM dbo.Customers INNER JOIN
   dbo.Orders ON dbo.Customers.CustomerID = dbo.Orders.CustomerID
  INNER JOIN
   dbo.[Order Details]
   ON dbo.Orders.OrderID = dbo.[Order Details].OrderID
  GROUP BY dbo.Customers.CustomerID, dbo.Customers.CompanyName
 END

 ELSE  -- return selected record
 BEGIN
 INSERT @temp
 SELECT dbo.Customers.CustomerID,
   dbo.Customers.CompanyName AS CustomerName,
   SUM(CONVERT(money, dbo.[Order Details].UnitPrice * dbo.[Order _
   Details].Quantity *
    (1 - [Order Details].Discount)))
   AS Total
  FROM dbo.Customers
  INNER JOIN
   dbo.Orders
   ON dbo.Customers.CustomerID = dbo.Orders.CustomerID
  INNER JOIN
   dbo.[Order Details]
   ON dbo.Orders.OrderID = dbo.[Order Details].OrderID
  WHERE Customers.CustomerID = @CustomerID
  GROUP BY dbo.Customers.CustomerID, dbo.Customers.CompanyName
 END

 INSERT @retOrderTotals
 SELECT CustomerID, CustomerName, Total
 FROM @temp
 RETURN
END
```

Calling the Function

All the code for calling the function is located in the On Open event of the report. If the form is open and a customer is selected, the ID of the customer is passed to the function, and only the single record is displayed. If no customer is selected or if the form is closed, the report is opened and all the records are displayed. Here's the code:

```
Private Sub Report_Open(Cancel As Integer)
    Dim strSQL As String
    Dim varID As Variant

On Error GoTo HandleErr
    varID = Forms!frmCustomerTotalsFunction!cboCustomer
    If IsNull(varID) Then
        strSQL = "SELECT * FROM fnCustomerOrderTotals(Null)"
    Else
        strSQL = "SELECT * FROM fnCustomerOrderTotals('" _
            & varID & "')"
    End If
    Me.RecordSource = strSQL

ExitHere:
    Exit Sub
HandleErr:
    Select Case Err
        Case 2450    ' the form is not open
            varID = Null
            Resume Next
        Case Else
            MsgBox Err & ", " & Err.Description, , "rptCustomerTotalsView"
            Resume ExitHere
    End Select
End Sub
```

Figure 12.23 displays the selection form and the report with a single customer record displayed.

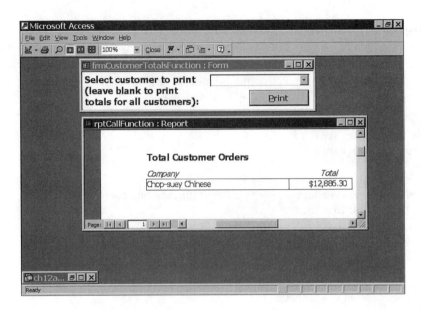

FIGURE 12.23
The results of a user-defined function displayed in a report.

Reporting in Access Databases

Reporting in Access databases (MDBs) hasn't changed much from earlier versions of Access—you can link to tables or views and base reports on them, or you can use pass-through queries. Generally speaking, pass-through queries are the best choice because you can run stored procedures, user-defined functions, or direct Transact-SQL on the server, returning only a resultset to the report. The fact that pass-through queries are read-only has no meaning for reporting because reports aren't used to update data anyway. Linking to tables or views goes through both Jet and ODBC on the way to retrieving the resultset, so you sacrifice both performance and flexibility. However, views can help users create their own reports without having to get too bogged down learning Transact-SQL or complex join syntax.

> **NOTE**
>
> If you use a Jet query as the RecordSource of a report in an Access database (MDB), avoid using heterogeneous joins (joins between Access tables and SQL Server tables), VBA functions, and expressions that will cause the data to be processed locally.

Basing Reports on Views

A report can be based on a view in the same way it can be based on a table. First, you have to link to the view (for coverage of linking to SQL Server data, see Chapter 5). Then you specify the view name in the RecordSource property the same way you would a table name. Alternatively, you can also use a SELECT statement with a view, the same way you can with a table. Figure 12.24 shows the Design view of a report based on a view.

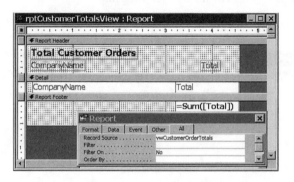

FIGURE 12.24
Design view of a report based on a view.

You can also assign the RecordSource property of a report at runtime, using a view, by writing code in the report's On Open event:

```
On Error GoTo HandleErr
    varID = Forms!frmCustomerTotals!cboCustomer
    If IsNull(varID) Then
        strSQL = "vwCustomerOrderTotals"
    Else
        strSQL = "SELECT * FROM vwCustomerOrderTotals " & _
            "WHERE CustomerID = '" & varID & "'"
    End If
    Me.RecordSource = strSQL
```

Basing Reports on Pass-Through Queries

A pass-through query in an Access database (MDB) allows you to send Transact-SQL statements directly to SQL Server, bypassing the Jet database engine.

Using Pass-Through Queries

As the name implies, pass-through queries are "passed through" to SQL Server for processing. Pass-through queries are not parsed by Jet, and the resultset is returned directly from SQL Server to the report. You can send raw Transact-SQL statements or execute stored procedures—with parameters, if necessary—from a pass-through query.

The main advantage of using pass-through queries is that you can base reports on stored procedures instead of linked tables or views. In addition to the performance benefits, pass-through queries allow you to run system stored procedures and perform many operations on the server that you could not otherwise perform from an Access database. For example, the following simple pass-through query returns the service name, the server, and the version:

```
SELECT @@servicename as Service,
  @@servername as Server, @@version as Version
```

A quick autoreport provides the results shown in Figure 12.25.

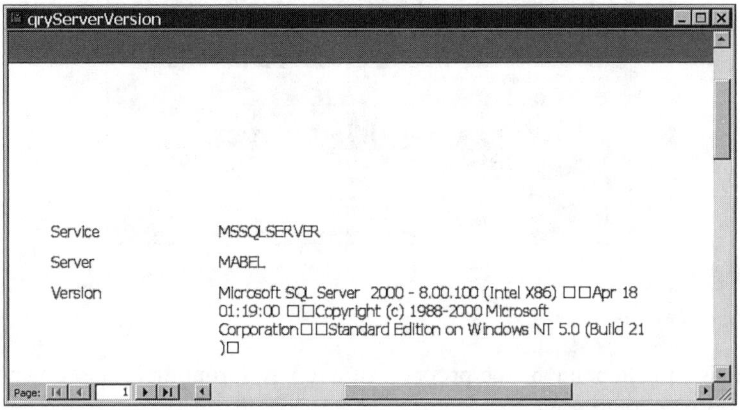

FIGURE 12.25

An autoreport based on a pass-through query.

You probably aren't going to need to put server information in most reports, but it does illustrate that a pass-through query is a gateway to reporting all kinds of information from your SQL Server that would be hard to get at using simple linked tables.

Pass-Through Queries and Stored Procedures

As shown in Chapter 5, you can create procedures to modify pass-through queries at runtime by supplying new definitions for the queries. This comes in handy when working with stored procedures because you can't pass parameters to stored procedures in a pass-through query the same way you would with a regular Access query.

The Stored Procedure

The stored procedure shown earlier in Listing 12.5 is a good candidate to be called from a pass-through query. The procCustomerTotals procedure has one optional parameter: @CustomerID. If no customer ID is passed to it, all the customer records are returned. If there is a customer ID, however, the selected customer record is displayed.

Setting Up the Pass-Through Query

The pass-through query needs to be set up with the properties shown in Figure 12.26. Use either a DSN or an ODBC connection string in the ODBC Connect Str property and set the Returns Records property to Yes. Type the name of the stored procedure in the SQL pane of the query and save the query.

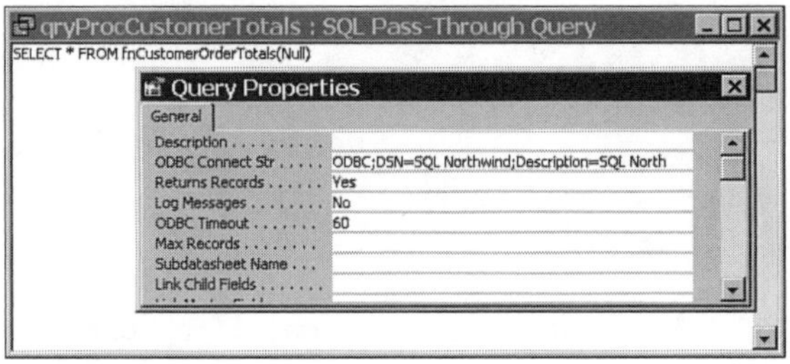

FIGURE 12.26
Setting up a pass-through query to call a parameterized stored procedure.

Because the parameter is optional, you can test the pass-through query by running it without supplying a parameter value. You should see all the records returned in Datasheet view.

Setting Up the Report

The report handles setting its own record source in the Open event. If it's opened from the form, it checks to see whether a company has been selected. If so, only the single company record is shown. If no company is selected, all records are returned. If the report is opened on its own with no form, all records are returned. Listing 12.9 shows the code for the Open event.

LISTING 12.9   The Open Event Procedure of a Report Based on a Parameterized Stored Procedure

```
Private Sub Report_Open(Cancel As Integer)
    Dim varID As Variant
    Dim strSQL As String

On Error GoTo HandleErr
    varID = Forms!frmCustomerParameter!cboCustomer
    If IsNull(varID) Then
        strSQL = "procCustomerTotals"
    Else
        strSQL = "procCustomerTotals " & _
            FormatString(varID)
    End If

    ' Process the pass-through query
```

LISTING 12.9   Continued

```
    Call PassThroughFixup("qryProcCustomerTotals", strSQL)

    ' Assign the RecordSource to the fixed-up query
    Me.RecordSource = "qryProcCustomerTotals"

ExitHere:
    Exit Sub
HandleErr:
    Select Case Err
        Case 2450    ' the form is not open
            varID = Null
            Resume Next
        Case Else
            MsgBox Err & ", " & Err.Description, , "rptCustomerTotalsProc"
            Resume ExitHere
    End Select
End Sub
```

The FormatString() function takes a single variant parameter and, if it's a textual string, surrounds it in single quotes. This function also replaces any single quotes embedded in the string with two single quotes so it can be parsed by Transact-SQL. This allows you to handle strings with apostrophes or single quotes (such as the name *O'Brien*). The code is shown in Listing 12.10.

LISTING 12.10   The FormatString Function

```
Public Function FormatString( _
  ByVal varInput As Variant) As Variant
    ' If input is null, returns NULL,
    ' else returns properly delimited
    ' value (used for strings and dates)

    Dim varTemp As Variant

    If Len(varInput & "") = 0 Then
        varTemp = "NULL"
    Else
        varTemp = "'" & Replace(varInput, "'", "''") & "'"
    End If

    FormatString = varTemp
End Function
```

The `PassThroughFixup()` procedure, shown in Listing 12.11, is the same one that appears in Chapter 5. It takes parameters for the name of the pass-through query to fix, the new SQL statement, and optional parameters for the connection string and the Returns Records property. It then modifies the query on which the report is based. Chapter 5 also includes a version of this function that uses ADO rather than DAO, but when you're working with Jet objects, as is the case here (the pass-through query is a Jet object), DAO is generally more efficient.

LISTING 12.11   The `PassThroughFixup` Procedure

```
Public Sub PassThroughFixup( _
  ByVal strQdfName As String, _
  ByVal strSQL As String, _
  Optional varConnect As Variant, _
  Optional fRetRecords As Boolean = True)

    ' Modifies pass-through query properties
    ' Inputs:
    '    strQdfName   Name of the query
    '    strSQL       New SQL string
    '    varConnect   Optional connection string
    '    fRetRecords  Optional returns records--
    '                 defaults to True (Yes)

    Dim db As DAO.Database
    Dim qdf As DAO.QueryDef
    Dim strConnect As String

    Set db = CurrentDb
    Set qdf = db.QueryDefs(strQdfName)
    If IsMissing(varConnect) Then
        strConnect = qdf.Connect
    Else
        strConnect = CStr(varConnect)
    End If
    qdf.Connect = strConnect
    qdf.ReturnsRecords = fRetRecords
    qdf.SQL = strSQL
End Sub
```

Figure 12.27 shows the form and report opened after a customer has been selected. Had no customer been selected, the report would have displayed all customer totals plus a grand total.

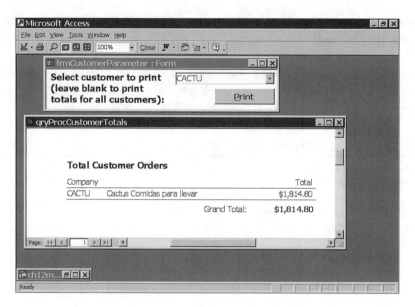

FIGURE 12.27

The form and the report based on the parameterized stored procedure.

Pass-Through Queries and User-Defined Functions

Working with user-defined functions that return tables is just a bit different from working with stored procedures. You create a pass-through query that invokes the user-defined function using SELECT syntax as though the user-defined function were a view. Parameter values are passed in parentheses, and the same single-quote delimiters apply for dates or string values. Here's an example:

```
SELECT * FROM fnCustomerOrderTotals(Null)
```

You then save the pass-through query and create the report. The report is identical in every respect to the previous example—except for the code in the Open event. And even that code isn't changed very much—the PassThroughFixup() procedure is called, but with a different string for the SQL statement:

```
varID = Forms!frmCustomerFunction!cboCustomer
If IsNull(varID) Then
    strSQL = "SELECT * FROM fnCustomerOrderTotals(Null)"
Else
    strSQL = "SELECT * FROM fnCustomerOrderTotals(" & _
      FormatString(varID) & ")"
End If
```

Everything else is the same, and the report opens displaying either all the records or just the record for the selected customer.

Reporting on OLAP Data

Normally when you read about reporting and OLAP (Online Analytical Processing, or *Analysis Services*, as it's now called in SQL Server 2000), Excel or some third-party tool is used as the reporting engine. However, it's possible to use Access to report on OLAP data—it just takes a little work. An Access MDB can't connect directly to an OLAP cube because Access uses ODBC, and OLAP cubes speak OLE DB. Access ADPs can only have a single connection to a SQL Server database, not an OLAP cube. The way around these obstacles is to use SQL Server's capability to link to external servers. Once you have a linked OLAP server in SQL Server, you can use views and stored procedures that point to the OLAP cube you want to query. Also, you can retrieve this data into Access reports in both MDBs and ADPs.

Before going into the details of how to accomplish this, here's a very brief overview of the basic OLAP concepts and how they are implemented in Analysis Services in SQL Server 2000.

OLAP Fundamentals

In SQL Server 7.0, Analysis Services was called *OLAP Services*. Although OLAP Services has been renamed and is now called *Analysis Services* in SQL Server 2000, the terminology used in SQL Server 7.0 is still around—one can still refer to an "OLAP cube" and be understood.

OLAP stands for *Online Analytical Processing*. The basic idea is pretty simple: You have a lot of data—maybe it's even in different databases—and you want to consolidate it all together so that you can query the whole thing. Maybe you want to get summaries of the data and then drill down into the detail layers. When your data is stored in relational databases, writing such queries is difficult, and with lots of data and complex aggregations, these queries run very, very slowly. What OLAP does is take the relational tables and construct a preaggregated array of values, called a *cube*, from all the raw data. The tradeoff is that you have the increased storage space of the cube balanced against the speed of querying it later, and you have the cost of purchasing and maintaining the OLAP server. In the past, OLAP servers were very expensive, costing in the tens of thousands of dollars. With SQL Server 7.0, Microsoft changed the economics of OLAP by including a powerful OLAP server in with the main product. To use Analysis Services, you do, however, need to own a full retail license for SQL Server—it isn't bundled with MSDE.

The Cube

The basic unit of storage and analysis in Analysis Services is the *cube*. OLAP databases are composed of one or more cubes. A cube can have three different modes of storage:

- *MOLAP (multidimensional OLAP).* All the data and aggregates are copied to the OLAP server. This gives the best query performance and takes the most storage.

- *ROLAP (relational OLAP).* The data stays in the relational tables, and a separate set of tables is used to store and retrieve the aggregate data. This takes far less storage but can be slower to query.

- *HOLAP (hybrid OLAP).* The data stays in the relational tables, but aggregations are stored on the server. HOLAP falls somewhere in between MOLAP and ROLAP in terms of storage and querying speed.

Cubes can also be partitioned, with different storage options for each partition. For example, a partition of a cube based on historical data could be stored using MOLAP because the data isn't going to change, and data that changes frequently could be stored using ROLAP or HOLAP. Partitions do not even need to be on a single server. You can also create virtual cubes, which are supersets of multiple cubes. This would allow you to derive statistics comparing your sales cube against your inventory control cube.

Cubes are ordered internally into dimensions, which come from dimension tables, and measures, which come from fact tables, that are discussed in the next section.

Working with Multidimensional Data

OLAP databases are often referred to as being *multidimensional*. It's not really helpful to think of the data schema of an OLAP database in the way you may be used to thinking of fields and tables in a standard relational database. The entire structure of an OLAP database is geared toward efficient retrieval and analysis, rather than efficient data entry and relational integrity, so many of the concepts you are used to don't apply.

Dimensions and Measures

In an OLAP database, the data is divided between *measures*, the facts you are analyzing, and *dimensions*, the categories you are using to slice and dice the data. For example, you have products that you sell. There are certain facts about these products—cost, units sold, total sales, and so on—that you want to report on. These facts in the multidimensional model are called *measures*. The measures can be evaluated using certain parameters—for example, sales by store, by country, and by product category. These parameters are called *dimensions*.

Each dimension can have several levels organized in a hierarchy. For example, the levels of a data/time dimension might by Year/Quarter/Month/Day/Hour. A location hierarchy could include Country/Region/City/Postal Code. Within each level, each dimension has members. The members of the Month level of the date/time dimension would be January, February, and so on. Members are the values that populate each dimension.

Somewhat like relational data, fact tables and dimension tables are related by foreign/primary key relationships. These related fact and dimension tables comprise the OLAP cube schema.

You can have multiple cubes in a single database, as in the sample FoodMart 2000 database, where you have several cubes, including the Sales cube shown in Figure 12.28. Inside each cube, the fact and dimension tables are organized into either a star schema, where all dimension tables are directly related to the fact table, or a snowflake schema, where some dimension tables are related indirectly to the fact table. The schema shown in Figure 12.28 is a snowflake schema because the Product_Class table is indirectly related to the central fact table by way of the Product table.

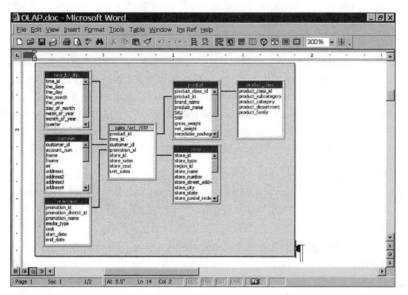

FIGURE 12.28
The schema for the Sales cube.

The MDX Query Language

MDX (Multidimensional Expressions) is the language that Microsoft has included with Analysis Services to allow access to OLAP data from client applications. It has many language elements in common with Transact-SQL, such as SELECT, FROM, and WHERE clauses, but it is not an extension of Transact-SQL. The main difference between the two is that Transact-SQL is designed to query standard two-dimensional relational data, whereas MDX is designed to query multidimensional data.

MDX can be used to create multidimensional queries, define cube structures, and, occasionally, even to change the data in the cube. This chapter focuses on selecting data. The general syntax for an MDX statement is as follows:

```
SELECT [<axis_specification>
       [, <axis_specification>...]]
  FROM [<cube_specification>]
[WHERE [<slicer_specification>]]
```

Here's a simple example using the Sales cube:

```
SELECT
    {[Product].[Product Category].Members} on COLUMNS,
    {[Measures].[Store Sales]} on ROWS
FROM Sales
```

In this SELECT statement, there are two sets, or *member selections*, defined on the Sales cube. One of these specifies a dimension, and the other specifies a measure. Each set is surrounded by curly braces ({}). You could also include a set of literal members. For example, {CA, FL, [Los Angeles], Miami} is a set composed of members of a geographic dimension. Square brackets ([]) are required when a member name has spaces in it, and commas separate the members of the set. Here is a brief overview of some other terminology you'll encounter when working with MDX queries:

- A *tuple* is a section of a cube that is defined when you have a set containing members from different dimensions, such as {(CA, 1999), (FL, 1998)}. A pair of parentheses surrounds each tuple.

- An *axis* is a collection of members from one or more dimensions organized as tuples. Axes are used to locate or filter values in a cube. The first five axes are called, respectively, COLUMNS, ROWS, PAGES, CHAPTERS, and SECTIONS. Axes are numbered starting with zero, so the first axis, COLUMNS, would be axis(0). You can't skip axis numbers or change their order in an MDX query.

- The Members function is used to define member sections. For example, {[Product].[Product Category].Members} would return {Drinks, Food, [Non Consumables]}. These are all the members of the Product Category level of the Product dimension.

- The Children function returns the members of a level beneath the current level. For example, {[Time].[1998].Children} would return {[Q1 1998], [Q2 1998], [Q3 1998] , [Q4 1998]}.

- The CROSSJOIN() function returns all combinations of the members of two dimensions.

- The slicer specification is defined in the WHERE clause of the MDX query and limits the resultset to a particular set of measures. To look at the average sales of FoodMart stores, based on the type of store and location, you would use this MDX query:

```
SELECT {[Store Type].MEMBERS} ON COLUMNS,
{Store.[Store City].MEMBERS} ON ROWS
FROM Sales
WHERE (MEASURES.[Sales Average])
```

Teaching you MDX is beyond the scope of this book, but you can use the MDX Sample Application, which you'll work with later in this chapter, to get started exploring some sample queries. MDX is fully documented in *SQL Server Books Online* under Analysis Services, MDX.

Another related technology that's not covered in this book is ADO MD. This is a library of ADO objects created specifically for working programmatically with multidimensional data. ADO MD is also covered in *SQL Server Books Online* and in any complete reference on ADO. Microsoft currently provides no support for using ADO MD to bring OLAP data into Access reports.

The Analysis Manager

Analysis Services has its own management application called *Analysis Manager*, which is a snap-in for the same MMC (Microsoft Management Console) framework used by Enterprise Manager. Figure 12.29 shows the Analysis Manager's main root node. Note you can run a tutorial that will take you through the basics. This tutorial also covers the new features in Analysis Services that were not present in the SQL Server 7/OLAP server, such as data mining.

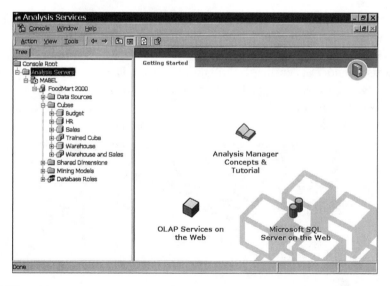

FIGURE 12.29

The Analysis Manager root node.

The FoodMart 2000 sample application installs with Analysis Services and serves somewhat the same role in OLAP that the Pubs and Northwind sample databases do in SQL Server. Another nice thing about Analysis Services is that, in addition to the tutorial, wizards are available to help you over the hump of getting started building your first cube.

Creating a New Database and Data Source

To define a new OLAP database, select the server name, right-click, and choose New Database from the menu. You will be prompted for the name of the database. Once it shows up as another node under FoodMart 2000, you can set up the data source by providing connection information to a SQL Server database. Simply right-click the Data Sources node and choose New Data Source. The Data Link dialog box will appear so that you can set the connection information for the data source.

Creating a New Cube

To create a new cube, right-click the Cubes node and choose New Cube, Wizard. The Cube Wizard will walk you through the process of setting up your fact tables and dimensions. Once you've created the cube, the Storage Wizard will help you decide on your storage options. When the cube is finished, a browser will let you perform *ad hoc* querying of the cube.

Browsing a Cube

To browse the data in a cube, right-click the cube and choose Browse Data from the list. This will load the Cube Browser with data from the selected cube. The Cube Browser shows the measures as columns and the dimensions as rows. It also gives you an All row to roll up totals aggregated across an entire dimension. To drill down to lower levels, simply double-click the plus sign at the level you want to expand. The minus sign in front of an item means that there are no further levels to drill down into. Double-clicking the minus sign collapses that level. Figure 12.30 shows the Sales cube in the FoodMart 2000 database.

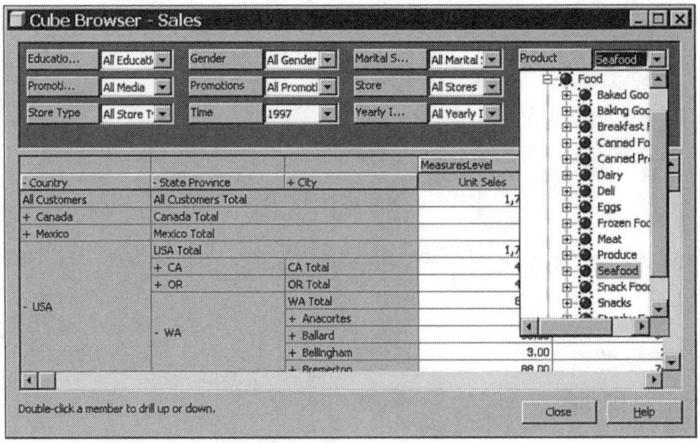

FIGURE 12.30
The Cube Browser in action.

The boxes at the top of the browser allow you to filter data. You can also drag and drop members back and forth between the top part of the browser and the bottom. You can drag to the column area at the left of the grid, to the row at the top of the grid, or back to the top area containing the unused dimensions.

Of course, you probably aren't going to distribute the Cube Browser as part of your application. You'll want to use other means to display data to your users. Microsoft Office 2000 contains data tools that let you easily export OLAP data to Excel or link to a cube from the PivotTable and PivotChart Web components. The Office Web components are discussed in Chapter 13, "Internet Features in Access and SQL Server."

The MDX Sample Application

The MDX Sample Application presents a graphical user interface for constructing MDX queries and testing MDX syntax. You can use this test application to explore the sample cubes in the FoodMart 2000 OLAP database or to test your own.

Load the MDX Sample Application from the Windows Start menu—it's located under SQL Server, MDX Sample Application. The actual files are installed in the \Program Files\OLAP Services\Samples\MDXSample folder. The MDX Sample Application (mdxsampl.exe) is nothing more than a compiled Visual Basic 6 project, and the source project is also included in the MDXSample folder (mdxsampl.vbp). This means that you can examine the VBA code behind the MDX Sample Application if you're interested.

After you launch the MDX Sample Application and connect to your OLAP server, the user interface loads. The toolbar displays a drop-down list where you can select prebuilt MDX queries, as shown in Figure 12.31. The Run Query button on the toolbar executes the selected query, and the results show up in the bottom pane.

The button on the far right of the toolbar is the Pivot Results button. This executes the same query but pivots the resultset, as shown in Figure 12.32.

You're not limited to the FoodMart 2000 database. If you have another OLAP database already built, you can select it in the DB drop-down list and build queries against it in the application. The MDX Sample Application gives you an excellent jumping off point for getting started reporting on an OLAP cube. You can refine the MDX syntax there until you have the results you want. The next step is to get the data into SQL Server by setting up an OLE DB connection to your OLAP database. Then you can query the cubes in that database by copying and pasting the MDX code from the MDX Sample Application into a view or stored procedure definition. (Or, of course, you could just write the MDX yourself from scratch if you are confident of the syntax.) You cannot, however, run MDX queries directly in Transact-SQL. Instead, you must use special Transact-SQL functions to send MDX statements to the OLAP server to be processed.

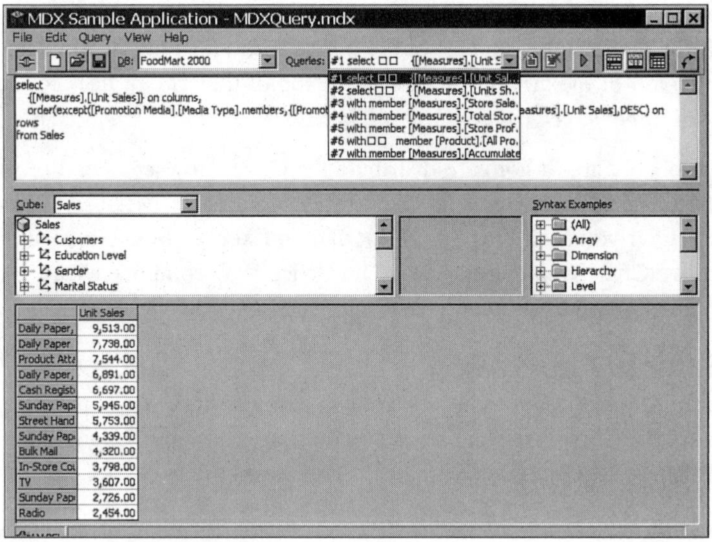

FIGURE 12.31
The user interface for the MDX Sample Application.

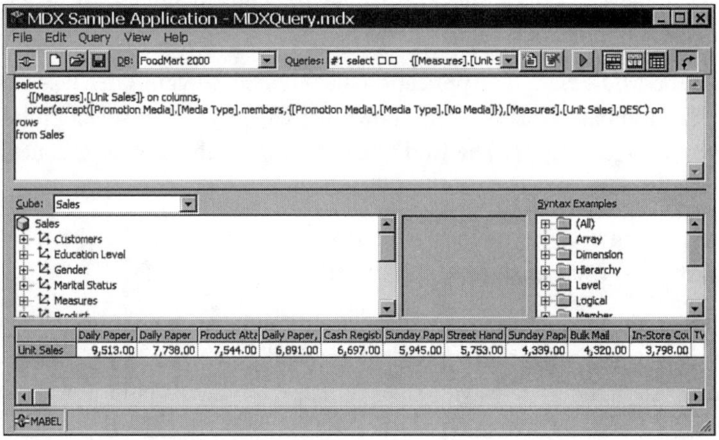

FIGURE 12.32
Pivoting the resultset.

Working with OLAP Data in SQL Server

Two Transact-SQL functions are capable of sending MDX (Multidimensional Expressions) as pass-through queries to an OLAP database:

- OPENROWSET. Lets you send a query to any OLE DB data source. OPENROWSET is good for a one-time-only *ad hoc* query because it doesn't require a linked server in order to work—you specify the connection to your OLE DB data source as part of the syntax. However, because the connection information is sent along with OPENROWSET, performance is slower than it would be with a linked server.

- OPENQUERY. Requires a linked server to an OLE DB data source and executes the specified query on the given linked server. The OPENQUERY function can be referenced in the FROM clause of a query as though it were a table name.

Setting up a linked server requires an additional step, but less overhead is involved in connecting to a linked server with OPENQUERY versus using OPENROWSET because the connection to the OLE DB data source has been preconfigured.

NOTE

In addition to OPENROWSET and OPENQUERY, OLAP supports a very limited Transact-SQL syntax for selecting data that uses a four-part name:

```
LinkedServerName.Catalog.Schema.TableName
```

However, this option is not recommended because SQL Server attempts to copy the contents of the entire fact table and then perform the calculations for aggregating the data itself, thus substantially increasing the query response time. Because cubes can be quite large, processing all that data locally instead of on the OLAP server would most likely prove unacceptably slow. The idea behind using MDX is that both OPENROWSET and OPENQUERY treat it as a pass-through query, and MDX is executed on the OLAP server, not locally in SQL Server.

Setting Up a Linked Server

You can set up a linked server in the Enterprise Manager or by executing a stored procedure. To set up a linked server in the Enterprise Manager, expand the Security node and right-click Linked Servers. Choose New Linked Server and fill in the properties. The linked server should look similar to the one shown in Figure 12.33.

The sp_addlinkedserver system stored procedure will also add a linked server. To re-create the linked server shown in Figure 12.33, you would type the following syntax in the Query Analyzer:

```
EXEC sp_addlinkedserver
    @server='FoodMart',
    @srvproduct='',
    @provider='MSOLAP',
    @datasrc='MABEL',
    @catalog='[FoodMart 2000]'
```

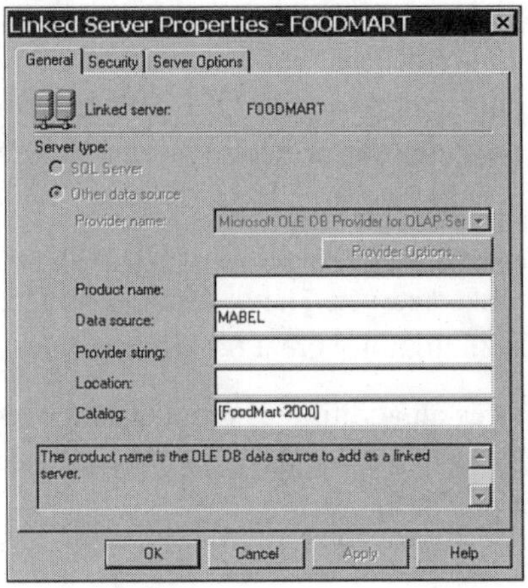

FIGURE 12.33
Setting up a linked server.

Once you've got the linked server set up, you can then write queries against it. In this example, `'Mabel'` is the name of the server; you cannot use `'(local)'`, even if your OLAP server is on the same machine.

> **NOTE**
>
> Linked servers are presented here as a means toward retrieving data from an OLAP database. However, you can use linked servers to get at any data that can be reached over an OLE DB connection, which includes all data for which you have either a native OLE DB provider or an ODBC driver. For example, if you need to work in SQL Server with data from an Oracle database, you can do so by using a linked server.

Querying the Linked Server

Other than using the MDX Sample Application, the best way to test out your MDX syntax is to write an *ad hoc* query in the Query Analyzer, using OPENQUERY with a linked server or using OPENROWSET to create an *ad hoc* connection to the OLAP server. Figure 12.34 shows an MDX query executed using the Query Analyzer.

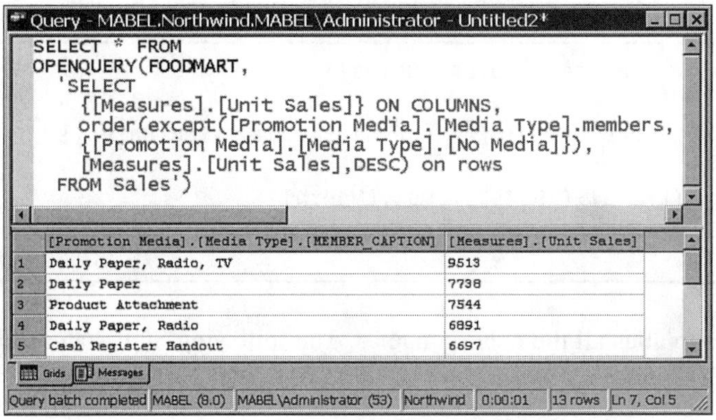

FIGURE 12.34

Running an MDX query from the Query Analyzer.

Note that the resultset column names are [Promotion Media].[Media Type].[MEMBER_CAP-TION] and [Measures].[Unit Sales]. These names can cause problems later because they don't conform to normal naming conventions for column names in SQL Server or Access.

Running the query in the Query Analyzer proves that it works. However, to get the resultset into an Access report, you need to create a view, stored procedure, or user-defined function. You'll learn each of these techniques for both Access projects and Access databases in this section, which also examines some of the benefits and pitfalls of each.

OLAP Reporting in Access Projects

In an Access project, you can base reports on SQL Server views, stored procedures, or functions that use OPENQUERY (or OPENROWSET) to connect to OLAP data sources. This section looks at the problems you'll run into if you attempt this and how to work around them.

Basing a Report on a View

A view created using the OPENQUERY syntax cannot be used as the RecordSource for a report. For example, the view shown in Listing 12.12 does not work because the column names cannot be parsed by the report.

LISTING 12.12   The vwAccumulatedSales View

```
CREATE VIEW vwAccumulatedSales
AS
SELECT * FROM
OPENQUERY(FOODMART,
  'WITH member [Measures].[Accumulated Sales]
```

LISTING 12.12 Continued

```
    AS ''Sum(YTD(),[Measures].[Store Sales])''
    SELECT
      {[Measures].[Store Sales],[Measures].[Accumulated Sales]}
      ON COLUMNS,
      {Descendants([Time].[1997],[Time].[Month])}
      ON ROWS
    FROM Sales')
```

What does work is to alias all the column names. The following SQL statement used as the `RecordSource` of a report does work:

```
SELECT [[Time]].[Year]].[MEMBER_CAPTION]]] AS Year,
    [[Time]].[Quarter]].[MEMBER_CAPTION]]] AS Quarter,
    [[Time]].[Month]].[MEMBER_CAPTION]]] AS Month,
    [[Measures]].[Store Sales]]] AS Sales,
    [[Measures]].[Accumulated Sales]]] AS Accumulated
FROM vwAccumulatedSales
```

However, there's still a problem with this approach. Figure 12.35 shows the report, as it would be printed. Note that the Sales and Accumulated Sales columns are not formatted. Both of these text boxes have the Currency format assigned, with two decimal places. These settings are completely ignored by the report.

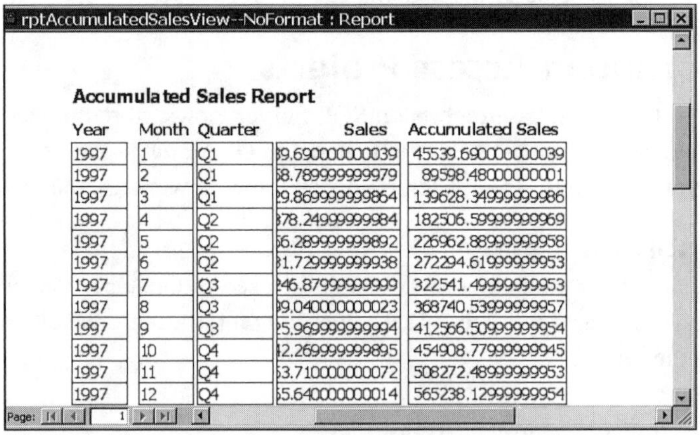

Year	Month	Quarter	Sales	Accumulated Sales
1997	1	Q1	9.690000000039	45539.690000000039
1997	2	Q1	8.789999999979	89598.48000000001
1997	3	Q1	9.869999999864	139628.3499999986
1997	4	Q2	78.2499999984	182506.5999999969
1997	5	Q2	6.289999999892	226962.8899999958
1997	6	Q2	1.729999999938	272294.6199999953
1997	7	Q3	46.8799999999	322541.4999999953
1997	8	Q3	9.040000000023	368740.5399999957
1997	9	Q3	5.969999999994	412566.5099999954
1997	10	Q4	2.269999999895	454908.7799999945
1997	11	Q4	3.710000000072	508272.4899999953
1997	12	Q4	5.640000000014	565238.1299999954

FIGURE 12.35
A report that can't be formatted.

The only way to get the Sales and Accumulated Sales columns formatted properly is to make the text boxes unbound and to format them in code in the Detail section's On Format event. This code is shown in the next example, which uses a stored procedure.

Basing a Report on a Stored Procedure

The same query can be wrapped up in a stored procedure as well as a view. Listing 12.13 shows the procAccumulatedSales stored procedure, which does basically the same thing as the vwAccumulatedSales view—it returns the data from the MDX query. Note that SET ANSI_NULLS ON and SET ANSI_WARNINGS ON have been added to the stored procedure. This prevents an error that can occur when these statements are omitted. The SET ANSI_NULLS and ANSI_WARNINGS options should be set automatically for any distributed query you're using OLE DB or ODBC to connect to the local SQL Server. Setting them in the stored procedure is insurance in case they may not be set to ON.

LISTING 12.13   The procAccumulatedSales Stored Procedure

```
CREATE PROC procAccumulatedSales
AS

SET ANSI_NULLS ON
SET ANSI_WARNINGS ON

SELECT * FROM
OPENQUERY(FOODMART,
    'WITH member [Measures].[Accumulated Sales] AS
    ''Sum(YTD(),[Measures].[Store Sales])''
    SELECT
    {[Measures].[Store Sales],[Measures].[Accumulated Sales]} ON COLUMNS,
    {Descendants([Time].[1997],[Time].[Month])} ON ROWS
    FROM Sales')
```

You can base a report directly on the procAccumulatedSales stored procedure with no problem. However, you still don't get any formatting if you try to apply it using the Format properties of the text boxes on the report's property sheet. All columns that you want to apply formatting to must be loaded in code into unbound text boxes and the formatting applied in the On Format event of the Detail section. In this example, the Month column is coded to display the month name instead of the month number:

```
Private Sub Detail_Format(Cancel As Integer, FormatCount As Integer)
    ' Format the columns
    Me.txtMonth = MonthName([[Time].[Month].[MEMBER_CAPTION]])
    Me.txtSales = Format([[Measures].[Store Sales]], "Currency")
    Me.txtAccumulated = Format([[Measures].[Accumulated Sales]], "Currency")
End Sub
```

Using User-Defined Functions for OLAP Reporting

In many ways, functions, which are new in SQL Server 2000, give you the best of both worlds. They can return a table (a set of records), so they can be used like a view. Yet, at the same time, they can accept parameters, and they have the performance benefits of stored procedures. This makes them the ideal mechanism for reporting.

Listing 12.14 shows the Transact-SQL statements used to create a function, fnPromotionUnitSales(), that returns the results of another MDX query. This user-defined function returns a table, @Promotions, that's defined at the start of the function, following the word RETURNS. To build the resultset, the function also uses a work table variable as a temp table (you can't use an actual temp table created with the # denominator). By defining the work table variable, @temp, with normal column names, you can insert the data from the OPENQUERY statement into it and thereby take care of converting the nonconforming column names. The data in the work table, @temp, is then inserted into the return parameter table, @Promotion.

LISTING 12.14   The Function fnPromotionUnitSales()

```
CREATE FUNCTION fnPromotionUnitSales ()

RETURNS @Promotions TABLE
    (Promotion nvarchar(50) primary key,
      Sales int NOT NULL)
AS
BEGIN
  DECLARE @temp TABLE (
    Promotion nvarchar(50) primary key,
    Sales int
    )

INSERT INTO @temp (Promotion, Sales)
SELECT *
FROM OPENQUERY(FOODMART,
  'SELECT
    {[Measures].[Unit Sales]} ON COLUMNS,
    ORDER(EXCEPT([Promotion Media].[Media Type].members,
    {[Promotion Media].[Media Type].[No Media]}),
    [Measures].[Unit Sales],DESC)
    ON ROWS
    FROM Sales') AS Prom

  INSERT @Promotions
  SELECT Promotion, Sales
  FROM @temp
  RETURN
END
```

To assign the function as the `RecordSource` of a report, use the following syntax in the property sheet:

```
SELECT * FROM fnPromotionUnitSales()
```

Running a report based on a user-defined function is noticeably faster than using a view or a stored procedure. If you attempt to write a stored procedure that uses a temp table to do the same processing, the Access report writer can't parse the table schema (see the example earlier in this chapter using crosstab queries). The user-defined function doesn't have this problem because the schema of the returned table is specified at the beginning of the function. For this reason, it is recommend that you use functions in this way, rather than views or stored procedures, to bring OLAP data into Access reports. Figure 12.36 shows the report based on the user-defined function in Print Preview mode.

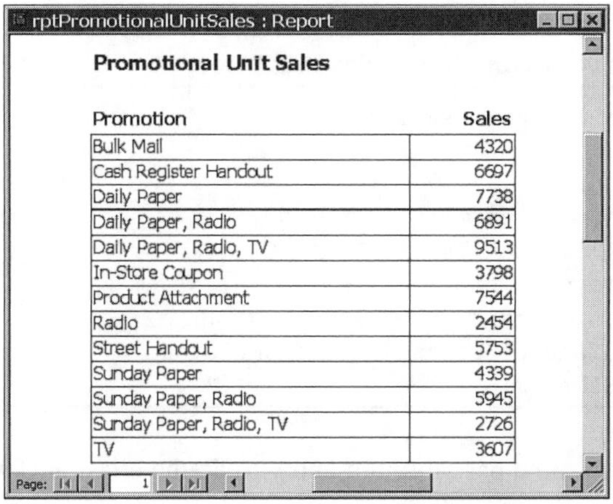
rptPromotionalUnitSales : Report

Promotional Unit Sales

Promotion	Sales
Bulk Mail	4320
Cash Register Handout	6697
Daily Paper	7738
Daily Paper, Radio	6891
Daily Paper, Radio, TV	9513
In-Store Coupon	3798
Product Attachment	7544
Radio	2454
Street Handout	5753
Sunday Paper	4339
Sunday Paper, Radio	5945
Sunday Paper, Radio, TV	2726
TV	3607

Page: 1

FIGURE 12.36
A report based on a user-defined function.

OLAP Reporting in Access Databases

Things are a little different when you use an Access database (MDB) to create reports based on OLAP data. Although you normally can link to views, views based on the `OPENQUERY` syntax can't be parsed by ODBC. Fortunately, there is a workaround. You just have to take care of aliasing those funny column names.

Basing Reports on Views in an MDB

If you try to link to a view based on an OLAP MDX query, you'll get an error message that goes something like this:

```
[Time].[Year].[MEMBER_CAPTION] is not a valid name. Make sure that it
does not include invalid characters or punctuation and that it is not too
long.
```

However, you can create a view that aliases the column names and link directly to it. In Access projects you can do the aliasing within the SQL of your RecordSource property, but to use an Access database you must handle the aliases within the linked view itself in SQL Server so that ODBC never has to see those invalid column names. Listing 12.15 shows the view vwAccumulatedSalesAlias, which selects from vwAccumulatedSales and simply aliases the column names.

LISTING 12.15   The vwAccumulatedSalesAlias View

```
CREATE VIEW vwAccumulatedSalesAlias
AS
SELECT
  "[time].[year].[member_caption]" AS Year,
  "[time].[quarter].[member_caption]" AS Quarter,
  "[time].[month].[member_caption]" AS Month,
  "[Measures].[Store Sales]" AS Sales,
  "[Measures].[Accumulated Sales]" AS Accumulated
FROM vwAccumulatedSales
```

Another alternative is to use a pass-through query to do the aliasing. The end result is the same—you just have one less saved view in your SQL Server database. The syntax would look like the following code snippet:

```
SELECT
  "[time].[year].[member_caption]" AS YearSold,
  "[time].[quarter].[member_caption]" AS QuarterSold,
  "[time].[month].[member_caption]" AS MonthSold,
  "[Measures].[Store Sales]" AS Sales,
  "[Measures].[Accumulated Sales]" AS Accumulated
FROM vwAccumulatedSales
```

Pass-through queries are covered in detail in Chapter 5. You have the same problem with formatting in an Access MDB as you do in an Access ADP. Assigning formatting directly from the property sheet doesn't work. Instead, you can use unbound text boxes and format them in the On Format event, as shown in the previous examples. Figure 12.37 shows the finished, formatted report.

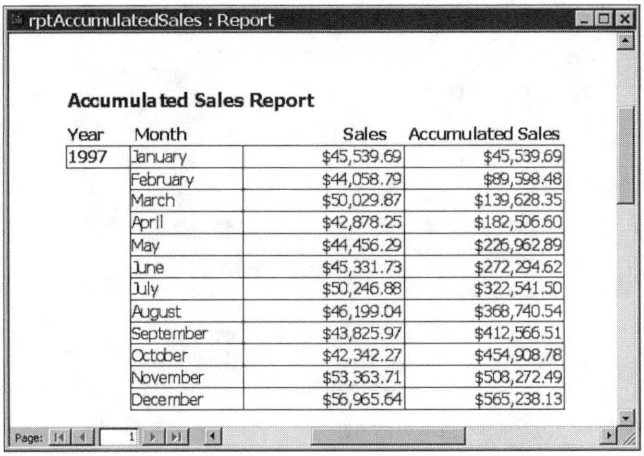
rptAccumulatedSales : Report

Accumulated Sales Report

Year	Month	Sales	Accumulated Sales
1997	January	$45,539.69	$45,539.69
	February	$44,058.79	$89,598.48
	March	$50,029.87	$139,628.35
	April	$42,878.25	$182,506.60
	May	$44,456.29	$226,962.89
	June	$45,331.73	$272,294.62
	July	$50,246.88	$322,541.50
	August	$46,199.04	$368,740.54
	September	$43,825.97	$412,566.51
	October	$42,342.27	$454,908.78
	November	$53,363.71	$508,272.49
	December	$56,965.64	$565,238.13

FIGURE 12.37

The finished, formatted report based on a view.

NOTE

You could, if you wanted to, do the formatting in the view, stored procedure, or function that the report is based on by writing a fair amount of Transact-SQL code. However, this is just going to slow down the query on which the report is based because the formatting functions have to be called for every row processed by the server. Because the report has to format every row anyway, it's much more efficient to keep your formatting code in the report.

Basing Reports on Stored Procedures and Functions in an MDB

If you're using an Access database, both stored procedures and functions are only available to reports through pass-through queries.

The pass-through query SQL to use for calling a function looks like this:

```
SELECT * FROM fnPromotionUnitSales()
```

The report's `RecordSource` property would then be set to the pass-through query. Figure 12.38 shows the report in Design view.

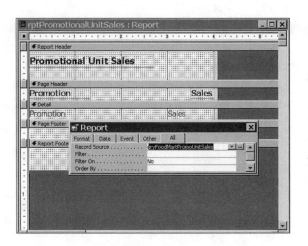

FIGURE 12.38
Design view of a report based on a pass-through query that selects from a function.

The finished report looks exactly the same as the one shown earlier in this chapter that was run in an Access project.

Summary

Reports benefit from indexing tables and fetching less data the same way forms do. Basing reports on views, stored procedures, or functions is efficient because data can be preaggregated on the server. Views allow users to create *ad hoc* reports without having to learn complex join notation. Views can be linked to like tables in an Access MDB. Stored procedures and functions are ideal for reports in both Access MDBs and ADPs because they are compiled and an execution plan is cached on the server. However, pass-through queries are needed in an Access MDB to access stored procedures and functions. The WhereCondition parameter of DoCmd.OpenReport will create efficient queries in both projects and databases. The Input Parameters and ServerFilter report properties in Access ADPs allow you to prefilter data for reports. The RecordSource property can be dynamically assigned in the report's On Open event. The WITH CUBE operator enables you to build multidimensional resultsets in Transact-SQL. Crosstab queries can be created in Access ADPs by taking advantage of temp tables in stored procedures. Multidimensional OLAP data from SQL Server's Analysis Services can be retrieved by setting up a linked server in SQL Server. Views and stored procedures can access data from the linked server by using the OPENQUERY Transact-SQL function. User-defined functions that return a table are ideal for OLAP reporting because it's easy to alias the column names in the body of the function.

Internet Features in Access and SQL Server

IN THIS CHAPTER

Access has never been a strong tool for creating Internet applications. If all you need is reporting, you may find enough there, but to build interactive data-entry applications that run over the Internet, you'll need to use other tools. Although Access 2000 introduces Data Access Pages (DAPs), the version 1 design environment and a restrictive licensing agreement that requires an Office 2000 license make them less than ideal for true Internet development. To use DAPs, clients must have Internet Explorer 5.0 or greater, and to bind them to data without a lot of extra work, the users must have access to the data over their local area or wide area network. The only way to use data-bound DAPs over the Internet is to set up Remote Data Services (RDS), which is difficult to configure (and explained later in this chapter). Having noted all that, however, DAPs do provide a way to build versatile user interfaces that can run in a browser, and many companies are using them successfully to enhance their intranets. Also, DAPs are bound to improve significantly in future versions of Access, so now's a good time to start learning the technology.

SQL Server has had system stored procedures and a wizard to support publishing data to the Web since SQL Server 7.0, but it would be hard to base much of a Web strategy on these features alone. SQL Server 2000 introduces new features that support XML functionality, which make it an XML-enabled database server that can both return XML from query requests and process requests that come packaged in XML updategrams. SQL Server 2000 also adds support for processing queries that come to the server over the HTTP Internet protocol. At first blush, it wouldn't seem like this XML support would do much for an Access application. However, using VBA code, you can easily take advantage of SQL Server's new XML functionality in Access by writing URL queries to fetch data to populate unbound forms. Updategrams allow you to post changes back to SQL Server.

This chapter covers how to publish SQL Server data to the Web using SQL Server tools and then introduces the XML features in SQL Server 2000. DAPs are also discussed, as well as other Access-specific Web functionality. Bear in mind that Web technology is changing by the day. You'll find enough here to get you started, but if you make the decision to implement solutions based on this technology, we encourage you to check Microsoft's Web site for the latest tools.

The XML features in SQL Server 2000 and the XML parser (MSXML) built into Internet Explorer are both being updated regularly by Microsoft and released over the Web. We also encourage you to learn about Active Server Pages (ASPs), which allow you to build true Internet applications that can be used to retrieve and modify SQL Server data from any browser. Visual Studio 6 includes a product called *Visual InterDev* for building ASPs, and the next version of Visual Studio will include support for an exciting new version called *ASP+*, which uses Microsoft's Common Language Runtime, part of the new .NET framework.

The easiest way to get started publishing SQL Server data to the Internet is to use the Web Assistant Wizard, and for simple data-reporting tasks, this may be all you need. Unlike the limited options that have existed in Access for publishing static HTML documents on demand, the SQL Server wizard allows you to create a schedule for generating the pages automatically or even for refreshing them anytime the data changes.

Publishing SQL Server Data to the Web

Publishing static HTML to the Web is accomplished in SQL Server in two ways: the Web Assistant Wizard and the Web system stored procedures.

The Web Assistant Wizard

The Web Assistant Wizard makes it easy to get started publishing SQL Server data to the Web. It walks you through the steps to create either a one-time HTML document or a job that can be scheduled.

The Web Assistant can publish data from table columns that you select, from the result set of a stored procedure, or from a Transact-SQL statement that returns records. The wizard also helps you format the finished page and set up scheduling for a job.

Launch the Web Assistant by choosing Tools, Wizards, Management, Web Assistant Wizard from the Enterprise Manager.

The first dialog box informs you that the wizard will perform the following tasks:

- Publish data from a server running SQL Server to a Web page
- Specify the frequency of Web page updates
- Specify the format of the published Web page

The next dialog box asks you to select the database to use, and the following dialog box asks you for the name of the Web Assistant job it will create. This wizard dialog box is also where you specify what kind of data source you'll be using. Here are the choices:

- Data from the Tables and Columns That I Select
- Result Set(s) of a Stored Procedure I Select
- Data from the Transact-SQL Statement I Specify

If you choose the first option, Data from the Tables and Columns That I Select, you'll be able to select the tables and columns, as shown in Figure 13.1. If you choose the second option, Result Set(s) of a Stored Procedure I Select, you'll be able to choose the stored procedure from a list of stored procedures in your database. If you choose Data from the Transact-SQL Statement I Specify, you'll be able to type in the Transact-SQL code. If you intend to use a Transact-SQL statement, it would be a good idea to create it ahead of time using a more user-friendly tool, such as the Query Analyzer, and then just paste the SQL code in the window.

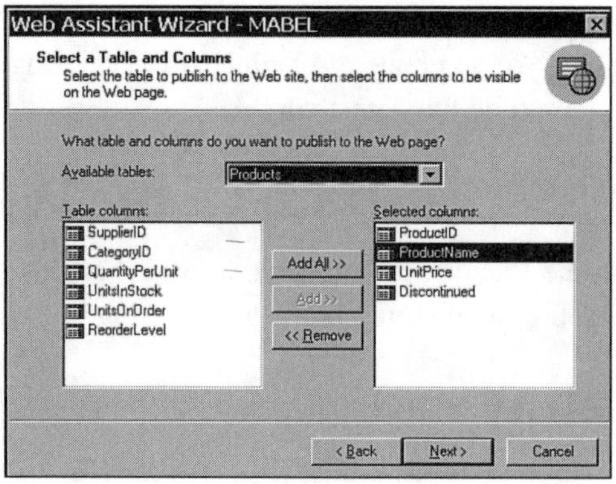

FIGURE 13.1
Selecting tables and columns from the Web Assistant Wizard.

The next dialog box gives you the option of publishing all the rows. Your other option is to choose to filter the data based on criteria that you select or a WHERE clause that you type in.

The next dialog box, shown in Figure 13.2, is where you can specify the frequency of updating the data and generating the Web page. Here are your options:

- *Only one time when I complete this wizard.*
- *On demand.*
- *Only one time at.* There are text boxes to fill in the date and time if you choose this option.
- *When the SQL Server data changes.* If you choose this option, the next dialog box will allow you to specify the data to be monitored.
- *At regularly scheduled intervals.* If you choose this option, the next dialog box will allow you to set up the schedule.
- *Generate a Web page when the wizard is completed.* This option generates a Web page when you're done with the wizard, no matter which other option you may have selected.

After you've set up scheduling or specified which tables and columns you want monitored, the following dialog box prompts you for a location for the Web page. Here's the default name and location:

```
C:\Program Files\Microsoft SQL Server\80\Tools\HTML\WebPage1.htm
```

You can change this to a location on your Web server, but the location needs to be available to SQL Server at all times if you've set up a schedule or chosen to generate a Web page when data changes.

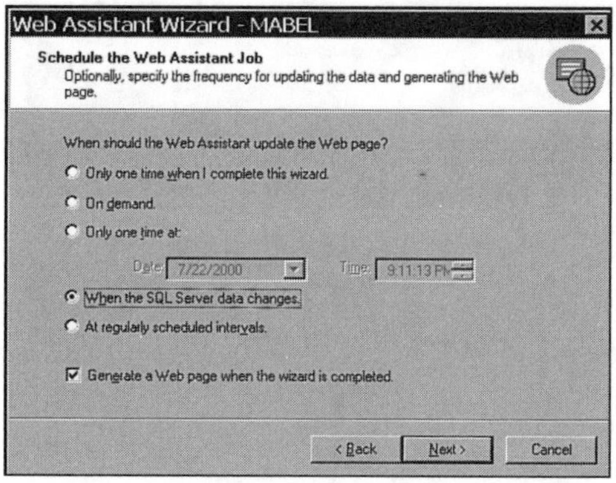

FIGURE 13.2

Scheduling the Web Assistant job.

The next dialog box asks whether you want the Web Assistant to help you format the Web page. Here are your options:

- *Yes, help me format the Web page.* In this case, you'll be able to select formatting options in the following dialog boxes.

- *No, use a template file from.* This option includes a text box for specifying the location of the template file. A *template file* is an HTML file with the marker `<%insert_data_here%>` to indicate where the query results should be inserted.

- *Use character set.* The default character set is already selected, but you can change it if you want.

If you selected Yes, Help Me Format the Web Page, the next dialog box, shown in Figure 13.3, lets you specify the title of the Web page and the title of the HTML table containing the page. You have several choices for the option What Size Should the HTML Table Title Font Be? Here are the available options:

- H1 - Largest
- H2 - Larger
- H3 - Large
- H4 - Medium
- H5 - Smaller
- H6 - Smallest

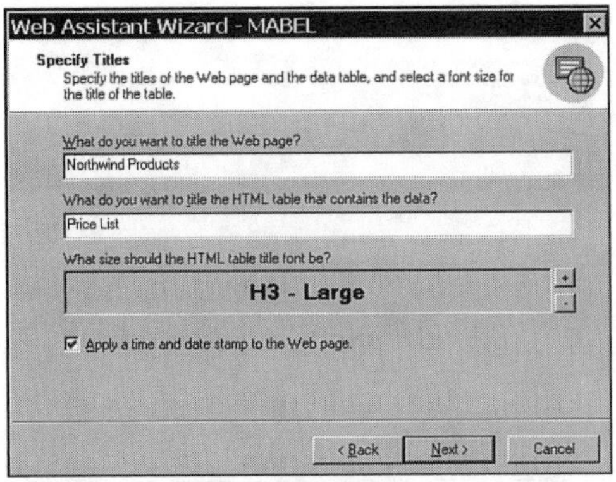

FIGURE 13.3

Formatting the titles for the Web page.

The next dialog box is for specifying how the table in the Web page will look, as shown in Figure 13.4. You can choose to display column names (or not), select font characteristics, and draw border lines around the HTML table.

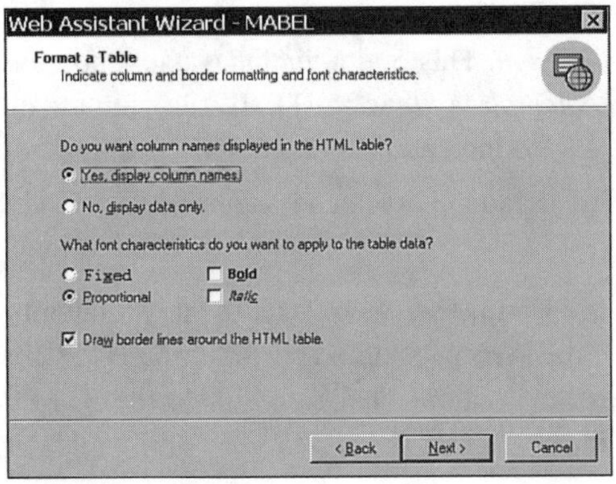

FIGURE 13.4

Formatting the table in the Web page.

After formatting the table, the wizard gives you the option of inserting additional hyperlinks in your Web page. Here are your choices:

- *No.* No hyperlinks will be added.
- *Yes, add one hyperlink.* In this case, you'll be able to fill in the hyperlink URL and the hyperlink label.

- *Yes, add a list of hyperlink URLs. Select them from a SQL Server table with the following SQL statement.* If you choose this option, you must already have a table containing the hyperlinks you want to use and supply the SELECT statement for the appropriate columns.

The next formatting dialog box allows you to limit the number of rows returned by SQL Server and also to specify whether all the data is placed on one scrolling page or on separate, linked pages, as shown in Figure 13.5.

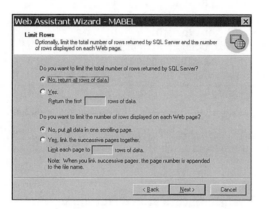

FIGURE 13.5
Limiting the rows and specifying scrolling or linked pages.

The last, and final, wizard dialog box displays a summary of the wizard options you've chosen. If you click the Write Transact-SQL to File button, a script will be created that you can use to re-create your Web job without running the wizard. That's right—everything you are doing with the wizard could also be done directly in Transact-SQL. Even if you're happy sticking with the wizard, go ahead and create the script so you can see the system stored procedure call that's being used to carry out your instructions. This system stored procedure is covered in the next section. When you click the Finish button, the wizard finishes up and the Web job is created.

The SQL Server Web Stored Procedures

After you finish running the wizard, open up the Transact-SQL file that was created in the final wizard dialog box. Listing 13.1 shows the script that was created. Note that the entire script executes one system stored procedure, sp_makewebtask. The input parameters are the options you selected when running the Web Assistant Wizard.

LISTING 13.1 The sp_makewebtask Stored Procedure

```
EXECUTE sp_makewebtask
  @outputfile = N'C:\Inetpub\wwwroot\NwindProducts.htm',
  @query=N'SELECT [ProductName], [UnitPrice] FROM [Products]',
  @fixedfont=0,
  @colheaders=0,
  @HTMLheader=3,
  @webpagetitle=N'Northwind Products',
  @resultstitle=N'Price List',
  @dbname=N'Northwind', @whentype=10,
  @datachg=N'TABLE=Products COLUMN=ProductName,UnitPrice',
  @procname=N'NorthwindProducts',
  @codepage=65001,@charset=N'utf-8'
```

Note the parameter @procname. If you look in the Northwind database, you'll find a new stored procedure named NorthwindProducts. Listing 13.2 shows the definition of the NorthwindProducts stored procedure, which simply selects the data columns you specified in the wizard.

LISTING 13.2 The NorthwindProducts Stored Procedure

```
CREATE PROCEDURE [NorthwindProducts]
  AS
  SELECT [ProductName], [UnitPrice]
    FROM [Products]
```

If you run the wizard and choose the option When the SQL Server Data Changes, the three triggers shown in Listing 13.3 are added to the Products table. This ensures that when a product is inserted, updated, or deleted, the NorthwindProducts Web task will be executed by running the sp_runwebtask system stored procedure, thus creating an updated Web page.

LISTING 13.3 The Triggers Added to the Products Table

```
-- Trigger to run web task when a new product inserted
CREATE TRIGGER [NorthwindProducts_1]
  ON [Products]
  FOR INSERT
AS
  IF UPDATE([ProductName]) OR UPDATE([UnitPrice])
    BEGIN
      EXEC sp_runwebtask @procname =  N'NorthwindProducts'
    END

-- Trigger to run web task when a product is updated
CREATE TRIGGER [NorthwindProducts_2]
  ON [Products]
```

LISTING 13.3   Continued

```
FOR UPDATE
AS
  IF UPDATE([ProductName]) OR UPDATE([UnitPrice])
    BEGIN
      EXEC sp_runwebtask @procname =  N'NorthwindProducts'
    END

-- Trigger to run web task when a product is deleted
CREATE TRIGGER [NorthwindProducts_4]
  ON [Products]
  FOR DELETE
AS
  BEGIN
    EXEC sp_runwebtask @procname =  N'NorthwindProducts'
  END
```

The sp_runwebtask procedure takes the name of the stored procedure used for retrieving the data (NorthwindProducts) as its first argument, and it runs that stored procedure to fetch the updated data from the Products table and push it out to a new Web page. Here's the procedure:

```
sp_runwebtask [ [ @procname = ] 'procname' ]
    [ , [ @outputfile = ] 'outputfile'
```

The finished Web page looks like the one shown in Figure 13.6, unless you choose to embell-ish it by using an HTML template.

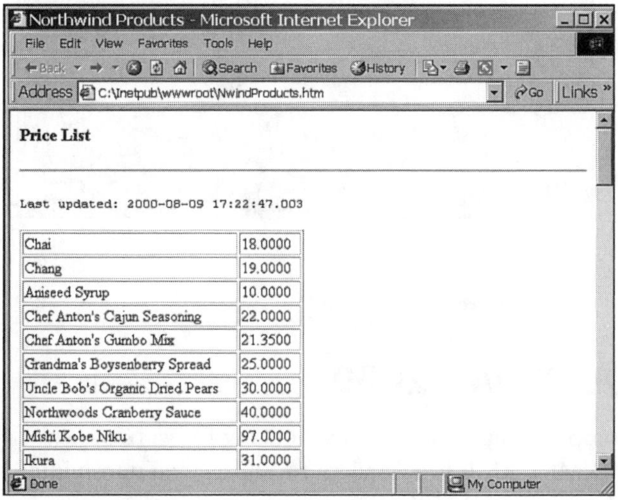

FIGURE 13.6
The completed Web page.

The `sp_dropwebtask` stored procedure deletes the Web task and the associated Web page:

```
sp_dropwebtask
  @procname = 'NorthwindProducts',
  @outputfile = 'C:\Inetpub\wwwroot\NwindProducts.htm'
```

This will execute dropping the stored procedure, cleaning up the triggers in the Products table and deleting the `NwindProducts.htm` file. If you only specify the `@procname` parameter, the HTM file will not be deleted.

The Web Job

If you choose any of the scheduling options while running the wizard, a job will be created. Unlike in SQL Server 7, there is no Web Publishing node created under the Management node—the Web jobs have been relocated under the SQL Server Agent node. To edit the job properties, expand Jobs, right-click the job, and choose Properties. This opens the dialog box shown in Figure 13.7. The Steps tab shows you the single step that the Web job consists of, which is executing the `sp_runwebtask` stored procedure. You can edit the step or add additional steps to the job. The Schedules tab lets you alter the schedule, and the Notifications tab allows you to send notifications upon job success, failure, or completion. SQL Server Agent, which is a powerful tool for defining, scheduling, and running all kinds of tasks in SQL Server, is covered in Chapter 15, "Deployment, Tuning, and Maintenance."

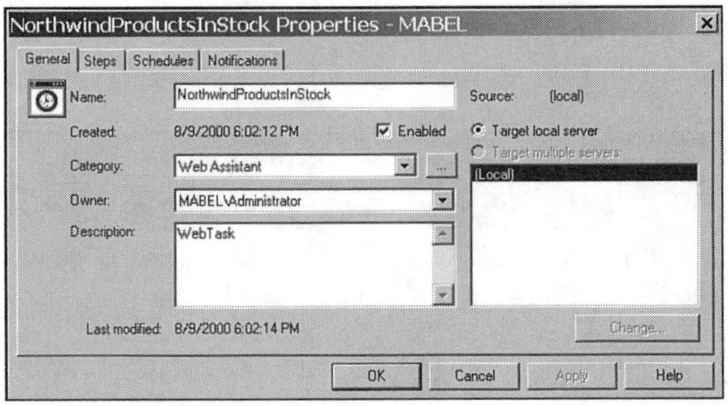

FIGURE 13.7
Editing the Web job after it has been created by the wizard.

XML in SQL Server 2000

SQL Server 2000 supports important new functionality for working with data using Extensible Markup Language (XML). XML is a standard for storing and transmitting data in a format that includes not only the data itself but also a description of its structure.

A Brief Introduction to XML

Since computers first came into widespread use, companies have had to deal with the problem of sharing data between disparate, unrelated systems. From its humble beginnings in SGML, the Standard Generalized Markup Language used to allow formatted documents to be shared, HTML (Hypertext Markup Language) emerged as a universal Internet standard when it was endorsed by the World Wide Web Consortium (W3C) as the standard for Web pages transmitted over the Internet and viewed in a browser. HTML documents use a standard set of tags, such as <p> for *paragraph*, that are used by browsers to render Web pages. XML allows you to create and codify your own set of tags focused not on formatting but instead on the structure of your data. Here's an example of a simple XML document:

```xml
<?xml version="1.0" encoding="UTF-8"?>
<products>
    <product id="P70" unitprice="15.00">
        <name>Outback Lager</name>
        <supplier id="S7">Pavlova, Ltd.
            <city>Melbourne</city><country>Australia</country>
        </supplier>
        <category id="C1">Beverages</category>
        <unitquantity>24 - 355 ml bottles</unitquantity>
    </product>
    <!-- repeat the product element for each item -->
</products>
```

Perhaps the most confusing part of reading XML is figuring out why some data is represented as attributes that are contained inside the tags, such as the product ID and unit price in the example, and some data appears as text elements between tags, such as the Outback Lager name. XML theorists debate whether attributes or elements are appropriate in different situations, but you'll see them both used, often without any apparent reason why. Other than that, however, XML is quite readable, and its meaning is usually obvious. Without knowing anything about XML, it is possible to understand quite a bit from reading this document, not just about the Outback Lager product but also about how this database is organized. It would be hard to find a better way of communicating all this information as clearly in a simple text file, and for that reason XML has been heartily embraced by just about every vendor and consumer of data and database management systems.

The preceding XML document shows only part of the story. Separate documents are created that define the allowed structure—for example, specifying that every product must have an ID and a unit price, expressed as attributes, and a name expressed as element text. The original standard for this was Document Type Definitions (DTDs), which are SGML documents that are rather abstruse and hard to work with. Most importantly, the DTDs are not, themselves, in XML format. To remedy this, a new way of defining structure using XML has been developed called *schemas*. The W3C is now in the final stages of completing a formal recommendation

13

for a schema standard, known as XSD. The XSD recommendation may already have been finalized by the time you are reading this. The full details of all W3C recommendations can be found at `http://www.w3c.org`.

Because XML documents can contain data from multiple sources, there is a need to resolve naming conflicts. For example, two different vendors may both use a `<product>` tag, but each could use it in a completely different way. You need some way to distinguish one kind of "product" from the other completely different item also called "product". To handle this, XML allows you to use the `xmlns` attribute to define namespaces, which can be assigned a unique identifier, often based on a Web address. Here's an example of one way that two namespaces could be defined to distinguish between two different kinds of product:

```
<products>
  <prd1:product xmlns:prd1="urn:acmeproducts.com:productinfo">
    <prd1:productid>1234</prd1:productid >
    <prd1:name>gizmo</ prd1:name>
  </prd1:product>
  <prd2:product xmlns:prd2="urn:zenithproducts.com:catalog">
    <prd2:productnumber>321</prd2:productnumber>
    <prd2:name>widget</ prd2:name>
  </prd2:product>
</products >
```

To work productively with XML data, you need tools for parsing the document and extracting or manipulating the data it contains. The W3C has recommended a standard Document Object Model (DOM) that supports programmatic access to XML data. The DOM works with XML as a hierarchy of nodes, allowing programmers to navigate through a document and read or modify it as needed.

Another programming tool that's commonly used, even though it is not a formal W3C standard, is the Simple API (Application Programming Interface) for XML (known as *SAX*). Unlike the DOM, SAX doesn't load the entire document into memory and allow you to navigate around within it. Instead, SAX is a protocol for running through the document and responding to what you find along the way. It lacks some of the flexibility of the DOM, but it runs much quicker and consumes much less memory.

In addition to using the DOM and SAX, another way of finding information in an XML document is *XPath*, a protocol for creating expressions that locate data according to its position within an XML hierarchy. XPath is analogous to the DOS standard of using expressions such as `C:\ Documents\*.doc` to locate all the Word files in a certain directory. So, to retrieve the name of a particular employee, you might use an XPath expression such as this:

```
/Employees[@EmployeeID=1]/@Name
```

Sometimes you need to transform data from one XML format into another. One common example of this is transforming XML data into a form that looks good in a browser, by enclosing the data within HTML table tags. Another example would be transforming data received from a vendor or customer into a form that matches your company's own database structure. In HTML, *stylesheets* are used to transform a document by applying formatting. This concept was generalized for XML to support stylesheets that can transform an XML document into any type of text file. The resulting document could be formatted HTML, or a new XML document conforming to a different schema, or even a plain text file without any tags. This W3C standard for transforming XML documents is called *XSLT*.

All these terms and concepts come into play when you work with the XML features in SQL Server 2000. Microsoft has embraced XML and has been active in both developing and accepting the standards recommended by the W3C.

Microsoft BizTalk Server is a product that provides useful tools for orchestrating the exchange of XML documents among business partners. Among other things, BizTalk allows you to map data visually from one XML structure to another by simply drawing lines between fields and to automatically generate an XSLT stylesheet that performs the defined transformation.

XML Features in SQL Server 2000

SQL Server 2000's new XML features include the following:

- The ability to access SQL Server through a URL (a Uniform Resource Locator, or simply a Web address) over HTTP. Your query would look something like the following:

  `http://IISServer/VirtualRoot?sql=SELECT+*+FROM+Customers+FOR+XML+AUTO`

  If you enter this in a browser and your server has been properly configured, you'll get back an XML document containing the results of the query. SQL Server 2000 also allows you to create special files, called *templates*, that can be called from a URL to run Transact-SQL that's stored in the template. By using templates, which can be sent parameters, you are able to avoid exposing your T-SQL within the URL.

- Support for XDR (XML-Data Reduced) schemas and the ability to specify XPath queries against these schemas. XDR is an interim schema format that Microsoft developed for use while the WC3 was working on a formal standard. When that standard, called *XSD*, becomes a W3C recommendation (which may already have happened by the time you read this), Microsoft has said that it will support the XSD standard. In the meantime, the XDR schemas that were in use in SQL Server 2000 when it shipped can be used without causing future problems, because they are a proper subset of the emerging XSD standard. Annotated schemas can allow your XML-based client applications to view relational SQL Server data as if it were one big XML document rather than multiple related tables.

- The ability to retrieve and write XML data. SQL Server 2000 enables you to retrieve XML data using a SELECT statement with a FOR XML clause, to read and write XML data using the OPENXML rowset provider, and to retrieve XML data using XPath query expressions.

- Enhancements have been made to the SQL Server 2000 OLE DB provider that allow XML documents to be set as command text and to return result sets in a stream. These extensions were applied to ADO as well.

- A standard for using specially formatted XML documents, called *updategrams*, to send data-modification commands to SQL Server. Updategrams can be used to insert, edit, or delete records in your SQL Server tables.

Before You Start

Before you start trying to use XML in SQL Server 2000, you should already be familiar with HTTP methods, URL syntax, and XML in general. To process XML documents, you'll also probably need familiarity with the MSXML parser, the Document Object Model (DOM), XPath expressions, and XSLT stylesheets. When it comes to exchanging data with other programs, you'll need a DTD or schema that describes your data structure.

One step that is absolutely indispensable if you want to work with XML in SQL Server 2000 is to set up a virtual root directory that's associated with your SQL Server instance, in Internet Information Services (IIS).

Creating a Virtual Directory (The Virtual Root)

To set up a virtual directory, use the IIS Virtual Directory Management for SQL Server utility. The following steps create a virtual root named Nwind that's associated with the Northwind database in SQL Server:

1. Create a folder named `nwind` in your `\Inetpub\wwwroot` directory with two subdirectories under it named `template` and `schema`.

2. From the Windows Start menu, choose Programs, SQL Server, Configure SQL XML Support in IIS.

3. Expand a server, right-click the Web site you want, and choose New, Virtual Directory, as shown in Figure 13.8.

4. Set the following options and click OK when finished:

   - *General tab.* Type the name of the virtual directory (`nwind`) and the path created for it in step 1 (`c:\Inetpub\wwwroot\nwind`).

   - *Security tab.* For the account type, choose SQL Server and supply a login and password that has access to the Northwind database.

   - *Data Source tab.* For the server name, enter the name of your server. For the database name, enter **Northwind**.

   - *Settings tab.* Check all options to allow URL queries, template queries, and XPath options.

- *Virtual Names tab.* This is where you create virtual names for the template and schema types that map to the subdirectories created in step 1. Click the New button to create the virtual names for each, setting the properties and filling in the paths to the two directories. Figure 13.9 shows the Virtual Names tab with the options already set for the schema and template. Click OK when done.

FIGURE 13.8
Creating a new virtual directory to use with SQL Server.

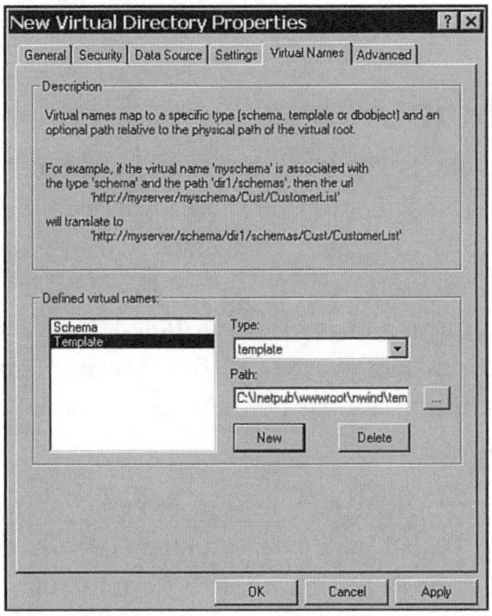

FIGURE 13.9
Setting the virtual names for the virtual root.

To verify that everything is working properly, type the following SQL statement in your browser and press Enter (make sure you enter your IIS server name, without the angle brackets, instead of the placeholder text <ServerName>):

```
http://<ServerName>/nwind?sql=SELECT * FROM Employees WHERE EmployeeID = 1
  FOR XML AUTO
```

The results are shown in Figure 13.10.

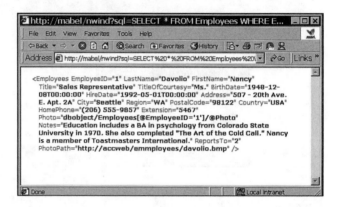

FIGURE 13.10
Testing the XML and the virtual directory.

Using URL Queries in Access

One of the problems with Internet or intranet applications in general is that they usually are limited to using a Web browser for the user interface. Although this makes the application easy to deploy, it also makes it harder to create a sophisticated user interface. If users are familiar with the forms they get with an Access or VB application, working with forms on a browser can be a real letdown. If you already have Office installed, there's no reason why you can't use unbound forms and URL queries sent over HTTP from Access to provide a more user-friendly user interface. This section covers the basics of how to get started creating an unbound Access front end for your Web application.

As you've seen, you can write a URL query in your browser by specifying the server name, virtual directory name, and a SELECT statement with the FOR XML clause. However, getting the data into a browser isn't the same as getting it into a form in your Access application. In order to write a URL query, you need to set a reference to the Microsoft XML type library, which is included with Internet Explorer. The XMLHTTP object in that library lets you write URL queries to fetch XML from SQL Server. SQL Server 2000 includes extensions to Transact-SQL that allow you to specify the XML format that you want returned from a query, and SQL Server also now includes system stored procedures for handling XML processing.

Creating an XML-Returning Stored Procedure

Listing 13.4 shows a query that returns an XML document containing the data from a single row in the Products table, based on the input parameter ProductID.

LISTING 13.4   Creating a Stored Procedure to Return XML

```
CREATE PROCEDURE procXMLProductParam
 @ProductID int
AS
  SELECT '<ROOT>'
  SELECT ProductID, ProductName, UnitPrice
  FROM Products
  WHERE  ProductID = @ProductID
  FOR XML AUTO
  SELECT '</ROOT>'
```

The FOR XML clause causes SQL Server to format the query appropriately. In order for the results to be processed properly, <ROOT> and </ROOT> tags are added to delimit the XML document returned by the query. SQL Server doesn't ever create complete XML documents on its own. Instead, it creates XML fragments that can be assembled into documents. For an XML document to be well formed, it must begin and end with tags delimiting a root node. Those tags don't actually have to be called ROOT. For example, the sample XML presented earlier in the chapter used <PRODUCTS> and </PRODUCTS> as the root node delimiters. The word ROOT is used in these examples as a generic delimiter for the document to make it well-formed XML.

To call the stored procedure from your browser, use the following syntax. The server name is mabel, the virtual root is nwind, and the @ProductID parameter value being passed in is 1. Plus signs are used instead of spaces when typing the Transact-SQL command. Here's the URL call to the stored procedure:

```
http://mabel/nwind?sql=execute+procXMLProductParam+1
```

Figure 13.11 shows the results of the query. Note that there are tags surrounding the values. The <ROOT> and </ROOT> tags delimit the root node. The <Products ProductID="1" ProductName="Chai" UnitPrice="18" /> tag indicates the one row returned by the stored procedure, representing all the data as attributes. This is the result set that will be returned when you call the stored procedure from Access.

Loading XML Data in Access

After you've set the reference to the Microsoft XML type library, you can create a procedure to execute the stored procedure and display the row of data on a form. Figure 13.12 shows a simple form based on the procXMLProductParam stored procedure. It opens with no product loaded. The user types in a ProductID value and clicks the Load button, which fetches the data.

FIGURE 13.11

Executing a parameter query from the browser.

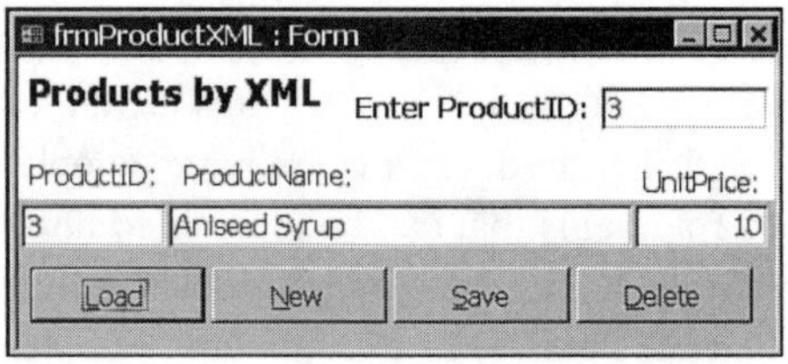

FIGURE 13.12

A simple form for working with XML.

The cmdLoad_Click() event procedure starts off defining some variables that will be used to process the XML. The XMLHTTPRequest object is used to execute the query, and DOMDocument is used to process the raw XML returned by the query. Here's the code:

```
Private Sub cmdLoad_Click()
    Dim oXMLHTTP As XMLHTTPRequest
    Dim oDOMDoc As DOMDocument
    Dim varProdID As Variant
    Dim strURL As String
    Dim ctl As Control
```

First, the data is validated—the ProductID needs to be a numeric value in order for the stored procedure to run:

```
    If Not IsNumeric(varProdID) Then
        MsgBox "Enter ProductID", , "ProductID Required"
        Me.txtEnter.SetFocus
        GoTo ExitHere
    End If
```

Then the query string is defined for the URL query. This looks the same as the string used in the browser, with the exception that the varProdID variable is used to concatenate in the @ProductID parameter value:

```
strURL = _
  "http://mabel/nwind?sql=execute+procXMLProductParam+" _
    & varProdID
```

The Open method of the XMLHTTPRequestobject is then called. The first argument, bstrMethod, is set to "GET". Other valid values are "POST", "PUT", and "PROPFIND", corresponding to the standard HTTP options. The second argument is the URL, and the final argument specifies that the code should wait for a response before continuing. The Send method sends the URL query to the server. Here's the code:

```
Set oXMLHTTP = New XMLHTTPRequest
Call oXMLHTTP.Open( _
  bstrMethod:="GET", _
  bstrURL:=strURL, _
  varAsync:=False)
oXMLHTTP.send
```

Once the URL query has run, the results have to be processed. This is where the DOMDocument object comes in. The DOMDocument object, based on the W3C standard DOM, allows you to work with the different elements in the XML. The string returned by the URL query is loaded into the DOMDocument variable, oDOMDoc, and then each text box on the form is assigned its corresponding node value. Each text box on the form has a name corresponding to the name of a column in the table. Because the data in this XML document is implemented as attributes, the code uses the getNamedItem method of the Attributes property of the target node to retrieve data from the document. If the document for some reason does not load successfully, then the text boxes are emptied. Here's the code:

```
Set oDOMDoc = New DOMDocument
If oDOMDoc.loadXML(oXMLHTTP.responseText) Then
  For Each ctl In Me.Controls
    If TypeOf ctl Is TextBox Then
      ctl.Value = _
        oDOMDoc.childNodes(0).childNodes(0).Attributes.getNamedItem _
        (ctl.Name).nodeValue
    End If
  Next ctl
Else
  For Each ctl In Me.Controls
    If TypeOf ctl Is TextBox Then
      ctl.Value = Null
    End If
  Next ctl
```

13

INTERNET
FEATURES IN
ACCESS AND SQL
SERVER

```
    MsgBox "Unable to load the specified product."
End If
```

Returning data as attributes is the default behavior when you use FOR XML AUTO. However, that's not your only option. SQL Server also supports FOR XML AUTO, ELEMENTS, which will return the data in the form of elements (text between tags) rather than attributes (text within tags). In addition to XML AUTO, you can also use FOR XML RAW, which uses attributes for data but does not support hierarchical nesting. A third choice, FOR XML EXPLICIT, supports a complex syntax that provides very granular control over the formatting of the returned XML.

Once the data is displayed in the controls, the user is free to edit it on the form. Any changes can be saved back to SQL Server, which is where updategrams come in.

Modifying Data Using Updategrams

Updategrams were not included in the first shipping version of SQL Server 2000. They were made available almost immediately after the product's debut, as a Web release. You can download the DLLs, documentation, and sample applications to work with updategrams. The central location for obtaining information and updates is the XML Developer Center (http://msdn.microsoft.com/xml/default.asp).

Updategrams work by using XML to describe the state of the SQL Server data before and after the change being described. The XML to implement this description consists of a <sync> node that contains a <before> node, showing the current data values, and an <after> node, showing the proposed new data, or both. Here's how it works:

- For editing data, you need both a <before> and an <after> block.
- For inserting data, you need only an <after> block.
- For deleting data, you need only a <before> block. The lack of an <after> block for deletions indicates that you expect there will be no data left that matches the <before> block.

Multiple <before> and <after> blocks are permitted within a <sync> block, and multiple <sync> blocks are permitted within an updategram document. The only restriction is that if you use multiple <before> and/or <after> blocks within a <sync> block, they must be in pairs, with one <after> block following every <before> block.

Updategram Syntax

The updategram syntax nests <before> and <after> blocks inside of the <sync> blocks. To avoid ambiguity, place an explicit reference to the updategram namespace in the root node of your document, and define a prefix to be used with all your updategram tags. Here's an example:

```
<ROOT xmlns:updg="urn:schemas-microsoft-com:xml-updategram">
 <updg:sync>
    <updg:before>
        <TABLENAME [updg:id="value"] col="value" col="value"…../>
    </updg:before>
    <updg:after>
        <TABLENAME [updg:id="value"] [updg:at-identity="value"]
         col="value" col="value"…../>
    </updg:after>
 </updg:sync>
</ROOT>
```

Editing Data

Because updating the Products table requires sending parameters, one or more values are replaced with named parameters designated by $ParameterName. Parameters are easily passed to an updategram contained in a template, which is an XML document stored in your template directory in the virtual root. The template used to update the UnitPrice is named UpdateProduct.XML. The template provides the mappings for the data changes. The <updg:param name="ProductID"/> parameter will be used to locate the row to be changed, and the <updg:param name="UnitPrice"/> parameter will be used to indicate the value to be changed. These values are plugged into the $ProductID and $UnitPrice parameters at runtime. Here's the code:

```
<ROOT xmlns:updg="urn:schemas-microsoft-com:xml-updategram">
<updg:header>
  <updg:param name="ProductID"/>
  <updg:param name="UnitPrice"/>
</updg:header>
  <updg:sync >
    <updg:before>
        <Products   ProductID="$ProductID"/>
    </updg:before>
    <updg:after>
        <Products   UnitPrice="$UnitPrice"/>
    </updg:after>
  </updg:sync>
</ROOT>
```

This is an example of what's called a blind update. The price for this item will be updated even if another user modified the record since you edited it. The <before> tag could be used to provide greater concurrency control by specifying other fields besides ProductID that would also have to match for the update to be executed.

To send an updategram from Access to SQL Server that updates the data in the UnitPrice field, you can use the XMLHTTPRequest object:

13

INTERNET
FEATURES IN
ACCESS AND SQL
SERVER

```
Private Sub cmdSave_Click()
    Dim oXMLHTTP As XMLHTTPRequest
    Dim varProdID As Variant
    Dim varUnitPrice As Variant
    Dim strURL As String
```

Using a template simplifies the client code—the string used merely specifies the template name and location and provides the parameter values. It is then executed using the XMLHTTPRequest methods Open and Send:

```
strURL = "http://mabel/nwind/template/UpdateProduct.xml?ProductID=" _
    & varProdID & "&UnitPrice=" & varUnitPrice
Set oXMLHTTP = New XMLHTTPRequest
Call oXMLHTTP.Open( _
    bstrMethod:="GET", _
    bstrURL:=strURL, _
    varAsync:=False)
oXMLHTTP.send
```

Adding New Data

To add a new product, the AddProduct.xml template for the updategram would have just the after tag along with parameter values for each column in the row to be inserted in the Products table:

```
<ROOT xmlns:updg="urn:schemas-microsoft-com:xml-updategram">
<updg:header>
  <updg:param name="ProductName"/>
  <updg:param name="UnitPrice"/>
</updg:header>
  <updg:sync >
    <updg:after>
      <Products   ProductName="$ProductName"
       UnitPrice="$UnitPrice"/>
          </updg:after>
  </updg:sync>
</ROOT>
```

The code to save the new record would look like this:

```
strURL = "http://mabel/nwind/template/UpdateProduct.xml?ProductID=" _
    & varProdID & "&UnitPrice=" & varUnitPrice
Set oXMLHTTP = New XMLHTTPRequest
Call oXMLHTTP.Open( _
    bstrMethod:="GET", _
    bstrURL:=strURL, _
    varAsync:=False)
oXMLHTTP.send
```

The form could then fetch the new ProductID, using the ProductName as a parameter. At the time of this writing, no technique was yet documented for returning the new ProductID without making a separate trip to the server.

Deleting Data

Deleting a product entails creating a parameterized DeleteProduct.xml template with just the before tag and a parameter for the records to be deleted:

```
<ROOT xmlns:updg="urn:schemas-microsoft-com:xml-updategram">
<updg:header>
  <updg:param name="ProductID"/>
</updg:header>
  <updg:sync >
    <updg:before>
       <Products   ProductID="$ProductID"/>
    </updg:before>
  </updg:sync>
</ROOT>
```

The lack of a corresponding after tag tells SQL Server that the matching rows are to be deleted. Because ProductID is the primary key, only that one row will be deleted. The template is then executed with the ProductID that is passed to it:

```
strURL = "http://mabel/nwind/template/DeleteProduct.xml?" _
   & "ProductID=" & varProdID
Set oXMLHTTP = New XMLHTTPRequest
Call oXMLHTTP.Open( _
  bstrMethod:="GET", _
  bstrURL:=strURL, _
  varAsync:=False)
oXMLHTTP.send
```

Of course, retrieving, editing, updating, and inserting data can much more easily be accomplished using ADO, and it is even possible to run ADO over an Internet connection using Remote Data Services (RDS), which is discussed later in this chapter. The advantages of working with XML become most apparent when you need to be able to share data among disparate systems. Unlike ADO, which is based on proprietary Microsoft technology, XML is based on international standards that a fast-growing number of software vendors all support. Microsoft, too, has seen the advantage of using XML, and most new products from Microsoft rely on it heavily. With a couple of partners, including IBM, Microsoft has developed the Simple Open Access Protocol (SOAP), which allows programs built on any platform to communicate over the Internet using XML. SOAP is in the process of becoming a formal W3C recommendation. As time goes by, SQL Server's support for XML will grow in its versatility and in its importance to your development efforts.

13

INTERNET
FEATURES IN
ACCESS AND SQL
SERVER

Using OPENXML in Transact-SQL

Chapter 8, "Introduction to Transact SQL (T-SQL)," shows how OPENROWSET can be used to retrieve data from any OLE DB data source. OPENXML is similar, but instead of being geared toward OLE DB data sources, it allows you to retrieve data from XML documents. This can be quite a challenge because the relational, rectangular row/column data structures that SQL Server normally works with are very different from the hierarchical, nested organization of data used by XML.

OPENXML addresses this challenge by providing a way to create relational rowsets based on hierarchical XML data, enabling you to query XML documents and, when appropriate, insert the retrieved data into SQL Server tables.

The first step in using OPENXML is to run a stored procedure that loads an XML document into SQL Server's memory and returns a handle in the form of an int output parameter. You use this number to refer to the XML document later in your code. In the following line of T-SQL, @doc is a varchar parameter that holds the text of an XML document, and @idoc is a variable that will be assigned a number when the stored procedure runs:

```
Exec sp_xml_preparedocument @idoc OUTPUT, @doc
```

Now that @idoc holds a reference to the in-memory DOM representation of your XML document, you can feed that value into OPENXML. Here's the syntax for using OPENXML:

```
OPENXML(idoc int [in],rowpattern nvarchar[in],[flags byte[in]])
[WITH (SchemaDeclaration | TableName)]
```

The first parameter, idoc, is the handle to your XML document. This is the number you got from running xml_preparedocument. The second parameter, rowpattern, is an XPath expression that defines which node or nodes in the document will be retrieved. The final parameter, flags, which is optional, can be used to specify whether an attribute-centric or element-centric mapping should be used when applying the XPath pattern. The default is to use attribute-centric mapping.

The WITH clause of OPENXML determines the format of the rowset that is returned. You have two options here. If the columns you are extracting from an XML document exactly match the columns in an existing SQL Server table, you can just give the name of the table. If you need a custom set of columns for this rowset, you can list their names and data types, similarly to the way you would in a CREATE TABLE statement. If necessary, you can also use an XPath expression for each column to tell SQL Server where to find the data. If the data is in the same location specified by the XPath expression in your OPENXML parameter, rowpattern, you can just use a name and data type to define each column in the SchemaDeclaration parameter. If you omit the WITH clause altogether, your rowset will be in a format called an *edge table*, which is basically a dataset containing columns that represent the entire structure and content of an XML hierarchy, using a numeric Id and parented column for each node to express the hierarchy.

Here's an example of Transact-SQL code that loads an XML document into memory and then uses OPENSQL to extract a portion of it. In this example, the XML is created inside the code using a varchar(1000) variable, but the XML could also be passed into a stored procedure in a varchar input parameter:

```
DECLARE @idoc int
DECLARE @doc varchar(1000)
SET @doc ='
<Products>
  <Product ProductID="123" ProductName="Widget">
      <Supplier SupplierID="ACM" SupplierName="Acme Supply"/>
  </Product>
  <Product ProductID="567" ProductName="Gizmo">
      <Supplier SupplierID="ZEN" SupplierName="Zenith Products"/>
  </Product>
</Products>'
--Load the XML document into a DOM in memory
EXEC sp_xml_preparedocument @idoc OUTPUT, @doc
-- Execute a SELECT statement that uses OPENXML
SELECT * FROM OPENXML (@idoc, '/Products/Product')
 WITH (ProductID int,
 ProductName varchar(50))
```

Here's the result set:

```
ProductID ProductName
--------- --------------------
123       Widget
567       Gizmo
```

To return SupplierName and ProductName, you would need to extract data from two different levels of the hierarchy. To do that, use an XPath expression to locate the data when defining the columns in your WITH clause:

```
SELECT    *
FROM      OPENXML (@idoc, '/Products/Product/Supplier')
          WITH (SupplierName  varchar(50) '@SupplierName',
                ProductName varchar(50) '../@ProductName')
```

Just as in DOS, two dots are used in XPath to move up the hierarchy to the parent "directory" node. In this case, the expression '../@ProductName' instructs SQL Server to move up a level from Supplier to Product and extract data from the ProductName attribute.

13

INTERNET
FEATURES IN
ACCESS AND SQL
SERVER

When you have finished working with the XML document in your T-SQL code, release the memory that it was consuming:

```
EXEC sp_xml_removedocument @idoc
```

Running `sp_xml_removedocument` is the functional equivalent of setting an object variable to `Nothing` in VBA.

As e-commerce becomes integrated into more and more business applications, it will become common for your applications to be receiving data in the form of XML documents. `OPENXML` gives you an alternative to parsing those documents in your application before you send the data to SQL Server. With `sp_xml_preparedocument` and `OPENXML`, you can use Transact-SQL to load the document into a DOM memory structure and parse out the data you need.

In addition to e-commerce applications, you may want to take advantage of `OPENXML` to allow you to send your own hierarchical data to a stored procedure in the form of XML. In the examples in Chapter 11, "Scaling Up with Unbound Access Applications," a string is used to pass order detail rows into `procOrderInsert` and `procOrderUpdate`, as a single parameter, along with the parameters for fields such as CustomerID and OrderDate in the Order table. An alternative would be to package all that data into an XML document and parse it out in the stored procedure using `OPENXML`. Be careful, however, to test this technique for its impact on performance, because XML processing will consume extra memory and processing resources.

Access Internet Features

Access 97 was the first version of Access to have any Internet functionality. It included the Hyperlink data type, the Hyperlink properties on controls, and the Publish to the Web Wizard. The Publish to the Web Wizard is gone from Access 2000, replaced by a dialog box that comes up when you choose File, Export and then select a file type of either Microsoft Active Server Pages (*.asp) or HTML Documents (*.html, *.htm). A third Internet format is also presented for backward compatibility: Microsoft IIS 1-2 (*.htx, *.idc). This is a very outdated Internet Database Connector format, which was replaced by Active Server Pages. You can also export to these formats from VBA code using `DoCmd.OutputTo`.

Creating HTML and Active Server Pages from Access

The following line of code will create a Web page based on the Categories table in the `OutputFile` location in HTML format:

```
DoCmd.OutputTo _
  ObjectType:=acTable, _
  ObjectName:="Categories", _
  OutputFormat:=acFormatHTML, _
  OutputFile:="c:\Inetpub\wwwroot\Categories.html", _
```

```
AutoStart:=False, _
TemplateFile:=""
```

Exporting to one of the Web formats through the Access user interface or by using
`DoCmd.OutputTo` is an easy way to reach a similar result in Access to what is possible in SQL
Server with the Web Assistant Wizard or its associated system stored procedures. The advantage in Access is that you can base your output on forms and reports in addition to tables and
queries. The advantage in SQL Server is that you have a rich set of built-in scheduling options.

The Active Server Pages that Access 97 created were dependent on an ActiveX control called
the *Layout Control*, which provided a nice user interface but limited the browsers that could
open your page. Since then Microsoft has dropped support for the Layout Control. In Access
2000, you can use File, Export or `Docmd.OutputTo` to create Active Server Pages that run on
the server and dynamically fetch the latest data and format it into HTML tables. This data is
read-only. Active Server Pages are capable of providing data-entry capabilities, but you would
have to use a tool other than Access to create such pages.

To address the need for richer Web application options in Access, Microsoft introduced Data
Access Pages, which leverage the Dynamic HTML (DHTML) support in Internet Explorer 5.*x*.
Although DAPs are of limited value for a public Internet application, where you have no control over the users' browser, they are very well suited for intranet applications where you can
ensure that everyone has the Microsoft files and licenses needed to make them work.

Access 2000 Data Access Pages (DAPs)

New in Access 2000, Data Access Pages (DAPs) allow you to create bound Web pages. The
data source for DAPs can be either Access or SQL Server data. DAPs can be created in both
Access MDBs and Access ADPs. DAPs work by using DHTML data binding, implemented by
a hidden ActiveX control, the Microsoft Office Data Source Control. DAPs also have pretty
heavy client requirements: An Office license and IE 5 are required on the client machines. A
SQL Server database is the best choice if you are deploying Data Access Pages on a Web
server for the same reason that SQL Server is the best choice for any business application—
scalability, reliability, maintainability, and security. With SQL Server, all processing takes place
on the server rather than on the client machines, as it would if you deploy a DAP/Jet application.

DAPs are not saved within Access, like forms and reports. They are saved in separate HTM
files, with only the link information saved in Access. This makes deployment interesting,
because any time a DAP is moved, the link information must be updated in the Access database. But that only comes into play if your users are running your DAPs from within Access.
The alternative that makes DAPs so useful is that they can be opened directly from Internet
Explorer rather than from within Access. Unlike other browser-based solutions, such as ASP,

DAPs don't even require you to use a Web server. As long as the users can connect to the SQL Server data, all that's required for them to run your DAP is the browser, because data binding is handled by an ActiveX control that runs on the client. Later in the chapter, you'll learn how to use Remote Data Services (RDS) and Internet Information Services (IIS) to connect on the server and ship recordsets back and forth over the Internet.

For a comprehensive and in-depth look at DAPs, we recommend the *Access 2000 Developer's Handbook, Volume 2*, by Litwin, Getz and Gilbert, which gives a thorough treatment of the topic, covering everything from scripting to deployment. Another excellent resource if you need help with a specific DAP question or problem is the `microsoft.public.dataaccesspages` newsgroup.

Creating Simple DAP Solutions

DAPs allow you to present live, attractively formatted data on demand. Also, subject to a few limitations, the data can also be edited, making DAPs a browser-hosted hybrid between forms and reports. If you want to enter or edit data, you must create a simple DAP, with no hierarchical grouping levels. Figure 13.13 shows editing a product using a DAP.

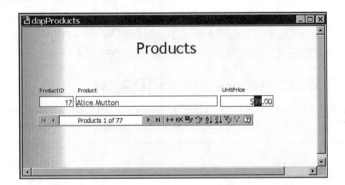

FIGURE 13.13
Editing data in a DAP.

If you elect to display more than one record at a time or use grouping, the DAP will be read-only, as shown in Figure 13.14, where the products are grouped by category.

These are simple examples that you can easily create yourself by using the Data Access Page Wizard. There are more sophisticated examples in the Northwind database that ships with Access, which add impressive Excel-like features by using the Office Web Components.

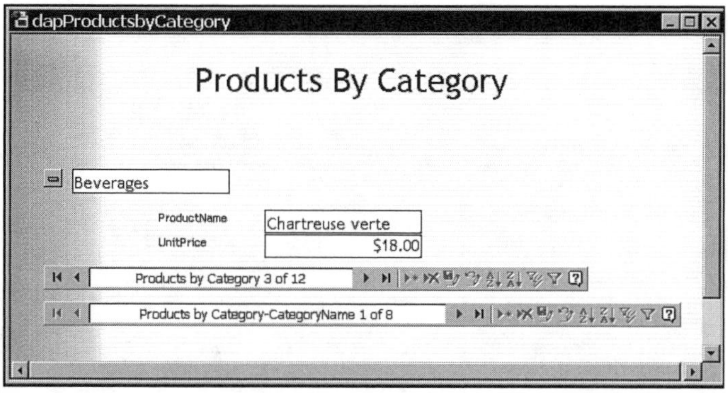

FIGURE 13.14
A DAP with a hierarchical grouping, such as Categories/Products, is read-only.

Using the Office Web Components

The Data Access Page Control Toolbox contains three controls provided by the Office Web Components. A fourth, hidden Web Component, the Data Source control, is always used behind the scenes in DAPs. The Office Web Components are a set of ActiveX controls that allow you to provide your users with interactive access to data. Here are the visible controls available:

- *The Office Pivot Table.* Can be used to sort, group, outline, or pivot data dynamically at runtime.
- *The Office Chart.* Displays data in graphical format and is similar to the Graph control in Access forms and reports.
- *The Office Spreadsheet.* A simplified version of an Excel worksheet.

The Northwind sample database, located in your \Program Files\Microsoft Office\Office\Samples directory, has several examples of DAPs that use the Office Web Components. These examples work against Access data, but they could just as well work against SQL Server data. The Analyze Sales DAP shown in Figure 13.15 uses the Pivot Table control, and the Sales DAP uses the Pivot Table control synchronized with the Chart control.

The Office Web Components are thoroughly documented in Dave Stearns' excellent book *Programming Microsoft Office 2000 Web Components*, from Microsoft Press.

Here's an example of how you can incorporate Web Components into your DAPs to provide flexible interactive analysis of OLAP data using SQL Server's Analysis Services. OLAP and Analysis Services are also covered in Chapter 12, "Building Access Reports from SQL Server Data."

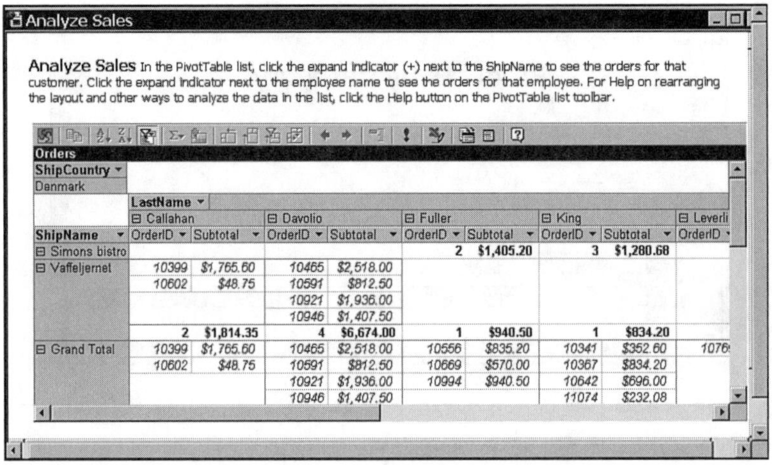

FIGURE 13.15

The Analyze Sales DAP in the Northwind sample database uses the Pivot Table control to support sales analysis.

Creating a Pivot Table Based on the FoodMart 2000 Sales Cube

To create a standalone DAP that isn't associated with a particular Access application, choose File, New Data Access Page from the Access file menu. There aren't any wizards to help you out when you create a DAP this way—the first thing you'll be prompted for is a data source. In this example, you'll connect to the Analysis Services sample database FoodMart 2000, so click Cancel on the Connection dialog box. The DAP can only be connected to a SQL Server or an Access data source. You could use SQL Server views, stored procedures, or functions that employ OPENQUERY or OPENROWSET to connect over an OLE DB connection to an OLAP data source, as presented in Chapter 12. However, you can more easily connect to an OLAP data source using the Office Web Components. Follow these steps to insert a pivot table using OLAP data on your DAP:

1. Choose Insert, Office Pivot Table from the menu bar. This will place a blank pivot table in your DAP.

2. To connect the pivot table to a data source and click the Property Toolbox on the Pivot Table toolbar. Expand the Data Source option and select the Connection option. Click the Connection Editor button. This will load the Data Link Properties dialog box.

3. On the Provider tab, choose the Microsoft OLE DB provider for OLAP Services 8.0.

4. On the Connection tab, type the name of your server in the Data Source box. The location is FoodMart2000. Make sure to check the Use Windows NT Integrated Security option and set the initial catalog to FoodMart 2000, as shown in Figure 13.16. Click OK when you're done.

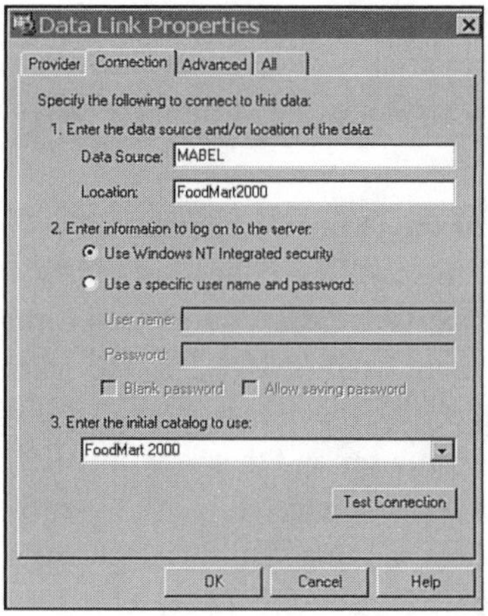

FIGURE 13.16

Setting up the Data Link properties for the FoodMart 2000 OLAP database.

5. Back in the Pivot Table Property Toolbox, set the Use Data From option to Data Member and select the Sales cube from the drop-down list.

6. Also on the Pivot Table Property Toolbox, expand the Show/Hide option. This allows you to configure what gets displayed on the pivot table. Make sure to select the Field List option. This allows you to drag and drop the different elements of the Sales cube onto the layout. Figure 13.17 shows the pivot table in Design view, with the Pivot Table Field List and the Pivot Table Property Toolbox loaded.

FIGURE 13.17

The Pivot Table Property dialog box and the Field List are both used to configure your pivot table.

7. Expand the Advanced option. Here's where you configure whether you want the user to be able to work with the pivot table interactively at runtime. Choosing the Lock Filters and Lock Row/Column Fields options will limit the users to the options you design at runtime.

This only scratches the surface of the Office Web Components, but as you can see from the preceding example, it's not that difficult to produce a sophisticated report using OLAP data from Analysis Services. The Office Web Components aren't limited to Access and other Office applications—you can also use them from ASP pages. The advantage here is that the code in an Active Server Page runs on the server, whereas in a DAP it runs on the client. This also means that you can use any Web browser and that you only need a license for the components on the Web server machine. The disadvantage is that the user experience isn't quite as rich because the Web Component is just sending GIF files (bitmap images) back to the browser, rather than providing a live, interactive control. The *Access Developers Handbook, Volume 2* gives several good examples of how to use the Office Web Components in ASP pages.

Although the Office 2000 Web Components are part of Office 2000, they can also be used with Office 95 and Office 97 applications. There is no code in the Web Components that depends on any part of Office 2000 being installed, although you do need to have purchased a license for Office 2000. That, however, is a legal requirement, not a technical one. Deployment with earlier Office versions is a little more complicated than simply deploying Office 2000 itself (which is the easiest way to go about it), because you need to use the Web Installer utility. See *Programming Microsoft Office 2000 Web Components* by Dave Stearns for the details on using the Web Installer utility to implement the Office Web Components in earlier versions of Office.

Deploying Data Access Pages

When you view a DAP in Access, IE 5 is being hosted in an Access window. You can deploy the DAPs without requiring them to be hosted in an Access MDB and instead make them available on a Web server or simply on a file server. There are several scenarios for deploying DAPs:

- *Single computer*. All files are installed on a single computer, either by copying to a local folder or to a local Web server. Pages are opened directly through the file system or through an HTTP URL to the local Web server.

- *Network file share*. Files are copied to a network file share, and default connections are used to connect users to the pages. Pages are opened using mapped drives or by UNC (Universal Naming Convention) paths.

- *Web server with two-tier data access*. Pages are published on a Web server running IIS (Internet Information Services) and SQL Server. Pages are opened using an HTTP URL.

- *Web server with three-tier data access.* This is similar to two-tier data access in that pages are published on a Web server running IIS (Internet Information Services) and SQL Server. Pages are opened using an HTTP URL. However, both the DAP and the Web server are configured to support Remote Data Services (RDS), which allows safe data access both inside and outside a firewall.

Two-tier data access for DAP deployment is much like a traditional client/server application. The client, or first tier, opens the page either through the file system or HTTP, connecting directly through an OLE DB provider to the database server (the second tier). The security context for accessing the database is dependent on the current user's identity, making it vulnerable to scripts that can exploit the current user's connection. This makes it inappropriate for Internet deployment.

Three-tier data access uses RDS running on IIS as an intermediate agent, which handles data access between the client and the database components. In other words, the client is no longer directly connected to the database. The benefit is that the RDS component establishes the security context for accessing the database, and it does not allow cross-domain data access attempts. This is really the only way to deploy DAPs over the Internet (rather than an intranet), because the client application running in the user's browser no longer needs a direct connection to SQL Server. The client connects to the Web server, and your RDS component on the Web server opens a connection to SQL Server. Figure 13.18 diagrams the difference between the two-tier and the three-tier data-access architectures.

13

INTERNET FEATURES IN ACCESS AND SQL SERVER

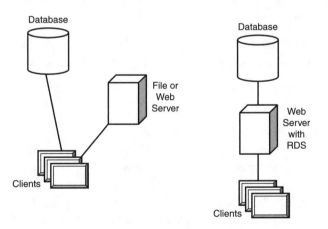

FIGURE 13.18
Two-tier architecture allows the client to be directly connected to the database, whereas three-tier architecture using RDS does not.

Using RDS and a Web server to implement three-tier data access is the most secure. It's also, unfortunately, the most difficult to set up correctly, as you'll see as you wade through the next section of this chapter. However, it is your only choice if you wish to deploy DAPs safely on the Internet.

> **NOTE**
>
> OLAP, or Analysis Services, data must be accessed through the two-tier data access method if you are connecting using Web Components, because the Pivot Table Service uses the OLE DB for OLAP provider, which doesn't support three-tier data access. However, you can use a linked server in SQL Server as a workaround if you are willing to create views or stored procedures in SQL Server to access the multidimensional data. See Chapter 12 for details.

Configuring a DAP to Use RDS

Make sure that all users have IE 5 and the ability to install the Office Web Components.

In order to use a DAP with RDS, you need to set the UseRemoteProvider property. However, you don't want to do this until you are ready to deploy the page, because once you set this property to True, you won't be able to view the page in Browse view, from the file system, or from the Database window. Follow these steps when you're ready to set the UseRemoteProvider property:

1. Click the title bar of the DAP or choose Edit, Select Page to select the entire page.
2. Choose View, Properties from the menu bar and select the Data tab.
3. Set the UseRemoteProvider property to True, close the dialog box and save your changes.

Database Security, Authentication, and DAPs

RDS gives you a way to expose your data over the Internet. That, of course, is a two-edged sword. Providing worldwide access to your data means that you must take security very seriously. Database security is configured separately from your DAPs. Both Integrated Security (Windows NT/Windows 2000 authentication) and SQL Server logins can be used to secure the SQL Server database being accessed through the DAP. Permissions are then assigned to database roles, which control data access. If you use Windows NT/Windows 2000 Integrated Security, only authorized Windows NT/Windows 2000 accounts will be allowed to open or work with the database. SQL Server security is covered in Chapter 3, "Understanding SQL Server Security."

If you desire a single level of access for all users who connect to the database through the DAP, add the Internet Guest user account as a logon to the SQL Server and add it as a user of the database being accessed. Use Anonymous Access authentication on the IIS server. With this configuration, users will not be prompted to log onto the database after the DAP is opened. However, SQL and IIS must be located on the same machine for this to work.

Defining the Level of Access for the DAP

For SQL Server databases, create a SQL Server user account that has access to the necessary data or use Integrated Security. Create a role that has the necessary permissions to work with the data underlying the DAP and assign users to the role so that they inherit the necessary permissions.

Disabling User ID and Password Saving in the DAP

No matter how a user is connecting to the database, one important point is to prevent the user ID and password from being saved with the page. This is important even if you are using Windows NT/Windows 2000 authentication. Follow these steps to prevent security information from being saved with the DAP:

1. Open the DAP in Design view and choose View, Field List from the menu bar.
2. On the Database tab, right-click the database name and then click Connection.
3. Clear the Allow Saving of Password check box under the Enter Information to Log on to the Server option.
4. Click OK to save changes.

Setting the UseRemoteProvider Property

When you're ready to copy the DAP to the IIS machine, set the UseRemoteProvider property to True.

Configuring the IIS Server

HTML pages published on an IIS server support three different forms of authentication:

- *Anonymous access authentication.* This authentication type provides an anonymous user (guest) account for all users. If your database is located on another computer, make sure that your guest account can connect to it. You'll need to enable a login on the SQL Server for this account and create a guest account in the database.

- *Windows NT Challenge/Response authentication (or Integrated Windows authentication in IIS 5.0).* This authentication type uses Integrated Security and works best in Windows NT 4 only if IIS and the SQL Server database are located on the same computer and the RDS component is using a local address to access the database. If you're running Windows 2000 and your SQL Server and IIS servers are on different machines, you can use Kerberos authentication.

- *Basic authentication*. This authentication type prompts the user for an account name and password before opening the page. Basic authentication is not recommended because it sends user account and password information across the network in an unencrypted format. To get around this, you'd need to configure a Secure Sockets Layer (SSL) encrypted connection (using the HTTPS protocol) to publish the DAP on your IIS server.

You need to define which form of authentication to use or coordinate this with your Web server administrator.

Configuring RDS Settings on IIS

To set up and configure the RDS components, follow these steps:

1. Launch the Internet Services Manager, select the MSADC virtual directory node, and click Properties.

2. Set the Read and Execute permissions as shown in Figure 13.19.

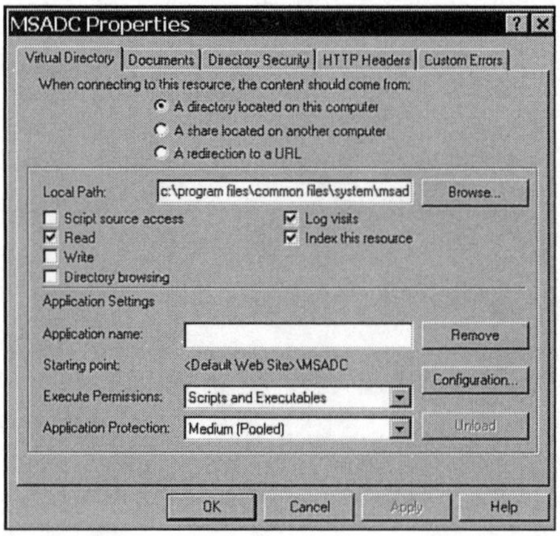

FIGURE 13.19

Configuring RDS in the IIS Services Manager.

3. On the Directory Services tab, configure the settings to match the virtual directories that hold the DAPs.

4. If you're upgrading from an earlier version of MDAC (2.0 or earlier), your RDS configuration might not be configured for safe mode. Run the following Registry entry file to correct this:

```
C:\Program Files\Common Files\System\msadc\handsafe.reg
```

When RDS is running in "safe" mode, a default custom handler named MSDFMAP.Handler protects databases from unsafe exposure to Web clients that use OLE DB providers to access the file system and shell commands. The MSDFMAP.ini file (located in the WINNT directory) that controls these settings needs to be modified so that users can connect to the database. The INI file contains four sections:

- *Connect.* Used to specify connection string mappings.
- *SQL.* Used to specify command string (SQL statement) mappings.
- *UserList.* Used to override default access permissions for a list of users.
- *Logs.* Used to specify the name of a file for error-logging purposes.

The [connect default] section should look like the following:

```
[connect default]
Access=NoAccess
```

Create a new [connect] section that uses local to connect to a server. Use (local) to reference the SQL Server in the first line of the [connect] section:

```
[connect (local)]
```

If you're using Windows 2000 with Kerberos delegation, the [connect] section can reference the server by name, as shown here, where the server name is Mabel:

```
[connect Mabel]
```

The second line sets access to be read-only. If you want read/write, use ReadWrite instead:

```
Access=ReadOnly
```

If you're not using Kerberos delegation, you need to set up a connection alias and provide connection information in the third line, as shown here, where the alias is MyDB:

```
[connect MyDB]
Connect=Provider=SQLOLEDB.1;Data Source=(local);
Initial Catalog=Northwind;Integrated Security=SSPI;
```

Maintaining the DAP After Publication

There are several different methods of updating pages once they're published:

- If the IIS computer and your computer can use the same connection information, you can view and modify the page in Design view in Access and save it.
- Set the UseRemoteProvider property to False and change the data source information. Copy or replace the file, setting the UseRemoteProvider back to True when it's back on the IIS machine.

Setting up and configuring DAPs to use RDS for three-tier data access is rather complicated. The good news is that Microsoft has done a good job of documenting the steps you need to follow. For more information, see the Microsoft.public.data.ado.rds newsgroup or download

13

INTERNET
FEATURES IN
ACCESS AND SQL
SERVER

"Deploying Data Access Pages on the Internet or Your Intranet" by Mark Roberts. It can be found at `http://msdn.microsoft.com/isapi/msdnlib.idc?theURL=/library/techart/deploydap.htm`.

Summary

SQL Server's Web Assistant Wizard makes it easy to publish SQL Server data to the Web. It lets you schedule publication of Web pages or automatically publish pages when data changes. The SQL Server Web stored procedures give you control over the publishing of Web pages from Transact-SQL. SQL Server 2000 has native support for XML. You can create XML documents directly from SQL Server by using the `FOR XML` clause in Transact-SQL. In addition, SQL Server data can be directly accessed through URL queries from client applications. Data can be modified through updategrams. Since Access 97, Access has had the ability to save data using the hyperlink data type. It also allows publication of static HTML, HTX/IDC, and ASP pages. In Access 2000, Data Access Pages (DAPs) allow you to create bound Web pages. The Office Web Components provide additional functionality for your DAPs. DAPs can be deployed to run on a Web server in a three-tiered architecture using Remote Data Services (RDS), which is difficult to deploy but does allow you to safely expose your data over the Internet.

Architecting Distributed *n*-Tier Applications

IN THIS CHAPTER

Overview of *n*-Tier Development

n-tier development breaks an application up into logically distinct parts to make it easier to deploy and maintain. For example, in the old DOS days, all the pieces of your application had to be compiled into a single, large executable, taking time and resources and requiring the entire file to be modified for every little change. Modern software is composed of many different pieces that interact with each other dynamically as they run and that can separately be revised and replaced. Microsoft realized that most people would rather spend their time and money writing custom business logic than spend it on writing complex code for sharing resources and monitoring distributed transactions. Therefore, Microsoft came up with a strategy for creating a generic framework for distributed applications. This framework has had several names over the years, the latest being the *Windows Distributed interNet Applications (DNA) architecture*. DNA includes many technologies never mentioned even once in this book and sometimes seems to include everything but the kitchen sink when Microsoft's marketing machine gets rolling. However, the core technology behind all of DNA is COM, or the *Component Object Model*.

COM began as a desktop-publishing specification for allowing software applications to communicate with each other so that documents from one application could be embedded within the documents of another. From this humble beginning, it has evolved into a pervasive standard for allowing software components to work together.

Explaining COM (Component Object Model)

COM manages to be both the Microsoft specification for writing reusable software that runs on component-based systems and a sophisticated infrastructure that allows clients and objects to communicate across process and computer boundaries. The programming model is based on object-oriented programming (OOP) concepts, whereby clients communicate with components by binding to them at runtime. At the programming level, these components consist of class modules, but they are packaged as binary objects.

COM-based applications are language independent, communicating with each other through their standard interfaces, or public methods and properties. In other words, you can write a COM component in VB, C++, Java, FORTRAN, or any language that implements the basic interfaces that Microsoft has mandated.

Interfaces are at the heart of COM, exposing the application's functionality without exposing the source code. This allows the COM-based component to function as a black box. As long as you don't change the interfaces, client applications that are dependent on the component will not break. Developers can write a middle-tier business object to encapsulate business logic or data-access code that, once implemented, does not require client recompilation or redistribution later when changes are made. When everything is working right, a new version of a COM component can replace an old version without the client applications that use it having to change in any way.

For example, many different applications at a company could all use a COM component that calculates customer credit limits. Anytime the company needs a credit limit, it passes a customer ID to this component and gets back a dollar figure. If the company decides to change its credit policies, all it has to do is replace the component with a new version that now will return different numbers to the client applications. Those applications won't have to change in any way.

Pre-COM applications were built by sending source files to a compiler, which built one monolithic executable file. Large applications tended to have long build times and to compile gigantic executables. All code used by the application had to be contained in the executable, and any modification caused the whole project to be rebuilt. This made team development problematic, to say the least.

The first version of COM shipped in 1993, solving many of the problems inherent in monolithic applications by allowing teams to ship a set of binary files rather than source code. Any of the binary files could be updated independently of the others—which leads us to the concept of two-tier, three-tier, and *n*-tier applications.

Two-Tier Applications

The traditional architecture for a classic client/server application is the two-tier model, where applications are directly connected to a database server, as shown in Figure 14.1.

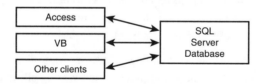

FIGURE 14.1

The two-tier application architecture.

The two-tier application model has some significant shortcomings:

- Presentation code, data access code, and business logic are all intermingled, making two-tier applications difficult to maintain. Distributing changes to the two-tier model often requires rewriting code on both the client and the server.

- Deploying a two-tier application to a client requires that each client have the server-specific drivers, client licenses, and other associated DLLs installed. If you want to change database servers—for example, move from Oracle to SQL Server—a system administrator would need to visit each client machine and install the appropriate software. Such maintenance might even be necessary when you install a new version of your existing database management system. This is both time consuming and expensive. The problems only increase if your client applications need to access multiple data sources.

- It is difficult to spread transactions across multiple data sources in a two-tier model, or if the data is stored in multiple formats. Also, each client runs in a separate process, so you can't share process-specific resources such as threads and memory. This inability to share resources across a set of users limits the performance and maintainability of the system.

- It is difficult to scale out to support distributed applications spanning different geographic locations. Two-tier applications are almost all limited to being located on the same local area network (LAN). This also becomes a problem as more and more users are working in disconnected, or infrequently connected, scenarios.

- Two-tier applications are platform specific, usually requiring the same operating systems and application software on all computers.

COM to the Rescue

The solution to the problems of two-tier applications is to introduce a third tier (or several additional tiers), built using COM components. Client code doesn't need to be hard-coded to work with one particular file in a specific location. Objects can be created in different processes or different computers without client code being affected. Because COM objects use interfaces (standard sets of properties and methods) to communicate, a new object can replace an old object with no client code changes as long as the interfaces don't change. This is probably the most attractive aspect of COM development.

This is not to say there aren't problems with COM. It takes a lot of work to design a scalable architecture in COM to support reusable components that work well in any environment.

n-Tier Applications

n-tier applications are also referred to as *three-tier* and *multi-tier* applications. These three terms all mean pretty much the same thing: A system includes components that have been added to middle tiers.

n-tier applications typically split the processing between at least three logical components, as shown in Figure 14.2, where there are clean lines of separation between the client, the middle-tier business objects, and the database. The client will typically contain code and user interface objects for interacting with the users. Unlike the two-tier model, the client application has no direct connection to the database. The middle-tier object contains data-access code and, optionally, business rules. There is no hard-and-fast rule about where to put business rules. Some developers prefer to put as much as possible in stored procedures on the database server, where they are enforced for multiple clients and where data security and integrity is ensured. Other developers prefer to place business rules in middle-tier objects, making the database tier vendor independent. In other words, if business logic is in a middle tier and not on the server in stored procedures, then changing from Sybase to Oracle will involve only minor changes in the middle tier, not a major rewrite of stored procedures. According to this philosophy, only the four primary operations of inserting, updating, retrieving, and deleting data are performed by the database server.

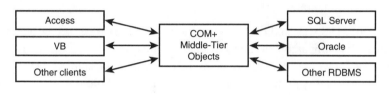

FIGURE 14.2
The n-*tier architecture.*

The *n*-tier architecture is essentially a logical separation, not necessarily a physical one. In other words, the deployment model might vary, with components located on different computers or on the same computer. For example, a middle-tier object and the SQL Server database might be located on the same computer, or the client and the middle-tier object might be located on the same computer, or the SQL Server database, middle-tier object, and the client application might all be located on separate computers.

Regardless of how you implement the *n*-tier architecture logically and physically, its main virtue is that it hides the details of its implementation from the client. Working with COM objects also gives developers the ability to write code once in a COM object and reuse it with multiple clients. For example, you could have an Access client, a Visual Basic client, and a browser client all happily using the same COM objects. None of these clients needs to know or care that it's working against multiple database platforms. Plus, none of these clients needs to contain code encapsulating business rules. Changes to the infrastructure take place in the COM objects, which can serve many different clients, making them reusable and flexible.

COM Communications

COM was designed to transcend process boundaries, allowing interprocess communication to extend across computer boundaries. This support is based on Remote Procedure Call (RPC), which is an industry standard that Microsoft has enhanced with object-oriented extensions. COM uses RPC to serve up objects across a network and to call methods on remote computers.

Microsoft Transaction Server (MTS)

Microsoft Transaction Server was introduced just after Windows NT 4.0 to provide the ability to perform high-performance transaction processing and object brokering. MTS doesn't replace or modify COM. It is a supportive runtime environment for COM objects, providing useful services that would be hard for individual objects to manage. MTS allows middle-tier objects to run and control distributed transactions from the middle tier. It acts as a traffic cop, adding support for distributed transactions, integrated role-based security, thread pooling, and improved configuration and administration.

The first version of MTS was sold by Microsoft for about $15,000 per server license, which was competitive with comparable products available at that time. In typical Microsoft fashion, the product eventually was used to add value to the company's flagship products. The second version (1.1) was bundled with the Enterprise version of Visual Studio 97, which also included VB 5.0. In version 2.0, MTS was made a free addition to the NT 4 operating system, as part of the same option pack that included Internet Information Server (IIS). In Windows 2000, MTS is an integrated part of COM+ services.

Unlike database transactions, which are confined to changes within a particular database management system, MTS transactions can span multiple database systems and non-database objects. With MTS you can mandate that five different component-based operations running in five separate systems must all either succeed or be aborted. The object brokering in MTS makes efficient use of computer resources by allowing objects that were instantiated by one client to also be used by other clients who need the same objects.

Because MTS is not strictly part of COM, developing efficient MTS/COM applications took an understanding of both models. Techniques that worked well in pure COM didn't necessarily translate well when used with MTS. Plus, the name caused confusion because MTS wasn't just about distributed transactions. All middle-tier objects implemented on Windows NT Server should be run in the MTS environment, regardless of whether they implement transactions, because MTS also acts as a traffic cop, managing how objects consume resources and generally speeding things up. Another obstacle that developers faced was that MTS was not actually part of NT 4.0—you had to endure a separate installation of the NT 4 Option Pack.

Many of these difficulties have been overcome with the implementation of COM+ in Windows 2000.

COM+

COM+ in Windows 2000 integrates all the features of MTS and adds new ones. COM+ isn't an option that you install later, as MTS was. Instead, it's part of the operating system. Microsoft changed the name to eliminate the confusion that the MTS name generated among developers, who believed that one needed to implement interobject transactions to make use of MTS. Here's a list of the features supported by MTS and also by COM+:

- Automatic thread pooling
- Automatic database connection pooling
- Automatic transaction enlistment
- Declarative security
- Shared property management
- Object request brokering

Here's a list of the new features introduced in COM+ that did not exist in MTS and a brief description of what each provides:

- *Queued Components (QC)* provides a set of COM interfaces that permits a remote server object's methods to be executed at a later point in time than the client invocation. What this means is that you can have disconnected users whose transactions are queued and can be implemented at a later time. Queued components are covered in the next section of this chapter, which discusses Microsoft Message Queue (MSMQ).
- *Loosely Coupled Events (LCE)* allows one or more threads or processes to be notified of a change in state of another process or thread. Publishers provide event notifications to one or more subscribers.
- *Object pooling* can improve performance by creating a pool of objects already created and ready for use (or reuse). This is more efficient than creating and destroying objects on demand.
- *Asynchronous object creation* is a mechanism for ensuring that the client gets the first object that becomes available, whether it was just returned to the pool or was just created. (Both object pooling and asynchronous object creation are COM+ features unavailable to Access/VB programmers, since they require free-threaded components. VB.Net will open up these features to the world of Visual Basic programmers by supporting free threading.)
- *Compensating Resource Managers (CRM)* makes it possible for nontransactional resources to participate in two-phase commit transactions.

Microsoft Message Queue (MSMQ)

MSMQ is a part of the COM+ infrastructure that provides message queuing services. Along with Queued Components, MSMQ supports asynchronous execution of middle-tier COM components. MSMQ uses Remote Procedure Calls (RPC) to place a message into a queue, returning a response immediately to the client so that the client can continue working without waiting for a response. Eventually, when the message is sent and a response is received, the originating component is notified. You could think of MSMQ as providing "email" for components. The biggest conceptual difference between a message queue and a standard RPC call is that the message moves in only one direction, whereas an RPC call involves both a request and an immediate response. The problem is that *immediate* doesn't always mean *right away*, and sometimes a more loosely coupled model is more appropriate. The originating component might be happy to continue going about its business once it knows for sure that the message will be delivered, without having to suspend all further processing until a response has been received.

MSMQ is useful for the many applications where you don't want to keep a client application waiting around for a response. A client can send messages even if the server application is offline. It also means that the server can respond when all the clients are offline as well—the messages in both cases simply get placed in a local queue. Cached local messages are automatically forwarded when the destination queue becomes available.

If you don't need concurrency, and requests can be serialized, then message queuing provides a good solution. For example, you might have an order-entry system in which the most important goal is for orders to be entered quickly. These orders, then, eventually get filled as resources become available. Any business process where "eventually" is good enough is a good candidate for message queuing. MSMQ provides extra infrastructure support to ensure that messages will indeed eventually reach their destination, thus eliminating the lost message problems that affect applications based on RPC or HTTP.

One of the most useful benefits of implementing message queues with MSMQ is its support for transactions, which allows you to create a single atomic operation that includes queued operations. For example, a transaction might involve sending separate messages to different queues, and this transaction completes only if all the messages are added to their respective queues. If there's failure at any point (a message doesn't get added to its queue), the transaction is rolled back and all the messages are pulled out of their queues.

Like MTS, MSMQ is part of the NT 4 Option Pack, or, if you're running Windows 2000, part of the core install. Choose the Queued Component Services option during the Windows 2000 setup or add it in later (it's not one of the default selections) by going into the Control Panel and choosing the Add/Remove Windows Components option.

Microsoft Internet Information Services (IIS) and Active Server Pages (ASP)

IIS is Microsoft's Web server. In Windows NT 4.0, it was a part of the Option Pack. With IIS version 5.0, it's a part of Windows 2000 and does not require a separate install. IIS handles incoming HTTP requests sent by client applications. It exposes the Internet Server API (ISAPI) for C++ developers who want to program ISAPI extensions and ISAPI filters that intercept and handle HTTP requests. The alternative for VB developers is a framework known as *Active Server Pages* (ASP), which is an ISAPI filter that allows developers to code server-side logic using scripting languages such as JavaScript and VBScript. From within that script code, COM objects can be instantiated to provide the performance benefits of running compiled code rather than interpreted script. Microsoft's Visual InterDev product makes it possible to build entire Web sites implemented using ASP. ASP is tightly integrated with COM+, making it easy to create and run middle-tier objects from an ASP page. Many companies have found that using ASP with Visual Basic COM components offers a good balance between productivity, maintainability, and performance.

The next version of ASP, called ASP+, is implemented as part of the .Net Framework. ASP+ allows compiled code to be written as part of the server pages, rather than forcing a choice between script and external components. ASP+ also supports standard VB-style event handlers that respond on the server to user-triggered events on the client, and it allows these event procedures to be completely separated from the HTML formatting instructions for the page.

Web-Based Architectures

Chapter 13, "Internet Features in Access and SQL Server," presents a simple example that uses IIS as part of a middle-tier platform for retrieving and updating SQL Server data over HTTP. SQL Server 2000 includes its own ISAPI filters to support HTTP communication with the database, and the new support for XML makes integration with Web applications much smoother than has been possible in the past.

XML, HTTP, SOAP, and .NET

With a couple of partners, including IBM, Microsoft has developed the Simple Object Access Protocol (SOAP), which allows programs built on any platform to communicate over the Internet using a standard protocol based on XML (Extensible Markup Language). As time goes by, SQL Server's support for XML will grow in its versatility and in its importance to your development efforts. For now, you can get started by using the XMLHTTP and XMLHTTPRequest objects provided by the XML parser in Internet Explorer to communicate with SQL Server over the Internet using HTTP requests and XML documents as the medium of exchange, as explained in Chapter 13.

Microsoft is developing a new set of technologies, broadly referred to as *.NET*, which will overcome many of the shortcomings that have become apparent in COM. Versioning, security, interoperability between languages and platforms, as well as a more thoroughly object-oriented infrastructure are all advantages that the new .NET framework will offer over older COM technologies. Microsoft has developed a Common Language Runtime (CLR) that will allow objects to be created in any language that conforms to simple published guidelines. Unlike

14

ARCHITECTING
DISTRIBUTED *N*-
TIER APPLICATIONS

with COM, which just allows objects to invoke each other's methods, objects created with the CLR will be able to customize each other's methods using standard object-oriented techniques. The CLR also supports a rich role-based security model that pervades its component framework down to the method level. Using SOAP and the next version of Active Server Pages, *ASP+*, you can easily expose your components over the Internet as Web Services that any application can consume. The .NET framework is fully integrated with COM+ services and is not intended to replace them.

Marshalling Data

One of the biggest challenges in Web development today is how to marshal data between the tiers. There are several approaches:

- Disconnected ADO recordsets
- Arrays
- Strings
- XML

Each has its strengths and weaknesses, but the last item in this list, XML, is the most appealing because it can serve as a *lingua franca*, allowing disparate systems on incompatible platforms to communicate using a standard format. Chapter 13 shows several ways to use XML with SQL Server 2000. The sample application shown later in this chapter uses XML to provide local storage for a client application. ADO 2.5 and later provide strong support for sending XML in binary streams, a technique that is used in the sample application.

Where Does Access Fit In?

Access was originally designed and implemented as the ultimate single-tier database. In that niche, it has outperformed and outsold all its competition over the years. In this role, it is superb—its millions of users attest to the fact of its success. The vast majority of all Access applications are *bound* applications, based on either native or linked tables. That is, Access internally handles all the mechanics of moving data from database tables to forms and back, or to reports, without any need for the developer to write code. A user-friendly, all-Access application is easy to create quickly.

However, speed in development doesn't necessarily translate into speed or scalability at runtime. The bound techniques that work so well when the data is in Access tables and shared by just a few users often fall down miserably when you move the data to SQL Server. Although Access can technically support a maximum of 255 concurrent users, in actuality the real maximum for concurrent users who are editing data is closer to 15 or 20. The challenge comes in trying to create an efficient Access front end for a SQL Server back-end database that does not impose the limitations of Access on the SQL Server database, while at the same time taking advantage of the unique features Access has to offer as a client application and as a development environment.

It's at this point that many application developers decide to leave Access and look to other products with a lighter footprint, such as Visual Basic, for constructing their front ends. If the original Access application is not modified in any way when the data is moved to SQL Server (that is, forms remain bound to large connected recordsets, Access queries are used instead of stored procedures, and static data for combo boxes is loaded from the server each time a form is opened), then performance might actually be worse with the data located in SQL Server than it ever was when the data was located in Access. Both the server and the network can become overloaded with too many client requests, causing performance to suffer. When blocking and deadlocking errors occur with increasing frequency, Access gets blamed. However, it's not really Access's fault—Access is only a tool, and it can be used efficiently as long as you are willing to reconsider the old ways of doing business.

The alternatives involve understanding the differences between the way Access and SQL Server work with data. There's no reason why Access can't be a good citizen in an *n*-tier world, requesting only needed data and working in an unbound mode, relying on middle-tier components running under MTS to handle the actual data access. There's also no reason why Access can't work with the same SQL Server database as other clients, such as Active Server Pages or Visual Basic front ends. You can use Access as a client in an *n*-tier application, accessing COM components as needed, instead of being tied to the server in a two-tier model.

Designing an *n*-Tier Application Around Access

Designing and planning an *n*-tier application is a daunting process. It's a given that no matter how good the original design is, it won't be the one that actually gets implemented. Application designs change repeatedly during the application development lifecycle, and being prepared for those changes is half the battle. Of course, if you don't have a plan at all, the battle is lost before you even begin.

Advantages of Access

With that in mind, consider the advantages of using Access to prototype and build an application:

- It's easy to get an application up and running quickly. Chances are if you are reading this book, you already know Access well, so there is no learning curve involved with getting up to speed on a new product.

- Access shares the VBA programming language with Visual Basic, so code that is not Access specific is easily portable.

- Code in Access class modules is very portable to Visual Basic. This means that a middle-tier data-access class can be prototyped and tested using Access and then ported to a Visual Basic ActiveX DLL project later. You'll see an example of this later in this chapter.

- Access can connect to, and utilize, middle-tier objects as well as any other client. It can happily exist in an *n*-tier world as one more client among many.

Design Goals: ADPs Versus MDBs

In Chapter 11, "Scaling Up with Unbound Access Applications," the concepts for creating an unbound application were covered. However, both of the examples were essentially two-tier applications—code in the Access application connected directly to SQL Server stored procedures using ADO objects or pass-through queries. In an *n*-tier Access application, Access never has a direct connection to SQL Server; instead, all data access occurs through the middle-tier objects, which can also serve other applications. Both Access databases (MDBs) and Access projects (ADPs) can be used this way, although Access projects really like to be directly connected to SQL Server. Once you sever that connection, projects lose most of the advantages they might hold over MDBs. Access ADPs are designed to function in two-tier mode, and it's difficult to get the same functionality when working in disconnected, *n*-tier mode. We expect that future versions of ADPs will include more support for *n*-tier data access using COM objects and XML. But in Access 2000, MDBs offer the solution with the most flexibility and options.

The Logical Architecture

The logical architecture for your *n*-tier Access application consists of three parts:

- *The Access client.* All the forms and reports, as well the code that supports these user interfaces, are located in the Access client application. You might also make use of local tables for temporary storage. As far as the users are concerned, everything looks and feels the same as the Access database used in Chapter 11. In the version of the application shown later in this chapter, however, there are no local tables at all—only a few XML files to cache lookup data—and there is never a direct connection with SQL Server.

- *The Access class modules.* All data access is handled by class modules that connect to SQL Server and move data in the form of strings, arrays, disconnected ADO recordsets, or XML back and forth to Access objects. Although the class modules are physically located in Access, there is a logical separation that would enable an easy physical separation later in the development process. You'll learn how to make that logical separation and the physical transition in this chapter.

- *The SQL Server stored procedures.* All data requests go through SQL Server stored procedures. This gives you the maximum amount of control and security over what the client application is allowed to do.

Implementing the logical architecture first in Access allows you to test and debug your prototype before implementing the physical separation. The advantage here is that testing and debugging can take place on a single machine in a single application—you don't have to worry about multiple platform issues and where the bugs are coming from. The following sections will cover creating the class modules and mapping them to stored procedures in the Northwind database. The forms and stored procedures are the same as those shown in Chapter 11. What's different is the code that connects them and how it can be partitioned from the rest of the application.

Data Access with Class

By wrapping up all data access in class modules, you gain the benefit of encapsulation. All the code that directly interacts with SQL Server is located in one logical tier instead of being spread out all over the application. The reason it's important to use class modules is that these are the vehicles that Microsoft gives to VBA developers to allow them to create COM objects. Only with class modules do you stand a chance of deploying your code to a pooled middle tier that is hosted in MTS or COM+. Once moved to a separate middle tier, code updates can be done independently of the Access application. Because Access class modules are virtually identical to Visual Basic class modules, they can be easily ported to Visual Basic when the time comes to physically implement a middle tier as a set of ActiveX DLLs. Even if you're not planning a move to an *n*-tier architecture, writing your code this way today will make it easier to maintain, more portable, and easier to scale up to support more database traffic.

However, not all components are created equal. To achieve maximum scalability, you need to take particular care when creating your Access class modules that you create stateless components.

Stateless Versus Stateful Components

A class module is nothing more than a template, or blueprint, for an object. That object is created in memory at runtime, possibly in many concurrent instances. Any properties or methods publicly declared in the class module then become available when the object is instantiated, thus allowing applications to manipulate the object and consume its services.

Objects can work in two basic ways. Consider the following code, which implements a `Tool` object:

```
Dim oTool As Tool
Set oTool = New Tool
```

```
oTool.Name = "Hammer"
oTool.Category = 2
oTool.Price = 7.95
oTool.Update
```

The `Tool` object's properties are `Name`, `Category`, and `Price`. `Update` is a method that updates the existing `Tool` object. In order for the `Update` method to work properly, the `Tool` object needs to maintain state between the different statements that set its properties and call the `Update` method. Think of each line of code as a separate remote procedure call to the `Tool` object. If the `Tool` object didn't remember the property settings between those calls or know who it was hearing from, then the `Update` method couldn't do its work. This is a *stateful* component.

On the other hand, a *stateless* object has no properties at all. The `Update` method of a stateless object does not rely on previously set property values—all the information it needs in order to do its work is passed in as parameters, and everything it needs back is received right away. Here's an example:

```
Dim oTool As Tool
Set oTool = New Tool

Call oTool.Update( _
  Name:="Hammer", _
  Category:=2, _
  Price:=7.95)
```

Both implementations of the `Tool` object achieve the same goal—to update the object—but how they do it is important. The stateless, method-only `Tool` object is designed to be used once and thrown away. It does not need to retain any data in order to function. Stateful objects that use properties to hang on to data between calls consume more memory, which is a finite resource on any machine. They require the application to ensure that a series of calls will return to the same object. Building stateless components is the only way to achieve maximum scalability.

Mapping Class Modules to SQL Actions

Your class modules are designed to function as a logical middle tier. As such, they will handle all the requests for data that flow from the Access application to SQL Server. Think of the middle tier as a virtual PBX switchboard, routing calls between your Access client application and SQL Server database.

Figure 14.3 shows a diagram of the relationship between SQL Server, the data class modules, and the Access user interfaces (the client). Note that Access invokes the methods of the data class, using `Add`, `Edit`, `Delete`, and `Retrieve`. The data class translates these to the relevant

Transact-SQL actions—INSERT, UPDATE, DELETE, and SELECT. Every invocation of a method is mapped to an equivalent action in SQL Server.

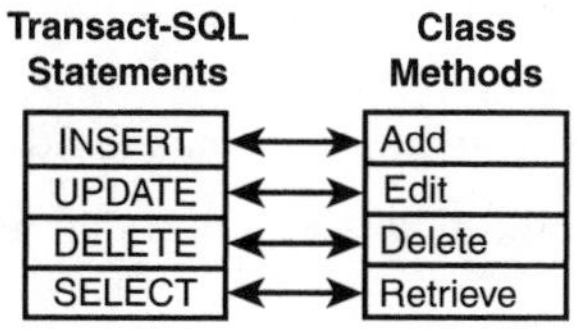

FIGURE 14.3
The data class sits between SQL Server and Access, mapping methods to their equivalent SQL Server actions.

Handling Returned Data

ADO recordsets provide strong data typing, are very efficient, and are flexible enough to be used in many different ways. This makes them the ideal choice for returning data from SQL Server. Optionally, you could use arrays, but they do not have the built-in support for handling data that is found in recordsets.

ADO has many features, allowing you to handle multiple recordsets and disconnected recordsets as well as to persist recordsets to files. ADO recordsets are reliable, and when used properly, they have a very low overhead. Recordsets can be passed across COM boundaries and do not need to keep a direct connection to the server. Every method that needs to get data from SQL Server should return it in the form of a Recordset object. XML is quickly gaining on recordsets, and the next version of ADO, a part of the .NET framework called *ADO+*, uses a new set of objects that are XML based. But for now, unless you need to save your recordset data to a persistent format or exchange data with business partners on disparate systems, recordsets still have the edge over XML. The sample application in this chapter uses recordsets directly and also uses them to create and consume XML.

How Stored Procedures Work with Data Classes

On the SQL Server side, you set up your stored procedures so that they work logically with the methods of the data-access class. Each stored procedure has specific parameters that map to the parameters of its related method in the data class. For standard tasks, generic class methods can be used with multiple stored procedures. Sometimes, complex stored procedures—for example, ones that return output parameters as well as recordsets—are more efficiently handled by class methods tuned for a particular stored procedure. Here's a quick review of some guidelines for working with stored procedures.

14

ARCHITECTING DISTRIBUTED *N*-TIER APPLICATIONS

Setting Up Stored Procedure Parameters

Every stored procedure that performs an action query should have two return parameters:

- *A numeric value.* Returns True if the stored procedure succeeds and False if it fails. Alternatively, you can create a return value that returns zero for success and an error number for failure. Whichever you choose, you should be consistent.

- *A message string.* Returns additional information that extends the return value.

Having success/failure information returned from every stored procedure keeps the client up-to-date—the last thing you want to have happen is to have an application perform a critical task and not be able to confirm whether it succeeded or not.

In addition to the return value and return message string, each stored procedure type needs to have the parameters shown in Table 14.1, depending on the type of action it performs.

TABLE 14.1   Additional Parameters Needed for Action Stored Procedures

Action	Parameters Needed
INSERT	Every column in the table needs to have a matching parameter for data to be inserted. All parameters should have a default null value, even if it corresponds to a required field in the table. This allows the procedure to validate parameters without having to deal with errors. The error code and an error message return string are returned if the validation fails. If a column is not required and has a default value specified in the table, then having a default null value for it means that it can be omitted from the parameter list when the stored procedure is called. Identity columns are handled with an output parameter to return the new value.
UPDATE	Every column in the table needs to have a matching parameter for data to be edited. All parameters, even required ones, should have a default null value. As with INSERT stored procedures, validation occurs, and the appropriate return values and messages are returned.
DELETE	Parameters for a DELETE stored procedure are those that uniquely identify the record to be deleted. Often this is the primary key, although a larger range of records can also be deleted with less-restrictive parameters. The return value and message string indicate whether the deletion succeeded or failed.

Return values from stored procedures are part of a SELECT statement at the end of a stored procedure and can be handled easily through ADO recordsets on the client or with an ADO command object's Parameters collection.

Because SELECT queries don't perform data manipulation the way action queries do, you don't really need to have return values and return messages for stored procedures that simply select data. Any errors encountered retrieving a recordset will be self-evident—either the recordset will show up on your doorstep, or it won't. The most common occurrence of specifying parameters for a SELECT stored procedure would be for a WHERE clause, to prevent the "SELECT * FROM MillionRowTable" kinds of queries.

Designing the Sample Application

Now that you've seen some general comments on implementing the various components, the next step is figuring out how to make it all happen in Access. The example used in this chapter combines features from the Access database and the Access project applications used in Chapter 11. It's intended to be a prototype and not a complete application—all it does is provide a facility for entering and editing order information in the Northwind SQL Server database and for finding orders.

The Login Form

The application as a whole centers around the order form, which is used for entering orders. However, the first thing the users see is the login form, which gathers information used by the data-access class to log on to SQL Server, as shown in Figure 14.4.

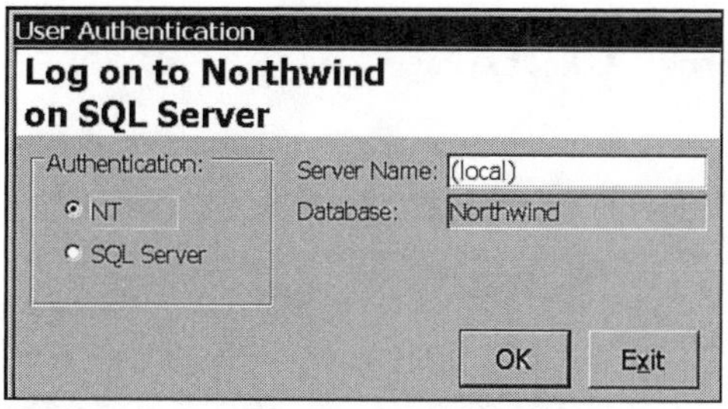

FIGURE 14.4

Logging on to the Northwind SQL Server database.

The user can choose the method of authentication used to access the SQL Server Northwind database. This information is cached in the form in a module-level variable that's exposed through a read-only property:

```
Option Compare Database
Option Explicit

Private mstrOLEDBConnect As String
Public Property Get OLEDBConnect() As String
    OLEDBConnect = mstrOLEDBConnect
End Property
```

The code attached to the Click event of the OK button calls a method of the middle-tier `DataAccess` object to check whether the generated connect string can be used successfully to log on to SQL Server, as shown in Listing 14.1. All connections with SQL Server are handled by middle-tier objects, implemented in the `DataAccess` and `SalesOrder` class modules.

LISTING 14.1   How the Login Form Handles Connection Information

```
Private Sub cmdOK_Click()
    ' Log on to SQL Server and open Order Form
    On Error GoTo HandleErr
    Dim da As DataAccess
    Dim fOK As Boolean

    Select Case Me!optAuthentication
        Case 1          ' NT authentication
            mstrOLEDBConnect = "Provider=SQLOLEDB.1;" & _
                "Data Source=" & Me!txtServer & ";" & _
                "Initial Catalog=" & Me.txtDatabase & ";" & _
                "Integrated Security=SSPI"
        Case 2          ' SQL server authentication
            mstrOLEDBConnect = "Provider=SQLOLEDB.1;" & _
                "Data Source=(local);" & _
                "Initial Catalog=" & Me.txtDatabase & ";" & _
                "User ID=" & Me!txtUser & _
                ";Password=" & Me!txtPwd
    End Select

    ' Check Connection
    Set da = New DataAccess
    fOK = da.CheckConnection(mstrOLEDBConnect)
    If fOK Then
        Me.Visible = False
        DoCmd.OpenForm "frmOrder"
    Else
        ' Connection failed.
        ' User can try again or
        '   close the form (and possibly exit).
        If MsgBox( _
          "Connection attempt failed." _
          & vbCrLf & vbCrLf _
          & "Do you want to try again?", _
          vbQuestion + vbYesNo, _
          "Unsuccessful. Try again?") _
          = vbNo Then
              DoCmd.Close acForm, Me.Name
        End If
```

LISTING 14.1   Continued

```
    End If
ExitHere:
    Exit Sub
HandleErr:
    Select Case Err.Number
        Case -2147217843   'OLE DB error. Failed to connect
          Resume Next
        Case Else
          MsgBox Err.Number & ": " & Err.Description, _
            Title:="Error Connecting"
    End Select
    Resume ExitHere
    Resume
End Sub
```

The CheckConnection method of the DataAccess class does the actual connecting to SQL
Server, as shown in Listing 14.2. It creates an ADO connection object and ensures that the
user can connect to SQL Server with the information provided in ConnectionString. If the
user can't connect to SQL Server, there's no point in continuing the application, unless the user
wants to try again.

LISTING 14.2   The CheckConnection Method of the DataAccess Class

```
Public Function CheckConnection( _
  ConnectionString As String) As Boolean

  On Error GoTo Handle_Err

  Const conProcName = conModuleName & _
    ".CheckConnection"

  Dim cnn As ADODB.Connection
  Set cnn = New ADODB.Connection
  cnn.ConnectionString = ConnectionString
  cnn.Open
  CheckConnection = (cnn.State = adStateOpen)

Exit_Here:
  ' Ensure that connection is closed and released.
  If Not cnn Is Nothing Then
      If cnn.State = adStateOpen Then
          cnn.Close
      End If
      Set cnn = Nothing
```

LISTING 14.2   Continued

```
  End If
  Exit Function

Handle_Err:
  Select Case Err.Number
    Case Else
        CheckConnection = False
        Err.Raise Err.Number, _
          conProcName, Err.Description, _
          Err.HelpFile, Err.HelpContext
  End Select
  Resume Exit_Here
  Resume
End Function
```

The order form then opens if the middle-tier object successfully connects to SQL Server.

Error Handling in COM Components

You might have noticed that the error-handling code in this procedure differs from the pattern used in most client-side Access code. (You do use error handling, right?) It is common to see error handlers, including the ones in most of the code in this book, that open a message box alerting the user when a runtime error occurs. In COM objects that will be used in middle-tier components, you should never include any user interface elements such as message boxes because the code might well end up running on a server in a closet somewhere, and nobody will be around to click the OK button. Instead, the standard pattern is to use Err.Raise in the error handler to raise the same error that originally caused the error handler to run, or sometimes to raise a custom error. Because the procedure's error handling is disabled inside the error handler itself, the raised error will simply be passed back to the application that called the method in your middle-tier component. This lets the client application deal with the error, where presumably there is a user sitting in front of the machine to click the OK button on the message box. Of course, this presumes that the calling procedure will have its own error handler in place to trap and deal with the error you raised and passed back.

The Order Form

The order form opens displaying an empty form. The combo boxes in the header section are filled from local XML files—the option to refresh them is located on the frmRefreshLocalData form. Figure 14.5 shows the order form opened, before any orders are loaded.

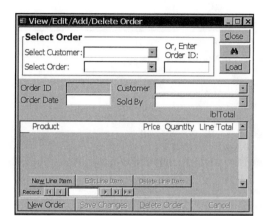

FIGURE 14.5
The order form opens without any orders being loaded.

Loading an Order

As you can see, the user interface looks exactly the same as the user interface for the sample application shown in Chapter 11. What's different is the way the data is fetched. Instead of connecting directly to SQL Server, all data access goes through the `SalesObject` middle-tier object. The following code fragment from the Load button's `On Click` event shows creating a new `SalesOrder` object and calling its `GetRstOrder` method, passing in the connection string and the order ID of the order to be fetched:

```
Set so = New SalesOrder
Set rst = so.GetRstOrder( _
  ConnectionString:=Forms!frmLogin.OLEDBConnect, _
  OrderID:=lngOrderID)
```

Listing 14.3 shows the code in the `GetRstOrder` method. This calls the `DataAccess` method `GetRstFromSPwSingleInputParam` (a generic method to get a recordset from a stored procedure that takes one input parameter, a common task), passing along the connection string, the name of the stored procedure to execute, and the recordset locking to be set on the recordset that `GetRstFromSPwSingleInputParam` will return.

LISTING 14.3   The `GetRstOrder` Method of the `DataAccess` Class

```
Public Function GetRstOrder( _
       ConnectionString As String, _
       OrderID As Long) As ADODB.Recordset
```

LISTING 14.3   Continued

```
      On Error GoTo Handle_Err
      Const conProcName = conModuleName & _
        ".GetRstOrder"
      Dim rst As ADODB.Recordset
      Dim da As DataAccess

      ' Use another middle-tier object to
      '    run a stored procedure and return
      '    a disconnected, read-only recordset.
      Set da = New DataAccess
      Set rst = da.GetRstFromSPwSingleInputParam( _
        ConnectionString:=ConnectionString, _
        StoredProcName:="procOrderSelect", _
        RstLockType:=adLockReadOnly, _
        ParamDataType:=adInteger, _
        ParamSize:=4, _
        ParamValue:=OrderID)
      Set GetRstOrder = rst
      Set rst = Nothing
      Set da = Nothing

Exit_Here:
  Exit Function

Handle_Err:
  Select Case Err.Number
    Case Else
        Err.Raise Err.Number, _
          conProcName, Err.Description, _
          Err.HelpFile, Err.HelpContext
  End Select
  Resume Exit_Here
  Resume
End Function
```

The GetRstFromSPwSingleInputParam method, shown in Listing 14.4, has all the information it needs supplied in its parameters. It can run any stored procedure that takes a single parameter, returning a recordset based on the options specified in its input parameters. This eliminates the need to have multiple methods, each calling a separate stored procedure.

LISTING 14.4   The GetRstFromSPwSingleInputParam Method of the DataAccess Class

```
Public Function GetRstFromSPwSingleInputParam( _
      ConnectionString As String, _
```

```vb
            StoredProcName As String, _
            RstLockType As LockTypeEnum, _
            ParamDataType As DataTypeEnum, _
            ParamSize As Long, _
            ParamValue As Variant) As ADODB.Recordset

    On Error GoTo Handle_Err

    Const conProcName = conModuleName & _
      ".GetRstFromSPwSingleInputParam"
    ' Return a disconnected
    '   recordset based on a
    '   stored procedure and one
    '   input parameter.
    Dim cnn As ADODB.Connection
    Dim cmd As ADODB.Command
    Dim rst As ADODB.Recordset

    Set cnn = New ADODB.Connection
    cnn.Open ConnectionString

    Set cmd = New ADODB.Command
    With cmd
      .Parameters.Append .CreateParameter( _
        "@Param", _
         ParamDataType, _
         adParamInput, _
         ParamSize, _
         ParamValue)
      .CommandText = StoredProcName
      Set .ActiveConnection = cnn
    End With
    Set rst = New ADODB.Recordset
    With rst
      .CursorLocation = adUseClient
      .LockType = RstLockType
      .Open cmd, Options:=adCmdStoredProc
    End With
    Set rst.ActiveConnection = Nothing
    Set GetRstFromSPwSingleInputParam = rst
    Set cmd = Nothing
    Set rst = Nothing

Exit_Here:
    ' Ensure that connection is closed and released.
```

14

LISTING 14.4 Continued

```
If Not cnn Is Nothing Then
    If cnn.State = adStateOpen Then
        cnn.Close
    End If
    Set cnn = Nothing
End If
Exit Function

Handle_Err:
  Select Case Err.Number
    Case Else
        Err.Raise Err.Number, _
          conProcName, Err.Description, _
          Err.HelpFile, Err.HelpContext
  End Select
  Resume Exit_Here
  Resume
End Function
```

Retrieving the Order Details

The order details are handled similarly to the ADP example shown in Chapter 11. However, there is an important difference in that the recordset is opened on SQL Server data by a middle-tier object, disconnected, passed back to Access, and then reconnected to the subform by setting the recordset's ActiveConnection property to CurrentProject.Connection. This makes it possible to bind the form to the recordset.

You cannot bind a form to a disconnected recordset. As soon as the form's Recordset property has been set to the ADO recordset, ActiveConnection can again be set to Nothing, thus severing the dummy connection to CurrentProject.Connection. At no time is the recordset connected both to SQL Server and to the form. The local Jet connection is used just briefly to trick Access into allowing the form to be bound. The ADO recordset doesn't care if its ActiveConnection property is set to a database other than the one it was opened against. The ActiveConnection property is set back to Nothing right after the form is bound to the recordset. The recordset is updateable due to the optimistic lock type that was used when it was opened, but unfortunately Access cannot directly update it through the user interface of the form. The application uses a separate unbound subform to gather data for edits and inserts to the order details recordset. Listing 14.5 shows the complete LoadLineItems procedure contained in the subform.

LISTING 14.5   The `LoadLineItems` Procedure in the Subform

```
Public Sub LoadLineItems()
    On Error GoTo HandleErr
    ' Use middle tier object to
    '    return a disconnected recordset.
    Dim so As SalesOrder
    Dim rst As ADODB.Recordset
    Set so = New SalesOrder
    Set rst = so.GetRstLineItems( _
      ConnectionString:=Forms!frmLogin.OLEDBConnect, _
      OrderID:=Nz(Me.Parent.txtOrderID, 0))

    ' The recordset must have an active connection
    '    to be bound to the form.
    ' Otherwise, error 7965 is raised.
    ' The local Jet connection works fine.
    Set rst.ActiveConnection = CurrentProject.Connection
    Set Me.Recordset = rst
    ' Once the recordset is bound to the form,
    '    the connection isn't required
    Set rst.ActiveConnection = Nothing
    ' Don't need the recordset variable anymore.
    Set rst = Nothing
    Set so = Nothing
ExitHere:
    Exit Sub

HandleErr:
    Select Case Err
        Case -2147467259 'Error trying to connect
            MsgBox "Unable to Connect", , _
              "Can't connect to the database."
            Forms!frmLogin.Visible = True
            DoCmd.Close acForm, "frmOrder"
            Forms!frmLogin.SetFocus
            Resume ExitHere
        Case Else
            MsgBox Err & ": " & Err.Description, , "LoadLineItems() Error"
    End Select
    Resume ExitHere
    Resume
End Sub
```

14

ARCHITECTING
DISTRIBUTED *N*-
TIER APPLICATIONS

Populating Combo Boxes

This application fills all its combo boxes using the same techniques shown in the section on ADPs in Chapter 11. The only difference is that all the recordsets are created by calling methods of the DataAccess class module.

The Select Order combo box on the order form (cboOrder) still uses a Microsoft Forms 2.0 ActiveX control and populates it using an ADO recordset. However, instead of opening the recordset directly, the code calls the GetRstFromSPwSingleInputParam method of the DataAccess class:

```
Set da = New DataAccess
Set rst = da.GetRstFromSPwSingleInputParam( _
  ConnectionString:=Forms!frmLogin.OLEDBConnect, _
  StoredProcName:="procOrderListForCustomer", _
  RstLockType:=adLockReadOnly, _
  ParamDataType:=adWChar, _
  ParamSize:=5, _
  ParamValue:=Me.cboCustomer)
```

The other combo boxes are all filled using the UseLocalFile callback function, which calls the HandleLocalStorage function to open ADO recordsets and to manage XML files for caching data. In the Chapter 11 code, the data is fetched, when necessary, using a global ADO connection object that is kept open. In this chapter's example, the code instead calls the GetXMLfromCommandText method of the middle-tier object, DataAccess:

```
Set da = New DataAccess
Set stm = da.GetXMLfromCommandText( _
    ConnectionString:=Forms!frmLogin.OLEDBConnect, _
    CommandText:=ctl.RowSource)
```

That middle-tier method handles connecting to SQL Server and opening a recordset based on the row source text that it receives as a parameter. It then saves the recordset in XML form to an ADO stream object, which is passed back as the return value of the method. Here's the code:

```
Dim cnn As ADODB.Connection
Dim rst As ADODB.Recordset
Dim stm As ADODB.Stream
Set cnn = New ADODB.Connection
cnn.ConnectionString = ConnectionString
cnn.Open
If Not cnn.State = adStateOpen Then
    GoTo Exit_Here
End If
Set rst = New ADODB.Recordset
Set stm = New ADODB.Stream
```

```
With rst
  .CursorLocation = adUseClient
  .LockType = adLockReadOnly
  .CursorType = adOpenStatic
  Set .ActiveConnection = cnn
  .Source = CommandText
  .Open
  .Save stm, adPersistXML
End With
Set GetXMLfromCommandText = stm
```

The ADO stream object was introduced in ADO version 2.5 to provide an efficient way of transmitting binary information. Earlier versions of ADO could only save recordsets to XML on disk. Being able to save instead to an in-memory binary stream is much more efficient and scalable. The stream is then saved to disk by the client code in HandleLocalStorage, so that the data can be reused locally later, and a client-side recordset is opened against it. Here's the code:

```
stm.SaveToFile strFile, adSaveCreateOverWrite
' Open local recordset based on the new file.
rst.Open Source:=strFile, Options:=adCmdFile
```

Saving Records

The validation routines for saving records are the same as they were in the Chapter 11 example, as is the logic for determining whether the record is a new record or a saved record. The only difference is that the middle-tier SalesOrder object is called. Here's the call to the Add method of the SalesOrder object when a new record is added. All the necessary information to add a new order is passed along via its arguments:

```
Set so = New SalesOrder
Call so.Add( _
  ConnectionString:=Forms!frmLogin.OLEDBConnect, _
  CustomerID:=Me.CustomerID, _
  EmployeeID:=Me.EmployeeID, _
  OrderDate:=Me.OrderDate, _
  LineItems:=strLineItems, _
  OrderID:=lngOrderID, _
  ReturnCode:=lngReturnCode, _
  ReturnMessage:=strReturnMessage)
```

Listing 14.6 shows the complete listing for the SalesOrder object's Add method, which executes the procOrderInsert stored procedure. Again, the main difference here is that the middle-tier object is executing the stored procedure and not the client application.

LISTING 14.6 The SalesOrder Object's Add Method

```
Public Sub Add( _
        ByVal ConnectionString As String, _
        ByVal CustomerID As String, _
        ByVal EmployeeID As String, _
        ByVal OrderDate As String, _
        ByVal LineItems As String, _
        ByRef OrderID As Long, _
        ByRef ReturnCode As Long, _
        ByRef ReturnMessage As String)
    On Error GoTo Handle_Err
    Const conProcName = conModuleName & _
      ".Add"
    Dim cnn As ADODB.Connection
    Dim cmd As ADODB.Command

    Set cnn = New ADODB.Connection
    cnn.Open ConnectionString
    Set cmd = New ADODB.Command

    With cmd
        Set .ActiveConnection = cnn
        .CommandText = "procOrderInsert"
        .CommandType = adCmdStoredProc

        .Parameters.Append .CreateParameter( _
          "RETURN_VALUE", adInteger, adParamReturnValue)
        .Parameters.Append .CreateParameter( _
          "@CustomerID", adWChar, adParamInput, 5, CustomerID)
        .Parameters.Append .CreateParameter( _
          "@EmployeeID", adInteger, adParamInput, , EmployeeID)
        .Parameters.Append .CreateParameter( _
          "@OrderDate", adDBTimeStamp, adParamInput, , OrderDate)
        ' The maximum size of 1000 for this parameter is arbitrary.
        '  It needs to match the size used in the stored procedure,
        '    which is limited only by the amount of memory on the server.
        .Parameters.Append .CreateParameter( _
          "@OrderDetails", adVarChar, adParamInput, 1000, LineItems)
        .Parameters.Append .CreateParameter( _
          "@OrderID", adInteger, adParamOutput)
        .Parameters.Append .CreateParameter( _
          "@RetCode", adInteger, adParamOutput)
        .Parameters.Append .CreateParameter( _
          "@RetMsg", adVarChar, adParamOutput, 100)
```

LISTING 14.6   Continued

```
        .Execute
        OrderID = .Parameters("@OrderID")
        ReturnCode = .Parameters("@RetCode")
        ReturnMessage = .Parameters("@RetMsg")
    End With
    Set cmd = Nothing

Exit_Here:
  ' Ensure that connection is closed and released.
  If Not cnn Is Nothing Then
      If cnn.State = adStateOpen Then
          cnn.Close
      End If
      Set cnn = Nothing
  End If
  Exit Sub

Handle_Err:
  Select Case Err.Number
    Case Else
        Err.Raise Err.Number, _
          conProcName, Err.Description, _
          Err.HelpFile, Err.HelpContext
  End Select
  Resume Exit_Here
  Resume
End Sub
```

If a record is being edited, the `Edit` method of the `SalesOrder` object is called:

```
Set so = New SalesOrder
Call so.Edit( _
  ConnectionString:=Forms!frmLogin.OLEDBConnect, _
  OrderID:=Me.OrderID, _
  CustomerID:=Me.CustomerID, _
  EmployeeID:=Me.EmployeeID, _
  OrderDate:=Me.OrderDate, _
  LineItems:=strLineItems, _
  ConcurrencyID:=lngConcurrencyID, _
  ReturnCode:=lngReturnCode, _
  ReturnMessage:=strReturnMessage)
```

Listing 14.7 shows the `SalesOrder` object's `Edit` method, which executes the `procOrderUpdate` stored procedure.

14

ARCHITECTING DISTRIBUTED *N*-TIER APPLICATIONS

LISTING 14.7 The `SalesOrder` Object's Edit Method

```
Public Sub Edit( _
        ByVal ConnectionString As String, _
        ByVal OrderID As Long, _
        ByVal CustomerID As String, _
        ByVal EmployeeID As String, _
        ByVal OrderDate As String, _
        ByVal LineItems As String, _
        ByRef ConcurrencyID As Long, _
        ByRef ReturnCode As Long, _
        ByRef ReturnMessage As String)

    On Error GoTo Handle_Err

    Const conProcName = conModuleName & _
      ".Edit"
    Dim cnn As ADODB.Connection
    Dim cmd As ADODB.Command

    Set cnn = New ADODB.Connection
    cnn.Open ConnectionString
    Set cmd = New ADODB.Command

    With cmd
        Set .ActiveConnection = cnn
        .CommandText = "procOrderUpdate"
        .CommandType = adCmdStoredProc

        .Parameters.Append .CreateParameter( _
          "RETURN_VALUE", adInteger, adParamReturnValue)
        .Parameters.Append .CreateParameter( _
          "@OrderID", adInteger, adParamInput, 4, OrderID)
        .Parameters.Append .CreateParameter( _
          "@CustomerID", adWChar, adParamInput, 5, CustomerID)
        .Parameters.Append .CreateParameter( _
          "@EmployeeID", adInteger, adParamInput, , EmployeeID)
        .Parameters.Append .CreateParameter( _
          "@OrderDate", adDBTimeStamp, adParamInput, , OrderDate)
        ' The maximum size of 1000 for this parameter is arbitrary.
        '  It needs to match the size used in the stored procedure,
        '    which is limited only by the amount of memory on the server.
        .Parameters.Append .CreateParameter( _
          "@OrderDetails", adVarChar, adParamInput, 1000, LineItems)
        .Parameters.Append .CreateParameter( _
          "ConcurrencyID", adInteger, adParamInputOutput, 4, ConcurrencyID)
```

LISTING 14.7   Continued

```
        .Parameters.Append .CreateParameter( _
          "@RetCode", adInteger, adParamOutput)
        .Parameters.Append .CreateParameter( _
          "@RetMsg", adVarChar, adParamOutput, 100)

        .Execute
        ReturnCode = .Parameters("@RetCode")
        ReturnMessage = .Parameters("@RetMsg")
    End With
    Set cmd = Nothing

Exit_Here:
  ' Ensure that connection is closed and released.
  If Not cnn Is Nothing Then
      If cnn.State = adStateOpen Then
          cnn.Close
      End If
      Set cnn = Nothing
  End If
  Exit Sub

Handle_Err:
  Select Case Err.Number
    Case Else
        Err.Raise Err.Number, _
          conProcName, Err.Description, _
          Err.HelpFile, Err.HelpContext
  End Select
  Resume Exit_Here
  Resume
End Sub
```

All the other processing for checking the ConcurrencyID property is handled the same way as it was in Chapter 11. There are no further changes to the client code for saving a record.

Deleting a Record

Deleting a record is handled by a call to the Delete method of the SalesOrder class, passing along the OrderID property of the record to be deleted:

```
Set so = New SalesOrder
Call so.Delete( _
  ConnectionString:=Forms!frmLogin.OLEDBConnect, _
  OrderID:=Me.OrderID, _
  ReturnCode:=lngReturnCode, _
  ReturnMsg:=strReturnMessage)
```

Listing 14.8 shows the `SalesOrder` object's `Delete` method, which calls the `procOrderDelete` stored procedure.

LISTING 14.8   The `Delete` Method of the `SalesOrder` Class

```
Public Sub Delete( _
     ByVal ConnectionString As String, _
     ByVal OrderID As Long, _
     ByRef ReturnCode As Long, _
     ByRef ReturnMsg As String)

  On Error GoTo Handle_Err

  Const conProcName = conModuleName & _
    ".Delete"
  Dim cnn As ADODB.Connection
  Dim cmd As ADODB.Command

  ' Run stored procedure to delete an order,
  '    and return output parameters.
  Set cnn = New ADODB.Connection
  cnn.Open ConnectionString
  Set cmd = New ADODB.Command
  With cmd
      Set .ActiveConnection = cnn
      .CommandText = "procOrderDelete"
      .CommandType = adCmdStoredProc

      .Parameters.Append .CreateParameter( _
        "RETURN_VALUE", adInteger, adParamReturnValue)
      .Parameters.Append .CreateParameter( _
        "@OrderID", adInteger, adParamInput, , OrderID)
      .Parameters.Append .CreateParameter( _
        "@RetCode", adInteger, adParamOutput)
      .Parameters.Append .CreateParameter( _
        "@RetMsg", adVarChar, adParamOutput, 100)

      .Execute

      ReturnCode = .Parameters("@RetCode")
      ReturnMsg = .Parameters("@RetMsg")
  End With

  Set cmd = Nothing
```

LISTING 14.8 Continued

```
Exit_Here:
  ' Ensure that connection is closed and released.
  If Not cnn Is Nothing Then
      If cnn.State = adStateOpen Then
          cnn.Close
      End If
      Set cnn = Nothing
  End If

  Exit Sub
Handle_Err:
  Select Case Err.Number
    Case Else
        Err.Raise Err.Number, _
          conProcName, Err.Description, _
          Err.HelpFile, Err.HelpContext
  End Select
  Resume Exit_Here
  Resume
End Sub
```

Code Organization and Logical Separation

The code in the sample application is broken logically into different components. Figure 14.6 shows a view of the VBA project window. All the code that relates to the user interface is stored in the form class modules, the two standard modules (basLocalData and basUtility), and the two class modules for filling combo boxes with XML (ControlToFillLocally and ControlsToFillLocally). Code that communicates with SQL Server is stored in the class modules DataAccess and SalesOrder, which comprise the logical middle tier.

All data retrieval and modifications take place through the methods defined in DataAccess and SalesOrder. There is never any direct communication between Access and SQL Server— everything goes through these two classes. Their methods map directly to stored procedures in SQL Server.

By placing all code that communicates with SQL Server in separate class modules, you make it easier later on to separate the code and move it to a Visual Basic ActiveX DLL project. Code in the existing Access class modules will work with no modification. Right now there is only a logical separation, but implementing the logical separation at the outset makes the physical separation easier when the time comes to migrate. At that time, all existing modules will remain in Access, except for the class modules DataAccess and SalesOrder, which will be moved to new Visual Basic 6 ActiveX DLL projects.

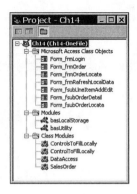

FIGURE 14.6
The VBA project window.

All data and requests for data pass through the middle tier, whether it is physically located in Access or in a separate middle-tier DLL. Application logic would continue to be located in Access while all data rules would be implemented in stored procedures in SQL Server, making the middle-tier objects very lightweight and fast.

> **NOTE**
>
> This example doesn't implement any business rules in the middle tier, which is used only for communication with the server. Another important use of middle-tier objects is to encapsulate business rules, such as the credit limit example given at the start of this chapter. When business rules are implemented in middle-tier objects, they can be shared by multiple-client applications. If the rules change, the change can be made efficiently to the shared middle-tier objects rather than you having to dig into the code of each client application.

The logical separation of middle-tier functionality into separate class modules is the first step toward the implementation of an *n*-tier architecture. The next step is to create your middle-tier component, as covered in the next section.

Once you've implemented the two data class modules as ActiveX DLLs, you can leverage your code to work with other clients besides Access, without having to modify the middle-tier code.

Creating Middle-Tier Components

The next step involves physically separating the middle-tier class modules from the Access application and moving them to Visual Basic, where they can be compiled in COM component DLLs.

Using Visual Basic to Create COM Components

You cannot create and compile an ActiveX DLL in Access 2000 to use as a middle-tier, object—creating DLL in Office. VBA is only supported for COM add-ins. This limitation mandates using another product, such as Visual Basic 6.0. Creating and compiling a middle-tier component will allow you to set a reference to it in Access or in any other COM-compliant programming environment, including any application that hosts VBA or VBScript. In Access, once the reference has been set, you work with the objects with no changes to your existing form or local module code.

Moving Data Classes to Visual Basic

In the case of the existing application, the two class modules, DataAccess and SalesOrder, are implemented as separate DLLs. This is necessary for them to run successfully under COM+ in their current form. The reason for this is that the SalesOrder object creates an instance of the DataAccess object by using the New method, which causes problems in COM+ if the objects are located in the same project. That's fine here because the DataAccess methods are generic ones that could be used for many different purposes, whereas the SalesOrder code is very specific to working with orders in the Northwind database. It makes sense to keep them separate. But this need for separation could easily be overcome, if necessary, by using a more MTS-friendly method of instantiating objects: ObjectContext.CreateInstance. Here's the generic syntax for using this method:

```
' in a method of ComponentA
Dim ObjCtx As ObjectContext
Set ObjCtx = GetObjectContext()
Dim ObjectB As ComponentB
Set ObjectB = ObjCtx.CreateInstance("MyDLL.ComponentB")
```

When you are ready to move your Access class modules in Visual Basic to be turned into COM components, here are the steps to take to accomplish the physical separation:

1. Create a new ActiveX DLL project in Visual Basic 6.0.
2. Import or copy the class module from the Access database into the Visual Basic project.

3. Delete the `Option Compare Database` statement from the Declarations section, because that is an Access-specific directive to VBA, instructing it to use the host Access database's collation for string comparisons.

4. Remove these two class modules from the Access database.

5. Set the following properties for the class modules:

Property	Setting
Name	DataAccess or SalesOrder
Instancing	Multi-Use

6. Set the following properties for the project on the General tab:

Property	Setting
Project Names	Ch14Data for DataAccess, and Ch14Business for SalesOrder
Project Description	Ch14 Data Access or Ch14 Sales Order
Unattended Execution	Checked
Retained in Memory	Checked
Threading Model	Apartment Threaded

7. Set any required references. In this example, both the Ch14Data and the Ch14Business projects need a reference to ADO. The Ch14Business object needs a reference to the Ch14Data object, so you need to compile the Ch14Data DLL first.

8. Once you've compiled Ch14Data, create a new folder and copy the DLL into it. Return to the Ch14Data properties and set the Binary Compatibility option on the Components tab, pointing to the copy of the DLL. Save the project.

9. Open the Ch14Business project and set a reference to Ch14Data. Save and compile the DLL.

10. Copy the Ch14Business DLL to a new folder and set the Binary Compatibility option on the Components tab, pointing to the copy of the DLL. Save the project.

11. Delete the two class modules from the Access database, if you haven't done so already. In a code module, choose Tools, References and set a reference to both the Ch14Data and the Ch14Business libraries, as shown in Figure 14.7.

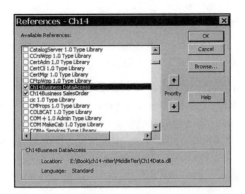

Figure 14.7

Setting a reference to the DLLs in your Access database.

Registering COM Components

When you compile your DLLs on your machine, they get automatically registered. To register your DLLs by hand on another client machine, you can run the `regsvr32.exe` command-line utility, as follows:

```
regsvr32 c:\MyDLLs\Ch14Data.dll
```

This method of registration is a less scalable alternative to the COM+ installation method described in this chapter, and it will not provide you with the services of MTS. To manually unregister a DLL that has been registered using this method, use the `/u` switch:

```
regsvr32 /u c:\MyDLLs\Ch14Data.dll
```

Put the Access database through its paces. It should perform exactly as it did when it was an all-Access application.

If you've achieved complete logical separation in your code, the physical separation is a piece of cake, and the Access database application should work with no modifications whatsoever. Once the objects are physically separated and the reference is set in the Access client to the ActiveX DLLs, the application will continue to work with no changes on the client. In other words, if you write the code this way to begin with, later on you won't need to rewrite it when you want to scale up to supporting more users or just want to gain the maintainability and reuse benefits of sharing components among multiple client applications.

14

ARCHITECTING DISTRIBUTED *N*-TIER APPLICATIONS

Installing the Middle-Tier Components in COM+

The good news is, unless you are using interobject transactions, there is nothing to change when you want to install your two DLLs in COM+.

In Windows 2000, choose Programs, Administrative Tools, Component Services from the Start menu. This will load the dialog box shown in Figure 14.8. Expand the nodes under Computers until the COM+ Applications folder objects are exposed. You will see the applications installed in the COM+ folder, some with little spinning balls in the center of their packages.

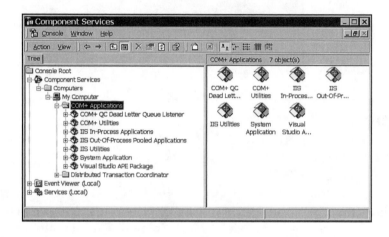

FIGURE 14.8

The Component Services window.

Here are the steps to install your application in COM+:

1. Right-click the COM+ Applications node and choose New Application from the list. This will launch the COM Application Install Wizard.

2. Click the Next tab. You'll see two options, as shown in Figure 14.9. Choose the Create an Empty Application option.

3. This will load the dialog box shown in Figure 14.10. Create a name for the application and set the Server Application option. Click Next when done.

4. The next dialog box lets you set security. Choose the Interactive User option. This will use the logged-on user's authentication for the package.

5. The final dialog box invites you to click the Finish button. The Ch14 application will now show up in the window along with the other applications, but it won't do much because it's not pointing to the DLLs yet.

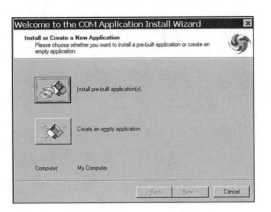

FIGURE 14.9

Installing an application.

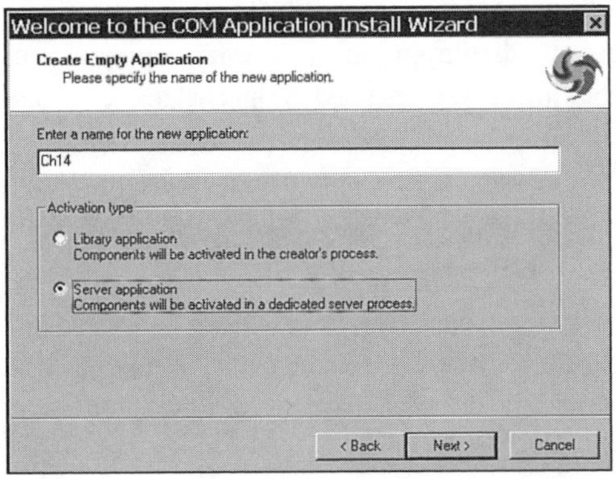

FIGURE 14.10

Naming and setting options for the application.

Here are the steps to finish the installation:

1. Expand the Ch14 object and right-click the Components folder. Choose New Component. This will load the Component Install Wizard. Click the Next button after reading the introductory screen.

2. On the Import or Install a Component dialog box shown in Figure 14.11, choose the first option: Install New Component(s). Theoretically, you should be able to choose Import Component(s) That Are Already Registered, but due to a bug in MTS/COM+, this choice will not always result in correctly registered components. Of course, we hope and expect that this will be fixed in a future version.

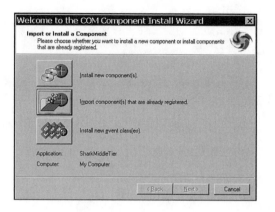

FIGURE 14.11
Importing a component.

3. This will display the Choose Components to Import dialog box, which might take a little while to load because it's displaying all the components on your computer. Select the Ch14Data.DataAccess and Ch14Business.SalesOrder components, as shown in Figure 14.12.

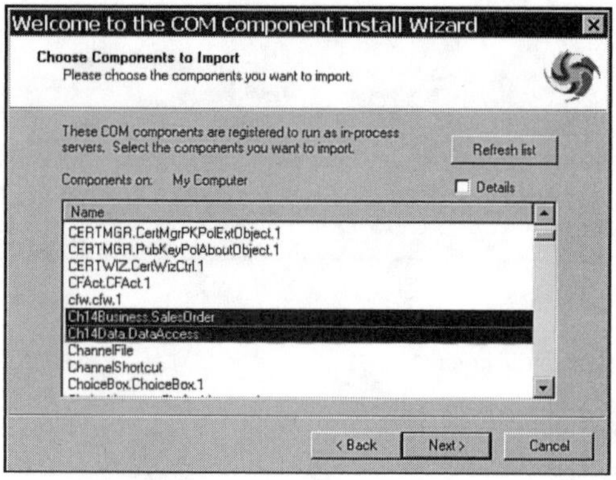

FIGURE 14.12
Selecting the SalesOrder and DataAccess components.

4. The next dialog box prompts you to click the Finish button. Your components are now installed in COM+, ready to roll (literally!). You can watch them in action by viewing them in the Component Services window, as shown in Figure 14.13. When the components are in use, the little marbles inside the package icons will roll around.

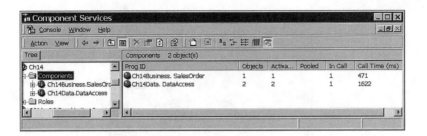

FIGURE 14.13
Monitoring object use in the Component Services window.

Client Setup

The first step in undertaking a client setup is to export the package by right-clicking the Ch14 object in the Component Services window and choosing Export. This will load the Export Wizard, which will guide you through the steps of exporting the package to a MSI file. This is useful if you need to export the package for other developers to use or for when you want to move it to the production server.

Setting Up in VB for Remote Use

The easiest way to create a client installation package is to use the Package and Deployment Wizard in Visual Basic, but first you need to take a couple of steps. Both of the DLL project files need to be configured for remote use by setting the Remote Server Files option on the project's Component dialog box, as shown in Figure 14.14. This tells the Package and Deployment Wizard that this component might be installed remotely.

When you compile the DLL again, this tells VB to create an external TLB file (type library) in addition to keeping one internally. A file with a VBR extension is created in the same directory as the DLL, which contains all the proxy/stub registration information. The VBR and TLB files install locally on the client; the DLLs install remotely on a server.

During the installation process, the contents of the VBR file are merged into the client machine's system registry. COM uses this information to set up remote connections between the client code and the code running in the COM+ application across the network.

14

ARCHITECTING DISTRIBUTED *N*-TIER APPLICATIONS

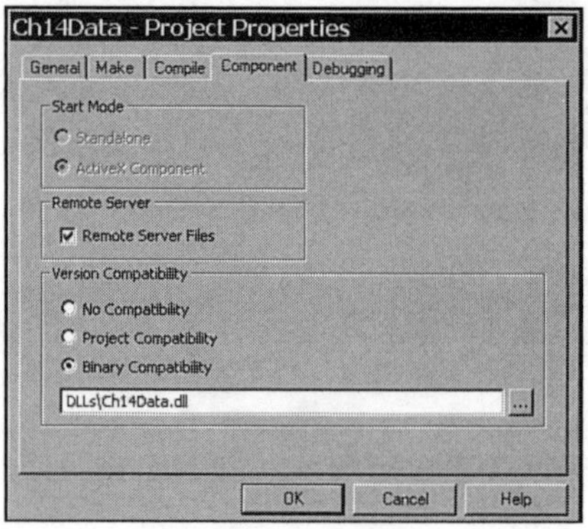

FIGURE 14.14

Configuring the project for remote use.

Deployment to Clients

The Package and Deployment Wizard will create a setup package for the client and package the full application, taking care of remote dependencies. Load the Package and Deployment Wizard by choosing Add-Ins, Add-In Manager and checking the Load/Unload box next to the Package and Deployment Wizard option. Then follow the steps to create a new package.

One vitally important step you need to take in the Package and Deployment Wizard is to remove each DLL and add a VBR file, as shown in Figure 14.15. If you omit this step, the application won't work on the client machine.

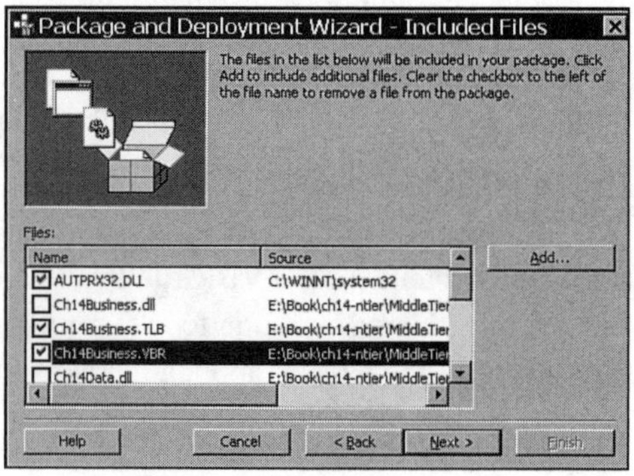

FIGURE 14.15

Adding the VBR file and removing the DLL in the Package and Deployment Wizard.

Removing the DLL ensures that the package won't create a local component that will run in place of the remote one.

Resource Pooling of Middle-Tier Components

Installing components in COM+ and watching the marbles in the packages spin around is all a lot of fun, but you might be wondering why it is worth the bother. One advantage is obvious from stepping through the client setup. You have taken code that previously existed separately in each copy of the front-end Access database and moved this code to a single, centralized location that can be accessed by all your client applications. If you need to make a change, you can do so in one place. If you don't change any of the COM interfaces (the names and data types of your objects and methods) and if you use Binary Compatibility in VB when you recompile, your client applications won't have to be touched.

Another important benefit—perhaps more important to your database application—is that your data access code will now automatically take advantage of a feature of COM+ called *resource pooling*. The resources that you are most concerned about if you are supporting a lot of users are the connections to SQL Server. Once your components have been installed in COM+, your ADO connections will be pooled. Connection pooling is not specific to COM+ applications—it happens anytime you use OLE DB connections. However, COM+ allows many users to share a common pool of objects, and thereby to share a common pool of connections. Without COM+, your connection pooling would affect only multiple connections made by each user.

When one user closes an object that opened a connection, the object will actually linger in memory for a little while waiting for another user to come along. Instead of opening a second connection for the next user, COM+, which is intercepting all calls to your object, will immediately give the object and its connection to the new user. This means that a few connections could support dozens of users, and dozens of connections could support hundreds of users.

The application example was specifically coded to take advantage of connection pooling. Connections are only kept open for the short time they are needed to execute a command or to open a recordset. Then, at the end of every procedure, they are closed and set equal to `Nothing`. The code to do this is placed in the `Exit_Here` section of each procedure to ensure that, even if a runtime error occurs, the connection will be closed (if it was open) and released:

```
Exit_Here:
    ' Ensure that connection is closed and released.
    If Not cnn Is Nothing Then
        If cnn.State = adStateOpen Then
            cnn.Close
        End If
        Set cnn = Nothing
    End If
    Exit Sub
```

14

ARCHITECTING DISTRIBUTED *N*-TIER APPLICATIONS

When the connection is released in this way, it is not actually closed. Instead it remains available in memory until another client requests an identical connection or until its timeout period expires. This timeout defaults to 60 seconds, and prior to AD0 2.5 it could not be adjusted. Using ADO 2.5 or later versions, the connection pooling timeout can be adjusted by adding a DWORD value called SPTimeout, containing the desired number of seconds, to the Class ID registry key for the OLE DB provider being used. This registry key is found at HKEY_CLASSES_ROOT/CLSID/ClassID, in which ClassID is the CLSID of the OLE DB provider. For most purposes, the default timeout value of 60 seconds works fine.

Security and Connection Pooling

Another important part of ensuring that connection pooling occurs is to use exactly the same connection string for each connection object. If the connection string is even slightly different from any available connection object in the pool, a new object will be created. This means that if users are authenticated with a SQL Server login that is different for each user, the benefits of connection pooling will largely be lost. Each individual user's connections might be pooled, but connections will not be pooled across users.

Even using a Windows login with integrated security will require different connections for different users if they are logged in to the operating system under different accounts. Using integrated security, you might think that the connection string would be consistent, always containing Integrated Security=SSPI rather than a username and password. However, the actual credentials of the user must be passed to the database somehow, and the connection object is tailored to each set of credentials.

Another way to ensure consistent connection strings is to use application roles in your connection code rather than using data supplied by the user. The user might get authenticated to use your application, but once he or she is in, the application role would be used for connecting to SQL Server. Application roles are covered in Chapter 3, "Understanding SQL Server Security."

There are pros and cons to using application roles with your application. When an application role is activated by using the sp_setapprole stored procedure, only the permissions explicitly granted to the application role, as well as any permissions granted to the public role and the guest user (if any) are applied. All other implicit permissions, including those of the sysadmin and owner roles, are ignored for the duration of the connection that activated the application role. Application roles can enormously simplify the process of administering security when all you need is one set of permissions to be applied for the entire application. However, there is another issue to consider: authentication.

Application Roles and Authentication

Applications employing an application role need some form of authentication to get through to the database and activate the application role. Your choices are to use integrated security with Windows NT/Windows 2000 authentication, or to create a SQL Server login in order to gain access to the server. If you choose integrated security, then the activities of individual users can be monitored and logged under their own logins even while the application role is active. On the other hand, if you chose to use a single SQL Server login for the application role, then Windows NT/Windows 2000 logging is not available.

However, connection pooling adds another consideration to your choice of authentication mode. The plus side of using a single SQL Server login is that the connection string used for that login is identical for all users, aiding connection pooling. Be aware that SQL Server logins are not considered to be quite as secure as Windows NT/Windows 2000 logins because they are stored in SQL Server itself, and the strings used for the name and password must of necessity be embedded in, or somehow supplied by, the application that uses them. You will need to balance your requirements for security and user tracking against the advantages provided by connection pooling.

Summary

COM is the underlying Microsoft architecture for supporting communication between software components. MTS in Windows NT 4 and COM+ in Windows 2000 provide a runtime environment for components that increases the efficiency of resource usage, supports cross-object transactions, and makes it easy to deploy components remotely. You can use Access to build an application that scales to an *n*-tier architecture by creating a logical separation between the data-access components and the client application code. All middle-tier code should be encapsulated in stateless class modules. Class modules can be easily copied or imported into a VB 6 ActiveX DLL project, compiled, and installed under COM+ Component Services. COM+ will take care of object brokering and resource pooling, with no additional code if there are no interobject transactions. Deploying the middle tier is easily accomplished by exporting the application and using the VB Package and Deployment Wizard to build a client setup program. Pooling of ADO connections occurs automatically if all connection objects are properly closed and released, and if consistent connection strings are used.

Deployment, Tuning, and Maintenance

IN THIS CHAPTER

As an Access developer, the maintenance part of the job is easy—compact your database regularly to keep it from bloating, make sure to back it up regularly, and you're done. You can even create shortcuts to compact and repair a database as well as use a third-party backup product to schedule regular backups. Tuning an Access database is also pretty straightforward—if a query or a report is too slow, you check whether there's an additional index you can add to help speed things up. Or, perhaps you add some temp tables to speed up reports. However, maintaining a SQL Server database is not quite so simple. SQL Server has more maintenance requirements because there might be much bigger databases supporting a larger number of users. SQL Server is a far more complex product, and it is often deployed in enterprise-wide solutions where there's zero tolerance for data loss or downtime. Plus, there's the added complexity of ensuring database consistency and making sure that the transaction log is backed up in addition to backing up the database.

In versions of SQL Server prior to SQL Server 7.0, it often took a full-time database administrator to tune, administer, back up, and ensure database consistency in a SQL Server installation. The administrator, or *DBA*, did no programming or application development; the DBA's responsibility was to protect the data and make sure the server was always up and running smoothly. With the advent of SQL Server 7, Microsoft introduced the concept of the *self-managing server*. Tools to introduce some smarts into the day-to-day tasks of managing and maintaining a SQL Server were added so that in many cases a full-time DBA is not necessary. Administering a SQL Server database is much easier than it has ever been in past versions of SQL Server. It's much easier in SQL Server than it is for other server database products, but it's still more difficult than managing an Access database. If you're an Access developer taking on this dual role of developer/DBA, then understanding how to use the tools that SQL Server provides for maintaining and backing up your databases is essential to being able to successfully fulfill your new role. Even if you're not acting as a DBA, understanding the tools provided will help you design and implement more robust solutions.

This chapter also discusses the options available to you for deploying your Access/SQL Server application.

Tuning

There are many different elements that affect the performance of your SQL Server application: the application design, the amount of system resources it consumes, performance of the network, and so on. Tuning isn't one-stop shopping—there are several places you need to look when trying to improve overall performance:

- Make sure that the problem isn't with the client application. In other words, don't open a form based on a million-row-plus table. Always fetch only the data needed. Many of the chapters in this book discuss ways to work efficiently with SQL Server data.

- Tune the database by refining its logical and physical design. A normalized database design is a good starting point.

- Tune the server by evaluating the storage design and server configuration options.

- Tune the hardware by adding more memory, processors, or computers. For example, SQL Server performs better if it's located on its own computer and doesn't have to share processing with other applications. Get faster hard disks or increase network performance.

Tuning isn't something you do only once and then forget about. The first time you'll think about tuning is when you're designing the database, then again when testing, and yet again after it's been deployed. And the process continues thereafter as you schedule ongoing maintenance and monitoring.

This chapter discusses the tools that SQL Server provides to help you tune and monitor your database—the Windows System Monitor, and the SQL Profiler. Also covered is backing up and restoring your database, plus strategies and techniques to use when deploying. The tools for tuning queries were discussed in Chapter 9, "Creating and Optimizing Views."

Monitoring Performance

When working with an Access/SQL Server application, you need to be able to find answers to questions about how SQL Server is handling your data. You might encounter problems that it would be hard to solve without knowing more about what's going on behind the scenes. Enter the SQL Server Profiler. It records activity against your SQL Server by running a *trace*, which is a definition of the events you're interested in monitoring. You create traces either from scratch by selecting events to capture, by customizing one of the sample traces provided, or by using the Create Trace Wizard. SQL Server Profiler intercepts the traffic between your Access client application and your SQL Server, keeping a copy in the trace file for you to analyze later.

Getting Started with the SQL Server Profiler

The SQL Server Profiler provides a graphical user interface on top of a set of extended stored procedures. This is a lot easier than using these extended stored procedures directly. It also means that you could write your own performance-monitoring tool by building your own graphical interface that calls these stored procedures in the background. You'll probably, however, be quite happy with what you can do in Profiler, which received a number of new features in SQL Server 2000. The SQL Server Profiler enables you to perform the following actions:

- Monitor the performance of your SQL Server.

- Step through queries and stored procedures to debug or find the cause of a problem.

15

DEPLOYMENT,
TUNING, AND
MAINTENANCE

- Find and diagnose slow-running queries.

- Capture a series of SQL statements in a trace file. The saved trace can then be used to replicate a problem on a test server where the problem can be replayed and diagnosed.

- Audit and record security activities, including the success or failure of login attempts and attempts to execute statements or to access objects. If a user tries to so something that he doesn't have permission to do, you can find out about it.

Profiler Concepts

The Profiler in SQL Server 2000 introduces some concepts that will be familiar to users of SQL Server 7.0, plus a few new ones. Here's a review of the terminology and concepts that you'll encounter when working with the Profiler:

- The SQL Server Profiler runs *traces* that record activity on your SQL Server.

- Traces are created from a *template* that defines the data you want to collect. A trace collects data by monitoring the events defined in the template. When you create a template, you specify which events, data columns, and filters to use.

- An *event* is an action generated within the SQL Server engine. For example, the start of a Transact-SQL batch triggers an event as does acquiring a lock on a database object.

- An *event class* is a generic description of the type of event that was produced by the SQL Server engine. The Profiler displays the event classes and data columns while the trace is running, and can optionally log them for playback later.

- An *event category* refers to the way events are grouped together. For example, all lock event classes are grouped within the Locks event category, transaction event classes are grouped within the Transaction event category, and event classes relating to stored procedures are grouped within the Stored Procedures event category.

- A *filter* lets you either include or exclude data. Filters are necessary because trace files can become quite large if too many events are being monitored, and the data you want can be hidden among a lot of clutter. For example, you're probably not interested in displaying events that the Profiler itself generates, so the default filter in all of the built-in templates is defined not to monitor events raised by the Profiler. You might also want to look at a specific application's events only. For example, mightbe you want to examine events raised by Access, and you don't care about events raised by the Query Analyzer. You can set up a filter so that only events raised by Access are displayed.

After defining the trace template, save it and launch a trace. The settings you defined in the trace will determine the data that is captured by the trace. This data can be viewed in real-time in the Profiler window, or captured to a file or database table. Traces can also be replayed, allowing you to re-create events in the Profiler at a later time. This can be a big help in troubleshooting a wide range of problems, such as slow-running queries, deadlocks and blocking issues, or security breaches.

Working with Events

There are many more event classes than you would ever want to work with in a single trace. They are organized by event category so that you can find the ones you need. Here's the list of the event categories you have to work with:

- Cursors
- Database
- Errors and Warnings
- Locks
- Objects
- Performance
- Scans
- Security Audit
- Sessions
- Stored Procedures
- Transactions
- TSQL
- User Configurable

When you create a new trace, it is defined with a set of default event classes. You can remove these event classes and add others when you create new traces. Unless removed explicitly, the default event classes are present each time you create a new trace. These are the default event classes:

- Audit Login Event. Collects all new connection events since the trace was started.
- Audit Logout Event. Collects all new disconnect events since the trace was started.
- ExistingConnection. Detects activity by all users connected to an instance of SQL Server before the trace was started.
- RPC:Completed. Indicates that a remote procedure call (RPC) has completed.
- SQL:BatchCompleted. Indicates that a Transact-SQL batch has completed.

You're not stuck with the event classes defined in the default trace. The Profiler templates make it easy to create your own custom traces.

15

Creating New Traces

Launching the Profiler can be a bit disconcerting since it launches a blank window. The Create Trace Wizard, which was in the SQL Server 7.0 version of the Profiler, is gone. There is no easy way to get started with using the Profiler unless you already know what you are doing.

Click the File, New menu; there are two choices for creating a new trace, Trace and Trace Template. The Trace option loads the Trace Properties dialog box where you can create a trace based on the standard template. The Trace Template option lets you create and save a trace template.

If you choose New Trace, the Trace Properties dialog box loads, as shown in Figure 15.1, where the General tab is displayed. Set properties for the trace, such as the filename of the .prc file that will record trace events, and its maximum size.

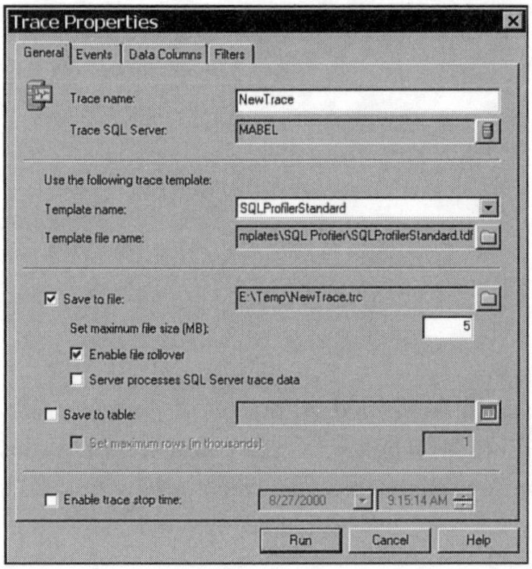

FIGURE 15.1
Creating a new trace loads the Trace Properties dialog box, where you can configure your trace.

The Events tab displays the event categories for the available events. Expand the event category to display the individual event classes that you can configure for your trace. Figure 15.2 shows the event classes for the default trace selected, with the Security Audit event category expanded. Add the trace events you're interested in by clicking the Add button.

The Data Columns tab shown in Figure 15.3 lets you configure the columns that are displayed in the trace. If you select a column name, a brief explanation of the column is displayed at the bottom of the dialog box.

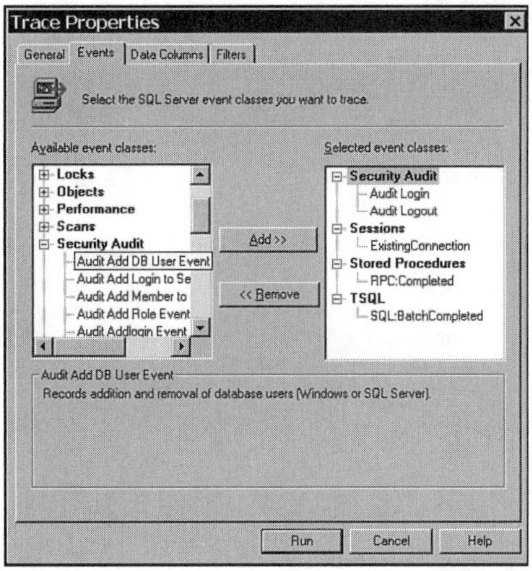

FIGURE 15.2
The event classes determine which SQL Server events will be monitored by the trace.

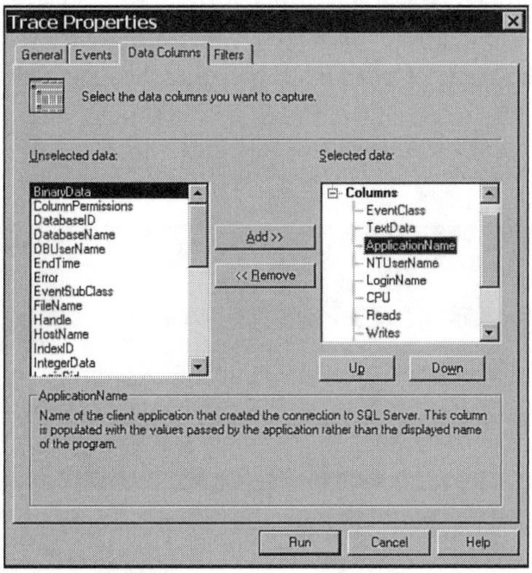

FIGURE 15.3
The Data Columns tab lets you select the columns to display in the trace output.

The Filters tab enables you to filter the information displayed. The default filter screens out events that the Profiler itself generates when it runs. Figure 15.4 shows filtering the Profiler output to watch activity on the Northwind database for user Dudley, and excluding the dbo user.

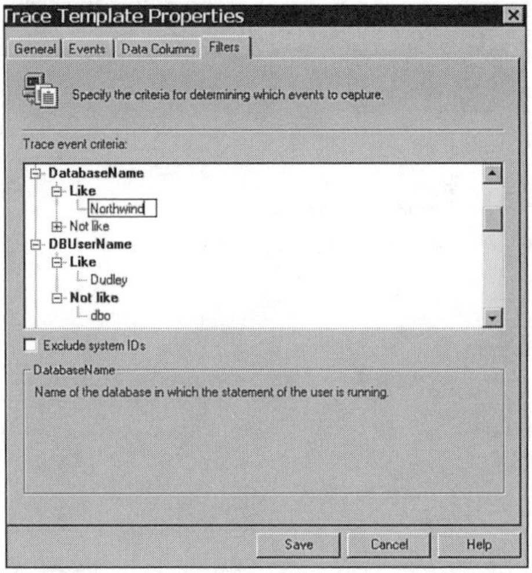

FIGURE 15.4

The Filters tab lets you filter the Profiler results.

Clicking the Run button launches the trace. Since a filter was set in the trace to track user Dudley, all statements and applications used by Dudley show up in the trace results. Figure 15.5 shows the results of the trace after Dudley has launched the Query Analyzer and run a SELECT query. Each row in the trace shows the SQL statements or commands issued to the SQL Server.

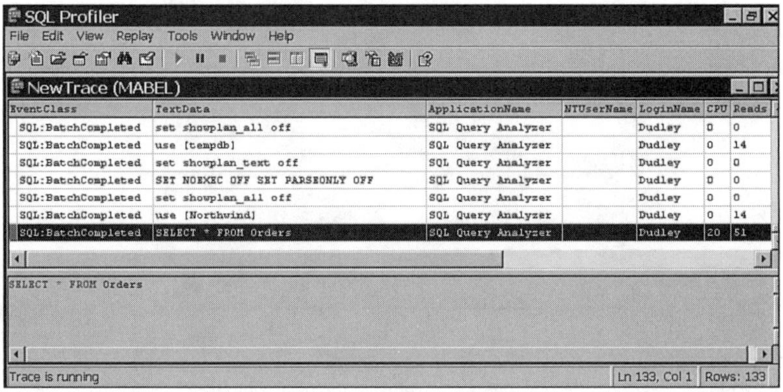

FIGURE 15.5

Viewing trace results in real-time.

Press the Stop toolbar button or choose File, Stop Trace from the menu to stop the trace. If you saved the trace to a file, you can load the file by choosing File, Open Trace File and selecting the saved trace. You can then replay the trace by choosing Replay, Start or Replay, Step from the menu. Single-stepping enables you to walk through the trace a line at a time. Figure 15.6 shows the replay options. If you choose to replay events in order, you can examine a progression of activity, viewing or single-stepping through the events in the order they occurred.

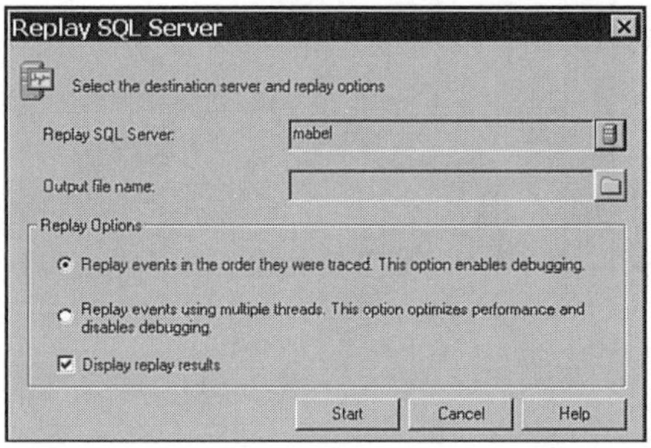

FIGURE 15.6
The Replay dialog box lets you set options for replay.

Working with Trace Templates

The SQL Server Profiler ships with some default trace templates, which you can use to design your traces. You can also save your own trace templates. The existing trace templates are available when you choose File, Open Trace Template from the menu.

When you select a trace template, you can configure its properties in the same way you configure trace properties for a new trace. However, instead of loading the default trace template, more specific trace classes are selected. The trace templates provided with SQL Server 2000 provide a good starting point for you to create and save your own templates. The General tab on the Trace Template dialog box provides a Save As button. If you save your version of the template under a new name in the same folder as the built-in templates, it will always be available. Figure 15.7 shows the Save As file location:

```
\Program Files\Microsoft SQL Server\80\Tools\Templates\SQL Profiler
```

You can't run the trace from the template dialog box. When you're done defining and saving the trace template, you need to choose File, New Trace to run it. Select the template from the Template name list box and click the Run button.

Using Profiler as a Development Tool

Besides using Profiler as a tool to troubleshoot problems and identify performance bottlenecks, the Profiler is also extremely useful in showing you what's really going on behind the scenes

15

when your application communicates with SQL Server. For example, what really happens when you base an Access form on a stored procedure in an ADP? Or when you use ODBC to link to a view in an Access MDB?

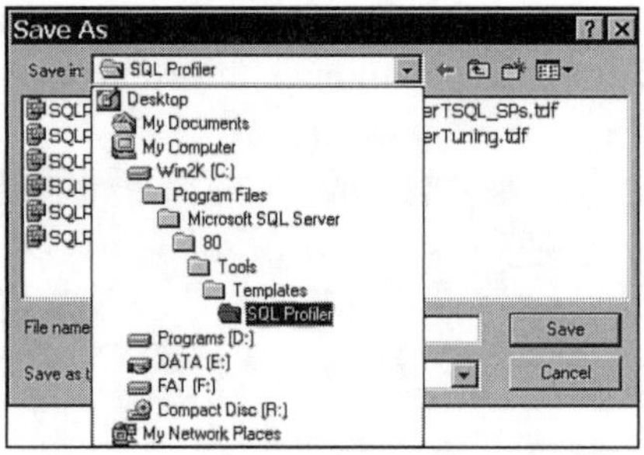

FIGURE 15.7

Trace templates provide a way of saving and re-running specific traces.

The built-in template, SQLProfilerTSQL.tdf, gives you the basic Transact-SQL statements sent to SQL Server. Create a new trace, basing it on the SQLProfilerTSQL template, choose the Save To Table option, and name the table AccessTrace. This will create a table that you can easily query using the Query Analyzer, eliminating the need to scroll through multiple lines of Profiler output. The columns displayed by the template are RowNumber, EventClass, TextData, SPID, and StartTime. Here's how you can observe the behind-the-scenes activity of your Access ADP or MDB application:

1. In an ADP based on the Northwind database, create a stored procedure that selects data from the Categories table, and then base a form on the stored procedure.

2. Start the trace running, if you have not already done so.

3. Open the form in the ADP, edit the first record, and save your changes.

4. Go back to the Profiler and press the Pause button on the toolbar. The first SQL statement you see executes the stored procedure:

   ```
   EXEC "procCategorySelect"
   ```

5. The second statement, SET ROWCOUNT 0, turns off counting rows so that all rows are returned.

6. The next statement uses a series of parameters to execute the UPDATE statement directly on the underlying Categories table:

   ```
   exec sp_executesql N'UPDATE "northwind".."Categories" SET
   "Description"=@P1 WHERE
   "CategoryID"=@P2 AND "CategoryName"=@P3', N'@P1 ntext,@P2 int,@P3
   nvarchar(15)',
   N'Soft drinks, coffees, teas, beers, and ales.', 1, N'Beverages'
   ```

This illustrates the fact that even though the form is based on the stored procedure, which is executed when the form is opened, Access is sending back an UPDATE statement directly to the base table, Categories. That can have profound implications. For example, it means your users would need update permissions on the table, not just execute permissions on the stored procedure.

Now follow these steps to see what's going on in an Access MDB:

1. Create an MDB and link to a view that selects columns from the Categories table. MDB forms based on stored procedures (using pass-through queries) aren't updateable, but forms based on views are. Create a form and base it on the view.

2. Clear the trace window by selecting Edit, Clear Trace Window from the menu. Start the trace up again.

3. Open the form in Access and update a record, saving your changes.

4. Return to Profiler and pause the trace. Here's the first SELECT statement processed—note that it only selects the CategoryID from the view. When the view was linked, CategoryID was identified as the primary key.

   ```
   SELECT "dbo"."vwCategorySelect"."CategoryID" FROM "dbo"."vwCategorySelect"
   ```

5. The next line of output shows creation of a prepared statement to select data from the view:

   ```
   declare @P1 int set @P1=-1 exec sp_prepexec @P1 output, N'@P1 int',
   N'SELECT
   "CategoryID","CategoryName","Description"  FROM "dbo"."vwCategorySelect"
   WHERE "CategoryID" = @P1', 1 select @P1
   ```

6. The following statement executes the prepared statement to retrieve data:

   ```
   exec sp_execute 3, 1
   ```

7. This statement updates the data:

   ```
   UPDATE "dbo"."vwCategorySelect" SET "Description"=N'Soft drinks,
   coffees, teas, beers, and ales'  WHERE "CategoryID" = 1 AND
   "CategoryName" = N'Beverages'
   ```

8. The last line commits the transaction:

   ```
   IF @@TRANCOUNT > 0 COMMIT TRAN
   ```

The Profiler is indispensable as a developer tool, showing you in detail each statement the way that SQL Server executes it. For example, you might try several different strategies for running a dynamically filtered Access report and see exactly how each is being implemented in Transact-SQL.

You can run multiple traces from the Profiler simultaneously. However, remember that in its role of intercepting SQL Server traffic, the Profiler consumes resources, placing an additional load on the server.

15

DEPLOYMENT,
TUNING, AND
MAINTENANCE

The Profiler isn't the only device in your toolbox for monitoring performance. The Profiler menus and toolbar also allow you to launch the Windows Performance Monitor.

Using the System Monitor/NT Performance Monitor

The Windows NT Performance Monitor has been renamed the System Monitor in Windows 2000, but for simplicity's sake we'll continue to refer to it as the Performance Monitor. The Performance Monitor can intercept traffic over your entire network and can monitor other applications besides SQL Server. It's a Windows NT/Windows 2000 tool, not simply a SQL Server tool. However, when you install SQL Server on either Windows NT or Windows 2000, SQL Server counters get installed in the Performance Monitor. The Performance Monitor uses counters to do its work. You can use these counters to monitor the following SQL Server activities:

- SQL Server I/O
- SQL Server memory usage
- SQL Server user connections
- SQL Server locking
- Replication activity

Configuring the Performance Monitor

The Performance Monitor can be launched from the Windows Start menu as well as from the Profiler.

The first step in using the Performance Monitor is to select some counters. Right-click on the chart area of the Performance Monitor and select one of the SQL Server counters from the Performance object drop-down list. Figure 15.8 shows SQL Server Locks with the different lock counters in the Select counters from list box.

Once selected, the counters are added to the chart and displayed as colored lines. Figure 15.9 shows the chart with several SQL Server lock counters selected.

Bear in mind that both the System/Performance Monitor and the SQL Server Profiler consume system resources themselves—you won't want to leave them running all of the time. However, using each tool for its intended purpose at selected times will help you identify performance bottlenecks and tune your server, your database, and your applications accordingly.

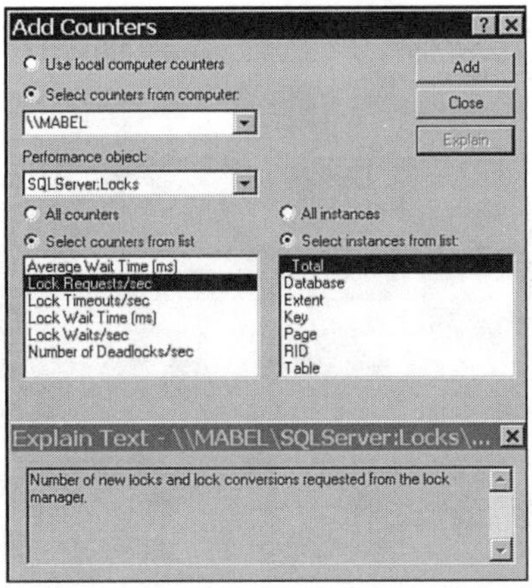

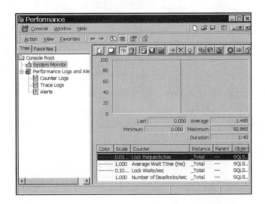

FIGURE 15.8
Selecting counters in the Performance Monitor.

FIGURE 15.9
The Performance Monitor at work.

Creating Alerts

The capability to set up alerts is one of the most useful features of the Performance Monitor because it's highly unlikely that you'll want to sit in front of your monitor the whole time it's running, looking at the little colored lines flowing by. To set up an alert to occur when a dead-lock arises, for example, follow these steps:

1. Expand the Performance Logs and Alerts node and right-click on the Alerts icon. Choose New Alert Settings and type in a name.

2. In the General tab, type in any comments for the alert and select the counters you want added by clicking the Add button, as shown in Figure 15.10 where the Locks/Total

number of deadlocks(sec) counter has been selected. This counter displays the number of lock requests that resulted in a deadlock.

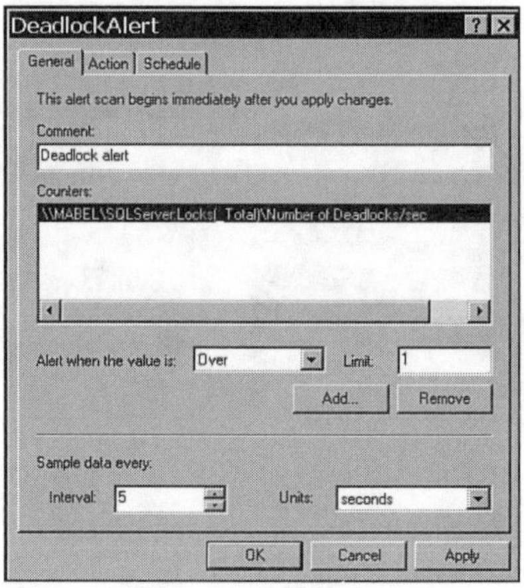

FIGURE 15.10

Selecting the counter for a deadlock alert.

3. On the Action tab, specify the type of action to take. Figure 15.11 shows your options: to create an entry in the application log, to send a network message, to start a performance data log, or to run a program. In this case, a message is being sent to AndyB, and an entry is being made in the Windows application event log.

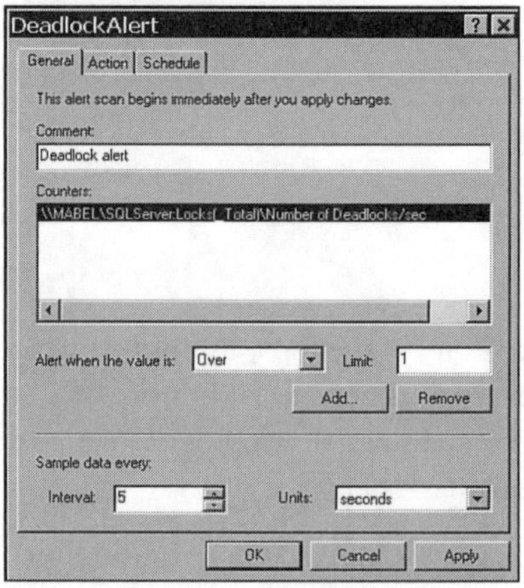

FIGURE 15.11

Taking action for an alert.

Once you've set up the alert in the Performance Monitor, it will automatically take the specified action. However, you can also set up alerts in SQL Server that allow you more flexibility in choosing the kinds of events that will trigger alerts—you're not limited to specific Windows NT/Windows 2000 performance counters.

The following section on the SQL Server Agent discusses setting up SQL Server alerts.

Using the SQL Server Agent

The SQL Server Agent is responsible for running SQL Server tasks at scheduled intervals, alerting someone that a certain condition exists, and handling replication tasks. The SQL Server Agent and the Performance Monitor can be configured to work hand in hand. Here are the three parts to the SQL Server Agent:

- *Jobs*. Jobs are objects consisting of one or more steps to be performed. Steps are defined in Transact-SQL statements and can be scheduled.

- *Alerts*. Alerts are actions to be taken when specific events occur. Alerts can be set to react to errors or to other conditions. Alerts can be configured to send email, to page an operator, or to run a job.

- *Operators*. Operators are people. They are identified through their network account or email ID, so that they can receive alerts through email, a pager, or a net send network command.

Accessing the SQL Server Agent in the Management folder of the Enterprise Manager is the easiest way to go about setting up jobs, alerts, and operators. The definitions of jobs, alerts, and operators are stored in the msdb system database, which is queried by the SQL Server Agent at startup. The SQL Server Agent will then execute jobs on schedule, receive alerts sent by SQL Server, send SQL Mail requests to SQL Server, or net send commands to Windows.

Configuring the SQL Server Agent

To configure the SQL Server Agent, expand the Management folder, right-click on the SQL Server Agent node, and select Properties. This will load the SQL Server Agent Properties dialog box. Figure 15.12 displays the General tab. The top part of the dialog box defines the account the SQL Server Agent service will run under. The middle part enables you to specify a mail profile to use for sending email messages. (This requires SQL Mail.) The bottom section specifies the error log and location. You can include additional information by checking the Include Execution Trace Messages check box.

The Advanced tab, shown in Figure 15.13, enables you to autostart SQL Server or SQL Server Agent, to forward event handling to another server, and to execute jobs during idle times, which are defined in the bottom part of the Advanced dialog box.

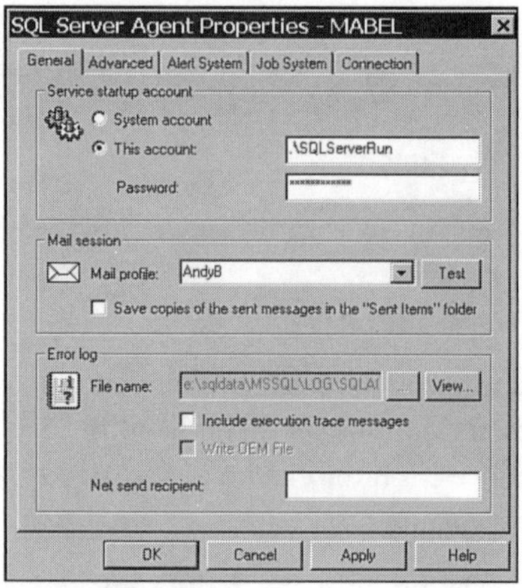

FIGURE 15.12

FIGURE 15.12

Configuring general properties for SQL Server Agent.

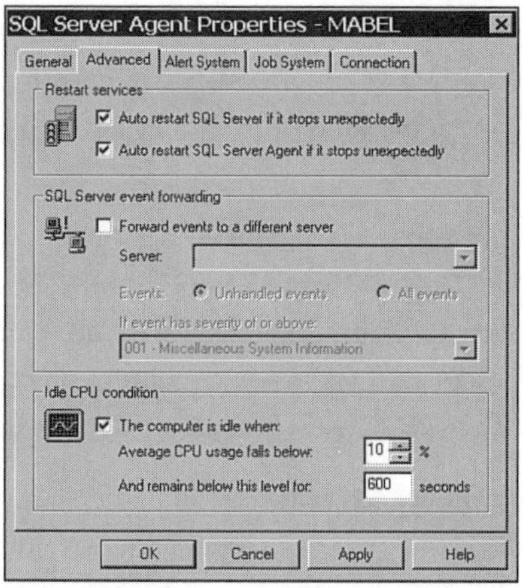

FIGURE 15.13

Setting advanced options for the SQL Server Agent.

The Alert System dialog box, shown in Figure 15.14, enables you to specify message properties for email and pager. The bottom part of the dialog box enables you to designate a failsafe operator. In this case, the operator AndyB will be notified by email. It's recommended that you always designate a failsafe operator. If an operator defined for a particular alert can't be reached, the failsafe operator will be notified.

Each job executed by the SQL Server Agent is logged. The Job System tab of the SQL Server Agent Properties dialog box is shown in Figure 15.15, setting limits on the size and maximum number of entries allowed. The middle part of the dialog box specifies a wait interval, and the bottom section enables you to place limitations on jobs using Active Scripting or CmdExec. This option is important for security reasons because the SQL Server Agent service itself must run with administrative privileges. Any user can create a job and have it executed, in effect granting him or her access to all the resources on the server. Enabling the option to restrict Active Scripting or CmdExec to administrators closes this security loophole.

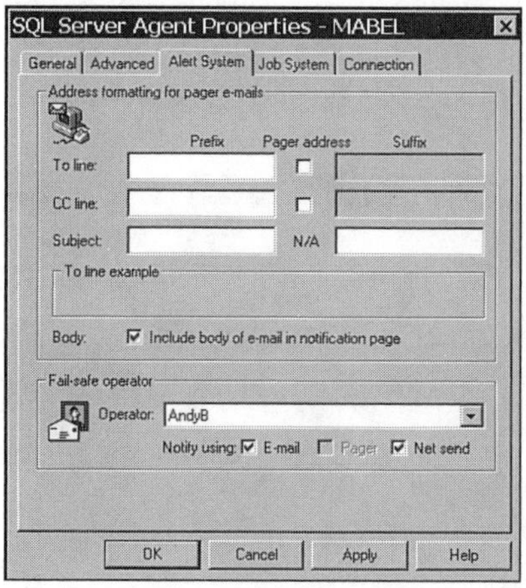

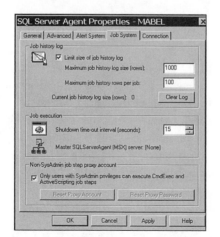

FIGURE 15.14

Specifying notifications in the SQL Server Agent.

FIGURE 15.15

Make sure to restrict access to execute CmdExec and Active Scripting tasks to administrators only.

The Connection tab enables you to configure the account that the SQL Server Agent uses. The default is the account that was used for the services to run under when you installed SQL Server.

Setting Up Operators

Before you create any alerts or jobs, you need to set up operators to receive notifications when things happen. To create an operator, right-click the Operators icon and select New Operator. Figure 15.16 displays creating a new operator named AndyB. Different operators can be created and assigned to different alerts. As noted earlier, if an operator is not available, the fail-safe operator will be notified. This prevents alerts from falling through the cracks.

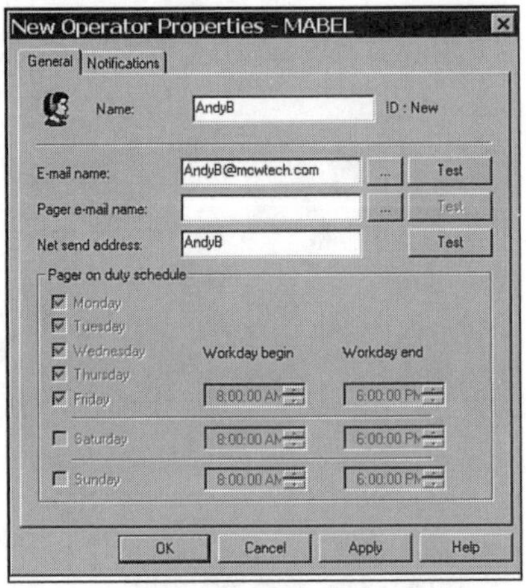

FIGURE 15.16
Creating a new operator.

The Notifications tab, shown in Figure 15.17, enables you to specify which notifications a given operator receives. The bottom part of the dialog box shows the last time that operator was sent a message—in this case, "never" is displayed because the operator is just being created. The "Demo" alert names you see listed in the Alert Name list box are predefined alerts that ship with SQL Server, most of which are based on SQL Server error numbers. New alerts can be added at any time to the existing alerts by right-clicking on the Alerts node and selecting New Alert and filling in the options in the New Alert Properties dialog box. Alerts can be based on SQL Server error numbers, or on your own user-defined errors.

Running the Create Job Wizard to Create a SQL Server Agent Job

The easiest way to create a job is to use the Create Job Wizard. Select Tools, Wizards, Management, Create Job Wizard from the Enterprise Manager menu.

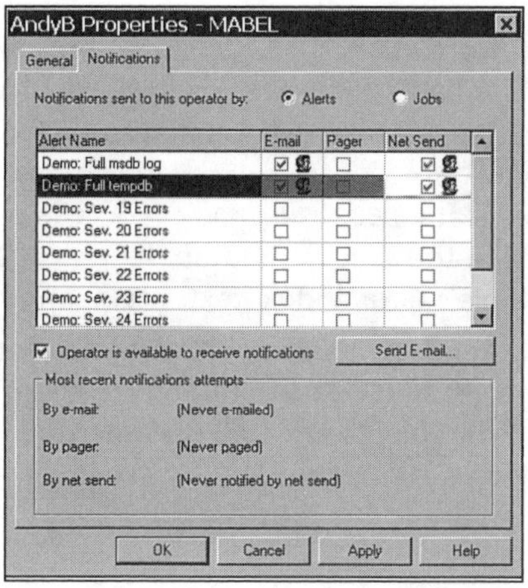

Figure 15.17

Sending notifications to an operator.

The first wizard dialog box asks you what kind of job you'd like to create. Here are your choices:

- Transact-SQL Command
- Operating System Shell Command (for example, run a batch script or invoke an application)
- Active Script (for example, VBScript or JavaScript)

If you select Transact-SQL Command, the next dialog box, shown in Figure 15.18, enables you to specify the Transact-SQL command to be executed. In this case, the Northwind database will be shrunk to allow 10% of free space using the DBCC SHRINKDATABASE command. (DBCC stands for *database console command.*) Ten percent is specified as the amount of free space to be left after the database has shrunk. DBCC statements check the physical and logical consistency of a database, fix detected problems, and perform other related actions, in this case, shrinking the Northwind database. Click the Parse button to check your syntax before proceeding, and then click the Next button.

DBCC

DBCC (*Database Consistency Checker* in older versions of SQL Server, and now described in Books Online as *Database Console Command*) statements check the physical and logical consistency of a database, and some can even fix detected problems. There are several classes of statements covering maintenance, status checks, validation, and miscellaneous statements, such as enabling row-level locking or removing a dynamic-link library (DLL) from memory. DBCC statements take input parameters and return values. Some, such as DBCC DBREPAIR, are included for backward compatibility only and might not be supported in future versions of SQL Server. Others, such as DBCC CHECKDB and DBCC CHECKTABLE, are fully supported as the recommended way to check the integrity of your data. DBCC CHECKDB checks the allocation and structural integrity of all the objects in the specified database, and DBCC CHECKTABLE checks the integrity of a particular table's data, index, text, ntext, and image pages.

Running DBCC statements tends to be both CPU and disk intensive because DBCC must read each data page. It's best to run DBCC when there is little activity on the system. The various DBCC statements are well documented in Books Online. As SQL Server has evolved, many operations that required manual intervention in the past are now performed automatically, but DBCC is still a very necessary tool for the diligent database administrator.

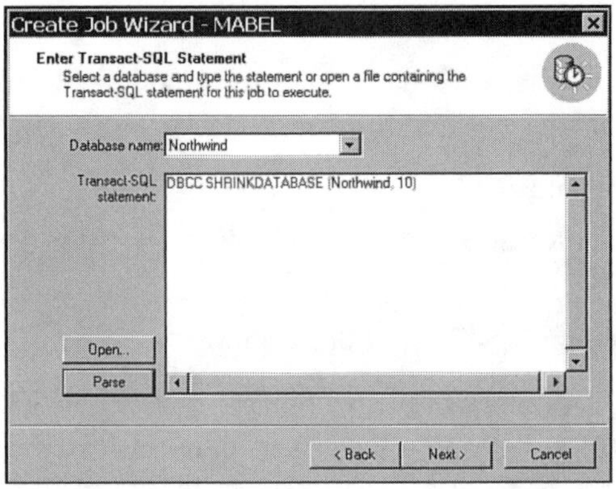

FIGURE 15.18
Entering and parsing a Transact-SQL statement in the Create Job Wizard.

The following wizard dialog box is for specifying when the job will be run. Here are your options:

- Now
- One Time
- Automatically when SQL Server Agent Starts
- When the Computer Is Idle
- On a Recurring Basis

If you choose the last option, On a Recurring Basis, click the Schedule button to load the Job Schedule dialog box, shown in Figure 15.19. Set up your schedule and click OK to continue.

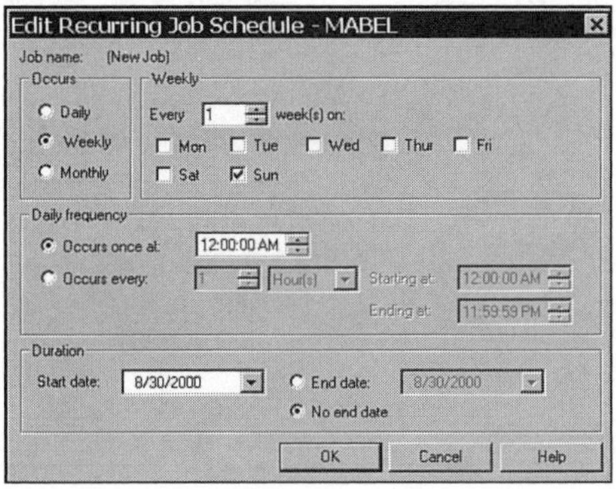

FIGURE 15.19
Scheduling a recurring job.

The next wizard dialog box enables you to specify an operator to notify, and the last wizard dialog box summarizes your options. Click OK to finish.

Modifying Jobs

Once you've created a job, it shows up in the Jobs folder under the SQL Server Agent folder in the Enterprise Manager. Right-click the job name and select Properties to edit the job. Figure 15.20 shows the Steps tab, where you can add new steps to the job created by the wizard. You can also modify the schedule and add notifications.

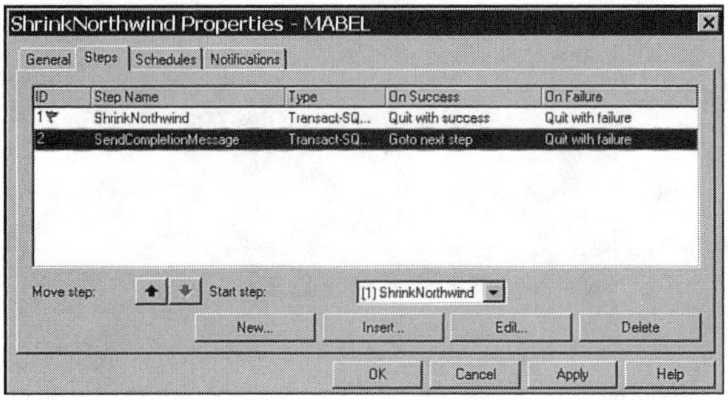

FIGURE 15.20
Modifying an existing job.

To edit an existing step, click the Edit button. This loads the Edit Job Step dialog box, as shown in Figure 15.21. The On success option on the Advanced tab is where you determine the action to take when a step is completed. This dialog box also enables you to configure retry attempts, to specify the action to take on failure, and to enter Transact-SQL command options.

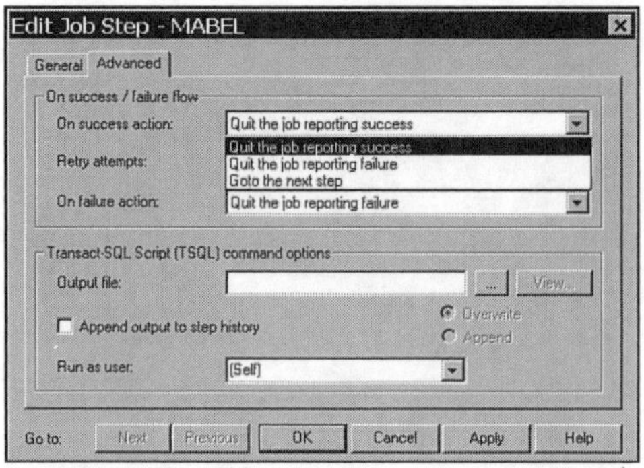

FIGURE 15.21
Adding a step to a job.

Configuring Alerts

Alerts are triggered for two types of events: error messages generated by SQL Server and a Performance Monitor threshold being reached. Built-in alerts are preconfigured in SQL Server Agent for errors that occur with severity levels of 19 and higher. They don't have any actions associated with them by default, but you can add any actions and notifications you want.

To associate an action with an alert, double-click the alert in the Alerts folder. This will load the Properties dialog box for the alert, shown in Figure 15.22. The Response tab is where you configure operators to be notified, jobs to run, and additional messages to be included in the response. In this instance, an operator (AndyB) will be notified by pager, email, and net send when any error occurs with a severity level of 19.

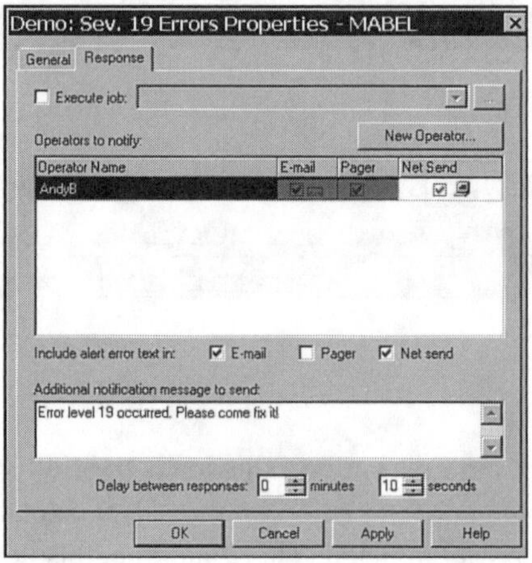

FIGURE 15.22
Taking action in the event of an alert.

To create an alert using a wizard, choose Tools, Wizards, Management, Create Alert Wizard. This will walk you through the steps of creating an alert. Alternatively, simply right-click the Alerts icon, choose New Alert from the menu, and fill in the required fields.

Backup and Maintenance

Data can be lost in many different ways and through all kinds of disasters—from power spikes to fires and floods, viruses, incompetent or malicious users, damage to the physical disk device, or theft. Advance planning is the key to handling these calamities—afterward is too late.

One of the main reasons that developers move to SQL Server from Jet is the need for reliable and regular backups. This is especially necessary when the database must be up and running 24 hours a day, seven days a week. Although there are third-party tools to copy all the data from a Jet database while it's running, they can't guarantee that the backed-up data will be in a consistent state if the database is being updated while the backup occurs. The only way to get a reliable Access backup is to shut down and copy the files. A SQL Server database can be backed up to a consistent state while it is still being used.

SQL Server has added enhanced functionality to the Enterprise Manager to automate backing up and restoring your SQL Server databases. But first, a word on how SQL Server uses the transaction log.

Transactions and Data Consistency

As discussed in Chapter 10, "Programming Effective Stored Procedures," SQL Server uses transactions to update data. When a transaction begins, the database is in a consistent state. The transaction makes updates to data, and as the updates are processed, they are either committed or rolled back, leaving the database in a consistent state once again.

How the Transaction Log Works

Every transaction is recorded in the transaction log before it is written to disk so that if something happens in the middle of a transaction, before it is either committed or rolled back, there is enough information in the log to either roll back (undo) or roll forward (redo) a transaction. If the server stops for any reason, the next time it starts it will automatically recover all outstanding transactions. It does this by writing all completed but uncommitted transactions still in the log to disk, and by rolling back any transactions that had not been completed at the time the server went down. When you restore a backup, all outstanding uncommitted transactions at the time the backup was made are also restored.

15

DEPLOYMENT,
TUNING, AND
MAINTENANCE

How to Determine Backup Needs

There are several types of database backups:

- *Full database backups*. The entire database is backed up, including portions of the log.
- *Transaction log backups*. Only the transaction log is backed up. The transaction log records all the transactions since the last full database backup.
- *Differential backups*. Only data modified since the last full database backup is backed up. Differential backups save time in the restore process since it's not necessary to apply all of the transaction logs or previous differential backups to bring the database to a consistent state.
- *File (or filegroup) backups*. Only data located on the designated filegroup is backed up. This is useful for very large databases where it might take too long to back up the entire database.

The type of backup you perform and how often you back up depends on the volume of transactions and the amount of work that might be lost in the event of a crash, as well as on how difficult it would be to re-create the results of that work. If you have a database with a high volume of transactions, you might want to back up the full database daily and back up the transaction log hourly. If your database is used primarily for decision support and the data does not change frequently, you might only need to back up weekly and have the transaction log backed up daily. You might use a differential backup where data loss isn't critical, and you don't feel it necessary to implement log backups.

Recovery Models

SQL Server 2000 implements three different recovery models:

- *Full*. You have complete protection against media failure and can restore all committed transactions. The log is backed up in addition to the database files. This option enables you to implement full point-in-time recovery.
- *Bulk Logged*. You get the best performance and least amount of log memory usage for large scale or bulk operations, such as bcp, BULK INSERT, and CREATE INDEX. Because logging is minimal, data recovery is limited to the last backup.
- *Simple*. You have simplicity of use with limited recovery. There is no transaction log backup. In the event of failure, you will lose all data since the last backup.

The recovery model is set on the Options tab in the database properties dialog box, as shown in Figure 15.23.

The default recovery model used for new databases is determined by the settings for the model database. Change the model database settings from the Enterprise Manager or by using the ALTER DATABASE Transact-SQL syntax.

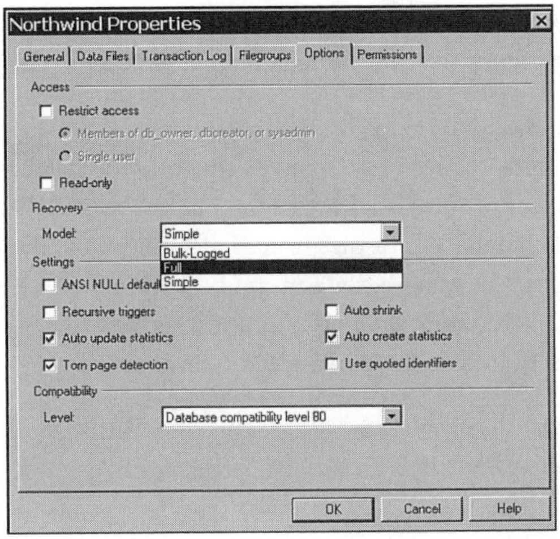

FIGURE 15.23
The recovery model.

It's important to consider the recovery options needed for your particular database and to choose the one which will give you adequate protection based on your needs.

What Gets Backed Up

A full database backup copies everything in the database, including portions of the log. A log backup only copies the log, which consists of all the transactions since the last full database backup. The backup file contains a snapshot of the database or log at the time the backup was made, containing copies of all the data pages and log images from a starting point to the end of the log at the time the backup finishes. A file backup backs up a single database file. Differential backups back up only data that has changed since the last full database backup.

The use of a transaction log in SQL Server is what enables a fully consistent backup to be made even while users are still modifying data. Even though it can take some time for the backup to be completed, you are assured that all transactions that have been committed at the time the backup ends will be included in the backup. This is why portions of the log are involved even in database backups. By adding a full backup of the transaction log, you add the capability to recover to a particular point in time, not just to the moment when the database backup was completed.

Filegroup Backups

You can back up individual files or filegroups if you have split your database into separate filegroups. This enables you to back up heavily used parts of your database more frequently by backing up your filegroups on different schedules. This saves time if the database is very large, but the actively used parts aren't necessarily that big. Another option is to create differential backups that contain only pages that have been changed since the last full database backup.

Differential Database Backups

Differential database backups record only changes made to the database since the last backup, thereby reducing the amount of time it takes for the backup to run. Differential backups can be performed against the full database or a filegroup. Differential backups should also be used after nonlogged transactions; otherwise, data might be lost in the event of a failure. By using a combination of database, differential database, and transaction log backups, recovery time and the amount of potential data loss due to failure can be minimized.

If you're performing any of the following actions during a differential backup, the backup will continue, but the operation will fail:

- Creating or deleting database files
- Creating indexes
- Running nonlogged operations
- Shrinking a database

Restoring from a Backup

When you restore from a backup, the backup copy of the database (or file, filegroup, or log) is restored. All data pages in the log are copied into the database, all transactions from the log pages are rolled forward and written to the data pages, and any uncompleted transactions from the log pages are then rolled back.

Restoring to Point of Failure

Restoring to point of failure involves backing up both the database and the log and choosing the Full recovery model.

To be able to restore to point of failure, you must back up the log periodically in between database backups. In the event of disaster, you restore the most recent database backup and then restore the logs in the same order in which they were written. If you lose a log backup, you can only restore to the log just before the lost one. In other words, you can't restore to any point beyond a break in the sequence of transaction log backups.

> **CAUTION**
>
> Certain operations, such as setting the Select Into/Bulk Copy option on or performing any nonlogged operations, cause a break in the transaction log. Immediately after such an operation you need to perform a full database backup and start the sequence of database backups and log backups anew if you are using the Full recovery model. This doesn't apply to the other recovery models.

Analyzing Your Backup Needs

You have several things to consider when deciding on a backup strategy. The type and frequency of your backups really depends on your business. How long can you afford to be down? How long does it take to perform the backup? You need to analyze your business requirements and your environment and then test out your backup and restore scenario to see which balance of data loss versus time consumed performing backups and restores is acceptable. Here are some questions you might ask yourself:

- Is the database you need to back up very large? In this case, an infrequent full database backup followed by incremental backups or log backups is probably best.

- How frequently does the data change? If very little changes, then infrequent full backups with regular log backups will probably suffice.

- Are some tables changed more often than others? If so, then file or filegroup backups might be in order if the tables are located in separate filegroups.

- Can lost data be re-created easily? If not, then point-in-time recovery might be necessary.

- How much data can your business afford to lose? An hour's worth? A day's worth? This is really the bottom line. If you can't afford to lose any data, then mightbe backup alone won't suffice. Standby servers or failover clustering might be in order.

- How important is it to never lose a single change? Log backups combined with incremental and full database backups are probably the way to go.

- Is there any particular time during production that is more critical than other times? Is the database more heavily used during certain time periods? Downtime is the best time for database backups.

- Do users need to access the database during backup operations? Changes made during backups will be recorded in the log, but not necessarily in a full database backup, so log backups are probably also required.

- Do you need to keep a rotating series of backups? In other words, do you need to restore further back in time if a problem is not detected for some time after it occurs? If so, then don't overwrite the backup files each time you make a new one.

There's no single backup and restore solution that fits every case because each business and each database is different. You'll need to carefully analyze your needs before making a decision. And then once you've developed a strategy, you'll need to test it to make sure that it's adequate.

Tape or Disk?

SQL Server supports the Microsoft Tape Format, which enables backups to share the same tape media with other programs' backups. For example, you could store both a Windows NT system backup and a SQL Server database backup on the same tape. You can also back up your databases on disk—although never on the same disk as the database itself because that would leave you with nothing in the event of a disk failure.

The time it takes to back up and restore depends a lot on whether you use tape or disk to store the backups. Backing up and restoring from disk is going to give better performance than from tape. You need to consult your device documentation to calculate the time it's going to take to back up your entire database. You will probably need to perform timing tests to figure out how long backing up and restoring is going to take because hardware and network configurations vary widely.

You have other options, if your backup needs go beyond those provided for by the standard SQL Server backup and restores. SQL Server also supports standby servers and failover clustering, as well as various implementations of RAID (redundant array of independent disks) for situations in which zero data loss and zero downtime are mandated. See SQL Server Books Online for more information on these options.

Don't Forget the System Databases

If you should be unlucky enough to suffer a system or disk failure, you'll need to restore the system databases as well as your user databases. The databases discussed in the following sections should be backed up based on the frequency with which they are used.

master

SQL Server will not start if the master database is damaged. The master database should be backed up after any procedure that changes information in the system tables, such as creating new databases. If you restore a version of the master database that existed prior to the creation of the new database, the restored master won't know anything about the new database.

If you can't restore master, you can rebuild it using the Rebuild Master utility, which also rebuilds the msdb and model databases as well. Make sure to specify the same sort order, code page, and Unicode collation as used previously. You won't be able to restore or attach databases with a different sort order, code page, or Unicode collation than the one these system databases were created with.

msdb

If you lose the msdb database, you lose scheduling information plus the backup and restore history for SQL Server, the Enterprise Manager, and the SQL Server Agent. If you can't restore it, you have to re-create this information from scratch.

distribution

If you lose the distribution database, all replication information used by the SQL Server replication utilities will need to be re-created.

model

The model database is used as a template for creating other databases. Any modifications you've made to the model database will be lost if you can't restore it.

Performing a Database Backup

When perform a full database backup, all the data in the database gets backed up regardless of whether it was changed since the last full database backup. Each database backup is self-contained and does not rely on any other backup medium to be restored. Consequently, it also uses the most storage space and takes the longest to both back up and restore. When you restore from a database backup, the database is re-created exactly as it was when the backup operation completed. There is no way to recover any changes made between the time the backup was made and when the restore is implemented.

Backing up from the Enterprise Manager is very easy. You can perform a complete database backup, a differential backup, a file and filegroup backup, or a transaction log backup.

The following methods all load the Backup Database dialog box:

- Right-click the Backup icon in the Management folder and choose Backup a Database.
- Right-click the database you want to back up and choose All Tasks, Backup Database.
- From the Main Console, choose Tools, Backup Database.

The General tab of the Backup dialog box enables you to specify the name of the backup, the type, and the destination. You can also specify whether a backup will be appended to an existing backup or will overwrite it. To create a new backup, click the New button and fill in the filename or the device name for the backup destination.

You can optionally schedule the backup by checking the Schedule box, which loads the Edit Schedule dialog box.

Click the Options button to set further options for the database backup. Verifying the backup on completion is a good idea because it checks the integrity of the backup and media so that you don't end up trying to restore from a bad backup.

If you're using tape instead of a file backup, you can elect to initialize the media (which will wipe out anything that was on the tape previously). If you don't schedule the backup, it will be performed immediately.

You can also use the Backup dialog box to back up the transaction log and perform a differential database backup. However, a better choice is to use the Database Maintenance Plan Wizard to create your entire backup plan. Although you can schedule backups from the backup dialog box, you'll probably want to set up a maintenance plan using the Database Maintenance Plan Wizard once you see the advantages that it offers.

15

DEPLOYMENT,
TUNING, AND
MAINTENANCE

The Database Maintenance Plan Wizard

The Database Maintenance Plan Wizard centralizes the tasks of scheduling regular backups for your databases and transaction logs. You can also use the Database Maintenance Plan Wizard to run database integrity checks and update database statistics as part of the plan. After the wizard has run, a plan is created. This plan is an object that shows up in the Enterprise Manager in the Database Maintenance Plans subfolder under the Management folder. Because the plan is an object, you can change any of your choices after the wizard has run by editing the properties of your database maintenance plan object.

To access the wizard, choose either of the following two methods:

- Select Tools, Database Maintenance Planner on the main console.
- Right-click the Database Maintenance Plans folder and select New Maintenance Plan. You can't create a new maintenance plan without running the wizard, but once the wizard has created the plan, you can make changes to it in a single tabbed dialog box that displays all of the options available in the wizard.

The first wizard dialog box is introductory, and it informs you that the Database Maintenance Plan Wizard can perform the following tasks:

- Run database integrity checks
- Update database statistics
- Perform database backups
- Ship transaction logs to another server

Adding Databases to the Plan

The second wizard dialog box enables you to choose which databases you want to back up. Here are your choices:

- All Databases
- All System Databases (`master`, `model`, and `msdb`)
- All User Databases (all databases other than `master`, `model`, and `msdb`)
- These Databases

It's up to you how you want to back up your databases. You can have a separate database maintenance plan for each database, or you can lump them all together under one master plan. Figure 15.24 shows creating a database maintenance plan for the Northwind database.

Updating Data Optimization Information

The top section of the Update Data Optimization Information dialog box, shown in Figure 15.25, configures the plan to reorganize data and index pages. Choosing to do this greatly enhances performance. The Remove Unused Space option shrinks database files by removing unused space. This is roughly comparable to compacting a database in Access. You can set the size that should trigger shrinking of the database, and the amount of free space that you want to leave remaining after the shrink. Your choice here will depend on how much growth you expect. SQL Server can grow the database dynamically as needed. Both growing and shrinking the database can impact performance, but shrinking is a much more expensive operation. You want to do it, but not too often when the database is in use. The Schedule pane at the bottom of the dialog box shows the default schedule. To modify the schedule, click the Change button at the bottom of the dialog box.

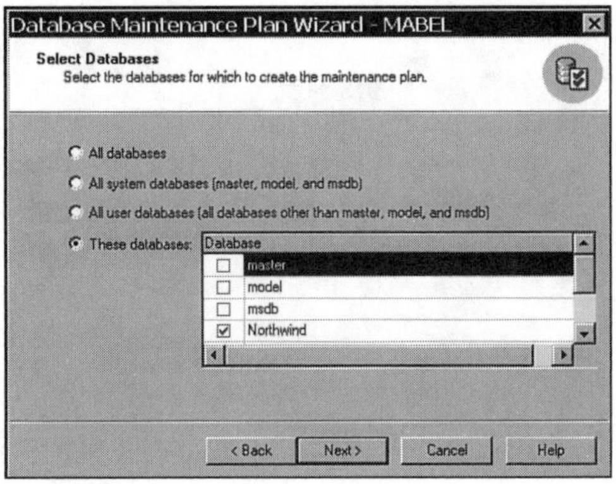

FIGURE 15.24
You can configure database maintenance plans in many different combinations.

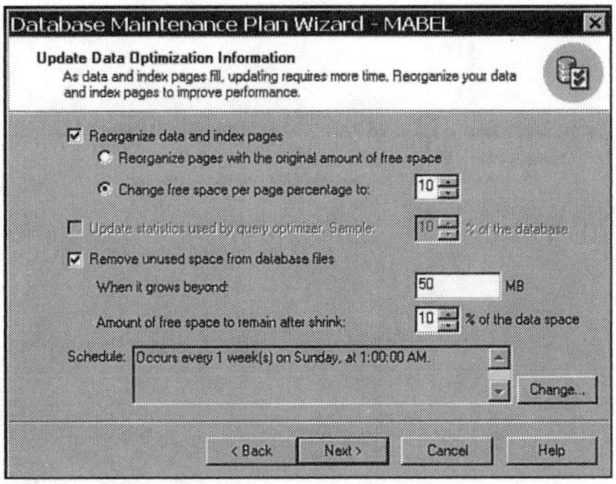

FIGURE 15.25
Reorganizing data and index pages, removing unused space, and scheduling with the Database Maintenance Plan Wizard.

15

DEPLOYMENT,
TUNING, AND
MAINTENANCE

Checking Database Integrity

Checking database integrity is a good idea prior to performing a backup—if there's any inconsistency or corruption (which might have been caused by electrical problems, among other things), you'll have a useless backup. The wizard will detect problems caused by hardware or software failures. Figure 15.26 shows checking the database and including the indexes. To modify the default schedule, click the Change button at the bottom of the dialog box.

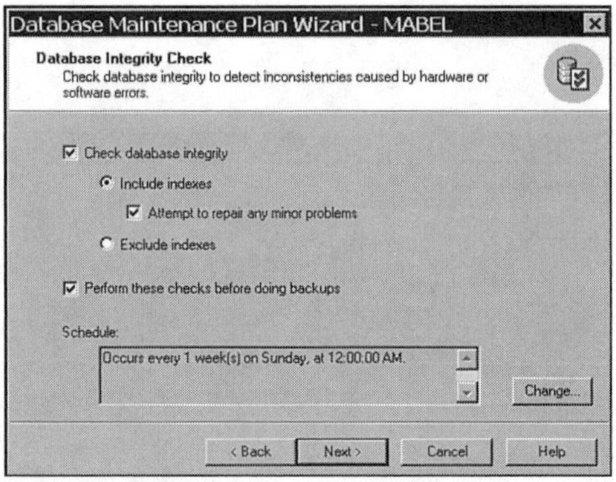

FIGURE 15.26
Checking database integrity with the Database Maintenance Plan Wizard.

Specifying the Database Backup Plan

Figure 15.27 shows the dialog box for specifying backing up the database as part of the database maintenance plan. If you have a tape backup devise, specify it here. Otherwise, you can back up the database to disk, but be sure to use a separate drive from the one that holds your data.

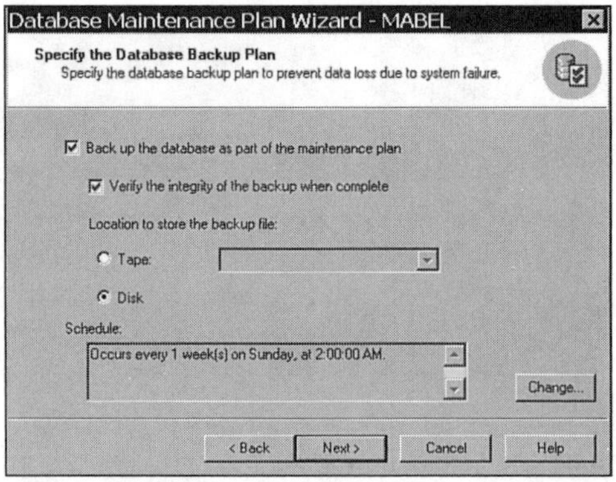

FIGURE 15.27
Specifying and scheduling the database backup plan.

Specifying the Backup Disk Directory

If you choose the Backup to Disk option, you'll be prompted for the location of the backup file. The default location, \mssql75\data\MSSQL\BACKUP, is not recommended. If you place the backup on the same device as either SQL Server itself or the SQL Server databases you're backing up, you will not be able to restore in the event of a total disk failure. Figure 15.28 shows backing up the Northwind database to a different location on the network. Creating a subdirectory for each database will help keep multiple backup sets organized. Files older than a set time can also be automatically removed by the plan. Naming files is automatic—you can't change that—but you can customize the filename extension.

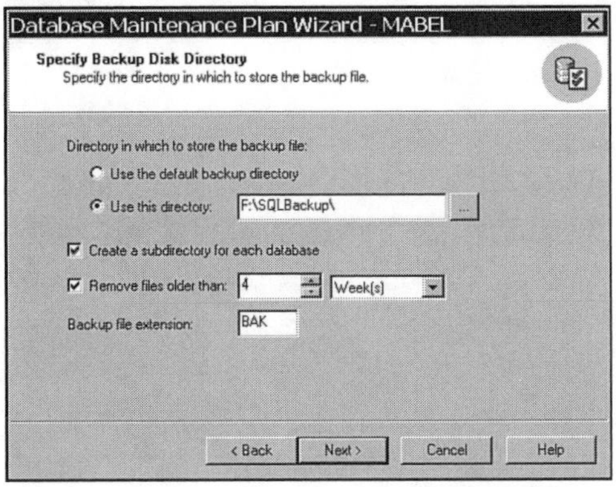

FIGURE 15.28
Specifying the backup directory.

Specifying the Transaction Log Backup Plan

Backing up the transaction log is an important part of your backup strategy, especially if you want to restore to a point in time. Usually, transaction log backups are performed more frequently than database backups because the contents of a transaction log backup contain only transactions since the last database backup or the last log backup, whichever is more recent. Figure 15.29 shows the options for backing up the transaction log. These are similar to the options for backing up the database. If you elect to back up to disk, you'll then need to specify the backup directory. The dialog box for doing this is similar to the dialog box shown in Figure 15.28 for specifying the disk directory for database backups.

Generating Reports

Reports generated by the plan include detailed information about the procedures performed in the database maintenance plan, along with any errors encountered (see Figure 15.30). You'll want to create reports so that you'll know if any problems are encountered.

15

DEPLOYMENT, TUNING, AND MAINTENANCE

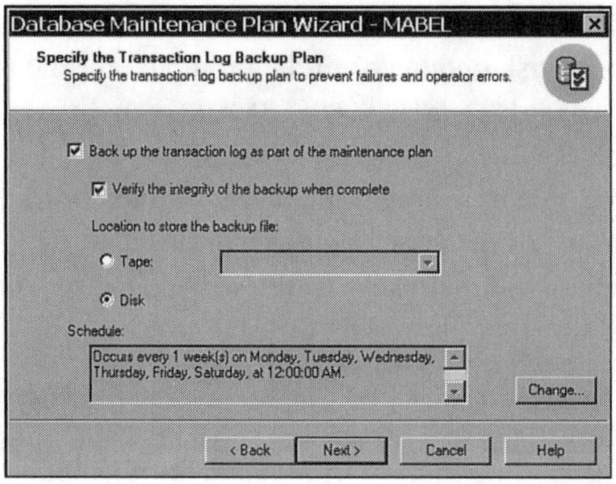

FIGURE 15.29
Specifying the transaction log backup plan.

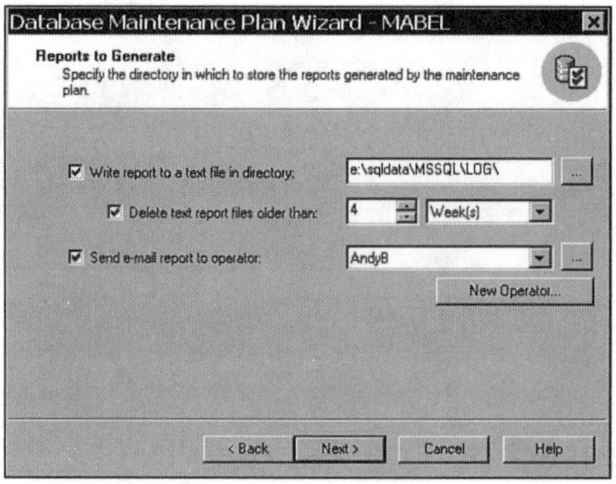

FIGURE 15.30
Generating reports.

Saving Maintenance History

SQL Server will write a detailed history of maintenance plan activity to the msdb system database on the current server or on a remote server, as shown in Figure 15.31. You can limit the size of the table in msdb to a certain number of rows. As the table fills up, older entries will be removed.

The final wizard dialog box enables you to name the database maintenance plan you've just created and summarizes the options you've chosen. Once you click the Finish button, the database maintenance plan will be created.

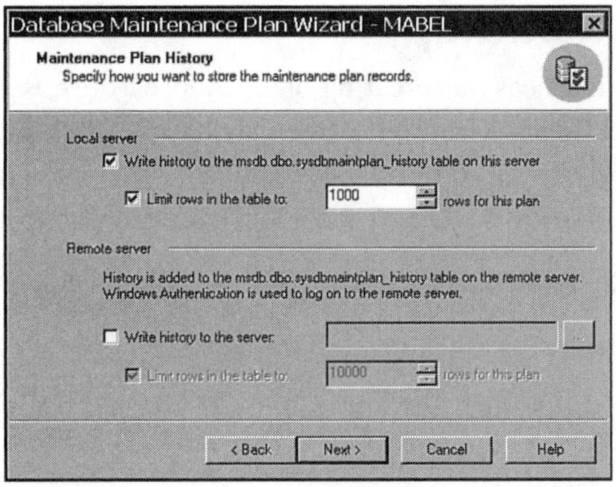

Figure 15.31

Saving maintenance history.

Modifying an Existing Database Maintenance Plan

You can modify the database maintenance plan at a later time simply by right-clicking the named plan in the Database Maintenance Plan folder and choosing Properties. This loads the dialog box shown in Figure 15.32. Note that the tabs on the dialog box correspond to the different dialog boxes the wizard presented. All the options you specified using the wizard can be modified should you ever need to change your plan.

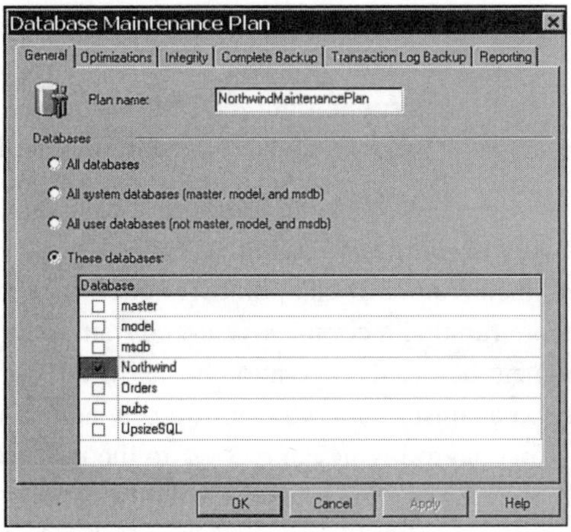

Figure 15.32

Modifying the database maintenance plan after it has been created.

Restoring from a Backup

Restoring from a backup is as easy as creating one. Choose Tools, Restore Database from the main Enterprise Manager menu or right-click the Databases folder and select All Tasks, Restore from Backup. If you want to restore the database to a different name, create an empty database by that name prior to restoring. You can only restore on top of an existing database.

The Options tab on the Restore Database tab enables you to specify the following options:

- Eject Tapes After Restoring Backup.
- Prompt Before Restoring Each Backup.
- Force Restore over Existing Database.
- Recovery Completion State. This option can be set to:
  - Leave the database operational. No additional transaction logs can be restored.
  - Leave the database nonoperational able to restore additional transaction logs.
  - Leave the database read-only and able to restore additional transaction logs.

When you click the OK button, the database will be restored according to the options you've selected. The Recovery Completion State option determines whether you can restore additional transaction logs after this restore operation has been completed.

Restoring to a Point in Time

The Restore Database dialog in the Enterprise Manager, shown in Figure 15.33, makes it easy to check off Point in time restore, and to enter a date and time. This will only be possible if your backup options were set to support point in time restores by saving transaction logs. On the Options tab, select, Leave database operational. No additional transaction logs can be restored.

SQL Server 2000 added a very useful new feature that enables you to mark and name a point in your transaction log, and then restore to that point without having to know the exact date and time. For example, before running a complex year-end transaction, you could mark the log and then restore to that moment before the operation began if it doesn't work out right. This can also be used as protection against operator error. If a new administrative assistant makes a boo-boo when running his first payroll, you can recover to the point in time before he messed up and let him try again. Although, running a restore will always disrupt your operations in a multi-user setting, it can be much easier than correcting complex or wide-reaching errors.

Inserting a named mark in your transaction log is done within your Transact-SQL code as part of creating a transaction. The BEGIN TRANSACTION statement now supports a new optional clause, WITH MARK [description]. The use of a description is optional. The name of the mark is equal to the name given to the transaction where it is declared. These transaction names do not have to be unique because in the log they are always combined with the date/time. The use of transactions in Transact-SQL is covered in Chapter 10. Here is what the first lines of a marked transaction might look like in a stored procedure:

```
BEGIN TRANSACTION 'PayrollTran'
WITH MARK 'Weekly Payroll Processing'
```

To recover to a marked point in the log requires that you use the Transact-SQL RESTORE LOG to perform the restore. The Restore Database dialog in the Enterprise Manager hasn't yet added support for this new feature. The Transact-SQL syntax you use depends on whether you want your restore to include the marked transaction or to include everything up to but not including that transaction. Depending on which you want, use one of these clauses:

```
WITH STOPATMARK='PayrollTran'
-- Or:
WITH STOPBEFOREMARK='PayrollTran'
```

But what if a transaction by that name appears many times in the log? SQL Server will stop at or before the first transaction in the log with that name, unless you add the optional AFTER clause:

```
AFTER '8/30/2000'
```

For full coverage of how to use Transact-SQL to perform backups and restores, see Books Online.

Deployment

There are two parts to deploying an Access-SQL Server application, deploying the Access application, and deploying the SQL Server database. Deploying Access is made easier by the Microsoft Office Developer edition (known as *MOD*).

Microsoft Office Developer (MOD) Features

Microsoft Office Developer (MOD) is the deluxe edition of Microsoft Office. It includes, among other developer tools, a redistribution license that enables you to distribute royalty-free copies of your Access application. This is the feature that's most useful to Access developers because it means that end users don't have to purchase a copy of retail Access. In addition, it includes a distributable version of Microsoft Data Engine (MSDE), which is covered later in this section. The edition of the MSDE distributed with MOD in Office 2000, uses the SQL Server 7.0 engine. However, you can also distribute the SQL Server 2000 Desktop Engine with your Access application once you own SQL Server 2000.

The only parts of MOD that are directly related to deploying your Access application are the Access runtime files, the redistribution license for Access and MSDE, and the Package and Deployment Wizard, but here's a complete list of what you get when you buy MOD:

- *COM Add-in Designer*. Used to create standalone COM add-ins (DLLs) in VBA.
- *Visual SourceSafe*. Version control and code management software. MOD includes both a source-safe add-in for VBA hosts and a copy of Visual SourceSafe. Note that Access has its own source code control add-in, so it won't use the one that ships with MOD, but the software itself adds a lot of value to MOD.
- *Error Handler add-in*. Adds error handling to your code. You can use this add-in to quickly create standard error handlers in every procedure.
- *Code Commenter*. Adds comments to your code. You can use this add-in to create standardized headers for each of your procedures.
- *Code Librarian*. Enables you to reuse code and code snippets from a centralized code library.
- *VBA Multi-Code Import/Export*. Used to import code without having to cut and paste. This is similar to the import facility of the Visual Basic development environment itself, but it enables you to select more than one module to import at a time.
- *String Editor*. Used to build SQL strings.
- *Data Environment Designer*. Used to create ADO objects with a graphical user interface.
- *Data Binding Manager*. Used to bind objects and handle interactions between data consumers and sources (not for use in Access forms and reports).
- *Data Report Designer*. Used to generate reports that can also be exported to HTML or text files. This is the same designer that ships with Visual Basic 6.0 and probably won't be useful for an Access application in which you have the Access report designer available.
- *ADO Data Control*. Used to bind to data through ADO/OLEDB. This is used for Office applications other than Access, which uses its own data binding.
- *Hierarchical Flexgrid Control and Data Repeater Control*. Used to display data on non-Access forms.
- *FrontPage 2000*. Used to create your own Web site.
- *Web Components*. Used to publish spreadsheets, charts, and databases to the Web (covered in Chapter 13, "Internet Features in Access and SQL Server").
- *Clip Gallery*. Provides pictures, sounds, and animated clips.
- *HTML Help Workshop*. Used to develop custom help in Windows HTML format.

- *Office assistants*. Used to create your own custom assistants with the Agent software development kit.
- *Package and Deployment Wizard*. Used to package applications for installation and deployment. This is based on the wizard that VB uses, so it should look familiar if you've used VB. However, the MOD version has additional features to find all the files in an Office application. For example, it will automatically search for data access pages used by your Access database or project.
- *Printed documentation and examples*. A hard copy of the *Microsoft Office 2000 Object Model Guide* and the *Microsoft Office 2000/Visual Basic Programmer's Guide* and a special edition of the MSDN CD library with sample files.

Not a bad package, but MOD is probably not of much value to most Access developers unless you want Visual SourceSafe or need to distribute runtime versions of your application.

The Access Runtime

The Access runtime environment is completely different from the normal Access environment. Your Access application launches in a hidden window, which means you have to provide your own user interface by designating a startup form plus any menus or toolbars you want your users to have available. In addition, all design surfaces are hidden or disabled. The Access runtime isn't a separate executable and creating a runtime edition of your application doesn't compile it, make it smaller, or make it run faster. It uses the same executable file, `msaccess.exe`, and entries in the licensing section of the Windows Registry. When your runtime application starts, it checks the licensing key to determine whether to run using retail Access or the runtime. If no licensing key at all is present, the application won't load.

The Access runtime has the following features:

- All design interfaces, including the database window and object lists, as well as design views of your forms and reports, are completely hidden.
- The Visual Basic Editor is not accessible.
- Certain features, such as Filter by Form and Server Filter by Form, as well as all the wizards, are not available.
- Built-in menu commands involving designing objects, and all toolbars are not available.
- All unhandled errors, whether in macros or VBA code, cause your runtime application to abruptly terminate.

You can simulate the runtime environment in the retail version of Access by using the `/Runtime` command-line switch in a shortcut, which will launch Access in runtime mode. This enables you to test your application without having to install it separately on another machine that does not have retail Access installed.

15

Runtime Security

The Access Runtime does not guarantee any kind of security on your Access database. There's nothing to prevent a user from copying the MDB or ADP file to a machine and opening it using the retail version of Access. However, there is a way to protect your application code and user interface design: Compile your Access application as an MDE (for Access databases) or as an ADE (for Access projects).

Compiling Your Access Database as an MDE

When you compile an Access database as an MDE file, all your modules are compiled, all editable source code is removed, and the database is compacted. This means you can't view or edit any of your VBA code, and the size of the database will be reduced. The process of compiling a database as an MDE also optimizes memory usage and improves performance slightly.

Once you've compiled into an MDE, you won't be able to view, modify, or create forms, reports, or modules, modify object library references, or do anything at all in VBA because the MDE no longer contains nor can contain any source code. The code that existed in your application still runs as it did before conversion, but it is compiled into a form that is inaccessible. Tables, queries, data access pages, and macros are unaffected.

You must save the original Access database (MDB) file if you want to be able to make changes later—there's no way to reverse-engineer the MDE formatting. To create a new version, you need to recompile and redistribute a new MDE from the changed MDB file. The MDE file also cannot be upgraded to future versions of Access, so make sure you save your MDB file.

Creating the MDE File

To create an MDE file, choose Tools, Database Utilities, Make MDE File from the menu bar. If you haven't got the database opened, you'll be prompted for the database name and location. Once the MDE file is created, none of the forms, reports, data access pages or modules will be editable in the new file, but your original file is left unchanged. The options for Design and New in the MDE will be disabled in the Objects list, as shown in Figure 15.33.

Distributing an MDE offers your application real protection, while simply distributing a runtime version of Access with a standard MDB file does not. Be aware, however, that any sensitive data, like usernames and passwords, embedded in your VBA code will still be stored in the MDE file as plain text. They'll be hidden among a jumble of meaningless characters, but someone who knows what to look for could find them. To prevent this exposure, encrypt the database before you convert it, or encrypt the MDE, and implement user-level security to prevent users from being able to decrypt it. To encrypt or decrypt a database, a user must either be the owner of the database or a member of the Admins group, and must have Open Exclusive permission on the database.

FIGURE 15.33
The Objects list in an MDE.

Compiling Your Access Project as an ADE

The ADE is the Access project equivalent of the MDE file format for Access databases. When you choose Tools, Database Utilities, Make ADE File, all your VBA Source code is stripped away, just as it is for an MDE. You'll no longer be able to see or revise the design of any of your Access objects. Because Access encryption uses the Jet database engine, Access projects cannot be encrypted, but strings in your code are not stored in ADE files as plain text the way they are in MDE files.

Compiling your project file as an ADE is a good way to protect your source code and application design. However, once you've made an ADE file, you (or your users) can no longer use it to create forms, reports, or modules. To make changes to your Access project, you need to use the original Access project file (ADP), make changes there, and recompile a new version of your ADE.

Guidelines for Developing an Access Runtime Application

If your users will be running your Access application using a runtime version of Access, there a few design considerations you should bear in mind. Remember that users won't have any user interface at all unless you develop it for them. The following guidelines will help you develop and debug your Access runtime front end, whether you're using an Access project or an Access database:

- Build and debug the application around forms. Although you can also create command bars with menus and toolbar buttons, forms are the most versatile Access user interface, and all features should be discoverable through your forms.

- Error handling is essential because untrapped runtime errors will cause your Access application to terminate. Include error-handling code in all your VBA procedures, so that a runtime error won't bring the application to a screeching halt. The error handler add-in that ships with MOD is a great way to add error handling to any procedures that need it, and it provides a `model` of how good error handling code should be written.

- Don't use macros at all, unless you need an AutoKeys macro to trap certain keystrokes globally in your application. Even an AutoExec macro can be replaced with code that is called in the Open event of a startup form (use the Tools, Startup dialog to select a startup form). There's no way to implement error handling in a macro.

- Create menus, toolbars, and any Help files or other documentation your application needs. You're not allowed to distribute any of the Help files that ship with Access.

- Don't rely on any Access wizards. Your runtime license doesn't include the right to redistribute them.

- Test the application using the `/Runtime` switch in the command-line option of a shortcut to simulate how it will behave after `distribution`. Create a shortcut using syntax like the following in the command line:

```
C:\AccPath\msaccess.exe C:\MyApp.mdb /runtime
```

- Use the Package and Deployment Wizard to create the installation package. Test it on a clean machine that does not have—and has never had—Access or Office installed. Remember that you already have all the necessary Registry entries and DLLs on your development machine, so you might not be able to spot a problem that will only show up on a "clean" machine.

User-Proofing and Security

Data security in your Access/SQL Server database is best handled on SQL Server. For application security, the best solution is to compile the front end as an MDE or ADE, as discussed earlier in this chapter. User-level security is available in an Access database if you want to enable or disable forms and reports based on the current user, or if you need to prevent users from decrypting the application or setting a database password. If simple user-proofing is your goal, here are some techniques you can employ to prevent users from tampering with your application if they do happen to open it in retail Access:

- Make sure your customized menus and toolbars do not include any options giving users access to any security options, design views, or macro and module windows.

- Set the `AllowBypassKey` property to `False` to disable the Shift key when the database opens. In the runtime environment, this is automatically disabled for an Access MDB. You must create this property programmatically before you can set its value. Here's VBA code that uses DAO to create the property in the current database and set its value to `False`:

```
Public Sub PreventBypass()
    Dim dbs As DAO.Database
    Dim prp As DAO.Property
```

```
    Set dbs = CurrentDb
    Set prp = dbs.CreateProperty( _
        Name:="AllowBypassKey", _
        Type:=dbBoolean, _
        Value:=False, _
        DDL:=True)
    dbs.Properties.Append prp
End Sub
```

The DDL parameter of the DAO `CreateProperty` method enables you to specify that this property can only be set by users who have dbSecWriteDef permission on the object you are adding the property to; in this case, the database object. This is documented in the help topic for `CreateProperty`, but unfortunately it is not mentioned in the help topic for `AllowBypassKey`, and that DDL parameter is not set in the example code there. So, many experienced Access programmers don't know about it. Using this DDL parameter is very important because without it any knowledgeable user could run VBA code to set the property to False and then use the Shift key to bypass your startup settings.

It is possible to create and set the `AllowBypassKey` property using ADO like this:

```
Application.CurrentProject.Properties.Add "AllowBypassKey", False
```

Unfortunately, however, the ADO method doesn't enable you to set that critical DDL parameter.

- Configure your startup properties to disallow using the Access Special Keys, Viewing Code After Error, Display Database Window, and Allow Toolbar/Menu Changes options. Although these options are disabled if you distribute your application using the runtime, they will protect it if a user opens it on a machine that has the full retail version of Access installed.

Simple user-proofing might be enough to protect your application because data security is handled by SQL Server, not Access.

Running the Package and Deployment Wizard

There are two steps to rolling out your Access application:

- Creating the package, which contains the files needed by your runtime application
- Deploying the package by making it available on `distribution` media or a Web site so that users can install it

The Package and Deployment (P&D) Wizard has replaced the old Setup Wizard of past versions. The P&D Wizard guides you through the steps of creating compressed cabinet (CAB) files and packaging them for installation by end users.

Launch the P&D Wizard from the Add-Ins menu in the Visual Basic Editor. Choose between the three following options:

- *Package*. Creates CAB files and a setup program for installation.
- *Deploy*. Used to deliver and deploy the package to the `distribution` media.
- *Manage Scripts*. Used to view and edit previously saved scripts. Each time you use the wizard, you have the option to save your selections in a script.

> **TIP**
>
> When you install Microsoft Office Developer, the Access runtime files are not copied to your computer. Copy them to your `\Program Files\Microsoft Office\ ODE Tools\V9\Runtime` folder prior to launching the P&D Wizard so that the wizard will be able to find them without prompting you for their location while you're in the middle of creating your package.
>
> If you're running Office SR1 with MOD SR1, then you need to take a couple of extra steps. Create the Runtime directory in the `\Program Files\Microsoft Office\ ODE Tools\V9\` folder. Locate the ACCESSRT folder on the MOD SR1 CD. Note that there are two folders inside of it: FULL and MIN. If you want a full installation of IE5, then copy the contents of the FULL folder to the Runtime folder on your hard drive. If you don't need all of IE5 (perhaps your users already have it on their desktops), then copy the contents of the MIN folder instead. This new choice between FULL and MIN file sets was introduced in SR1 to address the concerns of developers who were shocked at the size of an Access runtime installation. The FULL set runs about 150MB while the MIN set is "only" about 50MB, still a far cry from the old days when Access runtime setup files could be distributed on a few floppy disks.

Creating a Package

Click the Package button to start the process of creating the package. You need to determine which files are required in order for your project to install correctly and work. The wizard will guess many of the required files, but it must include all the project files and any dependency files before it can succeed. Make a list before you start so that package creation will run smoothly, and all the files you need will be included. However, if you do omit a file, you can rerun the wizard using a script created during a previous run.

Next, you need to choose the type of package to create. Standard Setup Package is usually the best choice. If you choose the Dependency File option, information about your components will be saved, but a setup program won't be created. This is useful if your using a third-party setup tool and want to use the P&D Wizard just to create the dependency file to feed to that tool.

The location for the package should be a separate folder, not the folder your application already resides in. The wizard will suggest a subfolder called Package to hold all the files it needs.

You'll then need to specify all the files to be included. If you have a file that does not show up on the list, click the Add button to include it. The wizard will automatically find all the files referenced from your application, including controls, Data Access Pages, and linked databases, as shown in Figure 15.34.

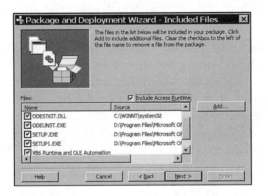

FIGURE 15.34
Including files in the Package and Deployment Wizard.

You'll then be prompted for a title for the installation package and any optional commands you want to run when the installation is finished. Use this option to automatically set up the MSDE if your application is going to be distributed using MSDE. MSDE is covered later in this chapter.

The next dialog box enables you to configure the location of the menu groups and other items that the installation will create on the user's machine.

You can modify the locations as needed.

The wizard enables you to specify the installed files as *shared* on the next dialog box. What this means is that the files will not be removed during an uninstall if other programs are using them.

The final dialog box prompts you for a name for the setup package. The next time you run the P&D Wizard, you can load the setup package and not have to choose every option from scratch. Once you click the Finish button, the package will be created in the folder you specified earlier in the wizard.

Deploying a Package

Once the setup package is created, you can test deploying the package by running the setup program the P&D Wizard created for you. You can deploy the package to disks, folders, CDs, or to the Web. Because the Access runtime itself is so large, you'll want to use a network folder or a CD-ROM deployment.

Test deploying your application on a computer that does not already have Access installed. Click the Deploy button on the first P&D Wizard screen and follow the steps. If you elect to deploy to the Internet, you'll be able to specify a Web site and also add or remove files from the file list.

When the setup program in your installation package (setup.exe) runs, all the necessary files for the setup program will be copied to the computer's hard drive. If the Visual Basic components the setup program needs are not already installed on the computer, the setup program will copy them, and the user must reboot. After rebooting, the user has to start the setup program again. If neither the Access retail nor runtime files are present on the target computer, those files will be installed. The user then selects either the Typical or Custom setup option. The computer will then reboot, and the setup will continue after the reboot.

When you finish the deployment portion of the wizard, it will also save a script. If you make changes to your package, you can just run this script to update the deployment.

Other Deployment Issues

Microsoft Internet Explorer 5.0 is a necessary component of the Package and Deployment Wizard as well as Access 2000 if you are using Data Access Pages. It will be installed on the target computer as part of the deployment process, if you use the FULL directory of runtime files. However, it will become the default browser only in the case where an earlier version of Internet Explorer was already present on the computer.

If the target computer does not have either Internet Explorer 5.0 or Microsoft Office 2000, there will be two restarts of the computer during the installation process.

Deploying an Application Using the Desktop Engine

Deploying your application to users who do not have access to a full version of SQL Server is possible by distributing the Desktop Engine as a component of your application. The Desktop Engine is a redistributable version of the SQL Server relational database engine and has all of the core functionality available in SQL Server. However, it does not come with any client tools, such as the Enterprise Manager or Query Analyzer. You can install your SQL Server database on a Desktop Engine server, and users can access it the way they would access a full installation of SQL Server.

The Desktop Engine dynamically manages its configuration and resource use, minimizing the need for any administration by the user.

After installing the Desktop Engine, either the application setup program or the application itself can use SQL-DMO (Distributed Management Objects) or Transact-SQL to create and configure the database. VBA code for using SQL-DMO to install a database is presented later in this chapter.

Installing the Desktop Engine

Use the Windows Installer service to install the Desktop Engine, or use your own installation program.

The Windows Installer comes with Microsoft Windows 2000 and is available for Windows NT 4.0, Windows 98, and Windows 95. The SQL Server 2000 Desktop Engine is supplied as a set of Windows Installer merge modules in the Windows Installer. You can use these merge modules to integrate the SQL Server 2000 Desktop Engine Setup into the application's Windows Installer setup. The merge modules let you reduce the disk footprint of your application by customizing the setup so that it does not install components you don't need, such as replication and SQL-DMO.

If you use your own setup program, then use the Setup.exe file that the SQL Server 2000 Desktop Engine provides. This Setup.exe program operates as a shell that calls Windows Installer to install the SQL Server 2000 Desktop Engine merge modules.

The Windows Installer can also be called directly, using command-line switches or an ini file to specify settings and define the way the Setup.exe installs the SQL Server Desktop Engine.

The full syntax is

```
setup [/?]
  [
    [   /i package_file
        [ /settings ini_file ]
        |   [   [ TARGETDIR="executable_folder_path"]
                [ DATADIR="data_folder_path" ]
                [ INSTANCENAME="instance_name" ]
                [ COLLATION="collation_name" ]
                [ CALLBACK=Dllname!CallbackFunctionName ]
                [ USEDEFAULTSAPWD | SAPASSWORD="sa_password" ]
            ]
        ]
    | [ /x package_file ]
  ]
  [ /L*v [filename] ]
  [ /qn | /qb ]
```

Your setup program should ensure that the proposed instance name for the Desktop Engine is not already being used by another instance of SQL Server, and that the computer does not

15

already have more than 16 instances (or 15 named instances) installed. SQL Server 2000 supplies two API functions, NumInstalledInstances and IsInstanceNameValid, to perform these checks.

Deploying an Application Using MSDE (SQL Server 7.0)

If you distribute your application using MSDE (Microsoft Data Engine), you are using SQL Server 7.0, not SQL Server 2000. The redistributable version of MSDE has the same core engine as the version of MSDE included in the Premium edition of Office 2000, but it lacks the user interface tools for editing server-side objects. This is the only version of Office 2000 that provides the license to freely redistribute MSDE. Other versions of Office 2000 that include MSDE do not provide the license to redistribute applications. Only one instance of MSDE can be installed and running on a computer at a time.

If you're going to distribute MSDE, you need to set up MSDE for packaging before running the Package and Deployment Wizard. The files located in the MSDE folder on the Office 2000 Developer CD make up a template that you can modify for your specific use. The MSDEx86.dep file lists dependencies for MSDEx86.exe, as follows:

```
; Dependency file for MSDEx86.exe

; Default Dependencies ----------

[MSDEx86.exe]
Dest=$(AppPath)\MSDETemp
Uses1=MSDEInst.iss
Uses2=MSDEInst.bat

[MSDEInst.bat]
Dest=$(AppPath)\MSDETemp
Uses1=

[MSDEInst.iss]
Dest=$(AppPath)\MSDETemp
Uses1=
```

The MSDEx86.dep file is designed to tell the Package and Deployment Wizard the installation location of the files on the target computer. You can modify the \MSDETemp location to reflect the actual location.

The MSDEInst.iss file should also be modified for your requirements, as discussed in the next section. At runtime, it should be changed to point to the correct drive install location.

Copy the MSDEx86.exe, MSDEx86.dep, MSDEInst.bat, and MSDEInst.iss files to your machine in a separate folder and modify them as necessary.

When you create your package with the Package and Deployment Wizard, you need to include the MDF file associated with your SQL Server database, along with all the files included in the folder with `MSDEx86.exe`. Uncheck any dependencies that might already be on the end user's machine, such as `SQLDMO.rll`.

As discussed earlier, the Package and Deployment Wizard has an option to run an executable file at the end of the setup process. This option can be used to launch a batch file to extract and install the redistributable version of MSDE on the target computer. On the Installation Options dialog box, select the Run This Command when Installation Is Finished option and specify the following batch file:

```
MSDETemp\MSDEInst.bat
```

The batch file contains the following line of code:

```
start /wait msdex86.exe -s -a -fl "sql70ins.iss"
```

The `sql70ins.iss` file is a default ISS file that's contained within `msdex.86.exe` along with all the product defaults. You can also use a custom ISS file, specifying it with a command like this:

```
start /wait msdex86.exe -s -a -fl "c:\progra~1\adp1\MSDETemp\MSDEInst.iss"
```

You need to modify the `adp1` folder name to reflect the name of your product. The statement silently installs MSDE to the target computer hard drive, using the `MSDEInst.iss` file for instructions. More detailed information on modifying the ISS file is available on the Platform SDK on MSDN. The `start /wait` parameter lets the installation complete before returning control to the batch file.

At the end of the installation process, you need to launch MSDE to load the SQL Server database on the target machine. There are two ways to do this:

- Use the following command-line statement for Windows NT/Windows 2000:
  ```
  net start mssqlserver
  ```
- Use the following SQL-DMO code. Note that you need to have a reference to the SQL-DMO Object Library. You'll also need a reference to the Microsoft Scripting Runtime Library when you load the database. Here's the code:
  ```
  Sub TurnOnMSDE()
  Dim oSvr As SQLDMO.SQLServer

      Set oSvr = CreateObject("SQLDMO.SQLServer")
      On Error GoTo StartError
      oSvr.LoginTimeout = 60 ' this needs to be high to avoid time-out _
      errors.
  ```

15

```
        oSvr.Start True, "(local)", "sa", ""

    ExitSub:
        Exit Sub

    StartError:
        If Err.Number = -2147023840 Then 'This error is thrown when the server
    is already
        running, and Server.Start is executed on NT
            oSvr.Connect "(local)", "sa", ""
            Resume Next
        End If

    End Sub
```

Once you've started the MSDE engine, you need to load the database into MSDE on the target computer. The code assumes that the setup program copied the MDF file to the same folder as the ADP file and that the current directory contains the MDF file. It also assumes that the MDF file will go in the MSSQL7\Data folder. Here's the code:

```
Sub ConnectData()
Dim strMsg As String
Dim strCurDir as String
Dim FSO As Scripting.FileSystemObject
Dim oSvr As SQLDMO.SQLServer

    Set FSO = CreateObject("Scripting.FileSystemObject")
    Set oSvr = CreateObject("SQLDMO.SQLServer")

'Log onto database
    oSvr.Connect "(local)", "sa", ""

'Copy File to data folder
    strCurDir = CurDir & "adp1sql.mdf"
    FSO.CopyFile strCurDir, "c:\mssql7\data\adp1sql.mdf", True

'Attach to database
    strmessage = oSvr.AttachDBWithSingleFile("DemoDatabase",
    "c:\mssql7\data\adp1SQL.mdf")

'Display the success or failure message
    MsgBox strmessage

    oSvr.Disconnect
    Set oSvr = Nothing

End Sub
```

For more information, see "Creating and Deploying Access Solutions with the Microsoft Data Engine" by Scott Smith, Microsoft Corporation. This white paper is available at `http://msdn.microsoft.com/library/techart/msdeploy.htm`.

Copying or Moving Your SQL Server Database

There are several methods for copying or moving a SQL Server database. You can use the `sp_detach_db` and `sp_attach_db` system stored procedures, the Enterprise Manager menus, or the Copy Database Wizard. The wizard, which is new in SQL Server 2000, is the easiest way to copy a database from server to server.

Copying a Database from Server to Server

Since copying or moving databases from one server to another was always a problem in earlier versions of SQL Server, Microsoft has provided a graphical interface for copying databases in the Enterprise Manager called the Copy Database Wizard. The wizard enables you to create logins on the destination server and to move supporting objects, jobs, and error messages, in addition to just copying a database. To launch the wizard, choose Tools, Wizards, Management, Copy Database Wizard from the Enterprise Manager menu and complete the information in the wizard dialog boxes.

Detaching and Attaching Databases

In order to copy or move a database, you need to detach it, copy the database and log files, and then attach it in its new location. SQL Server 2000 has added support in the Enterprise Manager menus for detaching and attaching databases.

Note that you can't perform this process if users are connected to the database.

To detach the database, right-click on it and choose All Tasks, Detach Database. This will load the Detach Database dialog box, shown in Figure 15.35. Select the Update statistics checkbox to make sure that all of the statistics for the database are current.

FIGURE 15.35
Detaching a database.

The database can now be safely moved to its new location by copying its associated .mdf, .ldf, and .ndf files.

To attach the new database at the destination, right-click on the Databases node and choose All Tasks, Attach Database. This will bring up the Attach Database dialog box, shown in Figure 15.36. Fill in the name and location of the MDF file, the name of the database, and specify an owner. If you choose 'sa', then the database will be owned by dbo.

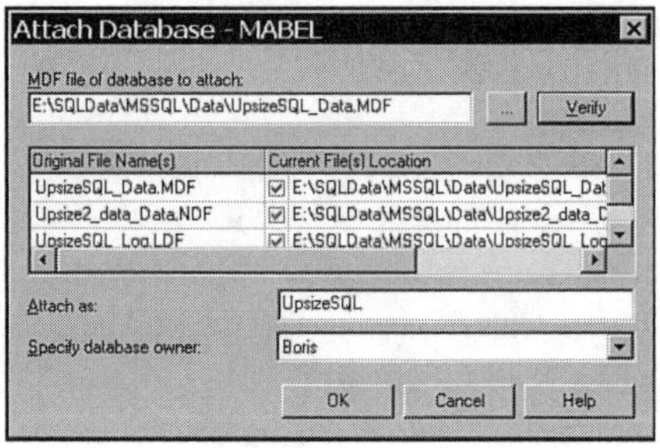

FIGURE 15.36
Attaching a database.

You can use the two system stored procedures, sp_detach_db, and sp_attach_db, to copy or move your SQL Server database. Whether you're copying or moving the source database, you need to run the sp_detach_db system stored procedure first, to allow it to be copied or moved. The sp_detach_db system stored procedure has two parameters: @dbname, which is the name of the database, and @skipchecks, which if set to False runs UPDATE STATISTICS. Set this to False and let UPDATE STATISTICS run only if you're moving the database to read-only media. Here's the syntax that detaches MyDB and skips updating the statistics:

```
sp_detach_db @dbname = 'MyDB', @skipchecks = 'True'
```

Then manually copy the database and log files (.mdf and .ldf extensions) to the new destination. If you're copying the database and want to keep the original database in its original location, after you run sp_detach_db and copy the files, run the sp_attach_db system stored procedure to reattach it. Run sp_attach_db on the database in its new destination as well. This creates the necessary entries in the system tables in the master database in the destination SQL Server. Here's an example:

```
sp_attach_db @dbname = 'MyDB',
    @filename1 = 'c:\mssql7\data\MyDB.mdf',
    @filename2 = 'c:\mssql7\data\MyDB_log.ldf'
```

Summary

SQL Server databases require a lot more attention than Access databases when it comes to monitoring, maintenance, and backups. However, there are tools in SQL Server 2000 that make automating these processes much easier than has been the case in past versions of SQL Server. The SQL Server Profiler and the Performance Monitor can help you track down problems at the database level and at the system level. The Database Maintenance Plan Wizard assists you in creating a comprehensive plan for checking database consistency and backing up your databases and transaction logs. When it comes time to deploy your application, the Microsoft Office Developer provides the Package and Deployment Wizard to assist you in creating and deploying your application setup files. The Microsoft Office Developer also provides a version of MSDE that you can redistribute for users who don't have a full SQL Server license. MSDE uses the SQL Server 7.0 engine. To take advantage of features in SQL Server 2000, distribute the SQL Server Desktop Engine. SQL Server databases are transferred from one server to another using the Copy Database Wizard, or by detaching and re-attaching them using the Enterprise Manager or using Transact-SQL.

Resources

IN THIS APPENDIX

Books

Access 2000 Developer's Handbook, Vols. 1 & 2, by Paul Litwin, Ken Getz, and Mike Gilbert. Sybex.

Visual Basic Language Developer's Handbook, by Ken Getz and Mike Gilbert. Sybex.

Inside SQL Server 7.0, by Ron Soukup and Kalen Delaney. Microsoft Press.

Hitchhiker's Guide to Visual Basic and SQL Server, by William Vaughan. Microsoft Press.

Visual Basic Developer's Guide to ADO, by Mike Gunderloy. Sybex.

Programming the Microsoft Office 2000 Web Components, by Dave Stearns. Microsoft Press.

Professional Visual Basic 6 XML, by James Britt and Teun Duynstee. Wrox Press.

SQL for Smarties, by Joe Celko. Morgan Kaufman.

Programming Distributed Applications with COM and Microsoft Visual Basic 6.0, by Ted Pattison. Microsoft Press.

Transact-SQL Programming, by Kevin Kline, Lee Gould, and Andrew Zanevsky. O'Reilly.

Data & Databases: Concepts in Practice, by Joe Celko. Morgan Kaufman.

Designing Relational Database Systems, by Rebecca Riordan. Microsoft Press.

Programming ADO, by David Sceppa. Microsoft Press.

Database Design for Mere Mortals, by Michael J. Hernandez. Addison-Wesley.

Jet Database Engine Programmer's Guide, by Dan Haught and Jim Ferguson. Microsoft Press.

Doing Objects in Microsoft Visual Basic 6.0, by Deborah Kurata. Sams.

An Introduction to Database Systems, by C. J. Date. Addison Wesley.

Web Sites

Microsoft SQL Server site:

http://www.microsoft.com/sql/

An index on everything that's available on Microsoft's SQL Web site:

http://www.microsoft.com/sql/index.htm

The best gateway to SQL Server support:

http://support.microsoft.com/support/

Microsoft Office Developer site:

http://msdn.microsoft.com/officedev

Microsoft Knowledgebase Search site:

`http://support.microsoft.com/support/search`

Michael Hotek's Web site for SQL Server:

`http://www.mssqlserver.com`

The Professional Association for SQL Server (PASS):

`http://www.sqlpass.org`

Bill Vaughn's Web site for information on ADO:

`http://www.betav.com`

Able Consulting's site for the ADO FAQ:

`http://www.able-consulting.com/ADO_FAQ.htm`

Dev Ashish's Web site for Access developers:

`http://www.mvps.org`

The Swynk.com Web site, with newsletters, discussion boards, and job listings:

`http://www.swynk.com`

Formerly Ntfaq.com, this site has a SQL Server section:

`http://www.windows2000faq.com`

The authors' Web site:

`http://www.mcwtech.com`

Useful Downloads

Migrating Your Microsoft Access Database to Microsoft SQL Server 7.0:

`http://www.microsoft.com/sql/interopmigrate/accessmigration.htm`

Migrating from DAO to ADO and Using ADO with the Jet Provider:

`http://www.microsoft.com/data/ado/adotechinfo/dao2ado.htm`

Creating and Deploying Microsoft Access Solutions with the Microsoft Data Engine (MSDE):

`http://www.microsoft.com/sql/productinfo/msde.htm`

Microsoft Access 2000: Choosing Between MSDE and Jet:

`http://www.microsoft.com/sql/productinfo/msdejet.htm`

Access 97 Upsizing Wizard and Help File:

`http://www.microsoft.com/AccessDev/ProdInfo/AUT97dat.htm`

Magazines and Journals

SQL Server Magazine:

`http://www.sqlmag.com`

Advisor publications:

`http://www.advisor.com`

Pinnacle:

`http://www.PinnaclePublishing.com`

Office VBA Web site, sponsored by Informant Communications Group:

`http://www.OfficeVBA.com`

Visual Basic Programmer's Journal:

`http://www.vbpj.com`

INDEX

SYMBOLS

A

Q

Hey, you've got enough worries.

Don't let IT training be one of them.

Get on the fast track to IT training at InformIT,
your total Information Technology training network.

 | **www.informit.com** | **SAMS**

■ Hundreds of timely articles on dozens of topics ■ Discounts on IT books from all our publishing partners, including Sams Publishing ■ Free, unabridged books from the InformIT Free Library ■ "Expert Q&A"—our live, online chat room with IT experts ■ Faster, easier certification and training from our web or classroom-based training programs ■ Current IT news ■ Software downloads ■ Career-enhancing resources